D1532819

PANZER

A Revolution in Warfare, 1939-1945

PANZER

A Revolution in Warfare, 1939–1945

ROGER EDWARDS

ARMS AND
ARMOUR

Left: Tigers and Pz Kpfw IVs of Panzer Group West roll forward to face the invading Allies on D-Day. Panzer action at Villers-Bocage ended any hopes of an early British Second Army break-through to the south.

About this book

The thematic structure of *Panzer* is intended to advance the exploration of a radical military concept and its implementation in battle; an arrangement that I believe to be of greater benefit to the reader in saving time tracing specific aspects of the revolutionary ideas than that afforded by a more conservative and wholly chronological plan.

A preamble establishes Hitler's rise to power, noting the Führer's influence as a national leader fostering rearmament and in particular the armoured idea in Germany after 1933, giving rise to the Second World War. The military role of Hitler's subordinates and some anti-tank developments of significance are also introduced at this stage.

In reviewing the progress of the German Army restoring (or acquiring) the mobility denied it by the Versailles Treaty of 1919, Part 1 takes as its starting point the endeavours of British tank pioneers seized upon and expanded by German devotees; a formative phase in panzer force history succeeded by campaigning experience gathered in Europe and Asia over a period of five and a half years.

So broad a view of panzer force history as that required of Part 1 in furnishing a rounded picture of an Army exploiting exceptional mobility in early campaigns but falling apart in operations after spring 1943 is enlarged upon in Part 2 by a review of the structure of the panzer force and in particular by profiling the wartime movement of all panzer and panzer grenadier divisions.

Fighting the mobile battle in Part 3 is also a thematic exploration of the role and combat effectiveness of panzer force elements, while in Part 4 the decisive influence of the air force shaping the capability of ground forces is revealed for what it was – the key to panzer success or failure.

But it is in the war action of panzer armies, the supreme expression of panzer force organization and mobility, originating in pre-existing panzer corps and panzer groups, that true success or failure of the panzer revolution is to be sought. With this point in mind, Part 5 is constituted as a visual guide to panzer force operations: twenty maps, organizational tables and commentaries reveal the aims and scope of panzer leaders serving as force commanders.

Their progress in battle is elaborated in Part 6, a chronological review of all campaigns undertaken by Panzer armies and their predecessors the panzer corps and panzer groups of the early wartime era upon whose experience in Poland, France and, to a lesser degree, the Balkans these same commanders and their successors drew so deeply.

Hitler's influence on panzer operations and the problems encountered by panzer leaders, not the least of which was the Führer's inability as self-proclaimed warlord to leave operational matters to the judgement of those on the spot, is clearly apparent in these day-to-day chronicles of panzer battles on all fronts, but more especially during the Allied invasion of north-west Europe, Pz-AOK5 (Europe), June 1944.

The post-war history of armoured forces is not included in the scope of this book; I nevertheless believe that no modern army can escape indebtedness to the panzer revolution for leading the way to effective battlefield mobility. What this book makes clear is that the Wehrmacht failure to modernize its armed services in time for more protracted battles than those entailed in *Blitzkrieg* sounded the death knell of the panzer force before even the inplacable will of Hitler's enemies brought about the downfall of an inglorious Third Reich.

First published in Great Britain in 1989 by Arms and Armour Press, Artillery House, Artillery Row, London SW1P 1RT.

Distributed in the USA by Sterling Publishing Co. Inc., 387 Park Avenue South, New York, NY 10016–8810.

Distributed in Australia by Capricorn Link (Australia) Pty. Ltd, P.O. Box 665, Lane Cove, New South Wales 2066, Australia.

British Library Cataloguing in Publication Data
Edwards, Roger
Panzer.
1. Germany. Heer. Armoured combat vehicles: Panzer tanks, 1939–1941
I. Title
623.74'752
ISBN 0-85368-932-6

Designed and edited by DAG Publications Ltd. Designed by David Gibbons; edited by Michael Boxall; layout by Anthony A. Evans; typeset by Typesetters (Birmingham) Ltd; camerawork by M&E Reproductions, North Fambridge, Essex; printed and bound in Great Britain by Courier International, Tiptree, Essex.

Acknowledgements

My gratitude is due to the following for their very kind help in the preparation of this book:

To Walther Nehring and Fritz Morzik, General Officers respectively of armoured troops and transport fliers whose helpful advice based upon events of the period enabled me to devise a suitable format for the project.

To Oberst a.D. Heinrich Nolte Ia 18th Panzer Grenadier Division July 1940 – February 1943; Oberst a.D. Friedrich von Hake CO, 4th Panzer Regiment September 1942 – June 1944; Major a.D. Hans Sittig CO, 16th Panzerjaeger Bn; Peter Strassner battalion adjutant S. S. Wiking and others whose comments on technical and other aspects of panzer force history broadened my concept of mobility.

To the librarians and archivists who guided me through their collections at the Bundesarchiv Coblenz; Imperial War Museum, Lambeth; Museum of Army Flying, Middle Wallop; Royal Corps of Signals, Blandford Forum; RAF Museum Hendon and Ministére de l'Armée, Paris.

My gratitude is also due to those professionals whose skills served me in turning ideas into print; translators Beryl Osmond and Petra Becker, cartographers Jane Pugh and Anne Duffy, photographer Malcolm Slater, secretaries Anne Cowlin and Wendy Newman. The AFV profiles were drawn by Mr Geoffrey Boxall and the project was advanced editorially by Chris Westhorp, David Gibbons and Michael Boxall of Arms & Armour Press. I must also place on record my appreciation of the help that I have received at various times from the historical institute of the Bundeswehr, the Militärgeschichtlichen Forschungsamt, Freiburg. I am especially grateful to Doctors Friedrich Forstmeir and Horst Rohde.

Lastly my thanks to those family members and friends who provided seemingly endless hospitality while writing, an area of support encouraged by a wife whose commitment to the project never wavered. Thank you then Patricia, Christopher and Margaret, Linda and Timothy, Peter and Janet, Sara, Jonathan, David and Marylyn and Timothy Walker. I am grateful to you all.

Roger Edwards

Contents

Key to Panzer Battles

Right: ***Die Woche*, Berlin 1935, and the Führer is pictured sharing a friendly moment with Dr Joseph Goebbels. Appointed Minister for Propaganda in 1933, Goebbels performed his duties enthusiastically, dominating the media and ensuring absolute government control. Teams were attached to service headquarters to take front-line pictures, items which are now stored in official archives.**

Prelude: the road to war

GERMANY UNDER HITLER

During the years 1933 to 1945 the political and military fortunes of the German Army, like that of the German people, became inextricably bound-up in the obsessions and aspirations motivating a single individual.

Adolf Hitler, leader of the National Socialist movement in Germany, came to power in January 1933 following moderate success at the polls. Winning popular support with 196 out of 584 parliamentary seats – 75 more than his nearest rival, the future dictator and commander-in-chief of the German armed services was accepted as Chancellor of the Third Reich by President Hindenburg. Using fresh elections to consolidate his position, Hitler suspended the constitution of the outgoing Weimar administration and in its place substituted government by personal decree. So unassailable did he proceed to make himself as a dictator that for the next twelve years (he died in April 1945) Hitler alone determined the political, economic and military future of Germany. Secret plans for German re-armament and economic advance, already in train when Hitler came to power, were speeded-up then followed by open steps to war, but not until 1939 did the Western powers resort to military action to stop Hitler's progress.

The Chancellor's approach to war was clear for all to see. Military conscription was introduced early in 1935 and the Rhineland re-occupied in 1936. This stretch of German territory adjoining France had been declared a demilitarized zone under the terms of the Treaty of Versailles and all German military presence excluded. Two years later, in March 1938, Hitler incorporated Austria into the Third Reich and in October of the same year ordered the occupation of Czech Sudeten (border) territories where German-speaking inhabitants predominated. In the same year Hitler ordered the re-occupation of Memel, another strip of former German territory, also forfeited under 'Versailles', this time adjoining East Prussia on the Baltic Coast and previously awarded to Lithuania. When Hitler decided that possession of more Czech territory, including the city of Prague and the western provinces of Bohemia and Moravia, was vital to the strategic interests of the Reich, they were annexed. Hitler's moves to rally the German people after their defeat in 1918, were foreshadowed in *Mein Kampf*, published in 1925. This was a personal programme to raise Germany to the level of supreme power in Europe. By restoring the nation's pride and extending its living-space or *Lebensraum* (Germany was the most populated country in Europe), Hitler proposed by his actions to unit all German-speaking people into a single Greater Germany – Gross Deutschland – knowing full well that war was a likely consequence.

Moving purposefully at a time of wide-spread unemployment, when Germany lay in the grip of economic recession, Hitler espoused many causes to increase his popularity. A road-building programme, partially inherited from the previous administration, created a motorway (*autobahn*)

Left: After Hitler's conscription decree and the unveiling of the Luftwaffe in March 1935, three panzer divisions were raised in October. In November *Die Woche* focused public attention upon a new, national war flag which was hoisted over Berlin on the 7th of that month.

network destined for the rapid transit of military personnel. Work organized by a National Labour Service (Reichs Arbeits Dienst or RAD) provided employment for 200–300,000 workers every year. More of the unemployed were absorbed into armament industries which, despite shortages of steel and other critically important materials, supplied countless, if inadequate numbers of weapons, vehicles and aircraft to the expanding armed services. Pursuing mobilization through sport, including Party flying and motoring clubs, physical education and sporting activities were widely promoted in Hitler's Germany. When the time came for full mobilization the armed forces would benefit substantially from such pre-service training. As time progressed, the nation became increasingly and irreversibly regimented for war. Boys of upper school age, assisted by the Army in their training, were recruited into the Hitler Youth Organization. Their seniors were inducted into pre-service work schemes organized by RAD. Girls joined a separate society; juniors enrolled in the Jungvolk.

Above all, Hitler was determined to re-vitalize the armed services and in particular to re-establish the air force whose fledgling military presence within the Air Ministry (RLM: Reichsluftfarhtministerium), would remain an official secret until 1935. Thereafter the air force would receive a higher

Above: Printed propaganda published in Berlin in 1936 which instructed the German people to be grateful to the Führer for his outstanding leadership.

proportion of re-armament finance and resources than the other two services. After 1938 its ranks would include all parachute troops of the Wehrmacht. On land, the Treaty of Versailles imposed on Germany by the victorious Allies, permitted the army no general staff, no tanks and no heavy artillery. Furthermore, the Reichsheer under General von Seeckt, the army of the Weimar administration, a force of seven infantry and three cavalry divisions, was limited to 100,000 men served by a handful of motor transport battalions. A 'state within a state', the German Army enjoyed a privileged and influential position in German society. Without its support no government could hope to survive. Hitler would eventually come to terms with it, but only after much anguish and the 'surrender' of the party's million-strong private army, the Sturmabteilung (SA).

SA leader Ernst Roehm and others, at the head of this force with its own general staff and training facilities, were opposed to Hitler's support for an Army High Command view that the basis of government power should lie solely with the Army. Hitler ordered Roehm's murder and that of a hundred others. The fateful event known as the 'Night of the Long Knives' took place on 30 June 1934. The new German Army, Hitler insisted, would possess a strength of thirty-six divisions. By September 1939 this had risen to one hundred and seven including fifteen tank and motorized formations of a type still undergoing development in foreign armies. Simultaneously the German air force, disbanded under 'Versailles' rules, but secretly re-organized and created for army support, would reach a strength of 4,000 front-line aircraft deployed in thirty-eight (incomplete) Geschwader (equivalent of RAF Group); this was double the strength of either the Royal Air Force or l'Armée de l'Air. Neither Army nor Air Force planned to reach optimum operational levels until 1942. When war did come in 1939 neither service was fully equipped for it. The German Navy, of which only a token 15,000 men remained in service after 1918, would before September 1939 under Admiral Raeder commission two battleships, *Scharnhorst* and *Gneisenau*, three 'pocket battleships', *Admiral Scheer, Deutschland* and *Graf Spee*, two heavy and six light cruisers, twenty-two destroyers and forty-nine U-boats with more on the stocks.

Hitler's massive reconstruction of German armed strength, coupled with his repudiation of the widely resented Treaty of Versailles and the steps taken to reduce unemployment became a significant part of Nazi appeal to the electorate, and plans for the future of Germany. When President Hindenburg died in 1934 the field marshal's death left Hitler undisputed Leader (Führer) of the German people. But, unsatisfied with supreme political office and unconvinced of the loyalty of the Army, he decided in 1938 to consolidate his hold on the armed services by establishing a supreme command – Oberkommando der Wehrmacht (OKW) – nominating himself as Commander-in-Chief. Taking advantage of a scandal involving senior army officers (War Minister, General von Blomberg and Army Commander-in-Chief, General von Fritsch), Hitler, whose military endeavours during the First World War were limited to the rank of corporal, proposed henceforth to direct the nation's military affairs in person. The war minister's office (Wehrmachtsamt) had until then been supervised by General Wilhelm Keitel whom Hitler promptly appointed professional head of OKW. But Keitel would discover all too soon that his advice, like that of other senior officers and staffs, would more often than not be ignored. OKW would serve Hitler as a personal staff; he alone would decide the action. In later years this situation would prove wholly disastrous as a means of initiating and directing a successful war strategy.

Certainly there were times when Hitler's military decisions would benefit the services, particularly those taken against advice from generals who for years before 1940 had been cautious about endorsing National Socialist expansionist plans – a caution that planted ineradicable seeds of distrust in Hitler's mind. The Führer's 'standfast' order in the winter of 1941 undoubtedly saved the army on the Eastern Front, yet more often than not Hitler as Commander-in-Chief interfered in local matters and destroyed service efficiency by forbidding and inhibiting initiative. In later years, with events in the field taking catastrophic turns, the 'gentlemen' of the general staff became a frequent target for Hitler's jibes and reproaches. Following the opening of a third front in the west in 1944, the general staff, appalled at the destruction threatening the Reich on all sides, plotted the assassination of the leader whose amateurish military intutition was (mis)directing their campaigns. On 20 July a group of Generals all but succeeded in their attempt on Hitler's life. He was saved by chance when a briefcase bomb planted at his feet during a conference at Rastenburg was accidentally removed out of effective range. His retribution was swift and ruthless. Five thousand victims of his unrestrained vengeance – including eminent and popular army leaders – were condemned to death when their part in the plot was uncovered or suspected by the SS. With Hitler in full control, the war continued on a savage and fanatical course; an unbridgeable rift now divided Commander-in-Chief from general staff with the Führer's jibes degenerating into vilification.

HITLER'S SUBORDINATES

The first of several subordinates to be awarded high office after Hitler came to power, and directly concerned with the armed services, was Hermann Goering, a flying ace of the 1914–1918 war. Goering had served Hitler and the Party more or less from the outset. Appointed Special Commissioner for Aviation in February 1933, he was to continue as Air Minister in March of the same year when his commissariat was expanded into a ministry which started secretly to organize a German air force. When this was revealed by official announcement in March 1935 Goering, with the rank of general, assumed the title Commander-in-Chief of the Air Force. He was also to benefit in stature from important political and economic planning responsibilities including the 1936 four-year plan to make Germany self-sufficient in raw materials. Promoted Generalfeldmarschall in 1938, Hitler would again reward this staunch supporter in 1940 when, following a successful conclusion to the campaign in France, the Field Marshal was created Reichsmarschall.

Pre-eminent among Goering's advisers and responsible for air force policy (opting mostly in favour of concentrated offensive support for the army) were three former Flying Corps officers: General Erhard Milch, Goering's deputy, Secretary of State for Air and Chairman of Lufthansa, who was promoted Generaloberst in November 1938; General Walter Wever, first Chief of Air Staff, transferred in 1933 from a comparable post in the Heeresamt; and Colonel (later Generaloberst) Ernst Udet, appointed Director, Technical Department of the Air Ministry in 1936 and thereafter, in 1939, Director-General, Air Force Equipment. Wever's death by accident in 1936 robbed the fledgling Luftwaffe of an able organizer and policy-maker. His successor, Generaloberst Hans Jeschonnek, appointed in 1937 from Chief of Operations (Ia) to the Air Staff, succeeded to Wever's post in February 1939. In that year Generaloberst Milch became Inspector-General of the Air Force, an appointment that he retained until January 1945. These developments allied to the rise and fall of the Luftwaffe are elaborated in Part 4. The Air Force's failure to subdue the RAF during and after the Battle of Britain, or to keep pace with foreign technical development and prevent the destruction of German industries by Anglo-US air power, was to cost Goering his credibility and Udet and Jeschonnek their lives at their own hands; Udet in 1941, Jeschonnek in 1943. Goering, in 1945, was to make an unsuccessful bid to supplant Hitler as head of state, thus prompting an outraged Führer to order the Reichsmarschall's arrest. The distinction of succeeding Hitler, albeit for as little as seven days, was instead accorded to Admiral Doenitz.

Surpassing Goering in power and influence was Reichsführer SS, Heinrich Himmler. He was appointed by Hitler in January 1929 to organize a dependable Party protection troop (SS or Schutzstaffel) responsible, above all, for the Leader's security. Hitler promoted Himmler in June 1936 to organize and preside over the centralized criminal and secret police forces. Himmler's powers were greatly extended in 1943 as Minister of the Interior. This allowed him to streamline control of the secret police (Gestapo), Party troops (SS) and the security services (Sicherheitsdienst or SD). The latter were inaugurated in 1931 by Reinhardt Heydrich (assassinated in Prague, May 1942). As a consequence of the generals' attempt on Hitler's life in July 1944, Himmler was immediately given control of military counter-intelligence, the Abwehr. With so vast an apparatus of surveillance at his command, few aspects of German life could escape the notice of Reichsführer SS. Wherever Himmler's jurisdiction held sway, at home or in the occupied

Below: An outing to Nuremberg on Party Day 1936. Members of the League of German Girls (BDM), a quasi-military organization which, like the Hitler Youth (HJ) movement, would prove a valuable source of recruitment for the services in time of war.

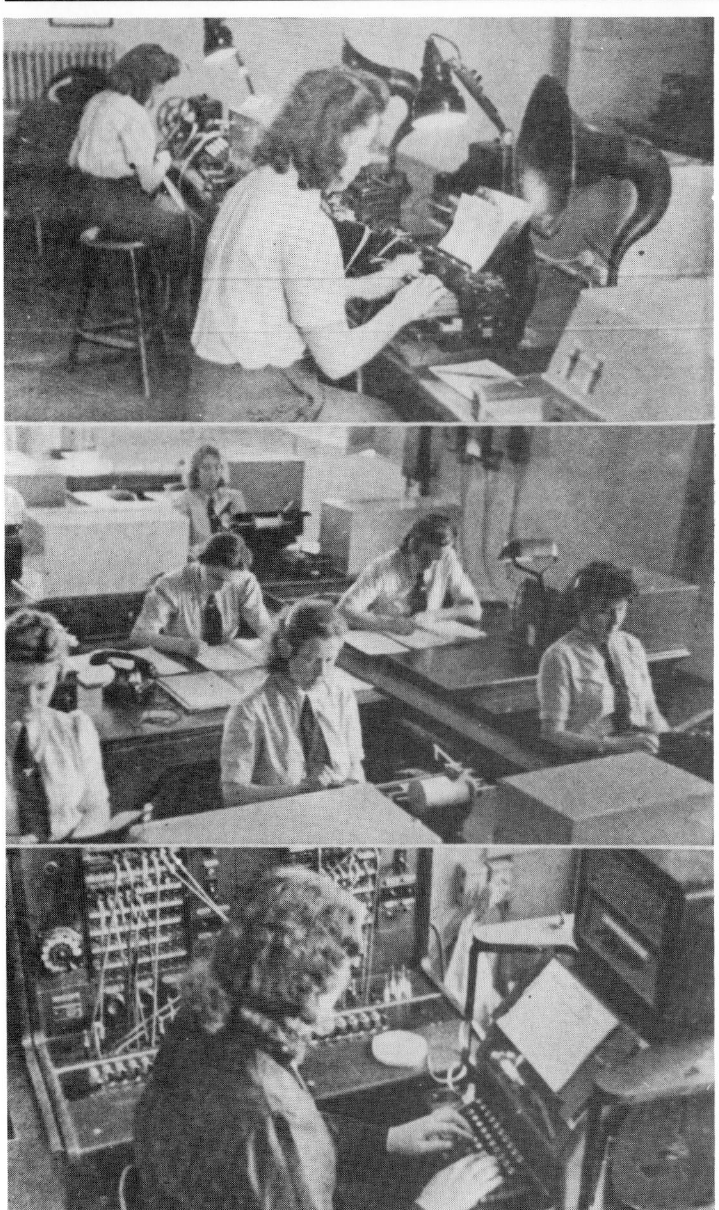

Above: Luftwaffe air defence teletype trainees and army signals personnel at work in 1941. Women served widely in flak commands, army headquarters and in industry.

territories, Jews and Slavs – Poles, Czechs and Russians – the main targets of a National Socialist obsession with racial purity, were ruthlessly repressed and annihilated. Fear and hatred of German domination spread throughout Europe. With the war in full swing, Himmler's powers continued to grow. Elevated to command of the Reserve Army in 1944 and responsible for army personnel and supplies, Himmler followed this new appointment with the active command of an army group on the Vistula – a post for which he proved totally unsuited and quickly relinquished.

Himmler's name is also linked with a 1935 development of considerable significance in subsequent German military success; the creation of an 'armed' or 'Waffen' SS. Pursuing instructions received from Hitler, and notwithstanding the Führer's 1933 pledge that the Army alone should bear arms, Himmler recruited from ideologically and physically qualified SS or others, an élite SS 'Verfügungstruppe'. The nucleus of this body (guard) was the Leibstandarte SS Adolf Hitler, established in Berlin in March 1933, with a strength of 120 men under the command of 'Sepp' Dietrich. An ex-Reichswehr general, Paul Hausser, was recruited to train and imbue the new corps with military confidence. By 1939 four motorized regiments, including the Leibstandarte, were ready to join in the invasion of Poland.

Other Reichswehr professionals joining the SS at this early stage included Majors Felix Steiner and Wilhelm Bittrich. The force expanded in later years to embody volunteer or drafted personnel from all over Europe including the eastern territories. Thus, legions of 'Germanic' Danes, Dutch, French, Flemish and east-European 'Volksdeutsche' entered into service with the SS to campaign ruthlessly alongside army formations. Swearing personal loyalty to Hitler and dedication to National Socialism, the SS Verfügungstruppe (SS-VT) was placed under operational control of the Army in 1938 and renamed Waffen SS in 1940. By June 1944, swelled by the influx of foreign recruits, it had risen in total to 21½ SS divisions serving with 257 Army divisions. SS numbers would continue to grow and ultimately reached close on a million. In the process of expansion, the Waffen SS raised fifteen exceptionally powerful armoured and motorized divisions; their military prowess and reputation as Hitler's élite guaranteed them a wide measure of respect on the battlefield. At times shouldering a disproportionately high share of the fighting, the finest of them were equal to the best of the Army formations, but SS loyalty to Hitler would prove small compensation for his military interference prompted by the, more often than not imagined, shortcomings of Prussian-German generals and the general staff.

After February 1942 armament production became the concern of Albert Speer, promoted to succeed Fritz Todt who was killed in an air crash. Speer proved a gifted organizer, advancing industrial and tank output to record levels. A former architect and town planner, he created grand city designs for Hitler, including the Chancellery. Speer was a war leader – there were others, including active army commanders – who, by disobeying orders in 1945 when Hitler was insisting that Germany be destroyed rather than surrender, were able to moderate the consequences of the Führer's increasingly fanatical directives. Other prominent leaders of the German war effort included Dr. Joseph Goebbels, Hitler's propaganda Chief, and Rudolf Hess, Hitler's deputy, who flew to Britain in 1941. Hoping to arrange a peace settlement, Hess achieved nothing. Instead he was interned and eventually sentenced to life imprisonment. Martin Bormann won distinction as the senior Party administrator, working in Berlin while the Führer spent his time at field headquarters. Bormann deputized as Party boss, organizing the civilian war effort through the work of Gauleiters whose territories or *Gaue* became Reich Defence Districts in 1942; their bosses were known as Reich Defence Commissioners. At the end of the war many of Hitler's immediate subordinates were committed for trial by an international military tribunal at Nuremberg; their minions being indicted at lesser courts elsewhere. Many of the twenty-one found guilty of war crimes at Nuremberg in September 1946 were sentenced to death, including OKW

Left: *JB*, Munich 1939, and the special issue which marked the defeat of Poland in a campaign lasting eighteen days.

chiefs Keitel and Jodl. Others received terms of imprisonment including life sentences. The SS, without exception, was accused of unmitigated terror and criminal aggression on and off the battlefield. It was condemned as a criminal organization thereby tarnishing for all time the outstanding combat achievements of the Waffen SS.

The end for Hitler came in May 1945, four months after his return to Berlin, in mid-January, from field headquarters in the west. Working from an underground bunker in the shattered city, the Führer took his own life, thereby escaping Allied retribution just hours before Russian armies closed in on the Chancellery. Goebbels died with Hitler; Himmler and Goering were taken into Allied captivity, but were also to die at their own hands and thus avoid being hanged. After more than forty years' incarceration in Spandau prison, Berlin, Hess died there in 1987. Bormann, although officially declared killed while escaping from Berlin in 1945, continues to excite Press attention, as does the fate of other

Right: *Die Wehrmacht* 1940, another special issue to celebrate the fall of France. Hitler is conferring with the Army Commander-in-Chief, von Brauchitsch (left), and chief of OKW, Keitel (right).

missing Nazi officials whose whereabouts are unknown (mostly presumed dead but some still hunted by Israeli agents if thought to be living in exile).

Armoured fighting troops of the Third Reich, the tank and motorized formations raised by the Army (and later Waffen SS) were known collectively in 1938 as Schnelltruppen (fast troops), renamed in 1943 as Panzertruppen. These troops became the decisive force in the country's aggressive expansion, and its subsequent defence. Concentrated into powerful spearheads with air force support, their moment came in September 1939 when Hitler called for the return of Danzig and transit rights across territories ceded to Poland; his demands were rejected outright. He invaded and conquered Poland, and Denmark, Norway, Holland, Belgium, France, Yugoslavia, Greece, the Baltic states and western tracts of the USSR. This run of victories fell in rapid succession, bringing much of Europe under the domination of the Third Reich, was, above all, the consequence of a new military doctrine. In daring to exploit the power and flexibility of fast armoured troops, deployed in conjunction with an equally powerful and flexible air force, Germany had created a decisive weapon out of the tank. This was due in no small measure to the persistent initiative of panzer generals, especially Heinz Guderian, who inspired a generation of gifted professional soldiers to combine traditional tactical skills with new armoured (and aviation) technology. German superiority on the battlefield was to prevail until such time as opponents with greater material resources could correct their mistakes and, by the narrowest of margins, reverse the situation.

The German Army of 1939 was otherwise not dissimilar to its traditional rivals in Europe, being largely infantry based and horse-drawn. Its overwhelming advantage, strengthened by a proficient general staff, lay in well-trained tank crews, gunners, signallers, engineers, motorized infantry and support services teamed for self-contained combat in co-operation with the air force. Early German victories which pioneered the flexible deployment of fast troops to conduct offensive operations were christened *Blitzkrieg* by the Press. In more analytical vein we might regard them as prime examples of co-ordinated action by land and air forces working to out-manoeuvre their opponents and defeat them by superior pace and power. Yet for all their apparent conclusiveness, as successive chapters will testify, these early victories would yield no lasting profit for the victors.

FACING UP TO THE OPPOSITION

German success with the panzer arm inevitably provoked countertactics and weapons. Pre-war anti-tank schemes, especially those of Anglo-French origin, relied for effect upon fixed installations; they thus erred in one vital respect: they failed to provide mobile forces to complement their static defences. By not possessing mobile forces capable of responding flexibly to the panzer threat – which was totally misjudged by Allied military commanders – the Allied armies were to suffer grievous consequences. Concrete bunkers and barricades shared defensive lines with impromptu devices such as flame-traps and flame-barrages. These were installed by the thousand in areas threatened by invasion – for instance the land frontier between France and Germany protected by The Maginot Line, or the south coast of England in the summer of 1940 when invasion was expected hourly. Such measures were intended to restrict panzer movement, allowing anti-tank squads to get to close quarters and artillery fire to destroy immobile targets. In the event the French defences were rapidly outflanked and the viability of British schemes went unchallenged after the German invasion plan 'Sea-lion' was abandoned late in 1940. In the east, the Red Army proposed the same solution as Britain and France. By siting minefields and earthworks, digging ditches and erecting barricades to create tank-proof localities, they hoped to channel panzer units into zones where the defence could concentrate against them. Such rudimentary measures would, it was hoped, win time in which more efficacious methods of combating the panzer menace could be developed. Anti-tank armouries in 1939 – and in this the German Army was no exception – were poorly served by small-calibre, 2pdr or equivalent 37mm weapons. Yet the inexhaustible energy of ordnance staffs, searching for effective weapons with which to counter armoured assault, would be rewarded by noteworthy progress in Britain, the United States, Germany and the Soviet Union; all, however belatedly, producing outstanding contributions to anti-tank technology.

Above: Service chiefs pictured in *Signal*, 1940, conferring over Hitler's map table. From left to right: Reichsmarschall Goering, Hitler and Keitel.

Significant trends in this sphere of design, upon which came to depend, if not the outcome of the war, then certainly a large measure of Allied (and German) success in defeating armoured attacks after 1942, are evident in several critical developments, one of the most significant being the self-propelled anti-tank gun. A German innovation, attributable directly to von Manstein, the mounting of direct-fire artillery weapons (7.5cm and later 8.8cm guns) on tank chassis, thereby improving rapid deployment against selected targets (*see* Part 2, Sturmgeschütze), would be matched by the Red Army who showed a remarkable capacity for employing even heavy-calibre guns up to 15.3cm in the role of tank destroyers; a weapons development programme in which Anglo-US ordnance teams would follow suit. Self-propelled anti-tank artillery would consequently evolve in a wide range of models and variants, entering service with all combatant forces.

Artillery improvements to strengthen the anti-tank protection of infantry would be marked by the introduction of British 6- and 17-pounder weapons which, combined with developments in armour-piercing technology, would halt panzer attacks at ever-increasing ranges, posing a threat even to the Tiger at 500 yards and notably hampering panzer operations in North Africa and subsequently in Italy and Europe. When fitted into Shermans and Valentines the 17-pdr would prove a formidable opponent as would the more powerful 9cm gun mounted by the US Ordnance Department on Sherman tank chassis and issued in 1944 as the M10 Tank Destroyer. No less potent in defeating panzer attacks would be an entirely new class of weapon modelled upon the 'Bazooka', a shoulder-fired 2.36in rocker-launcher introduced by the US Army in time for Operation 'Torch', the invasion of North Africa in November 1942. This extremely clever device, combining rocket propulsion with a new type of warhead to create a portable anti-tank weapon of undeniable power, would spawn a host of variants both Allied and German. Their distribution to forward companies would add immeasurably to the confidence of infantry expecting assault by armoured fighting vehicles. Easy to manufacture, like the *Panzerfaust* which would move significantly into this category in 1944, hand-launched rockets together with airborne systems were to prove indispensable in anti-tank combat.

Below: Berlin, 1945; a chilling reminder of the consequences of Hitler's warmongering. The victorious Red Army unfurls its banner over a ruined city. 'No bomb will ever fall here,' Goering had boasted in 1940.

Infantry defence would focus otherwise upon a variety of purpose-built and extemporary weapons including mines, grenades and projectiles, certain traditional forms of which could be extended in range by use in conjunction with projectors; the British projector infantry anti-tank (PIAT) was one such device.

But the greatest German respect for the opposition it was to encounter on an ever-increasing scale after 1942 was to be reserved for Allied air power. This weapon above all was to reverse the tide of panzer success, highlighting in the process an astonishing flaw in German planning – one no less deep-seated in its implications than the complacency exhibited by Allied commands in pre-1939 appreciations of German progress in armoured and airborne warfare. Hitler's inability as supreme commander to recognize the underlying strength of the opposition and his failure to appreciate the true potential of air power – matched by an equally evident failure of the high command when confronted by air force demands for more and better equipment to see further than army/air operations – was to bring these services to their knees. The army that had achieved outstanding success in applying new technology and tactical innovation in swift moving campaigns would discover all too late that its days were numbered by opponents purposefully and methodically exploiting more potent developments. Nevertheless, German progress in the design and construction of armoured fighting vehicles, in particular the Panther and its heavy counterpart the Tiger, both armed with high-velocity guns, is immediately traceable in the armoured establishment of every modern army. Equally influential in setting the trend of post-war armoured technology was panzer force success with armoured personnel carriers and, at a tactical level, the battle group integration of all arms into flexible, self-contained units.

This legacy, like that of the Luftwaffe's pioneering of ground attack, air reconnaissance and transportation methods to confer exceptional mobility on ground forces, is as relevant today in planning mobile operations in the harsh conditions of a nuclear age as in any previous era when the principles underlying the panzer revolution – decentralization of initiative, speed and flexibility in fire power and manoeuvre – proved indispensable to any would-be ruler of the battlefield.

Part 1. Restoring mobility to the German Army

1. 'Other things being equal, the most mobile side must win.' (J. F. C. Fuller, 1917)

The story of German involvement with armour leading to the creation of a panzer force, the armoured fighting troops of the Third Reich, can be said to have started during the First World War when the 'tank' idea was first formulated. A war of movement started by the German Army in August 1914 had brought the Kaiser's armies sweeping through Belgium and France to within fifty miles of Paris. Stalemated by September, both sides lay deadlocked. Lines of entrenched infantry seeking protection from the shattering effects of artillery fire, stretched from the Channel coast to Switzerland. Artillery and machine-gun dominated the battlefield. Sited in heavily protected fieldworks, so thickly secured with barbed wire entanglements that 'daylight could scarcely be seen', the machine-gun cut deep swathes in assaulting infantry. Offensives stumbled to a halt, casualties reached appalling levels.

A solution to the problem was put forward by a British Officer, Colonel E. D. Swinton, serving with the British Expeditionary Force. In a memorandum to the War Office during the closing months of the year, the Colonel recommended the construction and employment of a fighting vehicle; its purpose being to combat machine-gun nests and break the trench deadlock. Tracked for mobility, constructed of armour plating to withstand rifle or automatic fire, the revolutionary machine would open a path for the infantry by flattening the wire and crushing the machine-gun. Mobility would be restored – at infantry pace. Looking to the future, Colonel Swinton and later British tank enthusiasts envisaged the tank speeded-up, reinforced with infantry and artillery and deployed in mobile formations to the extent where armies, corps and divisions became the decisive weapon in land warfare. By April 1916, following an intensive period of trial and experiment in Britain, 150 28-ton machines, to be known in the interest of security as 'tanks', were ready for use or in production. Two companies each of twenty-five Mk I vehicles were sent to the Western Front. In mid-September they were used by British Fourth Army (Rawlinson) in action at Flers; of fifty machines on establishment, eighteen finally taking part in support of an infantry attack. Twelve months later three tank brigades each with two battalions had been formed.

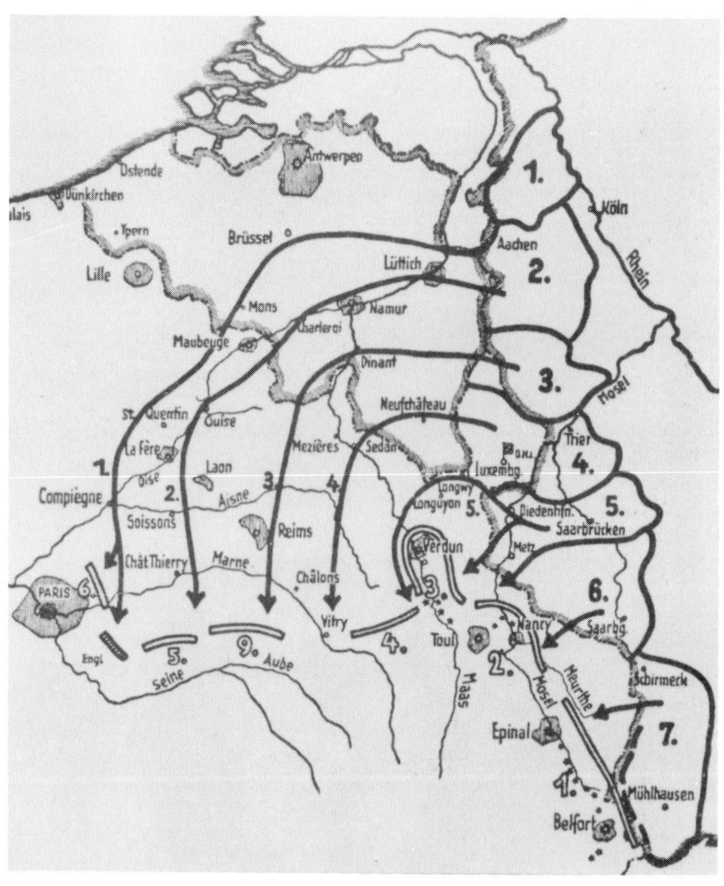

Disappointment attended the early efforts of the British pioneers when tank attacks in appalling conditions slewed to a halt. The lumbering steel giants working in two and threes impeded by shell craters, hampered by thick mud and heavy rain, quickly bogged down or otherwise failed to keep their schedules. At this early stage the tank idea might well have foundered, but a British success eighteen months later

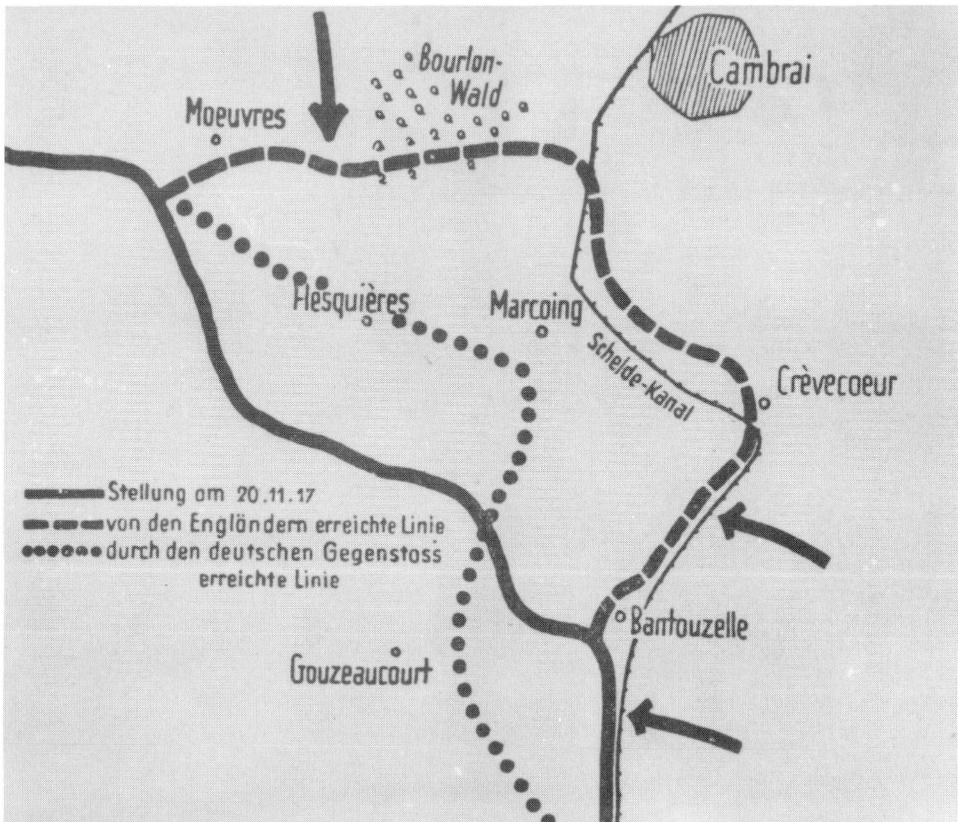

Right: Cambrai, November 1917, was the first true tank offensive of the war. It was launched by the British Fourth Army led by Rawlinson and was intended to break the trench deadlock. After gaining ground the British discovered they lacked the means to exploit it and quickly forfeited much of it to German counter-attacks.

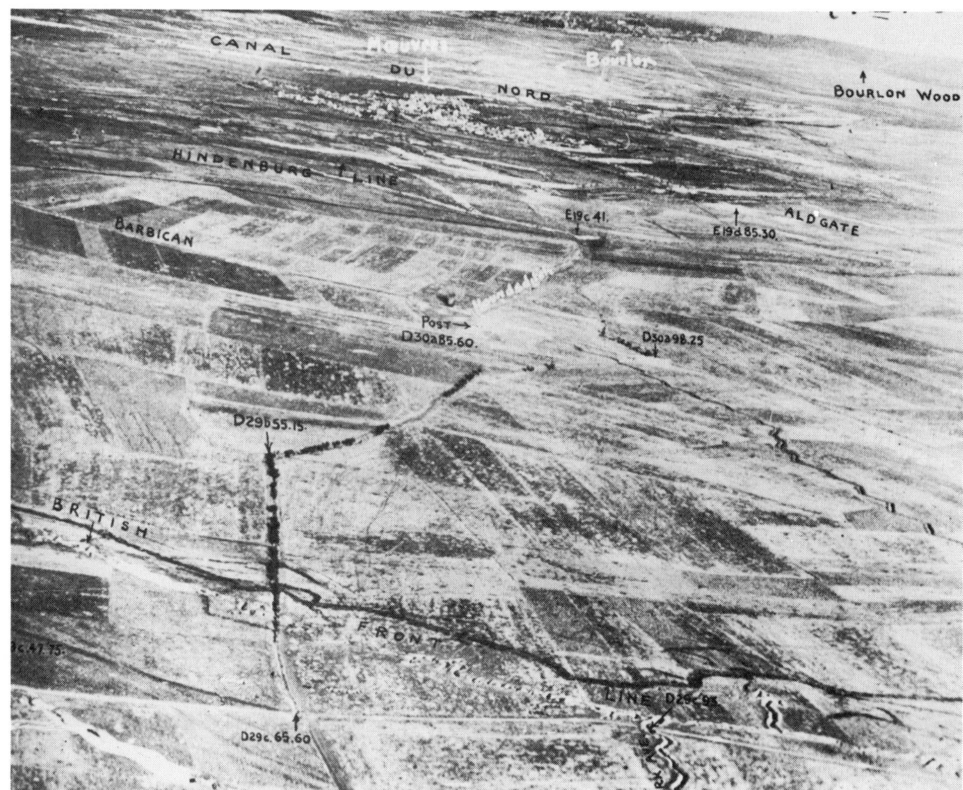

Right: This reconnaissance shot of the Cambrai battlefield reveals the British tank objectives. The Hindenburg Line was a stretch of concrete and steel shelters secured with barbed wire.

Left: Winter 1914 and Germany's railways transport the seven armies considered necessary by Count Alfred von Schlieffen for the decisive offensive against France. His plan envisaged the German Army investing Paris and trapping French forces against the Swiss frontier. The bold scheme failed when von Kluck, commanding First Army on the outer wing of the offensive, swung his troops off line and east of Paris in order to maintain contact with second army on his left. Soon the battle lines were drawn and the war became one of stalemated trench warfare.

Left: Amiens, August 1918; the tanks went in again. These tanks, visible next to uncompleted sections of the Hindenburg Line, breached the German lines in October.

Left: Lorry-borne infantry reinforcements for the shattered German front.

in a new tank offensive showed what could be achieved. Success in November 1917 lay to a great extent in the thorough preparations carried out by the newly appointed Chief of Staff of the Tank Corps, Lieutenant-Colonel J. F. C. Fuller. Using improved tanks *en masse* for the first time in history and fighting over ground specially chosen for the attack, objectives were clearly defined and accompanying infantry drilled in tactical support. In this way, on 20 November at Cambrai, four hundred or so Mk IVs of the British Army broke the German line in a surprise move. The planners' reward was a clear indication of the future role of armour.

German Second Army (Marwitz), defending this sector of the heavily protected Hindenburg Line, were stunned and demoralized by the appearance of tanks flattening their wire and, with infantry following in file close behind, thrusting towards their artillery positions. But the breach remained unexploited and the true fruits of the offensive, the paralysing effect of armoured troops driving deep into rearward areas, interrupting lines of communication, isolating and destroying headquarters and nerve-centres, was lost. Whereas future Allied tank offensives would employ modified Mk IVs as light pursuit tanks to move infantry and supplies forward in support of fighting tanks, no such vehicles were available in 1917. Instead, unprotected cavalry falling inevitably to the machine-guns, demonstrated their declining powers on the battlefield.

Allied plans for 1918 and 1919, however, were to develop on the basis of an all-mechanized force, initiated by Colonel (later Major-General) Fuller and elaborated by other creative British proponents of the new weapon, notably Captain (later General) Gifford le Q. Martel and Captain (Sir Basil) Liddell Hart. Fuller's proposals and his later writing would do much to influence post-war, particularly German, theories and practice of armoured warfare, but sadly for him and the defence of the west in general his ideas were to be largely disregarded by the British military hierarchy whose enthusiasm for the tank was to degenerate into complacency. Meanwhile, light tanks, a British-designed 14-ton Whippet and later the French 6-ton Renault FT – the first with a revolving turret – both intended for an exploitation role on the battlefield, were leaving the drawing-board for action in 1918. German counter-attacks starting on 30 November but without the benefit of armoured fighting vehicles, had recovered much of the ground lost to British initiative at Cambrai. During the counter-offensive a hundred or more tanks were retrieved by Second Army and, with some French machines taken later, prepared for German service.

In France, where the authorities were unaware of British progress in mobile technology, armoured fighting vehicles were evolving at two levels: a heavy trench-crossing vehicle, the 17-ton Schneider, fostered commercially by Colonel J. E. Estienne, and a competitor sponsored by the French General Staff, the 23-ton Saint-Chamond. The first of these French machines saw action at Berry-au-Bac on 16 April 1917, but neither design was a success. By agreement between the Allies, it was left to the Renault Company to build the first effective French tank, the Light FT, of which several variants would remain in service for more than two decades, some finding their way into both German and foreign service after the fall of France in 1940 (*see* Part 2, satellite armour). The immediate reaction of the German High Command to the British and French tank attacks was to study and improve anti-tank measures. Trenches were widened and the first infantry anti-tank weapon, a 13mm Mauser (tank) rifle, was swiftly designed and produced. A light mortar designed to fire at low angles, and armour-piercing shells for use by the field artillery were also developed. Within the Imperial War Ministry the Allgemeine Kriegsabteilung 7, Verkehrswesen (A7V) was set up in 1916 to advise on the design and construction of tanks and armoured vehicles, and British and French machines captured at Cambrai and Berry were studied, repaired and pressed into service. Up to that time neither the Austrian nor German governments had displayed much interest in 'gun vehicles running on moving tracks' as proposed as early as 1911 by the Austrian, Leutnant Burstyn.

The first example of A7V departmental work was a 32-ton turretless machine, based on a Holt tractor, with a crew of eighteen, six machine-guns and a 5.7cm gun mounted forward. In December 1917 twenty of these were completed and formed into two companies. In March 1918 this all-German tank detachment, deployed in conjunction with four companies of captured vehicles, mainly British Mk IVs, went into action with air support at St-Quentin. The A7V design was unsatisfactory at trench crossing, and after these wartime operations the Germans had no further use for it, but their experience of army-air co-operation – no less progressive than that of the Allies' – proved timely in focusing General Staff attention on critical developments. It was left chiefly to British tank pioneers to demonstrate the true value of tanks in breakthrough and, to a lesser extent, exploitation battles with a great Allied offensive in August 1918. Encouraged by results with sixty Mk V tanks introduced against German Second Army at Hamel on 4 July, 500 mainly British tanks, including 96 Whippets, were concentrated at Amiens on 8 August for a renewed assault eastwards against the Hindenburg Line. The Allied plan of attack, based on a scheme of Colonel Fuller's, was to push improved fighting tanks, Mk VI infantry- (machine-gun) carrying tanks and lightly armoured exploitation Whippets deep into the German lines, disrupting communications and destroying headquarters. Specially designed Mk IX supply tanks, projected as early as 1916, remained factory bound, their place being taken by modified Mk IVs. An armoured car battalion was to be made available to maintain the tempo of the attack.

The great Allied tank offensive unrolled on 8 August 1918. Supported by bombing and strafing attacks – much as earlier in the year the Germans had supported their March offensive at St-Quentin – the Royal Flying Corps neutralizing the defence with machine-guns and bombs, the tank force ripped a ten-mile breach in the defenders' positions. In the words of General Ludendorff, 'August the 8th was a black day for the German Army.' Least satisfactory were the results achieved by the light tanks committed under command of the cavalry. Pushing forward after the breakthrough to a depth of eight miles, they were frequently pinned down and halted by heavy counter-fire. Nevertheless, a single Whippet handled with much verve achieved spectacular results, shooting up artillery batteries, cavalry patrols, barracks, motor transport and more. The armoured cars, four-wheeled Austins with twin machine-gun turrets, proved their worth in dashing sorties against rear headquarters. Ludendorff records the German plight. 'British Fourth Army broke deep into our front, divisional staffs were surprised in divisional headquarters by hostile tanks. Our divisions allowed themselves to be completely overrun, six or seven divisions of good fighting troops were completely smashed. At many points officers lost control.'

German morale now evinced signs of collapse. Within three months the war was at an end, the Allied offensive at Amiens having contributed significantly to German defeat. The Treaty of Versailles imposed harsh conditions on Germany. No tanks were permitted to the Reichsheer, the army of a new (Weimar) administration, no General Staff and no heavy artillery. All German research in the important field of tank development was brought to a halt. The Imperial Air Force was ordered to disband. Britain and France, on the other hand, and indeed the United States too, in the person of Lieutenant-Colonel George Patton who, from January to September 1918 (with British and French equipment), had formed and operated an independent tank force on British lines, renewed their research into the capabilities of the new weapon. All had gained a wealth of experience in wartime operations, not only in the construction of tanks and their tactical employment with air support, but also in wireless control of tank formations introduced by the British Army with mixed results as early as 1916. Plans for mechanized infantry were continuously formulated.

Ground-attack bombers and fighters, including forward-firing and lightly armoured models, had demonstrated their merits in action on both sides and if, as was the case with wireless, considerably short of perfection, had progressed to a point of departure for the future. The antecedents of *Blitzkrieg* and developments associated in the post-war years with new weapons and technology – culminating in an irresistibly powerful German fusion of armoured fighting vehicles and ground-attack aircraft – are all too evident in the great confrontations of March and August 1918. In amalgamating foreign innovation with tactical tradition and creative power, turning the resulting weapons system to sound operative account, the German Army of 1939 would be first to capitalize on 1914–18 experience.

In Britain the tank idea continued to be fostered by Major-General Fuller and those who succeeded him in command of the Tank Corps or at the War Office; British state of the art advancing in 1927, 1931 and 1934 with experiments at brigade level on Salisbury Plain – the learning process promoted by tank and motorized infantry exercises and radio control of tank formations. New British contributions to the theory of armoured warfare appeared in works published by Captain (Sir Basil) Liddell Hart and Major-General Fuller. The views of these gifted British theorists concerning the viability of long-range operations helped immeasurably in shaping post-war thinking; but nowhere would their ideas make more impression or gain wider acceptance than in Germany, albeit at first limited to a narrow circle of professional officers prominent among whom was the young Captain Heinz Guderian, generously acknowledged by colleagues as creator of the panzer force.

British endeavours during the post-war period would lead to no more than the creation of two incomplete armoured divisions – light all-tank formations intended for the dual purpose of strategic reconnaissance and exploitation; one at home, the other in Egypt. A brigade of 24-ton 'I' tanks, 'Matildas', was also raised, for infantry support at walking pace. Professional circles in Britain no less than in France and the United States, and by no means excluding Germany, where conservative General Staff views on the primacy of infantry held sway, allowed infantry tanks and the infantry-support idea to dominate strategic and tactical thinking. Although presaged by Allied wartime experience and post-war experiments, opportunities for infantry-bound armies to create mobile forces capable of independent, that is to say self-contained, action through the inclusion of all arms in a fighting formation were neglected. Not only was this so in Britain and France, but also in Russia where embryonic tank and air forces were under development. The Russian General Staff, disposed towards new ideas under its chief of staff, Mikhail Tukhachevsky, later Deputy Commisar for War, was quick to recognize the growing importance of aircraft as a means of combating tanks. But Tukhachevsky, with other marshals, generals and brigadiers 'disappeared' in the Stalinist purges of the Red Army. Not before 1942 and the Battle of Stalingrad would the Red Army prove itself theoretically and materially ready to contend with high-powered aggression of the kind that it faced in 1941.

Above: Ground-attack aircraft from both sides caused havoc among troop concentrations and trench systems.

Above: An infantryman writing of his experiences of trench warfare on the Somme in 1917 spoke of German positions so thickly protected by barbed wire that daylight was scarcely to be seen.

Right: German ground-attack squadrons (Schlachtgruppen), flying the Halberstadt two-seater, played a significant role in assisting tank and infantry attacks.

2. 'If the tanks succeed, then victory follows.' (Guderian, 1937)

Left: By March 1918 the German A7V tank, mounting a 5.7cm gun and manned by a crew of eighteen, was to be seen in action at St. Quentin alongside captured British and French machines.

Only in Germany, encouraged by Hitler's arrival on the scene in 1933, were revolutionary military ideas to germinate into a strike force of exceptional power. Forbidden all but the most limited of resources in the aftermath of defeat, the German Army's Truppenamt, a substitute for the forbidden General Staff (responsible to the Commander-in-Chief of the Reichsheer, General Hans von Seeckt) was determined to circumvent by every possible means, Allied intentions of destroying German capacity for military resurgence. Concealing armament stocks and production centres from Versailles 'observers', von Seeckt and his colleagues resolved secretly to build a new German Army in which motorization would play a crucial part and foreign ideas particularly in the employment of tanks would be most enthusiastically reviewed and adopted.

Captain Heinz Guderian, encouraged in 1922 by the Inspector of Motor Transport Troops, General von Tschischwitz, to study motor repair and workshop practice in the Motorized Transport Department of the Inspectorate of Transport Troops (In 6) to which Guderian was seconded, was one of many pioneering spirits who in the next decade would evolve plans for creating a new German armoured force, despite hostility of the kind expressed by Tschischwitz's successor as Inspector, Colonel von Natzmer – 'To hell with fighting, you're supposed to carry flour.' Guderian moved out of the department in 1924 transferring to Stettin where he instructed staff candidates in military history. From practical understanding of motorization, through lecturing on tactics and in due course leading armoured formations in the field, Guderian's enthusiasm more than any other would motivate a generation of panzer leaders. Promoted major in 1927, Guderian's work as a staff instructor was followed by employment in the troop transport department of the Truppenamt until 1931. Meanwhile, in a notable change of emphasis inaugurated by von Vollard-Bockelburg, appointed (third) Inspector of Kraftfahrtruppen in 1926, succeeding von Natzmer, no time was lost in broadening Kraftfahrtruppen into Kraftfahr(kampf)truppen.

Left: Dummy tanks taking part in secret training sessions in Germany, 1929. Made of wood and steel, these 'vehicles' drew their motive power from Austin Seven-type runabouts formed into Motor Transport Battalions. Such events gave rise to Polish worries as to the true nature of the panzer threat.

Extending the scope of his duties to lecture on tank tactics, Guderian studied and reported on progress in foreign armies; made visits abroad, digested published works including British training manuals and worked out new ideas. It was during this period of the late 1920s that the structure and handling of a panzer division firmly crystallized in Guderian's mind. From teaching military history for three years (especially Napoleon's campaign of 1806 – the one in which Berlin was occupied) to staff candidates and then as tactical instructor on courses organized for the Army by the Fahrlehrstab (motor transport instruction staff) at Döberitz, forty miles west of Berlin, Guderian progressed to practical application.

Commanding No. 3 Motor Transport Battalion at Berlin in 1931 – one of the seven allowed to Germany under 'Versailles' – Major Guderian used dummy tanks and wooden artillery to represent fighting vehicles and anti-tank guns, experimenting with various tactical configurations. Similar work was undertaken in other 'transport' battalions doubling as combat units; No. 6 at Münster, for instance, where Captain Walther Nehring commanded No. 1 (motor infantry) Company. During 1931 command and staff changes instituted by von Hammerstein, one of von Seeckt's successors, laid the foundations of a tank force that would enjoy outstanding success in the conflict to come. In April of that year Guderian was promoted colonel and posted as chief of staff to a new Inspector of Kraftfahr(kampf)truppen, General Oswald Lutz. Lutz had succeeded yet another incumbent at the head of In 6, General Otto von Stülpnagel; Vollard-Bockelburg having moved up to promote army motorization. Major Walther Nehring, drafted to the staff of In 6 to serve as Guderian's deputy, arrived soon afterwards, replacing vehicle design pioneer, Major Werner Kempf. Kempf was posted to Munich as OC, No. 7 Motor Transport Battalion. These three officers – Lutz, Guderian and Nehring – were to prove zealous proponents of the tank idea, ably supported by like-minded staff; Captains Hermann Breith, Chales de Beaulieu, Ritter von Hauenschild and Walter Hünersdorff all energetically promoted German involvement in armoured technology – creating step by step a panzer force as yet little in evidence, untried and unbloodied, but destined in the space of ten years to dominate Europe.

In November 1933 training courses originating in 1925 and progressively expanded were established at a new school in the garrison area of Wûnsdorf-Zossen, thirty miles south of the capital. This Panzer School 1 was the first of many to be established over the next fourteen years. Tank-gunnery was taught separately at Putlos, a training facility in Holstein on the Baltic coast north of Hamburg. Ironically, by encouraging the German High Command to collaborate in establishing secret experimental stations at Kazan and Lipetsk deep in the Russian hinterland, the technical development of German tanks and aircraft was promoted by the Soviet Union as early as 1926. Both stations were surrounded by ample space for training and development and the arrangement was to prove advantageous to officers of both countries, but it was brought to an end by Hitler in 1933. At Kazan, otherwise known as 'Kama' from its proximity to the river of that name, General Lutz, one of the key figures, founded a programme for evolving and testing a new generation of German (and Russian) tanks and aircraft. Among future panzer army commanders to benefit from training at Kazan were Ritter von Thoma and Josef Harpe; von Thoma rising to lead the Condor Legion's tank component in Spain in 1936 before promotion to Waffen general (Schnelletruppen) 1940, command of DAK and briefly GOC, Panzer Army Afrika in 1942. Generaloberst Harpe was to become GOC, Fourth Panzer Army in 1944. Wilhelm Bittrich, another student at Kama, was destined for command of an SS panzer korps. The crucial aircraft and aviation technology upon which a future Luftwaffe would find strength and direction was pursued equally enthusiastically at Lipetsk where many of the Luftwaffe's future leaders contributed to the process of founding a new air force. Aviation developments are elaborated in Part 4.

In Berlin during the 1920s, when Captain Heinz Guderian (major, 1927), destined for the highest office as a panzer leader, was going about his instructional duties with the

Kraftfahrlehrstab, the Heereswaffenamt had placed contracts with private firms not only for new tanks, but for halftrack vehicles to move artillery and assist the mobility of other panzer support arms. When the projected tanks – Panzerkampfwagen (Pz Kpfw), intended for trial at Kazan, a 23-ton medium machine armed with a 7.5cm gun and a lighter model fitted with a 3.7cm gun proved slow to evolve, a Carden-Loyd chassis was indirectly purchased from Britain and taken as the basis for a new 6-ton training tank, the Pz Kpfw I built by Krupp. A second 10-ton vehicle, Pz Kpfw II, equipped with a 2cm gun and coaxial machine-gun was developed and manufactured by MAN. In 1934 these new armoured fighting vehicles, the first of their kind, would go to equip panzer regiments forming at Zossen and Ohrdruf, but when establishments failed, tanks were supplemented by tractors used for training. Within the year, six panzer regiments (four battalions of four companies, 32 Pz Kpfw each) – paired in panzer brigades – were raised and incorporated into three panzer divisions.

Recruits were provided initially by the cavalry, an arm of service with its own ideas on the role of army motorization and one that would raise partially armoured 'light' divisions for cavalry tasks. Contrary to expectation, the production of halftracks, in 1-, 6-, 12- and 18-ton models, crucial to the mobility of the supporting arms of the panzer force, soon lagged behind schedule. Shortages in this and other vital areas of motorization, particularly in the provision of cross-country transport for the infantry, would weigh heavily against future success in trackless terrain – such as might be expected in Russia. Better progress was recorded in the important sphere of training. At Wünsdorf-Zossen instructional courses pioneered by the Kraftfahrlehrstab were expanded by General Lutz and the first 'research and technical exercises', commencing as early as 1932, continued to be held annually. Theoretical knowledge benefited from publication of *Der Kampfwagenkrieg*, an Austrian study of tank tactics. The author of this work, General Ludwig Ritter von Eimannsberger, recommended the massing of tank wedges at the decisive point (*Schwerpunkt*) of the battle. A more significant contribution, to warfare in general, *Command of the Air*, by Italian air force General Giulio Douhet, pointed the way to the strike role of the bomber. Douhet also argued the case for the air force being used as a weapon to break civilian morale by intensive raids against population centres.

Above: General Heinz Guderian was responsible more than any other individual for the training and subsequent success of the panzer force. He served in Signals from 1914 to 1918, and lectured on mobility from 1924 to 1929; in 1931 he was appointed Chief of Staff, Kraftfahrkampftruppen. He followed theory with practice and commanded XIV Panzer Corps in February 1938. In November 1938 he became Chief of Mobile Troops, then led XIX Panzer Corps in 1939 before Pz-Gruppe Guderian was formed in 1940. In 1941, until Hitler placed him on the reserve list, he was GOC, Second Panzer Army. Recalled in February 1943, Guderian was made Inspector-General of Armoured Troops; his last appointment was Chief of the General Staff in July 1944.

With Hitler installed as Chancellor in 1933 and taking a special interest in tank development, the year to come would record a milestone in the progress of armoured troops. Visiting the army depot at Kummersdorf where new equipment, including tanks, was displayed and exercised in conjunction with infantry and aircraft, the future C-in-C of the Army was impressed to the point of declaring. 'That is what I want – and that is what I will have.' Twelve months later, on 15 October 1935, the vital step taking Hitler on the high road to power followed the conclusion of annual exercises – the first in which an embryo panzer division (von Weichs) was put through its paces – a panzertruppen command was established. The date is regarded in the German Army as the armoured troops' birthday; the new panzer command (Lutz) absorbing the old Kraftfahrlehrstab, cavalry and motorized infantry (Schützen) – the future panzer grenadiers. The event was significant not only in creating a nucleus of armoured forces for future offensive tasks, but also in affirming recognition at the highest political level of strategic potential in mechanization – a potency by no means universally accepted among the upper echelons of the German military establishment. The Army Chief of Staff, General Ludwig Beck, a former cavalry officer, was only one of many senior and influential officers not wholly in tune with Lutz and Guderian's ideas on the independent role of armoured divisions in battle; a situation not unknown abroad where horse and army were to prove inseparable.

For example, the position of tank development and employment in the French Army, the largest and potentially most powerful army in Europe (4.4 million, 1939), is revealed in the French General Staff's handbook on tank warfare published in 1930. In this work, tank formations

Above: Colonel (later General) Walther Nehring served Guderian as his deputy on the staff of the Kraftfahrkampftruppen in 1931, a partnership which continued into the war. Pictured here serving with Panzer Gruppe Guderian in 1940 (Guderian on the right and C-in-C von Brauchitsch on the left), he went on to command 18th Panzer Division that year. In 1942, serving with DAK, he was promoted to General after the fall of Tobruk. He subsequently served in the east as GOC, XXIV Panzer Corps (1943), GOC, Fourth Panzer Army (1944) and finally, in March 1945, as GOC, First Panzer Army.

are relegated to an infantry support role. A contrary stand was taken by Colonel Charles de Gaulle. Far-sighted like Lutz, Guderian and Fuller, De Gaulle realized that independent tank divisions would become a decisive weapon of the future, but not until the autumn of 1939 did the French Army actively set about establishing *divisions cuirassées* with tank brigades of 174 tanks, motorized infantry, artillery, armoured cars and motor cycles organized on German lines. Until then the French Army of the 1930s placed its faith in three 'armoured' divisions of a different kind; motorized cavalry formations (*divisions légères mécaniques*), each with a strength of about 170 tanks. In the forthcoming Battle of France, three *divisions cuirassées,* three *divisions légères mécaniques* and a handful of independent tank brigades dispersed over a wide front would be divided in support of infantry. The 31-ton Char B, at the core of French armoured formations in which the 11-ton Hotchkiss and 20-ton Somua predominated, would nevertheless prove superior in construction to German types while at the same time, the Somua was better armed (4.7cm) and more numerous than the Pz Kpfw III (3.7cm) deployed in the panzer divisions. A fourth, incomplete, *division cuirassée,* raised under de Gaulle after the commencement of hostilities, would serve with equally little influence on the course of events.

German armoured progress in the thirties, in contrast to developments abroad where, in Britain for instance, General Staff orthodoxy coupled with financial constraints continued to inhibit evolution of the tank idea, was rapid, and in emphasizing the need for balance in structuring armoured formations, distinctively different. Guderian only hints at this in his preface to the most important and frequently reprinted German work on the subject, Fritz Heigl's 1938 *Handbook of the Tank*: 'The difference of opinion concerning the value of tanks and their employment in battle is greater than ever,' he writes. 'Memories of the battles of the First World War [a reference to the origination of the tank in support of infantry] are now fading. The most recent fighting in Spain so far as this concerns tanks, was carried out on a relatively limited field and on too small a scale to allow accurate assessments to be made.' In referring to Spain (map 1), where companies of German and Italian tanks assisted General Franco's Nationalist army to defeat Soviet-supported Republican forces, Guderian is deceptively indifferent to opportunities for the collective training of tanks, infantry and aircraft.

The Spanish civil war in fact provided a German expeditionary force, the Condor Legion, with immensely beneficial training facilities. Flying old and new machines, improving ground-attack methods and equipment, Luftwaffe tactics and technology in later European campaigns would owe much to the unhappy Spanish conflict; air force action in particular illuminating a terrifying trend towards area bombing and the unconstrained use of air-power. Fulfilling its first major engagement in support of a Nationalist offensive against Bilbao on the northern front in April 1937, the Condor Legion laid waste the town of Guernica five miles behind the front and midway to Bilbao. Co-operating with White brigades seeking to breach and outflank a determined Republican defence, the Legion set out to inhibit rearward movement. Waves of Ju 52 transports, doubling as bombers until such time as the He 111 would arrive in squadron service, co-ordinated their attacks with Italian formations supporting the offensive with Savoia Marchetti S 81s flying under Legion command.

Guernica's importance to both sides lay in its road and rail connections to and from the front and its position on a river crossing at a point where Republican troops threatened with envelopment might be expected to slip the net and regroup. For two hours or more, led by He 111s of the Legion's bombing trials squadron, thermite incendiary and high-explosive missiles rained down upon the town, reducing historic timbered buildings to smoking ruins, destroying the railway station and blocking all movement for 24 hours – but leaving the vital river crossing in the suburbs undamaged. The devastation revealed to journalists was exploited to outstanding propaganda effect by Republicans alleging terror bombing as the prime motive for the attack. The incident provoked world-wide comment and diplomatic intervention by the British and French governments. Responsibility for the Luftwaffe-directed attack lay with Legion commanders, General-Major Sperrle and Chief of Staff Oberst Wolfram Freiherr von Richthofen. Von Richthofen had previously served at home and in Spain, leading air force technical research projects – and would eventually continue as the Legion's commanding officer. Both they and their accusers would be familiar with Douhet-inspired philosophy that wars could be won by inducing terror in the enemy's civilian population. Whatever the truth of the incident, the plight of Guernica's civilian population would be repeated a thousand-fold as bombing of this description, elevated into a strategy distinct from that of *Blitzkrieg*, spread across Europe giving rise to multi-national research and development programmes seeking ever new and efficient means of delivering incendiary and high-explosive material against area targets.

In attacking Guernica so ruthlessly, and it was not the only Spanish town to suffer uncompromising bombing attacks on this scale, the Luftwaffe gave notice that in exploiting military opportunities civilian centres could no longer expect exclusion; henceforth all cities could expect to become front-line cities. The Luftwaffe's challenge did not go unheeded in Britain where counter-measures undergoing development included radar, a novel radio wave transmitting and echo-recording system for detecting approaching aircraft, and the Supermarine Spitfire which the RAF would introduce into combat service in time for the 1940 Battle of Britain. In this future conflict, Field Marshals Kesselring and Sperrle (2nd and 3rd Air Fleets) would face Air Vice-Marshal Sir Hugh Dowding, creator of Fighter Command. The consequences for the Luftwaffe are noted in Part 4. In fact, so effective in attack would the RAF and its ally the USAAF become that by 1942 it would prove capable of neutralizing the power of the panzer divisions in North Africa and by 1944 in Normandy of destroying every threat by the German Army to concentrate panzer forces for a counter-offensive. In France, on the other hand, the Armée de l'Air would neglect either to develop the dive-bomber, to advance army-air co-operation or to organize an adequate system of air defence.

German advantage in the experimental use of new weapons in Spain was further demonstrated when the fighting spread east of Teruel in February 1938. In these battles the Legion introduced the hitherto secret Ju 87A (Stuka) in support of ground troops. Designed to deliver a 250kg, or when flown as a single-seater, a 500kg high-explosive bomb in a near vertical dive, the Stuka would prove capable of pin-point accuracy with devastating effect. Focusing on fixed targets, generally bridges and road-crossings or redoubts and resistance points, the Luftwaffe hammered home its superiority; a novel system whereby forward observers were linked to their ground-attack headquarters by wireless strengthening contact between ground forces and dive-bombing (Stuka) squadrons contributed notably to forward progress. From its experience in Spain, the Luftwaffe was to nurture developments of profound importance to mobile warfare, improving wireless range and performance in particular. For the future of a shock force intended for deep penetration, closing around the enemy in swift co-ordinated manoeuvres, like that taking shape in Germany where the momentum of fast troops would be dubbed *Blitzkrieg*, such developments were crucial.

Above: A dive-bombing squadron of the Condor Legion tests the Ju 87 on active service. Later versions of this aircraft were assigned to tank-busting roles while more advanced ground-attack aircraft such as the Fw 190 replaced them in service with Schlachtgruppen.

Meanwhile in German workshops new vehicles for infantry cross-country work, wireless command and signal trucks, repair, artillery and engineer vehicles were undergoing development and, like the new ground-attack and reconnaissance aircraft coming into service were progressively reaching the formations for which they were intended; but never in adequate numbers and far from ideal in form. A greater obstacle to the creation of a panzer force than either design or supply deficiencies was the General Staff's strongly conservative attitude. Guderian's deeply rooted views on the need for a panzer command to control the development and

Above: Ju 52s over Burgos, their base at the time of the infamous bombing of Guernica. The Ju 52 served as a temporary bomber with a 1,200kg load while the purpose-built He 111B was being prepared for service.

Below: The work-horse of the Kampfgruppen, the He 111B could carry a bomb-load of 1,500kg. It flew in Spain in 1937 and remained on active service on other war fronts until 1945.

training of all armoured and motorized units, including the mobile units that the cavalry and infantry would raise between 1935 and 1938, were not universally shared. Traditionalists lead by General Beck, the Army Chief of Staff, considered infantry and cavalry as the main battlefield arms. Guderian's concept of centralized development for mobile forces – placing them on equal footing with infantry and cavalry – would consequently remain unfulfilled until late 1938 and only then at Hitler's insistence would a token gesture be made in this direction. Yet despite equipment and material shortages, motorization of the German Army in the middle thirties continued to gain momentum – encouraged by Hitler, whose enthusiasm for the idea dated from the time that he had witnessed the new force in embryo at Kummersdorf shortly after taking office.

Panzer divisions, light divisions (a cavalry concept) and motorized infantry divisions – the nucleus of a panzer force requiring substantial numbers and types of vehicles – had been progressively raised and trained since 1935. Vehicle production, however limited by production resources, was to benefit from rationalization into a manageable programme, but at the expense of quality. In the absence of Army-designed trucks, many commercial trucks proved all too flimsy for sustained military use. During this late period in the development of the panzer force Guderian, whose bluff approach was not always helpful in promoting the panzer cause, served in command of 2nd Panzer Division at Würzburg and also as chief of staff to XVI Corps – formerly the panzertruppen command still lead by General Lutz. Comprising three panzer divisions: 1st, von Weichs; 2nd, Guderian and 3rd, Fessman, XVI Corps represented the fullest expression to date of German armoured progress. Promoted Generalleutnant in February 1938, Guderian's next challenge was in succeeding Lutz as corps commander; both Lutz and Army Chief of Staff Beck – equally critical of

Left: Reconnaissance flying between the wars assumed critical importance for the future of the panzer force. This Hs 126 observer doubled as a photographer; when not in use his cameras were stored behind the gun-mounting.

Hitler's war aims – were among many seniors about to be retired or transferred when the Führer took command of the armed services (4 February 1938) following the resignation of the Army Commander-in-Chief, von Fritsch, and the dismissal of the State Defence Minister, von Blomberg; events that were engineered by Hitler's supporters within the supreme leadership and turned by him to advantage.

In March 1938, within days of this radical change in the high command (Beck was a strong critic of 'independent' panzer development), Hitler fostered the 'Union' of Austria with the Third Reich and in October ordered the occupation of Czech Sudetenland. The uncontested, 400-mile advance of XVI Corps into Austria, in which the Leibstandarte Adolf Hitler (the Führer's bodyguard from Berlin) took part, helped the panzer training process and valuable lessons were learned; not the least of which, given that numerous vehicles broke down on the road to Linz, was the importance of repair and maintenance.

Guderian's philosophy on the employment of tanks – shaped in no small measure by the widely disseminated

Left: Colonel (later Generalfeldmarschall) Wolfram Freiherr von Richthofen, looking relaxed while observing the effects of a ground attack by a Legion squadron. He became the Luftwaffe's leading exponent of this type of warfare and in 1938 succeeded General Helmuth Volkmann as Legion commander. During the war he was GOC, Flieger Division zbv in Poland and then commander of VIII Air Corps in France, the Balkans and Russia before becoming GOC, 2nd Air Fleet Italy in 1943.

Right: The key to mobility: wireless equipment for transmitting orders and information between panzer leaders, subordinates and rear headquarters. The picture shows Guderian in his command vehicle; also visible is the famous 'Enigma' machine which encoded classified messages. The breaking of these codes at Bletchley Park in England compromised many German actions.

views of British tank theorists, Martel, Fuller and Liddell Hart, and by British Army training manuals – had crystallized in the late twenties before his promotion as Chief of Staff to General Lutz. Out had gone the notion that the tank was a secondary weapon intended solely for infantry support. Now he believed that the tank should be regarded as the key component of a panzer force possessing the capacity for independent action, proceeding at its own rate of advance; pace and power, and intimidation of the enemy by fear of encirclement, being relied upon to carry the day. In his book *Achtung! Panzer!*, outlining the composition and employment of armoured forces, published in 1938, Guderian expanded his philosophy – the kernel of *Blitzkrieg*. If armoured potential is to translate into dynamic and effective power on the battlefield, runs his argument, all arms of the service must unite to form a carefully composed, balanced and versatile, fighting machine – the panzer division; a formation of all arms in which tanks, infantry, engineers, anti-tank, signals, motor-cyclists, artillery and other troops with logistical support, are trained for self-contained action and employment *en masse*. In the war to come, Guderian's was the decisive formula for German success. Impeded by higher authority and reactionary arms of the service at every stage in translating ideas into practice, the indomitable general provided the army and consequently the nation with a touchstone of unparalleled military power. By the end of 1938 the number of panzer divisions had increased to five with a sixth still forming. Nearly 500 armoured fighting vehicles mostly 35(t) tanks acquired when Hitler annexed Bohemia and Moravia in March 1939, were followed by improved 38(t) models armed with a reliable 3.7cm gun. The tank production capacity of Czech armament and vehicle industries would prove immensely beneficial to new panzer divisions raised in time for action in France in May 1940.

More significantly, in October Hitler issued a vital instruction in the interests of armoured progress. Guderian would be promoted general of panzer troops on 20 November; his brief – to supervise all mobile troops, designated Schnelltruppen. The Light divisions, hitherto raised and trained by the cavalry, and motorized infantry divisions formed by the infantry, were henceforth his nominal responsibility as Chief. Yet despite the clear logic of Hitler's intentions there was to be no *carte blanche* for Guderian to train and organize all mobile forces. Not in fact until 1943, in the aftermath of two disastrous campaigns in Russia, would this far-sighted and creatively inspired professional achieve a position from which to co-ordinate and unify the development of panzer forces. Instead, with an allotment of two staff officers, an adjutant and the assistance of a working-party representing anti-tank, motorized infantry and cavalry interests, Guderian, who theoretically was answerable for all questions of army mechanization, prepared training manuals and disputed endlessly with the cavalry and High Command over his proposals to re-organize the former. Even this limited success was short-lived. Within the year, on the outbreak of war, Guderian's 'command' was dissolved and he was transferred, not without 'difficulty', to head XIX Motorized Corps; in his place, but as an Inspector comparable to those of other arms of the service supported by an appropriate department in the General Army Office, came General Friedrich Kühn, hitherto Wünsdorf school commandant (Schnelltruppen-schule, June 1941). Kühn's successor, appointed from command of 5th Light Division in the summer of 1942, was to be General-Major Johannes Streich, once Guderian's colleague, teaching tactics in the early days of the Fahrlehrstab. At a higher level, serving panzer interests at OKH, General Ritter von Thoma, the veteran of panzer action in the Spanish Civil War, was appointed Waffen General in March 1940.

When the Führer celebrated his 50th birthday with a grand parade in Berlin on 20 April 1939, the event was described in the German Press as the 'greatest display in the world'. Members of the new panzer force joining in the march-past sported distinctive black berets and uniforms. But as the war progressed, the beret would be replaced by more practical headgear, the peaked fieldcap – once reserved for mountain troops, soon to become general issue. In the same four-and-a-half-hour parade, paratroops, united under Luftwaffe control since December 1938, when the Army gave up its experimental battalion, made their first public appearance. Meanwhile, Army Group IV Headquarters, established in Leipzig in 1937 under von Brauchitsch (Army

Below: *Die Wehrmacht*, **1938. This was the issue in which Guderian and Nehring publicized their concept of the panzer division: 'A formation of all arms teamed and trained for mobile warfare.' Foreign military Intelligence took little notice of these comprehensive plans offered by** ***Blitzkrieg*****'s leading exponents. The cover shows a tank crashing a barbed wire obstacle, drawn by Theo Matjek.**

3. Victory without profit, 1939–41

Above: Field Marshal Gerd von Runstedt GOC (Generaloberst), Army Group South, Poland 1939; Army Group 'A', France 1940; Army Group South, 1941 and OB West 1944 (*See* maps 2, 3, 7 and 16).

The earliest opportunity for the panzer force to show its paces in action five years after the setting-up of the first tank regiments and their incorporation into panzer divisions or independent panzer brigades though not equipped to the scales laid down, came in September 1939. Many divisions still lacked a variety of equipment – medium tanks, 20mm Flak and more; certain panzer regiments made do with the Pz Kpfw 38(t). A tabulated growth of the panzer force is included in Part 2. For Operation 'White', the campaign against Poland (map 2) fifteen mobile divisions – six panzer, four light, four motorized (infantry) and an impromptu panzer division (Kempf) apportioned between two army groups were allotted air support of two Air Fleets (Kesselring and Löhr) with 1,900 aircraft. The German Army assembled some 3,000 armoured fighting vehicles, mostly Pz Kpfw I and II series. These light tanks, little better than training machines, were supported by a small number of Pz Kpfw IIIs and IVs, and armoured cars, principally of the Type Sd Kfz 222. The Commander-in-Chief of the German Army in 1939 was von Brauchitsch who from his early days as a colonel in the Truppenamt had encouraged motorization developments, first by organizing army–air co-operation exercises and later, as group (IV) commander in Leipzig, supervising the tactical co-ordination of tank and motorized divisions in corps exercises – to which Guderian's XIV Corps had been subordinate.

Against the panzer divisions of two army groups, the Poles could bring only two tank brigades with some five hundred armoured fighting vehicles and an air force of fewer than five hundred serviceable machines. Not only did the country possess fewer tanks and aircraft than the Germans, but many of the tanks were British-inspired designs, light Carden-Loyds and Vickers Armstrongs built under licence. They were too few in number and under-armoured. They were also ineffectually commanded. Polish propaganda, misleading its forces into believing that the mass of German armour consisted of runabouts built for training purposes, was no help in the situation. The result, a military disaster for the Poles. German armies in a double encirclement strategy lead by powerful tank thrusts were supported by the Luftwaffe which, striking hard at the opposing air force and destroying much of it on the ground, also greatly hampered Polish reserve movement by all-out assault on communications. In no time, panzer divisions penetrated the Polish lines, breaking through into open country. Large number of Polish infantry, with their supporting tanks, were cut-off, trapped and destroyed in ever-tightening rings.

When Brest-Litovsk, east of Warsaw and deep in the Polish rear, was reached by Guderian's XIX Corps leading the northern wing of the offensive fifteen days after the start of the campaign, the issue was virtually decided. Two days later, on 17 September, when von Kleist, striking from Czechoslovakia, made contact with Guderian east of Warsaw, the encirclement of Polish forces was complete. In the capital itself, armoured action by 4th Panzer Division fighting in built-up areas proved less effective. Warsaw held out to capitulate on the 27th day of the campaign. The

C-in-C, 1939 in succession to von Fritsch) followed by von Reichenau, exercised training and operational command over motorized units organized into mobile corps: XVI (Panzer) Lutz–Guderian; XV (Light) Hoth; XIV (motorized infantry) von Wietersheim. Equipment for the panzer divisions – the 20-ton Pz Kpfw III and 25-ton Pz Kpfw IV in particular – was nevertheless slow in reaching panzer regiments, fourteen of which, comprising mainly light battalions, were formed and, with few exceptions (7th, 8th, 11th and 25th Panzer Regiments) organized by OKH into panzer brigades of four battalions – the organic tank component of five panzer divisions raised by April 1939. A sixth panzer division (10th Panzer) incorporating 8th Panzer Regiment, taken from 4 Panzer Brigade, one of only two brigades serving at the time as Army troops, followed in time for action in September 1939.

contribution of the panzer force working in conjunction with Luftwaffe close-support groups proved decisive. SS participation in the thrust from East Prussia involved a motorized regiment, SS Standarte Deutschland, in action with Army Group North. The regiment formed part of a mixed Army and SS 'Panzer Division Kempf'. At the same time 'Adolf Hitler' moved from Lodz (Eighth Army) to Warsaw (Tenth Army) and 'Germania' (both in Army Group South), joined in the advance to Lemberg.

The Polish campaign vindicated a strategy of grand manoeuvre unique in the annals of military history. Exceeding in pace and power any offensive yet seen, the Wehrmacht took the military establishments of the world by surprise. Panzer divisions leading the infantry in concentrated thrusts while working in fast-moving battle groups supported by air force ground-attack formations – von Richthofen's Stukagruppen in particular – isolated resistance, demoralized the defence and created alarming envelopments on a battlefield extending across several thousand square miles. *Blitzkrieg* had triumphed, not exactly in accordance with Guderian's precepts, by independent free-ranging formations, but by motorized (panzer) corps allotted to infantry armies; their spearhead role coordinated by superior infantry army headquarters. Nevertheless these same tactics when repeated in the west against armies unable to adjust to the pace of a renewed German offensive would produce correspondingly successful results.

Using the knowledge which it had gained as a result of the fighting in Spain and Poland, the Army High Command (OKH) started to remould its panzer force. The light divisions, consisting principally of motorized infantry with a single tank battalion, were reformed as panzer divisions. Panzer regiments were strengthened with a greater number of better-armed tanks, the Pz Kpfw III and IV and supported by an increase in motorized infantry. But there was little time to introduce much new equipment before the forthcoming campaign in France. The Pz Kpfw I and II series were of necessity retained as the main types, while some of the Pz Kpfw III series were to be upgunned by rearming them with a 5cm weapon. The Pz Kpfw IV series too, when fitted with a new (long) 7.5cm gun, would prove even more of an asset; but production of these 'specials' was to be delayed until early 1942. More of the infantry units accompanying the tanks, the future panzer grenadiers, would be mounted in armoured personnel carriers, Schützenpanzerwagen (SPWs). The first of these vehicles, issued only in small numbers to 1st Panzer Division, had proved their effectiveness; less well-provided formations retained standard trucks to lift their motorized infantry as far forward as possible. Heavier armour was incorporated into new SPWs and weapon shields fitted to their on-board machine-gun. Henceforth, in numerous variants, these vehicles would become an indispensible part of the panzer force, conferring exceptional power and mobility on its motorized infantry. Panzer regiments would benefit increasingly from this partnership. In battle groups operating in close or wooded country, the escorting infantry would often fight ahead of the armour or on its flanks. Overcoming river barriers, clearing villages and so on, motorized infantry would prove their merits in countless situations where tanks alone would prove highly vulnerable to counter-measures by infantry and anti-tank detachments.

Above: Field Marshal Fedor von Bock, GOC (Generaloberst), Army Group North, Poland 1939; Army Group 'B', France 1940; Army Group Centre, 1941 and Army Group 'B', 1942 (*See* maps 2, 3, 7 and 10).

The first assault guns – Sturmgeschütze – turretless tracked vehicles fitted with a powerful low-velocity gun and intended for use in an infantry support role also made their appearance in the Polish campaign. They too were retained and expanded in numbers. In later operations they would often be used as substitutes for tanks. The white cross emblem painted on all German armoured vehicles as an identification mark was replaced by the straight-edged black cross.

At 0535 hours on 10 May 1940, Hitler launched Operation 'Yellow', (panzer order of battle and map (3)) with a force of more than 2,000 tanks formed into ten panzer divisions. Deployed as hitherto, in battle groups, the divisions advanced through Belgium and Luxemburg to lead the attack on France. Holland was also invaded. The ratio of opposing forces was 120 German divisions including ten panzer divisions with 2,574 tanks opposed by 83 French, nine British, 22 Belgian and ten Dutch divisions with a total of 3,600 tanks; a marked difference in armoured strength.

Above: Field Marshal Erich von Manstein, when chief of staff (Generalleutnant) to von Runstedt in Poland and France. He was credited with Plan 'Yellow' which employed the panzer divisions on the opposite axis to the von Schlieffen Plan which Hitler and OKH originally intended to repeat. Thereafter as Corps, Army and finally Army Group Commander, he reaffirmed his reputation as the Wehrmacht's leading strategist (see maps 3, 7, 10, 13 and 14).

Superior German leadership, tactics and inter-service co-operation, particularly between army and air force, would more than offset the disparity in numbers. Once again, a key feature of the German plan would be to win immediate air supremacy, destroying the enemy air force on the ground and over the battlefield. This the Luftwaffe would do with notable success, hindering in the process every attempt by Allied land forces to concentrate for counter-attacks against the invading Army Groups.

As hitherto, the Commander-in-Chief of the German Army was von Brauchitsch. His forces, Army Group 'B' (von Bock) with three panzer divisions would attack Holland and Belgium, Army Group 'A' (von Runstedt) strongest in armour with seven panzer divisions and the bulk of the German forces would strike at France through Luxemburg. Army Group 'C' (Leeb) would take up defensive positions in front of the Maginot Line. Applying the tactics successfully demonstrated in Poland, panzer spearheads raced to lightning victory while the French General Staff, believing in the impregnability of the Maginot Line, but more significantly clinging to the notion that the role of the tank was first and foremost to provide support for non-motorized infantry, was outmanoeuvred and brought to defeat, its tanks ineffectually spread in small numbers across a wide front.

In marked contrast to Allied dispositions, powerful concentrations of German armour with Luftwaffe support – especially Panzer Group von Kleist at the point of main effort – forced crossings of the River Meuse notably at Sedan and Monthermé, pausing only to consolidate before striking west through France and rupturing the defence on a narrow front. Wheeling north to isolate demoralized and outmanoeuvred Allied armies, the panzer divisions were followed by motorized and marching infantry; their task being to maintain the tempo of the attack, and line the shoulders of the 'corridor' created by the panzer divisions, freeing them for further operations. In secondary action upstream across the Meuse at Dinant, less powerful armoured spearheads with varying degrees of air force support reinforced the offensive (map 3).

Allied staffs expecting a repeat of Schlieffen's 1914 manoeuvre when the German Army swept through Belgium towards Paris, had moved the bulk of their forces north into Belgium to oppose von Bock's Army Group 'B' deceptively threatening invasion. But it was Army Group 'A' that struck the decisive blow, moving against France through Luxemburg; von Bock's infantry divisions pressing forward at an appropriate moment to complete the encirclement of the Allies armies.

The principal phase of Operation 'Yellow' lasted no more than eleven days following von Kleist's storming of the Meuse on the 13th. The greater part of Belgium and much of northern France was occupied by the 24th and the British Expeditionary Force was penned into a pocket totally cut off from its Atlantic coast bases at Cherbourg and Brest. With no mobile counter-attack force in reserve and unable to comprehend the magnitude of the defeat facing them, the armies of Britain, Belgium and France proved incapable of effective resistance and were shattered in the process. Holland had already fallen to an assault in which parachute and glider troops lead the way. Salvation for the BEF and a fraction of the French Army lay in escape through the Channel port and beaches of Dunkirk to England.

British and French forces that succeeded in crossing the Channel from Dunkirk owed their deliverance to Hitler's order halting the panzer divisions fifteen miles away. On 24 May, fearing that British or French counter-attacks might succeed in cutting the Flanders (panzer) 'corridor' (map 4) and thereby separate oncoming infantry divisions from the panzer spearheads, Hitler supported by von Runstedt, called a halt. The Royal Navy, with the support of hundreds of small boats, was quick to seize the opportunity of evacuating what it could of the defeated Allied armies. When Dunkirk was closed by air action, men were taken from the beaches.

At Goering's suggestion, the Luftwaffe attempted to finish off the embattled defenders. The plan was unrealistic; an overstretched air force, unable to meet the commitment, failed to prevent the escape of 3,300 mostly British troops. Total victory eluded the panzer force and Hitler's hopes of putting a swift end to the war faded, for good. Daring in concept, swift, precise and economical in

Above: Paratroops of 7th Air Division leading the way into Holland to secure key points on the western axis of von Bock's Army Group 'B' (*see* map 3).

execution, the German plan of attack carried the day. The decisive stroke delivered by von Kleist's Panzer Group, a phalanx of three panzer corps with 1,260 tanks concentrated into a powerful spearhead, had smashed through French Second Army on the Meuse and then bypassed or outflanked all other opposition. With Guderian's XIX Corps in the lead, the panzer group exceeded all but executant expectations. On 20 May Guderian's 2nd Panzer Division (Veiel) was first to reach the Channel at Abbeville.

The panzer divisions created such alarm and confusion by their surprise deployment in deeply echeloned attacks out of the Ardennes, a ravined and forest-bound area, considered impassable to tanks, that the opportunity for mounting a determined counter-offensive was never seized and the panzer columns with their powerful air support rolled to an astounding victory – prostrating the armies of four nations.

The success of *Blitzkrieg* in the west was virtually decided in its first phase when the German forces covered 160 miles in seven days to reach Abbeville, splitting the Allies and sealing the fate of the British Expeditionary Force. Prompt support by the Luftwaffe in impeding British and French counter-attacks on the flanks of German columns strung along the panzer 'corridor' contributed substantially to Allied defeat. Although French troops went on to offer resistance during the second phase of the fighting, when regrouped German armies in Operation 'Red', once again spearheaded by armoured troops, wheeled south to encircle Paris, they were no match for the panzer divisions and failed to halt the advance. On 14 June 1940 Paris surrendered. On the 22nd an armistice was signed and on the 25th, the guns fell silent.

Despite Hitler's misgivings over the safety of flanks, the deft handling of the panzer divisions combined with the maximum possible air support proved decisive in German victory. Panzer commanders and staffs at all levels contributed to the success. Many would capitalize their experience in senior command or staff appointments in later campaigns: Colonels Eberbach, von Manteuffel and Breith leading the offensive across the Meuse at Maastricht (map 3), Major Rothenburg, Rommel's panzer commander at Dinant (killed in action, 1941), Colonel Balck, whose motorized infantry paved the way for Guderian at Sedan; Generals von Kleist, Guderian, Hoepner, Reinhardt and Hoth, foremost in command at crucial stages in the battle.

Elsewhere at the time, Generalleutnant Walter Model served as Chief of Staff, Sixteenth Army, Colonel Walther Nehring was Chief of Staff to Panzer Group Guderian, while Major Fritz Bayerlein served in the same Group as 1a (Ops). Colonel Erhard Raus, the future GOC Fourth, First and Third

Panzer Armies, held a staff appointment outside the panzer force until 19 July. All served vital apprenticeships leading to high-ranking careers in Africa or Russia. Major-General Erwin Rommel, in command of 7th Panzer Division, crossed the Meuse at Dinant before sweeping on through Flanders leading his formation (like Heinz Guderian at Sedan) from the front. Given command of Deutsches Afrika Korps and subsequently Panzerarmee Afrika, Rommel would prove a wily and resourceful adversary in the Western desert.

The Waffen SS played a small but busy role in this campaign. The motorized regiments (excluding the Leibstandarte) that had fought in Poland and now formed part of an SS Verfügungs Division (SS-V) were lead by Paul Hausser. All joined in the attack on Holland (Eighteenth

Right: Motor-cycle troops preceding the main body of Army Group South *en route* through Poland. This is a typical early picture of a panzer division vanguard.

Army) advancing to Rotterdam, Amsterdam and beyond. Thereafter in Flanders, particularly around Arras and Dunkirk, they and a new motorized division, SS Totenkopf (Theodor Eicke) raised from state security personnel, supported the panzer groups, driving the BEF back to the Channel.

In the 'Red' phase of the battle for France, a partly motorized SS Polizei Division (Pfeffer von Wildenbruck) came into action across the Aisne; building bridgeheads to assist Guderian's southward advance while SS-V and SS Totenkopf served Panzer Group von Kleist.

The successful outcome of the battle for France, concluded on 25 June, found the German High Command with no contingency plans for continuing the land war against Britain; the BEF had escaped from Dunkirk by the narrowest of margins – thanks to tireless efforts by the Royal Navy and Royal Air Force – and returned home in a much depleted state. However, a German plan to pursue the BEF and thereby complete the humiliation of the British army quickly materialized. On 30 June 1940, in a war aims memorandum submitted to Hitler by General Jodl (OKW chief of staff), the idea of invading Britain was established at the highest level. By 12 July, Jodl's notes were being shaped into Operation 'Sea-lion' and plans to involve all three services in summer assault operations across the English Channel were initiated; Army Group 'A' (von Runstedt) consolidating on the Channel coast was directed by OKH to develop the Army side of the operation. Von Runstedt was to be responsible for two armies disembarking simultaneously in three waves between Worthing (Ninth Army) and Hythe (Sixteenth Army).

Assault infantry in the first wave, landing on open beaches from improvised landing craft, were to be followed in the second (principal) wave of the invasion by four panzer and two motorized divisions divided between Hoth (XV) Ninth Army and Reinhardt (XXXXI) Sixteenth Army. They too practised open coast landings in case no suitable harbour was available (*see* Third Panzer Army, July–October 1940). Armoured support for first wave infantry would be provided additionally by three panzer battalions equipped mainly with Pz Kpfw III (Tauchpanzer) submersible battle tanks, and a fourth equipped with flame-throwers. Primary operations would focus upon Brighton, Folkestone and, above all, Dover where parachute landings to secure the flanks of the invasion force might equally be expected to accelerate the capture of port facilities needed for handling heavy equipment and follow-up waves.

Despite prodigious efforts by the Luftwaffe to win air superiority as a pre-requisite for success, *Blitzkrieg* against England was never to achieve reality. Goering failed and the German Navy under Admiral Raeder, ill prepared for such an eventuality,* baulked at transporting and re-supplying in safety an invasion force opposed by a much superior Royal Navy and an undefeated Royal Air Force. These and degenerating weather in the Channel prompted Hitler in October to postpone and early in 1941 to cancel the projected operation. 'Sea-lion' divisions were instead re-deployed and in common with others required to give up one of their two panzer regiments as cadres for new formations (Panzer Divisions 11–21), re-organizing for action against Russia. The next *Blitzkrieg* commitment for the panzer force, Operation 'Marita' (map 6) came in 1941 after Italian Army attacks from Albania against the Greek Army had failed to produce results. German forces were then drawn into a Balkans campaign to rescue an ally. Once again panzer divisions headed a German offensive. When the friendly state of Yugoslavia unexpectedly turned against the Axis that country too was included in a hastily inaugurated German plan of attack. On 6 April 1941 Luftwaffe raids against Yugoslav Army headquarters and transport installations in Belgrade signalled the simultaneous invasion of both Greece and Yugoslavia. Roumania, Bulgaria and Hungary all provided jumping-off points for the attacking force. Nevertheless, one-third of the panzer divisions intended for the operation, the responsibility of Field Marshal List's Twelfth Army and at the last moment von Weichs' Second Army, were not needed. Air opposition

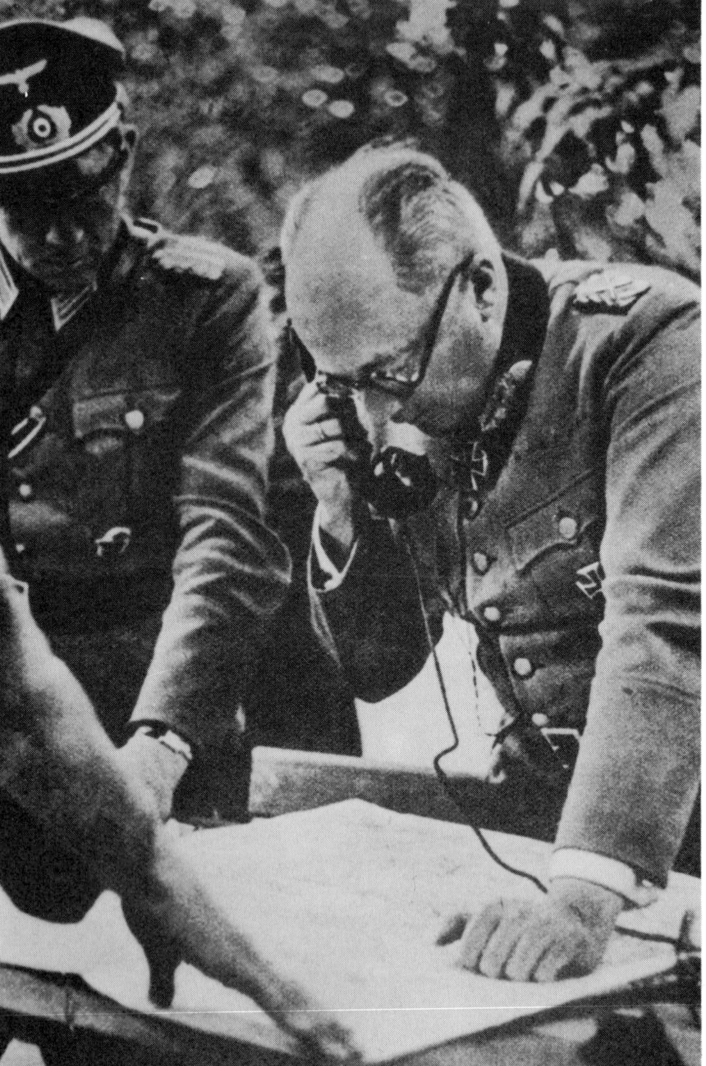

Above: Field Marshal Hans von Kluge, GOC (Generaloberst), Fourth Army in the battle of France, led the strongest of von Runstedt's armies – at the crucial assault stage. Thereafter in 1941 he commanded Army Group Centre, in 'Barbarossa' and in August 1944 he replaced Rommel at Army Group 'B' before committing suicide (*see* maps 3 and 7).

*German capital ships out of commission: *Scharnhorst, Gneisenau, Lützow* (formerly *Deutschland*) torpedoed. *Graf Spee* scuttled. *Bismarck, Prinz Eugen* and *Tirpitz* not expected in service before spring or autumn 1941.

was negligible. Twelfth Army's Panzer Group von Kleist supported by von Richthofen's VIII Air Corps thrusting via Nish to the Yugoslav capital brought swift surrender.

A southwards advance by Twelfth Army into Greece where a British expeditionary force from Egypt had arrived at Piraeus and Volos on 7 March, made equally rapid progress. The panzer divisions aided by mountain troops, the first of many collaborations, turned the Metaxas Line – fortified frontier heights protecting Salonika. 2nd Panzer Division, striking out on a daring and successful 130-kilometre thrust into the city and unnerving the defence, contributed notably to success. Further west a turning movement southwards through Skopje giving List control of strategic north–south rail connections and access to mountain routes leading into the heart of the country further imperilled the defence. On 21 April the largely immobile Greek Army capitulated; disaster threatened the British expeditionary force. But the German advance through Greece in the direction of Athens faltered at Thermopylae when British and Empire troops with Matildas diverted from Egypt held the advance at bay. Taking to the road and retreating via the Peloponnese, 45,000 troops reached Crete where a further reverse at the hands of General Student's (XI) Parachute (and glider) Corps was waiting. A British seaborne evacuation followed and the German campaign in the Balkans was over.

The war in the Mediterranean (map 5) was nevertheless far from finished. Other German forces in the shape of Rommel's DAK, had been committed to North Africa, once again bolstering Italian forces. Mobile operations over vast

Right: Rommel inspecting units of 7th Panzer Division. It was during the Battle of France that both commander and division won a reputation for thrustfulness.

Above: The ubiquitous Ju 87, employed against ground targets, opened the way for advancing panzer divisions, notably at Maastricht and Sedan (*see* map 3).

Left: The Me 110 was deployed in 1939 as a long-range fighter and issued to certain Jagdgeschwader following successful outings in Spain. In Poland and France it flew ground-attack missions; later versions flew as night fighters.

Opposite page, top: The results of dive-bombing and artillery fire on a fixed installation, the Namur fort on the Belgian–German frontier, is all too evident.

Opposite page, bottom left: Colonel Georg Rothenburg, CO, 25th Panzer Regiment, 7th Panzer Division, leading Rommel's armour across the Meuse at Dinant (*see* map 4).

Opposite page, bottom right: Colonel Eugene Meindl who became CO, Assault Regiment of XI Air Corps. In May 1940 constituent glider units served Captain Koch (Sturmabteilung) and Oberleutnant Witzig (Pionierzug) in their seizure of Fort Eben Emael which opened the way for Fourth Panzer Div/ Sixth Army. Meindl later played a distinguished part in defending St-Lô in Normandy.

distances would take on new and greater dimensions stretching the panzer force to its limit and diverting men and equipment needed for operations against Russia. German armour committed in support of the Italian adventure into Albania and Greece had triumphed over admittedly inferior opponents. Superior skills and mobility prevailed in taking panzer divisions the length of the peninsular through rugged terrain under gruelling conditions. When units were obliged to replan operations resulting from the high wastage rate of their equipment, panzer troops learned valuable lessons in improvisation. The Luftwaffe, by delaying the movement of enemy reserves and reinforcements and combating active opposition, supported the Army as it had earlier in the west, assisting the forward progress of panzer divisions and corps directly and indirectly through VIII Air Corps attacks against resistance centres and road and rail communications.

The Leibstandarte SS Adolf Hitler raised to brigade strength and SS Das Reich Division, both motorized, also supported Army panzer divisions in the Balkans offensive. Das Reich, under the leadership of Paul Hausser, future GOC, German Seventh Army in Normandy in 1944, strengthened Panzer Corps Reinhard, the northern arm of Panzer Group von Kleist thrusting to Belgrade. A battle group from Hausser's division ceremoniously accepted the surrender of the city on 13 April. The Leibstandarte, reinforced with an assault gun battery and commanded by 'Sepp' Dietrich, future commander of Sixth SS Panzer Army in the Ardennes in 1944, waged a bitter campaign through Greece, assisting 9th Panzer Division in the drive south outflanking the British forces. On 9 April Dietrich's brigade stormed the Klidi Pass, winning a gateway for the continuation of the offensive, then quickly secured the Klissura Pass, another key defile, and Yanina, a communications centre in the rear of Greek armies fighting in Albania. Pushing on south, Dietrich followed these successes with a crossing of the Corinth Canal in Hussar style while paratroops of 2nd Paratroop Regiment (Sturm) seized the Corinth bridge on the 25th, but failed by 24 hours to trap retreating British, Australian and New Zealand units. List pushed his divisions further into the Peloponnese; 5th Panzer reached Kalamata on the 28th. Protected by rearguards, the Allied troops embarked at Nauplion and other ports for Crete. But however successful and daring the small panzer force had proved, thrusting the length of the peninsula against more or less immobile opponents, the largely unforeseen Balkans Campaign – considered essential to the security of oil-fields in Roumania and Hungary by putting them out of range of the RAF, and the bolstering of the Italian Army struggling in Albania to defeat the Greeks – was to effect delay in the opening of Operation 'Barbarossa', the invasion of Russia, for which plans had been made since July 1940. 'Barbarossa' would be fatally compromised by the delay. When the panzer divisions were eventually re-deployed for their new task, only one month separated the two campaigns.

Starting at 0300 hours on 22 June 1941, 'Barbarossa' (map 7) would rank as one of the great military misadventures of the Second World War, a trial of strength for German and Russian forces; the death-knell of the panzer force. Estimates put Russian opposition at 150 infantry divisions (15 motorized) 32 cavalry divisions and 36 motorized brigades; with 10,000–20,000 tanks supported by 10,000 aircraft. On the German side the forces deployed in three army groups, North, Centre and South, totalled some 153 divisions of which 140 were actually German, with 3,417 tanks. Each army group was supported by an air fleet. The German armoured force consisted basically of nineteen panzer divisions, ten motorized infantry divisions, three motorized SS divisions and one motorized SS brigade. A reinforced Gross Deutschland motorized infantry regiment and a small number of independent (Army) assault-gun batteries, heavy artillery, anti-aircraft and anti-tank units supported the deployment. The SS contribution would rise to fifteen panzer or motorized divisions; about one-third of the panzer force.

Whatever the precise tally of the Russian land and air forces, their gross underestimation by Hitler and the General Staff was to prove disastrous to German hopes of quick victory. General Franz Halder, Chief of Staff to the Army High Command, would record in his diary at the end of November: 'No fewer than 360 Russian divisions have so far been identified.'

The Red Army, erroneously concluding from its experience in the Spanish Civil War, where several hundred light tanks had been committed by both sides, that large armoured units could not carry out independent tasks, had consequently based its pre-war tank organization on the French infantry-support model. Not until the battle for France did the Russian General Staff make belated attempts to reorganize on German lines. Thereafter Russian armoured forces would improve out of all recognition in armament, tactics and above all, in heavy armour. The later preponderance of tracked heavy weapons – tanks and tank destroyers – would prove a decisive element in defeating the panzer force. Tank production would also prove markedly superior. Marshal Sokolovsky records: 'At the beginning of 1945, the Red Army had eight times as many

Below: General (later Generaloberst) Kurt Student conferring with General Ringel, OC, 5th Mountain Division, during the Battle of Crete. This was the first strategic deployment (Operation 'Mercury') of paratroops and glider-borne troops (*see* map 6).

Above: A 3.7cm anti-tank gun deployed on the road to Leningrad. When faced with the T34 and KWII only larger calibres, generally 7.5cm, could provide effective protection.

tanks as it had possessed in December 1941.' Soviet emphasis on heavy tanks had started as early as 1939 with the manufacture of the 44-ton KV–1 and 53-ton KV–2A running parallel with the medium 26-ton T34. From the time that they were first encountered all proved superior to German models. As early as mid-1940 these unknown new Russian tanks including 1,000 T34s were arriving in border defence zones. The planned output for 1941 was 5,500 a year!

At the start of the campaign four panzer groups, including all the available motorized SS formations, were deployed to lead the armoured thrusts of Army Groups North, Centre and South. Their commanders were, respectively: von Leeb, von Bock and von Runstedt. None of the panzer groups handling a burgeoning number of panzer divisions and corps were allowed total operational freedom. In the north, Hoepner's Fourth Panzer Group was allotted to von Leeb. Von Bock was provided with Second and Third Panzer Groups commanded by Guderian and Hoth respectively, while in the south, First Panzer Group led by von Kleist was given to von Runstedt. The two panzer groups of Army Group Centre had the largest combined strength in tanks – about 1,800 in all. The strategic objectives of the army groups were set out in Hitler directives giving the army groups Leningrad, Moscow (direction), Kiev and subsequently Rostov as their targets. The panzer groups would be committed on widely divergent courses, their objectives lying hundreds of miles distant and hundreds of miles apart. Despite the distances involved, the panzer force would come close to success; a startled world taking little comfort in the extent to which the Wehrmacht was so evidently overstretched. Planned to end in weeks (but in the event destined to last close upon four years), the unusually harsh winter of 1941–2 would take a savage toll of increasingly worn-down and exhausted panzer divisions. Within months of the start of the campaign, battle losses were severely depleting the panzer force. Frostbite and a hostile winter climate paralyzed its operations. Evidence of defects in equipment and the unsuitability of panzer force vehicles for operations in exceptionally roadless conditions soon became apparent. The toll inflicted by stubborn Russian resistance, the aggravation of excessive demands by the Army High Command for advances to Leningrad and Moscow, taking the panzer force well out of reach of its railheads, jeopardized its future.

In the offensive against Leningrad, Hoepner's panzer group, beating off counter-attacks at Rossieny where the heavy Russian KV–1 made an unexpected appearance, swiftly overcame the River Duna, a major obstacle in its path, and within a week reached the shores of Lake Peipus. By mid-July von Leeb, developing plans to encircle the city, had captured the Schlusselberg, a fortress guarding the eastern approaches to the city. The position was taken on 8 September by which time the slower infantry units had caught up with the leading panzer divisions. But Hitler postponed the capture of Leningrad, instead ordering the transfer of much of the investing panzer force to the centre, leaving the infantry armies around the city to pursue only partial investment. A desperate but unsuccessful attempt to snap the ring tight would be made later with Hitler ordering a link with the Finns. In the centre, where Panzer Groups 2 and 3 lead by Guderian and Hoth fought their way towards Moscow, German double encirclement tactics resulted several times in the capture of large Russian forces, near Bialystok, Bryansk and Smolensk. Smolensk fell on 15 July. But in August Hitler announced a new plan. Instead of Moscow the emphasis of the assault would be on the wings of the offensive. The advance towards the Soviet capital by Army Group Centre was postponed in favour of supporting Army Group North attacking Leningrad and Army Group South aiming to capture Kiev and the Donetz industrial basin. Guderian's panzer group, forging east in the centre, was swung south and west behind Kiev, joining with a northward-circling von Kleist; Hoth Group was partially diverted to assist von Leeb's Leningrad offensive.

With 13th Panzer Division leading Panzer Group von Kleist to the outskirts of Kiev by mid-July, the invasion of the south had made steady if unspectacular progress. But in consequence of Hitler's change of plan and a fruitful collaboration between Panzer Groups von Kleist and Guderian, creating an envelopment of major Russian forces

Below: The 7.5cm long-barrelled Pz Kpfw IV, introduced in 1942 (seen here in Tunisia), was a match for most early opposition encountered by the panzer force.

in the Kiev region, the occupation of the city by Army Group South on 18 September brought an end to the greatest of all German encirclement battles; enormous booty being taken from annihilated Russian armies. Renamed First Panzer Army, von Kleist's group, then struck out across the Dnieper towards the Sea of Azov and on 20 November captured Rostov, von Kleist's gateway to the Caucasus and Russian oil. But Russian flank attacks in the north, forcing the army group into untimely retreat to the River Mius, was to bring Rostov-on-Don once more into Russian hands.

Meanwhile, launching Operation 'Typhoon' (map 8), in the centre of the eastern front, Hitler resumed the advance to Moscow. Redeploying Panzer Groups 3 and 4 (the latter withdrawn from Leningrad) and pushing hard for the Soviet capital while Panzer Group 2 (Guderian) joined the action from the south-west, the great advance was re-started. But all too late. The momentum of the sweeping advances was lost. Autumn mud slowed the offensive; snow with 30° of frost, blizzards, undernourishment, decrepit vehicles and unserviceable equipment including tank turrets that failed to traverse, rendered operations well-nigh impossible. Winter clothing and supplies failed. Frost-bite and counter-attacks took a deadly toll. Exhaustion brought the offensive to a halt. All movement north and south of Moscow intended to bring about the fall of the city failed utterly.

With winter conditions, snow especially, restricting German mobility to the few serviceable roads, fresh Russian armies transported from the east, equipped and experienced in winter warfare, their presence only vaguely suspected by the General Staff, pressed home their advantage. For the

German Army the situation deteriorated daily in mid-winter. Panzer divisions thrusting to within twenty miles of Moscow, were unable to find the power required to fight their way forward; even to extricate themselves required a super-human effort. *Blitzkrieg* strategy had failed and on this front would never restart. Moscow would not again experience a threat to its security. A Russian counter-offensive, starting on 5 December, swung purposefully into action. Cutting deep swathes into the central front, the German armies facing Moscow under von Bock and his successor, von Kluge, were brought within an ace of collapse. Hitler's response on 16 December was a stand fast order – the first of many. Bitter disputes over unscheduled withdrawals consumed Guderian and von Kluge, the army group Commander. Stalled in exposed positions north of Tula on the south-west approaches to Moscow, Guderian had been unable to find the strength to advance further. Seeing that Red Army attacks were a constant menace the prudent general pulled back to better positions. On Hitler's orders he was relieved of his command and transferred to OKW's officers' pool on 26 December. Other generals disobeying Hitler's instructions to stand fast were similarly dismissed.

For the Luftwaffe, no less than for the Army, its airfields blanketed in deep snow and barely a machine flying in leaden skies, supplies of all kinds dried-up. So traumatic became the onset of deep winter that for both services the period was one of agonizing adjustment to defensive operations and a new strategy. Towns and villages were organized for all-round defence in a 'hedgehog' system. Tanks, what few remained, were formed into counter-attack detachments. Tankless crews found themselves employed as infantry. The home front had meanwhile been active, but tank production showed little sign of upward movement and would remain virtually static for a further twelve months. Technical development had nevertheless resulted in the long-barrelled tank gun. New tank designs, a Pz Kpfw V Panther weighing 43 tons and a 56-ton Pz Kpfw VI Tiger were developed to counter the T34 and its heavy partners. The contribution of these new machines to the battlefield fighting alongside increasing numbers of Pz Kpfw IVs would prove effective by the middle of 1943. Hitler, eager as always to promote technical progress in tank design, ordered the construction of a new super-heavy tank (Mouse) weighing 170 tons.

Assault-gun production was increased and armour skirting introduced to improve the protection of vehicles such as the Pz Kpfw IV. Of equally far-reaching importance to the panzer force was a decision to mount the 8.8cm gun, hitherto employed in anti-aircraft and ground defence roles, in the Tiger. The first half-company of this new tank would be introduced into trial service on the Leningrad front within a year (September 1942). It was there and also on Guderian's sector in the early days of the invasion that the panzer groups discovered to their consternation that not only were their opponent's T34s and KV–1s heavily armoured and dangerous, but largely impervious to German 3.7cm and 5cm anti-tank guns. The need for improvements in anti-tank defence was self-evident. More 7.5cm and 8.8cm guns were essential. Until such time as they were available, preferably mounted in self-propelled form as Panzerjaeger (tank destroyers), captured Russian 7.62cm guns would be improvised to serve on Czech 38(t) mountings. One advantage of Russian weapons, and this included the T34, was simplicity of construction. Most needed little servicing, but were vulnerable to the Stuka dive-bomber. By contrast many of the German weapons, and in this the tanks were no exception, were liable to break down because of their complicated design. Then too there was the problem of their high petrol consumption; for example, the Panzer IV, with a fuel tank holding 470 litres, had a maximum range of only 150 kilometres.

Steadily mounting air attacks by the Red Air Force making good its disastrous losses at the start of the invasion, emphasized the need for motorized anti-aircraft detachments to escort armoured formations. The experience lead to the inclusion of an additional AA company in the motorized infantry and panzer regiments. Negligence in the provision of adequate anti-aircraft protection for panzer columns would prove a significant factor in later reverses. As more and increasingly powerful air forces out-matched the Luftwaffe east and west, the panzer force would discover all too late that it possessed too few effective means with which to combat the menace. Panzer engineers engaged in lifting mines, demolishing tank-traps, bridging rivers and laying roads in the trackless eastern hinterland, proved themselves indispensable in early operations, although the speed of the German advance frequently gave the defenders no time to destroy bridges. For engineers in the forefront of the action, improved protection became a matter of priority. Special armoured vehicles for engineer use or captured ones

Above: The famous '88', an anti-aircraft gun deployed by Flakkampfgruppen which could also protect against tanks and other ground targets.

Above: **In Russia manhandling anti-tank guns was a problem for both armoured troops and infantry. The heavier calibres were naturally the most cumbersome, requiring self-propelled mountings.**

until such times as purpose-built machines could be produced were a necessity. During the first year of the campaign submersible tanks, originally intended for the invasion of Britain, were used by the panzer force to cross the River Bug.

The setbacks and severe losses suffered by the German Army in the winter of 1941–2 emphasized a clear need for new and improved equipment of all types. The Army's order of battle for the period shows that of twenty-one panzer divisions on establishment, only eight were then fully operational and with production running at a low ebb, not all could be rebuilt. Moreover, instead of renewing the advance on Moscow, as soon as the Russian counter-offensive had spent itself at the end of spring 1942, Hitler decided that the axis of the 1942 attack should be switched from Moscow to oil-fields in the Caucasus. For these reasons, panzer divisions allotted to First and Fourth Panzer Armies (expanded panzer group headquarters) spearheading Army Groups 'A' (List) and 'B' (von Bock) in Operation 'Blue', the new offensive, were given priority in supplies and equipment. The Pz Kpfw IIIs and IVs, although no match for the heavier T34s now appearing in masses on the front, had been upgunned in an effort to restore the balance.

4. Outrunning resources, 1942

With no hint of the disaster soon to befall it at Stalingrad, Hoth's Fourth Panzer Army, re-enacting the tactics that had won the battle for France, raced into Voronezh (map 10). Renewed German attacks also brought success for von Kleist whose First Panzer Army recaptured Rostov-on-Don. The industrial basin of the Donetz also succumbed and a tank drive by von Kleist in the direction of Maikop and Mozdok threatened oil towns of the eastern Caucasus. The panzer army's main objectives, Soviet oil centres at Tiflis, Grozny and Baku, lay 400 miles across the Kalmuck Steppe. Within weeks the German drive into the Caucasus, seizing outlying towns and pressing forward into the foothills of the range, reached Malgobek (SS Wiking) and the outskirts of Ordzhonikidze (23rd Panzer). There German progress ended – the panzer force once again at the end of its resources. Maikop destroyed by retreating Russians, would never contribute oil to the German war effort and the thrust would never be resumed. A Red Army counter-offensive encircling Stalingrad in the North and threatening von Kleist's rearward services would finally seal the fate of Operation 'Blue/Brunswick'. The great advance had been enormously hampered; trucks standing idle for want of fuel, supplies drying-up and putting a brake on progress. Von Kleist's strength was either dissipated in drawn-out engagements or creamed off for action at Stalingrad and elsewhere. The offensive in the south slowly stalled. Persia and its oil-fields, long coveted by Hitler as a contributor to the nation's economy, would remain an unattainable dream. And then, too, the Russians had learned to evade the encircling panzer thrusts and no great losses had been inflicted by von Kleist or Hoth on Russian forces deployed in the land corridor between the Donetz and the Don.

Faced with vehicle shortages in operations across the Europe/Asia frontier, the panzer force turned to the camel as a pack-animal. Cossacks and other martial races of the regions were recruited as allies; a Cossack cavalry regiment serving with an over-extended First Panzer Army. The Cossacks screened the panzer army's open flank on the Kalmuck Steppe. But events on the Volga where Fourth Panzer Army was supporting Sixth Army (Paulus), attacking Stalingrad in the course of Hitler's eccentric offensive, pursued simultaneously with von Kleist's advance into the Caucasus, would turn all too soon into unmitigated disaster, forcing both panzer armies into retreat.

The battle for Stalingrad had begun well enough (maps 10 and 11). Army Group 'B' had crossed the Don and panzer divisions leading Sixth Army (Paulus) forward on 23 August had reached suburbs on the Volga immediately north of the city. A concentric attack by Fourth Panzer Army approaching from the south-west also had eventually carried through bitterly contested suburbs to the centre. Yet by late October, hampered by a lack of fuel and unrelenting Soviet

Below: Panzer grenadiers assisting the tanks in their fighting tasks as the platoon commander observes a river crossing operation. The vehicle is an Sd Kfz 251 mounting a 3.7cm anti-tank gun.

Right: September 1941; Stuka crews wait on the northern front for orders to attack. Their machines were to prove progressively obsolete against Russian air opposition and by 1943 they were outclassed.

resistance, only two-thirds of Stalingrad city was in German hands. Heavy fighting to reduce the town continued with slow German progress. A strong Russian counter-offensive launched with the benefit of a snowstorm at dawn on 19 November enveloped the city. Sixth Army and much of Fourth Panzer Army were isolated. A Luftwaffe promise of resupply, despite prodigious efforts by aircrews and ground staff operating at a great disadvantage in a second winter of appalling conditions, would go unfulfilled. Within weeks Paulus, forbidden by Hitler to break out, was surrendering his entire army conscious of an even greater disaster threatening Army Group 'A' as the Red Army lunged west to endanger Rostov and von Kleist's lifeline into the Caucasus. Immediate withdrawal of First Panzer Army from the jaws of a gigantic trap was vital if a greater catastrophe were to be avoided.

Weakened by battle losses and diversions – Gross Deutschland transferred to the west and 23rd Panzer and Wiking sent north to assist Hoth in an Army Group plan to relieve Stalingrad and stiffen the outer defences of Rostov – the depleted panzer army (which had also given up much of its air cover) started the long return trek to Rostov, hoping to negotiate the 'gateway' before the Red Army could seize it. In this endeavour von Kleist was successful, but an attempt by Fourth Panzer Army to relieve Stalingrad was to end in failure (map 12). On 2 February 1943 Stalingrad and Paulus's entire force totalling 250,000 men of 22 divisions, six of them mobile, fell to the investing Russians. Panzer General Hube, succeeding von Wietersheim as Corps Commander of the first panzer contingent to reach the Don at Kalatsch and help in the fighting for the northern suburbs of the city, was flown out before the collapse. Three panzer and three motorized divisions were lost in the capitulation – the worst in German history, a turning-point in Wehrmacht military fortune.

Viewed in retrospect, the summer battles leading to disaster at Stalingrad had seen German fighting spirit and leadership in battle as strong as ever. In seizing Voronezh, *Blitzkrieg* renewed had taken the opposition in its stride.

Left: Terrain factors increasingly entered into the operational planning of panzer leaders; in this picture Guderian has halted for a progress report.

Left: Whenever marshland threatened to delay the advance, panzer engineers were called forward to lay temporary roads. Guderian's staff car can be seen displaying the identifying 'G' of his Gruppe and a corps headquarters tactical sign.

Left: During summer, the movement of heavy weapons was not a problem. Here a 15cm howitzer SFH18 is drawn by an 8-ton purpose-built machine, the Sd Kfz 7. Artillery was generally moved well forward to play a crucial role in defeating enemy attacks, usually before they could reach the main battle line.

Above: The autumn and spring rains turned the ground to mud which led to a loss of mobility for even the light Volkswagen 82.

First and Fourth Panzer Armies, leading the summer offensive, pressed home their attacks in conjunction with powerful air support, working tirelessly, yet to no real advantage. For the Russians, preliminary battles at Issyum had resulted in a repetition of large-scale losses. Tank actions of rare ferocity had been fought out on the Ukranian Steppe; in the Don bend in particular. Fourth Panzer Army in action with VIII Air Corps, the best-equipped of the available Luftwaffe ground-attack forces, had been constantly engaged; first in the eastwards thrust to Voronezh and then southwards in the Don corridor to Stalingrad, while simultaneously First Panzer Army pressed into the Caucasus. Such victories as these proved worthless. The 250,000-strong German Sixth Army, including six mobile divisions, had been lost at Stalingrad and no significant envelopment achieved. Nothing could hide the fact that 1942 had not produced the expected decisive victory.

No review of the changing fortunes of the panzer force can ignore the fighting in North Africa (map 5). In Libya, as hitherto in the Balkans, German forces were deployed in the role of 'fire brigade', assisting the Italian Army which was facing disastrous military setbacks.

At first only two panzer divisions served to create the Deutsches Afrika Korps progressively organized into Panzerarmee Afrika under General Rommel; 5th Light, converted to 21st Panzer and shortly afterwards 15th Panzer. Two light divisions, 90th and 164th, fighting alongside Italian infantry and armour substantially improved the offensive capacity of Rommel's desert force. German strength in North Africa was also to benefit from the timely deployment of 2nd Air Fleet in Sicily and finally the arrival of a third, 10th Panzer Division in Tunisia. Rommel's armoured divisions, 15th and 21st, were basically equipped to the same scale as divisions fighting on the eastern front. Three Italian armoured divisions: Ariete, Littorio and eventually Centauro, contributed more in numbers than power to the panzer army. But the African theatre was never considered more than a side-show by OKW. Consequently Rommel, who might have linked-up with von Kleist pushing through the Caucasus and on through Persia, was starved of the resources that could have taken him to Suez and beyond.

The tanks used in the earliest days of desert fighting were standard Pz Kpfw I, II and III series. Later came the much respected Pz Kpfw III and IV 'specials' with long-barrelled 5cm or 7.5cm guns respectively. These and other armoured fighting vehicles, including 8-wheeled armoured cars, unlike Italian armour serving with Ariete and Littorio, were on a par with if not superior to those in service with the British Army, the Matilda and 'Cruiser' tanks. But an influx of new American equipment into the theatre, Honeys, Grants and, above all, the formidable, 30-ton Sherman, armed and armoured to match the panzer 'specials', would go far towards tipping the armoured balance in favour of Eighth Army.

Broadly speaking, the 'African' panzer divisions – according to reports released by Wünsdorf technical centre and Panzer School I – were reasonably satisfied with the performance of their armoured vehicles. Motor cycles and 'soft' transport were less well regarded. All suffered the scouring effect of sand on engine performance. In respect of numbers, regimental strengths, like supplies in general, gave much less cause for optimism. War establishments were rarely fulfilled; reinforcement and supplies mostly ended up at the bottom of the Mediterranean – intercepted as a result of outstanding British Intelligence successes with 'Ultra' (*see* Part 2, Panzer signals and 'Ultra'). Yet despite such unfavourable circumstances, Rommel's more often than not inspired handling of armour, demanding and mostly receiving the highest level of support from subordinate commanders and staffs, would force British opponents to the brink of collapse. But Axis air power in North Africa was never able more than fleetingly to challenge the supremacy of the RAF or later the combined RAF and US air forces in Tunisia. Rommel's supreme disadvantage in the air was also fatally matched by Italian inability to guarantee the security of a long and constantly interrupted German supply line stretching back through the desert across the Mediterranean to Naples, or alternatively through Greece into Germany itself, the source of replacement engines and new vehicles. After twice outmanoeuvring British Eighth Army, inflicting savage defeats and reducing Tobruk in June 1942 (map 9), Rommel reigned supreme, forcing British commanders back upon Cairo and a battle of attrition. At El Alamein the Desert Fox was beaten; a tenacious British defence and an overwhelming counter-stroke tearing the heart out of Panzerarmee Afrika.

The Luftwaffe, eclipsed in air battles and unable to push its ground organization forward at the same rapid pace as the Panzerarmee, left Rommel particularly short on air reconnaissance and at the mercy of Allied air power. Lacking air support of his own, and resources with which to fight a mobile battle, Rommel could do no more and, after conflict with Hitler over intentions, turned about. The British counter-stroke 'Lightfoot' followed by 'Supercharge', starting on 23 October 1942 and directed by General Bernard Montgomery, had been a set-piece armour and infantry assault supported by massive air force and artillery concentrations. Montgomery had 'crumbled' Rommel's infantry. Starting with a superiority of more than four to one in (German) armour – a preponderance of Grants and Shermans tipping the balance in Eighth Army's favour and easily outnumbering Rommel's few Pz Kpfw IV 'specials' and lesser support – all that remained for the Panzerarmee after 4 November, when Montgomery's offensive had reduced the combined German-Italian tank strength to fewer than twenty machines, was a long fighting withdrawal to Tunisia. There, more than 1,500 miles away under Fifth Panzer Army, a newcomer to the German order of battle, a fresh German build-up was bringing new divisions to Africa – Hermann Goering, 10th Panzer, a Tiger battalion and more – which, had they been made available earlier, would have totally changed the picture for Rommel's panzer army.

But more unrewarding battles, command changes and conflict with higher authority leading Rommel into short-lived command of Army Group Africa before departing the desert for higher employment in the Balkans and Italy signalled an end to the Field Marshal's African career. Thereafter as inspector of coastal defences western Europe and C-in-C, Army Group 'B', Rommel would plan the defence of the west-European seaboard including Normandy where his experience of Allied air power pinning the panzer force to the ground before and after Alamein would all too strongly shape his views on the vulnerability of armoured formations to air attack. In consequence Rommel was to stress to Hitler the need to subject the defensive movement

Left: Wehrmacht supply columns, transferring from the eastern to the western theatres, frequently broke down as a result of water-logging; the provision of half-tracks helped to ease this problem.

of panzer divisions to the least possible degree of intervention; a warning destined to fall upon deaf ears. With operational control in North Africa passing to Army Group Tunis (von Arnim), the combined German and Italian force in North Africa enduring concentric pressure in consequence of the Anglo-US invasion of Morocco and Algeria (Operation 'Torch') proved unable to stave off disaster and collapsed. By the middle of May 1943 the war in Africa was over. DAK, three panzer, four motorized divisions, and 230,000 infantry went into Allied prisoner-of-war camps. Before the collapse, some personnel did manage to escape to Sicily or Italy. Of those that did, elements of Herman Goering and 15th Panzer without heavy weapons, many were to rejoin rear echelons to be reconstituted; HG was to be rebuilt, 15th Panzer converted to a panzer grenadier division and, like HG, deployed in support of Italian infantry divisions in Sicily. Both divisions would strengthen the defence of mainland Europe.

Right: The T34, which Second Panzer Army first encountered at Mzensk on the road to Moscow, came as an unpleasant surprise to Guderian who demanded increased firepower to counter it.

Right: Rail-borne supplies were no safer from attack, this time by partisans, and local defence units had to be raised to protect them.

5. Decline and fall of the panzer force, 1943–5

The disastrous consequences for the German Army of overwhelming Allied victories absorbing and destroying panzer divisions piecemeal in Africa and southern Russia during the winter of 1942–3 had been compounded by an unsuccessful Fourth Panzer Army attempt to raise the siege of Sixth Army which, together with a substantial part of Fourth Panzer Army, had been locked into Stalingrad since 19 November 1942 (map 12). Hoth's urgently assembled relief force of three panzer divisions – 23rd taken from von Kleist in the Caucasus, a refitted 6th railed from France to join 17th brought down from Army Group Centre – in the hands of experienced LVII Panzer Corps commander, Friedrich Kirchner, struggled forward despite midwinter conditions; Sixth Panzer (Raus) leading.

Opposed by a Red Army equally determined to halt the relief attempt, Kirchner thrust to within 48 kilometres of the city at which point, on 19 December, a new threat emerged close by, giving von Manstein, GOC, Army Group Don, cause for grave concern. Crumbling Italian resistance to renewed Russian attacks launched on an adjoining front along the River Chir started the rot. Faced with danger to Stalingrad's resupply points, von Manstein called off the relief operation and the exhausted panzer divisions were redeployed to cope with the new crisis which, should it result in the loss of Tazinskaya and Morovskaya, would destroy all continuity in air transport operations sustaining Sixth Army. Despite a successful intervention by panzer divisions sealing off the Russian spearheads on the very outskirts of the resupply points, von Manstein's worst fears were realized; the crucial airfields were lost and Paulus, deprived of supplies and unable to offer further resistance, surrendered an entire army.

So great a reverse shamed Hitler into action. He dismissed the Chief of the Army General Staff, Franz Halder, and replaced him with Kurt Zeitzler, a current favourite. He also shunned his generals and, distrustful of Prussian-German leadership of the Army, agreed with Himmler on expansion and strengthening of the Waffen SS with panzer divisions; quarrels developed between Zeitzler and Jodl over resource allocations and a general air of despondency seized the supreme military leadership. Strategically, the thrusting emphasis of *Blitzkrieg*, notwithstanding plans to break the Red Army at Kursk in July, would change to aggressive counter-action in self-defence; the Army, contending with counter-offensives, benefiting from arms and equipment deliveries from the west. Panzer divisions instead of sweeping forward in tightly co-ordinated mass would re-learn their tactics, turning individual mobility to account – sealing-off break-through offensives, organizing relief columns and adopting new measures to contain the progress of massive Russian motorized penetrations. At Hitler's senseless insistence, panzer divisions would succumb time and again defending ground unnecessarily.

The sacrifice of so many troops in coming months as Red Army Fronts deployed tanks and motorized forces in manoeuvres surpassing even the best of *Blitzkrieg* operations, would rarely win benefits for the defence. In passing from years of sweeping victory in Poland and France, where the panzer force had swept all before it, future action would degenerate into desperate battles for survival. German belief in victory, despite the menacing power of the Red Army and its increasingly sophisticated methods of warfare, no less so than that of the Red Air Force, revitalized and secure in new production localities in the Urals, would remain unshaken.

Left and right: Russian resistance necessitated close contact between the advancing German armour and fighting troops; panzer grenadiers were lifted into combat in semi-tracked armoured carriers (SPW) which assumed increasing importance on the battlefield. The work-horse in this area was the Sd Kfz 251 which was produced in a variety of forms with the needs of commanders, mortar crews, medical teams, etc., all provided for.

But of gave concern to the General Staff was a host of new Russian equipment, including aircraft deliveries from the Western Allies, legions of tanks and armoured fighting vehicles, not the least of which were powerful assault guns copied from the German model and soon to take effect on the battlefield. In another Russian development, increased fire-support from the 'Stalin organ' – a fearsome multi-barrelled rocket-launcher which the Army would counter with its own projector, the six-barrelled *Nebelwerfer* – would raise artillery concentrations to new levels.

In response to challenging conditions at the front, a new generation of German armoured fighting vehicles and transport machines bred in the harsh conditions of Eastern Front operations were shortly to enter service. Yet mounting evidence of Hitler's failure to provide effective war direction was to surface in unending retreat, vehicle, weapon and equipment shortages, declining fuel supplies and in crisis situations a general disregard for the views of commanders on the spot. Reporting divisional tank strength in December 1942 during the attempt to relieve Stalingrad, 17th Panzer Division listed fewer than thirty armoured vehicles on establishment. Above all, the absence of the Luftwaffe, drawn-off for action to defend the Reich from increasingly effective Anglo-US bombing or cleared from the skies by the Red Air Force, would accelerate the demise of the Wehrmacht. But all was not yet lost and the German Army was to demonstrate in future battles its remarkable resilience. Following the catastrophe at Stalingrad, von Manstein in particular would succeed with First and Fourth Panzer Armies in restoring the southern front (map 13). The spring of 1943, moreover, would witness a new milestone in the history of the panzer force.

On the unemployed list since December 1941, General Guderian was recalled by Hitler in February 1943 and appointed to a new post – that of Inspector-General of Armoured Troops; Panzertruppen – hitherto Schnelltruppen. The Inspector-General's responsibilities covered technical development of weapons and vehicle production planning, training and replacement programming for the Army, Waffen SS and Luftwaffe. Motorized infantry, renamed panzer grenadiers, were also included in the shake-up. With characteristic zeal Guderian set about the crucial task of revitalizing the worn-down panzer force. With combat efficiency at a low ebb, following years of action and

Below: Rail routes were also defended by well-sited anti-aircraft and anti-tank guns, often mounted on platforms on the trains themselves.

Above: An improvised ferry carrying a motor-cycle unit across the Dnieper. The motive power comes from a 20-man engineer assault boat lashed to a pneumatic infantry model driven by an outboard motor. Rafts were constructed to carry heavier items; these were made from assault boats and pontoon decking.

crippling losses in men and material, both in Africa and Russia, Guderian's neglected expertise was a dire necessity. Inaugurating a new training command with programmes at Wünsdorf and Krampnitz (the Schnelltruppen School's re-designated Panzertruppenschule I and II) and collaborating with Albert Speer, the Armaments Minister, Guderian proposed to reduce the number of tank models to a minimum. Speer and Guderian were to prove remarkably successful in rationalizing tank design and raising production – increasing Pz Kpfw output by 30 per cent in 1943 and more than doubling it from the 1942 level of 4,278 vehicles to a high peak of 9,161 in 1944. Losses, on the other hand, continued to increase faster than production so that by the end of 1944 the actual surplus would amount to a disappointing 15 per cent.

Reviewing equipment tables and personnel strengths of panzer and panzer grenadier divisions, the new Inspector-General paid special attention to the need for better self-propelled artillery and anti-tank weapons – Panzerjaeger and Jagdpanzer – predominantly turretless Pz Kpfw III/IV vehicles mounting a 7.5cm gun to combat the menacing power of Russian armour. An increase in heavy (turretless) self-propelled weapons to assist in attack or defence, and easier to produce than tanks, was decided upon as an urgent requirement. Production of these weapons, the Pz Kpfw III/IV assault gun (Sturmgeschütz) in particular, consequently increased elevenfold. From 788 vehicles produced in 1942, numbers rose to 3,406 in 1943 and would continue to expand at a faster rate than tank production – a true measure of change in store for the panzer force. In the aftermath of German failure at Stalingrad, Russian exploitation had continued for 300 miles between the Don and the Dnieper across the Donetz until von Manstein's (Army Group Don) counter-stroke had brought the offensive to a halt (map 13); the re-capture of Kharkov by SS Panzer Corps Hausser under command of Fourth Panzer Army proving the culminating point of von Manstein's achievement. During the course of the action, planned and executed in high *Blitzkrieg* fashion (*see* Part 4, Stukagruppen – Schlact-gruppen), skillfully combined army-air operations inflicted grievous damage on Russian armour. When von Manstein had disposed of the Russian winter threat, the focus of OKW attention in the east swung to plans for a great summer offensive Operation 'Citadel' – the battle for Kursk. The German armoured build-up to 'pinch out' this threatening Russian bulge was prodigious (map 14).

Concentrating panzer and panzer grenadier divisions on abnormally narrow sectors and in greater numbers than at any time since the invasion began, the point of main effort would lie with Hausser's SS Panzer Corps deployed north of Bjelgorod in the centre of the southern build-up. North of the bulge, Ninth Army (Model) disposed of a near equivalent number of armoured formations. Forty-three divisions, including eight panzer divisions, Gross Deutschland and supporting units with 2,700 tanks and assault guns, were drawn up to face 100 Russian divisions (five tank armies with 3,306 tanks and assault guns). The most violent and decisive tank battle in history, Operation 'Citadel', opened on 5 July 1943 with considerable success attending the early efforts of the panzer force despite bad weather. New tanks and self-propelled guns, Panthers, Tigers, Ferdinands and Hornets, the product of hard-won Eastern Front experience were brought into service – not all with Guderian's approval. Some, such as the Panthers and Ferdinands were committed prematurely with disappointing results. Shortcomings in most cases were made good, but the SP 'Ferdinand', renamed 'Elefant', failed totally and the surviving vehicles found future employment in defensive battles either in Italy (Anzio) or in the east where operations would increasingly favour delaying action involving tanks and SP guns in ambush-like situations.

The battle for Kursk, coinciding with Operation 'Husky', the Allied invasion of Sicily on 12 July, ended in total German disaster. After losing more than a thousand tanks and three hundred assault guns in the attempt to force six successive lines of defence, and counter a new Russian offensive ploughing into Second Panzer Army (which had long since given up most of its armour), Hitler called it off. The power of the panzer force, into which everything had been committed at Kursk, faded in a welter of engagements. Soviet tanks and aircraft striking against the flank of Hoth's Panzer Corps at Prochorowka on 12 July finally put an end to panzer progress – despite the intervention of Luftwaffe ground-attack squadrons flying the newest Hs 129 and breaking up concentrations of enemy armour (a significant development, discussed in Part 4, Stukagruppen – Schlact-gruppen), German offensive power was never to recover from the setback at Kursk although in the following year a dozen or so SS and Army panzer divisions would be deployed in the west contesting Operation 'Overlord', the Allied invasion of Normandy; the losses in trained crews and fighting machines at Kursk and its aftermath would never be made good.

At the conclusion of 'Citadel' with the strategic initiative swinging irretrievably in favour of the Red Army, the forward progress of the panzer divisions was finally halted. In the air, Luftwaffe resources were increasingly diverted to defend the Reich and no great Army reliance could be placed upon an air force mainly dependent upon obsolete and inadequate machines; the Ju 87s of Spanish Civil War days proving unable to cope with modern Russian types – their successors, the Fw 190 and Hs 129 in short supply. Russian air power on the other hand, gaining strength from new manufacturing locations hidden deep in the Urals and well out of reach of a Luftwaffe lacking a four-engined bomber, imposed its authority with much improved fighter and ground-attack types including tank-busting Stormo-vicks. Pursuing summer and autumn offensives to encircle Manstein (with four armies deployed west of the Donetz and south of Pripet), the Red Army struck powerful blows at Kharkov and Kiev; Fourth Panzer Army holding grimly on to Kharkov for a time while to the south First Panzer Army fought without success to retain Krivoi Rog and Nikopol. Despite local successes in counter-attacks, the retrograde movement of the panzer divisions continued unchecked.

Carrying the war into 1944, the Red Army would strike again with concentrated force at Army Group South before turning its attention to Army Groups Centre and North, trapping the panzer force time and again and exhausting its energies. A timely operation by II SS Panzer Corps in the spring of 1944 (map 15) rescued First Panzer Army, reduced to thirty tanks and encircled with a Leibstandarte divisional battle group at Kamenets Podolsk in North Ukraine. Disaster on the scale of Stalingrad was narrowly averted. Only weeks earlier First Panzer Army in the relief of Cherkassy, fifty miles to the east, had organized the escape of SS Wiking surrounded on the Dnieper. One of the most formidable German divisions on the Eastern Front, Wiking lost all its equipment in the débâcle; the Luftwaffe played a vital role in transporting supplies to encircled formations. (*See* Part 4, New Horizons in Transport.)

In the Mediterranean, where collapse of Axis resistance in Tunisia was followed by the Allied invasion of Sicily on 12 July 1943, panzer divisions were to fight tough delaying battles. The action in Italy is summarized in Part 6. In France, the Western Allies compounded German problems by opening a third front in Normandy, bringing Fifth Panzer Army (Europe) into action. Demands on the panzer force were now set to increase out of all proportion to available resources. Despite Guderian's efforts to rebuild divisions for limited offensive roles there would be too little equipment and, given the overwhelming presence of Allied air power, too few opportunities for their concentrated use in counter-attacks.

Above: The great turning-point of Stalingrad as seen from a Stuka, with burnt-out fuel tanks visible on the right bank of the Volga. The devastation for the Wehrmacht was total with some 200,000 troops taken prisoner (*see* map 11).

In a year of destiny for Hitler and the Wehrmacht, June 1944 marked the beginning of the end for the panzer force. Starting on 22 June, the third anniversary of Hitler's invasion of Russia, four Russian army groups (Fronts) deploying 5,000 tanks and 6,000 aircraft would henceforth allow no respite for Army Group Centre which collapsed almost at once under the hammer blows of tank and infantry attacks; defensive actions such as that forced upon Third Panzer Army holding the line at Vitebsk, demanded great sacrifice in the flux of disaster. Understrength panzer divisions lacking even the most basic of vehicles and weapons, as the year progressed, were switched between sectors and fronts, from west to east and back again. Schools were combed out by OKH, and truly impoverished formations, with grandiose names, Clausewitz, Muncheberg and others, were raised for action in daunting circum-stances. All would serve to the best of their limited abilities.

On the Russian side, tank armies bolstered by masses of transport delivered by the Western Allies and benefiting from tank production soaring to new levels made sweeping

Right: A panzer battle group passes a burning T34.

Right: The '88' on a Pz Kpfw IV chassis (Hornet) provided much needed support for those divisions expected to cope with a new breed of Russian tanks and assault guns.

advances through German fronts stretched between Baltic and Danube. Leningrad was prised free of Army Group North by Russian Fronts clearing a way through Estonia and Lithuania, while at Jassy and Debrecen panzer battles flared as other Fronts driving through Roumania and Hungary closed on Budapest (map 19). Operation 'Bagration', the Red Army's June offensive against Army Group Centre, carried to Warsaw and the Vistula, progressing a distance of 200 miles in four weeks, culminating in battles for the Polish capital. Reorganizing its tank and motorized forces on German lines, the Red Army, although lacking sophisticated infantry personnel carriers of the German type, exploited heavy fire power and manoeuvrability to remarkable effect.

In this fifth year of war, with Berlin itself threatened east and west, there would be a marked change of emphasis in German armament production – switched from the all-out manufacture of tanks to the production of defensive armoured fighting vehicles, notably Jagdpanzer. In tabling strengths for 1945 panzer divisions, Guderian's concept would be wholly defensive; the tank complement of a future panzer regiment amounting to no more than 54 vehicles, a far cry from pre-war tank strengths when in 1935 a panzer brigade comprised 561 tanks. Suffering the consequences of Hitler's war direction, with its maladroit insistence on rigid defence, tying the Army to first one string of 'fortress' towns – Vitebsk, Kowel, Tarnopol, Bobruisk, Minsk – and then another, panzer battles to shield or relieve immobile infantry sapped every sinew of the once formidable panzer force – mortally weakening the defensive capacity of the Wehrmacht. During the summer of 1944, Army Group Centre alone suffered the loss of 28 infantry divisions. And not only in the east was the army saddled with Hitler's mismanagement leading to the wasteful employment of panzer divisions in unsuitable defensive tasks.

The return of vast new Allied armies to the continent, in Operation 'Overlord' on 6 June had heralded a renewal of panzer operations in the west (map 16). In month-long battles of attrition the panzer force was bled white. The Führer's uncompromising attitude towards winning the war

Above: A graveyard of wrecked Russian armour of passing interest to the inquisitive.

(which he directed from East Prussia), allowing no respite for the armed services, accelerated the destruction of two complete armies, Seventh and Fifth Panzer including eleven Army and SS panzer divisions. Contending with land, sea and air opposition arrayed against them in overwhelming strength, the panzer divisions fought the Battle of Normandy to the point of extinction.

Jagdpanzers, a new category of self-propelled defensive vehicles – including the formidable King Tiger making an appearance on the battlefield in Normandy – were too few to do more than fleetingly sustain the powers of resistance needed by panzer divisions enduring day and night assault by US, British, French and Polish armour sweeping forward to the Seine and beyond. Allied air power, destroying German tanks and transport in vast numbers while sealing the Normandy battlefield against reinforcement, robbed the panzer force of its vitality. Rommel's views on the need to avoid unnecessary movement by deploying panzer divisions close to the beaches and thereby counter constant air surveillance and attack were ignored by Hitler and the High Command – with grievous consequences. Panzer divisions were decimated by air power. Anti-aircraft tanks, Whirlwind and Ostwind, that might have protected the panzer divisions, were only belatedly entering service. Without them and in the absence of air cover, Fifth Panzer Army under General Eberbach, was rendered impotent. Aided by a brilliant deception plan focusing Hitler's attention on the wrong (Pas-de-Calais) invasion area, Field Marshal Montgomery's strategy of attrition followed by the sweeping advance of US armour led by General Patton proved decisive. In this situation, verging once more on total disaster, the Army leadership in Normandy was obliged to defer its professional responses in favour of instructions coming direct from Führer Headquarters in East Prussia; none of the senior commanders on the spot, von Runstedt, Rommel or von Kluge, being allowed to make even the slightest alteration to counter-offensive plans conceived over a map table in Rastenburg. The predictable result was a disaster greater even than Stalingrad. Forty-three German divisions were sacrificed in a strategy of unyielding defence; none of the mainly SS panzer divisions escaping across the Seine with more than ten tanks! (Model).

At the height of the battle on 20 July 1944, a number of disaffected Generals made an unsuccessful attempt on Hitler's life. In its aftermath General Guderian, enjoying Hitler's grudging respect, was promoted Chief of the General Staff in succession to General Zeitzler, and Field Marshal Model arrived in the west to take command of the theatre. Opting to continue the evacuation of Normandy, Model withdrew the broken Wehrmacht across the Seine to the western frontiers of Germany. Dramatic battles such as the defence of Arnhem (II SS Panzer Corps) and fighting around Aachen, would steal newspaper headlines bolstering German morale, but a panzer force equipped and organized for swift, effective, retaliatory action no longer existed. All attempts by the new Chief of the Army General Staff Guderian to assembles such a force on the Eastern Front were to end in frustration. In the west Hitler was planning a counter-strike to recapture Antwerp so as to isolate Allied armies in Holland and north-west Germany. Allowing little respite for the panzer divisions, Hitler's new offensive, 'Autumn Mist' starting on 15 December, would destroy much of what was being committed within 5th Panzer and a new Sixth SS Panzer Army (map 17).

Despite protests from von Runstedt, C-in-C, West, recalled from retirement to direct the offensive, Hitler gambled with nine re-equipped panzer divisions to restore the Army's fortunes. Lead by Generals von Manteuffel and Dietrich, the panzer armies were to be launched against US forces, surprising them in rest sectors of the Ardennes and catching them off-balance. But 'Autumn Mist', materializing west of the Rhine in the short daylight hours of December and benefiting from the bad weather which grounded British and US air forces, was thwarted by American troops holding

Right: Equipment became heavier and more powerful after Stalingrad with steel skirts, as seen here, fitted to protect assault guns and medium tanks.

Right: A towed 7.5cm Pak. This gun allowed German crews to engage marauding Russian armour at longer ranges and with increased effectiveness.

out in Bastogne and turning other towns into strong points. Five or six hundred priceless tanks and assault guns, Germany's last reserve diverted from hard-pressed armies in the east, were sacrificed in the attempt. The armies involved were extricated with difficulty. In the east, where Soviet progress had brough the Red Army to the Vistula opposite Berlin and through Roumania to the Danube, Hitler decided upon a new move. In January 1945 Sixth SS Panzer Army was transferred across Europe not to defend Berlin but western Hungary where the Red Army, having encircled Budapest, was threatening the Wehrmacht's oil-producing centre at Nagykanizsa – more important than ever to the economy after the loss of Roumanian capacity at Ploesti (map 19). Nevertheless the vital oilfields were soon lost with dire consequences (*see* Part 4).

Unable to halt the Red Army driving for Berlin and Vienna in January 1945, the heartlands of Germany were exposed to attack from offensives launched on all sides. On the Eastern Front, 12½ panzer divisions were all that remained to serve two army groups deployed between the Carpathians and the Baltic. Fourth Panzer Army, holding the line south of Warsaw, collapsed leaving Panzer Corps Nehring and others to survive in a moving pocket before contacting Gross Deutschland Corps, sent from Lodz to relieve them (map 18). Protracted and ferocious battles for Berlin and Vienna absorbed panzer divisions, independent panzerjaeger battalions, assault-gun brigades and a new but ineffectual Eleventh (SS) Panzer Army, also the rumps of First and Fourth Panzer Armies and, fighting for Budapest, a re-deployed Sixth SS Panzer Army (map 19). All confronted the enemy in suicidally small numbers on fronts crumbling into nothing. In north-west Europe, powerful Anglo-US armies lead by armoured and motorized divisions at full strength, extended their drive to encircle the Ruhr, the heart of German industrial power in the west. In the process, Fifth Panzer Army was trapped and destroyed. The Red Army sweeping through Hungary, overruning Poland and isolating East Prussia, surged uncontainably through Pomerania and Silesia, closing up to the Oder less than a hundred miles from Berlin (map 20).

Panzer divisions in continuous action on all fronts were reduced to battalion and company battle groups with handfuls of vehicles and men, contesting step by step every new Russian or Allied advance. Third Panzer Army on the Oder defending Stettin, make-shift armoured units serving Ninth Army at Küstrin and Frankfurt, and Fourth Panzer Army deployed along the Neisse at Cottbus, Spremberg and Bautzen, recorded local successes, all dearly bought. Depleted battle groups standing four-square in the path of the Red Army's ruthlessly conceived offensive against Berlin, survived through grim determination, closing on enemy armour with the deadly *Panzerfaust* – a hand-held, anti-tank rocket-launcher modelled on the American Bazooka and, like anti-tank mines in determined hands, used to crippling effect. Reporting on a week's fighting during march 1945, OKW recorded 300 Russian tanks destroyed in eight days, 135 of them in close combat. The armoured fighting troops that had once so triumphantly sown the seeds of victory for Hitler and the Third Reich, finally reaped a whirlwind of annihilation. When tanks and transport were stranded for want of fuel, their crews destroyed them before joining mixed formations of all kinds to fight on foot until they too were swept into defeat; the Luftwaffe, stretched in all directions, would occasionally find the strength to re-supply encircled formations, at the same time supporting 'fortress' cities such as Breslau, holding out for three months and counting the days to capitulation.

In this desperate hour panzer divisions, gravely weakened by years of action taking a heavy toll of experienced commanders and units, counted for no more than symbols on enemy situation maps. When the Red Army broke into Pomerania, Third Panzer Army possessed fourteen tanks and 164 assault guns with which to oppose six Russian armies. In the ruined shell of Berlin, no more of a safe haven for Hitler than any other of Germany's shattered towns and cities, where battle raged before fuel supplies dried up completely, single-vehicle combat by SS and Army battle groups was the order of the day. Sharing the defence with Volksturm veterans of the First World War, Hitler Youth and refugees from the eastern provinces – many of them women and girls – with swastikered armbands declaring allegiance to a state on the verge of collapse – battle groups continued the fight; bicycles serving as transport for anti-tank auxiliaries. The life expectancy of junior leaders in those grim days was forty-eight hours. For the defenders of the city, isolated from all landward connection with the interior of Germany after 27 April, the situation was hopeless. The efforts of Muncheberg and surviving battle groups, including those of SS Nordland and SS Charlemagne fighting in the Tiergarten only blocks away from Führer HQ, were doomed to failure. Yet Hitler, wrecked in mind and body, following years of treatment for health disorders and never properly

Below: Emulating Germany's success with self-propelled weapons, the Red Army introduced a similar range of heavily armoured vehicles using the T34 chassis. The 30-ton SU-85, pictured here, required a crew of four, carried an 8.5cm gun and had a road speed of 34mph.

recovered from the attempt on his life in July 1944, was determined to fight on – obsessed with map flags and disputing with Guderian (who had wanted to re-deploy Sixth SS Panzer Army in defence of Berlin but had been overruled) how best to make use of meagre and failing resources. Bitter recrimination followed. Guderian fell from favour and was sent on indefinite leave to be replaced by General Krebs. Directing operations from a command bunker sited beneath a garden of the Chancellery, Hitler took his own life in Berlin on 30 April.

For the Panzer troops and others of the German armed services bolstering armies and army groups of indifferent size and power, fighting in defence of Courland, East Prussia, Berlin and Alpine Germany, the end came officially nine days later on 9 May 1945. Campaigning the length and breadth of Europe, von Seeckt's Kraftfahrtruppen, the motor supply troops of the twenties, Guderian's Schnelltruppen of the thirties – Hitler's Panzertruppen – had witnessed triumph wither into defeat. In *Blitzkrieg* against unprepared and incompetent opponents the panzer divisions

Below: An upgunned version of the same vehicle carrying a 12.2cm howitzer.

Bottom: The 45-ton Josef Stalin JSU-152 required a crew of five. It carried a 15.2cm gun howitzer and could travel at 23mph.

Left: Rocket weapons raised the power of artillery fire to new levels and were used to good effect by both sides on the Eastern Front. The multi-barrelled 'Stalin organ' was matched by a six-barrelled 15cm Nebelwerfer towed into action and a ten-barrelled self-propelled version.

Left: A later version Pz Kpfw III assault gun with rounded gun mantlet and close-defence machine-gun. Production gradually overtook tank output and in 1945 it had equal importance in the panzer divisions.

had reigned supreme, principally in the battle for France. But in later campaigns, bolstering infantry with no adequate anti-tank or anti-aircraft protection of their own and thus easy prey to the *Blitzkrieg* tactics of their opponents, the panzer and panzer grenadier divisions suffered the consequences of Hitler's maladroit war direction (self-appointed Army C-in-C, December 1941). Seldom willing to accept professional advice on the need for concentrating panzer divisions in a counter-attack role – exploiting their potential for rapid intervention in a crisis – Hitler instead allowed that power to be frittered away in generally wasteful defensive tasks; a doctrinaire insistence on 'not one step back' proving no substitute for a strategy of flexible defence.

Von Manstein's recovery of Kharkov in 1943 and less spectacular success by other army group commanders, counter-attacking the Red Army as it smashed a way through Roumania, Poland and Hungary at Jassy, Wilomin and Debrecen in 1944, all demonstrated effective mobile intervention. Nevertheless, in conceiving air power as a strike weapon more potent than the tank, Hitler's implacable enemies broke the Wehrmacht and its panzer force to pieces. With an advantage in high-grade Intelligence pinpointing targets in 'Ultra' detail, Allied air power secured the defeat of the panzer divisions, nailing them to the ground and sealing their fate. The Third Reich assailed from all sides collapsed in the process.

Part 2. The grand design

1. Panzer and panzer grenadier

Starting with three panzer divisions raised in October 1935, the German Army put into the field in the space of ten years, 86 panzer and panzer grenadier divisions, thirty or more panzer corps and eight panzer armies of which, one – Fifth Panzer Army following its destruction in North Africa in 1943 – was reformed for action in Normandy 1944. Subordinate armoured units including panzer regiments and battalions were raised in varying numbers to serve these formations or to fight independently as Army and Corps troops at the disposal of relevant headquarters. At the highest operational level stood the Panzer Army (abbreviated to PzAOK=Panzer Armee Oberkommando) which according to the German system was essentially a command body of specialist officers controlling combatant units and formations allotted in accordance with changing operational needs. Panzer armies were identified by number or name, and made their first appearance in action against the Red Army on the Central Front in 1941 – their role being to control increasingly complex mobile operations and a burgeoning number of panzer divisions in the battle for Moscow. Raised in a separate series from the normal type of army (AOK), their numbers, First, Second, Third and Fourth, were expanded to include Panzer Army Afrika (PzAOK 5) (Tunisia 1943, reformed Normandy 1944), Sixth (SS) in action on main fronts east and west, and Eleventh (SS) mostly engaged by the Red Army in Pomerania and the battle for Berlin in 1945. A war chronology of these formations, featuring subordinate panzer corps and divisions, also panzer action in Italy where the highest regular armoured formation to take the field was the panzer corps – two of which serving regular armies were deployed in defence of the peninsular – is provided in Part 6.

At each panzer army headquarters, evolving with (SS) exceptions out of *ad hoc* panzer groups whose origins lay in pre-existing panzer corps, permanently appointed personnel were supervised by a chief of staff whose main branches – Operations (1A), Supply and Rear Services (1B) Intelligence (1C) – were supplemented by Army supply, signals, field security, legal, cartographic and other ancillary personnel. An army artillery commander (Arko) and air liaison officer (Koluft), also with subordinates, worked alongside permanent headquarters staff. Executive assistants (ordnance officers, e.g., 01 Ops, 03 Intelligence) and additional technical and administrative officers, including anti-tank specialists and translators, might also be seconded to a headquarters when operations so required. Upwards of 600 officers and men served at a panzer army headquarters. A panzer group (Panzergruppe) like any other group (or gruppe) whether Armeegruppe, Korpsgruppe or Battalion Kampfgruppe was essentially an impromptu battle formation whose 'standing' was indicated by the rank of its commanding, commissioned or non-commissioned, officer. Generals(Obersten) von Kleist, Hoth and Guderian, in France in 1940 and afterwards in Russia together with Generaloberst Hoepner, all operated panzer groups (controlling armoured, motorized and regular infantry corps) within the framework of higher (Army) operations until their own commands were upgraded to panzer army. Panzer and panzer grenadier divisions organized into regiments and battalions all created Kampfgruppen (battle groups) within their permanent structure. The composition and strength of these *tactical* units depended upon whatever operational tasks were required of them; numbers if deficient being made up by 'outside' units.

The battle group system employed by tank (and infantry) formations was a means of concentrating and balancing a formation's powers where it was most needed. In so far as the panzer division was concerned, this more often than not entailed the creation of Kampfgruppen around the division's three principal combat units: the panzer regiment, with divisional armour concentrated into a powerful strike force; the panzer grenadier regiment, organized for action in a less demanding, usually supportive role; and the panzer reconnaissance battalion, equipped and organized for skirmishing and, like other units, reinforced when necessary with extra weapons from support companies. A prime early example of the battle group system in Africa during Operation 'Scorpion' is provided in Part 6 by Panzer Army Africa, 21 May 1941. A later example of battle groups in action (at Falaise in the closing stages of the war in Europe) is provided by 12th SS Hitler Jugend deployed in defence of Normandy (*see* Fifth Panzer Army, 8 August 1944 (D+63)). Battle groups, incidentally, posed considerable problems for Allied Intelligence staffs. With units of mixed kinds finding their way into battle groups, particularly in the

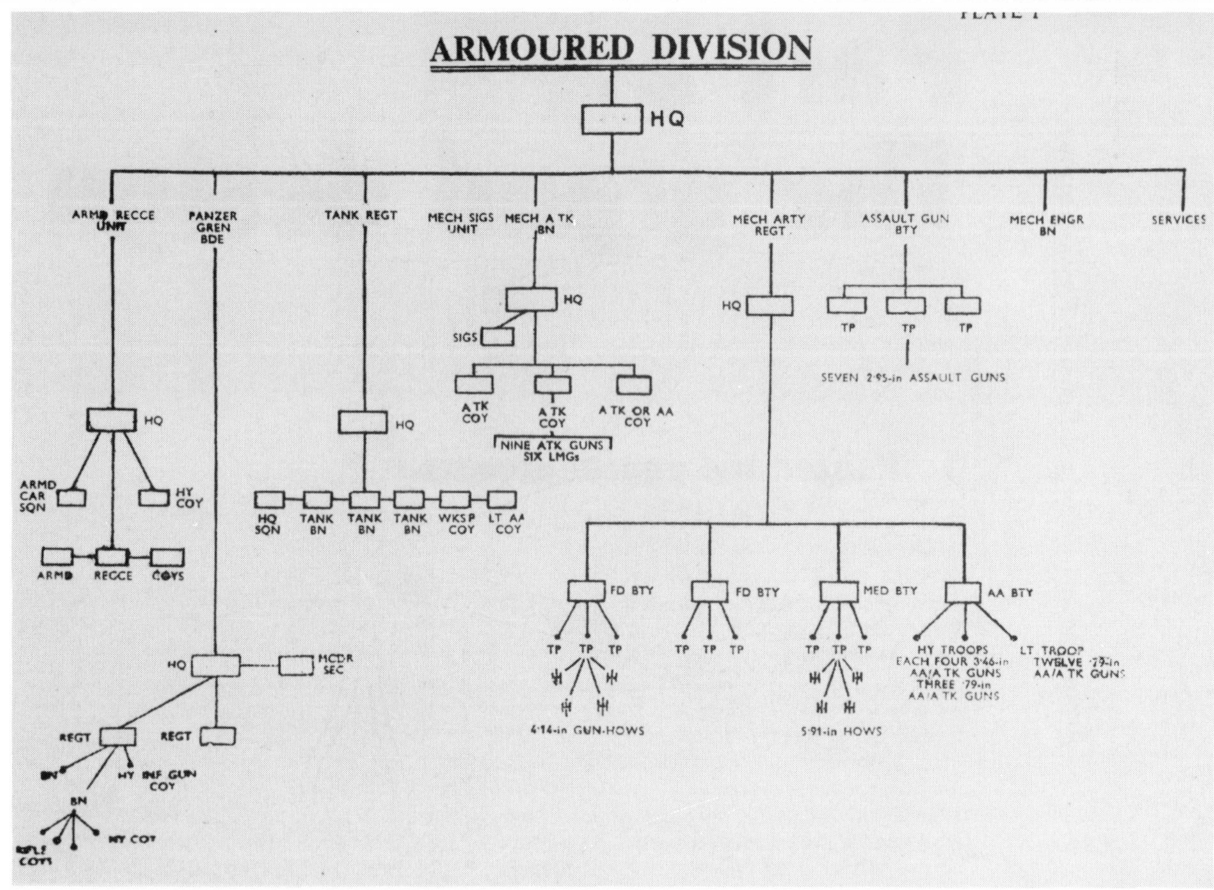

Above: Layout of an armoured (panzer) division comprising two panzer grenadier regiments and three tank battalions. In practice, by the end of 1943, most divisions were fighting with only a single panzer grenadier regiment and only one or two tank (or assault gun) battalions.

confusion of battle, the Intelligence officers' task of building a picture of a German order of battle could prove both difficult and time-consuming.

Panzer corps (Pz-Korps abbreviated to PzK) originated in the motorized armee-korps serving regular armies in the 1939/early 1940 campaigns. Throughout the war, divisions of any type, not only panzer and panzer grenadier, but also infantry divisions, might be allocated to a panzer corps in the light of changing operational needs; numbers varying usually from two to four, often daily. At times in later campaigns panzer corps consisted solely of infantry divisions. The number of panzer corps in the German Army, no more than four (motorized corps) at the start of the campaign in Poland and twelve at the outset in Russia, grew ultimately to about thirty, not all of which were in action at the same time (twelve on 1 January 1943, fifteen on 10 December 1944, including four Waffen SS), some having been lost in action. As the war progressed, these corps, particularly those of the Waffen SS, were favoured with extra heavy weapons; by mid-summer 1944, Tiger or King Tiger and Werfer (mortar) battalions were notably strengthening corps establishments and firepower. If required, additional engineers (Pioniere), medical (Sanitäts) and observation (Beobachtung) units would be available to corps commanders 'on loan' from Army (OKH) reserve. Other Army troops (Heerestruppen) at OKH disposal, included heavy bridging columns, road construction, railway artillery, heavy anti-tank and tank destroyer (Panzerjaeger and Jagdpanzer) battalions and companies. Gross Deutschland (two battalions) the Leibstandarte SS Adolf Hitler and three other SS regiments, all motorized, plus two independent panzer brigades were included in this category in 1939. Support units of this kind could expect to operate with any formation, working alongside its 'organic' units.

The panzer division – the German Army's most powerful regular combat formation with a permanent establishment of weapons, vehicles and personnel – whose individual roles are elaborated in Part 3 – varied substantially in strength and composition over the years depending upon war organization tables in use or simply material availability. Identified by number or name, starting with three formations in 1935 (numbers 1 to 3), the panzer division was initially founded upon two (brigaded) panzer regiments – reduced to a single regiment by June 1941 in order to create additional divisions – one Schützen (panzer grenadier) brigade of two motorized infantry regiments (each of two Schutzen battalions with motor cycle companies), one reconnaissance battalion of three companies (one motor cycle), one anti-tank battalion, one artillery regiment, signals, engineers and supporting services.

The first three panzer divisions undergoing training in 1938 with XVI (mot) Corps, forerunner of Panzergruppe 4 in1941 (later Fourth Panzer Army) were followed over the years by divisions numbered 4–27, 116, Gross Deutschland, Panzer Lehr, Feldherrnhalle and, in 1944/45, divisions of lesser stature – FBD, FGD, Clausewitz, Holstein, Muncheberg and others, none more powerful than brigade or regimental battle groups. Following no regular pattern of expansion, but raised in expectation of operational needs, the original 1935 panzer divisions were joined by three more in September 1939. This total of six panzer divisions plus a mixed (Division Kempf) joined in the campaign against Poland (map 2). By May 1940 in time for the Battle of France, the total stood at ten (map 3). In June 1941 at the start of the campaign against Russia (map 7), by the over-simple expedient of halving divisional tank strengths, the total was more than doubled to twenty-one; subsequent progress was less dramatic and after June 1941 the number of regular Army panzer divisions as distinct from the seven contributed from 1943 onwards by the Waffen SS, and to which an increasingly high proportion of new equipment was diverted, would not rise above twenty-nine. Impromptu panzer divisions raised in 1945 increased the total by ten. Certain divisions destroyed in action like those that had served Sixth Army at Stalingrad in 1942 (14th, 16th and 24th) or in the same year lost with Fifth Panzer Army in Tunisia (15th and 21st) were subsequently reformed. A handful of reserve Panzer Divisions, 155th, 178th, 179th, 233rd and 273rd, ended by providing personnel for the refitting of front-line divisions. None of the late 1944/45 divisions raised from panzer schools or war remnants with the outstanding exception of Panzer Lehr, formed basically from Panzer School 2 cadres at Krampnitz, exceeded battle group status. But it must be said that in times of crisis on the Eastern Front, following the collapse of Army Group Centre in June 1944, culminating in the battle for Berlin in 1945, these and other 'scratch' panzer formations of indifferent size and power, made a much needed contribution to the over-strained and rapidly diminishing resources of the panzer force.

Panzer grenadier divisions raised by the Army and Waffen SS, no more than twenty-one in the 1943 order of battle and rarely exceeding fifteen in action at any one time, were originally termed motorized (mot) infantry divisions. Unlike their more powerful panzer division counterparts, panzer grenadier divisions were neither designated nor numbered in a separate series, but their establishments varied similarly in accordance with changing organization tables and availability of equipment and personnel. Several, mostly SS, panzer grenadier divisions, were converted to SS panzer divisions. Independent panzer brigades, consisting basically of two battalions (one panzer, one panzer grenadier) were a 1944 emergency measure to create new defensive formations in the wake of catastrophes on both main fronts. Numbered 101–113 and of limited strength (35 tanks, twelve assault guns), they were mostly too weak and were incorporated into panzer or other divisions. In contrast to the declining number and power of Army panzer divisions as they were exhausted or destroyed in action was the growing contribution of the Waffen SS. Providing OKW with seven SS panzer, eleven SS panzer grenadier divisions, four SS panzer corps and two SS panzer army headquarters, the Waffen SS shouldered a burden of heavy and continuous fighting in later years. SS panzer divisions, notably those with Tiger companies on establishment, were exceptionally powerful formations. At their head, elevated from panzer grenadier status in 1943, were 1st Leibstandarte SS Adolf Hitler, 2nd SS Das Reich, 3rd SS Totenkopf and 5th SS Wiking. Prior to their up-grading, all were superior even to Army panzer divisions. With the advent of 9th SS Hohenstaufen, 10th SS Frundsberg and 12th SS Hitler Jugend in 1944, the number of SS panzer divisions increased to seven. All were regularly kept up to strength, but as the quality of recruits declined and establishments were reduced, differences between SS and Army panzer divisions in strength and composition became less pronounced.

SS panzer grenadier divisions other than those converted to panzer status and mostly expanded from motorized infantry regiments serving on the Eastern Front included 4th SS 'Polizei', 11th SS 'Nordland', 16th 'Reichsführer'-SS and 17th SS 'Goetz von Berlichingen'. Less prominent formations by virtue of late or incomplete establishments were 18th SS 'Horst Wessel', 23rd SS 'Nederland', 27th SS 'Langemarck' and 28th SS 'Wallonien'. SS panzer corps (I–IV) served east, west and briefly in northern Italy (II) but never entered North Africa. The first SS panzer corps formed under Paul Hausser, designated II SS Panzer Corps, took control of the Leibstandarte, Reich and Totenkopf in the battle for Kharkov in 1943 (map 13). In Normandy in 1944 (map 16), 'Sepp' Dietrich lead I SS Panzer Corps until his promotion to GOC, Fifth Panzer Army; Felix Steiner commanded III (Germanisches) SS Panzer Corps in Courland and Pomerania before a new appointment brought him command of Eleventh (SS) Panzer Army. Herbert Gille also served only in the east, bringing IV SS Panzer Corps through 1944–5 campaigns east of Warsaw and west of Budapest (map 19). Two SS panzer armies were raised and deployed late in the war. Sixth SS Panzer Army (Dietrich), spearheading 'Autumn Mist', Hitler's 1944 Ardennes offensive (map 17), was – on Hitler's instructions and contrary to the general situation at the time – fully equipped with heavy weapons, tracked and wheeled vehicles; it controlled I and II SS Panzer Corps, and more, in battles for Brussels and Antwerp. The other, Eleventh SS Panzer Army (Steiner), a hybrid Army SS Headquarters, defended Pomerania and outer Berlin before redeployment in the Hartz Mountains took the Army briefly to the west in 1945.

The Luftwaffe created an air-mobile intervention force for OKW in 1943, by rebuilding its premier (1st and 2nd) Fallschirm Divisions and concentrating them at Istres in Provence, later raising by stages the powerful Hermann Goering (Fallschirm) Panzer Division – intended partly for commitment by air – a scheme that never materialized. The Panzer Division demonstrated sterling worth in Italy. The Luftwaffe's ultimate contribution to the panzer force, Fallschirm Panzer Corps HG, comprising HG 1st (Panzer) and HG 2nd (Panzer Grenadier) Divisions, campaigned vigorously in both East Prussia and Silesia, counter-attacking Russian spearheads at crisis points in battles for Königsberg and Berlin.

Panzer and panzer grenadier divisions raised by the Army, Waffen SS and even the Luftwaffe in 1943, spearheaded all critical German attacks and counter-attacks from 1939 to 1945. Concentrating heavy fire-power in their panzer regiments, the panzer divisions constituted the core of the German Army's offensive capacity – despite battle attrition, production shortages, terrain factors and changing tactical requirements frequently giving rise to modifications in equipment and organization. In later years these formations, instead of exploiting their flexibility and striking power to the degree apparent in *Blitzkrieg* campaigns 1939–41, were more often than not unable to break free from a day-to-day commitment to Hitler's linear 'no step back' strategy. They were, in any event, too few to win more than temporary respite from retreat. Ironically, as the war progressed and the number of panzer and panzer grenadier divisions increased, tank strengths declined. From four (brigaded) battalions with 324 tanks per panzer division in 1939, by 1944 the level had fallen to two battalions of 159 tanks per division. The 1944 panzer division then consisted of a single panzer regiment, a panzer grenadier (motorized infantry) brigade of two regiments and supporting reconnaissance, artillery, engineer, signals, anti-tank and workshop personnel – 13,833 officers and men. A further reduction of tank strength by two-thirds was planned for 1945 panzer divisions.

For the 1945 panzer division, establishment changes increasing the number of self-propelled (SP) weapons, would reduce the number of tanks to 54 plus 22 Jagdpanzer – shrinking the offensive power of a panzer division and reducing personnel strength to 11,500 effectives – the equivalent of a panzer grenadier division. Account should nevertheless be taken of powerful reinforcement available to divisions from higher formations. Tiger and flame-throwing tanks (Flammpanzer), multiple rocket-projectors (Flammen Werfer) supported by heavy SP anti-tank guns (Panzerjaeger and Jagdpanzer) being re-allotted by divisional commanders to battle groups in accordance with the latter's tactical needs. Motorized infantry (Panzerschützen) in regimental strength intended for the new German tank arm were raised from the cavalry or infantry as early as 1935. Their role was to serve as assault infantry alongside tank battalions. A Schützen regiment in the 1935 panzer division consisted basically of two lorry-borne battalions and a motor cycle battalion. By the end of 1943, 47 such regiments were serving with Army panzer divisions.

The motorized division, forerunner of the panzer grenadier division, evolved in stages out of motorized infantry regiments raised by the infantry and trained independently of panzer divisions. By 1939, four such divisions supplemented by four light divisions – motorized infantry with a single tank battalion (88 tanks) intended for strategic reconnaissance and raised by the cavalry, stood ready for action either alongside panzer divisions in mixed panzer/motorized infantry corps or in separate army corps (mot). Responsibility for forming and training motorized divisions lay initially with XIV Corps at Magdeburg. Light divisions were raised and trained at Jena by XV Corps, expanded in 1940 into Panzer Gruppe 3, the 1941 Third Panzer Army. By October 1943, thirty-one light or motorized divisions had been raised by the Army and Waffen SS, some converted to full panzer status, others lost in action. Following General Guderian's appointment as Inspector-General of Armoured Troops in February 1943, and the consequent reorganization of Panzertruppen to which these troops would henceforth belong, two motorized divisions reverted to the infantry arm. At this time twenty-eight motorized infantry regiments, served twelve Army motorized infantry divisions; twenty-two served the Waffen SS. Sixteen more were to follow in 1944.

Renamed panzer grenadiers (the High Command's intention being to confer an élite infantry status upon such troops with a name derived from the original grenadier who threw his grenades and had to fight in advance of his unit armed only with the rifle), the motorized divisions would be re-equipped and re-organized to include tank or assault gun

Below: Layout of a panzer grenadier division of normal type. Certain 'ideal' divisions – Gross Deutschland and Leibstandarte for instance – were the equal of panzer divisions in strength and capability, but by 1945 a common organizational table had united them into a single formation equipped with self-propelled anti-tank guns equal in importance to tanks.

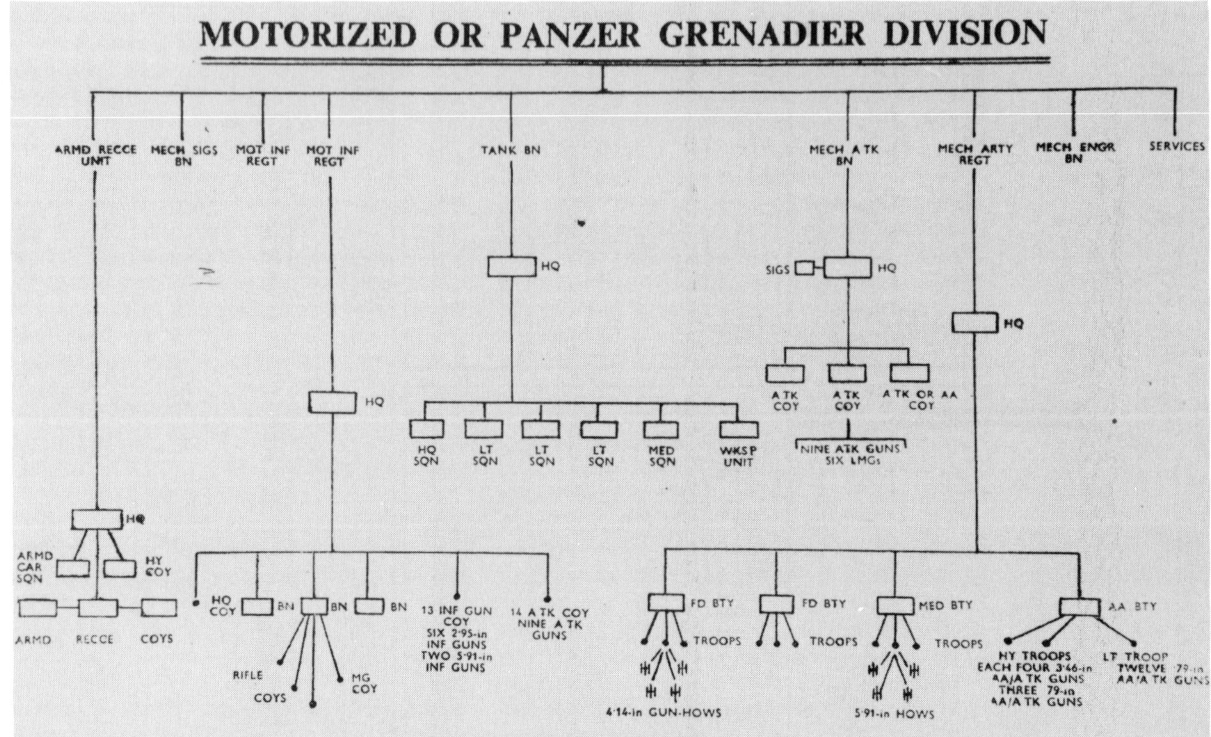

battalions. Armoured infantry carriers (SPWs) already in service would be scaled-up in numbers and provided in sufficient strength for one of the motorized infantry regiment's two battalions. The specially designed personnel carrier (Schützenpanzerwagen = SPW) was designed to improve fighting on the move. Until the advent of SPW companies, motorized infantry moved less effectively to the attack in standard trucks. Panzer grenadier companies benefited immensely from these specialized combat vehicles – a largely German innovation. Panzer grenadier divisions, including Gross Deutschland and Feldherrnhalle – 3rd, 10th, 15th, 16th, 18th, 20th, 25th, 29th, 90th, also Brandenburg and, after 1943, seven Waffen SS divisions – would constitute an integral part of the panzer force. The Brandenburg Division, after retraining and conversion to this mobile category, was OKW's special-purpose unit (800) of the early years, once entrusted with covert operations in Europe and North Africa – responsible to Abwehr Director, Admiral Canaris. The planned role of the panzer grenadier division was to work in conjunction with the panzer division, remedying the special weakness of the tank in its inability to hold the ground that it had won. More often than not the panzer grenadier division by virtue of its tank component would serve as a substitute for the panzer division. The 1944 panzer grenadier division, with a strength of 14,267 men, consisting of either one or two panzer grenadier regiments plus a tank or assault gun battalion of 42 vehicles and supporting arms, was completely motorized. Army commanders, in rearguard situations, relied greatly upon these mobile divisions to screen and support less well-endowed infantry. Panzer divisions were in theory retained for concentrated counter-strokes. After 1943, the planned war organization of panzer and panzer grenadier divisions was rarely fulfilled; divisions usually fought well below strength, in some cases little more than a brigade of one or perhaps two 'panzer' battalions supported by an equivalent number of trucked infantry battalions.

Mobility was restricted by petrol and other shortages, equipment was frequently lost in action and manpower deficiencies never made good. Regimental tank strengths declined and the once irresistible power of the panzer division waned in the face of opponents fielding more and overwhelming strength in ground and air forces. The distinction between panzer and panzer grenadier divisions became increasingly blurred, confusing their roles, resulting often in the misuse of the weaker division in mobile action.

2. Satellite contributions for the panzer force

Satellite support for the panzer force was in general limited, by out-of-date equipment and inexperience, to subordinate operations on secondary fronts; foreign contributions being particularly sought after by Hitler in the winter of 1941 when the Wehrmacht was pre-occupied with plans for 'Blue'/'Brunswick' (map 10) – the demand for numbers surpassing the need for proficiency. Germany's principal ally fighting in North Africa from September 1940 onwards – when Italian Tenth Army (Berti), comprising eight divisions and eight tank battalions (six light, two medium), crossed out of Libya into Egypt – contributed two armoured (Ariete, Littorio) and two motorized (Trento, Trieste) divisions to Rommel's 1942 offensive against British Eighth Army (map 5). The mobile divisions were supported by four–five non-motorized infantry divisions. At this time the Italian Army consisted of 61 infantry, four armoured (Centauro, Ariete, Littorio – one in embryo), two motorized (Trento, Trieste) and seventeen other divisions; a strength of 84 divisions. This order of battle was to remain broadly unchanged for the rest of the war; in Italy's case ending in September 1943. Before June 1940 when Italy entered the war, Ariete and Littorio Armoured Divisions had been grouped with two existing motorized divisions – Trento and Trieste – into an armoured corps. This, with a mobile (cavalry) and truck-borne corps formed Italian Sixth Army known as the Army of the Po; the main component of Ariete and Littorio being 'light' tank regiments consisting of 3½-ton (CV33) or experimental 6-ton (CR30) – eventually 6.8-ton (L6/40) vehicles.

By 1940, 11-ton medium tanks (M11/39) were in production, marginally enhancing the assault power of the armoured division. Centauro, deployed in Albania against the Greeks, had three light and one medium tank battalion; all fared badly, Centauro's place in the armoured corps being taken by Littorio converting to armour after fighting in Spain (map 1). In the 15-day Italian campaign against France – 10–25 June 1940, coinciding with the final stages of Operation 'Red' (map 3), when Italian Fourth and First Armies (north to south) crossed into France between Mount Blanc and Ventimiglia – Littorio and Ariete remained in reserve ready to exploit a break-through to Marseille. That break-through never came. Thereafter Littorio moved to Yugoslavia, eventually linking-up with Centauro, while Ariete moved to Libya in January 1941. Comando Supremo (Cavallero) still in the process of rebuilding its armour in 1941, after reverses in Europe and North Africa, then determined upon a new establishment for the tank regiments of armoured divisions – henceforth three medium and one heavy tank battalion; improved mediums (M14/40 and M14/41) making their appearance in North Africa with both Ariete and Littorio after the latter's redeployment from Yugoslavia. Captured Renault T35s of about 10 tons and Somuas of 18- or 21-tons also entered service with certain Italian tank battalions. But even with these improved mediums, the Italian armoured division as constituted in North Africa, with three medium battalions (165 tanks), was incapable of more than light assault. Trento and Trieste, it should be noted, were distinguished at times from other North African truck-borne infantry divisions by the inclusion – in common with the armoured division – of a Bersaglieri regiment; such formations normally consisting of two semi-motorized formations only.

Campaigning against Wavell before Ariete and Rommel arrived on the North African desert scene in February 1941 (map 5), Italian Tenth Army was obliterated, losing more than 100 M 11s in action at Beda Fomm. In this engagement an Italian army of ten divisions reinforced by an armoured brigade (Babini) withdrawing west from

Benghazi was finally intercepted by mobile forces under O'Connor and overwhelmed; 7th Armoured (Hobart) and 4th Indian Division (Tuker) leading the way. Twelve months later, defending Cyrenaica against 'Crusader' (*see* Panzer Army Africa, 18 November 1941) much the same could be said of Italian forces supporting DAK. Deploying obsolete artillery (half the range of British equivalents), fielding uncompetitive armour and failing with much other military equipment, the outcome of Italian failure in the desert was a predictable dependence on German support. On the advice of Wünsdorf specialists, the Italian armoured division was strengthened; SP guns, improved medium tanks, heavier supporting weapons and a Bersaglieri regiment being added to establishment. In the run-up to Alamein (map 5) these developments taken in conjunction with German support were to prove advantageous, but in southern Russia where Italian Eighth Army (Gariboldi) was barring the progress of SW Front in the concluding phase of 'Blue'/'Brunswick', the absence of German support was to prove catastrophic (map 12). Deployed in defensive positions on the Don north of Stalingrad, Eighth Army included the Italian expeditionary force in Russia – Corpo di Spedizione Italiano (CSIR) – which, under General Messe since the July days of 'Barbarossa', had campaigned vigorously with Army Group South on its Voronezh–Stalino axis.

Comprising 'Pasubio' and 'Torino' – neither more than semi-motorized and one other infantry division, the CSIR serving Eighth Army on the Don as XXXV Corps, was lost together with an Alpini and II Corps, ten divisions in total, when German reinforcement for Eighth Army was sucked into the battle for Stalingrad. By May 1943, reporting 130,000 dead, wounded and missing and 90 per cent of its equipment abandoned on the battlefield, the remnant of Italian Eighth Army was withdrawn from the front. This débâcle was immediately followed by another in Tunisia where Italian forces serving First Italian Army (Messe) were equipped and deployed to approximately the same scale as those in Libya; seven Italian and ten German divisions capitulating in the theatre on 12 May 1943. In the autumn of 1943, there occurred a 'peaceful' sequel to the catastrophes overtaking Italian arms in Russia and Tunisia, when in consequence of Italy's defection from the Axis, broadcast on 8 September, Centauro (Count Calvi) was disarmed in Rome. Re-equipped, at Mussolini's request, with new Pz Kpfw IIIs and IVs Centauro was one of seven Italian divisions including Ariete and Piave that were concentrated by Comando Supremo in the neighbourhood of the capital; their presence threatening German communications with the panzer and other divisions deployed in the south. A 'ceasefire' brought the crisis to an end without bloodshed. The Pz Kpfw IIIs and IVs were re-possessed (*see* Part 5, Panzer Action in Italy, page 202).

Much the same story of lamentably weak allies creating unforeseen, and ultimately irreconcilable difficulties for the Wehrmacht when these same allies defected from the German cause, unfolds in the case of Finnish, Roumanian, Hungarian and Slovak contingents; obsolete ground and air forces limiting their employment to secondary fronts and their eventual defection tearing gaps in German strength and dispositions that were impossible to make good. Equipped in pre-war days with AFVs purchased abroad or manufactured at home under licence (Skoda-Roumania, Ansaldo-Hungary, etc.) or fortuitously supplied by the Wehrmacht with captured Czech and French vehicles – satellite armies deployed in the east were to prove no match for the power of the Red Army. As the war progressed new German equipment came their way, albeit in small quantities; assault guns for the Finns supplementing either captured Soviet T34s and towing machines taken in Karelia, or imported foreign types, and heavier AFVs for the Roumanians, Czechs and others. In the Roumanian case, captured Renaults (T35s) and Hotchkiss H35s taken by the Germans from French and Belgian stocks in 1940 following the Battle of France found their way on to the strength of a Roumanian armoured division. This, and two cavalry divisions eventually converting to 'armour', were also allotted a small percentage of new German equipment. From the outset of 'Barbarossa' the Roumanians contributed two armies – Third (Dumitrescu) and Fourth (Ciuperva) – to Army Group South; neither were strong on motorization, anti-tank weaponry, artillery or signals equipment.

These same armies, in a strength of 25 divisions (one armoured) with their own air support, participated in 'Blue'/ 'Brunswick'. Arriving on the Don in October 1942, Roumanian Third Army reached the river north of Stalingrad deployed between the Italians (Gariboldi) left, and German Sixth Army (Paulus) right; Fourth Army (Constantin-Claps) traversed the Kalmuck Steppe to arrive south of the city on Fourth Panzer Army's right flank. The consequences of this deployment, despite the presence in reserve of German XXXXVIII Panzer Corps (Heim) – 22nd Panzer, 1st Roumanian Armoured – was to prove an unmitigated disaster (map 11).

The nucleus of Hungarian support for 'Barbarossa' was concentrated in a motorized corps (Szombathelyi) of three divisions (one cavalry). Equipped with 65 Italian 3½-tonners and 95 8½-ton Swedish-Hungarian Toldis, the corps served Seventeenth Army, Army Group South, advancing via Nikolaev to the Donez at Issyum. A subsequent Hungarian contribution to 'Blue'/'Brunswick' was provided by Hungarian Second Army (Jány) alone. In that fateful winter of 1942–3, when the Roumanians collapsed on the Don, the Army was deployed between Italian Eighth Army right and German Second Army (von Salmuth) left. Woefully short of anti-tank guns and with only a single panzer battalion (38ts) on hand to counter Voronezh Front (map 12), the Hungarians were overrun. The survivors, excluding 105,000 dead, wounded and missing, were withdrawn from the front on 24 January. The army returned home in March 1943. In September 1944, with the Red Army driving into Hungary, three Hungarian armies – First, Second (re-activated) and Third – were deployed under Army Group South Ukraine (Friessner) – from 24 September Army Group South – defending a Hungarian national redoubt. Heading the Hungarian order of battle were two 'armoured' divisions mostly equipped with German material (Pz Kpfw IIIs and IVs). Both divisions participated in battles for Budapest (map 19).

As regards a Bulgarian contribution to the panzer force, Guderian records that 138 Pz Kpfw IIIs and assault guns (intended for a Bulgarian armoured division?) were lost when that country changed sides at the end of August 1944.

Finally, in this summary of satellite support for the panzer

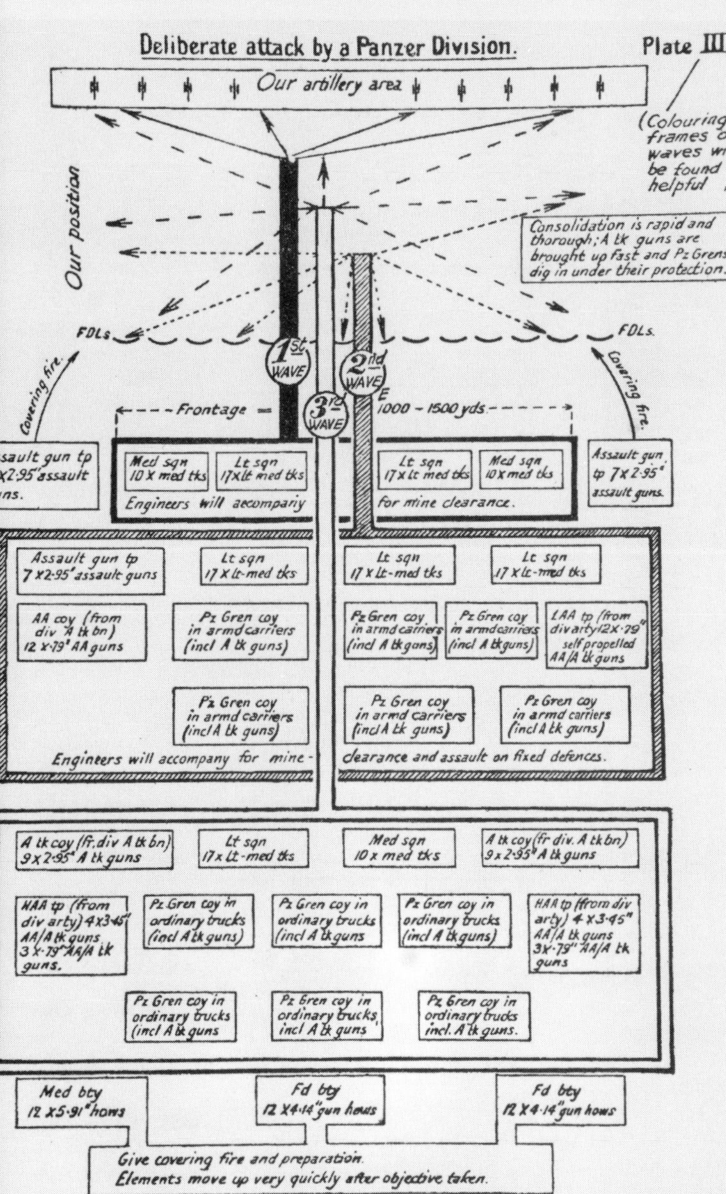

Above: Schematic plan for a 'deliberate attack by a Panzer Division'.

force, a short note on the Slovak 'Schnelle' Division (Turanec). Following Fourth Panzer Army into the Caucasus in 1942 (map 10), the division enjoyed a proportion of new German equipment replacing the division's – formerly Schnelle Brigade's – antiquated Pz Kpfw 38ts and 'Tatra' 4-wheeled armoured cars. By February 1943, however, the Slovak Schnelle Division had practically ceased to exist, having lost most of its equipment retreating from the Kuban across the Sea of Azov to the Crimea (map 11).

With action at Rostov, Maikop and Tuapse behind it, the Schnelle Division's 4,000–5,000 survivors were reformed into Slovak 1st Infantry Division (Jurech), continuing a presence in the area until October 1943 when at Kachovka, west of the Dnieper, the division again experienced the full weight of the Red Army, this time removing it from the German order of battle.

Spanish and French contingents consisted solely of infantry sent to the Eastern Front. The Spanish Blue Division (Munoz-Grandes), German-equipped when deployed under Eighteenth Army, Army Group North, in the Battle of Leningrad, served at first on the Volkhov, where the action was brisk, before returning home to Spain in October 1943; a Spanish Legion of 2,000 effectives being left in action on the Narwa until April 1944. That too was then withdrawn to Spain. 'Charlemagne' (Puaud), a French infantry contingent elevated in the autumn of 1944, to the status of an SS Waffen grenadier division, originated in a pre-existing volunteer regiment known as the Légion Volontaires Françaises (LVF). Incorporated into the German Army as 638th Regiment (7th Infantry Division), the LVF served Fourth Army in the battle for Moscow (map 8) before seeing action against partisans on the same Central Front in 1942–3. Re-constituted in 1944 as an SS division, some 7,000 French volunteers served briefly in two battle groups – one under Army Group Weichsel, surrounded in Pomerania and virtually destroyed there, the other including survivors from Pomerania defended Hitler in the Reichs Chancellery until forced to capitulate on 2 May 1945 (*see* Third Panzer Army, 16 April 1945).

Other foreign troops serving the panzer force included Osttruppen recruited in Russia as 'Hiwis' – (*see* Part 3, Panzer Supply) and those recruited and formed into certain SS panzer or panzer grenadier divisions (*see* Part 3, Divisional Profiles). Italy's defection from the Axis in September 1943, was matched by the exit of Hitler's other partners in the war on the Eastern Front. In August 1944 the Roumanians had changed sides to support the Red Army with 22 divisions in the advance through Hungary. Within days Bulgaria followed suit; nine divisions joining in the advance through the Balkans. Finland left Germany's side in September, turning from 'Waffenbrudder' to active hindrance of Twentieth Mountain Army (Rendulic) withdrawing south by road from the far north of the country, while in October an unsuccessful attempt by the Horthy government to negotiate a ceasefire with the Soviets lead to Hungarian desertions, a German take-over of Hungarian military forces and, in December, a declaration of war against Germany by a counter-regime established in Debrecen under Soviet auspices. By the end of the year, foreign support for the Wehrmacht outside the framework of regular Waffen SS divisions still being raised by Himmler as late as March 1945 and 'Hiwis', had faded into insignificance. In Italy just two or three non-motorized divisions continued in action with Tenth Army (OB, South West), while in Yugoslavia (OB, South East) a comparable number of German-Croat divisions served in two German mountain corps, supporting twelve national Croat divisions clustering in defence of Zagreb, Sarajevo and key Croatian localities. Only in Hungary, where twelve Hungarian divisions including the two panzer 'divisions' serving Army Group South (Wöhler in succession to Friessner), was there any significant concentration of Axis divisions deployed in support of the Wehrmacht, and much of this was of dubious value, some 'divisions' consisting of no more than 1,500 men; Hitler's grip on events in the theatre had long since faded into history.

3. Panzer force growth, 1939–45

1. GERMAN MOTORIZED INFANTRY AND PANZER GRENADIER DIVISIONS

1939	1940	1941	1942	1943	1944	1945
2 MotDiv*	2 MotDiv	[12]				
13 MotDiv*	13 MotDiv	[13]				
20 PzGrDiv*	20 PzGrDiv	20 PzGrDiv	20 PzGrDiv	20 PzGrDiv	20 PzGrDiv	20 PzGrDiv
29 PzGrDiv*	29 PzGrDiv	29 PzGrDiv	29 PzGrDiv[2]	29 PzGrDiv	29 PzGrDiv	29 PzGrDiv
1SS PzDiv A Hitler	**1SS PzDiv A Hitler**	**1SS PzDiv A Hitler**	**1SS PzDiv A Hitler**[2]	**1SS PzDiv A Hitler**[4]	**[1SS PzDiv A Hitler]**	
2SS PzDiv	**2SS PzDiv Das Reich**[1]	**2SS PzDiv Das Reich**[1]	**2SS PzDiv Das Reich**[1]	**2SS PzDiv Das Reich**[4]	**[2SS PzDiv Das Reich]**	
	3SS PzDiv Totenkopf[1]	**3SS PzDiv Totenkopf**[1]	**3SS PzDiv Totenkopf**[1]	**3SS PzDiv Totenkopf**[4]	**[3SS PzDiv Totenkopf]**	
	4SS PzDiv Polizei[1]	**4SS PzDiv Polizei**[1]	**4SS PzDiv Polizei**[1]	**4SS PzDiv Polizei**	**4SS PzDiv Polizei**	**4SS PzDiv Polizei**
		5SS PzDiv Wiking[1]	**5SS PzDiv Wiking**[1,2]	**5SS PzDiv Wiking**	**[5SS PzDiv Wiking]**	
	Gross Deutschland	Gross Deutschland	Gross Deutschland[2]	Gross Deutschland[4]	Gross Deutschland[5]	Gross Deutschland
		3 PzGrDiv	3 PzGrDiv[2]	3 PzGrDiv	3 PzGrDiv	3 PzGrDiv
		10 PzGrDiv	10 PzGrDiv	10 PzGrDiv	10 PzGrDiv	10 PzGrDiv
		14 MotDiv	14 MotDiv	(14 MotDiv)		
		16 PzGrDiv	16 PzGrDiv[2]	16 PzGrDiv	[116]	
		18 PzGrDiv	18 PzGrDiv	18 PzGrDiv	18 PzGrDiv	18 PzGrDiv
		25 PzGrDiv	25 PzGrDiv	25 PzGrDiv	25 PzGrDiv	25 PzGrDiv
		36 MotDiv	36 MotDiv	(36 MotDiv)		
		60 MotDiv	60 MotDiv[2]	60 MotDiv	[FH1]	
				90 PzGrDiv	90 PzGrDiv	90 PzGrDiv
				386 MotDiv		
				999 MotDiv		
				15 PzGrDiv	15 PzGrDiv	15 PzGrDiv
				Brandenburg	Brandenburg	Brandenburg
H Goering Div	H Goering Div	H Goering Div[3]	H Goering Div	[H Goering Div]	H Goering Div 2	H Goering Div 2
				9SS PzDiv HOH	**[9SS PzDiv HOH]**	
				10SS PzDiv FRU	**[10SS PzDiv FRU]**	
				11SS PzGr Div NDL	**11SS PzGr Div NDL**	**11SS PzGr Div NDL**
				16SS PzGr Div RSS	**16SS PzGr Div RSS**	**16SS PzGr Div RSS**
					17SS PzGr Div GvB	**17SS PzGr Div GvB**
					18SS PzGr Div HW	**18SS PzGr Div HW**
				23SS PzGr Div NED	**23SS PzGr Div NED**	**23SS PzGr Div NED**
				28SS PzGr Div WAL	**28SS PzGr Div WAL**	**28SS PzGr Div WAL**
					27SS PzGr Div LMK	**27SS PzGr Div LMK**
						PzGrDiv Kurmark
						+

(**Heavier type** indicates SS division.)
See also satellite contributions to the panzer force, page 66.

Key
[ ] Motorized infantry or panzer grenadier division converted to a panzer division.
( ) Motorized infantry division reverting to former infantry status.
\+ 1944–5: impromptu panzer grenadier divisions raised from schools, training or other units; 31SS Bohmen-Maren, 33SS 30 Januar and 38SS Nibelungen.
_ _ _ _ Motorized regiment expanded into a brigade or division.
____ Brigade expanded into a division.

* 1939 motorized infantry division deploying *three* motorized infantry regiments, each of *three* battalions (I Bn, Companies 1–4; II Bn, Companies 5–8; III Bn, Companies 9–12; plus Company 13, infantry gun; and Company 14, anti-tank) together with reconnaissance, artillery, anti-tank, engineer, signals, supply, administrative and medical services. In 1940 the motorized infantry division was reduced to *two* motorized infantry regiments of *three* battalions each; but see also the following notes.

1 1940–1/2 SS motorized infantry division retaining *three* motorized infantry regiments, usually with extra companies (e.g., 2SS in May 1941 deployed 16 companies in each regiment). After September 1943, SS motorized infantry divisions were reduced to two panzer grenadier regiments.

2 1942 motorized infantry division favoured with a panzer battalion (88 tanks in three companies) for the summer offensive (map 10). In September 1943 a panzer or assault gun battalion was provided for all motorized divisions plus an Army AA (Flak) battalion for the majority.

3 Air Force motorized anti-aircraft regiment reinforced with an Air Force jaeger battalion.

4 1943 divisional panzer battalion or 1SS, 2SS, 3SS panzer regiment reinforced with a Tiger company for the summer offensive (map 14). Note that Gross Deutschland had a Tiger battalion.

5 Gross Deutschland, the Army's most powerful panzer grenadier division, with an exceptional weapons establishment.

2. GERMAN PANZER AND LIGHT DIVISIONS

1939	1940	1941	1942	1943	1944	1945
1 PzDiv*	1 PzDiv*	1 PzDiv	1 PzDiv	1 PzDiv	1 PzDiv	1 PzDiv
2 PzDiv*	2 PzDiv*	2 PzDiv	2 PzDiv	2 PzDiv	2 PzDiv	2 PzDiv
3 PzDiv*	3 PzDiv*	3 PzDiv	3 PzDiv[1]	3 PzDiv	3 PzDiv	3 PzDiv
4 PzDiv*	4 PzDiv*	4 PzDiv	4 PzDiv	4 PzDiv	4 PzDiv	4 PzDiv
5 PzDiv*	5 PzDiv*	5 PzDiv	5 PzDiv	5 PzDiv	5 PzDiv	5 PzDiv
1 LtDiv[3]	[6 PzDiv]	6 PzDiv	6 PzDiv	6 PzDiv	6 PzDiv	6 PzDiv
2 LtDiv[3]	[7 PzDiv]	7 PzDiv	7 PzDiv	7 PzDiv	7 PzDiv	7 PzDiv
3 LtDiv[3]	[8 PzDiv]	8 PzDiv	8 PzDiv	8 PzDiv	8 PzDiv	8 PzDiv
4 LtDiv[3]	[9 PzDiv]	9 PzDiv	9 PzDiv[1]	9 PzDiv	9 PzDiv	9 PzDiv
10 PzDiv	10 PzDiv*	10 PzDiv	10 PzDiv	10 PzDiv		
Kempf		11 PzDiv	11 PzDiv[1]	11 PzDiv	11 PzDiv	11 PzDiv
		12 PzDiv	12 PzDiv	12 PzDiv	12 PzDiv	12 PzDiv
		13 PzDiv	13 PzDiv[1]	13 PzDiv	13 PzDiv	FH2
		14 PzDiv	14 PzDiv[1]	14 PzDiv	14 PzDiv	14 PzDiv
		15 PzDiv	15 PzDiv	[15 PzDiv]		
		16 PzDiv	16 PzDiv[1]	16 PzDiv	16 PzDiv	16 PzDiv
		17 PzDiv	17 PzDiv	17 PzDiv	17 PzDiv	17 PzDiv
		18 PzDiv	18 PzDiv	18 PzDiv	(18 PzDiv)	
		19 PzDiv	19 PzDiv	19 PzDiv	19 PzDiv	19 PzDiv
		20 PzDiv	20 PzDiv	20 PzDiv	20 PzDiv	20 PzDiv
	5 LtDiv[3]	[21 PzDiv]	21 PzDiv	21 PzDiv	21 PzDiv	21 PzDiv
			22 PzDiv[1]			
			23 PzDiv[1]	23 PzDiv	23 PzDiv	23 PzDiv
			24 PzDiv[1]	24 PzDiv	24 PzDiv	24 PzDiv
				25 PzDiv	25 PzDiv	25 PzDiv
				26 PzDiv	26 PzDiv	26 PzDiv
				27 PzDiv		
		90 LtDiv[3]	90 LtDiv[3]	[90 LtDiv]		
			164 LtDiv[4]	164 LtDiv[4]		
				H Goering	H Goering 1[2]	H Goering 1[2]
					FHH1	FHH1
					Norwegen	Norwegen
					116 PzDiv	116 PzDiv
					Pz Lehr[2]	Pz Lehr
					1SS PzDiv A Hitler[2]	**1SS PzDiv A Hitler**
					2SS PzDiv Das Reich[2]	**2SS PzDiv Das Reich**
					3SS PzDiv Totenkopf[2]	**3SS PzDiv Totenkopf**
					5SS PzDiv Wiking[2]	**5SS PzDiv Wiking**
					9SS PzDiv HOH	**9SS PzDiv HOH**
					10SS PzDiv FRU	**10SS PzDiv FRU**
					12SS PzDiv HJ	**12SS PzDiv HJ**
					Führer Begleit	Führer Begleit
					Führer PzGr	Führer PzGr
						+

(**Heavier type** indicates SS division.)
See also satellite contributions to the panzer force, pate 66.

Key
[ ] Converted from light to panzer division.
[__] Converted from panzer or light division to panzer grenadier division.
(__) Reorganized as an artillery division.
+ 1944–5: Impromptu panzer divisions raised from schools, reserve units, etc.; 232, 233, Clausewitz, Donau, Holstein, Jüterbog, Muncheberg, Schlesien, Thuringien, Westfalen.

* 1939–40 panzer division deploying a brigade of *two* panzer regiments of 324 tanks in four panzer battalions (3 companies). 6, 7 and 8 Panzer Divisions deployed *one* panzer regiment of three battalions (9 Panzer Division two panzer battalions only) plus one motorized infantry (Schützen) regiment of *two* battalions (5 companies each), one motorcycle battalion (5 companies), reconnaissance, artillery, anti-tank, engineer, signals, supply, administration and medical services. In 1941 the panzer division was reduced to *one* panzer regiment of 196 tanks in two panzer battalions, but an increase in motorized infantry to *two* regiments of *two* battalions each. Many minor variations existed between divisions.

1 Certain 1942 panzer divisions had the panzer regiment strengthened to *three* battalions for the summer offensive (map 10). Beginning in mid-1942, an Army anti-aircraft (Flak) battalion was proposed for all panzer and certain motorized infantry divisions, limited at first to those taking part in the summer offensive.

2 1944 panzer divisions favoured with abnormal complements of weapons, vehicles and personnel. 1SS, 2SS, 3SS and 5SS had *two* panzer grenadier regiments with *three* battalions and extra weapons; Hermann Goering, Panzer Lehr and Gross Deutschland (nominally a panzer grenadier division but, like SS panzer grenadier divisions, originally superior to an Army panzer division).

3 Light division deploying a single panzer battalion of 88 tanks otherwise organized as a motorized infantry division (two regiments).

4 Light division with *no* integral panzer battalion.

4. Divisional profiles

1. Motorized infantry and panzer grenadier divisions, 1934–45

2ND MOTORIZED DIVISION

Raised **Oct 1934** at Stettin as 2nd Inf Div; 1937 motorized; Sept 1939 Poland (map 2); May 1940 France (map 3); July 1940 Germany; Jan 1941 reorg as 12th Pz Div (q.v.).

3RD PANZER GRENADIER DIVISION

Raised **Oct 1934** at Frankfurt/Oder as 3rd Inf Div; Sept 1939 Poland; Jan to Sept 1940 France; Oct 1940 Germany, reorg as 3rd Mot Inf Div; **June 1941** Eastern Front, Ostrov, Luga, Demjansk (map 7); Oct to Dec 1941 Moscow (map 8); Jan to April 1942 Gshatsk, Vyasma; May 1942 refit; July 1942 Voronezh (map 10), Don corridor; **Feb 1943** destroyed at Stalingrad; Mar to June 1943 at Lyon reform as Pz Gren Div incl. 386th Mot Div and 103rd Pz Bn; July 1943 to July 1944 Italy (Rome occup. 9 Sept 1943); Aug 1944 Mosel, Metz; Dec 1944 to Feb 1945 Ardennes (map 17); **Mar 1945** Cologne; April 1945 destroyed in Ruhr pocket.

10TH PANZER GRENADIER DIVISION

Raised **Oct 1934** at Regensburg as 10th Inf Div; Sept 1939 Poland; June 1940 France; Oct 1940 Germany, reorg as 10th Mot Inf Div; **June 1941** Eastern Front, Bobruisk, Smolensk (map 7); Oct to Dec 1941 Gomel, Kiev, Bryansk, Tula (map 8); Jan to Dec 1942 Mozaisk, Juchnow, Demjansk; **Jan to Mar 1943** Demjansk, Orel; April 1943 renamed 10th Pz Gren Div; July 1943 N. Kursk (map 14); Aug 1943 Bryansk inc. 239th Assault Bn; Oct to Dec 1943 Dnieper; Kanev (Bukrin) bridgehead, Kremenchug, Kirovograd inc. 7th Pz Bn; Jan to July 1944 Dnieper/Bessarabia; Aug 1944 practically destroyed serving Sixth Army at Husi; Sept to Oct 1944 reform as battle group at Krakow; **Jan 1945** destroyed at Radom; Feb 1945 reform as battle group at Gorlitz; Mar 1945 Silesia; April 1945 Moravia; May 1945 surrendered to Russians at Olmutz/Deutsche Brod.

13TH MOTORIZED DIVISION

Raised **Oct 1934** at Magdeburg as 13th Inf Div; 1937 motorized; Sept 1939 Poland (map 2); May 1940 France (map 3); July 1940 Germany; Oct 1940 reorg as 13th Pz Div (q.v.); Nov 1940 Roumania.

14TH MOTORIZED DIVISION

Raised **Oct 1934** as 14th Inf Div; Sept 1939 Poland (map 2); Jan to Sept 1940 France; Oct 1940 Germany reorg as 14th Inf Div(mot); **July 1941** Eastern Front (map 7), Minsk, Smolensk; Oct to Dec 1941 Vyasma, Klin (map 8); Jan 1942 Velish; **Feb to Mar 1943** Rshev; April 1943 Neva; May 1943 revert inf status, retained East Front; 1945 E. Prussia, surrendered to Russians Stathof/Frisches Nehrung.

15TH PANZER GRENADIER DIVISION

Formed **May 1943** as Sicily Div from remnant 15th Pz Div (destroyed Tunisia), Army 215th Pz Bn and other troops in Italy; July 1943 renamed 15th Pz Gren Div, served in Sicily until June/July 1943, thereafter Tenth Army Salerno, Cassino, Anzio; Aug 1944 E. France; Sept 1944 incl. 111th Pz Bde; Dec 1944 Ardennes (map 17); **Feb 1945** lower Rhine Gennep–Reichswald; April 1945 Ems, Weser; May 1945 surrendered to British.

26/GS Publications/1073

Popular Guide to the German Army No. 1 *(This pamphlet supersedes Nos. 1 and 5 of 1941)*

The German Armoured Division (Panzer Division)
and
The German Motorized Division (Panzer Grenadier Division)

RESTRICTED

The information given in this document is not to be communicated, either directly or indirectly, to the Press or to any person not authorized to receive it.

Prepared under the direction of the Chief of the Imperial General Staff

THE WAR OFFICE

NOVEMBER 1943

Above: By November 1943 much of the mystique surrounding the panzer force had been dissipated and its invincible reputation broken. The diagram is one of a series of British and American Intelligence appreciations depicting panzer and panzer grenadier division layouts.

16TH PANZER GRENADIER DIVISION

Raised **Aug 1940** at Sennelager as 16th Inf Div(mot) from 16th and 228th Inf Divs; Dec 1940 France; **April 1941** Yugoslavia (map 6), Hungary; June 1941 Germany; July 1941 Eastern Front (map 7), Dubno, Nikolayev; Oct 1941 Kiev; Jan 1942 Kursk; July 1942 Voronezh (map 10); Aug 1942 Caucasus (map 10), Armavir, Maikop, Elista; **Jan 1943** Don, Rostov; Mar 1943 Stalino, Mius; June 1943 incl. 116th Pz Bn and renamed Pz Gren Div; Sept to Dec 1943 Zaporoshe/Krivoi Rog; Jan to Mar 1944 S. Ukraine, destroyed Uman serving Sixth Army, remnant to 116th Pz Div (q.v.).

18TH PANZER GRENADIER DIVISION

Raised **Oct 1934** at Leignitz, as 18th Inf Div; Sept 1939 Poland; June 1940 France; Oct 1940 Germany reorg as

18th Inf Div(mot); **June 1941** Eastern Front (map 7), Minsk; Aug 1941 Novgorod; Nov to Dec 1942 Volkhov, Tikhvin; **Jan to April 1943** Staraya Russa/L. Ilman; May 1943 incl. 18th Pz Bn and renamed 18th Pz Gren Div; Aug 1943 Yelnya; Oct to Dec 1943 Orscha; Feb to June 1944 Bobruisk, destroyed serving Fourth Army; Sept to Oct 1944 Silesia, reform as battle group; Dec 1944 to Feb 1945 practically destroyed E. Prussia; **April 1945** reform from Pz 'Div' Schlesien and Holstein (A Gp Weichsel); late April 1945 Berlin; May 1945 encircled and practically destroyed; break-out group to Twelfth Army, Tangermünde.

20TH PANZER GRENADIER DIVISION

Raised **Oct 1934** at Hamburg as 20th Inf Div; 1937 motorized; Sept 1939 Poland (map 2); May 1940 France (map 3); July to Oct 1940 preparing for 'Sea-lion'; Dec 1940 Magdeburg; **June 1941** Eastern Front (map 7), Bialystok, Minsk; Sept to Dec 1941 Tikhvin, Volkhov, Velish until May 1943; **June 1943** incl. 8th Pz Bn and renamed 20th Pz Gren Div; July to Dec 1943 Orel, Bryansk, Dnieper, Zhitomir; Jan to Feb 1944 Winniza; Mar to April 1944 Hube pocket (map 15); May to July 1944 Brody; Aug 1944 Baranov/Weichsel until Dec 1944; **Jan to April 1945** Weichsel (map 18), Silesia, Oder (Küstrin Seelow), late April 1945 Berlin; May 1945 Potsdam, break-out group to Twelfth Army, Tangermünde.

25TH PANZER GRENADIER DIVISION

Raised **April 1936** at Ludwigsburg as 25th Inf Div; Sept 1939 Saar; Jan 1940 France; Oct 1940 Germany reorg as 25th Inf Div(mot); **July 1941** Eastern Front (map 7), Zhitomir, Uman, Kiev; Oct to Dec 1941 Bryansk, Tula, Venev; Jan 1942 to May 1943 Mzensk, Orel; **June 1943** incl. 5th Pz Bn (delayed until Oct 1943) and renamed 25th Pz Gren Div; July 1943 to July 1944 Bryansk, Orel, Smolensk, Orscha, destroyed serving Fourth Army, remnant to 107 Pz Bde; Oct/Nov 1944 reform Grafenwöhr/ Baumholder inc. 107th Pz Bde; Dec 1943 Saar; Jan 1945 Saar; Feb to April 1945 East Front, Oder (Küstrin) then west to Oranienburg (27 April); May 1945 Mecklenburg, surrendered to US at Radelübbe.

29TH PANZER GRENADIER DIVISION

Raised **Oct 1936** at Erfurt as 29th Inf Div; 1937 motorized; Oct 1938 Sudetenland (8–15 Oct); **Mar 1939** Prague (15 Mar); Sept 1939 Poland, Radom, Modlin, Bug (map 2); May 1940 France (map 3); Nov 1940 to Feb 1941 Antwerp preparing for 'Sea-lion'; **Feb 1941** Germany; June 1941 Eastern Front (map 7), Minsk, Smolensk, Bryansk (Oct), Dec 1941 Tula; Jan to June 1942 Orel, Kharkov; July to Sept 1942 Don corridor to Stalingrad (map 10); **Feb 1943** destroyed at Stalingrad serving Sixth Army; May 1943 SW France reform, June 1943 renamed 29th Pz Gren Div incl. 345th Inf Div(mot); June 1943 Italy; Sicily (10 July), Salerno (10 Sept), Cassino (6 Nov); Feb 1944 Anzio (10–19 Feb), refit Florence, Rimini (4–28 Sept), Bologna, Po, Veneto until May 1945 surrendered to British Piave (Feltre).

36TH MOTORIZED DIVISION

Raised **Oct 1936** at Kaiserlautern as 36th Inf Div; Sept 1939 Saar; May 1940 Lux/France until Sept 1940; Oct 1940 Germany; Nov 1940 reorg as 36th Inf Div(mot); **July 1941** Eastern Front (map 7), Pleskau, Leningrad; Oct to Dec 1941 Moscow, Kalinin, Klin; Jan 1942 to Feb 1943 Rshev; **May 1943** practically destroyed serving Ninth Army at Dorogbusch; April–June 1943 rebuild for 'Citadel' (reserve); July 1943 committed N. Kursk and Orel sustaining heavy losses; Oct 1943 revert to inf status on Central Front; June 1944 destroyed at Bobruisk.

60TH MOTORIZED DIVISION

Raised **Oct 1939** at Danzig as 60th Inf Div; July to Oct 1940 Germany reorg at Grossborn as 60th Inf Div(mot); Nov 1940 Poland; Dec 1940 Vienna; **Jan 1941** Roumania; April 1941 Yugoslavia (map 6); July 1941 Eastern Front (map 7), Zhitomir, Uman, Rostov; Jan 1942 Mius, Stalino; Mar 1942 Kharkov; June 1942 incl. 160th Pz Bn; July 1942 Issyum; Aug 1942 to Jan 1943 Don corridor, Stalingrad (map 10); **Feb 1943** destroyed at Stalingrad serving Sixth Army; Mar 1943 reform SW France; June 1943 renamed Pz Gren Div Feldherrnhalle; Dec 1943 East Front, Orscha; Jan 1944 Vitebsk; July 1944 practically destroyed serving Fourth Army; Aug 1944 reform; Oct 1944 Hungary, Debrecen; Nov 1944 reorg as Pz Div Feldherrnhalle (q.v.).

90TH PANZER GRENADIER DIVISION

Raised **July 1943**, *see* 90th Light Africa Division.

386TH MOTORIZED DIVISION

Raised **Nov 1942** at Frankfurt/Oder; **Mar 1943** Lyon inc. into 3rd Pz Gren Div reform after Stalingrad.

999TH MOTORIZED DIVISION

Raised **Feb 1943** at Bizerta–Tunis from penal units; May 1943 destroyed Tunisia.

PANZER GRENADIER DIVISION BRANDENBURG (BR)

Raised **Oct 1939** at Brandenburg/Havel as Bau-Lehr-Kompanie zbv 800, responsible to OKH/Abwehr for covert ops; autumn of 1940 increased to three bns: Brandenburg, Düren, Vienna; Nov 1942 expanded to Div Brandenburg; **Oct 1943** NW Belgrade reorg as Pz Gren Div Brandenburg inc. Gross Deutschland cadre and part Festungs Div Rhodos; Nov 1944 inc. Pz Battle Group von Wietersheim (GD) bracketed with GD (E. Prussia) into Pz Corps Gross Deutschland; **Jan 1945** redeployed, with GD corps staff but not GD Div, from Rastenburg to Lodz and with HG1 committed to relief of XXIV Pz Corps Nehring at Petrikau (map 18); Feb 1945 rearguard action with HG1 to the Neisse (Görlitz); Mar/April 1945 retired Görlitz/Dresden; May 1945 encircled at Olmütz (Olomouc), remnant surrendered to US/Russians via Deutsch-Brod.

PANZER GRENADIER DIVISION FELDHERRNHALLE (FH), *see* 60th Motorized Division.

GROSS DEUTSCHLAND DIVISION (GD)

A panzer Grenadier division in name only, *see* Profiles 2. Expanded from mot regt (1939) to pz corps (1944), GD was unrivalled in stature among Army formations, surpassed in strength only by premier SS and HG divisions. In action at crisis points on Eastern Front only. Assoc formations raised with help of cadres from GD: Brandenburg; Führer Begleit; Führer Grenadier; Pz Gren Kurmark (all entitled to GD cuffbands).

HERMANN GOERING DIVISION (HG: HG1, HG2)

Mot div N Africa – Italy 1942–3; July 1943 Sicily, upgraded to pz div; Oct 1944 reorg as HG1 and HG2, eventually with weapons and personnel estab superior to any in Wehrmacht.

Raised **Feb 1933** at Berlin as mot police detach (Wecke) from Prussian police volunteers; from July 1933 responsible to Ministerpräsident Hermann Goering; Sept 1935 inc. into Goering's Luftwaffe, renamed Regiment General Goering and expanded to two bns one of which, Brauer, later became first Fallschirm (paratroop) bn, plus support and guard coys; 1936–8 reorg at Reinickendorf into three flak bns and a guard bn for Luftwaffe and Führer HQ protection; Mar 1938 Austria; **Mar 1939** Bohemia; Sept 1939 Berlin protection; May to June 1940 Belgium, France (map 3) reinforcing XVI Pz Corps (Hoepner) as Flak Regt 103 under II Flak Corps; **April 1941** inc. Jaeger bn, Balkans (map 6); June 1941 Eastern Front under Kleistgruppe Dubno, Zhitomer; July 1941 Uman; Aug 1941 Nikopol; Nov 1941 Orel; May 1942 Brittany, reorg as Bde HG; July 1942 Bordeaux reform as mot div; Nov 1942 to May 1943 Tunisia, Regtl Battle Group Koch, arty regt, flak regt, et al; **May 1943** practically destroyed serving Fifth Panzer Army, Tunisia; May to June 1943 reform S. France and Naples; July 1943 Sicily, renamed HG Pz Div (q.v.).

PANZER GRENADIER DIVISION KURMARK (KMK)

Raised **Jan 1945** at Cottbus from GD replacement personnel with one pz(v) and one pz Jaeger (Hetzer) bn; Feb 1945 Frankfurt/Oder; April 1945 narrowly escaped encirclement at Halbe, remnant retired Elbe, surrendering to US at Tangermünde.

2. Panzer and light divisions, 1935–45

LIGHT DIVISIONS 1–4 reorganized as panzer divisions after participating in Polish campaign (map 2): **1st Light Division** raised April 1938 became 6th Panzer Division Oct 1939 at Wuppertal. **2nd Light Division** raised Nov 1938 became 7th Panzer Division Oct 1939 at Gera. **3rd Light Division** raised Nov 1938 became 8th Panzer Division Oct 1939 at Cottbus. **4th Light Division** raised April 1938 became 9th Panzer Division Oct 1940 at Vienna.

5TH LIGHT AFRICA DIVISION

Raised **Feb 1941** Wünsdorf/Tripoli from 3rd Pz Div(Staff 3 Pz Bde, 5th Pz Regt; two pz bns only, recce, anti-tank and arty bn) also Army troops incl. 2nd, 8th, MG bns(mot) hvy anti-tank and flak bn; Mar 1941 'Sunflower' (map 5) Rommel's advance El Agheila – Sollum (May 1941); July 1941 reorg and renamed 21st Pz Div (q.v.), 2nd MG Bn transf to 15th Pz Div.

90TH LIGHT AFRICA DIVISION

Raised **Nov 1941** N. Africa as Afrika Div zbv with inf units flown from Germany, incl. 361st Afrika Mot Regt (former Fr Foreign Legion personnel) and Army troops; Jan 1942 'Theseus' (map 5); April 1942 renamed 90th Light Div; May to Oct 1942 Gazala, Tobruk (21 June) to El Alamein (23 Oct) (map 9); Nov to April 1943 in retreat west; **May 1943** destroyed in Tunisia; July 1943 Italy, reform Sardinia as 90th Pz Gren Div (q.v.); Oct 1943 reorg Tuscany, thereafter in action mainland Italy; **1945** surrendered to US N. Italy.

164TH LIGHT AFRICA DIVISION

Aug 1942 N. Africa inc. two pz gren regts of Festungs Div Kreta (formerly 164th Inf Div) redeployed by air from Crete, also Army troops but no pz bn; Oct 1942 practically destroyed at El Alamein (23 Oct) (map 9), thereafter in retreat west (map 5); **Feb 1943** reorg; May 1943 destroyed in Tunisia.

1ST PANZER DIVISION

Raised **Oct 1935** at Weimar from 3rd Cav Div; Sept 1939 Poland (map 2); May 1940 France (map 3); Sept 1940 E. Prussia, Soviet border; **June 1941** Eastern Front (Map 7), Dunaburg, Leningrad; Oct to Dec 1941 Moscow (map 7); Mar to Dec 1942 Rshev; **Jan to June 1943** refit France; July to Oct 1943 Greece; Nov 1943 East Front: N. Ukraine, Zhitomir (17 Nov); Feb 1944 Cherkassy relief; Mar 1944 Brody, 'Hube' pocket (map 15); Sept 1944 Carpathians; Oct 1944 Hungary: Debrecen, Nyiregyhaza; **Jan 1945** Budapest relief (map 19); May 1945 surrendered to US at Enns.

2ND PANZER DIVISION

Raised **Oct 1935** at Würtzburg; 1938 Vienna; Sept 1939 Poland (map 2); May 1940 France (map 3); July to Aug 1940 Germany; **Jan 1941** Poland; Mar 1941 Roumania; April 1941 Greece (map 6); June 1941 Germany; Aug to Sept 1941 France; Oct 1941 Eastern Front (map 8), Vyasma; Nov 1941 Klin, Krasnaya Polyana (31 Nov–5 Dec); Feb to Dec 1942 Rshev; **Jan to Mar 1943** Rshev; April 1943 Smolensk; July 1943 N. Kursk (map 14); Oct 1943 Kiev; Nov 1943 Gomel; Jan 1944 France (Amiens); June 1944 (D+6) Normandy (map 16); Aug 1944 practically destroyed in Falaise pocket (20 Aug); Sept 1944 refit Bitburg; Dec 1944 Ardennes (map 17); **early 1945** middle Mosel, Hunsrück/Rhine; April 1945 Karlsbad-Pilsen; surrendered to US at Kötzing.

3RD PANZER DIVISION

Raised **Oct 1935** at Berlin; Sept 1939 Poland (map 2); May to June 1940 Belgium/France (map 3); July 1940 Germany; **June 1941** Eastern Front (map 7); Smolensk, Kiev, Tula (map 8); Feb 1942 transf south to Kharkov; July to Dec 1942 Caucasus (map 10); **Jan to Mar 1943** Donets/Stalino (map 13); July 1943 S. Kursk (map 14); Aug 1943 Kharkov; Sept 1943 Kiev; Dec 1943 Cherkassy relief (map 15); April to July 1944 S. Ukraine; Aug to Nov 1944 Poland, Baranov; Dec 1944 Hungary; **Jan to April 1945** Hungary: Budapest relief (map 19); May 1945 Steirmark, Warsaw, reserve; surrendered to US at Enns.

4TH PANZER DIVISION

Raised **Nov 1938** at Würzburg; Sept 1939 Poland (map 2); May to June 1940 Belgium/France (map 3); July to Nov 1940 preparing for 'Sea-lion'; Dec 1940 Germany; **Feb 1941** W. France; April 1941 Balkans, reserve; June 1941 Eastern Front (map 7): Gomel, Kiev, Tula (map 8); Jan to Dec 1942 Orel (Severssk 7 Mar); **Jan to June 1943** Orel/Kursk; July 1943 N. Kursk (map 14); winter 1943–4 A Gr Centre: Bobruisk, Kowel; summer 1944 Latvia, Courland; **Jan to May 1945** refit Danzig for ops E. and W. Prussia, surrendered to Russians at Frisches Nehrung.

5TH PANZER DIVISION

Raised **Nov 1938** at Oppeln; Sept 1939 Poland (map 2); May to June 1940 Belgium/France (map 3); **Jan 1941** Roumania; Mar 1941 Bulgaria; April 1941 Yugoslavia/Greece (map 6); July 1941 Germany (Berlin OKH reserve); Oct 1941 Eastern Front (map 8): Vyasma; Nov 1941 Istra; Dec 1941 Moscow; Jan to Dec 1942 Gshatsk, Rshev; **Jan**

to Mar 1943 Gshatsk; April 1943 refit Orel; July 1943 Kursk (reserve); Sept 1943 Dnieper; early 1944 Dnieper: Bobruisk, Kowel, Minsk; Aug 1944 Lithuania, Courland; Nov 1944 E. Prussia; **Jan to April 1945** Königsberg, Pillau, surrendered to Russians Hela Peninsular.

6TH PANZER DIVISION

Raised **Oct 1939** at Wuppertal from 1st Lt Div(Poland) (map 2) (three pz bns only, with Czech 35(t) equip); May 1940 France (map 3); July 1940 Germany; Sept 1940 E. Prussia, Soviet border; **June 1941** Eastern Front (map 7), Ostrov, Leningrad; Oct 1941 Vyasma (map 8); Nov 1941 Klin; Dec 1941 Moscow; May 1942 Brittany; Dec 1942 Stalingrad relief (map 12); **Jan to Mar 1943** Donets/Kharkov (map 13); July 1943 S. Kursk (map 14); Mar 1944 Hube pocket (map 15); June 1944 refit with German equip Bergen; Dec 1944 Hungary, Danube (map 19); **Jan 1945** Budapest relief; April 1945 Vienna; May 1945 Moravia, surrendered to Rusians at Brno.

7TH PANZER DIVISION (THE 'GHOST' DIVISION)

Raised **Oct 1939** at Gera from 2nd Lt Div(Poland) (map 2) (three pz bns only, with Czech 38(t) equip); May to June 1940 Belgium/France (map 3); July 1940 preparing for 'Sea-lion' until Jan 1941; **Feb 1941** Bonn; June 1941 Eastern Front (map 7), Smolensk; Oct to Dec 1941 Kalinin, Dimitrov (map 8); Jan 1942 Rshev; June 1942 NW France, Niort, refit with German equip; Nov 1942 Vichy, Toulon (occup. 27 Nov); **Jan 1943** Donets (map 12); Feb 1943 inc. remnant 27th Pz Div; Mar 1943 Kharkov (map 13); July 1943 S. Kursk (map 14); Nov to Dec 1943 Kiev, Zhitomir; Mar 1944 Tarnopol, Hube pocket (map 15); Aug 1944 Lithuania, Courland; Oct to Nov 1944 Doblen, Memel; Dec 1944 evac to Danzig, Arys (E. Prussia) for refit; **Jan 1945** Vistula; Feb to Mar 1945 E./W. Prussia, Danzig, Hela; April 1945 evac to Swinemünde; May 1945 after refit Krampnitz remnant surrendered to British Schwerin/ Hangow.

8TH PANZER DIVISION

Raised **Oct 1939** at Cottbus from 3rd Lt Div(Poland) (map 2) (three pz bns only, with Czech 38(t) equip); May to June 1940 Belgium/France (map 3); July to Dec 1940 preparing for 'Sea-lion'; **Jan 1941** Germany; April 1941 Yugoslavia (map 6); June 1941 Eastern Front (map 7), Luga, Leningrad; Nov 1941 Tikhvin; 1942 Leningrad, Cholm, Smolensk, Velish; **Feb 1943** Vitebsk; April 1943 Orel; Oct 1943 Tarnopol, Kiev; Jan to Sept 1944 Winnitza, Brody, Lemberg, Carpathians (Dukla Pass); Oct to Nov 1944 refit in Slovakia; Dec 1944 Hungary/Budapest (map 19); **Feb 1945** Silesia (Lauban); Mar 1945 Moravia; May 1945 surrendered to Russians at Brno

9TH PANZER DIVISION

Raised **Jan 1940** at Vienna and lower Austria from 4th Lt Div(Poland) (map 2); May to June 1940 Holland/France (map 3); July to Sept 1940 refit at Vienna; Dec 1940 Poland; **Jan to Feb 1941** Roumania; Mar 1941 Bulgaria; April 1941 Yugoslavia/Greece (map 6); May 1941 Germany; July 1941 Eastern Front (map 7), Uman, Kiev; May 1942 Bryansk, Kursk; June 1942 Voronezh (map 10); Dec 1942 Rshev; **Mar 1943** Orel; April 1943 refit; July 1943 N. Kursk (map 14); late summer 1943 Dnieper, Stalino; Nov 1943 Krivoi Rog; Jan 1944 Nikopol; April 1943 S. France (Nîmes) reform by inc. 155th Res Pz Div; Aug 1944 (D+51) Normandy (map 16) Alençon, practically destroyed in Falaise pocket (20 Aug), then to Metz; Sept 1944 Aachen/Geilenkirchen; Nov 1944 refit Zanten inc. 105 Pz Bde; Dec 1944 Ardennes (map 17); **Jan 1945** Eifel; Mar 1945 Cologne, Remagen; April 1945 encircled Ruhr pocket, with remnant in Harz surrendered to US.

10TH PANZER DIVISION

Raised **April 1939** at Prague; Sept 1939 Poland (map 2); Oct 1939 to April 1940 Lower Silesia; May 1940 France (map 3); July 1940 to Feb 1941 preparing for 'Sea-lion'; **Mar 1941** Lower Silesia; June 1941 Eastern Front (map 7), Minsk, Smolensk, Moscow (map 8), Juchnow until April 1942; May 1942 NW France refit; Aug 1942 Dieppe; Nov 1942 Marseille (occup.); Dec 1942 N. Africa, W. Tunis (map 5); **Feb 1943** Kasserine; Mar 1943 Medenine; May 1943 destroyed defending Tunis.

11TH PANZER DIVISION

Raised **Aug 1940** at Neuhammer from 11 Schützen Bde, 5th Pz and other cadres; **Feb 1941** Roumania; Mar 1941 Bulgaria; April 1941 Yugoslavia, Belgrade (map 6); June 1941 Eastern Front (map 7), Uman; Oct 1941 Vyasma (map 8); Dec 1941 Moscow; Jan 1942 Gshatsk; June 1942 Voronezh (map 10); Aug 1942 to Jan 1943 Don/Donets (map 12); **Feb to Mar 1943** Donets/Kharkov; July 1943 S. Kursk (map 14); Sept 1943 Kremenchug; Jan 1944 Cherkassy relief (failed); Mar 1944 Hube pocket (map 15); April 1944 Jassy; May 1944 S. France refit inc. 273rd Res Pz Div; July 1944 Toulouse/Carcassonne; Aug 1944 Rhône valley; Sept 1944 Belfort refit inc. 113 Pz Bde; Dec 1944 Saar, Ardennes (map 17); **Jan 1945** Trier; Mar 1945 Remagen; May 1945 surrendered to US in Bavaria.

12TH PANZER DIVISION

Raised **Oct 1940** at Stettin from 2nd Inf Div(mot); **July 1941** Eastern Front (map 7), Minsk, Smolensk; Sept 1941 Leningrad, Tikhvin, Volkhov; Jan 1942 refit Pleskau/ Estonia; Feb 1942 to Feb 1943 Volkhov, Leningrad, Beliya, Vitebsk; **Mar 1943** to A Gr Centre: Gomel, Orel, Pripet until Jan 1944; Feb 1944 Leningrad, Luga, Pleskau; April 1944 refit Ostrov; July 1944 Bobruisk; Aug 1944 E. Prussia/ Courland, **April 1945** surrendered to Russians in Courland.

13TH PANZER DIVISION

Raised **Oct 1940** at Magdeburg and Vienna from 13th Inf Div(mot) thereafter 'instructional' duties Roumania; **June 1941** Eastern Front (map 7), Uman, Kiev, Rostov; Aug 1942 Caucasus: Armavir, Mozdok until Dec 1942 (map 10); **Jan 1943** Kuban; July 1943 refit Crimea; Oct 1943 to Jan 1944 Krivoi Rog; Feb 1944 Cherkassy relief (failed); April 1944 transf to Moldavia; May 1944 Kishinev, inc. Pz Gren Regt Feldherrnhalle; Aug 1944 practically destroyed serving Sixth Army at Husi (Roumania); Sept 1944 reform SE Vienna; Oct 1944 Hungary: Debrecen, Nyiregyhaza; Dec 1944 to Jan 1945 Budapest (map 19), encircled and again practically destroyed; **Jan 1945** reform as Pz Div Feldherrnhalle 2 (q.v.).

14TH PANZER DIVISION

Raised **Aug 1940** at Köningsbrück/Milowitz by reorg of 4th Inf Div; Nov 1940 to Feb 1941 Germany; **Mar 1941** Hungary; April 1941 Yugoslavia (map 6); June 1941

Germany; July 1941 to Nov 1942 Eastern Front (map 7), Don, Rostov, Mius, Stalingrad (map 10); **Feb 1943** destroyed at Stalingrad; Mar 1943 reform France (Angers); Nov 1943 Krivoi Rog; Dec 1943 Kirovograd pocket; Jan to Feb 1944 SW Cherkassy; Mar to April 1944 Bug/Dniester; May to June 1944 Moldavia: Jassy; July 1944 refit; Aug 1944 Lithuania: Tilsit, Schaulen; Sept 1944 Latvia: E. of Riga, Baldone (20 Sept); Oct 1944 Courland (Lithuania) 1st–3rd battles; **Jan to May 1945** Courland, 4th and 5th battles, surrendered to Russians at Libau.

15TH PANZER DIVISION

Raised **Nov 1940** at Darmstadt/Landau by reorg of 33rd Inf Div; **May to Aug 1941** North Africa (map 5), Tripoli, Derna, Libya/Egypt frontier; Nov 1941 to Jan 1942 in retreat ('Crusader' counter-action 24–27 Nov) to El Agheila; Jan 1942 renewed offensive 'Theseus'; May 1942 Gazala/Tobruk (21 June) to El Alamein (23 Oct) (map 9); Nov 1942 again in retreat to Tunisia; **Feb 1943** Mareth Line; Mar 1943 8th Pz Regt (Irkens) reinf by 5th Pz Regt (21st Pz Div) responsible to Pz Führer Afrika Irkens, later weak Pz Gr Irkens; May 1943 destroyed at Tunis serving Fifth Pz Army; July 1943 Sicily, remnant used to raise 15th Pz Gren Div (q.v.).

16TH PANZER DIVISION

Raised **Aug 1940** at Münster by reorg of 16th Inf Div; Dec 1940 Roumania 'training'; **April 1941** Balkans (map 6); June to Dec 1942 Eastern Front (map 7), Uman, Kiev, Kharkov, Stalingrad (map 10); **Feb 1943** destroyed at Stalingrad; Mar 1943 reform Brittany; June 1943 Taranto; Sept 1943 Salerno, Naples; Oct 1943 Sangro; Nov 1943 Bobruisk, Kiev; Feb 1944 Cherkassy relief; Mar 1944 Hube pocket (map 15), Vistula; Dec 1944 Kielce, reorg with 17th Pz Div into XXIV Pz Corps Nehring (map 18); **Jan 1945** Baranov (Kielce); Feb 1945 Glogau, Lauban; Mar 1945 refit inc. Pz Div Jüterbog; May 1945 Moravia, Tropau, surrendered part Russians/part US.

17TH PANZER DIVISION

Raised **Nov 1940** at Augsburg by reorg of 27th Inf Div; **June 1941** Eastern Front (map 7), Smolensk, Kiev; Oct to Dec 1941 Tula, Kashira (map 8); Jan to Nov 1942 Orel, then transf south; Dec 1942 Stalingrad relief (map 12); **Jan to Mar 1943** Donets/Kharkov; April to Sept 1943 Issyum (map 13); Oct 1943 to Jan 1944 Cherson, Winnitza; Feb 1944 Cherkassy relief; Mar 1944 Hube pocket (map 15); April to Aug 1944 E. Poland; Sept 1944 Baranov; Dec 1944 Kielce, reorg with 16th Pz Div into XXIV Pz Corps Nehring (map 18); **Jan 1945** Baranov (Kielce); Feb 1945 Oder, Glogau, remnant surrendered to Russians in Moravia.

18TH PANZER DIVISION

Raised **Oct 1940** at Leisnig from elements of 4th and 14th Inf Divs; in Germany until **June 1941** Eastern Front (map 7), Smolensk; Sept 1941 Bryansk; Dec 1941 Jefremov (map 8); Jan 1942 Suschinitschi relief; Feb to Dec 1942 Orel; **Jan to June 1943** Orel; July 1943 N. Kursk (map 14); Aug 1943 Bryansk, Orscha; Oct 1943 Vitebsk, virtually destroyed; reorg in Lithuania as 18th Arty Div; April 1944 destroyed there.

19TH PANZER DIVISION

Raised **Nov 1940** at Hanover by reorg of 19th Inf Div; **June 1941** Eastern Front (map 7), Minsk, Smolensk: Veliki Luki (20 July), Velish (22 July); Oct to Dec 1941 Moscow, Naro-Forminsk (map 8); Jan to Dec 1942 Juchnow, Orel, Beliya (8 Dec); Dec 1942 transf south to Kupjansk; **Jan 1943** Starobjelsk, Millerovo; Feb to Mar 1943 Donets, Kharkov; July 1943 S. Kursk (map 14); late summer escaped encirclement Graivoron (9 Aug) before joining GD in action at Achtyryka, Kiev, Kanev (Bukrin) bridgehead (25 Sept), Zhitomir, Kaments-Podolsk; Mar 1944 Hube pocket (map 15); June 1944 refit Holland; July 1944 Poland: Grodno, Bialystok; Aug 1944 to Jan 1945 Warsaw region SE and SW Warka/Magnuschev bridgehead (2–17 Aug); **Jan 1945** Radom; Feb to Mar 1945 Silesia: Breslau SW (9 Mar); April 1945 upper Oder: Rogau; May 1945 Slovakia, SW Olmütz (Olomouc), surrendered to Russians in Bohemia.

20TH PANZER DIVISION

Raised **Oct 1940** at Erfurt from elements of 19th Inf Div; **June 1941** Eastern Front (map 7), Minsk, Smolensk; Oct to Dec 1941 Moscow (map 8); Jan 1942 to June 1943 Gzhatsk, Orel, Beliya, Toropez; **July 1943** N. Kursk (map 14); Oct 1943 to Feb 1944 Vitebsk; Mar to July 1944 Bobruisk, practically destroyed serving Ninth Army; Aug 1944 Roumania; Oct 1944 to Jan 1945 refit Arys (E. Prussia); **Jan 1945** Hungary (map 19), Silesia; May 1945 surrendered to Russians at Görlitz.

21ST PANZER DIVISION

Raised **Aug 1941** in N. Africa by reorg and renaming 5th Light Africa Div (q.v.); Nov 1941 to Jan 1942 retreat and 'Crusader' counter-action (20–27 Nov) between Sollum and El Agheila; Jan 1942 renewed offensive 'Theseus'; May 1942 Gazala/Tobruk (21 June) to El Alamein (23 Oct) (map 9); Nov 1942 in retreat west to Tunisia; **Feb 1943** Kasserine (map 5); Mar 1943 reorg. Contributed Pz Kampfgruppe 5 to Pz Führer Afrika (*see* 15th Pz Div Mar 1943); May 1943 destroyed at Tunis serving Fifth Pz Army; July 1943 France, reform at Rennes from Schnelle Bde 931 and other units inc. Pz Regt 100, with French equip; June 1944 (D-Day) Normandy; Aug 1944 practically destroyed Falaise pocket (20 Aug); Sept 1944 Lothringa refit inc. 112 Pz Bde; Dec 1944 Saarpfalz; **Jan 1945** N. Strasbourg; Feb 1945 Oder, Lauban; April 1945 Görlitz, Halbe, surrendered to Russians at Cottbus.

22ND PANZER DIVISION

Raised **Sept 1941** in SW France, inc. Pz Regt 204, three pz bns with Fr, later Czech 38(t) and Ger (Pz Kpfw III and IV) equip; Mar 1942 Crimea, Feodosia; May 1942 Kertsch, Sevastopol; June 1942 Donets/Slavjansk; July 1942 Rostov except detached Kampfgruppe Michalik (reinf Pz Gren Regt 140) at Voronezh (used Sept as kernel 27th Pz Div (q.v.)); Aug to Sept 1942 Don crossing Kalatsch; Nov to Dec 1942 Chir, surrounded and practically destroyed serving Roum Third Army (map 12), thereafter Pz Kampf Gr Oppeln/Burgsthaler in action Donets/Dnieper; **Jan to April 1943** weak battle groups absorbed into 6th and 23rd Pz Divs (Burgsthaler).

23RD PANZER DIVISION

Raised **Oct 1941** in Paris region inc. Pz Regt 201 with Fr equip; April 1942 Eastern Front: Kharkov; Aug to Nov 1942

Caucasus (map 10); Dec 1942 Stalingrad relief (map 12); **April 1943** refit Stalino inc. elements 22nd Pz Div; summer to winter 1943 Dnieper; Jan 1944 Krivoi Rog; Feb 1944 Pz Bn to First Pz Army; April to July 1944 Jassy; Aug 1944 Vistula/Baranov; Oct 1944 Hungary: Debrecen, Nyiregyhaza; Jan 1945 Budapest (map 19); Feb to May 1945 Hungary/Austria, surrendered to British in Steiermark.

24TH PANZER DIVISION (THE 'LEAPING RIDER' DIVISION)

Raised **Nov 1941** at Stablack E. Prussia by reorg of 1st Cav Div; June 1942 Eastern Front, Kursk; June 1942 Voronezh (map 10); Sept 1942 Don corridor to Stalingrad; Oct 1942 to Feb 1943 Stalingrad; **Feb 1943** destroyed at Stalingrad; Mar to Aug 1943 reform France; Aug to Sept 1943 N. Italy security; Oct 1943 East: Ingulez/Dnieper: Nikopol, Krivoi Rog; Mar 1944 Nikolayev, airlifted to Kishinev 22 Mar; April to July 1944 Jassy; Aug to Sept 1944 Poland: Dukla Pass (18 Sept); Oct 1944 Hungary: Debrecen (Szolnok); Dec 1944 Slovakia; **Feb to April 1945** E. Prussia: Allenstein, Heiligenbeil Balga (26 Mar) reduced to weak battle group transp by sea to Schleswig Holstein; May 1945 surrendered to British at Eckenford.

25TH PANZER DIVISION

Raised **Feb 1942** in Norway as Mot Kampf Gp, Oslo (146th Mot Inf Regt, Pz Jaeg Coy, etc.), later Pz Bn 214; Mar to Oct 1942 additional cadres to full strength; **Aug 1943** France, training at Mailly-le-Camp; Nov 1943 Eastern Front: Fastov (7 Nov); Dec 1943 to April 1944 Zhitomir, N. Ukraine Hube pocket (map 15), practically destroyed except Lemberg, Kampf Gp Treuhaupt (inf, arty, two pz coys); May 1944 reform Varde (Esbjerg), Denmark, inc. Pz 'Div' Norwegen (q.v.); Sept 1944 Warsaw, Radom; Nov 1944 inc. 104 Pz Bde; **Feb 1945** Oder; April 1945 lower Danube; May 1945 surrendered to US at Passau.

26TH PANZER DIVISION

Raised **Sept 1942** at Amiens by reorg of 23rd Inf Div, occup. France until July 1943; **July 1943 to Aug 1945** Italy: Calabria, Salerno, Anzio, Cassino, Rimini, Bologna; **April 1945** surrendered at Imola.

27TH PANZER DIVISION

Raised **Oct 1942** at Voronezh from detach 22nd Pz Kampf Gp Michalik (Pz Gren Bn 140 and a pz bn) and Army troops (Pz Verband 700); Nov to Dec 1942 Rossoch (NE Millerovo) in rear It Eighth Army on Don. Practically destroyed there opposing Russian winter offensive; **Jan to Feb 1943** weak battle groups Oskol/Donets; Mar 1943 disband: units to 7th, 19th and 24th Pz Divs (France).

116TH PANZER DIVISION (THE 'GREYHOUND' DIVISION)

Raised **Mar 1944** in NW France by Fifteenth Army from reorg 179th Res Pz Div inc. remnant 16th Pz Gren Div; mid-July 1944 Normandy (map 16), released to Fifth Pz Army (Caen); Aug 1944 Mortain (7 Aug) and action with 9th Pz Div to halt US drive on Alençon (map 16), practically destroyed in Falaise pocket (20 Aug); Sept 1944 Aachen; Oct 1944 refit inc. 108 Pz Bde; **Dec 1944 to Jan 1945** Ardennes (map 17); Feb to Mar 1945 lower Rhine/Kleve, Wesel; April 1945 encircled in Ruhr pocket serving Fifth Pz Army. With elements in the Harz, surrendered to US.

232ND PANZER DIVISION

Raised **Feb 1945** in Slovakia from Pz Feldausbildungs Div Tatra: two pz gren regts only; Mar 1945 destroyed at Raab.

233RD PANZER DIVISION

Raised **April 1945** at Aarhus/Viborg, Denmark by renaming 233rd Res Pz Div (reconstituted prev Feb after having provided cadres for Pz Div Holstein (q.v.)); security Denmark until capitulation; Battle group to 'Clausewitz' at Lübeck.

1ST FELDHERRNHALLE PANZER DIVISION (FHH1)

Raised **Sept 1944** in Hungary by reorg of Pz Gren Div Feldherrnhalle (60th Mot) (q.v.); Oct 1944 Debrecen, inc. 109 Pz Bde, and renamed Pz Div FHH; Dec 1944 Danube, serving Pz Kampf Gp Pape; **Jan 1945** Komorn, Budapest (map 19), practically destroyed; Feb 1945 joined Pz Div Feldherrnhalle 2 (13th Pz Div) (q.v.) in Feldherrnhalle Pz Corps (formerly IV Pz Corps); Mar to April 1945 E. Hungary, Gran, lower Austria; May 1945 surrendered to US in upper Austria.

2ND FELDHERRNHALLE PANZER DIVISION (FHH2)

Raised **Feb 1945** by renaming 13th Pz Div elements outside Budapest, plus elements of FHH1 (q.v.), both divs otherwise destroyed defending Budapest (map 19); Feb 1945 Komorn; May 1945 surrendered to US in upper Austria.

FÜHRER BEGLEIT PANZER BRIGADE (FBB), LATER FÜHRER BEGLEIT PANZER DIVISION (FB-D)

Originally Führer Begleit (mot escort) Bn **(Oct 39)**; Regt (June 1944); Brigade Nov 1944 E. Prussia/Cottbus, two pz (or assault gun) bns, three pz gren bns with GD personnel; Dec 1944 Ardennes (map 17); **Jan 1945** Division: Feb 1945 Stargard offensive; Mar 1945 Troppau/Ratibor; April 1945 encircled and practically destroyed at Spremberg, remnant surrendered to US.

FÜHRER PANZER GRENADIER BRIGADE (FGB), LATER FÜHRER PANZER GRENADIER DIVISION (FGD)

Brigade: raised **July 1944** at Cottbus from GD replacement bde, two pz (or assault gun) bns, three pz gren bns; Oct 1944 E. Prussia; Dec 1944 Ardennes offensive (map 17); **Jan 1945** Division: Feb 1945 Stargard offensive; Mar 1945 Stettin, Küstrin relief (failed); April 1945 Vienna; May 1945 surrendered to US/Russians.

GROSS DEUTSCHLAND PANZER GRENADIER DIVISION (GD), LATER GROSS DEUTSCHLAND PANZER CORPS

A pz gren div in name only, GD developed as the army's premier armoured formation, comparable to 1SSLAH and HG. Progressively expanded from Regt to Division and finally Corps, by July 1944 the weapons estab incl. a pz regt (Aug 1943) with a third (Tiger) bn, six pz gren bns (two regts of 16 coys), an assault gun bde (three battys) and an arty regt (I–IV Bns). **Oct 1939** raised at Grafenwöhr as Inf Regt (mot) GD by expand and reorg Wacht (guard) Regt (formerly Wachttruppe Berlin (1933)) inc. part Inf Demo Bn Döberitz; Aug 1939 provided cadre for Führer Begleit Bn; May 1940 France, Sedan (map 3); **April 1941** Balkans (map 6); June 1941 Eastern Front (map 7), Minsk, Smolensk, Jelnya, Konotop, Romny (Kiev); Oct 1941 Bryansk (map 8), Orel, Tula; Jan 1942 Oka; April 1942 expand to inf div mot; May 1942 Orel; June to July 1942

Voronezh/Don corridor (map 10); Aug to Dec 1942 Rshev; **Jan 1943** Bjelgorod; Mar 1943 Kharkov, recapt Bjelgorod (map 13); June 1943 renamed Pz Gren Div GD; July 1943 S. Kursk (map 14); Aug 1943 transf to A Gp South, Achtyrka; Sept 1943 Kremenchug bridgehead; Oct 1943 Krivoi Rog, Kirovograd; Jan to end April 1944 in retreat S. Ukraine to Carpathians, Jassy, Targul Frumos; July 1944 refit; Aug 1944 E. Prussia: Gumbinnen for counter-offensive E. and then N. to restore contact between Army Gps Centre and North at Tukkum (failed at Doblen); Oct 1944 Schaulen, Memel bridgehead (evac 26 Nov); Dec 1944 Rastenburg reorg with Brandenburg Div (q.v.) into Pz Corps GD (never in action together); **Jan to April 1945** practically destroyed with HG2 defending Königsberg, evac Balga (29 Mar) to Pillau, remnant transp by Baltic to Schleswig-Holstein; May 1945 surrendered to British.

HERMANN GOERING FALLSCHIRM (PARATROOP) PANZER DIVISION (HG: HG1 (ARMOURED), HG2 (MOTORIZED), LATER HERMANN GOERING FALLSCHIRM PANZER CORPS

Raised **July 1943** in Sicily as Pz Div HG from replacement personnel, staff and cadres from HG Div (practically destroyed in Tunisia). Reform S. France and Naples (*see* Div Profiles 1). Sept 1943 Salerno; Oct to Nov 1943 rearguard action Volturno, Garigliano; Nov 1943 refit Frosinone to exceptional estab (21,0000 field effectives, Pz Regt two bns plus assault gun bn, two pz gren regts with four bns, recce and support units). Guard Regt Berlin, Replacement Regt Holland, battle school, etc. Battle group action Monte Maggiore, Monte Troccio.

Jan 1944 renamed Fallschirm Pz Div HG; Anzio (22 Jan) until early Mar; refit Lucca/Pisa; May 1944 Valmonte (US Anzio breakout); June to July 1944 Chiusi, Arno; 15 July redeployed to Warsaw; Aug 1944 Volomin (NE) Magnuschev (SE); Sept 1944 Bugmunde (NW); Oct 1944 Modlin reorg as HG1 (two pz bns, five pz gren bns) and bracketed with new HG2 Pz Gren Div and corps troops (pzjaeg bn, Sturm bn, eng bn, flak regt) into Fallsc Pz Corps HG; until mid-Jan 1945 redeployed E. Prussia defending Königsberg E. At Nemmersdorf; **Jan 1945 HG1** redeployed south to Army Gp Centre. In action Lodz-Petrikau with Brandenburg (Pz Corps GD) to relieve encircled Pz Corps Nehring (map 18); rearguard action Oder/Neisse to Muskau; Mar 1945 upper Silesia, Neisse, Gorlitz; April 1945 Bautzen/N. Dresden. In action with Fallsc Pz Corps HG survivors (HG2); evac Heiligenbeil by Baltic after abortive defence E. Prussia; May 1945 most remnant surrendered to Russians, others to US.

HOLSTEIN/CLAUSEWITZ* PANZER DIVISION

Raised **Feb 1945** as Kampfgruppe Holstein from principal combat units 233rd Res Pz Div; East: Pomerania, Stargard Baltic coast; Mar 1945 encircled with Korpsgruppe Tettau at Horst before leading breakout (10 Mar) to west at Stettin; redeployed Oder near Küstrin inc. with Schlesien (Döberitz) into 18th Pz Gren Div; April 1945 Berlin, Potsdam, surrendered to US at Tangermünde.

April 1945 Holstein HQ personnel posted Lüneburg, S of Hamburg as kernel Pz Div Clausewitz (pz bn ex-Putlos, two coys eleven Pz Kpfws each plus mot inf bns and support units); 12–21 May in action S. of Lüneburg against flank of Allied drive to Elbe; May 1945 surrendered to US at Lauenburg.

KEMPF PANZER DIVISION (K)

Raised in **Sept 1939** in Poland, improvised from Staff 4 Pz Bde, 7th Pz Regt, SS Deutschland Regt, SS arty regt, recce, anti-tank and support units (map 2).

NORWEGEN PANZER DIVISION (NWN)

Raised in **Sept 1943** at Oslo after departure of 25th Pz Div (q.v.) to France; June 1944 transf to Varde (Esbjerg) Denmark and absorbed into 25th Pz Div.

PANZER LEHR DIVISION (PL)

Raised in **winter of 1943** at Bergen, Germany from Pz Schools 1 (Bergen) and 2 (Krampnitz); an exceptionally well-equipped formation, both pz gren regts in SPWs, a Tiger bn and Goliath coys; Feb 1944 France; Mar 1944 Hungary; June 1944 (D+2) Normandy (map 16); Aug 1944 practically destroyed in path of US breakout ('Cobra'); Sept 1944 Germany (Swabia) refit; Dec 1944 Ardennes (map 17); **Jan 1945** Eifel; Feb 1945 Wesel; Mar 1945 Remagen, Siegen; April 1945 Ruhr pocket serving Fifth Pz Army, surrendered to US.

TATRA PANZER DIVISION

Raised **Oct 1944** *see* 232nd Panzer Division.

CLAUSEWITZ[1]*, COURLAND[2], DONAU[1], JÜTERBOG[1], MÜNCHEBERG[1], NIBELUNGEN[3], SCHLESIEN[4], THURINGIEN[1], WESTFALEN PANZER DIVISIONS

In Feb, Mar and April 1945, impromptu pz divs (Kampfgruppen of one/two pz coys, one/two pz gren bns and support units) raised mostly for action in the east.

3. SS panzer and panzer grenadier divisions, 1933–45

1ST SS PANZER GRENADIER/PANZER DIVISION LEIBSTANDARTE ADOLF HITLER (AH, LSSAH)

Raised **Mar 1933** in Berlin as SS Stabswache (Führer mot escort coy); Sept 1933 designated Leibstandarte SSAH; 1938 expanded into mot regt; Mar 1938 Austria; Oct 1938 Sudetenland; **Sept 1939** Poland (map 2); May 1940 Holland, France (map 3), Dunkirk; Aug–Dec 1940 expanded into bde inc. heavy (assault gun) coy; **Mar 1941** Balkans; April 1941 Greece (map 6); June 1941 expanded into inf div (mot); June 1941 Eastern Front (map 7): Uman, Perekop, Rostov, Mius; Aug to Dec 1942 France, reorg as pz gren div; Toulon occup. (21 Nov); **Feb 1943** Donets, Kharkov (map 13); April 1943 refit Bjelgorod; July 1943 S. Kursk (map 14); Aug 1943 N. Italy; Oct 1943 Milan occup. and reorg as pz div; Nov 1943 Zhitomir (Brusilov); Feb 1944 Cherkassy relief; Mar 1944 Hube pocket (Skala) (map 15), Tarnopol; April 1944 Belgium refit; June 1944 (D+19) Normandy (map 16), Caen; Aug 1944 Mortain (7 Aug), practically destroyed in Falaise pocket (20 Aug); Sept 1944 refit Siegburg; Dec 1944 Ardennes (map 17); **Feb 1945** Hungary: Gran (Estergom) bridgehead; Mar 1945 Stuhl-

[1]Inc. schools, training and replacement personnel. *See* *Holstein.
[2]Remnant 14th Pz Div and others.
[3]Inc. SS Junker School Bad Tolz: *see* 38th Pz Gren Div (Divisional Profiles 3).
[4]*See* Holstein.

weissenburg (Szekesfehervar) (map 19); April 1945 St Polten; May 1945 surrendered to US at Linz.

2ND SS PANZER GRENADIER/PANZER DIVISION 'DAS REICH' (R, V)

Raised **Oct 1939** at Pilsen as Verfügungs (mot) Division inc. SS Standarte (regiment) Deutschland (Poland), Germania (Poland) and Der Führer; May 1940 Holland (map 3), Flanders; June 1940 Soissons, Orléans, Bordeaux/SW France; July to Dec 1940 Holland; Dec 1940 renamed 'Reich'; **Mar 1941** Balkans (map 6): Belgrade (12 April); June 1941 Eastern Front (map 7), Brest-Litovsk; Sept 1941 Romny; Oct 1941 Borodino; Nov to Dec 1941 Istra/Moscow (Der Führer destroyed W. of Rshev); July to Dec 1942 refit NW France inc. new Regt Langemark; **Feb 1943** Donets/Kharkov (map 13); June 1943 refit; July 1943 S. Kursk (map 14), Mius; Oct 1943 reorg as pz div; Nov 1943 Fastov/Zhitomir (R. Teterev); Jan 1944 Shepetovka; Feb 1944 France, refit Montauban leaving Battle Group (Weidinger) Hube pocket Proskurov (map 15), Tarnopol; June 1944 (D+9) Normandy (map 16) via Oradour-sur-Glane; Aug 1944 Mortain (7 Aug), practically destroyed in Falaise pocket (20 Aug); Nov 1944 refit; Dec 1944 Ardennes (map 17); **Feb 1945** Hungary: SE Komorn (map 19); Mar 1945 Stuhlweissenburg (Szekesfehervar), Raab; April 1945 Vienna, St Polten; May 1945 surrendered to US at Pilsen.

3RD SS PANZER GRENADIER/PANZER DIVISION 'TOTENKOPF' (T)

Raised **Nov 1939** at Dachau as SS Totenkopf (part mot) Div from 'Totenkopf' personnel; May 1940 Cambrai, Arras, Dunkirk (map 3); June 1940 Loire, Lyon; July 1940 to April 1941 occup. SW France, full motorization; **May 1941** Germany; June 1941 Eastern Front (map 7), Kaunus, Dunaburg; Aug 1941 Luga/Leningrad; Jan 1942 L Ilmen; Feb 1942 Denmjansk; Oct 1942 France, refit; Nov 1942 S. France occup.; **Feb 1943** Kharkov/Donets (map 13); July 1943 S. Kursk (map 14); Sept 1943 Mius; Oct 1943 reorg as pz div, Krivoi Rog/Dnieper; Jan to April 1944 in retreat Roum border; June 1944 Poland (Grodno); Aug 1944 Warsaw; Dec 1944 Modlin/W. Hungary (Komorn); **Jan 1945** Budapest relief (failed) (map 19); Feb 1945 Stuhlweissenburg; April 1945 Vienna; May 1945 surrendered to US/Russians at Linz.

4TH SS 'POLIZEI' PANZER GRENADIER DIVISION (P)

Raised **Sept 1939** at Wandern as SS Polizei Inf Div from police and specialist army personnel; May 1940 (part mot) Belgium, Flanders; June 1940 Aisne, Champagne; **June 1941** Eastern Front (map 7); Dunaburg, Luga, Leningrad, Volkhov; Jan 1942 to June 1943 Volkhov/Leningrad; **July 1943** onwards Bohemia reorg as pz gren div leaving battle group in action Leningrad; Mar 1944 Greece counter partisan; Sept 1944 Serbia, Belgrade; Oct 1944 Hungary, Debrecen (Szolnok); **Jan 1945** Stettin; Feb 1945 Stargard, Danzig; April 1945 Hela by sea to Swinemünde for refit Mecklenburg; May 1945 surrendered to US at Wittenberge.

5TH SS PANZER GRENADIER/PANZER DIVISION 'WIKING' (W)

Raised **Dec 1940** at Munich/Vienna as SS inf div (mot) from Dutch/Flemish volunteers for SS Standarte (regt) 'Westland' and Danish/Norwegian volunteers for SS Standarte 'Nordland', with 'Germania' as third regt; **June 1941** Eastern Front (map 7), Tarnopol, Zhitomir, Azov, Rostov, Mius; May 1942 inc. 5th Pz Bn (later Regt); July 1942 Rostov/Bataisk (map 10); Aug 1942 Maikop; Nov 1942 Terek/Malgobek S. of Mozdok; Dec 1942 Kotelnikovo (SW); **Feb 1943** Donets/Krasnoarmeyskoye (Kharkov) (map 13); April 1943 Don; July 1943 Kharkov; Sept 1943 Kiev; Oct 1943 reorg as SS pz div; Dec 1943 to Feb 1944 encircled and practically destroyed at Cherkassy (breakout 17 Feb); Mar 1944 remnant reform Debica; Mar to April 1944 Kowel (Battle Group Mühlenkamp); July 1944 Maciejov; Aug 1944 Warsaw; Oct 1944 Modlin; Dec 1944 Hungary; **Jan 1945** Budapest relief (failed) (map 19); Feb 1945 Stuhlweissenburg; Mar 1945 partly encircled SW of town; May surrendered to British at Furstenfeld.

9TH SS PANZER GRENADIER/PANZER DIVISION 'HOHENSTAUFEN' (HOH)

Raised **Mar 1943** at Mailly-le-Camp as pz gren div; June to Oct 1943 Amiens reorg as Pz Div; Feb 1944 Nîmes; March 1944 Poland; April 1944 Buczacz relief ops to save First Pz Army (map 15), Tarnopol ops to relieve garrison; June 1944 (D+19) Normandy (map 16), Caen; Aug 1944 practically destroyed in Falaise pocket (20 Aug); Sept 1944 Arnhem refit and counter-attack Br 1st Airborne Div ('Market Garden'); Siegen; Dec 1944 Ardennes (map 17); **Jan 1945** Hungary; Mar 1945 Stuhlweissenburg (map 19); May 1945 surrendered to US at Linz.

10TH SS PANZER GRENADIER/PANZER DIVISION 'FRUNDSBERG' (FRU)

Raised **Feb 1943** in the Charente (SW France); Oct 1943 reorg as pz div inc. 10th SS Pz Regt; Mar 1944 Poland; April 1944 Tarnopol/Buczacz relief ops to save First Pz Army (map 15); June 1944 (D+19) Normandy (map 16), Caen; Aug 1944 practically destroyed in Falaise pocket (20 Aug); Sept 1944 Arnhem refit and counter-attack Br 1st Airborne Div ('Market Garden'); Nov 1944 Aachen; Dec 1944 reserve Ardennes (map 17); **Jan 1945** upper Rhine: Haguenau forest, Strasbourg; Feb 1945 Stargard; Mar 1945 Stettin, Cottbus; April 1945 encircled and practically destroyed at Spremberg; May 1945 remnant surrendered to Russians at Shonau.

11TH SS FREIWILLIGE PANZER GRENADIER DIVISION 'NORDLAND' (NDL)

Raised **May 1943** at Grafenwöhr from German, Dutch, Norwegian, Danish and other volunteers (Freiwilliger) inc. 11th SS Pz Bn; Sept 1943 Croatia (Zagreb), counter-partisan; December 1943 Eastern Front: Orianenbaum (Leningrad); Jan to April 1944 Narwa bridgehead; Sept 1944 Courland; Tukkum; Dec 1944 transp. Baltic to Libau/Stettin after 3rd Battle of Courland; **Feb to Mar 1945** Stargard, Stettin, Altdamm bridgehead; end Mar 1945 refit Schwedt-Angermünde; April 1945 Berlin, Reichskanzlei, encircled and practically destroyed; May 1945 break-out group to Twelfth Army, surrendered to US Elbe.

12TH SS PANZER GRENADIER/PANZER DIVISION 'HITLERJUGEND' (HJ)

Raised **July 1943** at Beverloo (Belgium) as pz gren div from Hitler Youth members and cadres from ISSLAH; Oct 1943 reorg as pz div inc. 12th SS Pz Regt, again with help from ISSLAH; April 1944 Normandy (map 16): Evereux; June 1944 (D+2) Caen; Aug 1944 practically destroyed in Falaise pocket (20 Aug), Beauvais, Kaiserlautern; Sept 1944 Hirson, Meuse (Houx); Oct 1944 refit Oldenburg; Dec 1944 Ardennes (map 17); **Feb 1945** Hungary (map 19): Gran (Estergom) bridgehead; Mar 1945 Stuhlweissenburg; April 1945 Wienerwald; May 1945 surrendered to US at Enns.

16TH SS PANZER GRENADIER DIVISION 'REICHSFÜHRER SS' (RSS)

Raised **May 1941** in Berlin as Reichsführer SS Escort Bn; **Feb 1943** Debica, expand to RSS Sturm-Brigade with a gren regt, assault gun, flak and other detachments; July to Oct 1943 Corsica; Nov 1943 Lubljana reorg as pz gren div inc. assault gun bn; Feb to April 1944 Anzio battle group; Mar 1944 Debrecen; May to Dec 1944 Italy inc. SS Pz Lehr Bde: Grosseto, Pisa, Carrara, Bologna; **Feb to Mar 1945** Hungary (map 19): Nagykanizsa oilfield protection; Mar to April 1945 lower Steiermark and Yugoslav mountain pass security (battle group); May 1945 Klagenfurt, Villach, surrendered to US/British Steiermark.

17TH SS PANZER GRENADIER DIVISION 'GOETZ VON BERLICHINGEN' (GvB)

Raised **Oct 1943** at Tours; June 1944 (D+5) Normandy (map 16) US sector Carentan/Tribehou; July 1944 Savigny; Aug 1944 Mortain battle group (7 Aug), practically destroyed in Falaise pocket (20 Aug); Sept to Nov 1944 Metz inc. SS Pz Gren Bdes 49, 51 (raised Denmark) and SS Signals School Metz; Dec 1944 West Wall, Rheinheim/Habkirchen, refit Zweibrücken; **Jan to Mar 1945** N. Alsace, Lothringia, Rimlingen (11 Jan), Rhine bridgehead, Germersheim (25 Mar); in retreat SE to Nuremberg, Munich, Bad Tolz; April 1945 Donauwörth; May 1945 surrendered to US at Achenthal.

18TH SS FREIWILLIGE PANZER GRENADIER DIVISION 'HORST WESSEL' (HW)

Raised **Feb 1944** at Zagreb (Agram/Cilli), Croatia from 1 SS Inf Bde (mot) and Bashka Volksdeutsch volunteers inc. SS assault gun bn; Mar 1944 W. Hungary, counter-partisan; July to Nov 1944 Lemberg (battle group); Aug to Oct 1944 Slovakia/Hungary, then redeploy and refit SE of Budapest; **Jan to Mar 1945** upper Silesia, practically destroyed Ratibor, Leobschütz; May 1945 Silesia, surrendered to Russians at Hirschberg.

23RD SS FREIWILLIGE PANZER GRENADIER DIVISION 'NEDERLAND' (NED)

Raised **July 1943** as pz gren bde (two regts) from 'Germanic' Dutch volunteers 48 Gen Seyfard, 49 de Ruiter; Dec 1943 SE Hungary: Agram (Zagreb), counter-partisan; Jan to Dec 1944 Oranienbaum (Leningrad), Narwa bridgehead, Estonia, Riga, Doblen, Courland; transp Baltic to Libau/Stettin (Pomerania), some units sunk *en route*, after 3rd Battle of Courland; Feb 1945 Stettin, Altdamm reorg as weak pz gren div; deployed Staargard, Furstenwalde; Mar 1945 Schwedt; April 1945 encircled at Halbe, practically destroyed. Some escapees crossed Elbe, surrendered to US.

27TH SS FREIWILLIGE PANZER GRENADIER DIVISION 'LANGEMARCK' (LMK)

Raised **May 1943** at Debica (Poland) as SS Sturm-Brigade Langemarck, from Flemish volunteers; July 1943 Prague inc. Flemish bn and further Flemish volunteers (Freiwilliger); Dec 1943 completed training; Jan 1944 Zhitomir, encircled with 'Das Reich', loosing 60% strength; April 1943 refit Bohemia; July 1943 Narwa bridgehead (Courland) battle group (decimated); Nov 1943 reorg Lüneburg as incomplete Pz Gren Div Langemarck from Flemish, Todt, Luftwaffe, naval and other personnel; Dec 1943 Eifel battle group; **Jan to Mar 1945** Arnswalde, Zachan, Stargard, Stettin, Altdamm bridgehead; April 1945 Oder, Prenzlau; May 1945 Mecklenburg, Neustrelitz/Lübeck, surrendered to British.

28TH SS FREIWILLIGE PANZER GRENADIER DIVISION 'WALLONIEN' (WAL)

Raised **July 1943** at Wildflecken as SS Sturm-Brigade 'Wallonien'; Nov 1943 Dnieper bend under command SS Wiking; Jan to Feb 1944 encircled with Wiking at Cherkassy losing heavy weapons and transport during breakout (17 Feb); spring of 1944 refit at Wildflecken, interrupt by posting east: Narwa bridgehead, practically destroyed; summer 1944 Hanover/Hildesheim; Oct 1944 reorg from Walloons, Belgians, French and others as incomplete pz gren div; Dec 1944 Cologne; **Jan to Feb 1945** Stargard/Altdamm bridgehead battle group; Mar 1945 Stettin; April 1945 Prenzlau; May 1945 Lübeck, surrendered to British at Schwerin.

31ST SS FREIWILLIGE GRENADIER DIVISION 'BOHMEN-MAREN'

Raised **Oct 1944** in south-east: Hungary inc. Volksdeutsch units of 23rd SS Div 'Kama'; Nov 1944 Pecs, practically destroyed; Dec 1944 refit Steiermark S. of Marburg inc. schools personnel; **Feb 1945** Silesia: Striegau, Strehlen; May 1945 decimated units disbanded Königgratz.

32ND SS FREIWILLIGE GRENADIER DIVISION '30 JANUAR'

Raised **Jan 1945** at Grunow/Briesen (Kurmark) from SS arty, anti-tank and eng schools replacement units and Battle Group Schill; 25 Jan 1945 Frankfurt/Oder; Feb to April 1945 practically destroyed defending outer Berlin, encircled at Halbe, remnant Beelitz; May 1945 surrendered to US at Tangermünde.

38TH SS PANZER GRENADIER DIVISION 'NIBELUNGEN'

Raised **Mar 1945** at Freiburg/Schwarzwald then Grafenwöhr (Franconia) from Junkers School Bad Tolz, RAD and other personnel – six/seven part mot bns; April 1945 Neustadt/Kehlheim, Ingolstadt, Landshut; May 1945 surrendered to US at Reit-im-Winkel, upper Bavaria.

Part 3. Fighting the mobile battle

1. The panzer battle group

The thrusting tactics leading to encirclement of the enemy, a tradition taught to all combat arms of the German Army but for which panzer divisions in the early campaigns became particularly notorious, were put into effect by divisional battle groups (Kampfgruppen) varying in size and composition. The driving force in all such manoeuvres, as in any tank offensive, was provided by the panzer regiment employing tank battalions in close formation; a proportion of divisional and, if necessary, corps supporting arms assisted the tanks in their fighting task. Panzer artillery engaged fixed defences, engineers cleared obstacles, anti-aircraft troops protected bridges or other defiles on the axis of advance. The role of these specialists is explained in later sections. A regimental or supporting Kampfgruppe like those created around panzer grenadier and panzer reconnaissance battalions were organized by divisional commanders determined to exploit boldness and initiative, operating more or less independently along roads or across open country; battle group objectives, either enemy positions or terrain features, being dependent upon intentions and orders of higher commanders. But whatever the intended objective of a battle group, speed and surprise were vital considerations in every operational plan – fewer than twenty-five minutes being the time expected for a panzer regiment to shake-out from march order into attack formation; light tank companies in the lead.

The tank battalion of a regimental battle group advancing in waves, deployed its companies in wedge-shaped formation (Panzerkeil); at other times panzer battle groups adopted a bell-shaped formation (Panzerglocke), attacking with heavy tanks screened by medium or light vehicles. Liaison officers from ground attack, engineer and artillery units supporting the armoured movement, operated close to forward headquarters moving behind the leading tank wave

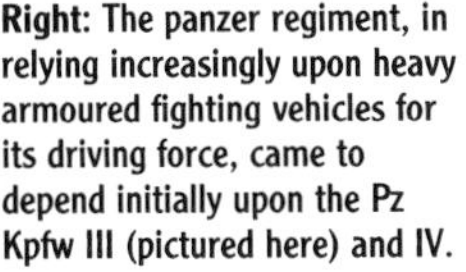

Right: The panzer regiment, in relying increasingly upon heavy armoured fighting vehicles for its driving force, came to depend initially upon the Pz Kpfw III (pictured here) and IV.

Above: The Pz Kpfw III and IV only featured during the earlier campaigns in limited numbers; here a Pz Kpfw III prepares to move into action (*see* map 3).

ready to summon immediate help as resistance developed. Divisional attacks, launched in waves of up to fifty tanks abreast on a 2,000–3,000-yard front, were carried out by regimental battle groups with two tank battalions forward. If the regiment had three battalions, the third battalion was held in reserve. Accompanied by engineer and other specialists, the first wave would drive deep into the enemy's artillery positions accompanied or followed by a second wave of panzer grenadiers mopping-up surviving resistance. A third wave of tanks and supporting infantry followed if necessary. The tank company, one of three or four in a battalion, moving with platoons in wedge formation, would have as its immediate objective enemy infantry, anti-tank and artillery positions which it would attack with high-explosives and machine-gun fire. Tank guns served equally as a major offensive weapon and as anti-tank protection. Flame-throwing tanks cleared positions immune to tank fire. Panzer engineers, assault artillery or other units reinforcing the attack, would be allotted to the leading tank wave or positioned close behind. In built-up or wooded areas panzer grenadiers fighting either from their vehicles or in dismounted action would lead the way. In operations to encircle the enemy when a breakthrough had been achieved, tank battalions changing to an appropriate formation would advance directly forward before bearing back in a wide circle to the original point of penetration; or two battalions starting on a narrow front would diverge after penetrating the enemy position and bear round in opposite arcs. Encirclement was complete when the forward tanks of either battalion met at a point approximately opposite the original breach. On a given wireless signal, the destruction of the enveloped forces would begin by simultaneous thrusts from four points 90° apart. The following dramatic account of Panzer action in 1942 is taken from the diary of an artillery officer in 33rd Artillery Regiment, 15th Panzer Division, attacking Tobruk in Rommel's second and successful attempt to capture the port (map 9).

'The attack began at 0520 hours with a few minutes of intense artillery fire from every type of gun. This was followed by a Stuka attack [numbers not stated]. At 0600 hours infantry and engineers advanced and after three-quarters of an hour had crossed the anti-tank ditch. This was bridged over and first one then two lanes were made in the minefield. The tanks advanced closely followed by artillery. At 0930 hours 15th Panzer Division reported to DAK that Ariete was lagging behind.'

'Ariete was offered the use of the way-in which had been established by 15th Panzer Division, but managed to get on with the help of Stukas. At 1630 hours 15th Panzer Division reached the Tobruk–Acroma road and turned left.' At 1815 hours the officer records that his troop opened fire on Solaro, a defended locality astride the road three miles from their objective. By nightfall it was considered that the battle was won. The diary then records: 'The English destroyed all arms and vehicles, but some "fanatics" were still resisting the next morning.'

Rommel, in the forefront of battle, epitomized the practice of trained panzer commanders leading from the front. The need to set a personal example was instilled into all ranks – leading to staggering losses in officers and NCOs. In only five weeks of fighting, from 22 June to 26 July 1941, one panzer division recorded the loss of 147 officers (35 per cent) and 367 NCOs (19 per cent). Even greater casualties were experienced by another panzer division whose losses

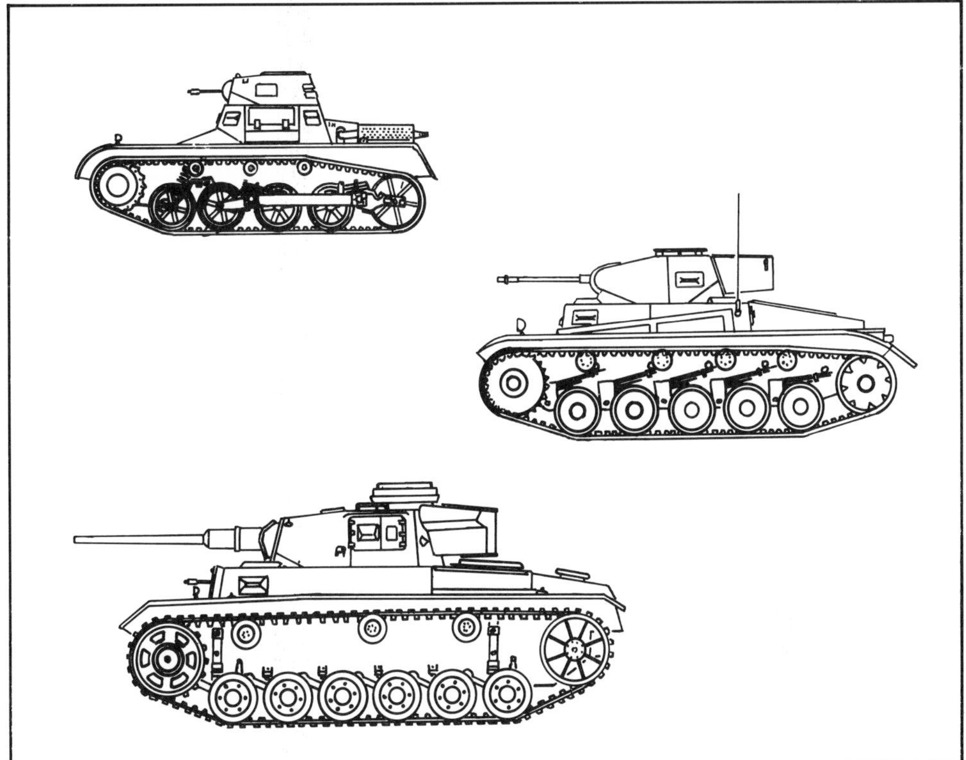

Right: The Pz Kpfw I, Sd Kfz 101, was armed with two machine-guns and crewed by two; it weighed six tons and could reach a speed of 32mph with a range of 95 miles.

Right: The Pz Kpfw II, Sd Kfz 121, carried a 2cm gun and a crew of two. The vehicle weighed ten tons, had a speed of 32mph, and a range of 112 miles.

Right: The Pz Kpfw III, Sd Kfz 141, had a 5cm gun and weighed 22 tons; it carried a crew of five and could manage a speed of 28mph over a range of 100 miles.

in dead or wounded during the period 22 June to 5 December 1941 reached a level of 351 officers (64 per cent) and 1,122 NCOs (47 per cent). Other divisions were to experience losses on a similar scale. Whenever a division was strong in assault guns (Sturmgeschütze) or other self-propelled artillery, the commander would move them well forward within battle groups. There they would engage likely targets over open sights at ranges of 1,000 yards or below. Anti-tank guns played an important role in tank battles. At first towed into action, later self-propelled (Jagdpanzer), they were intended to perform the same functions as destroyers in relation to battleships, to screen and protect the main body. Used at first in a static role countering advances by the opposing tank force, their employment in the Western Desert and eastern theatres developed into offensive action leap-frogging with tanks in the attack. Such tactics lead to heavy losses in British and Russian armour.

Heavy weapons of the Jagdpanzer and Sturmgeschütz type, able to attack and destroy their heavy opponents with 7.5cm or 8.8cm guns, equalled tanks in importance in the final (1945), establishment of the panzer division. The evolution of these weapons symbolized a distinct change in German strategic and tactical thinking, a measure of which can be read into the planned production of the new weapons, which in 1945 would have exceeded tank production by 350 per cent. During the closing stages of the war, Sturmgeschütz and panzer divisional battle groups were employed in direct support of infantry formations lacking basic tank protection. The practice served to increase the fragmentation of the panzer force, destroying its potential for swift and concentrated mobile intervention.

2. The panzer regiment

The strength of a panzer regiment, concentrated in battalions organized into three or four companies varied widely over the years and between formations; three was an average number of companies, but an SS panzer regiment in 1944 would contain up to five companies. Foreign vehicles, Czech (t) 35 and (t) 38 models in particular, served several regiments during the early years, constituting the core of 6th, 7th and 8th Panzer Divisions. At other times Sturmgeschütze were substituted for Panzerkampfwagen.

In 1935 a panzer regiment of two battalions would consist of four, light companies each of 32 vehicles. By 1939 this had changed to three light and one medium company, each of 22 vehicles. But by 1944 a panzer regiment at the peak of wartime development consisted theoretically of two tank battalions each with four companies of seventeen vehicles (reduced from 22 in 1943). Half of these companies, were Panthers and half Pz Kpfw IVs. Together with headquarter company vehicles, the tank strength of a regiment then totalled 159. A 1945 panzer regiment, reflecting the change to a defensive strategy in its establishment, was intended to have only 54 tanks supported by 22 Jagdpanzers.

Starting in 1935, panzer regiments were equipped with vehicles weighing between 6 and 25 tons – the Pz Kpfw I to IV series of which after 1943 only the Pz Kpfw IV remained in production. Although intended to be replaced by the Pz Kpfw V Panther, the Pz Kpfw IV would nevertheless remain to serve out the war – overshadowed

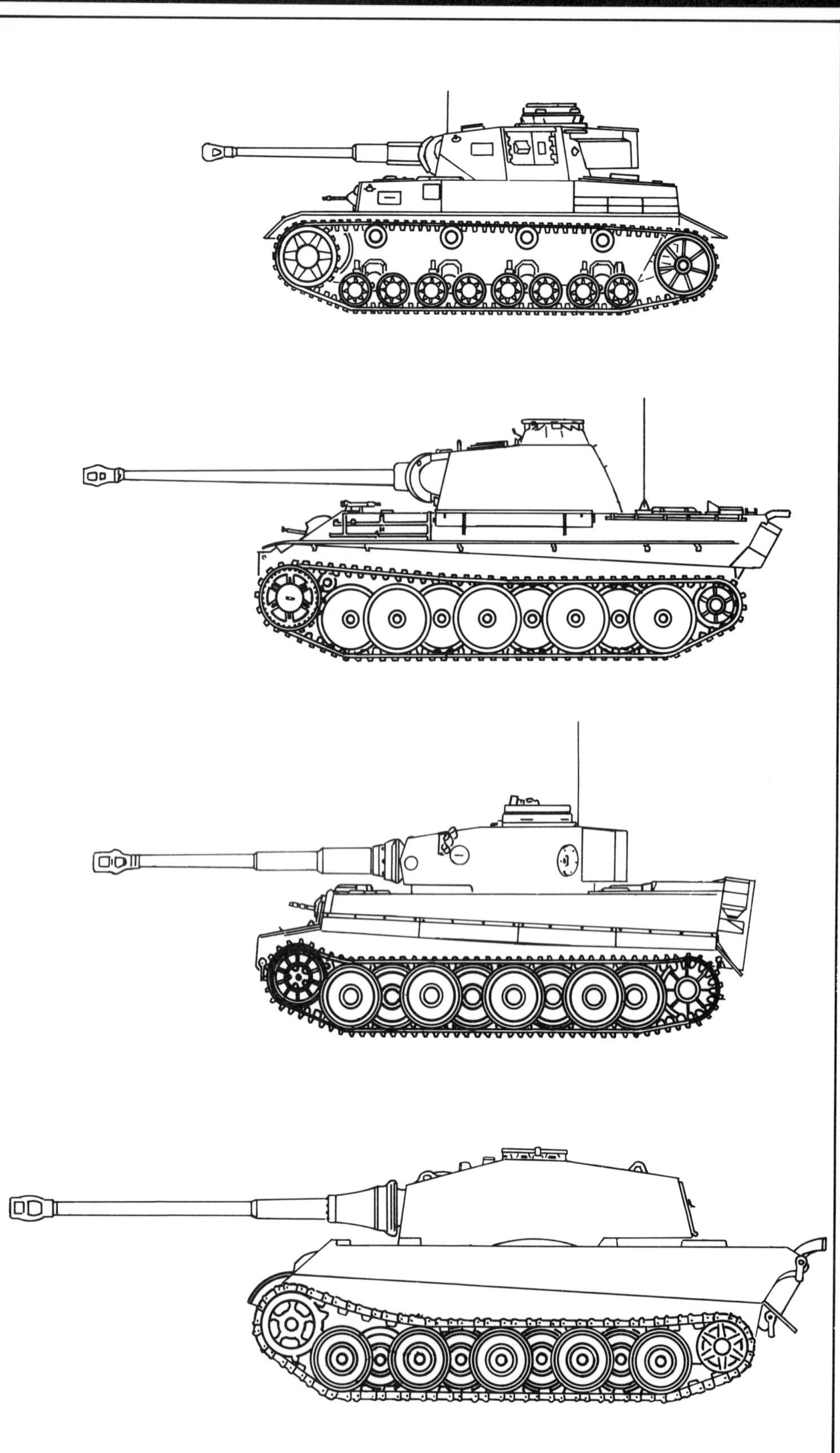

Left: The Pz Kpfw IV, Sd Kfz 161, was crewed by five men and armed with a 7.5cm gun. It weighed some 26 tons, but could still manage a speed of 30mph with a range of 100 miles.

Left: A Panther (Pz Kpfw V) Sd Kfz 171 armed with a 7.5cm 42 L/70 gun and manned by a crew of five. This mighty machine weighed 50 tons, had a speed of 35mph and a range of 60–120 miles.

Left: A Tiger (Pz Kpfw VI) Sd Kfz 181 armed with an 8.8cm 36 L/56 main armament and two 7.92mm MG 34s as secondary. It carried a crew of five, weighed 62 tons and could manage a speed of 25mph with a range of 50–80 miles.

Left: The King Tiger (Pz Kpfw VI IIB) Sd Kfz 182 had a crew of five. Its firepower was provided by an 8.8cm 43 L/71 gun; it weighed 70 tons and travelled at 15–24mph.

by more illustrious counterparts. Introduced into service in 1934, the Pz Kpfw I at 6 tons was the lightest German tank model. Like its contemporary, the 10-ton Pz Kpfw II, it was phased-out after 1943 – other than for command or training purposes.

The Pz Kpfw III, a 20-ton medium tank, and the Pz Kpfw IV, a 25-ton vehicle, served as the main battle tanks in early campaigns. Main armament was improved by substituting the long-barrelled 5cm gun for the 3.7cm in the Pz Kpfw III and a 7.5cm gun replaced the 5cm weapon in the Pz Kpfw IV. Both vehicles were adapted to commanders' use and as ammunition-carriers. Other roles included flame-throwing and armoured observation for panzer artillery. In Poland, France and in Russia until 1943, when mediums predominated in the panzer regiments, the ratio of medium to light tanks changed only slowly.

Regarded by many who knew it as the best tank of its generation, the greatly feared Panther, intended in 1942 as a replacement for the ageing Pz Kpfw IV, was introduced on to the battlefield at Kursk by Panzer Brigade Decker in mid-1943 (map 15). Teething troubles reduced the brigade's combat-ready vehicles from 200 to 40, but when

Right: This picture shows the Pz Kpfw IV.

Right: The increasing power of anti-tank weaponry inevitably led to heavier armour in an attempt to afford crews greater protection. After 1942 the panzer force was receiving tanks of up to 70 tons; pictured here is a 50-ton Panther which has halted at the roadside – note the protective skirt.

Left: A 62-ton Tiger moves into position in Normandy as members of the crew take a breather.

Left: A 70-ton King Tiger rolls through deserted streets on the Eastern Front.

overcome, the Panther served notably with tank regiments on all fronts. The Panther's powerful 7.5cm gun, high speed, heavy (122mm) sloping armour and easy manoeuvrability commended it highly to its crew of five. The Jagdpanther, a noteworthy variant of the Panther incorporating an 8.8cm gun, was issued to panzer divisions and independent SP anti-tank battalions. The Bergepanther was employed in the recovery sections of regimental workshop companies.

The Tiger, an early German answer to the T34, planned as early as 1940, was introduced prematurely in August 1942 along an unsuitable, forested axis near Leningrad. The units concerned, 1/502, in action at Mga east of the city lost all four of its vehicles. The Western Allies first encountered the Tiger in North Africa at Tebourba where in December 1943 British First Army's drive to Tunis was halted. Engagements between Tigers and T34s with disastrous results for the latter, started at Kharkov in 1943 when II SS Panzer Corps recovered the city. A redoubtable armoured fighting vehicle, the Tiger was issued to heavy (schwere) tank battalions in the Army series 501–510 and SS series 501–503 (formerly 101–103). In company and eventually battalion strength, Tigers were also issued as standard equipment to selected panzer divisions: Gross Deutschland, Leibstandardte SS Adolf Hitler, Das Reich and Totenkopf. Delivering a severe jolt whenever it appeared on the battlefield, the Tiger went on to become the most famous tank of the war, winning a fearful but undeserved reputation for invincibility. Designed on familiar squat German lines with heavy frontal armour (144mm) and equipped with a high-velocity 8.8cm gun, the Tiger required skilful driving and maintenance from well-trained crews. Tigers in panzer regiments or independent battalions served alongside Panthers or Pz Kpfw IVs on all war fronts. Slightly fewer than 1,500 vehicles were delivered to field and training units.

The King Tiger (Tiger II), a late development of Tiger I with heavier, sloped, armour and improved 8.8cm gun, made its first appearance on the battlefield in Normandy during August 1944 (a company from SS schwere Panzerabteilung 503) followed by action in the Ardennes and the Ruhr. By virtue of its great weight and low speed, the King Tiger was essentially a defensive weapon and in that capacity made its greatest impression. Fewer than five hundred were built during and after 1944 replacing Tiger Is in declining numbers mostly in Army and SS panzer corps heavy tank battalions. In company or lesser strength, on the Eastern Front, King Tigers reinforced the defence at crisis points in Hungary, Pomerania and in the final battle for Berlin (Panzerabteilung 503) Sturmtiger, *see* p 105.

	1 Sept 1939	10 May 1940	22 June 1941
Pz Bns	33[1]	35[2]	57[3]
Pz Kpfw I	1,445	523	180
Pz Kpfw II	1,223	955	746
Pz Kpfw III	98	349	965
Pz Kpfw IV	211	218	439
Others	218	469	1,187[4]
Total	3,195	2,574	3,417

[1]20 in five pz divs. [2]35 in ten pz divs. [3]47 in nineteen pz divs. [4]Includes 772 Pz Kpfw 38(t). The difference between pz bn total and numbers deployed in pz divs is accounted for by OKH allocations to light divisions (1939) and/or Army troops and pz divs in Africa (1941).

3. The panzer grenadier regiment

Fighting on the move from armoured personnel carriers, termed Schützenpanzerwagen (SPW) or, when the situation so required, fighting dismounted – clearing woods and villages or effecting river crossings – armoured (gepanzert) panzer grenadiers were organized into battalions of three or four (armoured) panzer grenadier companies. Deployed alongside panzer regiments and to complement tanks in action, panzer grenadier regiments were broadly comparable in mobility, but the second of the two panzer grenadier regiments in the establishment of a panzer division was usually motorized; élite SS panzer grenadier regiments and Panzerlehr excepted.

The medium weight, 3-ton Schützenpanzerwagen Sd Kfz 251, a lightly armoured and semi-tracked combat vehicle – not to be confused with the 1-ton machine used by panzer reconnaissance battalions – soon proved its value in action. In October 1943, following General Guderian's review of combat efficiency, no fewer than twenty-one variants of the Sd Kfz 251 were planned to meet differing needs of regimental units or support teams. Heavy weapon, engineer, signals, medical and other companies with specialized equipment were all provided for, but adequate numbers of SPWs were rarely available and although 16,000 were produced in numerous versions up to 1944, only a small proportion of the units for which they were intended actually received them. When SPWs were unavailable wheeled vehicles were substituted and the norm more often than not became a mixture of both types of transport.

Evolved in 1937 from artillery tractors undergoing trials for the army, the basic 3-ton SPW was issued from 1939 onwards, at first on a limited scale to 1st Panzer Division. Lifting twelve men including a driver and commander, 23 such vehicles were required to transport a panzer grenadier company of 190 officers and men. Deploying two 8.1cm mortars, seven 20mm AA guns, two 7.5cm guns, 30 light and three heavy MGs, the 1944 armoured panzer grenadier company, with or without the support of tanks, became a powerful influence on any battlefield.

The six (armoured) panzer grenadier companies of a 1944 panzer division, organized into *two* panzer grenadier battalions each incorporating a battalion heavy weapons company and supported by regimental infantry gun, flak and engineer companies, provided a panzer grenadier regiment at full strength with outstanding firepower and independence. More powerful SS panzer grenadier regiments, found in élite formations, were sometimes – like Army panzer grenadier divisions (three regiments) – composed of *three* battalions each of four companies numbered 1 to 12, possessing extra (i.e., SP anti-tank) companies numbered 13 to 16. A panzer grenadier regiment would operate by forming battle groups around battalions or companies and allotting individual objectives to them.

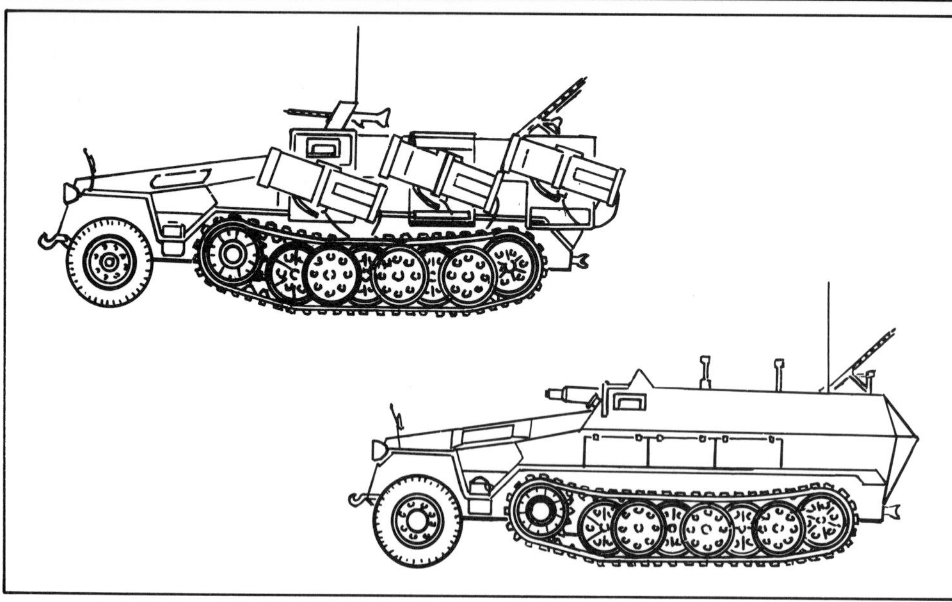

Left: Another SPW variant issued to panzer grenadiers was the 251/1 equipped with launching plates for 6.28cm rockets carried on frames inside the vehicle.

Left: A 251/9 SPW armed with a 7.5cm assault gun.

Below: Panzer grenadier regiments which fought on the move were served by numerous types of personnel carriers; pictured here is a medium-weight Hanomag 3-ton 251/10, armed with a 3.7cm anti-tank gun. This vehicle was issued to platoon commanders and this particular one was captured by the British in Libya.

Right: A rear view of a '251' deployed in the Balkans; it could carry twelve men including driver.

Medium SPW: Schützenpanzerwagen Sd Kfz 251 Variants
251/1: Standard vehicle
251/2: 8cm Mortar carrier
251/3: Radio vehicle
251/4: Ammunition carrier (for light infantry gun)
251/5: Assault engineer vehicle
251/6: Command vehicle
251/7: Engineer equipment carrier
251/8: Armoured ambulance
251/9: SP 7.5cm L/24 gun
251/10: SP 3.7cm A/T gun
251/11: Telephone/line laying vehicle
251/12: Survey section instrument carrier
251/13: Sound recording vehicle
251/14: Sound ranging vehicle
251/15: Artillery spotting vehicle
251/16: Flamethrower vehicle
251/17: SP AA vehicle, 2cm gun
251/18: Mobile observation post
251/19: Telephone exchange vehicle
251/20: Infra-red searchlight vehicle
251/21: SP AA vehicle with triple 1.5 or 2cm cannon
251/22: SP 7.5cm A/T gun

4. Panzer reconnaissance

Armoured reconnaissance battle groups leading a division or protecting vulnerable flanks flushed out and overcame light opposition. Advancing to contact, their role in addition to seeking Intelligence about the enemy was to smooth the way for oncoming armour. Such panzer Aufklärungsabteilungen (alternatively termed Vorausabteilungen, forward units) consisted of motor-cycle troops (Kradschützen), and infantry in wheeled or semi-tracked armoured vehicles accompanied by air, artillery and engineer liaison officers. But the all too familiar image of motor-cycle troops swarming along the roads ahead of an armoured division was relevant only to summer campaigns in the west and the early months of the war against Russia. Motor-cycle combinations, at first civilian machines of all types, sprayed uniformly dark-grey when employed in motor-cycle battalions, proved exceptionally manoeuvrable and capable of making 'U' turns within the width of a road. They were also exceptionally vulnerable to small-arms fire. Not until 1941 was a specially designed cross-country motor-cycle combination, with engine geared to both rear and side-car wheels introduced into military service with motor-cycle battalions. The BMW R75 and Zundapp KS750, both fitted with 2-cylinder, 4-stroke engines, were built in the same factory. Characteristic features included road and cross-country gearing, reversing gear, exceptionally strong frames, high positioning of engine and exhaust and large-profile tyres. Solo machines were only issued to dispatch riders. Their uses included traffic duty and road escort work.

Kradschützen armament included light machine-guns mounted on combination side-cars and mortars to provide covering fire whenever the two non-driving members of the 3-man crew were obliged to dismount. Dismounted riflemen in turn provided covering fire while the driver moved his machine out of hostile range. Kradschützen battalions were

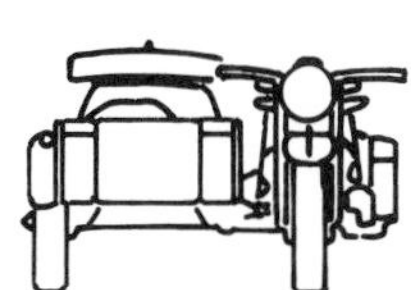

Above and right: Panzer reconnaissance battalions required fast and light vehicles with which to advance, to contact or protect the flanks of their division. The motor cycle served this purpose and depicted here is a Zundapp KS 750 with sidecar which was issued to motor cycle (m/c) recon' battalions during the early years of the war. It had a speed of 60mph and a range of 175–200 miles.

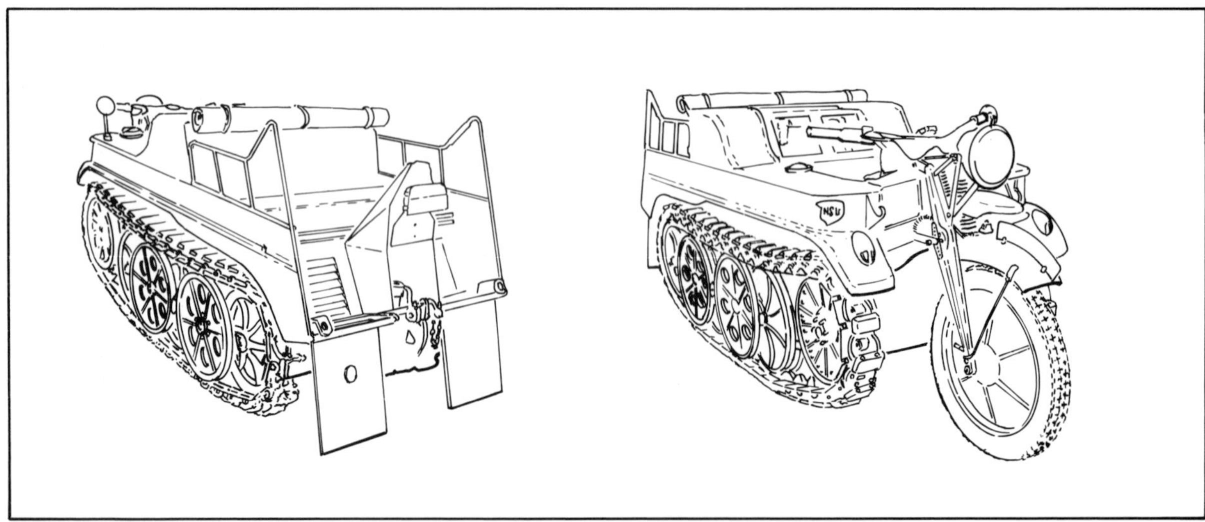

Above: Front and rear views of the NSU Kettenkrad Sd Kfz 2. It had a speed of 70mph, weighed 1.2 tons, and had a range of 120–150 miles.

kept up to strength with captured and newly manufactured stocks of French and Belgian machines, but quite early on in Russia, where mud and snow predominated during autumn and winter, conditions proved radically different from those prevailing in the west and it soon became evident that motor-cycles were not suited for work in such terrain. Neither did they prove of more than temporary value in the Balkans or Africa where their performance was badly affected by dust.

In order to offset the limitations of the motor-cycle, new types of vehicle were introduced into panzer service and the armed forces generally. They were, the easy to maintain VW Kubel (bucket) and its variant the VW Schwimmwagen (amphibian), both of which could be produced economically and in large numbers; also the Kettenkrad. Although less manoeuvrable than any of the motor-cycle combinations, the VWs had the advantage of being able to transport four or five men with extra weapons, ammunition and equipment. The Schwimmwagen, with its amphibious characteristics, certain of which detracted from its cross-country performance, was a great advantage in river crossings. So useful was the vehicle that it won the unofficial title of Kradschützenwagen.

The Kettenkrad, a small tractor with motor-cycle front, was equally versatile. Development commenced in July 1940, issues to reconnaissance companies beginning soon

Top left: Motor cycle troops waiting for orders to move off on a reconnaissance exercise. The symbols (lower left) identify the unit as No. 1 m/c Coy of Schützen Regiment 69, 10th Panzer Division.

Top right: The Russian countryside, and changing battle conditions, soon revealed the motor cycles' limitations, especially in mud and snow. The VW 82 Kubelwagen and its schwimm-wagen variant, VW 166, although not immune to the motor cycles' problems, improved the mobility and tactical resources of panzer grenadiers and recce units. The vehicle in this 1943 picture carries a Gross Deutschland emblem and a tactical sign which identifies it as that of the panzer grenadier regimental CO.

Right: Kettenkrads demonstrated excellent mobility and performed widely varying duties for all services on all fronts.

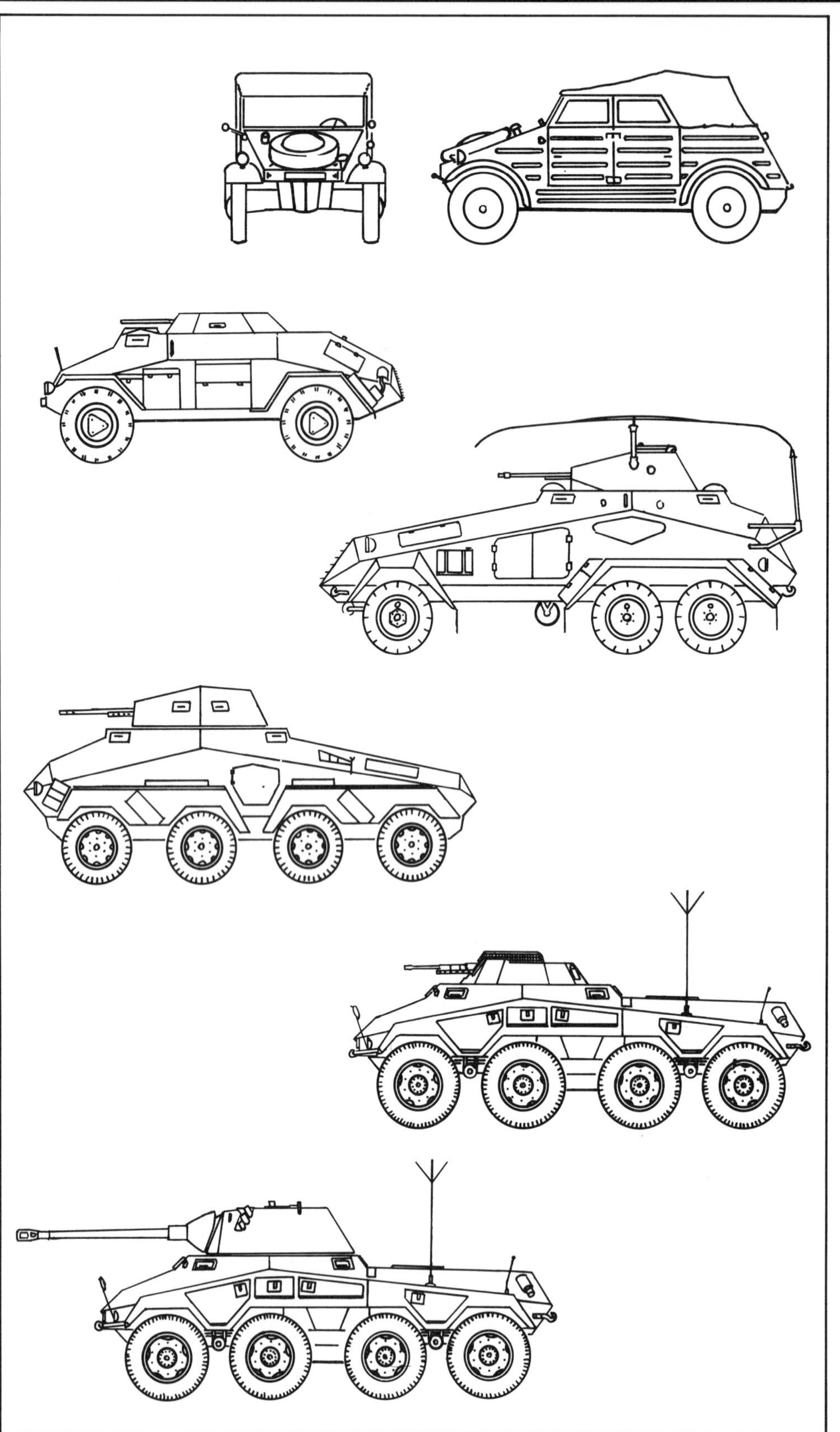

Left: A VW 82 Kubelwagen transporter could carry four to five men with weapons and equipment at a speed of 50mph. Some 37 variants existed for the use of army and Luftwaffe units on all fronts.

Left and right: Armoured cars serving reconnaissance companies varied in weight and battle-fitness. Both the light, four-wheeled Sd Kfz 221/2 and the heavy, eight-wheeled Sd Kfz 231 were retained in service for most of the war in one form or another, while the six-wheeled Sd Kfz 232 was not. Shown right is the Sd Kfz 221/2 four-wheeled armoured car which could mount a single machine-gun or 2cm gun and a coaxial MG (222), weighed 5 tons and had a speed of 50mph.

Left: This Sd Kfz 232 eight-wheeled armoured car (command model) had a 20mm armament, weighed 8.5 tons and had a speed of 50mph. It was a replacement for the six-wheeler.

Right: A Sd Kfz 232.

Left: Sd Kfz 234/1 mounting a 2cm KWK L/55 cannon.

Left: Sd Kfz 234/2 eight-wheeled armoured car mounting a 5cm KWK L/60 gun. Known as Puma, it was crewed by three, weighed 11 tons, and had a speed of 50mph.

Left: Some eight-wheeled armoured car variants mounting a single 20mm gun and a coaxial machine-gun.

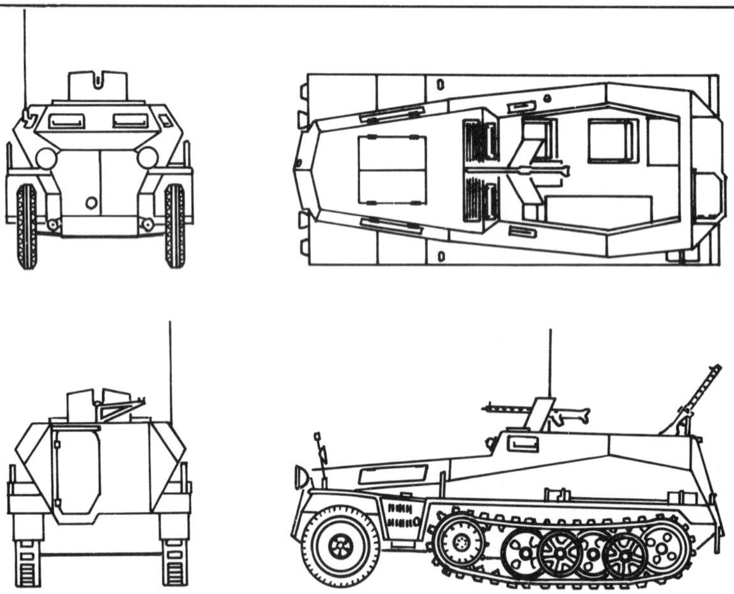

Left: Measures to improve reconnaissance mobility resulted in the production of a small armoured semi-track. The Sd Kfz 251 had fourteen variants which served specialist needs; this particular one is a Demag Sd Kfz 250/1 Light SPW. It weighed 1 ton, and transported six men at 37mph with a range of 200 miles.

Left: An Sd Kfz 250/7 armed with an 8cm mortar.

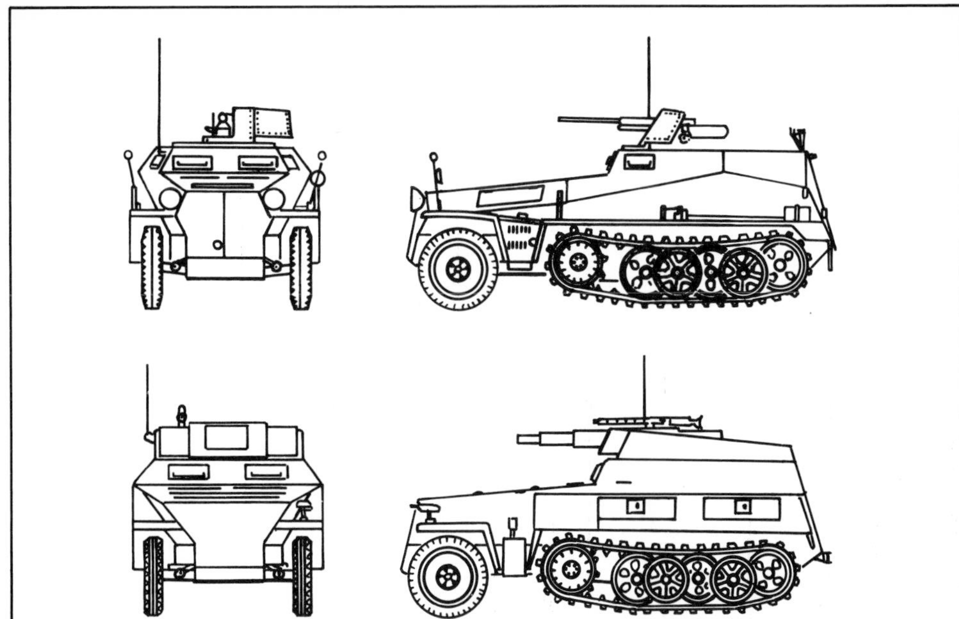

Right: An Sd Kfz 250/10 armed with a 3.7cm Pak.

Right: An Sd Kfz 250/8 armed with a 7.5cm assault gun.

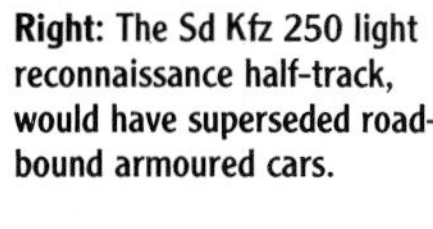

Right: The Sd Kfz 250 light reconnaissance half-track, would have superseded road-bound armoured cars.

Light SPW: Schützenpanzerwagen Sd Kfz 250 Variants
- 250/1: Standard vehicle
- 250/2: Telephone/line laying vehicle
- 250/3: Radio vehicle
- 250/4: Air support (Flivo) vehicle
- 250/5: Mobile observation post
- 250/6: Ammunition carrier
- 250/7: 8cm Mortar carrier
- 250/8: SP 7.5cm gun
- 250/9: Armoured reconnaissance vehicle
- 250/10: SP 3.7cm A/T gun
- 250/11: SP 2.8cm Panzerbüchse
- 250/12: Light survey instrument vehicle
- 252: Armoured ammunition carrier
- 253: Armoured mobile observation post

afterwards. The Kettenkrad was employed in many and varied roles, towing weapons, laying cables and transporting supplies. From Karelia to the Caucasus this diminutive workhorse served panzer troops, paratroops and most other arms of the services; 8,000 were produced up to the end of 1944.

Kradschützen were eventually absorbed into panzer grenadier or infantry reconnaissance battalions. By 1944 armoured reconnaissance companies replacing motor-cycle companies were transported either in 1-ton Sd Kfz 250 armoured troop-carriers or Volkswagens, leaving only a small proportion on motor-cycles. Battalion organization comprised one armoured car (Panzerspähwagen) company and three armoured reconnaissance companies. Issued to reconnaissance battalions in 1942, the '250' was to become the principal combat vehicle of the recce companies. Lightweight, fast across country, the basic '250' lifted a complement of six men; variants using the same semi-tracked chassis-mounted anti-tank and close-support guns.

By no means perfect, the '250', evolved in 1939 out of earlier light unarmoured vehicles designed for anti-tank or other weapon-towing duties, restored the prestige and fitness for purpose of the Auflkärungsabteilungen. by 1944 some 7,599 machines had been built for use in twelve versions. Armoured cars serving the recce companies included a light 4-wheeler, a 6-wheeler (quickly phased out) and a heavy 8-wheeler. All entered service before 1939; two remained largely unchanged, but in the trackless conditions of European Russia and opposed by increasingly effective anti-tank weapons, they too were superseded by semi-tracks, notably the 250/9 with a superior cross-country performance and a turreted 20mm gun.

The original Sd Kfz 222 4-wheeler mounted a 20mm automatic gun; other versions were armed with a single MG or were fitted our as radio vehicles (Sd Kfz 223) equipped with folding, overhead frame aerial.

The Sd Kfz 231 8-wheeler was developed in a limited number of variants: the Puma with a 5cm gun mounted in a turret (Sd Kfz 233) and a turretless version (Sd Kfz 234) armed with a 7.5cm gun. These and a signals variant equipped with the familiar overhead frame aerial became the principal types in service.

5. Panzer engineers

Panzer engineers (Panzerpioniere) working in support of panzer or panzer grenadier battle groups were carried into action either in armoured semi-tracked SPWs or wheeled vehicles. They were usually positioned well to the fore in assault formations, demolishing tank obstacles, clearing lanes through minefields or in defensive situations creating strong points. More often than not panzer engineers worked under heavy fire using specially developed assault equipment including armoured (SPW) flame-throwers, remote-controlled Goliath demolition tanks and, at times, a radio-controlled, explosives-filled Pz Kpfw IV. In the poorly drained countryside in Russia where streams and rivers with marshy banks frequently needed permanent crossings, engineer bridging responsibilities proved highly demanding. In the experience of 6th Panzer Division's engineer battalion, 153 bridges were required in 150 days of fighting during the division's advance to Leningrad in the summer of 1941.

Heavy bridging operations were supervised by a Commander, Armoured Engineers (Panzerarmee Pioniereführer) at Army Headquarters, at whose disposal were heavy bridging columns supplemented if necessary by columns from OKH Reserve. Panzer commanders deploying heavy armoured fighting vehicles frequently taxed the load-carrying capacity of bridging columns; the mobility of their heavy panzer companies being greatly impaired by bridging limitations only gradually increased from 40 tonnes to 60 tonnes and later to 90 tonnes. Panzer engineer battalions were reorganized several times during the course of their existence. Their work under fire as early as 1939 made the introduction of armoured troop carriers essential. Yet by 1943, when a panzer engineer battalion was organized into three companies, only one-third was lifted in armoured SPWs; the remainder being motorized.

Within days of the attack on Russia, a true 'mine-war' started for the panzer force – requiring an exhausting effort by engineers to push through seemingly endless minefields. LVII Panzer Corps recording progress on 12 July 1941 did so in the following terms: 'At the moment the advance can only proceed step by step because the enemy has blockaded all streets and roads with entanglements of trees and mines.' Similarly at the end of September, XXXXVII Panzer Corps, responsible to Second Panzer Army, reported: 'All streets in the advance area are mined. All bridges blown . . . six hundred mines lifted at one stream crossing.' In November, according to a report issuing from 3rd Panzer Division, mines were located in one town, '. . . in the main street, at the approaches to all bridges, on all access roads, at the railway station, in the town park, at the waterworks and water tanks, in all food stores and bakeries, around all public and corner buildings'. Anti-tank ditches arranged row upon row across their line of advance further slowed the progress of the panzer divisions. Between the ditches additional hazards such as buried heavy aerial bombs created long delays. Observers following the progress of panzer divisions in their lightning campaigns in Poland and the west might have been forgiven for believing that nothing could halt them, but in Russia skilfully sited obstacles and minefields, often concealed under a thick layer of snow and only discovered when the foremost vehicle ran on to them, effectively stopped tanks for long periods. Quotations from the war diary of another panzer corps demonstrate the extent to which panzer tactics were affected by minefields and the need of panzer engineers to neutralize them. 'Intensively mined areas are forcing us to attack, as if in an infantry action.' And, 'The tanks of 4th Panzer Division have not advanced but lie trapped in a minefield.' 'In three days' fighting from 1st–3rd December 1941, 21 Panzer Regiment lost no fewer than 10 tanks due to damage caused by mines.' Panzer engineers, in their efforts to reduce mine losses, performed a crucial service to panzer divisions often in the most hazardous of circumstances. In demolishing tank obstacles of all descriptions, neutralizing fortified positions, bridging water obstacles or anti-tank ditches, and helping the division through defiles, the engineers earned a reputation as the hardest of the hard men in the German Army.

Right: A prefabricated box girder bridge of 40-ton capacity, bolted together in sections and capable of spanning 64 feet, carried the Pz Kpfw IV to safety if needed. Fascine bundles were nevertheless essential in seeing the vehicles through swamp and over soft river banks.

Right: Recovering ditched vehicles was work for the tank recovery sections of the workshop companies.

Left: Panzer engineers were called upon to solve many assault and engineering problems in order to keep panzer divisions moving; bridging and ferrying were only two of the most frequent tasks undertaken by engineers in the trackless Russian interior.

6. Panzer artillery

Artillery that could advance with panzer divisions and provide equally mobile fire support was no less vital a part of Guderian's formula for a balanced force of all arms breaking through and operating in the rear of enemy positions than tanks or motorized infantry. The first tracked weapon of this kind was a 15cm heavy infantry gun sIG 33, mounted on a light tank (Pz Kpfw I) chassis. In 1942 a more stable version using Pz Kpfw II chassis was issued to the heavy infantry gun companies of panzer grenadier regiments and panzer artillery battalions.

A heavy (15cm) field howitzer SfH 18/1 known as Hummel (bumble-bee) increased the power of panzer artillery. Produced from 1943 onwards, the Hummel remained in service until the end of the war, by which time more than 600 had been built. Equally effective, serving at first with DAK (Deutsches Afrika Korps), was the SfH 13/1, an older heavy howitzer mounted on a French Lorraine chassis. But most popular of all panzer artillery weapons was the Wespe (wasp), a light, 10.5cm field howitzer mounted on the Pz Kpfw II chassis introduced in 1942 (Pz Kpfw II's principal use after February 1943). When production ceased in 1944 due to deteriorating economic and military conditions, more than 600 of these exceptionally useful support weapons had been produced for panzer service.

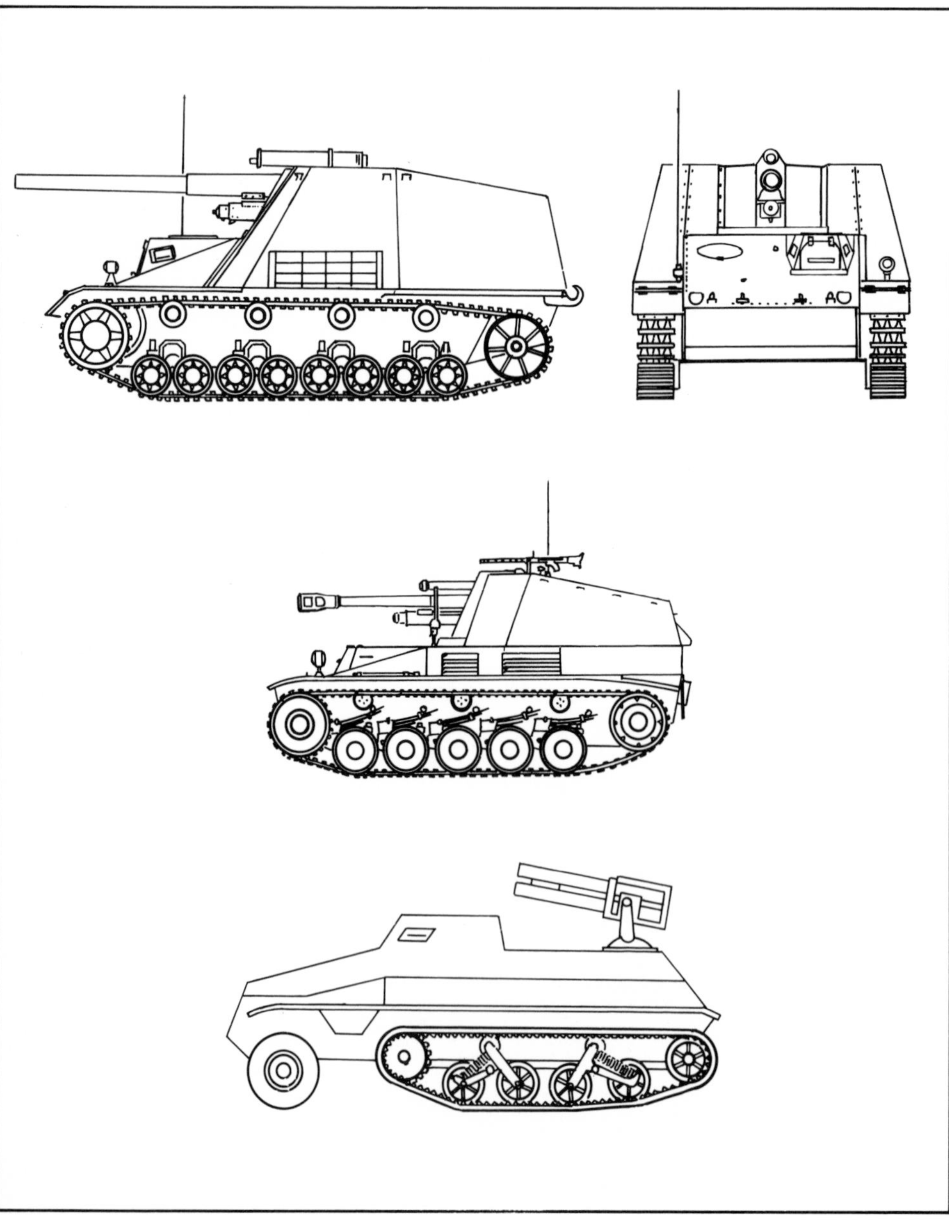

Left: A Hummel Sd Kfz 165 in profile. The 15cm field howitzer had a range of 14,000 yards, a crew of 6 and a weight of 26 tons.

Left: Wespe Sd Kfz 124 in profile. This 10.5cm field howitzer had a range of 14,000 yards, a crew of 5, and a weight of 12.5 tons.

Left: A Panzerwerfer 42, Sd Kfz 34/1, in profile. The ten-barrelled 15cm rocket projector was mounted on an Opel 'Maultier' (mule). It weighed 7 tons and had a speed of 25mph.

Right: Panzer artillery, deployed in mobile support of the panzer regiments, was a vital part of Guderian's concept of a mechanized force of all arms. Two of the most effective and widely used self-propelled artillery weapons were the Hummel and Wespe. Here a battery of Hummels (bumble bees) is in a firing position waiting for orders.

Right: A rear view of the Panzerwerfer 42, one of a growing family of rocket-launchers which matched the 'Stalin organ' in mobility and firepower. Its successor, the Nebelwerfer 42, could traverse through 360 degrees with a range of 7,000 yards, but its accuracy was less than that of conventional artillery weapons.

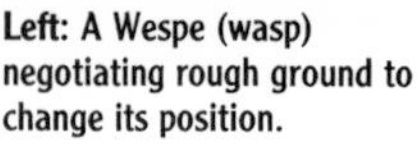

Left: A Wespe (wasp) negotiating rough ground to change its position.

7. Panzerjaeger and Jagdpanzer

The tracked anti-tank weapons of the panzer force, broadly classed as Panzerjaeger, started with anti-tank guns on improvised mountings, mostly tank chassis; crews were protected by an open armour-plated superstructure. More satisfactory were the fully enclosed, purpose-designed and produced weapons, Jagdpanzer, resembling tanks in appearance and at times in performance. In the first category, rushed into service in 1940 during the Battle of France, was the makeshift Marder series initially featuring a Czech 4.7cm anti-tank gun mounted on a German Pz Kpfw I chassis – Marder I. This was followed by Marder II mounting a (captured) Russian 7.62cm anti-tank gun on the Pz Kpfw II chassis. In turn, Marder II was succeeded in 1942 by Marder III employing first the Czech 38(t) mounting, but later substituting the French Lorraine chassis and armed with the German 7.5cm PaK, anti-tank gun, 40/3.

Of greater significance was the Nashorn (rhinoceros) formerly Hornisse (hornet) armed with the powerful 8.8cm PaK. 43 introduced during the Battle of Kursk, 1943. Other anti-tank weapons, either improvised armoured car chassis or mounted in SPWs, afforded basic protection for panzer grenadier companies. These same companies were also issued with the Panzerfaust, a hand-held rocket-launcher. A second and more elaborate category of weapons – Jagdpanzer (tank destroyer) – was a natural outcome of the first. Excluding a Sturmgeschütz III adaptation armed with a 7.5cm gun, the first true Jagdpanzer, Ferdinand, introduced in 1943 at Kursk, was a re-designed Porsche Tiger (Henschel being responsible for the production Tiger). Although armed with a powerful, long-barrelled 8.8cm gun, the vehicle's poor vision, mechanical unrealiability and lack of a machine-gun for close protection disappointed designer and user alike.

A turretless Jagdpanzer IV using Pz Kpfw IV chassis, Sd Kfz 162 followed in late 1943 and in two variants both armed with the 7.5cm PaK served out the war with the anti-tank battalions of panzer divisions. But not until the arrival of the Jagdpanther, armed with the 8.8cm PaK 43, was the panzer force provided with a truly successful tank destroyer design. Production of this fast, well-armoured, low-profile vehicle, carrying a crew of five, started in February 1944 and by April 1945 some three hundred had been delivered to anti-tank battalions.

Equally successful and produced in sizeable numbers (more than 15,000 by the end of the war) was a light Jagdpanzer, the Hetzer (baiter) using the Czech 38(t) chassis. Introduced in May 1944, for the use of infantry anti-tank battalions, the Hetzer was armed with the 7.5cm PaK 39. A variant entered service as a flame-thrower.

Finally, the Jagdtiger, Jgd Pz VI, a hunting version of the Tiger (B) armed with the formidable 12.8cm PaK 44, earned distinction as the biggest and most powerful fighting vehicle of the war. This distinction failed to translate into success on the battlefield and the few vehicles that entered service in 1945, notably with two companies of 512th Schwere Panzerjaeger Battalion during March against the US bridgehead at Remagen and, until capitulation, in the Ruhr pocket at Iserlohn (*see* Fifth Panzer Army, 14 April 1945), proved sluggish in manoeuvre and subject to unremedied mechanical faults.

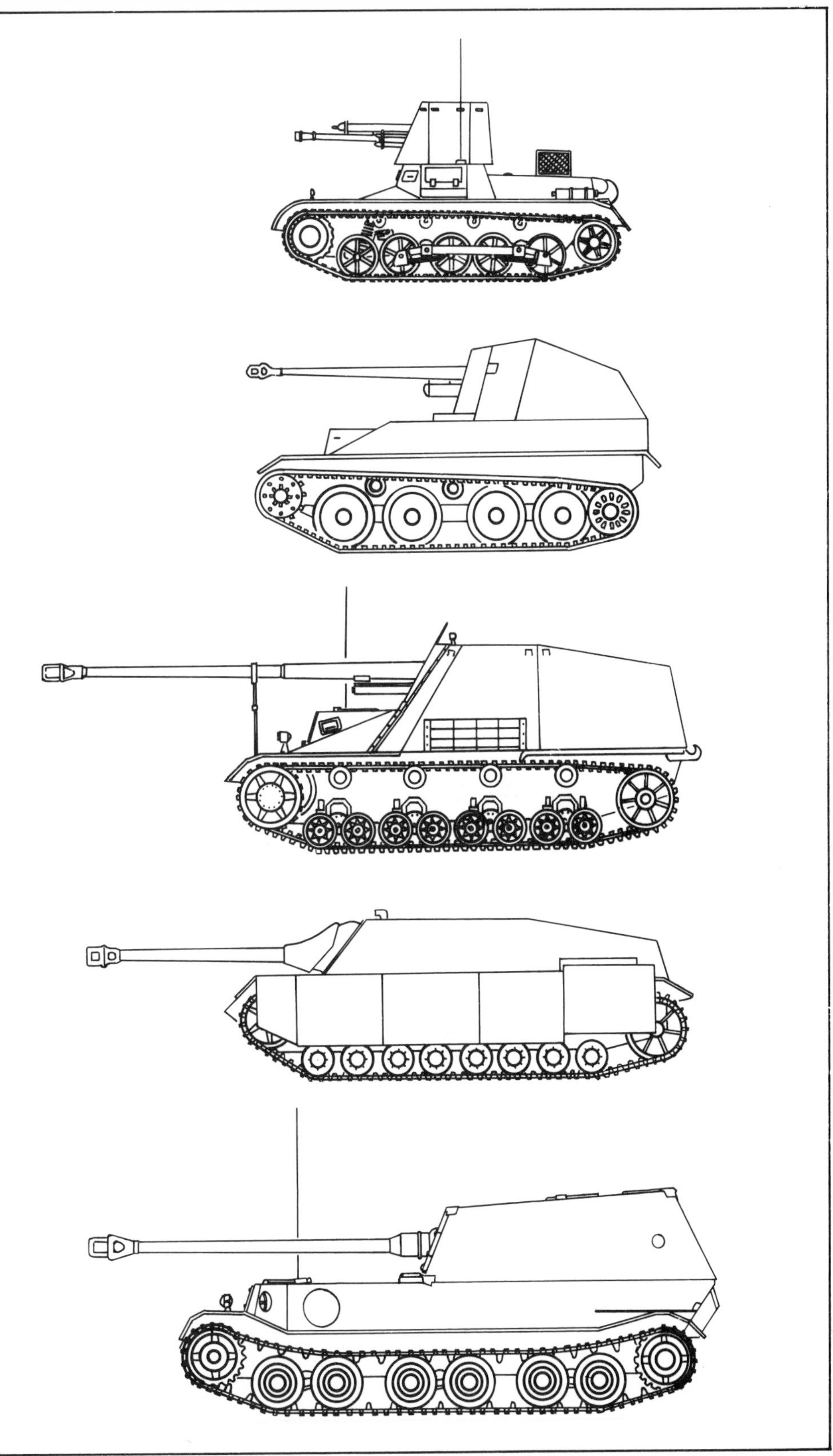

Right: Panzerjaeger and Jagdpanzer tracked anti-tank weapons and assault guns came to equal tanks in importance in the 1945 establishment of a panzer division. The principal types discussed in the text are illustrated here in profile.

Right: Marder I, 4.7cm Pak, weighed 6.4 tons and was crewed by three.

Right: Marder III, 7.5cm Pak 40/3 Sd Kfz 138, weighed 10 tons and was crewed by four. It had a speed of 26mph and a range of 115 miles.

Right: The Nashorn (rhinoceros) was an 8.8cm Pak 43, Sd Kfz 164, which weighed 27 tons and required a crew of five. It could manage speeds of 25mph with a range of 160 miles.

Right: Jagdpanzer IV 7.5cm Pak, Sd Kfz 162, had a crew of four, a speed of 24mph and a range of 160 miles; quite impressive for its weight of 28 tons.

Right: The Elefant (Ferdinand) 8.8cm Pak, Sd Kfz 184, weighed 68 tons and had a crew of six. It could reach speeds of 25mph with a range of 100 miles.

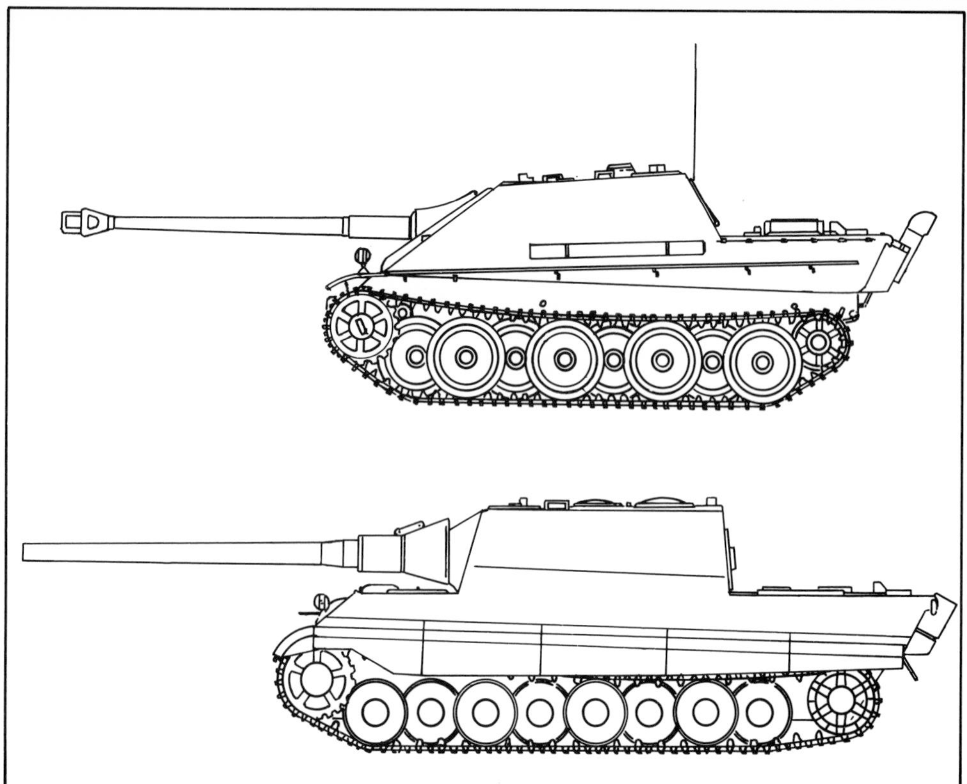

Left: The Jagdpanther 8.8cm Pak 43/3, Sd Kfz 173, was crewed by five and weighed 51 tons. It had a speed of 29mph and a range of 85 miles.

Left: The Jagdtiger 12.8cm Pak 44, Sd Kfz 186, weighed 77 tons and had a crew of six. It had a speed of 25mph, a range of 105 miles, and was the heaviest vehicle in panzer force service.

8. Flakpanzer

When enemy air opposition expanded to the point of sweeping the weak and overstrained Luftwaffe from the skies after 1943, anti-aircraft protection for panzer divisions at rest or on the move demanded urgent reassessment. In Russia, Italy and France enemy air forces hammered panzer columns unmercifully reducing them more often than not to blackened wrecks – destroying all efforts at swift concentration and counter-attack. Flakpanzer, tracked anti-aircraft weapons with power-driven turrets, to protect panzer formations against harassing low-flying attack were devised all too late. Of the types planned, few entered service. The first of an early generation of tracked anti-aircraft weapons to serve the panzer force was the Sd Kfz 140, a 20mm FlaK 30 mounted on a Czech 38 chassis. This was followed by two- (zwilling) and four- (vierling) barrelled versions of the gun on Pz Kpfw IV chassis. A more powerful 3.7cm gun belatedly entered service at Guderian's insistence in 1943. Nicknamed Mobelwagen (furniture van), this too was mounted on a Pz Kpfw IV chassis.

Anti-aircraft protection for panzer divisions had been part of German thinking from the earliest days but never to the extent necessary. Pre-war and early wartime production shortages delayed the introduction of 20mm dual-purpose weapons (into the anti-*tank* battalions) to all but a few of the panzer, motorized infantry, light as well as infantry divisions for which it was intended. When available the gun was employed against both air and ground targets; twelve to a flak company. Steps to improve matters brought Army flak battalions into panzer divisions re-equipped for the 1942 summer offensive (map 10). By 1943, flak battalions equipped with eight 88s and fifteen 20mm weapons were intended for all panzer and certain panzer grenadier divisions. At the same time a 20mm weapons company was introduced into panzer grenadier regiments serving both panzer and panzer grenadier divisions. But when SPWs similarly armed were distributed throughout the regiment, seven guns each to individual panzer grenadier companies, the need for this company became less pronounced.

Not until mid-1944 did the establishment of a panzer division provide for a panzer regiment with a flak section of eight Wirbelwind (whirlwind) or later (3.7cm) Ostwind (east wind) incorporating powered revolving turrets to deal with high-speed, low-flying attack.

Until the advent of Army flak battalions in 1942, reliance was placed largely upon anti-aircraft units allotted to panzer formations by the Luftwaffe; these, while tactically under Army control, remained Luftwaffe property (*see* Part 4). Luftwaffe units of this type equipped either with the 20mm Flak 30 standard light anti-aircraft gun, or the heavy 8.8cm gun first produced in 1934 to become the standard (mobile) anti-aircraft gun, accompanied the Condor Legion to Spain. Both guns quickly proved their effectiveness – in the role for which they were intended and in action against ground targets. The 8.8cm gun in particular produced devastating effects against tanks and fortified positions and was exploited to the maximum by crews firing over open sights. The '88' evolved as probably the most versatile weapon of the war, playing a crucial role in defeating tank attacks.

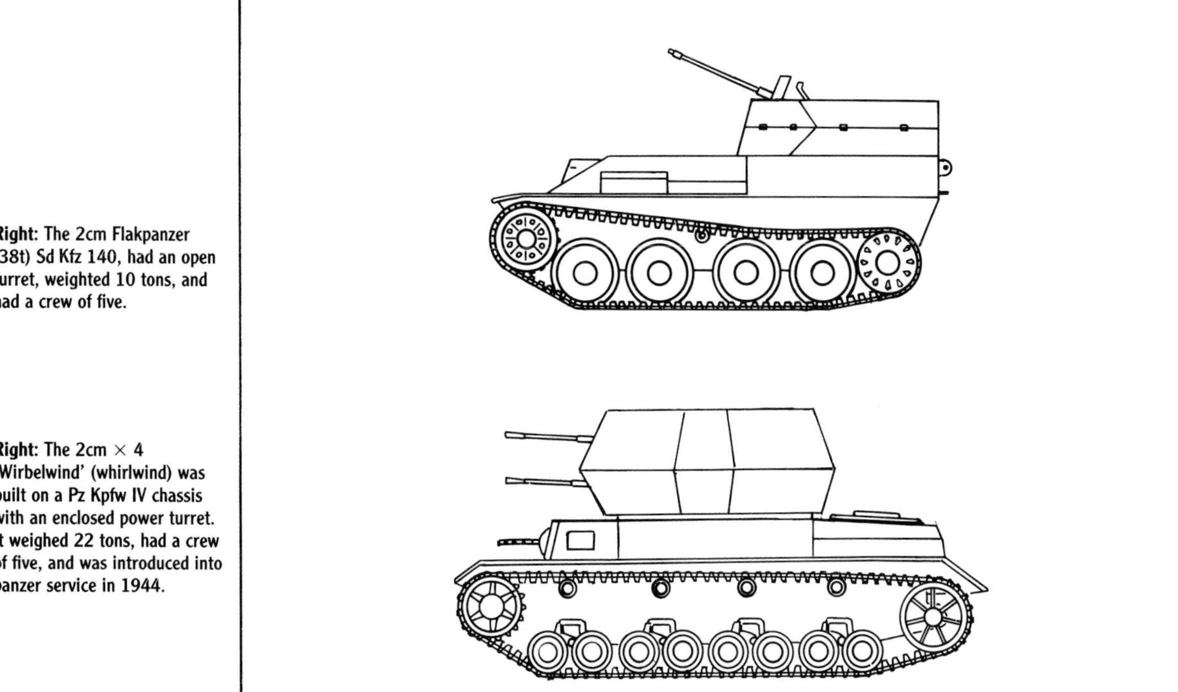

Right: The 2cm Flakpanzer (38t) Sd Kfz 140, had an open turret, weighted 10 tons, and had a crew of five.

Right: The 2cm × 4 'Wirbelwind' (whirlwind) was built on a Pz Kpfw IV chassis with an enclosed power turret. It weighed 22 tons, had a crew of five, and was introduced into panzer service in 1944.

Right: Flakpanzer, starting with the 2cm Flak, became an increasingly important class of self-propelled weapons. Used against both air and ground targets, the 2cm Flak seen here is deployed in a static role with its SS crew preparing their defence against low-flying attack. It was towed into action and had an effective ceiling of 3,500 feet.

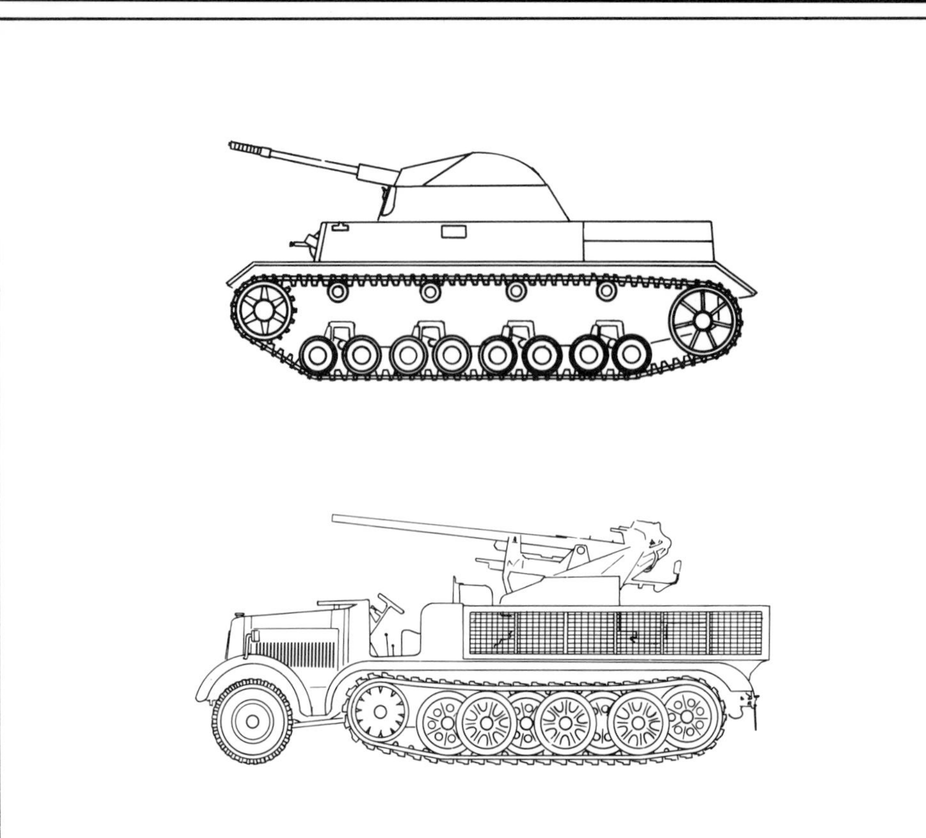

Left: The 3cm × 2 'Kugelblitz' was built on a Pz Kpfw IV chassis. This experimental Daimler-Benz model, with high-speed, enclosed power turret, weighed 24 tons and had a crew of five.

Left: The 3.7cm Flak mounted on a 5-ton half-track was replaced with an armoured model needing an 8-ton half-track which gave better protection to the crew of seven. It had an effective ceiling of 5,000 feet.

Above: An 8cm Flak in its travelling position. This weapon had an effective ceiling of 20,000–30,000 ft and together with two hundred or more types of tanks, assault guns, Sturmpanzer and other AFVs, made a notable contribution while serving the panzer force.

Left: The 2cm × 2 Flak mounted on a 5-ton halftrack provided poor protection for its crew of five, but was a useful mobile weapon.

9. Sturmgeschütze, Sturmpanzer and miscellaneous vehicle types

Considerably more than two hundred types of armoured vehicle were designed or planned to serve the panzer force during the period 1929 to 1945: 94 tanks, 42 SPWs, 19 armoured cars, thirteen Panzerjaeger, ten Jagdpanzer and twelve Flakpanzer. Among miscellaneous vehicle types introduced into panzer service during the course of the war the following were most prominent.

Sturmgeschütz, turretless, self-propelled assault guns not intended for panzer divisions but soon in widespread use were designed for infantry support; their role in the attack being to provide close assistance for assaulting infantry. In defence, especially against tank attacks, assault gun manoeuvrability and fire power greatly strengthened divisional capacity to resist. Organized as army/corps troops into assault gun battalions (Sturmgeschütze Abteilungen) (renamed brigades in 1943) with 21 guns in three batteries each of seven weapons, their numbers increased at the expense of tank production. By the spring of 1944, 45 assault gun brigades were serving in the east. A German innovation attributed to von Manstein during his service with the Truppenamt in 1935, the Sturmgeschütz, equivalent to a turretless tank with heavy frontal armour, introduced into service in 1939, required a crew of four and initially mounted a low-velocity weapon in the front hull. But as the war progressed other higher performance guns were substituted. Several variants using Panzer III chassis (no longer required for tank production after 1943) entered service; one, the Sd Kpfz 162 armed with a 7.5cm anti-tank gun, becoming the forerunner of the Jagdpanzer.

Sturmpanzer IV, Brummbär, 15cm Stu. Howitzer produced in small numbers and a handful of Sturmtigers armed with a massive rocket-projector were intended for street fighting. Introduced in 1944 the howitzer contributed to the fire power of panzer artillery and heavy weapons companies of panzer grenadier regiments. The Sturmtiger, of which no more than ten were built early in 1944 and divided between two companies, 1000 and 1001, served as Army troops to break Polish resistance in Warsaw 1944, before their transfer to the Ardennes (Fifteenth Army) followed by action in the Ruhr pocket in 1945.

Miscellaneous types of unarmoured vehicles developed in other categories included experimental weapon carriers (Waffenträger), ammunition carriers (Munitionsschlepper), armoured rocket-launchers (Panzerwerfer) and observation vehicles (Beobachtungspanzerwagen). Fuel delivery trucks and armoured recovery vehicles (Bergepanzerwagen) together with supply transport raised the wheeled and tracked complement of a 1944 panzer division to more than 3,000 vehicles, excluding tanks and SP artillery.

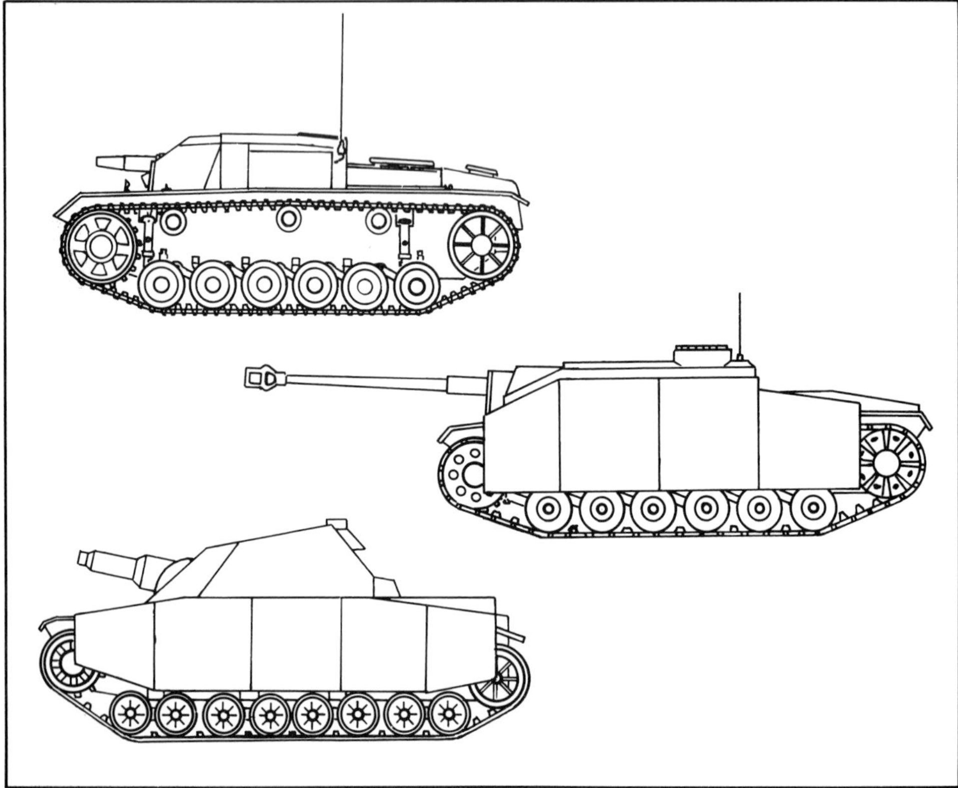

Left: The Sturmgeschütz III, 7.5cm L/24 Sd Kfz 142, turretless AFV. Intended as infantry support, the assault gun nevertheless served in panzer regiments and independent brigades. It weighed 22 tons, had a crew of four and a speed of 20mph. Higher performance guns were substituted in later models.

Left: Sturmgeschütz III, Sd Kfz 142/1, assault gun armed with the 7.5cm StuK 40 L/48 which remained in use until 1945.

Left: The five-man Brumbar (grizzly bear) 15cm howitzer, Sd Kfz 166, was based on the Pz Kpfw IV chassis and weighed 28 tons. A late development in the 'sturm' or close-support category, together with the more limited Sturmtiger, it was issued to panzer-grenadier heavy-companies and Army panzer battalions.

Left: Sturmgeschütz III, Sd Kfz 142/1, assault gun armed with the 7.5cm StuK 40 L/48.

10. Panzer signals (and 'Ultra')

The signals system of a panzer division was the responsibility of a divisional signals officer (Nachrichtenführer) with both line (telephone) and wireless companies at his disposal. The purpose of the system was to transmit instructions and information between commander, staffs and subordinate or attached units; the mobility of signal detachments particularly those on the move with a commander at battle headquarters being assured by transportation in wheeled or half-tracked vehicles. At rear headquarters the Nachrichtenführer co-ordinated all communications of the division, whether at rest or on the move, supervising links to rearward and neighbouring formations, and liaising continuously within units; a generous distribution of divisional wireless and telecommunications equipment achieving the desired results. At corps and army level the signals equipment included facilities for wireless Intelligence; panzer commanders, Rommel in particular, setting great store by the work of signals specialists who deduced enemy strengths, dispositions and intentions from radio intercepts. The importance of wireless communication directing and controlling mobility and firepower on the battlefield, had been recognized by those in authority from the earliest days of the panzer force.

During the early thirties a key figure guiding Army signals technology and organization was General Erich Fellgiebel, a 1914–18 veteran appointed Inspector of Signal Troops (In 7) in October 1934. Fellgiebel's experience of wartime communications began when he was a signals officer with 4th Cavalry Division. In charge of a signals detachment working with a reconnaissance troop, his duty was to advise headquarters of enemy movement through the use of rudimentary wireless equipment transported in a 6-horse wagon.

The fundamental step in the process of linking panzer commands to subordinates as required by Guderian, who was intent upon welding panzer divisions into ever larger battle formations, was the introduction into military service of ultra-short-wave radio – the brainchild of Colonel Gimmler, head of signals section 7 of the Heereswaffenamt. In 1938, when Guderian's XVI Corps epitomized panzer progress, the signals officer of that formation, Colonel (later General) Albert Praun, promoted from command of 2nd Panzer Signals Battalion, played a leading role in the development of wireless communication at command level. Following the attempt on Hitler's life in July 1944, Praun was to replace General Erich Fellgiebel as the Army's senior signals officer. Guderian, although inheriting a family tradition of infantry (Hannoverjaeger) service had, at his own wish, acquired a thorough understanding of wireless procedures and potential both prior to and during the course of the First World War, serving with a telegraph company in Coblenz (1912), a cavalry unit at the Battle of the Marne (1915), and in Fourth Army signal staff appointments (1915–17).

Spurred by foreign (notably British in 1931) experiments in the tactical control of armoured formations, Guderian's interest in wireless technology continued undiminished during the inter-war years. By 1940 thanks to Fellgiebel, Praun and Gimmler, progress in mobile communications had been so swift that, working from a suitably equipped armoured command vehicle, Guderian was able to keep pace with his units on the battlefield, ordering changes in deployment by wireless immediately such action became necessary – an advantage denied to his opponents until much later.

From a mobile battle headquarters, Guderian extended communications forward so that orders travelling via intermediate levels reached advance units and individual tanks whose wireless operators, with ultra-short-wave sets ranging up to six miles, worked under orders of the tank commander. During the course of battle, radio operators when not actually transmitting, would keep sets on 'receive'; in a crisis they were also expected to man the hull machine-gun. In addition to wireless equipment German tanks had an

Right: Panzer signallers on the move enjoyed the mobility and resources of specially designed armoured command radio vehicles. Pictured here are Gross Deutschland signallers at a static forward communications point; their equipment includes hand-sets and a ten-line exchange.

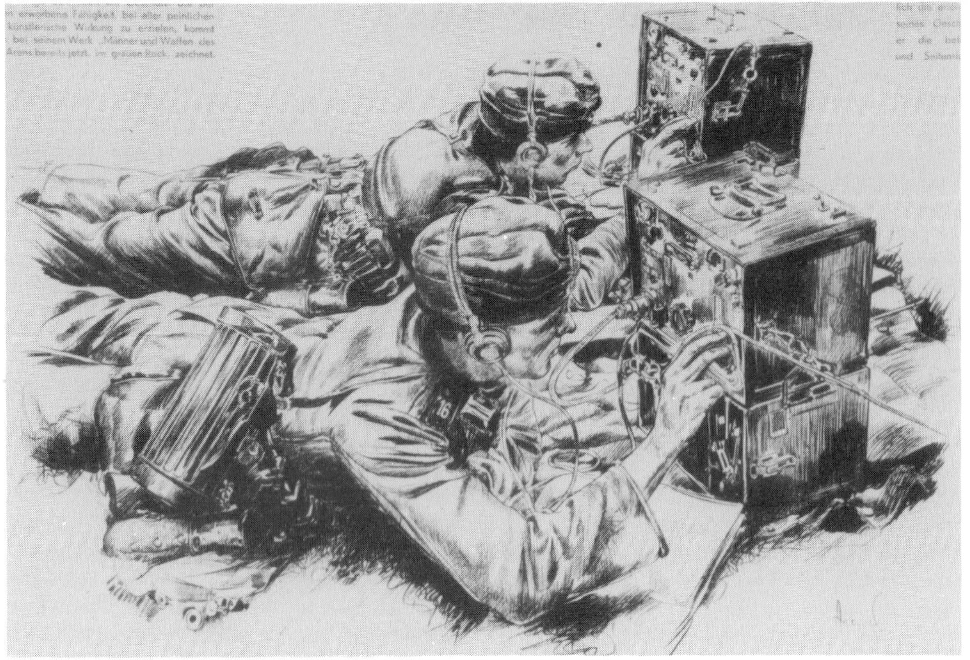

Left: Wireless communication between dismounted panzer grenadiers, their headquarters and mobile units was facilitated by portable W/T equipment (used in the illustration by men of 16th Infantry Regiment). More than thirty different types of transmitter and fifteen types of receiver were in use by signallers in 1941.

internal telephone system allowing tank commanders access to both driver and wireless operator and, by speaking-tube, to the gunlayer and loader. Individual tanks in wireless contact with platoon (and upwards through company) benefited from battalion links to other units and to supporting units such as artillery and engineers. During static periods, as an alternative to wireless, the telephone companies were expected to lay land-lines between units and thereby reduce wireless traffic to a minimum rendering communications 'silent'. When at such times, units were not actively mobile, a very complete telephone network was built up; dispatch riders or couriers supplementing land-lines proved essential when communications were interrupted by enemy action. The network of lines established by a formation such as DAK in North Africa, would typically comprise connections to individual staff officers, headquarter units, corps troops and main divisional formations. Lines were also laid to fixed exchanges at rearward points where further connection could be made to formations or units not directly under DAK control. The work of signals personnel at higher headquarters, for example that of an army signals regiment – two battalions each of three companies – included wireless interception analysis and direction-finding. In consequence the monitoring of enemy call-signs and the systematic logging of their orientation provided Intelligence staffs with invaluable information.

For a time, when Eighth Army, with a notable exception that was to prove Rommel's undoing (*see* Panzer Army Africa, 18 November 1941), was lagging behind German efficiency in this important sphere of Intelligence, the British order of battle, tank strength, equipment levels and tactical progress were as well known to the German commander as to his opponents; Rommel came to rely heavily upon signal Intelligence to supplement meagre photographic reconnaissance and laid plans accordingly, particularly at times when the air situation was not in his favour. Unfortunately for Rommel, total British awareness of Mediterranean transport movement – individual cargoes even – intended for Panzer Group Africa would contribute directly to defeat. At the heart of this success lay one of the Second World War's best kept secrets – the breaking of German Enigma ciphers. In early and widespread use by all three services, including the panzer force at appropriate levels, the Enigma cipher machine fell into British hands early in the war. Thereafter much of what was 'Ultra' secret being transmitted by Enigma link between Berlin, Rome and North Africa, more especially Flivo's requesting air support in Normandy (*see* Part 4), was read by the Government Code and Cipher School at Bletchley and passed to field commands. The consequence of this German security failure was a major factor in Allied victory.

A distinctive feature of a panzer division's wireless plan, 16th Panzer's, for instance, during the advance to Uman in 1941, was the allocation of a fixed call-sign for the exclusive use of formation commanders at division and above, enabling them to interrupt wireless traffic on any link and be immediately recognized.

In the important sphere of defensive planning, signals security required call-sign and frequency changes to be made at irregular intervals – often daily; the highest frequencies with least chance of interruption being reserved for tank regiments and air to ground traffic. Other defensive measures included long wireless 'silences' and jamming action. German army group information bulletins covering weather or the military situation in general, were regularly broadcast; programmes going on the air at set times. Lower formations were expected to listen-in two or three times daily. Air co-operation broadcasts served to transmit important reports quickly, and could be expected at any time. Such broadcasts, provided with serial numbers, helped recipients to check that none had been missed.

Right: Panzer repair and recovery teams operating within regimental workshop companies provided round the clock service to the panzer regiment. Here an armoured command vehicle is receiving a replacement engine at the hands of regimental personnel in Libya.

Far right, top: More elaborate workshop repairs necessitating heavy lifting gear were carried out in base workshops operating within panzer army transport/maintenance parks. In this photograph a Panther has come in for repair.

Far right, bottom: Recovery platoons collecting damaged vehicles, like this 'Marder' I anti-tank gun, would use the 22-ton low-loader; the towing machine is a 12-ton Sd Kfz 8. The restoration of armour to battle-fit condition was a crucial function.

11. Panzer recovery and repair

Tank repair and maintenance troops (Panzerinstandsetzungstruppen), not withstanding their limited distribution within a panzer division, provided services vital to maintaining the tempo of an attack. When replacement tanks were in short supply, as was generally the case, prompt action by repair and recovery units proved decisive. Damaged tanks were swiftly recovered and defective ones rehabilitated by repair and recovery sections of regimental workshop companies. Recovering battle-damaged tanks or other vehicles of a panzer regiment by collecting on low-loaders, or alternatively bringing them in behind suitable towing machines, was nominally the responsibility of regimental workshop tank recovery sections. But so great was the need at times of stress for armoured fighting vehicles to be returned into action with the least possible delay that *ad hoc* recovery teams were organized at short notice by fighting units on instructions from divisional commanders. Facing hazards of enemy air attack, working through undetected minefields or under constant shellfire, recovery teams laboured round the clock to maintain panzer strengths at the highest possible level. In Africa, where a tremendous toll of armour was taken by enemy ground and air action, twenty minutes was regarded as a good time for loading a damaged tank on to a low-loading transporter. At other times suitable vehicles were sent out to bring tanks in with hawsers.

Salvaged machines, including captured ones, were returned by day or night to assembly points at the rear where repair units could deal with them; captured vehicles constituting a high proportion of panzer division establishments. But the use of transporters became less and less frequent in all theatres until they were eventually confined to roads where they could maintain comparatively high speeds. Instead, tanks were regularly towed by standard towing machines of either 6- or 18-tons. For recovering heavy tanks like the Tiger, recovery sections were theoretically issued with a variant of the Tiger itself, the Bergpanzer Tiger equipped with spade and winch. In practice, two 18-ton towing machines were usually coupled and damaged Tigers hauled off in this way.

Bergepanthers and Pz Kpfw IIIs adapted to recovery roles were also employed in salvage operations. Tank repair, as distinct from tank recovery, sections were included in panzer establishments at company, battalion and regimental level. Tank crews were nevertheless expected to make their own running repairs – only heavy work being undertaken in regimental workshops. Equipped with mobile cranes and

recovery vehicles, regimental workshops were a crucial part of the German concept of an independent mobile force. Workshop companies at panzer army level undertook more difficult and time-consuming work; their equipment including heavy lifting gear. Ranged alongside panzer army heavy workshop companies were army motor transport parks and other specialist units allotted to panzer formations by OKH – including tank spares and motor tyre depots. Separate transport columns were sometimes allotted to panzer formations for transporting these essential stores. The repair and maintenance of wheeled vehicles belonging to a panzer division was the responsibility of a divisional workshop company; only in a crisis would this unit undertake tank repairs.

12. Panzer supply and transport

The supply and transport services of a panzer division were the responsibility of a Kommandeur der Divisions Nachschubtruppen, abbreviated to Kodina. At panzer army headquarters a 'Nachschubführer' with wider organizing and co-ordinating powers was ultimately responsible for all questions relating to supply and transport within the formation. Divisional supplies were usually brought forward by attached motor transport columns, each of standardized capacity, working between army railheads and divisional supply points. A light column, twelve or more vehicles, had a capacity of 90 tonnes and a heavy column, 22 or more vehicles, 120 tonnes. Although numbers of columns and vehicles varied considerably between divisions, four to six such columns were usual in a 1944 panzer division establishment. A keynote of the system was flexibility enabling army and divisional supply commanders to switch columns and concentrate them wherever they were tactically required.

Under army control, road tankers or more often 4–5-ton standard trucks supplemented Kodina's resources. Organized into columns of either 5,500 or 11,000 gallons capacity, they transported petrol in 200-litre steel drums filled from rail tankers at army railheads, bringing them to issue points in forward areas. In a crisis, standard supply arrangements were frequently varied; the movement of petrol, ammunition or rations then being undertaken by improvised columns or transport groups of the Luftwaffe. This later likelihood was catered for as early as April 1940 when panzer divisions in the west were advised of air supply procedures (*see* Part 4, New Horizons in Transport); crisis facilities becoming increasingly necessary in later years as divisions and entire panzer armies outran or were cut off from landward re-supply.

In 1943 a radical step was taken towards centralizing divisional supply services following Guderian's appointment as Inspector-General of Panzertruppen. Supply facilities were then concentrated in battalion supply companies attached to panzer, panzer grenadier and reconnaissance battalions – thereby gathering into a single unit the former rear echelon transport vehicles of fighting companies leaving company commanders with only their battle transport. Fighting company commanders, hitherto responsible for the movement of their own supplies, were consequently relieved of this administrative duty and freed to concentrate more upon tactical problems. The work of loading and unloading divisional supply columns was the responsibility of a divisional supply company. Theirs' was the primary duty of establishing supply points from which the new battalion supply companies using their own vehicles provisioned the combat companies for which they were responsible. A volunteer labour force of east Europeans and Russian prisoners-of-war, 'Hiwis' (Hilfeswilliges), many of whom were Georgians or Ukrainians, were used to augment supply company personnel. Hiwis accompanying transport drivers also assisted in handling supplies and setting up supply points.

Panzer corps were largely bypassed in the chain of supply until 'organic' panzer corps such as Gross Deutschland – consisting of a panzer and a panzer grenadier division – were being established in 1944–5. Only then, when a corps supply company became responsible for both organic divisions, did this intermediate level between division and army assume real importance in the chain of supply. Notwithstanding attempts by OKW to standardize transport and fighting vehicle production, a characteristic of all supply columns was the varied number and types of vehicles on establishments; multifarious German and foreign vehicles creating an exceptional problem for the workshop companies responsible for repair and maintenance. In 1944 upwards of 96 different types of vehicle could still be found in the wheeled complement of a panzer division; Panzer Lehr, for instance, in Normandy recorded 60 per cent of its transport as being of foreign origin. When autumn and spring rains turned the Eastern Front into a morass rendering vehicle movement impossible, peasant transport was commandeered and pressed into service. Horse-drawn *Panje* wagons, troikas, and sledges were gathered into panzer supply columns. Camel-trains served First Panzer Army in the south. In the west, where summer conditions prevailed during the early campaigns, panzer supply arrangements although not altogether satisfactory gave no great cause for concern. In Poland (map 2) supplies for Guderian's XIX Motorized Corps travelled barely more than 350 kilometres from East Prussia. Rail networks remained largely intact and compatible with the German gauge. Shortages that did occur were of a minor kind, and the mobile troops, although occasionally requiring air assistance, were never seriously hampered in their sweeping advance to Brest-Litovsk.

In France, on the other hand, supply lines were stretched considerably. Guderian's motorized corps pushing west from Sedan needed its supply columns to travel about 160 kilometres daily – clocking up 6,000 kilometres by the end of the campaign. First Panzer Division, advancing over good metalled roads south of the Aisne with Panzer Group Guderian in phase two of the battle for France (map 3), reported fuel shortages, but the deficiency was made good from captured stocks. Reporting ammunition shortages after a tank engagement, Panzer Group von Kleist also in the drive south with the equivalent of eight mobile divisions,

Right: The Bussing NAG 4.5-ton semi-track entered transport service during the autumn of 1943.

once recorded '. . . no sign of resupply . . .'. After this campaign OKH emphasized in training manuals the need for proper logistical administration, stressing that every movement and action of a panzer division required thorough preparation and servicing; a clear-sighted theoretical approach soon at variance with the realities of Operation 'Barbarossa'. In the view of many commanders the offensive started with hopelessly inadequate stocks of petrol, tyres, replacement engines, gearboxes and a host of other crucial war materials without which the panzer divisions would grind to a halt. Thrusting deep into Russia, panzer divisions rapidly out-stripped their supplies. OKH Chief of Staff Halder recorded in his diary, 'The number of supply trains is insufficient for a widespread attack. Because of a difference in railway gauges, only a limited volume of supplies can be moved forward until such time as the Russian wide gauge can be converted to the German standard.'

Manhandling supplies between gauges, until conversion work (moving one of the Russian rails 9cm inwards) was completed, despite the prodigious efforts of railway engineers and labour battalions, was only the start of the problem. When winter gripped the front in sub-zero temperatures, '. . . there were days when as many as a hundred locomotives broke down and water-tanking stations were totally unsuitable for the unusually cold spell'. So fundamental was this problem in occupied Russia that Hitler charged the German State Railways with responsibility for the entire railway system leaving General Gercke, chief of military transport, to concentrate on arrangements for road supply. With panzer divisions, follow-up infantry and other services, vying for the few available routes, the supply situation in the east degenerated to near collapse. Transport columns moving over vast distances struggled mightily to overcome their difficulties. Consequently, as panzer and other formations moved east their supplies were carried by transport columns using roads of deteriorating condition; roads becoming increasingly congested. In later stages of the advance to Moscow and Lenningrad, passing through remote hinterlands, roads were totally absent. Maps for service use frequently proved useless in this situation; Russian road classifications bearing little resemblance to Western standards.

A measure of the problem facing panzer supply staffs is recorded in the diary of 9th Panzer Division advancing with Second Panzer Army south-west of Moscow. Over a period of eight weeks the division required petrol for nearly 200,000 kilometres. Desperately trying to beat a harsh winter and reach the Soviet capital in December 1941, panzer armies were reporting: 'Troops could go no further from railheads than could be reached by horses and sledges.' Second Panzer Army, reduced to living from hand to mouth on local supplies, was defeated by the inability of transport columns either to negotiate seas of mud into which vehicles at first sank up to their axles, or snow-drifts into which both they and tanks with narrow tracks floundered uselessly. The result, by the end of 1941, was to bring panzer operations to a standstill; halted as much by climatic conditions and munitions shortages as exhaustion of men and materials. The vast quantities of petrol, oil and lubricants needed to ensure operational mobility of panzer divisions became overnight as important to the plans of panzer commanders as terrain or enemy strengths and dispositions. Success in battle came to depend as much upon considerations of supply as fighting capacity. And not only petrol, but oil consumption too proved much higher than expected. In trackless terrain vehicles were driven for long periods in first gear; LVII Panzer Corps reported as early as 6 August 1941 that vehicles required 20–30 litres of oil per 100 kilometres instead of the planned half-litre. The same division reported 50 per cent of its armoured vehicles engaged in the attack on Kiev falling out because of shortage of oil. Second Panzer Army recorded in late November that it was receiving 300,000 litres of fuel, whereas one million litres were required to sustain operational efficiency. From 22 June 1941 when Guderian's tanks crossed the Polish demarcation line until mid-November when Second Panzer Army approached Tula in a final bid to reach Moscow, many vehicles had travelled 4,000 kilometres and had served for weeks without maintenance.

Typical of panzer division states at the time was 4th Panzer Division reporting on 5 December: tanks down to 15 per cent of establishment, personnel reduced to 30 per cent, transports to 34 per cent and motor cycles no more than 10 per cent. Partisans directing their attacks against road and rail routes with increasing boldness and effectiveness aggravated the supply position. Endless stoppages were recorded in the rear of advancing panzer armies where territories were unoccupied or lightly held. The diary of Field Marshall Keitel confirms the experience of the field formations: '. . . more than a hundred stretches of railway line blown up in one night'. In mid-winter 1941 the entire German front opposite Moscow might have collapsed had it not been for Hitler's stand fast order of 16 December. During the following months panzer formations were rehabilitated and supply arrangements gradually improved. At key road and rail junctions supply bases were established and lines of communication, wherever they were exposed to guerrilla attack, wired-in and protected by local security groups, but never to the extent required. Tank tracks were widened, wheeled transport, especially motor cycles, were partially replaced. Tracked or semi-tracked machines were introduced into supply service – the diminutive Kettenkrad and the light Raupenschlepper-Ost. Heavier vehicles introduced in 1943 for transport duty in the east included a semi-tracked transport and towing machine, the Wehrmachtschlepper, and another semi-track, the Maultier (mule).

In occupied territories, especially in Russia, railway engineers, army personnel, prisoner-of-war construction battalions and locally impressed labour, worked continuously to maintain the railway system. Armour-protected locomotives with improvised ground and anti-aircraft protection using captured weapons or the ubiquitous 20mm AA guns were introduced in small numbers. But the menacing problem of supply shortages was never wholly eradicated; ammunition, food, fuel and a thousand other stocks continued in short supply. On any war front in the east, west, south-east, Italy or Africa, the total collapse of supply arrangements was never far from the thoughts of panzer commanders. Improvised air transport programmes played a vital role at times in supplying panzer formations and many of the problems facing supply staffs might have been resolved in this way but, as is made clear in Part 4, there were never sufficient transports available and an infrastructure for aircraft servicing and dispatch with a centralized command was instituted too late to become more than a qualified success.

Left: Early in the war Army and divisional transport columns placed their faith in commercial vehicles, but bad weather led to more robust vehicles being brought into service. The mobility of supply columns and divisional units was essential. The Opel 'Blitz' 3-ton general-purpose truck, improved with a 4-wheel drive, was suitable for the task.

Far left: The Mercedes-Benz 'Maultier' 4.5-ton halftrack adopted the Panzer II chassis and was introduced in 1943. Other halftrack transports were built by Ford, Opel, Magirus and French factories, while a Raupenschlepper Ost (light halftrack) served the infantry.

Near left: The Wehrmacht Schlepper sWS entered transport service during the autumn of 1943.

Left: A Bussing NAG 4.5-ton truck. This vehicle was the standard Wehrmacht heavy duty transport, and a forerunner of the sWS. Mercedes also produced a 4.5-ton, 4-wheel drive model for service with transport columns.

Part 4. Air support: the decisive factor

1. Key to victory

The shock tactics used by the German Army to extraordinary effect in eliminating opposition in Poland, France and the Balkans, or again in Russia until the Red Air Force gained supremacy, depended to a great extent upon co-operation with the Luftwaffe. Without this crucial component of mobile operations characteristic notably of the Wehrmacht, the rapid advance of the panzer divisions would have been unlikely to succeed.

Consider the plan for zero hour in the battle for France, when the mass of German armour was poised to strike across the Meuse on 13 May 1940. The level of support afforded by 3rd Air Fleet[1] to Panzer Group von Kleist leading Operation 'Yellow' (map 3) at this critical time can be gauged from orders issued to 1st Panzer Division by General Guderian, commanding XIX Panzer Corps. Concentrated with other attacking divisions in the neighbourhood of Sedan, 1st Panzer Division was deployed in battle groups ready to strike west.

'The point of main effort of our western offensive', reads Guderian's order, 'lies in the Sector von Kleist. Almost the whole of the German Air Force will support this operation. By means of uninterrupted attacks lasting for eight hours, the French defenders along the Meuse will be smashed. This will be followed by an assault across the river by Gruppe von Kleist at 1600 hours and the establishment of bridgeheads.'

Army High Command (OKH) orders rationalizing joint action by Army Group 'A' and 3rd Air Fleet into Operation 'Yellow', a 'Sichelschnitt' plan aimed at rupturing the Meuse defences on a narrow front, had been issued three months earlier and derived from an updated OKW (Hitler) directive of October 1939; von Kleist's orders came to him directly from the army group ('A') to which his group was initially subordinate. Lead by Panzer Group von Kleist the panzer divisions would exploit their break-through in a deep enveloping thrust to the west, isolating Allied armies from rearward support in France and Belgium and rendering them ineffective. Indirect support by 3rd Air Fleet restraining opposition air forces while at the same time dislocating command centres and communications over a wide area was an essential pre-requisite. Initiated by von Runstedt's chief of staff, Erich von Manstein, looking to exploit the surprise effect of an armoured offensive out of the Ardennes forest – a direction from which the Allies least expected attack – the sweeping manoeuvre was to succeed beyond the expectations of all but a few involved in its planning and execution. The role played by the Luftwaffe was decisive. Attacking on sectors of the Meuse where opposition by French Second and Ninth Armies was thinly concentrated, Sperrle's fighter and bomber groups lead by Stukas assailed the defenders in terrifying force, smashing artillery positions, scattering opposition and creating favourable conditions for the armoured columns to force the river and race 240 miles to the Channel at Dunkirk. Eleven days after the crucial break-through the campaign in France was virtually at an end. By 24 June, joint action by Army Group 'A' and 3rd Air Fleet with the advantage of surprise had provided the key to German victory; success, foreshadowed by similar events in Poland, had been swift and conclusive.

German experience of ground-attack operations as entailed in the Battle of France was rooted in war experience and secret trials stretching back more than twenty years via Poland and Spain to the First World War. Then, as early as November 1917, armour protected aircraft strafing Allied artillery and infantry with forward-firing – and in later models synchronized machine-guns, notably the Junkers CL-1 (1918) – supported German infantry in the attack. By March 1918 the number of battle squadrons supporting ground operations on the Western Front had risen to thirty-eight. On the British side the Sopwith Salamander (1918), another expressly designed ground-attack machine but less prominent in support of Allied military operations by virtue of fewer numbers, served the Royal Flying Corps in much the same role as the Junkers. Indirect support for land forces in the shape of bombing attacks to delay the movement of enemy counter-attack reserves, contributed to offensive success by both sides. By 1923 the German Army, in common with western counterparts, was once more experimenting with tactical schemes to advance army air

[1]At the start of Operation 'Yellow' (map 3), 3rd Air Fleet (Sperrle) was composed of two air corps (Fliegerkorps): II (Lörzer) deployed in support of Army Group 'A' (von Kleist) at Sedan, and V (Greim) supporting Army Group 'C' (von Leeb); 2nd Air Fleet (Kesselring) comprising XI Air Corps Landing, I, IV and VIII Air Corps supported Army Group 'B' (von Bock). From 13 May onwards, VIII Air Corps (von Richthofen) was co-operating with II Air Corps at Sedan – flying in support of Army Group 'A'.

co-operation; in the German case by secretly developing ground-attack machines – the Hs 51, and (modelled on the American Curtiss Helldiver), the Hs 123 – culminating in the notorious Ju 87 dive-bomber (Stuka) making an appearance on active service in Spain and winning early wartime victories for the Luftwaffe.

Dive-bombing in fact was to come as a very unpleasant shock to early German opponents none of whom had effectively developed this type of attack and, short of winning air supremacy for protection, were unable to deploy immediately effective counter-measures. Much of the credit for generating Luftwaffe enthusiasm for the dive-bomber lay with Germany's First World War ace, Ernst Udet. Early in 1931 this champion aerobatics pilot flew the American Curtiss Helldiver privately in the United States and thereafter tested the Hs 123 in trials in 1935. But the Hs machine handled uncomfortably and Udet expressed his dislike of it. Von Richthofen, director of research at the Technical Office of the Air Ministry, was unenthusiastic about dive-bombing and in consequence no real progress in design and development of Stukas leading to production of the Ju 87 was possible. But fortunately for Udet the situation changed when Goering persuaded him to take charge of the Office in 1936 – which he did; von Richthofen departing for Spain to promote operational research before becoming Chief-of-Staff to Hugo Sperrle (map 1).

The Luftwaffe's first dive-bombing unit was raised at Schwerin in 1936 (1-StukaGeschwader 162) equipped with the Hs 123. But it is to Spain following von Richthofen's career that we must turn for developments in dive-bombing. For three years, from July 1936 onwards, the Condor Legion under Hugo Sperrle and Chief of Staff Wolfram Freiherr von Richthofen, the Legion's last commander (29 November 1938), introduced wireless for transmitting target information from forward Luftwaffe observers to squadron headquarters, improved the machines and evolved the tactics that the Luftwaffe would use in Poland and France on a grand scale. The experience of these officers' pioneering army/air operations in Spain, including the notorious incident at Guernica (page 25) followed by action along the Ebro eastwards in the direction of Valencia and Barcelona, contributed notably to Luftwaffe progress in tactical flying. Von Richthofen was to emerge from these operations as the leading exponent of the new style of battlefield support for the Army – a lustrous career taking him from command of the Condor Legion (Generalmajor, November 1938) to command of 4th Air Fleet in Russia (Generaloberst, June 1942) and 2nd Air Fleet in Italy where he was promoted Field Marshal in October 1944.

Directing action against ground targets in Poland, the General gathered Stuka groups into an Air Division 'for special purposes' – the kernel of VIII Air Corps detailed to assist Panzer Group von Kleist in its sweeping advance through France. In these campaigns, forward observers were provided with wheeled (and eventually tracked) transport, facilitating mobility in the company of fast troops; ground-control systems were further refined and air force tactics for reducing or eliminating ground opposition greatly improved by massed concentration of dive-bombers. The technical accomplishments of *Blitzkrieg* – joint army-air operations, deciding in the space of short campaigns, the fate of powerful yet confused opposition, was most persuasively demonstrated during the Battle of France in 1940; but not to the full – communication between tank and air force commanders remained imperfect and not until 1941, when 'Barbarossa' burst upon Russia, would the technology reach an effective level of clear speech contact for the exchange of information and orders.

In the meantime mobile operations, including the campaigns in the Balkans and North Africa, would owe much of their effectiveness to wireless technology promoted by Guderian and von Richthofen's development of close-support techniques and communications without which *Blitzkrieg* would have been stillborn. Later proof of German success in uniting ground and air forces into powerful and flexible shock formations is evident in von Manstein's recovery of Kharkov in 1943 (map 13). By 1939, the Luftwaffe's dive-bombing strength had grown to a total of 219 aircraft deployed in nine groups; a group consisting theoretically of three squadrons, each of twelve Stukas. But the Hs 123 having proved unsatisfactory as a dive-bomber in Spain was scheduled for replacement by the Ju 87A. Deployed instead in a single ground-attack Schlachtgruppe (11/LG2, formerly Schlactgeschwader 100), the type was phased out of production in 1942. On the other hand, approximately 5,000 Ju 87s were to be produced for wartime service with the Luftwaffe. But Luftwaffe ground-attack units, subordinate to von Richthofen in his Air Division for special purposes (eventually VIII Air Corps) and deployed in support of the panzer divisions in *Blitzkrieg* campaigns, whether organized initially into Schlacht or Stuka squadrons – the difference is elaborated later – were not the sole representation of Luftwaffe presence on the battlefield. Air reconnaissance units working with the panzer force gathered crucial Intelligence. Observing and photographing troop movements and more, their contribution to panzer operations was to prove indispensable.

Above: Ground-attack flying played a key role in eliminating opposition to the panzer divisions. The Ju 87B Stuka was a principal ground-attack aircraft of the early war years and was capable of delivering 1,000lb of high-explosives with pin-point accuracy. It is seen here being prepared for active service.

As early as 1915 cameras were being carried in aircraft over the Western Front by both sides. Oscar Messter, a German film pioneer, experimented with semi and later fully automatic cameras. His apparatus, the prototype of much subsequent service equipment, produced overlapping aerial views easily adapted into maps, while a growing band of specialists, organized into (Army) photographic units (Stabsbildabteilungen) attached to air reconnaissance battalions for photo interpretation purposes, employed the stereoscope to reveal detail in overlapping prints. Defeat in 1918 might theoretically have been expected seriously to impede German progress in this important field of technology. Yet by 1935, following secret experiments at Lipetsk and the establishment of training schools at Brunswick and Hildesheim, the Luftwaffe's first air reconnaissance schools (Fliegerbildschule) were re-established at Cottbus, Münster and Göppingen, with five reconnaissance squadrons flying either Heinkel He 45 or He 46. A succession of reconnaissance aircraft types was developed beginning in 1912 with the primitive, low-wing Rumpler-Taube which served the army in a two-seater observation and ultimately photographic role. In 1913 the Albatross B11 arrived in service; the Rumpler C1 followed in 1916; the DFW CV in 1917; Heinkel He 45 and He 46, 1932–5 and Henschel Hs 126, 1935–41. The Focke-Wulf Fw 189 (Owl) also arrived in service in 1941. Fast single-seaters, basically fighter types, also provided reconnaissance data for the Army from 1917

onwards. This practice, matched by foreign air forces, would continue with the Me 109 flying photographic missions in 1940; the Fw 190 in 1942 and briefly in 1944–5 the jet-propelled Me 262.

A key figure in the promotion of photographic Intelligence during the inter-war years was Oberst Theodor Rowehl. His enthusiasm for reconnaissance flying motivated much of the Luftwaffe's pre-war progress in photographic work. The success of his organization, methods, and training given to aircrews and ground staff demonstrated a remarkably innovative approach to all questions of Intelligence during the Luftwaffe's formative years. Starting in reconnaissance as early as 1917, when he flew Rhombergs over England, a demobilized Rowehl exchanged a service career for private flying from Kiel. Using chartered aircraft for the purpose of nefarious Intelligence-gathering, Rowehl snapped Polish border fortifications for the Abwehr. In 'experimental' flying on subsequent missions he piloted a Ju 34 to heights approaching the world altitude record of 41,800 feet set by Walter Neuenhofen in May 1929. More flying for the Abwehr was followed by a return to air force service and in 1936 a move from Kiel to Staaken (Berlin West) where Rowehl's squadron (Fliegerstaffel zbV) was expanded three-fold and its name in the Luftwaffe order of battle changed to Aufklarungsgruppe OKW. A fourth squadron was added to establishment at the outbreak of war when Aufklarungs-gruppe OKW was re-designated Aufklarungsgruppe (F) OKL. Extending German Intelligence cover over Russia in the late thirties, Kronstadt, Leningrad, Pskov and Minsk were reconnoitred under guise of high-altitude research. Border defences, military and other installations located deep within Russia, France, Czechoslovakia and Poland were photographed, analysed and sorted into target files for the later use of bomber crews.

Intelligence flying continued in the late thirties with long-distance flights over Great Britain under the pretext of route-proving for Lufthansa. In 1937 Rowehl moved headquarters to Potsdam (Oranienburg). There a joint army/air force photographic centre (Hauptamt für Lichtbild) adjoining Luftwaffe headquarters and within easy reach of Berlin's Intelligence agencies, was placed under his control. These were the years in which Intelligence agencies flourished in Germany: Abwehr, OKW, OKL and OKH all demanding Intelligence of Rowehl who turned such opportunities to marked advantage. Co-opting commercial firms, leading Europe in optical technology, among whom Carl Zeiss was pre-eminent, or companies developing ideas in the air survey business, Rowehl created a Luftwaffe technical service in the forefront of Intelligence agencies – collecting, sorting and analysing a wide range of espionage data. Foremost of his colleagues whose progress was to influence the wartime performance of the Luftwaffe were those engaged in the business of Intelligence planning and liaison.

Above: A Stukaleiter (controller) in close proximity to panzer headquarters briefs pilots temporarily under his command. Targets, weather information, the position of friendly and enemy troops were typical of the data communicated direct by radio.

Dating from the era when von Seeckt as head of the Reichswehr established a desk for air Intelligence in the Truppenampt (T3), Major Hilmer Freiherr von Bülow directed Foreign Air Forces (5th Branch) over a period of ten years from the spring of 1927 to the autumn of 1937. Fifth Branch responsibilities extended not only to target evaluation, filed for the future briefing of bomber crews – for which purpose Rowehl's imagery was a prime source – but also appreciations of foreign military resources, notably in connection with air-war command. Von Bülow's successor, Oberst Hans Jeschonnek, held the post for little more than a year from the autumn of 1937 until February 1939 when promotion to Chief of Air Staff removed him to the High Command. Jeschonnek was followed by Oberstleutnant 'Beppo' Schmid. As head of Foreign Air Forces, Schmid held this key Intelligence post until October 1942 when reorganization drafted him to field command. That Luftwaffe Intelligence, notwithstanding its pre-war lead in reconnaissance technology, would prove unable to match the supreme challenge of wartime action after 1940 – failing time and again when information about enemy capabilities and intentions was vitally important to army and Luftwaffe alike – would soon become all too apparent. For example, during Schmid's tenure of office a faulty appreciation of RAF strength probably contributed to Luftwaffe failure in the Battle of Britain. In fostering OKW belief that the RAF was outstripping its resources, which it certainly was not, the Luftwaffe prelude to 'Sea-lion' (page 36) may have been prematurely suspended. Neither was the Luftwaffe aware at the time of the crucial role played by radar in controlling RAF fighter defence. Reconnaissance/Intelligence failures of this magnitude were soon to become commonplace.

A significant development in inter-service co-operation upon which the success of mobile operations depended and dating from the inter-war years was the installation of a senior Luftwaffe representative at OKH. General Paul Bögatsch was the candidate selected for this High Command appointment and it was he who in 1937 took the post of Luftwaffe General to the Commander-in-Chief of the Army von Brauchitsch (Fritsch having been replaced in February 1938 when Hitler promoted himself C-in-C). The General's title, Kommandeur der Luftwaffe, was abbreviated to Koluft. This liaison link between Army and Luftwaffe involving control of air reconnaissance units was further developed by appointing Koluft personnel downwards – officers and staff varying in numbers according to command level. Koluft personnel attached to army group and subordinate commands, including panzer and motorized corps when needed, were an important link in the chain of photographic reconnaissance support for the army. Flak detachments were also theoretically under Koluft control, but not ground-attack units. The Koluft arrangement was to continue unchanged until the winter of 1941–2. This was the critical phase of 'Barbarossa' when aircraft shortages and the overlapping dictates of army and Luftwaffe commanders frequently competing for the same Intelligence led to a wide-ranging review of reconnaissance procedures – to the advantage of both services. The change is summarized in The Army's Eye in the Sky, page 130.

By 1939 the Luftwaffe's photographic Intelligence effort was proceeding at two levels: 'H' (Heer = army) units served the tactical support needs of the army, mostly attached to mobile formations; 'F' (fern = distant) long-range units were deployed for strategic work with higher army and Luftwaffe commands. 'H' units comprising 29 squadrons served nine wings (provided also with eight F units), while three 'F' wings controlled an additional thirteen F squadrons. Rowehl's wing comprised four 'F' squadrons; leaving one other independent. Total: 29 'H' and 26 'F' squadrons, 342 'H' and 260 'F' aircraft respectively – 7 per cent of Luftwaffe strength. The aircraft selected pre-war for re-equipping 'H' units was the Hs 126, an open, two-seater biplane; other types dating from before the Spanish Civil War continuing to serve 'H' squadrons in small numbers. Long-distance reconnaissance units, flew the Do 17F, He 111, Ju 86P and later the K high-altitude series, also the Ju 88D an adaptation for photo-reconnaissance of the standard Ju 88 bomber. War production of reconnaissance aircraft included in the 113,515 all-types total of aircraft delivered to the Luftwaffe or satellite air forces from 1939 to 1945 amounted to 6,299 aircraft.

Pre-war German progress in optics and aircraft was matched by significant developments in radio equipment. By 1935 radio had moved from the 1914–18 era of Morse code to speech transmission and reception. Two-way contact between ground and air force units linking the two into flexible working teams was to prove the decisive step in mobile operations. Major von Richthofen, before taking up his Legion appointment in Spain, was one of the key figures promoting technical development in this field of technology.

As the Second World War progressed, robbing *Blitzkrieg* of momentum, air transportation emerged as a new and demanding form of military aviation. At the core of Luftwaffe transport operations from 1939 to 1945 stood the Ju 52 'Judula'. This work-horse of 1936 vintage was to play a key role – not only in refuelling and provisioning fast troops by providing air-landed and parachuted supplies – but also in sustaining encircled panzer formations. The transporting of infantry from North Africa to Andalusia during the Spanish Civil War (map 1) provided the renascent Luftwaffe with highly realistic training opportunities; testing aircrews, equipment and ground organization. The military début of the Ju 52 was followed in 1938 by experience in Austria when transport units flew infantry into Vienna at the time of the Anschluss. Hitler's annexation of Czechoslovakia proved another opportunity for rehearsing transport aircrews and ground organization. So too did Operation 'Green', a plan to seize Prague and the Sudetenland – by war action – carried out instead as an elaborate training exercise; political agreement at Munich having achieved Hitler's aims 'peacefully'. The taxing realism and complexity of 'Green' exercised the Luftwaffe in assembling, loading and operating a fleet of 250 Ju 52/3m under command of 7th Air Division (Student). The event marked a significant stage in air transport operations. Infantry Parachute Battalions I and II, two battalions of 1R16 and SA Regiment Feldherrnhalle organized into two regiments (six battalions) also participated in the action. Dispatched on a one-battalion to one-transport group basis, the modestly equipped infantry supported by mountain artillery were lifted over Czech border defences and landed – not dropped for security reasons – in the vicinity of Freudenthal. Here, reminiscent of action in Holland 1940 and the relief of First Panzer Army in the spring of 1944 (map 15), open-country landing arrangements played a significant part in success.

Also participating in the action under Student's command (Chief of Staff Oberst Jeschonnek) was Schlachtgeschwader 100 equipped with ground-attack Hs 123s and Ju 87s. Their protection was ensured by the inclusion of a fighter Group in Student's command. Such opportunities as 'Green' enabled transport groups to perform in war situations, advancing their planning, organization and procedures to an exceptional degree – especially in relation to parachute and air landing troops. (At the conclusion of 'Green', Student was nominated Inspector of Parachute and Air-Landing Troops (L In XI); a post held simultaneously with command of 7th Air Division – later XI Air Corps). The deployment of parachute and air-landing troops (Fallschirmjaeger and Luftlandetruppen) in campaigns against Denmark, Norway (Operation 'Weserübung'), Holland (Operation 'Yellow') (map 3) and Crete (Operation 'Mercury') (map 6) is outside the scope of this inquiry except to note them in passing as prime examples of transport enterprise and initiative.

Of greater relevance to mobile operations is transport action at a later date when, for instance, in the spring of 1944 First Panzer Army, encircled in the Ukraine, survived only through the efforts of air transport groups to resupply and maintain them; enterprise and resourcefulness being no less characteristic of transport flying at this late stage in the war than at earlier and more dramatic times in the first flush of airborne innovation in the west (*see* New Horizons in Transport). A common denominator in all air transport operations carried out by the Luftwaffe from 1936 to 1945 was the Ju 52/3m developed from a civil prototype. First flown by Junkers in 1932, the Ju 52 right from the start proved an exceptionally robust transport with a reputation for safe and reliable flying. Three engines and an all-metal construction commended it highly, not only to Lufthansa the state carrier with whom it entered service in 1933, but also to numerous foreign airlines, early versions carrying 15–17 passengers. When the Spanish Civil war erupted in 1936 and the Condor Legion required bombers, the Ju was converted to serve as a temporary (*behelfs*) bomber until purpose-built He 111s under test there at the time were declared operational. In its improvised role the Ju 52/3m could carry a maximum bomb-load of 2,300lb (1,500kg). As regards transport numbers and organization at the outbreak of war, twenty Ju 52/3m squadrons were deployed in five transport groups, each of *four* squadrons divided between two battle groups: KG zbV 1 (Morzik) at Stendal (three Wings, one detached at Gardelegn) and KG zbV 172 at Berlin Tempelhof (two Wings and a DFS 230 glider HQ). Contingency planning in 1938 also provided for Group staff, KG zbv 2 (Conrad), and a heavy weapons group to be found from flying schools' personnel and aircraft engaged on pilot and blind-flying training. At the disposal of these early transport groups stood upwards of 250 Ju 52/3ms including 145 of the improved radio version (gbe). Another 250 or so machines deployed in training schools or on courier service brought the 1939 service total of Ju 52/3ms to 552. Production continued until June 1944 by which time almost 3,000 'Judulas' had been delivered to Luftwaffe or satellite air forces.

Organized for Army support and committing 75 per cent of its strength to this activity during the Second World War, the Luftwaffe improvised methods and equipment to meet many and varied contingencies in air reconnaissance, ground attack and re-supply. But in furthering the effectiveness of panzer operations extending the length and breadth of Europe, Luftwaffe resources were rarely if ever adequate for such a high-priority task. Neither in the early days of the war, nor later, were there sufficient transports or adequate numbers of reconnaissance and ground-attack units. The deplorable shortages evident soon after the start of 'Barbarossa' were soon to become apparent on all other fronts. Disparities in equipment and organization, distinguishing Luftwaffe from RAF in 1940, were rooted in conflicting views and strategies determining the growth and uses of air power. Foreign air forces generally tended towards the German notion of maximizing close support for the army. Not so the RAF, pursuing a policy of 'independence'.

Formed in 1918 by merging the RNAS and RFC, the aviation agencies in Britain responsible for naval and military flying, the Royal Air Force (Trenchard) – itself a response to 'strategic' bombing of London by Gothas in 1917 – resisted every attack intended to deprive it of integrity and independence. Much of the opposition to current British policy of centralizing air power after 1918 was fostered by War Office and Admiralty critics who were greatly concerned over the loss of highly prized air-support arms. Many also doubted the value of 'strategic' bombing. Despite vitriolic differences of opinion, the RAF emerged from pre-war debate intact and while neglectful of army co-operation to an alarming degree, free to explore air war possibilities untrammelled by inward-looking army and navy close-support considerations. After 1938, fighter resources assumed a high priority in air staff deliberations – radar control of air formations in particular.

Independent status in the German case was conditioned by General Staff planning in the aftermath of 'Versailles'. These were the years from 1920 to 1933 when von Seeckt, or those who followed at the head of the Heeresleitung – Haye, 1926–30 or Hammerstein, 1930–4, controlled expansion of the army and military flying by allocating executive responsibilities mainly to army officers; those with General Staff training in particular. The key expansion project of the late twenties and early thirties, before Hitler arrived on the scene to take control, was a Russo-German training and research scheme operated secretly, 200 miles south-east of Moscow. This was the Lipetsk project started in 1925 and officially known as Fliegerschule Stahr; Major (aD) Stahr being the school commandant. By 1929 Stahr's command included more than 60 aircraft stationed at Lipetsk – predominantly Fokker D XIII single-seat fighters acquired from Holland plus a two-seater aircraft establishment that included a small number of Heinkel He 17 or even more venerable types. Aircraft and equipment intended for proving also passed through the hands of trials units at Rechlin and Staaken. Naval flying was pursued on the Baltic coast at Strahlsund and north of Hamburg at Travemünde. A command link uniting Lipetsk with the Heeresleitung (Seeckt, Haye, Hammerstein) lay with Fliegerstab Wilberg, a command staff set up within the Truppenamt and lead by Oberstleutnant Helmut Wilberg.

Wilberg's activities, illegal under the Treaty of Versailles, were progressively concealed in Truppenamt Sections T 2 IV and T 2 V (2) followed by a merger with the inspectorate of flying schools (von Mittelberger); the In 1 designation of this branch of the Heeresleitung, concealing the covert presence of a Luftwaffe executive – the inspectorate's chief of staff, Oberstleutnant Helmut Felmy.

Leading the development of von Seeckt's aviation programme at this time and founding future wartime careers for themselves mostly as distinguished field commanders, were Oberst Albert Kesselring, C-in-C, South 1944 (Field Marshal) Oberst Wolfram von Richthofen, C-in-C, 4th Air Fleet 1944 (Field Marshal) and Major Kurt Student, C-in-C, First Parachute Army (Generaloberst). But this step towards establishing an air force command within the Reischwehr was almost immediately overtaken by Hitler's decree of 15 May 1933; merging military (Luftschutzamt) and civil (Lufthansa founded in 1926) agencies into an Air Ministry – Reichsluftfarhtministerium (RLM) – under the control of Hermann Goering, hitherto Reichskommissar for air traffic. And not only did Hitler's decree centralizing air power remove aviation from the army's grip, but anti-aircraft units too were taken away and placed under Goering's control; the army's flak units would henceforth serve as Luftwaffe units leaving the army with a meagre tally of heavy machine-gun units with which to effect local anti-aircraft protection. At this critical stage in an accelerating programme of rearmament taking the fledgling Luftwaffe from a strength of sixteen squadrons in 1933 to 302 in September 1939, many more army officers arrived in service of the RLM – either posted by the Reichswehr or recruited from the reserve list. Setting aside conflict at the outset, military and civil sides of the RLM settled into a harmonious relationship; key posts would nevertheless remain in the hands of army or civilian heads of branches. Below Goering, Minister of State for Aviation and C-in-C, Luftwaffe, stood his deputy Milch, Secretary of State for Air and a former director of Lufthansa. A new Air Command Office (Luftkommandoamt) supervised inspectorates governing planning, and setting standards in all areas of equipment and training. Oberst Wever headed this important office. Oberst Kesselring took over administration; Oberst Wimmer, technical development, Oberst Stumpff, air personnel. Oberst Felmy continued in RLM service and so too did Oberst Wilberg, subsequently first commandant of the Air War Academy. Majors Student, von Richthofen and Hauptmann Jeschonnek were joined by others taking important posts and set to rise in the Luftwaffe. Their ranks included Josef Kammhuber, Josef Schmid and Hugo Sperrle, the Condor Legion commander, later GOC, 3rd Air Fleet.

In the aftermath of this and more open stages of expansion, when its existence was announced by the Führer in March 1935, there was to emerge an air force created in the image of an army and substantially dependent upon military tradition. Lead by a General (air) Staff incorporating the now defunct Luftkommandoamt and organized on military lines, i.e., air fleet – army group, air corps – army corps, and downwards even to include ground forces in the form of parachute infantry (Fallschirmjaeger), the Luftwaffe, like the army an offensive concept, was to be prematurely locked into a pattern of land warfare determined by Hitler's expansionist designs. But another important event was to shape Luftwaffe policy before war became inevitable in 1939 – the loss to the air force of its prime mover in 'strategic' bombing. General Wever's death by misadventure in June 1936 was to prove a most damaging blow to Luftwaffe prospects in later years. Coinciding with air-war developments in Spain, this resulted in strategic bombing being relegated to the background of air force policy, enabling army-support circles including von Richthofen to gain ascendancy in matters affecting equipment and employment of the air force.

A glance at the organizational difference between the Luftwaffe and the RAF in 1940 underlines the conflicting approach of opponents to air power. Whereas the RAF was split between functional commands, Fighter Command, Bomber Command, etc., and subsequently a Tactical Airforce Command, the Luftwaffe was divided territorially into operational commands headed by air fleets (Luftflotten). By 1938 three air fleets were spread across Germany: 1, Berlin; 2, Brunswick; 3, Munich, while a fourth with headquarters in Vienna following the incorporation of the Sudetenland and Austria into the Third Reich was added in March 1939. Three more air fleets appeared in the Luftwaffe's order of battle as the war spread across Europe: 5, Christiansand embracing Scandinavia; 6, Brest-Litovsk Eastern Front (Centre); and Luftflotte Reich, Germany after December 1943. Operational areas and headquarter locations of these air fleets varied with time and in accordance with military needs. Air formations (Fliegertruppen) allotted to air fleets were organized into air corps (Flieger Korps) by expansion of air divisions, Geschwader (Groups), Gruppen (Wings) and Staffeln (squadrons). The building-block of Luftwaffe strength – three to a Group – was the wing of three squadrons; each consisting of 9–12 similar types of aircraft. An air corps, on the other hand, was a composite command, allocated a geographical area within which it would support the army for specific operations, or for the whole or part of a campaign, with a varying number of bomber, dive-bomber, ground-attack, fighter and reconnaissance wings.

Battle groups (Gefechtsverbandes) organized for limited operations were also formed by air corps and others. Such short-term groupings of fighter or ground-attack units appeared during the Battle of France, in North Africa and subsequently in Russia, notably at Bryansk and Orel (*see* page 153). This was the organizational basis upon which the Luftwaffe founded its strike force. Excluded from the common framework until 1942 were air force 'H' and 'F' reconnaissance units supervised by Koluft. Flak too, when placed under army control, was nominally responsible to Koluft, but in practice mobile anti-aircraft units were left to determine their own course of action in conjunction with superior army formation headquarters. Motorized flak units – corps, divisions and regiments accompanying the army proved formidable adversaries. In action against ground and air targets in the course of mobile battles, for example, I Flak Corps/Panzer Group Guderian or II Flak Corps/Panzer Group von Kleist, June 1941, destroyed aircraft, concrete bunkers and armoured vehicles alike; all falling easy prey to 8.8cm mobile (towed) Flak. The tally of enemy tanks destroyed by such versatile units frequently exceeded the number of aircraft shot down. During the advance to Voronezh by Fourth Panzer Army (map 10) starting on 28 June 1942, 10th Flak Division reported 50 Russian aircraft and 66 tanks destroyed.

Another area of co-operation serving the army to advantage in 1939–40 was that of fire-support. The shortage of divisional artillery in the panzer division – 36 field and medium guns compared with 48 in an infantry division – and the relatively limited use expected to be made of it in the spearhead of the attack, could only be made good by the Luftwaffe; Stukagruppen in particular.

Luftwaffe inability to withstand long and ruinous campaigns, evident on all fronts by 1944, originated not only in the unprecedented capacity of Anglo-American air forces after 1942 to dominate air battles in general and eradicate key German industries – aircraft manufacture and oil production in particular – but also in the Luftwaffe High Command's (OKL) own shortcomings. Failures in aircraft replacement programmes by way of mishandled procurement, poor Intelligence about Allied (especially Russian) strength and production resources, but above all an Air Staff failure to convince the Supreme Command (OKW) – an army dominated directorate – of the need to allocate to the Luftwaffe resources consistent with the demands of air supremacy were root causes of defeat, leading in turn to the

Below: With the Ju 87 proving slow and vulnerable in battle by 1940, Stukagruppen demanded new equipment and the Fw 190 was eventually settled upon as a replacement. Fast and efficient though they were, the new attack machines nevertheless failed to materialize in the numbers that panzer divisions had expected.

army's failure. Add to this catalogue of misdemeanours Hitler's scorn for Reichsmarschall Goering as Commander-in-Chief of the Luftwaffe when 'Barbarossa' failed in December 1941, and his wavering control of Wehrmacht priorities – depressing Luftwaffe material and labour requirements into fifth place in September 1940 and second place to the army in January 1942 – and there emerges the formula for a catastrophic prosecution of the war. A formula for self-destruction was compounded by the narrowness of the nation's industrial base – one wholly incapable of sustaining growth in overlapping rearmament programmes upon which three competing services were totally dependent. For air staffs contemplating re-equipment programmes at any time in the war, the outlook was indeed bleak, but, given the prodigious efforts of a new armaments minister (Albert Speer), not entirely without high spots.

2. Stukagruppen-Schlachtgruppen

Swift action by ground and air forces acting jointly against centres of resistance was crucial to the success of panzer operations when tank thrusts were halted or in danger of delay. Yet despite appearances to the contrary fostered by swift and obviously successful military campaigns in Poland and France, Luftwaffe ground-attack responsibilities were surprisingly divided. Whereas Ju 87s entering service with dive-bomber Wings (Stukagruppen) from 1936 onwards were responsible to the bombing arm of the Luftwaffe, other types, particularly the Hs 123 and successors such as the Me 109, Me 110 and Hs 129, were formed into ground-attack Wings (Schlachtgruppen) answerable to the fighter arm. The result of this dichotomy was Luftwaffe failure to meet the challenge of expanding commitments. Training went unco-ordinated and technical developments upon which future potency depended remained at a low ebb. Not until 1943 – and then too late – did Air Staff appreciate the overriding importance of uniting Stukagruppen and Schlachtgruppen into a single ground-attack arm under a General of Ground Attack Flying. The mainstay of ground-attack operations in the early campaigns was the Ju 87 – organized into nine Wings (Gruppen). In Poland these Wings were more frequently engaged on Luftwaffe than army business. That is to say, Stuka targets were mostly short-range and 'strategic', aimed at winning air superiority for the Luftwaffe – by destroying opposition on the ground – leaving only a single Schlachtgruppe II/LG2 flying Hs 123s and performing more or less exclusive army tasks under Fliegerführer zbV (von Richthofen). Theoretically the Stukagruppen were answerable to von Richthofen for both army and Luftwaffe work, but in practice the prior needs of the Luftwaffe were answered before assistance was given to panzer divisions.

Introduced in 1936 as a dive-bomber, the elderly but robust Hs 123.A-1 biplane used for ground-strafing was armed with two 7.92mm machine-guns positioned ahead of the pilot. The Hs 123 could also deliver a single 500lb bomb from a centre-line rack beneath the fuselage. A more useful B variant was introduced in 1941 intended for action against enemy armour. Armed with two 20mm cannon, this version flew with a modified bomb-load. The Ju 87B, on the other hand, was capable of delivering twice the high-explosive load of the Henschel – one 1,102 pounder on centre-line and four small 50-pounders on wing racks. In addition to its bomb-load, the early Ju 87 (Stuka) was armed with two 7.9mm machine-guns located in the wing roots. Another (MG15) for defence was operated by the observer/radio operator in the rear cockpit. The D-1 version introduced in 1940 demonstrated a much improved performance with a new engine, better armour protection for the pilot and a greater bomb-load – 3,968lb. This version flew most of the Luftwaffe's ground-attack missions after 1940. A Ju 87 G variant, flying in 1943 with two 3.7cm cannon, was to win fame as a tank-buster, but this development explored later was limited by obsolescence to Eastern Front operations (*see* anti-tank operations, page 124).

In so far as the future of the dive-bomber was concerned, the Luftwaffe's early model, the Henschel Hs 123, relegated to ground-attack duties after a disappointing performance in the role in Spain, would remain in production until 1942. The Ju 87, by contrast, would maintain a continuous if at times precarious level of production until 1944, by which time some 5,000 various marks would have entered service with Stukagruppen and Schlachtgruppen.

In conditions of air supremacy achieved by the Luftwaffe at no great cost in Poland, France, the Balkans and, at first, in Russia, the Luftwaffe's machines and its highly trained personnel and organization performed well enough. Enjoying the benefits of pre-war planning and progress, particularly in army co-operation, the Luftwaffe created a strike force of immense power demonstrating its prowess in a spectacular run of victories. Opponents in Poland and France were surprised and overwhelmed by the combined efforts of army groups and air fleets. After the fall of France the Luftwaffe reigned supreme on the continent in 1940, but in the high summer of that year as the air war developed over Britain the fortunes of the Luftwaffe suffered a dramatic change. In operations clearing the way for 'Sealion' – bringing Stukas and their fighter escorts into conflict with the RAF – the Luftwaffe was outclassed, driven from the sky by resolutely handled Spitfires and Hurricanes.

Despite dedicated flying by experienced crews determined to press home pin-point attacks against RAF ground targets, the Stukagruppen concentrated under von Richthofen – VIII Air Corps/3rd Air Fleet (Sperrie); or Lörzer – II Air Corps/2nd Air Fleet (Kesselring) were outmanoeuvred and after suffering unacceptable losses withdrew from the conflict.

When VIII Air Corps entered the Balkans supporting von Kleist, von Richthofen's Stukagruppen and Schlachtgruppen were in no way stretched. Little or no interference being suffered from Greek or Yugoslav air forces chased off by the Luftwaffe (map 6). But when the Stukas joined in new offensives launched by Hitler in Africa and on the Eastern Front (maps 5 and 7) the situation again changed dramatically for the worse. So inadequate was the Luftwaffe in the face of its old adversary the RAF and in due course new opponents like the Red Air Force – struggling to win time and recover from invasion – or the USAF that it was

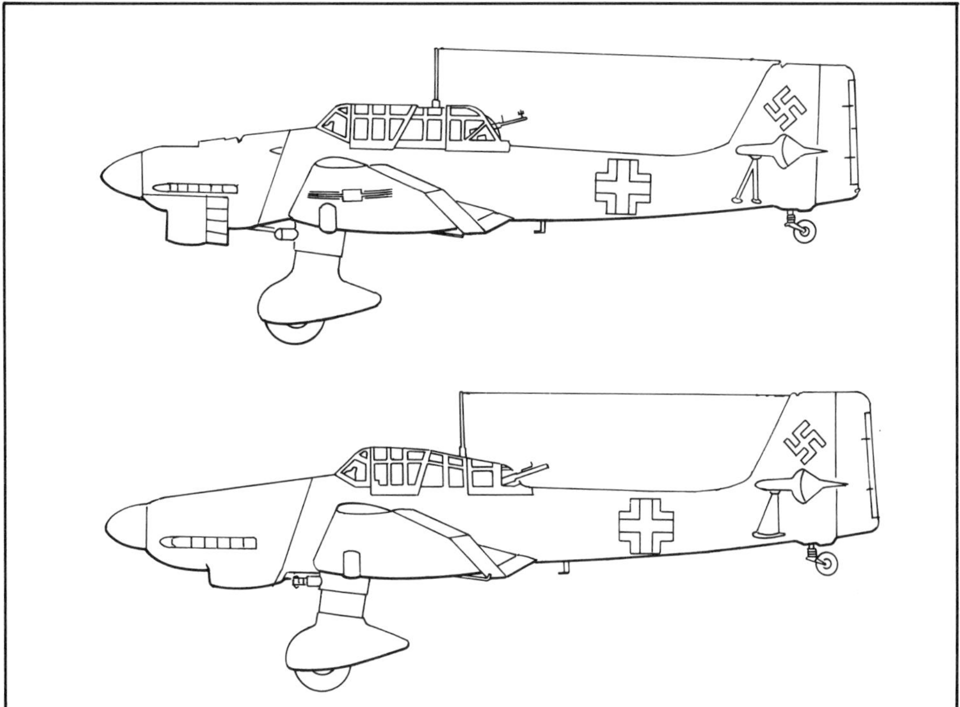

Right: The Ju 87B-2 was a two-seat dive-bomber armed with two 7.92mm MG17 machine-guns in the wings and one 7.92mm MG in the rear cockpit. It carried a bomb-load of one 1,102lb (500kg) bomb on the centreline and four 110lb (50kg) bombs on the wing racks. It had a speed of 242mph and a range of 373 miles.

Right: The Ju 87B D-1 improvement on the B-2 had twin 7.92mm MG81 machine-guns in the rear cockpit. The bomb-load increased to 3,968lb (1,800kg), speed to 252mph and range to 620 miles. Later versions were armed with two 20mm MG151/20 wing cannon.

to meet in action in North Africa, the Ju 87s could operate only with a strong fighter escort. In Tunisia in 1942–3, for instance, a squadron of 8–12 Ju 87s needed the protection of up to 30 Me 109s if it were to perform effectively. In Russia, at a time when the Red Air Force was relatively unprepared for invasion, the Stukas recorded better results; but the days of overwhelming support for the army in conditions of Luftwaffe superiority were drawing to a close. Few suitable replacements were on hand to assist the rebuilding of depleted Stukagruppen. The Fw 189 (Owl), having failed to measure up to Luftwaffe ground-attack requirements, had been diverted to air reconnaissance work (*see* page 134), other projects were late (Ju 87 D-G), abandoned (Me 210) or still on the drawing-board (Me 410). In this situation the Air Staff turned to ideas of employing fighters as fighter-bombers ('Jabos').

During the Battle of Britain and afterwards in the Balkans and North Africa, before the war turned east, the Me 109E flying with fighter Wings (Jagdgruppen) attacked RAF ground installations with 500lb high-explosive bombs.

The Me 110C, a 'heavy' twin-engined fighter flying in support of the Me 109 and deployed in destroyer Wings (Zerstörergruppen), could deliver twice that explosive load, while the much superior Fw 190, a fighter by design, but developed in G and F series as a ground-attack fighter-bomber, could unleash a devastating 3,968lb of high-explosives. Capable of speeds up to 400 miles per hour, the Fw 190 was eventually decided upoon as the ground-attack successor for the Luftwaffe's ageing fleet of Ju 87Bs – limited by engine performance to 255mph. Notwithstanding the remarkable capacity of one Fw 190 variant to obliterate any target with a massive weight of high explosives, the standard bomb-load of this, the Luftwaffe's best all-round tactical aircraft of the war, was to settle into a combination of one 500lb and four small 100lb, SC 50 bombs. Alternatively, the Fw 190 could operate with two 3cm anti-tank cannon (BK103) modifying a bomb-load supplemented by two 7.9mm machine-guns (MG17). In fact, no fewer than forty bomb, cannon and machine-gun alternatives were devised for the Fw 190 in close-support work. Production, including a late F9 variant armed with 8.8cm rocket-projectiles, continued until May 1945. The rockets were used to better effect against air targets than in operations against tanks where their effectiveness was much less a matter of note.

Somewhat less commendable than the Air Staff decision to replace its Ju 87s with new Fw 190s was a lack of motivation in developing tank-busting aircraft of the kind entering service with foreign air forces. In 1942, when the Red Air Force introduced the Bell P-39 Airacobra into its operations on the Eastern Front, and the new Ilyushin Il-2m3 Shturmovik appeared over the battlefield in droves, much to the consternation of the German Army, the Luftwaffe faced another unwelcome challenge to its authority. Received under a lend-lease arrangement with the USA, the P-39's principal armament was a reasonably powerful but low-velocity – later improved – 3.7cm cannon firing through the hub of the propeller. In its improved version, the Airacobra was to prove effective against all but the most heavily armoured ground targets; its speed of 360–376mph placing it in the fighter class. The Bell's Soviet-designed companion was a heavily armoured ground-attack (Shturmovik) Ilyushin (Il-2m3) equipped with two high-velocity 23mm cannon or any of several weapon packages. In the role of tank-buster, the Shturmovik proved superior to both the P-39 and Hs 123. In action against panzer columns, P-39s and Shturmoviks quickly made their mark. Flown by pilots whose skill and

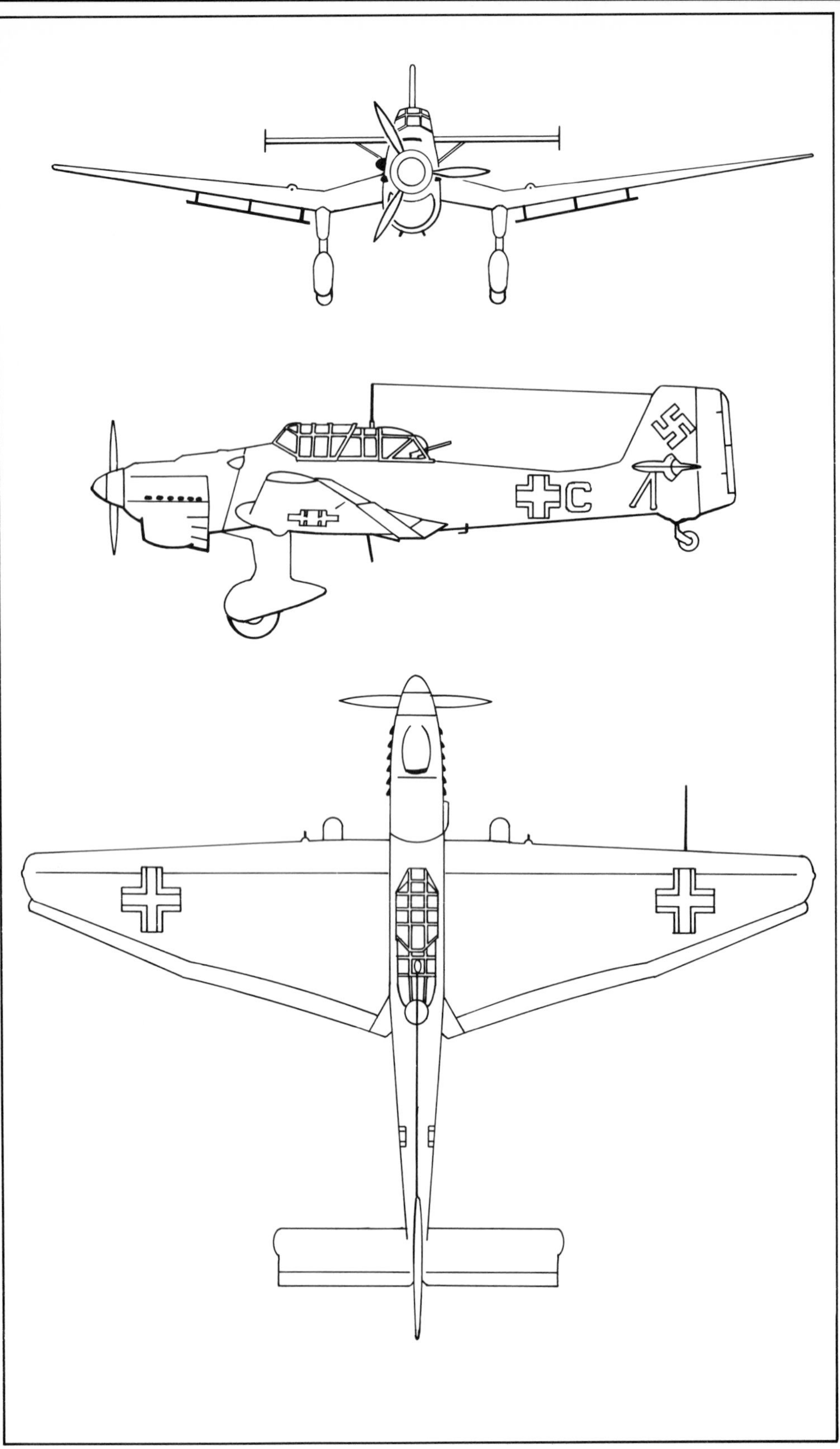

Left: A Ju 87-B1 three-view arrangement of the Luftwaffe's most famous and distinctive gull-winged dive-bomber. The term Stuka was dropped in 1943 in favour of Schlacht, meaning battle or ground-attack aircraft.

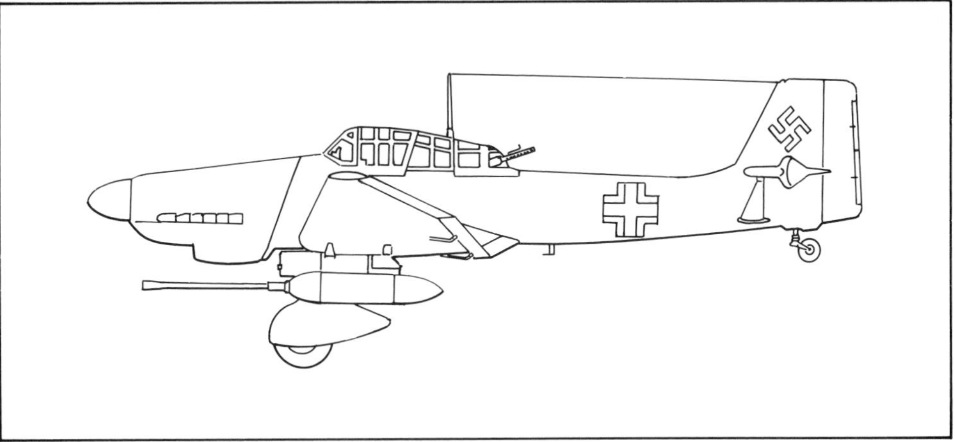

Right: The Ju 87-G tank-busting version of the Stuka was introduced into limited service in 1943. It was armed with two 3.7cm BK (Flak 18 or 36) cannon, or later six MG81 machine-guns, in underwing pods. The speed and range were significantly reduced by drag, but Hauptmann Rudel of Schlachtgeschwader 2 flew the Ju 87-G with enormous anti-tank success.

resolve matched their German opponents, the Bells and Ilyushins supported by one or two other close-support types raised the stakes in the air war. Luftwaffe response was to hinge on the new, heavily armoured twin-engined Henschel Hs 129B2 whose main armament consisted of one 3cm (ultimately 3.7cm) Mk 103 anti-tank cannon with two 7.9mm machine-guns; 841 Henschels of this type were built for service with the Luftwaffe. Experiments were also set in train to adapt the ubiquitous Ju 87 to a tank-busting role – armed with two 3.7cm Flak mounted in underwing fairings. When flown by Hauptmann Rudel, whose exploits in ground-attack are touched upon later, the G variant of the Stuka – despite a lack of aerodynamic finesse – was to become a renowned but largely illusory symbol of Luftwaffe power.

In the spring of 1942 with the Luftwaffe expanding its ground attack forces, in anticipation of Operation 'Blue/Brunswick' (map 10), II/LG2, the veteran army support wing of operations in Poland, France and the Balkans, was incorporated as II Gruppe in Shlachtgeschwader I. A second Schlachtgeschwader, SchG 2, was formed out of Stukageschwader 2 later in the year; neither formation being more than two Wings strong.

These Schlachtgeschwader supported by twelve to fifteen Stukagruppen equipped with the surviving Ju 87Bs and Ds, and various marks of Me 109, Fw 190 and Hs 129, were eventually to stage a qualified return to effective Luftwaffe ground-attack flying on the Eastern Front. The flare-up followed a period of Luftwaffe eclipse during which time the Red Air Force, drastically improved in numbers and equipment, dominated the Eastern Front. On the German side the ground-attack units that had accompanied the army into Belorussia, serving in offensives against Leningrad and Moscow and before supporting Eleventh Army in the Crimea, were more often than not concentrated at the point of attack under VIII Air Corps (von Richthofen). Progress, however, was rarely spectacular and when VIII Air Corps reached Stalingrad (map 12) the fiasco there was somewhat less than a triumph. But in two subsequent operations during and after 'Citadel' at Bjelgorod and Bryansk in 1943, the ground-attack Wings performed in worthy fashion; operations in which VIII Air Corps, subordinated to von Richthofen's 4th Air Fleet, played a key role. However, far from heralding a return to power of a pre-eminent Luftwaffe enjoying much improved equipment – welcome as this was to Stukagruppen and Schlachtgruppen starved of equipment and resources in 1941–2 – the new aircraft at the centre of operations served more to swell Luftwaffe pride than generate power at the heart of a reinvigorated air force. In this respect, army expectations of Luftwaffe battlefield support matching its own expanding commitments were to prove unfounded. In action against tank forces of much superior strength on at least two of its many fronts in 1944–5, but unprotected from opponents enjoying infinite

Right: The Hs 129 single-seat ground-attack fighter was usually armed with a 3cm MK101 canon, but other versions carried four MG17s, 551lb of bombs or a BK 3.7cm gun. An experimental model was provided with a 7.5cm gun, the muzzle of which projected eight feet in front of the aircraft! The versions depicted here and overleaf had a maximum speed of approximately 250mph. Hauptmann Bruno Meyer earned distinction with the Hs 129 in action with IV/SG9 against Russian armour at Kursk.

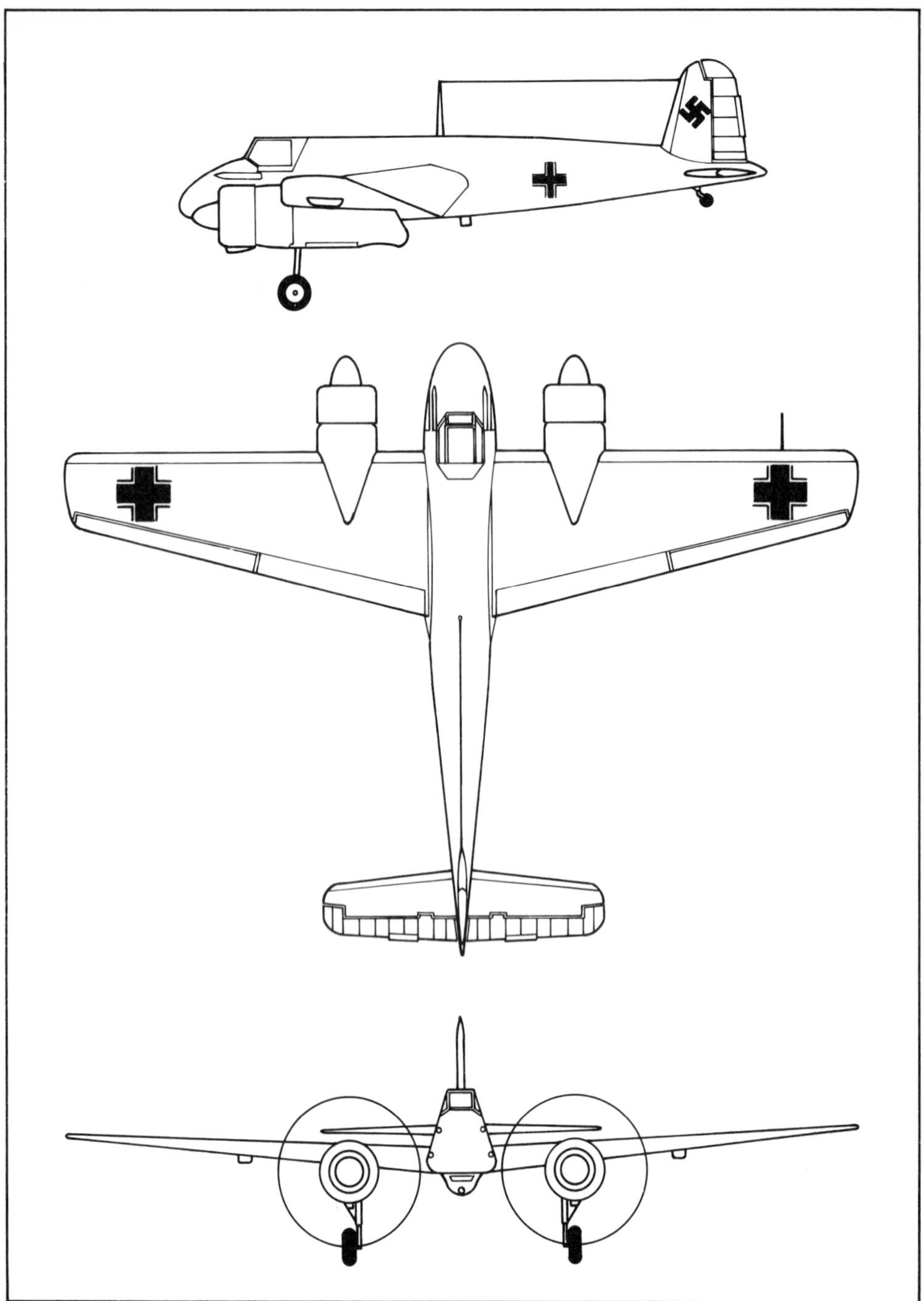

Left: The Hs 129 ground-attack fighter.

resources, the German Army would collapse; the panzer divisions unable to contend with modern air power simply melting away.

Consider the Luftwaffe's unexceptional progress in anti-tank warfare. Until September 1943, when close-support operations were completely reorganized under a General of Ground Attack Flying, Hs 129s served only in (panzer) squadrons numbered 4 and 8 in Schlachtgeschwadern SG1 and SG2. Each of these under-strength Geschwader, equivalent to an RAF Group (USAF Wing), comprised two instead of the normal three Wings (gruppen) although each consisted of four staffeln (squadrons). A fifth Panzerjaeger squadron operated with JG51. The first of these Panzerjaeger panzer squadrons – 4 and 8 SG1 – made their début on the central front in the summer of 1942, flying with VIII Air Corps/4th Air Fleet in operations against Voronezh (map 10). On this front they demonstrated a marked advantage over other types when attacking Soviet armour.

On the other hand, 4 (Pz) SG2, operating in North Africa during November 1942, served unremarkably with engine trouble plaguing operations. Thereafter ground-attack operations in Tunisia, where Fifth Panzer Army Africa faced the prospect of early defeat, was left to 8 (Pz) SG2, the Jabos of two Zerstörergruppen and Stukas of two other depleted units assembled under Stukageschwader 3.

At this point, in the spring of 1943, service trials at Rechlin and Bryansk under the supervision of Oberst Otto Weiss were devoted to testing the effectiveness of a variety of aircraft and weapons paired in anti-tank combinations. The Sonderkommando für Panzerbekâmpfung (Stepp) formed specially for the purpose by the air staff, was responsible for the field trials and, when a crisis developed in the Kuban during February and March 1943, a certain amount of operational flying. Air battles in this region of Russia, where 4th Air Fleet was engaged, brought test units and all five Hs 129 squadrons into action, before Stepp rejoined SG2. The best of the aircraft/weapon pairings tried out by the Sonderkommando were the Ju 87G, fitted with two 3.7cm anti-aircraft guns, and the Hs 129, tried out with a similar heavy-calibre weapon. Both Junkers and Henschel types were favoured as 'standard issue' to future panzer-jaeger squadrons, but the production capacity of the Luftwaffe being what it was in 1943, despite prodigious efforts by Armaments Minister Speer too few entered service. Other aircraft/weapon pairings included the Ju 88 (P-1) fitted with a 7.5cm anti-tank gun (PaK 40) which proved impracticable, and the Me 110, also fitted beneath the fuselage with a 3.7cm PaK, but which could not be spared from fighter production.

The saga of Luftwaffe anti-tank operations continued in 1943 with preparations for 'Citadel' (map 14), the battle in which Panzerjaeger were to make a distinguished contribution to an otherwise disastrous undertaking. Thereafter in a reorganizational sequel to 'Citadel', panzerjaeger would be re-grouped and all five panzer squadrons concentrated in IV/SG9 (Meyer). Only one other Wing was raised for inclusion in this formation. Furthermore, the few Ju 87Gs becoming available for service were distributed as a 10th squadron to four of the six Schlachtgeschwader created during the course of reorganization; the selected Geschwader being SG1, 2, 3 and 77; those not so fortunate, SG4 and SG10. This was the organizational tally of Luftwaffe progress in anti-tank operations.

After the spring of 1943 when the war against the Soviet Union resumed in earnest after the fall of Stalingrad (map 12) – a period of operations during the winter of 1942 in which any number of reserve and training aircraft had to be brought forward to sustain Luftwaffe front-line strength – ground-attack operations were to reveal a more revolutionary dimension of battlefield support. Equipped with new and improved aircraft types – the Fw 190, Ju 87D and Hs 129 – yet still requiring the veteran Hs 123 to make good their strength, Schlachtgruppen and Stukagruppen gave new tactical meaning to the notion of flexible response in a crisis. The recovery of Kharkov by 4th Air Fleet and Army Group South in March 1943 (map 13) illustrates the point to advantage; in this action the all-important air support arrangements leading to a re-enactment of *Blitzkrieg* were the responsbility of von Richthofen. No Luftwaffe commander possessed his experience in directing ground-attack operations. From the time of the Spanish Civil War onwards, von Richthofen's service career had been devoted almost exclusively to this area of flying. Under his tutelage, VIII Air Corps had been deployed at the point of attack in Poland, France, the Balkans, at Leningrad, Moscow, Voronezh and Stalingrad, evolving as the prime command for this form of warfare. However, the exigencies of the military situation being what they were at Stalingrad and then in the Kuban, VIII Air Corps was temporarily employed there as a transport command; notwithstanding which von Richthofen initiated a series of judicious moves to provide the best possible support for von Manstein preparing a counter-stroke against an over-extended Red Army pressing west from Stalingrad.

Re-grouping 4th Air Fleet, but excluding VIII Air Corps (IV Air Corps was used instead), von Richthofen created anew the condition for success that had eluded the Wehrmacht since the Battle of France (map 4). Concentrating close-support units in the shape of two air corps: I (Korten) at Poltava; IV (Pflugbeil) at Dnepropetrovsk; and an *ad hoc* Fliegerdivision Donets (Mahnke) at Stalino for the benefit of von Manstein's armies and Armeeabteilung Kempf (map 13), von Richthofen retained the air fleet's long-range bombers under personal command. On hand at headquarters with advice for von Richthofen if required was Oberst Weiss, the Panzerjaegerführer guiding trials of the anti-tank units assembled at Bryansk. The (proto)types available for action included the Ju 88-C (P) armed with a 7.5cm cannon. This unsatisfactory fighter-bomber was eventually discarded, but not before making something of a name for itself as a railway (Eisenbahn)-buster. The key to von Richthofen's close-support success is to be seen in its most advanced form in the recovery of Kharkov. Two aspects invite comment: concentration and flexibility. In the first place concentration was achieved by making dispositions that embraced every available aircraft; all being pressed into tactical service including his own long-range bombers. Secondly, flexibility was achieved by a policy of switching the main effort from one air corps to another in accordance with von Richthofen and von Manstein's reading of the tactical situation. The creation of *ad hoc* battlefield support groups, remarkably effective at Bjelgorod and Bryansk during 'Citadel' – the sequel to von Richthofen's battles for Kharkov, was to prove a significant factor in local success. With von Richthofen's full support for von Manstein, Kharkov was recovered and Russian spearheads destroyed.

One other praiseworthy contribution that von Richthofen made to the consolidation of army-air operations was the Panzerverbindungsoffizier or Stukaleiter (Stuka controller). By using a two-way (R/T) link making contact with battle groups flying temporarily under his control, the Stukaleiter allotted to a panzer regiment was able to direct or redirect Stukas to opportunity targets, theoretically ensuring their profitable employment. This concept of creating radio links between tanks and aircraft evolved out of von Richthofen's experience in the Spanish Civil War when he allocated forward observers to ground troops, linking them by wireless to their air force headquarters. By 1940 the arrangements had changed; a panzer commander needing air support notified an air liaison officer (Fliegerverbindungsoffizier – Flivo) serving divisional headquarters. Flivo in turn contacted the division's appointed close-support group commander who arranged the required sortie. In 1941 a more effective method of consolidating ground and air forces was developed within VIII Air Corps (von Richthofen) when an experienced Stuka pilot was appointed regimental tank liaison officer (Panzerverbindungsoffizier). He was allocated a Pz Kpfw III tank in which was installed Luftwaffe radio equipment (Fluggerate VII) capable of communicating directly with the Stukas. When they appeared overhead the controller took complete charge of the sortie, giving advice on approach, method of attack and confirming the target, which, more often than not, he was able to observe at close range; at times uncomfortably close. The Stukaleiter was not a Flivo and rarely usurped that officer's function at division or higher headquarters; liaison between army and Luftwaffe at these levels continuing unchanged.

British Intelligence, reporting the interrogation of a Stukaleiter from 7th Panzer Regiment, 10th Panzer Division, appointed by 5/StukaGeschwader 3 in Tunis, does so in the following terms:

'Medjez el Bab, 10th December 1942. On this the first day of the liaison officer's appointment, there was no activity on account of the unsuitable weather but on 11th December a conference was held in Tunis at the HQ of Generalmajor Harlinghausen (Fliegerführer Tunisia), attended by the panzer commander and commanders of the air formations.'

'It was decided to attack Medjez el Bab and the Stukas were given three targets which they were to destroy; one a battery, another an Allied tank concentration on the road, and a third a bridge at or near Medjez.'

'The liaison officer joined the tanks early morning and commenced by transmitting a weather report to the Fliegerführer. There was 5/10th cloud at 800 metres which was considered favourable for a Stuka attack.'

'When the attack was due to commence it was found that the battery had already moved, and the liaison officer therefore directed the Stukas to the Allied tank formations. He took up a point of vantage on a hill nearby where he could view the whole operation and sat on top of the tank to obtain a better view.'

'The Stukas arrived on the scene and were duly directed to their target, but dropped their bombs some 300 yards ahead of the tanks.'

Before considering developments in close-support at Bjelgorod and Bryansk during and after 'Citadel' in August 1943 – where Schlachtgruppen demonstrated a remarkable propensity for breaking up dangerous Russian counter-offensives – this change of emphasis in ground-attack operations is worth noting as a new and powerful contribution to the defensive resources of the Wehrmacht.

Launching Stuka and panzerjaeger attacks at short notice against Russian armour, the Luftwaffe would strike effective, if somewhat limited, blows – substituting for non-existent army group reserves. Successful actions of the kind to be witnessed at Bjelgorod and Bryansk, where von Manstein and Model faced grave problems with no reserves, were to become all too necessary as the war entered a critical phase and air corps at danger points were required to execute ground-attack operations – albeit on a diminishing scale – to protect armies facing crises on widely separated fronts. Consider the itinerary of Schlachtgeschwader 2 (Rudel) over a period of twenty months from September 1943 to May 1945. During this time, SG 2 flew ground-attack missions in the Ukraine, Roumania, Poland, East Prussia and Courland. After returning to Roumania, SG 2 moved to Hungary, Silesia and Pomerania, subsequently defending Berlin itself on the Oder at Küstrin. Only the American bombing of Czech airfields in support of the Red Army, brought the odyssey of SG 2 to a close, destroying most of III/SG2, the Geschwader's best equipped and most celebrated unit at Kletzen. From this secondary airfield north of Prague the 'Immelmanner' (as the personnel of this Geschwader were known in tribute to the 1914–18 air ace) flew their last Ju 87G and Fw 190 missions in aid of Army Group Schörner.

Close-support provided by the Luftwaffe for the armies at Bjelgorod and Bryansk during 'Citadel' (map 14) marked a significant development in ground-attack operations. From aircraft operating in small numbers against tanks, more or less at random during early campaigns, their employment developed to the stage where they were used *en masse* as a decisive weapon with which to counter superior enemy ground forces. In the first instance, at Bjelgorod, the panzerjaeger element of various geschwader subordinate to VIII Air Corps (Siedeman) flying with 1st Fleet/Army Group South, were committed in a powerful and remarkably effective *ad hoc* battle formation to destroy an opportunity target. Panzerjagdverband Meyer (so named after Hauptman Bruno Meyer) under whose command were 4 (Pz), 8 (Pz) SG1 and 4 (Pz), 8 (Pz) SG2, represented the most powerful concentration of anti-tank aircraft available to the Luftwaffe on the Eastern Front. The situation that Meyer turned to advantage arose out of the failure of III Panzer Corps to close up and protect the open flank of II SS Panzer Corps leading the Kursk offensive north of Bjelgorod; (Fourth Panzer Army, July 1943). Patrolling ahead of SS Liebstandarte, Meyer detected the presence of a Russian armoured brigade, raised the alarm and in an hour long engagement left fifty Russian tanks crippled or destroyed on the battlefield; the SS divisions were able to regroup and, under intensive pressure from Shturmoviks newly provided with 3.7cm cannon, eventually withdrew to their start-line. The subsequent retreat from Kursk was to lead within days to the second notable example of this form of anti-tank support for the army; this time, on 19 July, when at a point on Second Panzer Army's front a Russian penetration of the main battle line north of Bryansk threatened to split Army Group Centre. The German response was to assemble all available panzerjaeger and Schlacht units into Gefechtsverband Kupfer, a battle group responsible to the commanding officer of SG2 (Kupfer), comprising his own Ju 87G/Fw 190s and Meyer's Hs 129s. Co-operating with bomber and fighter units stripped from other sectors to reinforce 6th Air Fleet (Greim) in what is now recognized as the last significant concentration of Luftwaffe strength in the east, Kupfer's anti-tank group launched blistering attacks against Russian tank thrusts. Targeting T34s and KVs (I and II) with 3cm and 3.7cm cannon-fire, or dispersing supporting infantry with fragmentation clusters and high-explosives, Kupfer's combined force of Stukas, panzer-knackers and protective fighters played the key role in eliminating a dangerous and unexpected threat to Army Group Centre.

But these Panzerjagd and Schlacht units operating under Meyer and Kupfer, whatever their success in defeating Russian intentions at Bjelgorod and Bryansk, represented a waning fraction of declining Luftwaffe effort. In the wider

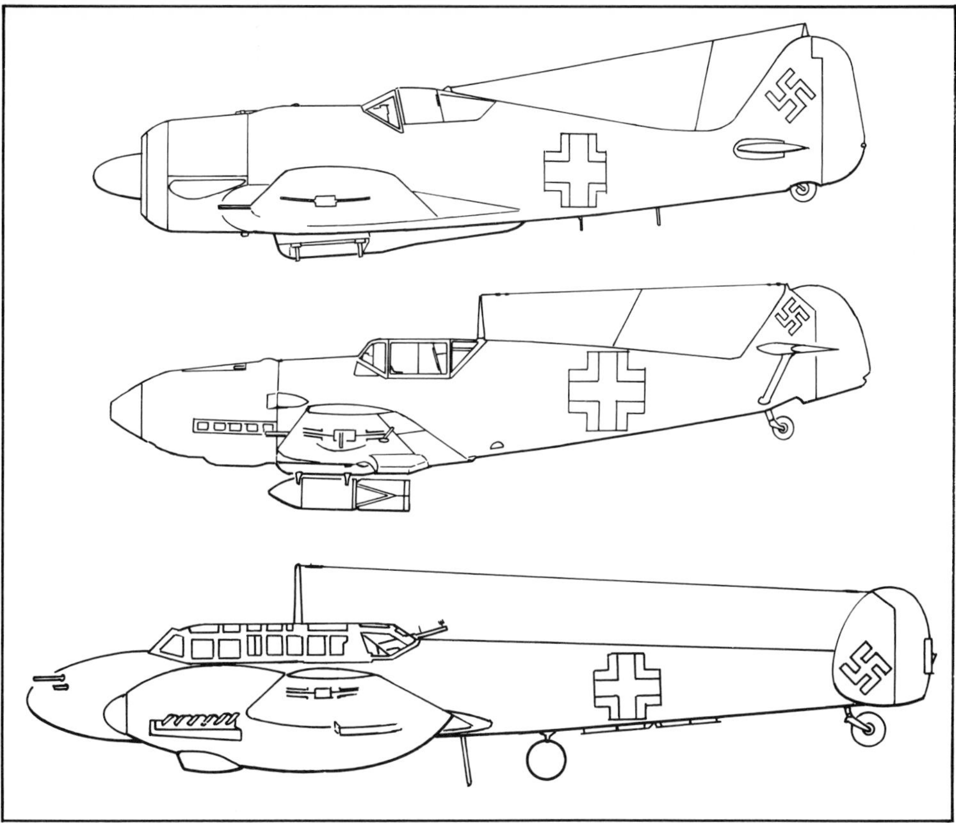

Right: The Fw 190A-7 single-seat fighter-bomber. It was armed with two 13mm MG131 above the engine, two 20mm MG151/20s in the wing roots and two 30mm cannon in the outer wings. The bomb-load was one 1,100lb (500kg) on the centreline, though other weapons packages were possible. It had a speed of 408–440mph and a range of 560 miles.

Right: With the Ju 87's poor performance highlighting the need for better equipment, especially for the Stuka units involved in the Battle of Britain in 1940, fighter types were pressed into service as fighter-bombers. One of the most prominent of those engaged in such missions was the Bf 109E-3B which carried a single 500lb or a greater number of smaller high-explosive bombs. Machine-guns and cannon supplemented the Messerschmitt's bomb-load which was curtailed in weight by a narrow undercarriage.

Right: The Bf 110-F twin-engined two-seat heavy fighter was another of the types which undertook ground-attack missions prior to the arrival in service of the Fw 190. Armament consisted of: one 1,000lb bomb on centreline (later versions with improved engine performance were able to carry two); two 20mm cannon and four 7.92 MG17 machine-guns fixed firing forward in the nose.

sphere of operations nothing could conceal Luftwaffe inferiority. Following a disastrous outcome to the war in Tunisia for which, in Hitler's eyes, the Luftwaffe was much to blame, and mounting evidence of Luftwaffe inability to protect the war economy or German cities – Hamburg alone suffering 50,000 casualties and almost ceasing to exist when attacked by RAF Bomber Command, 25 July–3 August 1943 – Hitler demanded changes. In this the Führer's judgement was correct; Goering's Luftwaffe on evidence accumulating from Russia and Tunisia was a declining asset – viewed either as an adjunct to land warfare or as protector of the Reich – nowhere capable of winning decisive superiority. Neither in the scale of its aid to army groups taking punishment in the east where Russian pressure was driving von Manstein back across the Don and Donetz to the Dnieper (map 15) – or defending Germany against increasingly powerful attacks on its cities and most sensitive economic targets, was the Luftwaffe living up to expectation. Industries of crucial importance to the war economy and Luftwaffe survival in particular – aircraft construction and oil production – topped Anglo-American target programmes. Streams of RAF and US (8th Air Force) bombers, flying unchallenged over Germany, were daily bringing destruction to the core of the Luftwaffe; attacking Junkers, Messerschmitt and Focke-Wulf plants in particular.

Hitler's reaction to so many Luftwaffe 'failures' dating back to the Battle of Britain now surfaced in command changes. Two dates point indirectly to progress in close-support flying. On 18 August 1943 the Chief of Air Staff was 'sacked' – permitted no option but to commit suicide. Jeschonnek's death was announced to the world as 'a consequence of chronic illness'. On 25 August 1943 his successor as Chief of Air Staff was named as Generaloberst Günther Korten. Elevated from command of 1st Air Fleet, Korten selected General Karl Koller as his chief of operations staff. Koller at the time was serving as Chief of Staff to Generaloberst Sperrle, 3rd Air Fleet, Paris. Unfortunately for Korten he was to be present in Rastenburg eleven months later to take the full blast of von Stauffenberg's briefcase bomb intended for Hitler; his successor, General Werner Kreipe, lasted only four months in office until Koller became Chief of Air Staff. Neither Korten nor Koller wasted time in reversing an air force policy that had maximized support for the army. Their new watchword was 'Reich defence' and Korten and Koller proceeded to create a fighter force for the defence of the homeland – at the expense of fighter protection for ground-attack Wings elsewhere. Air staff instructed to re-cast aircraft production priorities and to review training arrangements while also withdrawing fighters from the east, left Schlachtgeschwader under-equipped and painfully exposed.

On the other hand, in the course of re-appraising the responsibilities of his Inspectors, the Waffengenerale of various arms of the service, Korten provided for the appointment of a General of Ground Attack Flying. Oberstleutnant Dr Kupfer was promoted from command of the 'Immelman' Geschwader (SG2) and nominated for the new post with responsibility for uniting both Stukagruppen and Schlachtgruppen under a single authority. Henceforth Stukagruppen and Schlachtgruppen would be known only as Schlachtgruppen, abbreviated SG. More significantly, the process of converting Ju 87 squadrons to Fw 190s would be accorded greater momentum. The new chief of ground-attack flying was a veteran of Eastern Front operations. With more than 600 sorties to his credit, like his more famous subordinate, Hauptmann Hans 'Ulli' Rudel – Staffelkapitän, I/SG2 (major, March 1944, Oberst, January 1945) a pioneer of anti-tank operations and a future Geschwaderkommodore – Kupfer was proud of his distinguished war record. But whereas Rudel had the good fortune to survive innumerable crashes, injuries and forays to rescue shot-down colleagues, continuing to fly until May 1945, Kupfer within days of his appointment was posted missing in action on 6 November. A new 'Chief' was appointed; another Eastern Front veteran, Oberst Hitschold. Commended in May 1942 for distinguished service – leading 1/StG2 in operations to sink the destroyers *Kelly* and *Kashmir* in the battle for Crete and again in action defending Morovskaya at a crucial moment in the battle for Stalingrad in December 1942 (map 12) – Hitschold was to prove a worthy successor to Kupfer.

Rudel's claim to fame started in September 1941 with the sinking of the 23,600-ton Russian battleship *Marat* in the harbour at Kronstadt during the advance of Army Group North to Leningrad. Thereafter followed three-and-a-half years of distinguished flying on the Eastern Front – rewarded in January 1945 with Golden Oak Leaves to the Swords and Diamonds of his Knight's Cross – a unique decoration awarded to no other member of the Wehrmacht. The name of Ulli Rudel came to be particularly associated with the Ju 87G tank-buster. Flying this improvised panzerjaeger in operational trials with the Versuchskommando in the Kuban during the spring of 1943, and in action during 'Citadel', Rudel, to whom ground-attack flying was second nature, was to prove a master in the art of 'tank-busting'. In the course of 2,530 sorties he was credited with 519 tank kills – equivalent to two full-strength Russian tank corps. The exploits of this most highly decorated of Luftwaffe aces, were widely reported in journals and newsreels; Goebbels' media celebrating in no small measure a rare talent for ground-attack flying. Civilians and services thrilled to accounts of resolute flying, but success was illusionary. Dr Goebbels' outpourings, masked the unpalatable fact that the ground-attack arm was in terminal decline.

Deployed in the summer of 1944 along fronts stretching from Courland to Hungary, across Italy and, after 6 June, also committed to battle in the west, Schlachtgeschwader wherever they were present were fighting to the finish. In action against Russian armour threatening fronts at Husi and Jassy (First Panzer Army, 29 August 1944) – where Rudel flew his 2,000th sortie – or in defence of Kovno, Memel and in a score of other bitter contests where the German Army faced disaster, the indomitable Schlachtflieger and his Gruppe reduced the Red Army offensives to a shambles. But the pace of operations was unsustainable; Germany's ground-attack strength measured in aircraft numbers in the summer of 1944 sank to a level of 1,005 machines whereas, according to Luftwaffe estimates, opponents in the east could put up at least 5,120 and in the west, 7,270 ground-attack aircraft respectively. So, with air war losses escalating uncontrollably – no fewer than 11,074 aircraft (1,345 Schlacht types) being lost during the summer of 1944 and enemy air power destroying the infrastructure of production, there were few highlights to brighten the gloom of an air force degenerating uncontrollably. Up-dated pre-war types, the Ju 87G and the Hs 129B-3 in particular, were still furnishing ground-attack squadrons with a moderately successful generation of improvised tank-busters. Among new fighter-bombers was the Fw 190 'Panzerblitz'. This late 1944 variant of the Luftwaffe's most successful aircraft incorporated experimental anti-tank weaponry in the shape of (eight underwing) 8.8cm rocket-projectiles. There was a new 477mph DO 335 ground-attack type carrying with it a promise of better days; so too did progress in re-equipping Stukagruppen with Fw 190s – displacing Ju 87s for early re-organization into night-attack wings (Nachtschlachtgruppen).

By August 1944 all but four (two converting) of the fifteen or so Stukagruppen taken into the ground-attack arm were flying with a high proportion of F-8 or G-1 ground-attack variants of the Fw 190; most were equipped with auxiliary fuel tanks and a rich variety of weapon loads. The displaced Ju 87s, despite their obsolescence, were scheduled to enjoy a new lease of life in night-attack operations; protected marginally from prying fighters by darkness. Twenty-six squadrons were eventually formed into nine Nachtschlachtgruppen, adding materially to Luftwaffe resources. But these developments linked to improvements in training, navigational aids, weapon loads and battle organization – however welcome – were too few and too late to meet the needs of the army. On fronts collapsing east and west as concentric pressure mounted uncontainably, the effectiveness of combined Army/Luftwaffe operations plunged disastrously.

In mid-summer 1944 when the Red Army, launching its 'Bagration' offensive, sought to eliminate Army Group Centre, (Third Panzer Army, 22 June 1944) 6,000 Russian aircraft (700 long-range bombers) – the strike force of four air armies – were concentrated in support of four Belorussian or Baltic Fronts (2,715 tanks, 1,355 SP guns). From day one of the offensive, Ilyushin I1-2 Shturmoviks with Petlyakov Pe-2 and Yakovlev Yak 9B fighter-bombers descended on Army Group Centre in droves. In *Blitzkrieg* style, the Red Army carried its offensive to Warsaw and East Prussia, ripping a 250-mile gap in Army Group Centre defences.

At the focus of Luftwaffe operations, facing overwhelming odds, stood 6th Air Fleet (Greim) starting with no more than 800 aircraft in its order of battle. Deprived of fighters when Jagdgruppen were diverted to meet the demands of other fronts – including the west – Schlachtgruppen reinforced by SG4 (Italy), where the front was practically stripped of ground-attack units, were left to shoulder a heavy burden of fighting. By October 1944 re-deployment of Schlachtgruppen to the east was absorbing all available units: SG1, 2, 3, 4, 10, 77 and IV/SG9. In the west, where Sperrle's 3rd Air Fleet (HQ, Paris), deployed on the Channel coast against invasion (map 16), was downgraded within weeks to the status of Luftwaffenkommando West (Josef Schmidt), no better prospects lay in store. Anglo-American air power deployed in support of 'Overlord' (map 16) exulted in three tactical air forces in addition to a massive superiority in fighters and bombers. These ground-attack forces consisted of 2nd Tactical Air Force (RAF) deployed in support of the

Anglo–Canadian forces and US 9th Air Force divided between IX TAC (US First Army) and XIX TAC (US Third Army). In excess of 100 ground-attack squadrons (57 US, 51 RAF) equipped with Mustangs, Thunderbolts and rocket-firing Typhoons, also Mosquitoes and Spitfires supplemented by bombers in the Fortress class, shattered all German hopes of halting the Allied drive to the Seine and beyond. German armies in the west, reduced to a pitiful level of Luftwaffe support, were grossly under-resourced.

Generals Eberbach and Hausser, in common with panzer commanders on other fronts, lacked the vital air component needed to win battles – none more so than Panzer Group Eberbach, Fifth Panzer Army (Europe) seeking to counter Patton [D+62] or retreating without air cover [D+72]. At times like these panzer divisions deprived of support at Mortain and Falaise suffered unprecedented reverses. Six months later much the same can be said of operations by von Manteuffel, Fifth Panzer Army (Europe) and Dietrich, Sixth SS Panzer Army in the Ardennes. As soon as weather conditions permitted Anglo-American Air Forces their customary freedom of action the fate of these armies was sealed.

In 'Autumn Mist' (map 17), a single Schlachtgeschwader, SG4, on loan to Luftwaffenkommando West from Greim's 6th Air Fleet, Army Group Centre, deployed on the Vistula in critical battles for Berlin, contributed fewer than one hundred Fw 190s to the offensive. Sharing ground-attack duties with Jagdgruppen diverted from home defence, SG4 made little impression in the battle for the Meuse crossings. And neither were a handful each of Kampf and Nachtschlachtgruppen of much use. The outcome was all too predictable and after participating in 'Bodenplatte', the Luftwaffe's New Year's Day offensive against Anglo-US close support airfields in north-west Europe, SG4 and the Jagdgruppen were hurriedly redeployed east. Serving 6th Air Fleet SG4, like other depleted ground-attack units faced by the Red Air Force, enjoying a superiority of 6:1 in aircraft, contemplated the impossible task of delaying the disintegration of eastern army groups (map 20).

Most at risk was Schörner's Army Group Centre (First and Fourth Panzer Armies, 12 January–May 1945) and Rendulic's Army Group South (Second Panzer and SS Sixth Armies). But it was painfully clear that the Luftwaffe no longer possessed the omnipotence of early campaigns supporting the army while winning the air war. For allowing so deplorable a state of affairs to develop this self-appointed Commander-in-Chief could blame no one but himself. He had raged at Goering, Goering had been reduced to tears, and officials at the highest levels of procurement and operations had committed suicide. Udet in November 1941, Jeschonnek in August 1943. Operational losses had continued to plague the Luftwaffe – even in fighters which enjoyed the highest of the armaments minister's priorities. Speer's dispersal policy, distributing aircraft production to more than three hundred sites either at home or in occupied zones most certainly helped to put off the day when aircraft manufacture would cease completely, either through enemy occupation or destruction in air raids. Nevertheless, the most crippling factor in the history of army/air operations – beyond any help that Speer could give – was the total destruction of Germany's oil industry. Other than promoting the manufacture of jet aircraft using the lowest grade fuel, for instance, the Hs 162 fighter, Speer was powerless. By December 1944, following an interval in which stocks improved to the advantage of 'Autumn Mist', home production had been ravaged almost beyond repair and fuel stocks reduced to emergency levels.

Operational flying was consequently proscribed by OKL for all but 'decisive situations' – bringing Luftwaffe bombing operations to an end and imposing severe constraints on ground-attack flying. Schlachtgruppen still operational and capable of offensive action (like SG2, driven into Bohemia) were henceforth committed if and when the fuel situation permitted. Thus grounded for want of fuel, Luftwaffe units were of no more use to the Wehrmacht than panzer battalions halted with dry tanks. Ironically, the type of fuel required to keep the Ju 87 flying was available in substantially greater quantities than that required for the Fw 190; an argument used by Air Staff to retain the Ju 87 in service. But with or without improved versions of the Ju 87 to expand re-equipment schedules, any presumption on the part of the Air Staff of raising Schlacht units equipped with new Fw 190 variants, the Panzerblitz, Me 410 or later types including the Do 335 and Ar 334 were, to say the least, unreal. The fuel facts were stark. Eighteen months earlier an Anglo-American air offensive against synthetic (coal-related) fuel production plants in north Germany – Leuna in particular – had by September 1944 reduced the output of this region from 195,000 tons in May 1943 to less than 7,000 tons. No less catastrophic than the virtual destruction of the synthetic oil plants was the loss of crude oil output from eastern Europe; Ploesti, the most important centre in Roumania falling to 2nd Ukrainian Front on 31 August. Other centres were immediately threatened, especially Nagykaniska in western Hungary with related refineries at Komorn and Vienna. 'Spring Awakening', Hitler's last offensive in the east (map 19), was intended to forestall this loss of capacity, but the final nail in the coffin of Luftwaffe tactical and general flying was a resurgence of Anglo-American air attacks against production centres in Silesia followed by a return to Leuna and associated plants in January 1945; by April the industry was wrecked.

The effect of dwindling fuel stocks on Luftwaffe operations when aircraft were being lost at an irreplaceable rate and production resources were increasingly curtailed was to inhibit a successful prosecution of the war. Tactical flying faded for days a time. Replacement aircraft failed to arrive on schedule – abandoned in assembly plants east and west as they fell into enemy hands, and transport arrangements degenerated alarmingly. Command arrangements too suffered dislocation when headquarters moved uncertainly from one threatened locality to another. Reduced to impotence by the air war being waged against military and economic targets, battlefield support for the army ended in failure eclipsed by Allied air forces in all but a few significant aspects of research and development. A true reflection of the Luftwaffe's inability to meet the army's demands for close-support on the battlefield after 1941 can be read in an official German report, compiled by the Luftwaffe's own historical branch, in December 1944. 'In Italy fighter escorts could be provided for an average of only one ground-attack sortie per day . . . early hopes that the Fw 190 could operate without fighter protection were never realized.'

3. The Army's eye in the sky

Light aircraft organized into army close-reconnaissance squadrons (Heeres 'H' Staffeln) and at the request of panzer commanders making regular sorties to the limit of their range, observing and photographing hostile tank and infantry movements, would also spot for artillery or report the position of their own and neighbouring units. Other tasks included the gathering of topographical Intelligence to augment out of date or otherwise unsatisfactory official maps. Two types of aircraft flew this kind of operation, the Hs 126 and, after 1941, the Fw 189 (Owl). At higher army and Luftwaffe headquarters the work of the close-reconnaissance squadrons was supplemented by long-distance reconnaissance units (Fernaufklärungstaffeln) flying Dornier Do 17s and Ju 88s. The arrival of a photographic mission at (mobile) squadron headquarters was usually the signal for intense activity; roll film being taken from the aircraft's cameras, swiftly processed and wet negatives studied. Results were then compiled into Air Photo Interpretation reports and forwarded to Koluft or, following changes instituted in 1942, to Luftwaffe/panzer Intelligence staffs (Ic). For more elaborate second-phase viewing, prints were made in stereoscopic pairs; reports and prints being distributed to interested parties including Berlin Intelligence agencies for third-phase analysis and long-term storage. The practised ease with which in the early campaigns API reports were prepared by the Luftwaffe and acted upon by panzer commanders is indicative of the high standards achieved in pre-war training, equipment and liaison. Equally commendable was the trend towards clear speech contact between air and ground forces, developed through wireless technology in the shape of the VHF radio telephone (RT). An observer witnessing the progress of German Twelfth Army (List) through Yugoslavia in April 1941, most probably SS Liebstandarte Adolf Hitler, recorded a typical example of army/air co-operation in the early days of the war. '. . . the radio outfit and observer in the advanced unit was housed in a fairly heavy closed truck. I noticed that it contained both receiving and broadcasting equipment . . . Two German planes had previously been seen scouting west-wards for the road unit at low altitude . . . A closed car, preceded by a motor-cyclist came back towards us from the west, it was travelling fast along the road and had apparently been doing reconnaissance co-operation with the planes. Shortly afterwards the main body was moved up.' The observer then describes the deployment of four heavy guns positioned on each side of the road facing west, and the subsequent leap-frogging of motor-cycle units after which the planes were again noticed scouting over the road in the direction of a mountain pass.

These tactics were those most frequently encountered by British and Allied troops in the Balkans. British Intelligence, reporting the incident, noted the presence of a radio vehicle well forward in the column; commenting too that the radio sets employed were of very high frequency (42100–47800 kc/s) which limited their range and made interception difficult. Other units would also have been in radio contact with the scouting aircraft especially the artillery waiting to be given opportunity targets; all diligently displaying their own identity to the air-arm by using white or yellow strips and swastika flags spread out on vehicles. Air sentries too would have been posted to warn of the approach of enemy aircraft. In the words of a training memorandum issued at the time by Koluft at OKH (Bogatsch), the crux of army-air co-operation lay in '. . . the need to obtain the most complete possible picture of the enemy by the extremely close working of motorized ground and air co-operation squadrons. Commanders are advised to agree starting times for aircraft, reconnaissance limits and action in case of forced landing, also call-signs and the line of march of ground troops.' A reconnaissance sortie such as this would have been at the centre of a wireless 'star' disseminating information to both reconnaissance units and dependent headquarters. In addition to R/T speech, bringing air and ground units into contact, messages were often conveyed to the foremost tank or tactical headquarters in the form of marked maps or written messages. During a single day in France 1940, von Kleist Gruppe received no fewer than 22 dropped messages, all reporting the enemy situation on 19 June. A yellow smoker marker fixed to the message cylinder helped ground troops in its recovery. Other means of air-to-ground signalling followed a prearranged code involving the use of coloured flares or smoke signals. A green flare fired by an observer/pilot usually preceded a dropped message; red signified enemy anti-tank activity and blue/violet a warning – beware enemy tanks! For signalling their own presence or needs to the air force, ground troops were provided with national flags and white cloth strips. Displaying the strips in code would bring a resupply of weapons, ammunition and equipment – not always into the right hands.

Army/Luftwaffe success with reconnaissance sorties was short-lived however. The inability of the Luftwaffe to penetrate hostile air space in later years – a consequence of obsolete aircraft equipment and a loss of air superiority on all fronts – was to lead to a marked deterioration in the army's performance. Panzer commanders and staffs denied photographic Intelligence at critical times were all too often incapable of reading enemy intentions and thereby develop an effective counter-strategy or maximize tactical opportunities. In Normandy in 1944, Panzer Group West, facing the prospect of invasion, was gravely disadvantaged by the failure of Luftwaffe long-range reconnaissance missions to observe and photograph the build-up to 'Overlord' (map 16). Equally unsatisfactory was the subsequent dearth of battle reconnaissance which hampered effective counter-action. Defective surveillance – partially offset by an increase in wireless Intelligence (*see* Panzer Signals) – was nothing new to panzer commanders brought up on the Eastern Front. On a significant number of occasions formations there were surprised by the scale of Russian counter-offensives. In the closing stages of 'Typhoon' for example (Second Panzer Army, 5 December 1941), the undetected build-up of Red Army Fronts concentrating for action against Panzergruppen attacking Moscow was a consequence of air reconnaissance failures. The lack of such information compounded, to a disastrous degree, the tactical and supply problems facing exhausted panzer troops. Intelligence of this kind was normally to be read in an increase of traffic densities on lines of communication, on support air fields and in burgeoning supply and storage installations. Denied such Intelligence (assisted by Russian deception) and at the end of its resources, von Bock's Moscow offensive collapsed. (Hitler's obscurantism also contributed to the army's defeat in the battle for Moscow. In refusing to countenance any suggestion of Russian superiority – dismissing unfavourable appreciations of enemy strength as 'rubbish' – the Führer was to prove, as on many subsequent occasions, a potent factor in the army's downfall).

As regards aircraft, the mainstay of the 'H' squadrons accompanying the panzer force in Poland and France in 1939–40, thereafter in the Balkans and in Russia in 1941, was the Hs 126 supported to a lesser degree by the Fieseler Fi 156 Storch. Tested in Spain and selected for squadron service in 1938, the Hs 126 was to become standard aircraft equipment for army air co-operation, displacing an older He 46 and a small number of He 45s considered unfit for front-line service. But the high-wing Henschel, seating pilot and observer in a semi-enclosed cockpit, was soon to fail, being too slow and ill-adapted to a crucial role in mobile operations even in 1940. Production ceased early in 1941.

Below: The Luftwaffe High Command, January 1943. From right to left: Reichsmarschall Hermann Goering, General Feldmarschall Erhard Milch, and Generaloberst Hans Jeschonnek. The occasion for this unflattering group portrait was a visit to the Eastern Front on the Reichsmarshall's 50th birthday.

Surviving machines served in glider squadrons as towing machines for the DFS 230 and GO 240; others found employment in action against partisans where speed limitations were less of a handicap. Standard German cameras, as installed in the Henschel, included both hand and automatic models; a Reihenbild (serial picture) 50×30 apparatus being accommodated in the fuselage behind the observer, and a hand camera when not in use stowed beside the observer. Despite inter-war progress in wireless technology, early Henschels arrived in service without the all-important R/T speech facility (FuG VII) of later models. Nevertheless, by 1939 most of the thirty-eight 'H' squadrons – mustering 342 reconnaissance types – were flying the VII radio-improved Hs 126B. Until the Owl arrived in service (summer of 1941) or improvised types like the Me 109E or Me 110G served reconnaissance needs during the Battle of Britain, the usual mix of aircraft in 'H' squadrons allotted to headquarters of army, corps and divisions was six or seven Hs 126s and two or three Storche. These aircraft would be further deployed, for example to the divisional artillery when required for battery ranging or target identification work.

In the campaign against Poland (map 2) twenty-two 'H' squadrons, almost all of which were equipped with the Hs 126, were committed to army corps and divisions, leaving no more than a handful of squadrons in the west where the slower He 45s and He 46s were less of a liability. In May 1940, when army/air forces were regrouped for Operation 'Yellow' (map 3), the number of close-reconnaissance squadrons in army service increased to 34; deployment by squadrons following the pattern established in Poland. Similarly in the Balkans (map 6), although in that offensive fewer than twelve 'H' squadrons participated in the action against Yugoslavia and Greece. These early campaigns were marked by few losses or surprises to disturb reconnaissance routines. Not in fact before the Battle of Britain was the Luftwaffe seriously challenged. In that conflict with the RAF, reconnaissance flying over the Channel and south-east England revealed the extreme vulnerability of the Hs 126 to fighter attack and in consequence the need for better aircraft equipment in 'H' squadrons. Unfortunately the planned replacement, the Fw 189A-1 (Owl), intended in 1938 as a dive-bomber, but when revealed as inadequate during trials, decided upon as a substitute for the ageing Hs 126, was still unavailable; the reconnaissance squadrons on the Channel coast receiving instead a handful of Me 109E fighters adapted for photographic service. This stop-gap measure in the face of RAF superiority was helpful in reviving effective reconnaissance, but prospects for the 'H' squadrons, condemned by procurement failures to flying inferior aircraft in 1940, were to prove no better at the work twelve months later in North Africa and Russia. In fact, by the end of 1941, only nineteen of the original 56 'H' air reconnaissance squadrons accompanying the army into Russia were still intact.

The consequent decline in the army's ability to acquire tactical and topographical Intelligence, more necessary than ever in Russia, was sorely felt – in particular the photographic resources of attached squadrons with facilities for map-making at scales of 1:20,000. Their contribution to official mapping by way of providing amendments to out-of-date Russian reprints was irreplaceable. In a slightly

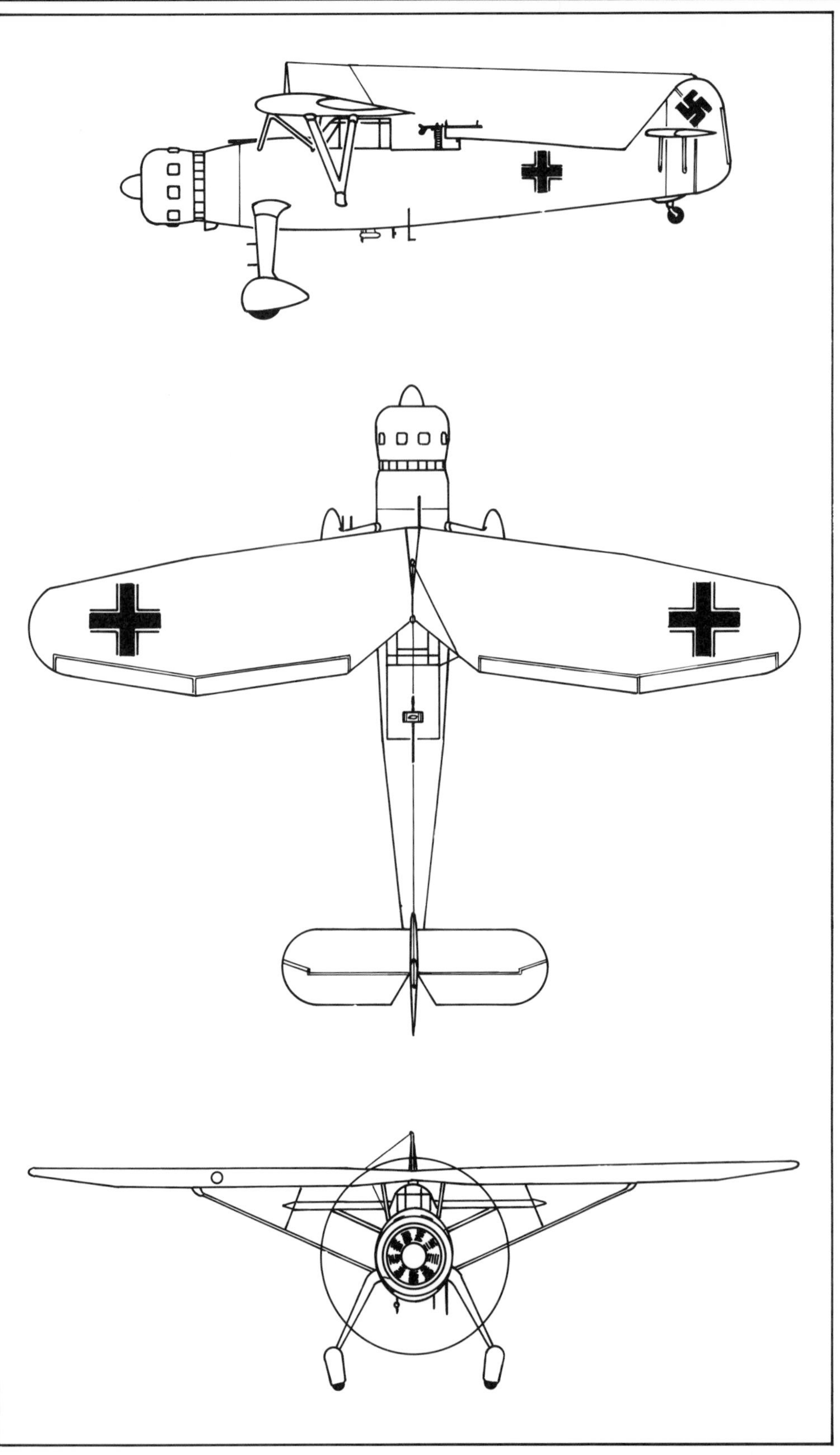

Left: When successfully undertaken, reconnaissance flights provided panzer commanders with details of enemy dispositions and movement. Their role was thus vital in terms of Intelligence. The Hs 126 (seen here in 3-view) was a two-seater observation and photographic machine which served close-reconnaissance wings on all fronts until air superiority was lost to the opposition. After 1941 their role was ceded mainly to the Fw 189 Owl which had superior speed – 326mph compared to 221mph.

different category to the ubiquitous Hs 126 work-horse of the 'H' squadrons was the slow-flying Fiesler Fi 156 Storch introduced to army service in 1937. This diminutive cabin monoplane with folding wings and capable of a remarkably short take-off and landing run, earned a well-deserved reputation for outstanding design; much admired – prized even – by opponents. An ideal performer in many battlefield situations, the Storch was especially welcome in liaison and communications work – exploiting its characteristic ability to operate in all weathers from improvised airstrips adjacent to operational headquarters. And although it was never intended that the Storch should serve photographic reconnaissance, it did in fact share such missions especially in later years with the purpose-built Henschels and the Fw 189 (Owl). The Storch's most attractive feature appreciated by those working aloft – normally a crew of two and passenger – were the sweeping views afforded by wrap-around plexiglass windows. In fact, so effective was the Fieseler Storch in surveillance roles, patrolling the battlefield or working forward with panzer reconnaissance detachments, that General Hasso von Manteuffel, later GOC, Fifth Panzer Army and one of Germany's leading panzer tacticians, expressed the view that the commander of a tank division should command in this way from the air.

Rommel in Africa was to spend much of his time aloft, assessing battle situations before arriving unexpectedly to liven up subordinates. Panzer headquarters to which a flight of one or two of the versatile Storche were allotted for command and staff use were generally encouraged to make full use of them. This they did, attending other headquarters and staff conferences or visiting forward positions, at times with disastrous results; the slow and easily recognizable Storch being frequently shot down. Generaloberst Model, GOC, Ninth Army, visiting Second Panzer Army in action at

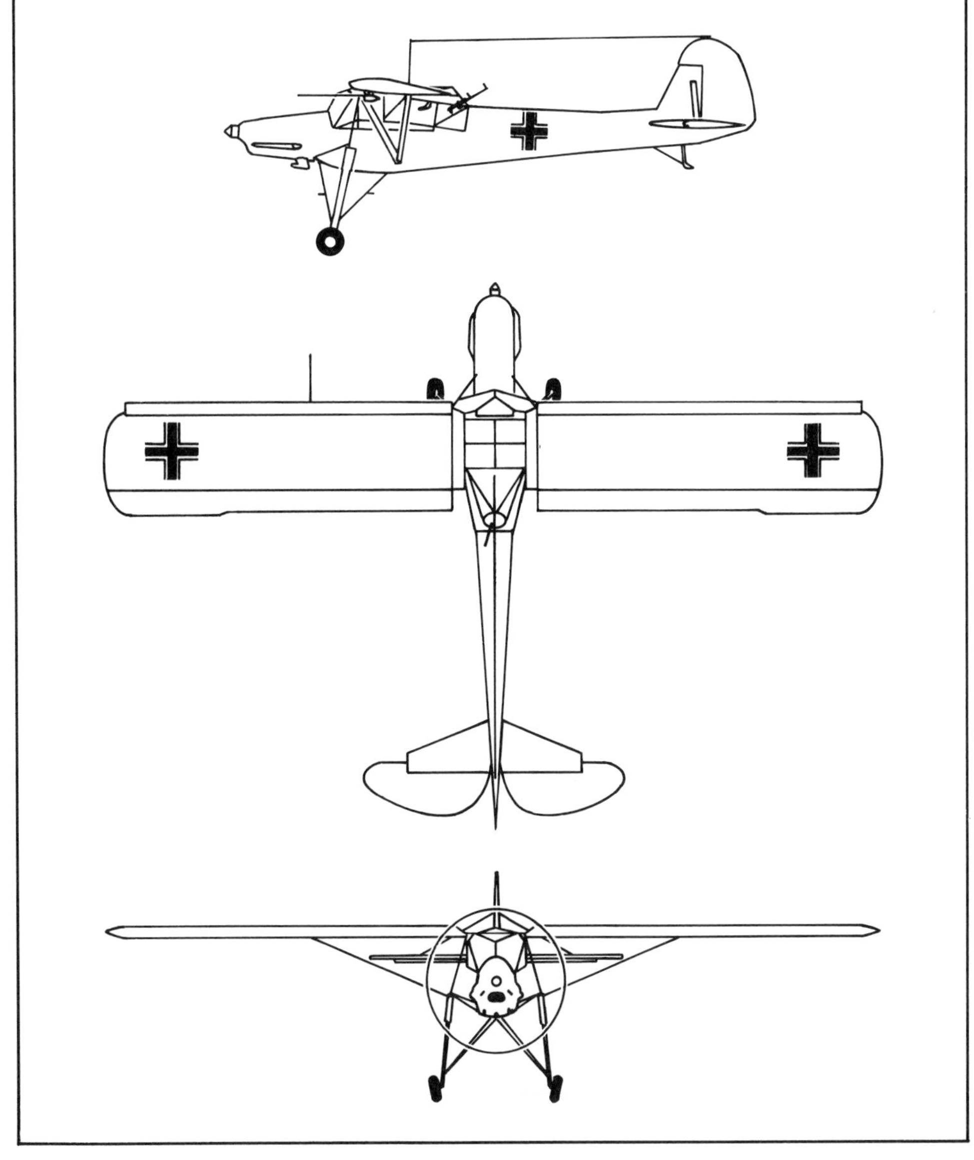

Right: Liaison flying enabled panzer commanders to maintain visual contact with forward troops, visit higher headquarters and personally reconnoitre the battlefield. The Fieseler Fi 156c Storch, seen here in 3-view, was ideal for such work with its low speed (32mph), short take-off run (213ft), its long range (600 miles) and its good all-round observation facilities.

Rshev opposite Moscow during May 1942, sustained leg injuries in this way. In a notorious incident a few weeks later, OKH plans for Operation 'Blue' were to fall like manna into the hands of Russian commanders when the Storch carrying Ia (Reichel) 23rd Panzer Division crashed in enemy territory when hit from the ground following a corps conference. In the western desert, too, accidents happened. In May 1942 General Crüwell was taken prisoner when his Storch was brought down by ground fire. Kesselring, von Richthofen and their senior army and air force colleagues all used Storches on liaison visits to outlying headquarters, and when the British Eighth Army commander, General Bernard Montgomery, was flown in a captured Storch he too admired the machine's versatile qualities. Storch production, including C1 and C2 variants produced for communications and reconnaissance work, reached a total of 2,549 peaking in 1943. Other roles for the Storch included that of medical transport courier, observation, and towing.

When the Fw189 (Owl), a twin-boom cabin monoplane with a built-in photographic facility, finally arrived in service during the late summer of 1941, the panzer force possessed a seemingly fast modern aircraft designed and produced especially for mobile operations. The Owl's camera position(s) were located in a fully enclosed and partially glazed cabin designed for a crew of three. Frontal areas were armour plated. Four machine-guns provided defence, but the extra weight told against performance and Soviet fighters would soon outclass the army's 'Flying Eye', the total production of which by 1945 reached fewer than 900 machines. Unlike the practice of British and American reconnaissance teams, committing Spitires (IV, X, XI) and Mustangs to high-speed and very often unarmed high-altitude reconnaissance work, the Luftwaffe's use of the fighter in a reconnaissance role was less than notable. The cumbersome Rb 50/30 camera at 160lb proving difficult to install in a narrow fighter fuselage. Fighter types were nevertheless employed increasingly on photographic work and the Messerschmit Me 190E introduced in 1940, followed by F and G variants into which small wing cameras were fitted, all flew Mediterranean or Eastern Front sorties in support of panzer armies; sluggish Henschels, easy prey for the RAF in North Africa, were instead redeployed to work with panzer formations in the east. But life for the Henschels

Top left: Flying in contact with ground reconnaissance units, the Storch extended a commander's ability to see and to plan ahead; two-way radio maintained a link between units while headquarters listened in.

Left: Many versions of the Storch were produced for specialized duties; here a medical Storch is evacuating casualties above a northern morass. The inhospitable terrain would have inhibited any other form of transport.

Above: Storchs frequently served on reconnaissance although this was not their intended role. A panzer detachment is pictured standing-by for information which it expects to be dropped in a metal tube if radio contact has not been established.

was to prove no more certain in the long term than their uneasy life left behind in Africa; newer types – Me 109Gs, Me 110Gs and 'Owls' – were consequently brought in during 1943 to replace them.

In the early campaigns, reconnaissance flights attached to panzer formations performed a variety of photographic, observation or communications duties, and to all intents and purposes were a formation's own. Following the invasion of Russia, however, the system of army/air co-operation was reviewed and instead of direct army control, reconnaissance flying was brought under Luftwaffe supervision. In place of Koluft staffs, air fleets appointed their own liaison officers and in the same shake-up air Intelligence personnel (Luftwaffe Ic) were posted to higher headquarters where their work entailed photo interpretation and air analysis. The Koluft system, supervised by General Paul Bogatsch since 1937, had removed reconnaissance flying from the framework of regular air fleet operations – necessitating the attachment of air force staff and signals personnel, to Army Group, Army and certain lower headquarters. Thereby Koluft could *order* photographic missions as and when required by the army commander to whom he was responsible. But such were the losses depleting 'H' squadrons in six months of operations in Russia that a policy review was inevitable and changes followed in March 1942. Koluft was consequently abolished and in a plan to rationalize army and air force reconnaissance all such activity was brought under control of General Günther Lohmann, nominated General of Reconnaissance Flying. Henceforth reconnaissance was to become a wholly Luftwaffe-controlled activity available to the army only *on request.*

In line with this development 'H' and 'F' squadrons were regrouped into Nahauflkärungsgruppen (NAG) for close-range and Fernaufklärungsgruppen (FAG) for long-range reconnaissance. In place of Koluft, Air Liaison Officers (Fliegerverbindungsoffiziere – Flivos) would forge new links between army and Luftwaffe, working in contact with locally deployed reconnaissance group commanders (Grufl). Under their new Chief of Reconnaissance Flying 'H' groups would continue tactical support for the army, making increasing use of fighters, while the long-distance groups, whose performance is reviewed in a concluding paragraph, served both army and Luftwaffe strategic requirements – flying improved Ju 88s. Despite a modest improvement in aircraft strength in time for Operation 'Blue' (map 10), reconnaissance numbers continued to dwindle at an alarming rate. During the Battle of Stalingrad alone, fourteen squadrons were destroyed or reduced to a nucleaus; 150 aircraft being totally written-off together with 400 aircrew and ground staff. Despite General Lohmann's preference for the new, fast fighter types, Me 109G-8s, Me 110Gs and 'Owls', as replacements for the Hs 126, the situation was never to improve to the extent of matching the Luftwaffe's deployment for 'Barbarossa' in 1941. With operations expanding into the farthest corners of Europe, new tasks came the way of reconnaissance units; traffic observation control and searching for evidence of partisans in particular.

On the central front especially, forest belts provided much needed sanctuary for guerrilla bands. Their tell-tale tracks, carelessly felled trees, removed to widen a field of fire, or smoke escaping from carefully camouflaged bunkers, revealing their clandestine presence. Fieselers or Henschels patrolling at low speeds were particularly suitable for this kind of observation work. In the forest regions around Minsk, bypassed in the drive to the east in 1941, partisans were especially active; their presence in large numbers requiring joint panzer army action to reduce or eliminate the threat to supplies and communications (*see* Second Panzer Army, March 1942 and Third Panzer Army, spring of 1943). Elsewhere in western Europe, in the Balkans, Italy and France, panzer detachments suffered damaging attacks aimed at carelessly guarded headquarters or beleaguered units, despite motor-cycle patrols designed to guard against such eventualities.

Most frequent were attacks by guerrilla bands, some armed with heavy weapons, seeking by day and night to disrupt supply traffic and requiring air surveillance patrols to warn of their presence.

The performance of the long-range reconnaissance groups (Fernaufklärungsgruppen) whose work at the centre of Luftwaffe Intelligence was initiated by Rowehl in the early thirties (*see* page 115) is an appropriate note on which to conclude this section. The 1939 establishment of a long-range reconnaissance group consisted basically of three squadrons of twelve aircraft in which the Do 17F and Ju 88D predominated. Converted from bombing to reconnaissance, the Dorniers and Junkers carried their heavy cameras installed for vertical photography in empty bomb-bays. Most operated close to their service ceiling, which in the case of the Do 17 approached 20,000 feet, and that of the Ju 88, 27,000 feet. German cameras although technically sound and easy to operate were mostly cumbersome and difficult to manipulate – the standard Rb 50/30 producing a 12in×12in negative weighing 160lb – and although not impossible to install in high-flying fighters, created a significant drag on performance. Camera development too, failed to match the technology evident in the best Allied equipment, particularly for high-altitude work; little or no use being made of colour or infra-red film. The Do 17 introduced into squadron service in 1937 performed well enough in Poland and France, but in reconnaissance over Britain in 1940 performance defects signalled an early end to an unremarkable career. Typical Do 17 activity at this time included port watching and the monitoring of shipping lane movement, also high-level surveillance of RAF installations to obtain evidence of target destruction by Kampfgruppen. But in carrying out these tasks the 'Flying Pencil' fell easy prey to Dowding's Fighter Command.

Despite improvements in Dornier Z and 215 variants taking the 'Flying Pencil' higher and faster than hitherto, none was to prove effective at avoiding interception. Neither was a follow-on type, the Do 217E, introduced in 1941 and capable of flying fast or high enough to escape the RAF's radar-directed fighters. More successful at avoiding interception on battle fronts east and west, was the versatile Ju 88. Pressed into Luftwaffe service in a variety of fighter, bomber and reconnaissance roles, production of variants for the latter purpose during the war reached 1,915 or 24 per cent of all Ju 88 production, totalling 8,000 machines. A better aircraft, designed for high-altitude Intelligence-gathering, was the Ju 86 (P and R series) developed from a pre-war civil prototype. Capable of carrying three cameras without difficulty and constructed around a pressurized cabin, facilitating operations up to 40,000 feet, the Ju 86 was introduced over Britain in 1940, frustrating RAF interception until August 1942 when it was countered by the high-flying Spitfire. In consequence of this development constraining Ju 86 P and R variants, operations in the Mediterranean and thereafter in the west, Luftwaffe intelligence was to fail in penetrating 'Overlord' security – arguably the gravest of all German Intelligence defeats during the Second World War.

This is not to say that the Luftwaffe was the sole cause of German failure to wake up to 'Overlord' in June 1944. Their inability to provide the High Command with positive evidence of 'Overlord' intentions and timing – the raw material of OKW defence planning – was matched by the equally unproductive efforts of every other German Intelligence agency. Nevertheless, in one vital area of its operations, namely signals security, the Luftwaffe was to make a notable contribution to its own defeat in battles for control of air space over Normandy, a defeat that – as Field Marshal Model was later to complain – robbed the land forces and Luftwaffe alike of a crucial element of power (however unwittingly effected); all at root cause down to 'Ultra'. When the code-breakers at Bletchley Park broke into Flivo cipher communications throughout the battle in Normandy – one of fifteen Luftwaffe 'keys' to succumb to

Below: The Fw 189 Owl was a robust, three-seat twin-engined, twin-tail aircraft. Intended as a dive-bomber, the Owl instead entered service with close reconnaissance 'H' squadrons in the summer of 1941. It remained in service until 1945, but reconnaissance had by then degenerated into a fiasco, leaving panzer commanders without 'eyes'.

Bletchley expertise – and continued to do so throughout the battle, the result was a devastating volume of highly rewarding Intelligence delivered, often currently, into the hands of Allied commanders. By decrypting Flivo transmissions, British Intelligence garnered every worthwhile detail of Luftwaffe deployment in Normandy, its order of battle, strength and intentions, particularly in respect of panzer operations. This vital data was most often obtained from Flivo traffic requesting reconnaissance coverage at critical stages in the battle. The consequence of security lapses such as these were without precedent (*see* Fifth Panzer Army Europe [*D+62*], 7 August 1944).

As German war performance degenerated in ever more disconcerting phases, leadership changes in directorates responsible for Luftwaffe reconnaissance and Intelligence became inevitable. After only nine months' service, Günther Lohmann, General of Reconnaissance Flying, appointed March 1942, was replaced by General Karl-Henning von Barsewisch, left to continue in office until the end of the war. By December 1943 Rowehl had retired from active service; his Aufklärungsgruppe ObdL having lost its identity in KG200 deployed on covert missions as well as pure reconnaissance. At 5th Branch, where Schmid had supervised air Intelligence operations since 1939, Oberst Josef Kögl, Schmid's successor for a year, was eventually followed by Oberst Walter Kienitz. Kienitz was succeeded as head of Foreign Air Forces, West by Major Hubert Owe, promoted from a sub-section; control of that section falling to Hauptmann Zetzschka who was to observe candidly, 'The German Ic service has in fact failed from 1939 to the end of the war.' Allied air forces proceeded to wreck the power of the Wehrmacht in Normandy, ending German domination of France and precipitating the retreat of burned-out and harassed divisions to the Rhine. Battles for the Reich itself were soon to begin, but with defeat of the Luftwaffe east and west, spelling an end to all but the most slender chances of a Wehrmacht revival, air reconnaissance missions sank to meaningless proportions.

4. New horizons in transport

By the spring of 1944, when 300,000 men of First Panzer Army (Hube) were trapped in the Ukraine (map 15), threatened with annihilation by Ukrainian Fronts, the years of aggressive panzer force action were clearly at an end. The armies that had once advanced powerfully as far as the Caucasus had been checked and forced into headlong retreat. In Hube's case, First Panzer Army was totally isolated and bereft of all landward means of resupply. In such catastrophic circumstances air transports alone could provide a life-line to keep supplies flowing; Hube's panzer divisions, if they were to survive, could rely only upon the efforts of the Luftwaffe to provision them. The process had been introduced into panzer operations on a very small scale as early as 1939 in Poland (map 2), when armoured troops of von Kleist Corps, outrunning supplies, were provisioned by Ju 52s landing with ammunition and fuel at forward airfields. By April 1940 the movement of supplies by air was recognized in panzer divisional orders. For instance, 10th Panzer Division making ready for the Battle of France: 'Aircraft can, to a certain degree, assure the transmission of supplies in small quantities partially by parachute, partially by landing. This method of supply must only be used in cases of emergency. Application must be made to division either by telephone or wireless. In the case of supplying by parachute, a Ju 52 can carry, in addition to 1,500kg of supplies, four containers to drop. The contents of a container can consist of fuel or ammunition to the following scale: 100 litres of fuel or 250kg of ammunition. Example – 6,000 rounds of SAA or 500 rounds for the 2cm tank gun or 150 rounds for the 3.7cm anti-tank gun, 20 rounds for the 7.5cm tank gun, 55 rounds for the 8cm mortar.' Divisional orders continued with instructions to save both parachutes and containers for return to army ordnance depots. During the campaign in France which followed, Panzertruppen made no exceptional demands for this facility.

Not, in fact, until much later did air transport operations expand to the point of provisioning encircled troops. Starting in mid-winter 1941 with the German Army at the end of its first eastern offensive and struggling to retain 'hedgehog' positions at Demjansk and elsewhere in the north, the Russian 1941 counter-offensive surrounded many infantry and ancillary units. Air supplies landed in the Demjansk pocket kept the force of 90,000 men intact, but the loss of more than 250 transports here and elsewhere on the front, so soon after sustaining equally high losses in Holland and Crete, was a blow from which the air transport groups would never recover. These operations also established a precedent that the Luftwaffe, when called upon to repeat it was soon to regret. Within the year, Sixth Army (Paulus), encircled at Stalingrad in December 1942, was for a time maintained and kept partly mobile by air transports. But the tonnage delivered proved much less than promised, failing utterly to sustain the needs of 250,000 men – a force of 22 divisions including three panzer and three motorized divisions (map 12). When dispatching airfields, notably 'Moro' (sovskaya) and 'Tazi' (nskaya), feeding supplies into Gumrak and Pitomnik under the supervision of VIII Air Corps, were finally overrun, Sixth Army surrendered unconditionally. Epidemics and intense winter conditions compounded the German problem. The panzer and motorized divisions were lost.

Similarly in the Mediterranean (map 5), so great was the loss of supply tonnage in sea transports attempting the crossing to Africa, that air transports were increasingly committed to the maintenance of DAK and Panzerarmee Afrika. When the battle moved into Tunisia the desert panzer divisions – 10th, 15th, 21st and 90th Light – if they were to retain even partial mobility, needed even more transport groups as a substitute for freighters and tankers that mostly went to the bottom, their fuel and ammunition lost to both air and ground operations in North Africa. At the root of Axis Mediterranean difficulties, compounded by 'Ultra' revelations to British intelligence of cargo manifests and timings, were British naval and air forces operating mostly from Malta in defiance of 2nd Air Fleet (Kesselring). Redeployed with II Air Corps from the Moscow Front to Sicily in December 1941 (twelve months after the arrival of X Air Corps), Kesselring was expected to eliminate all island-based opposition. Responsibility for subsequent air-bridge

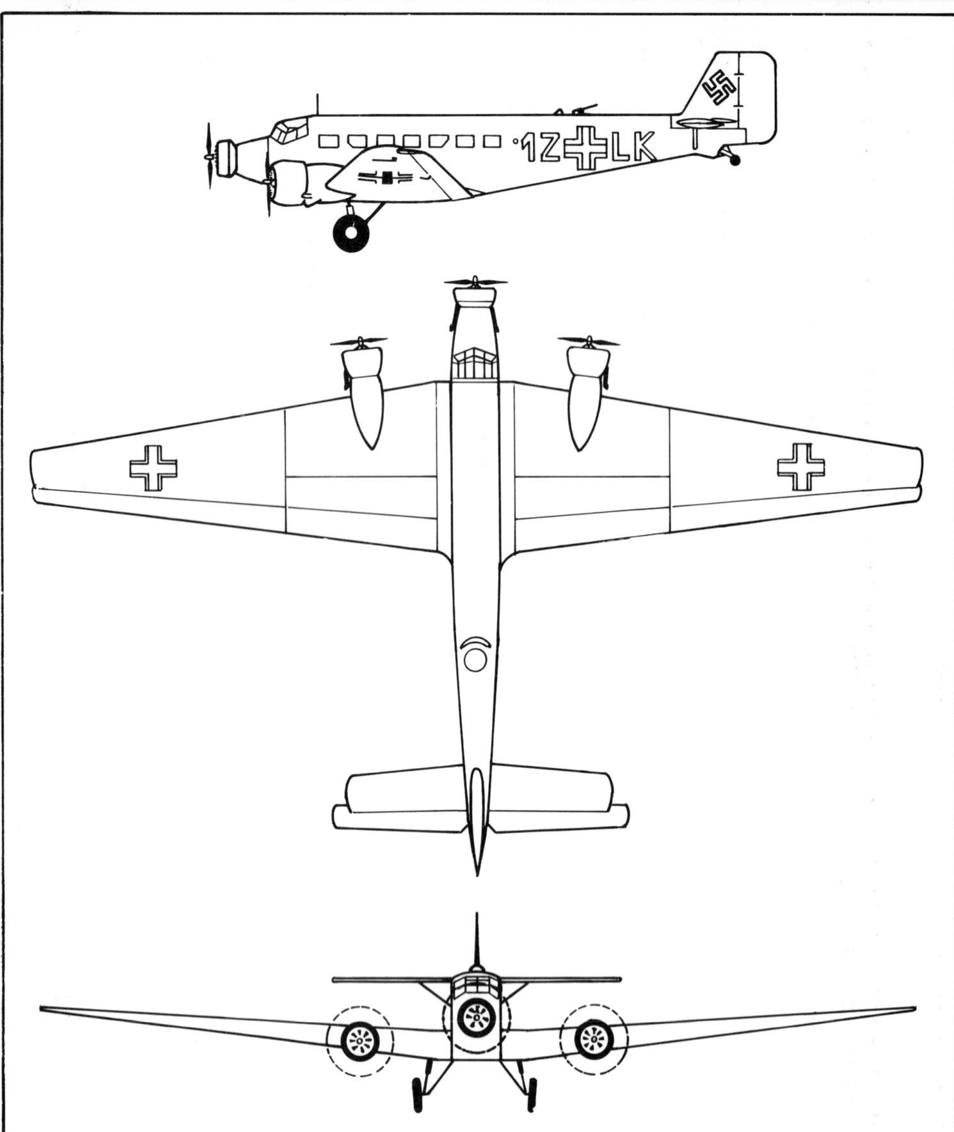

Left: This 3-view shows the Ju 52 three-engined transport (and temporary bomber if required) aircraft. It had a speed of 190mph, a range of 800 miles and a useful cargo capacity. It could carry seventeen fully armed men in addition to a crew of three, or a maximum bomb load of 3,300lb (1,500kg).

Right: The Luftwaffe undertook air transport operations in support of the army throughout the war, although after 1942 they still relied upon veteran aircraft of the pre-war era. The Ju 52 and Heinkel III were initially deployed in Kampfgeschwader zbv; the Ju 52, apart from its use as an assault transport in attacks on Norway, Holland and Crete, served ground troops in a variety of roles: transporting fuel, munitions and weapons to beleaguered garrisons such as Cholm, Demjansk and Stalingrad; evacuating casualties in all theatres; and maintaining the mobility of encircled panzertruppen (*see* maps 15 and 18).

operations linking North Africa and Europe (Catania-Tripoli) lay initially with III/KGzbvl whose commander, Oberst Starke, under X Air Corps, served also as Transport Commander, Mediterranean. Starke's Wing had been operating in the Mediterranean since December 1940 when Hitler answered an Italian request for air transport assistance; III/KGzbvl operating transport missions from Foggia to Albania.

As the Mediterranean war intensified and sea transport services for Rommel between Naples and Tripoli suffered mounting disruption by the Royal Navy and Air Force, more transport units were brought in from training schools in Germany and the Eastern Front. By the end of July 1942, following Rommel's success in capturing Tobruk, six transport Wings centred on Brindisi, Calabria or Heraklion (Crete) were ferrying supplies and reinforcements to Panzerarmee Afrika via Benghazi, Derna and Tobruk (HQ III/KGzbvl). The air-lift supplemented sea transports docking at Tripoli and Benghazi. But however valuable these contributions to panzer army strength and mobility were, so precarious was Rommel's supply situation, manifest in chronic fuel and food shortages, that all his attempts to outmanoeuvre and defeat British Eighth Army were gravely compromised, despite help from an unlikely source. In the summer of 1942 Panzerarmee Afrika, advancing from Gazala to Alamein, was refuelled by immense British stocks captured in the neighbourhood of Tobruk (map 9). British vehicles were also pressed into service, some with fighting units others in panzer supply columns; Rommel's transport strength then being 85 per cent British in origin. Largely on account of this windfall, a Luftwaffe plan ('Hercules') to invade Malta and eliminate the threat posed by the island to Mediterranean supply routes was cancelled.

But Rommel's advantage in captured petrol and transport was to prove short-lived with formations outrunning supplies as the advance continued to Mersa Matruh and beyond to Alamein. Tanks and transports with empty tanks were forced to a standstill. Panzer engagements were curtailed and battle refused or broken off. Rommel's diary records the panzer army's plight before and after the battle in October 1942 (map 9): 'The supply situation remained as wretched as ever, although petrol showed a slight improvement as a result of increased supplies brought across by air to Tobruk. The ammunition situation was as bad as it could be. Only 40 tons has reached Africa since the launching of the British offensive and we were being forced to the strictest economy.' On 15 November (three weeks after Alamein) the petrol crisis took an even more acute turn when several ships on their way to Benghazi were turned back. Added to this the Luftwaffe was still getting only very small quantities across. Rommel continues: 'Lack of petrol prevented the Afrika Korps from getting under way until midday and by evening it was halted again without a drop in its tanks. In motorized forces we were hopelessly inferior . . . quite apart from the fact that our petrol would not possibly run to a mobile battle.' Coinciding with Rommel's problems in the aftermath of the Battle of El Alamein, a new German build-up to counter Anglo-US landings in Algeria and Morocco in November 1942 were succeeding 1500 miles to the west in the neighbourhood of Tunis – thanks to rigorous efforts by air transport groups deployed in a new air-bridge operation.

The very fact that this could, or even should, be done was of immense concern to Rommel whose depleted panzer divisions withdrawing from Libya were in urgent need of assistance. After Alamein the Panzer Army possessed fewer than twenty tanks and was appealing for help, even to Hitler. Instead reinforcement ten times that number would soon be *en route* for Tunisia – the kernel of a new (Fifth) Panzer Army under command of General von Arnim. From the outset, the new air-bridge was gravely compromised by Luftwaffe inferiority in numbers. Organized by a new Transport Commander, Mediterranean, Generalmajor Bucholz, the hazardous work of moving men and materials from Europe to Africa was divided between transport groups based in Sicily and Naples. But the 200 or so Ju 52s and other types remaining in action (after withdrawals were taken to fly supplies into Stalingrad) suffered grievously working between Trapani in south-west Sicily and Tunis (or Bizerta) on the African coast – a much shorter distance than hitherto flown across the Mediterranean in support of DAK. The desperate shortage of Ju 52 transports in the Mediterranean theatre could only be made good as on other fronts by Heinkel He 111s and freight gliders. Those deployed for the operation included a new tail-loading Go 240 and the Me 323. A cavernous, 6-engined transport, developed from the glider of the same name, the Me 323 'Gigant' joined the transport force for the first time, to ferry weapons, equipment, troops and vehicles to the African battle zone. Twelve-ton towing machines and 8.8cm Flak were not unusual in Me 323 loads. Casualties, up to 130 at a time, were evacuated on return flights.

Defying exceptionally strong opposition put up by US and British fighters, the Luftwaffe pursued its Mediterranean transport operations with horrendous losses; transports flying with little if any fighter cover were written off in dozens. On 5 April 1943 no fewer than fourteen Me 323s were lost on a single supply sortie. Despite the sacrifice of so many transport and crews, a German collapse in Africa was inevitable and in May 1943 Army Group Tunis (von Arnim) capitulated to the Allies. Field Marshal Alexander's 'bag' included 230,000 German and Italian troops, three

Left and right: Resupply by parachute container was one means of delivering basic needs to encircled troops. A container would consist of three or four fitted compartments; each filled according to requirements. Alternatively, supplies were released from transports in drums and bundles.

Left: Freight gliders were introduced into Luftwaffe service in 1942 to supplement the resources of transport wings. A Go 242 tail-loader would lift 23 fully armed men or their equivalent; the Ju 52s were used as tugs.

panzer and four motorized divisions. Some panzer personnel were saved by sea and air for new assignments in Europe, and certain formations, notably Hermann Goering and 15th Panzer Division (reformed as a panzer grenadier division) redeployed in Sicily. For the transport groups fortunate enough to survive the rigours of Mediterranean action or at Stalingrad where some 500 transports of all types (266 Ju 52s) were sacrificed in a vain attempt to save Sixth Army (Paulus) there followed a period of rationalization under XIV Air Corps (Coeler). Coeler's headquarters at Tutow – until air raids forced it out to Rügen on the Baltic north of Berlin – enjoyed the status of a 'Transport Command' promoting air transport interests and guiding development in this specialized area of army-support flying. Under the new transport chief Coeler, simultaneously appointed Waffengeneral Transportflieger in October 1943, stood two air transport commanders: (1) Mediterranean, Bucholz and (2) East, Morzik. Theirs was the responsibility for conducting large-scale operations of the kind required in building the Tunisian bridgehead and maintaining Sixth Army at Stalingrad.

Henceforth, the Kampfgruppen zbV at the heart of Luftwaffe air transport operations would be referred to as Transportgruppen and incorporated into Transport Geschwader (Groups) 1 to 4, each of three Ju 52 wings and TG5 comprising two Me 323 or mixed units. In the spring of 1944, when heavy demands were being made on transport units – evacuating the Crimea and maintaining encircled divisions at Cherkassy and Kaments-Podolsk (map 15), the Luftwaffe's air transport strength comprised the same two transport commanders, six transport groups, 24 transport Wings (each with fourteen Ju 52s) and a number of independent squadrons flying the He 111, Me 323 or the Italian SM 81 and SM 82. The catastrophes during the winter of 1942–3 in Africa and Europe, had cast warning shadows over the campaign in South Russia where, in a third winter campaign, in January 1944, 5th SS Panzer Division Wiking, cut off from Eighth Army and trapped with other divisions on the Dnieper at Cherkassy–Korsun, was defying all Russian attempts to annihilate them (map 15). Starting on 31 January 1944 and continuing for twenty days, transport groups would brave appalling weather in search of improvised landing strips necessary for provisioning the Cherkassy–Korsun garrison of 54,000 men and a relief column driving towards them under III Panzer Corps (Breith). In this timely operation, air transport groups risked exceptionally precarious operations using frost-hardened landing strips prepared inside the pocket or adjoining the relief column's snowbound approach route. Notwithstanding the flying difficulties involved, the garrison's crucial supplies – originally consigned to the relief column in wheeled vehicles but failing to arrive – were successfully brought in by air. Whereas only the weather could hamper transports flying out of Uman, land transport floundering in thick snow or locked axle deep in morasses of mud and sleet failed totally. Three transport Wings, II, III/TG3 and I/TG1 – each 30 to 40 strong in Ju 52s – served VIII Air Corps (Seidemann) in the Cherkassy–Korsun action, flying an average outward distance of 75 miles. Their resolute flying was rewarded on 17 February when 30,000 of the troops besieged in Cherkassy–Korsun and lead by SS Wiking escaped the encircling Russians to join with III Panzer Corps at Lissjanka; none would have survived without air transports to provision them.

But German air transport problems in South Russia were by no means at an end. Within six weeks of Wiking's narrow escape, First Panzer Army withdrawing west was itself overtaken by the Russian 1944 spring offensive and trapped against the River Dniester at Kaments-Podolsk. Lead by Air Transport Commander, East (Morzik), organizer of the Demjansk and Stalingrad air lifts, transport units redeployed with him from the Crimea came to the rescue, preserving the strength and mobility of 300,000 men and saving them from extinction (map 15). Separated on 24 March 1944 by a distance of 180 miles from the main body of Army Group South/North Ukraine withdrawing into eastern Galicia, First Panzer Army would eventually fight its way into contact with II SS Panzer Corps thrusting from Lodz. Until that time, fourteen days after the panzer army's breakdown in supplies, a mixed force of transports and gliders (before the latter were diverted to relief work of greater urgency at Tarnopol) ferried ammunition, fuel, spares, weapons and medical equipment daily to the beleaguered army. Responsibility for provisioning the panzer army's 19 (nine panzer) divisions' 300,000 men – an exceptional problem by any reckoning – lay with Generalmajor Fritz Morzik, Transport Fliegerführer 2. When the call for air transports went out from GOC, 4th Air Fleet (Desloch), Morzik was in Odessa directing another air transport operation relieving the supply problems of Seventeenth Army (Jaenecke) cut off in the Crimea. Acting promptly on orders received on 25 March, Morzik moved headquarters to Krosno and established the signals and

ground-support facilities required for handling the new situation.

For this unprecedented task he was allotted four Ju 52 Wings: a He 111 Wing, a Wing of towed gliders (Schleppengruppe) (He 111s and DFS 230 gliders) and additional He 111 capacity; total 150 Ju 52s and 100 He 111s.

Despite wintery conditions inhibiting operations on the Eastern Front at the time, Ju 52s, mostly from Lemberg, transported more than 2,000 tonnes of supplies into the moving panzer army pocket. On return flights they evacuated 2,500 sick and wounded; seven hundred severe cases. Thirty-two Ju 52s were lost in the action, some defying a three-day blizzard, others attempting to evade interception. A small proportion of the losses fell to anti-aircraft fire; 113 more were withdrawn for extensive repair. In good conditions the air transports flew direct to serviceable airfields or improvised landing strips inside the pocket. Aircraft loads were picked up and distributed internally by unit transport. But when conditions deteriorated, making landing impossible, loads were parachuted in by container or dropped in free-fall from low altitudes; the cushioning effect of mud or deep snow being relied upon to absorb ground shock to cases, bundles and even 200-litre drums of fuel released a few feet above ground.

Morzik's air-bridge operation had started on 26 March, with He 111s from Krosno dropping container supplies to the panzer army while Ju 52s from Lemberg were landing at Proskurov – the only serviceable airfield remaining to the troops in the pocket. The operation continued until 10 April, two days after the army reached Buczac. At dispatching airfields around Lemberg the weather was often greatly different from that prevailing at bridgeheads in the pocket 180 miles away, so that even experienced flyers found difficulty in locating dropping zones. They frequently overshot and watched containers fall into Russian hands. When prevailing conditions over the pocket were at their best, anti-aircraft fire became intense and Russian fighters were drawn into the conflict. Morzik then resorted to night operations, with aircraft departing at 50-minute intervals on and after 28 March. Weather permitting, three or four flights were made in a single night. Despite the fixing of flight paths with radio beacons set up by 4-man teams sent in by the Fliegerführer, aircrews had great difficulty in locating the constantly moving pocket. Ground troops also joined in the reception activity, firing signal lights and arranging fires in agreed patterns of circles and crosses. Landing zones, indicated to incoming flights by radio at the last minute, were also helpful in guiding the transports in. But such tactics were soon detected by the Russians and, with their own fires and signals, they quickly replicated German communications to confuse the approaching transports.

By 2 April 1944 Proskurov airfield was lost, and supply containers, 11,000 in total – however uncertain their delivery by parachute – became the principal means of resupply. Night landings on strips less than 400 × 30 metres, laid out in the snow and illuminated by headlights, were attempted but soon abandoned. Only to the west of Kaments-Podolsk, were landing conditions marginally suitable for experienced pilots actually to set down their loads at a make-shift strip. The operation was concluded on 8 April 1944 by which time the panzer army was safe. Caught up in a deteriorating military situation, panzer formations east and west came to depend increasingly for survival upon the rapidly shrinking numbers of air transport Wings which by January 1945 totalled fewer than ten, of which only seven still possessed Ju 52s. On the Vistula (Weichsel) south of Warsaw during January 1945, when the Red Army aiming for Berlin broke out of its Baranov bridgehead, XXIV Panzer Corps (Nehring) deployed west of the river as a mobile reserve and threatened with annihilation, fought desperately to stave off disaster. Opposed on all sides by Russian armour, Nehring's weak 17th and 18th Panzer Divisions narrowly escaped the tightening ring (map 18). Isolated from connection with Fourth Panzer Army (the Corps's parent formation), the harassed divisions, hardly stronger than regimental battle groups, started a fighting withdrawal via Petrikau to the main battle line fast receding in the direction of the Oder.

Air transport groups, already facing an exhausting future conforming to Hitler's insistence on rigid defence and thereby obliged to contend with the resupply problems of beleaguered 'fortress' cities – Breslau, Posen and Schneidermühl, later Arnswalde, Glogau and Berlin itself, rose unstintingly to the occasion. Containers of petrol and ammunition were parachuted to the corps on the night of 21 January; eighty-two desperately needed canisters being dropped by eleven He 111s at Petrikau; the panzer divisions narrowly remained mobile. On 31 January, after nineteen days of bruising battle with 1st Ukrainian Front, Nehring brought his decimated divisions – swelled by units collected *en route* – into contact with Gross Deutschland Panzer Corps (von Saucken), a relief force first railed from East Prussia to Lodz and then pushed forward to find Nehring, despite Guderian's protests (as Chief-of-Staff) over the dire consequences of weakening Army Group Centre. Driving south-east from war-torn Lodz, von Saucken too received air transport assistance.

Two squadrons of He 111s were initially deployed on Gross Deutschland resupplying missions, 163 containers of ammunition being dropped to the Corps on 25 January; 91 containers of fuel and 25 containers of ammunition on the 26th. A day later fourteen Ju 52s supplied fuel and diesel oil in a direct landing operation; 114 wounded were flown out on the return flight. With the further help of a mixed fleet of 27 Ju 52s and 40 He 111s, Nehring and von Saucken regained the main battle line at Glogau, but with little power remaining for further action. In later weeks pursuing panzer operations in Silesia, Panzer Group Nehring (Fourth Panzer Army), like those of other war-weary panzer corps fighting in Pomerania, Courland and East Prussia, owed something of their mobility and battle-fitness to fuel and munitions flown to them by the few remaining air transports. In the east at the conclusion of hostilities these machines were for the most part concentrated under VIII Air Corps (HQ Prague). In the west, transport wings reduced to squadron strengths flew no less demanding missions provisioning Hitler's Atlantic coast 'fortresses'. Consequently few Ju 52s were left for the relief of Army Group 'B' encircled in the Ruhr. Supplies were nevertheless flown into the pocket by a Ju 52 squadron until 18 April when Model's capitulation ended all further need for air transport to provision them.

Left and right: The Me 232 'Gigant' originated in 1942 out of the freight glider of the same name. A six-engined transport of surprising capacity, the Gigant was nevertheless slow and vulnerable. The ponderous five-man machines flew transport missions on main fronts, most notably in support of the panzer armies in north Africa where, in action between Sicily and Tunisia, Gigant squadrons suffered grievous casualties ferrying 130 fully armed men, 88s complete with towing-machines or munitions to von Arnim.

Part 5. Panzer action in maps

Explanatory note.

Maps 1–20 with their supporting text and data concerning panzer order of battle and comparative military strengths, require little further elucidation except to note that taken as a whole they illustrate not only the operative involvement of panzer divisions at crucial stages in the great campaigns and battles of the Second World War, but they also serve as a visual index of the ensuing panzer army histories (Part 6). And although not every action in which panzer divisions participated is mapped and tabulated in this way, most are included in Part 6 where the Chronology includes tank battles by armies on adjoining fronts, e.g., Pz-AOK4, 2 August 1944 *[Ninth Army defending Warsaw]* or Pz-AOK5 (Europe), 25 July 1944 *[Seventh Army shattered by 'Cobra']*. When a panzer army included in the map text is named in brackets and followed by a date, e.g., map 3: Hoth (Third Panzer Army), 13 May 1940, it is to the history of that panzer army at that date in Part 6 that the reader

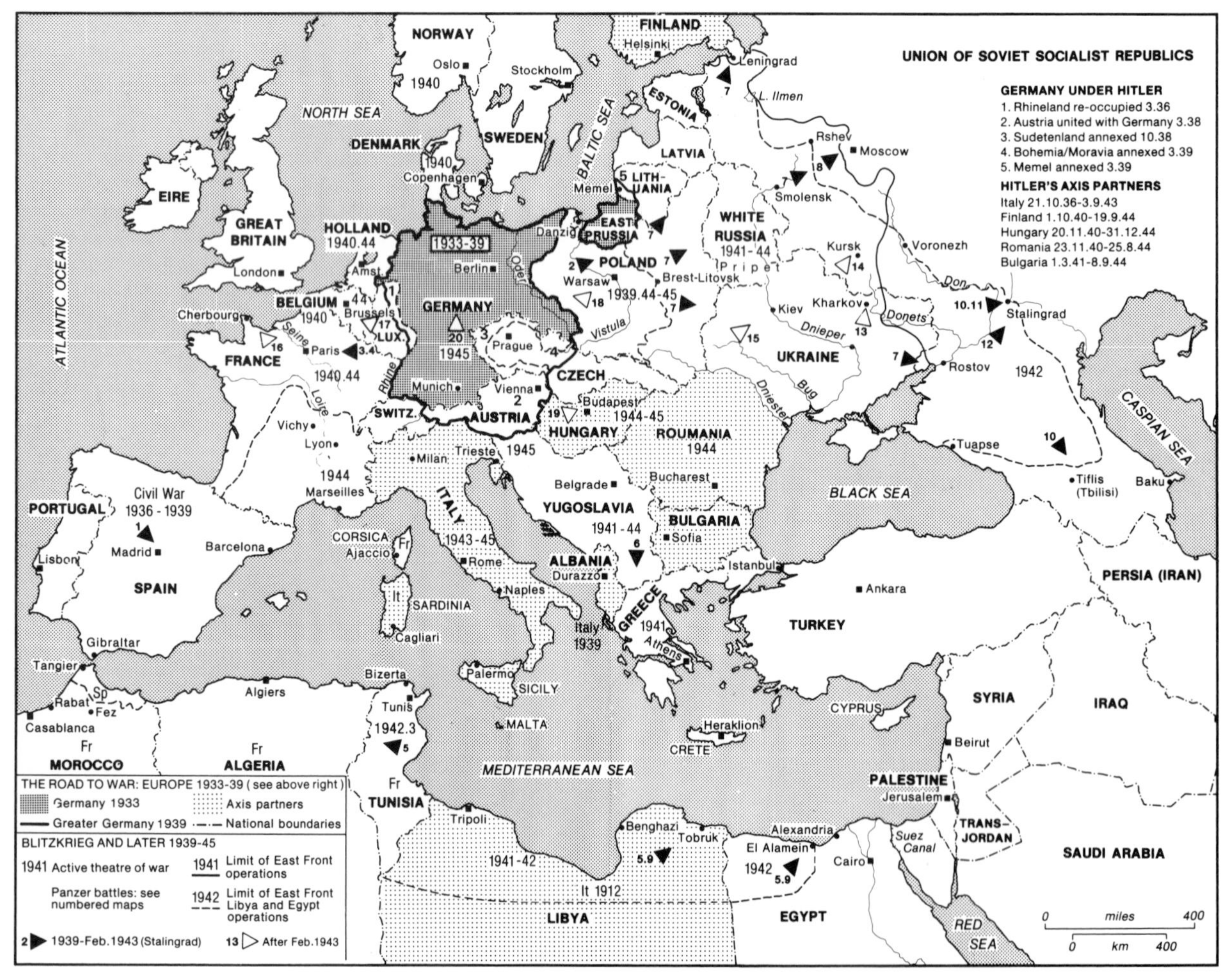

should turn for elaboration; the panzer corps or panzer group serving the commander (Hoth) at the time having been upgraded at a later date. Transliteration of map place names conforms, in general, with English practice. Minor place names, e.g., Narwa, reflect German map traditions and, like the symbols used for army corps, army and group, are consistent with the official Wehrmacht usage.

1. Testing Time in Spain, 1936–9

The Spanish Civil War is seen by certain foreign governments as a unique opportunity to test and develop new military equipment under active service conditions: Germany and Italy support General Franco's Nationalists, Soviet Russia the Republicans; motorized forces and tanks are committed in small numbers on both sides.

A German armoured contingent – Panzer Bn 88 (Colonel von Thoma) – is deployed in conjunction with a Luftwaffe expeditionary force – the Condor Legion. Consisting of three light mainly Pz Kpfw I companies, transport, anti-tank (3.7cm) and signal units, the battalion serves basically as a Nationalist training cadre.

Italian involvement in the civil war north-east of Madrid is headed by 'Littorio' a motorized division serving General Gervasio Bitossi. The division is accompanied by 60 light tanks (*see* Part 2, Satellite contributions for the panzer force).

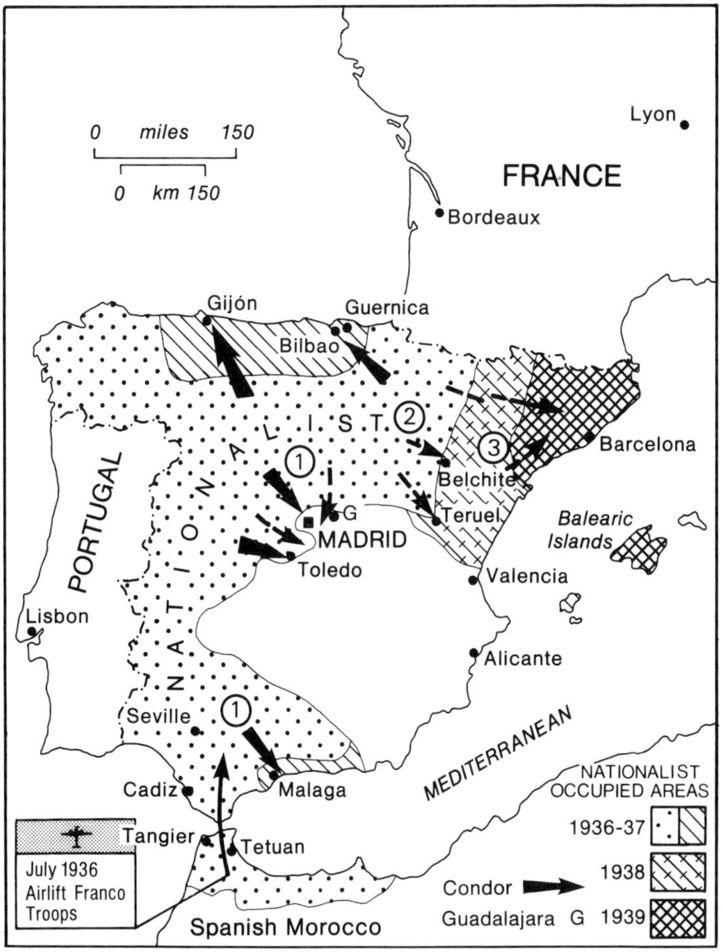

A lightly equipped Russian contingent fighting on the Republican side is equipped with 500–600 BT and T26 type tanks led by General Dimitri Pavlov. Italian and Russian national contingents are both accompanied by air force detachments. Action is generally limited to company schemes planned in conjunction with infantry attacks.

Hitler 1 July 1936, approves the use of Ju 52 transports to move 13,000 Franco troops from Tetuan to Seville. Four months later the Condor Legion (Major-General Hugo Sperrle) arrives from Germany. Chief of Staff and eventually Sperrle's successor (29 November 1938) is Colonel Wolfram Freiherr von Richthofen. Initially 4,500 strong, the Legion remains on active service for three years. By rotation of personnel 18,000 officers and men gain war experience in Spain.

Sperrle, Richthofen ❶ After capturing Bilbao and Malaga with Legion support, Nationalist armies link up north and south. *See* Guernica 26 April 1937 page 000. In April 1937 Madrid is partially invested but 'Littorio', assisting a Nationalist attack from the north-east, is repulsed at Guadalajara.

Volkmann, von Richthofen ❷ Action towards Valencia east of Teruel and along the Ebro east of Belchite is marked by an increase in dive-bombing and ground-attack missions flown here and elsewhere in the north-east by the Legion.

Von Richthofen ❸ The Nationalist offensive continues in the direction of Barcelona.

19 May 1939, the Condor Legion stages a victory parade through Madrid. The Condor Legion, constituted principally from Luftwaffe aircrews and ground staff, comprises three squadrons of Ju 52 transports, three of He 51 fighters, a dive-bombing (Hs 123), reconnaissance (He 45/70) and a bombing research (HE 111) squadron. The Legion is eventually re-equipped with improved aircraft types, notably the He 111, Ju 87 A (Stuka) and Me 109 fighter.

Three heavy and two light anti-aircraft batteries support the Legion with (towed) 8.8cm and 20mm flak. The guns engage both ground and air targets.

2. Panzer action in Poland, 1939

In Operation 'White', Hitler commits the German Army and Luftwaffe to the invasion of Poland. When two Army Groups, North and South, strike concentrically at a weak opponent – mostly infantry divisions deployed within fifty miles of the frontier, Polish forces are encircled and within seventeen days the campaign is virtually at an end. Warsaw, unsuited to armoured attack, continues to resist until 27 September. German double encirclement strategy and previous experience gained from Condor Legion operations in Spain prove decisive.

Hoth and Hoepner (Third and Fourth Panzer Armies) 1 September 1939. The main weight of Panzer assault lies

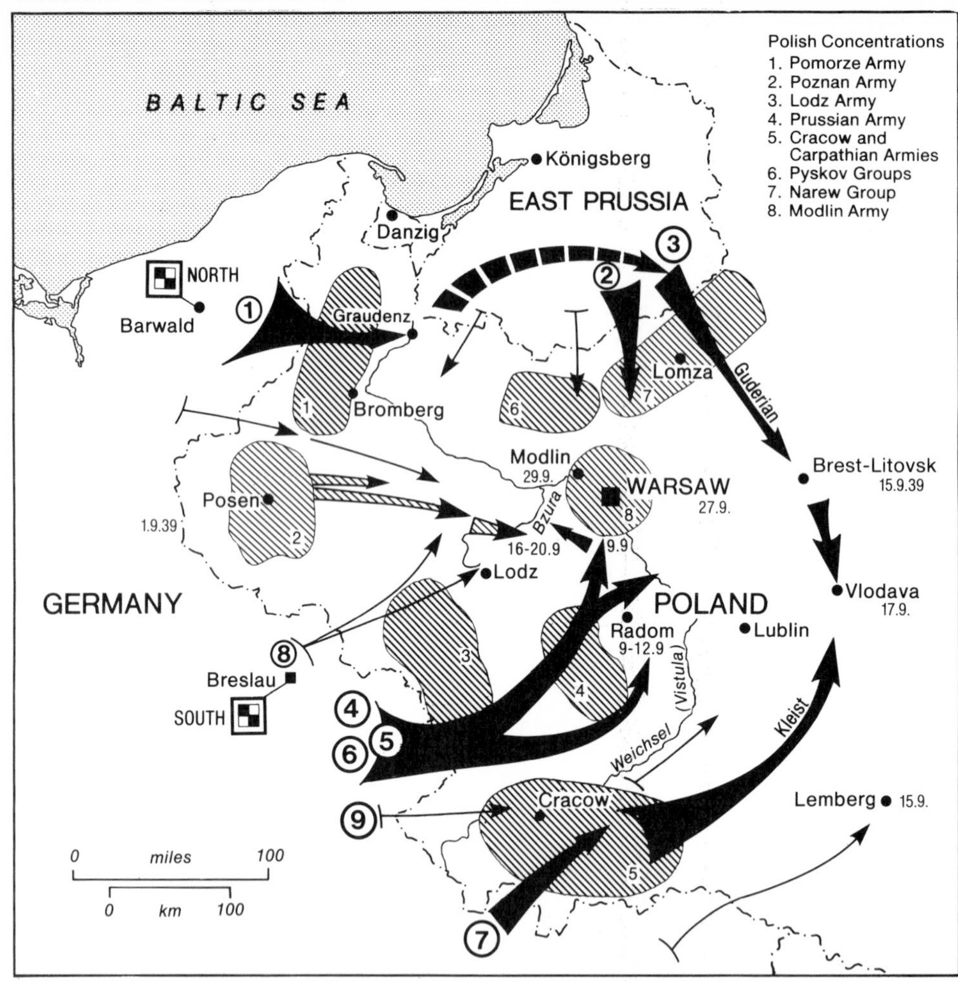

with the three motorized corps, XIV, XV and XVI, spearheading German Tenth Army (von Reichenau).

Von Kleist and Guderian (First and Second Panzer Armies) 1 September 1939, also deployed in conjunction with infantry armies, operate on the wings of the offensive.

Operations are led by six panzer divisions, including a 'mixed' division (Kempf), four light divisions, and four motorized divisions. Included in the invasion force are SS Regiments: Adolf Hitler (SSLAH), Deutschland and Germania.

Guderian ❶ XIX MotK: 2nd, 20th MotDivs; 3rd PzDiv
Kempf ❷ PzDiv Kempf: 7th PzRegt, SS Regt Deutschland, etc.
Guderian ❸ Redeployed XIX MotK: After 7 September includes 10th PzDiv
Von Wietersheim ❹ XIV MotK: 1st LtDiv, 13th, 29th MotDivs; and later 5th Pz Div
Hoepner ❺ XVI MotK: 1st, 4th PzDivs; two InfDivs
Hoth ❻ XV MotK: 2nd, 3rd LtDivs; 25th PzRegt
Von Kleist ❼ XXII MotK: 2nd PzDiv; 4th LtDiv
❽ (Eighth Army) XIII AK includes SS Regt Leibstandarte Adolf Hitler before transfer to Tenth Army
❾ (Fourteenth Army) VIII AK includes SS Regt Germania
A Gr North/South von Bock/von Runstedt; 37 infantry, three mountain, fifteen mobile divs, 3,195 tanks
Polish Army 38 infantry divisions, eleven cavalry, two motorized brigades, 600–700 light tanks (500 battle-fit)
Luftwaffe Kesselring 1st Air Fleet-A Gr North; Löhr 4th Air Fleet-A Gr South, 1,550 aircraft
Polish Air Force 750 aircraft (500 battle-fit)

3. Victory in the West, 1940

In Operation 'Yellow', Army Groups 'A' and 'B' with Luftwaffe support, smash across the Meuse and in ten days outmanoeuvre the Western Allies whose armies, including a British Expeditionary Force of nine divisions, serve a French commander-in-chief – General Gamelin, replaced 19 May 1940 by General Weygand.

Schmidt and Hoepner (Fourth Panzer Army) 10 May with two panzer corps ❶ and ❷ allotted to Army Group 'B', lead a decoy offensive into Holland and Belgium where airborne operations under General Kurt Student aim to reduce key defences astride the Army Group axis of advance.

Von Kleist and subordinate Guderian (First and Second Panzer Armies) 13 May attack west across the Meuse at Sedan–Monthermé ❹, ❺, ❻ initiating the main armoured movement of Operation 'Yellow' – a westward thrust by two panzer and one motorized infantry corps under Panzer Group von Kleist (K) – the vanguard of Army Group 'A'. See also Panzer break-through, France (map 4).

Von Kleist leads German Twelfth Army (List), but under pressure from superior headquarters, limits subordinates to a narrow range of action. Despite this, the panzer group pushes ahead until Hitler's nervousness at the danger to the resulting panzer 'corridor' and technical considerations finally halts the armour.

Hoth (Third Panzer Army) 13 May starting from a Meuse crossing at Dinant – ❸ – also strikes west, reinforcing von Kleist.

A total of ten panzer divisions, six and two-thirds motorized infantry divisions support Army Groups 'A' and 'B'. The panzer force is swiftly regrouped for phase two of the battle – Operation 'Red'* commencing 5 June 1940.

Schmidt ❶ XXXIX PzK: 9th PzDiv; SS Verfügungs Div; After 13 May LSSAH

Hoepner ❷ XVI PzK: 3rd, 4th PzDivs; 20th InfDivMot; SS Totenkopf

Hoth ❸ XV PzK: 5th PzDiv; 7th PzDiv

(K) Reinhardt ❹ XXXXI PzK: 6th PzDiv; 8th PzDiv

(K) Guderian ❺ XIX PzK: 1st PzDiv; 2nd PzDiv; 10th PzDiv; Inf Regt Mot-Gross Deutschland

(K) Von Wietersheim ❻ XIV MotK: 2nd, 13th, 29th InfDivs Mot

***Hoth** ❼ XV PzK: 5th, 7th PzDivs; 2nd InfDiv Mot

***Von Kleist Gr** ❽ XIV PzK von Wietersheim: 9th, 10th PzDivs; 13th Inf Div Mot, SS Verfügungs Div, InfReg Mot-Gross Deutschland. After 12 June SS Totenkopf Div

XV! PzK Hoepner: 3rd, 4th PzDivs; Reserve LSSAH

***Guderian Gr** ❾ XXXIX PzK Schmidt: 1st, 2nd PzDivs; 29th InfDiv Mot

XXXXI PzK Reinhardt: 6th, 8th PzDivs; 20th InfDiv Mot

German Army Von Brauchitsch: 120 infantry divs, 16⅔ mobile divs, 2,574 tanks

A Grs 'A', 'B' Von Runstedt 45⅓ divisions; von Bock 29⅓ divisions

Luftwaffe Kesselring 2nd Air Fleet-A Gr 'B'; Sperrle 3rd Air Fleet-A Gr 'A': 2,750 aircraft

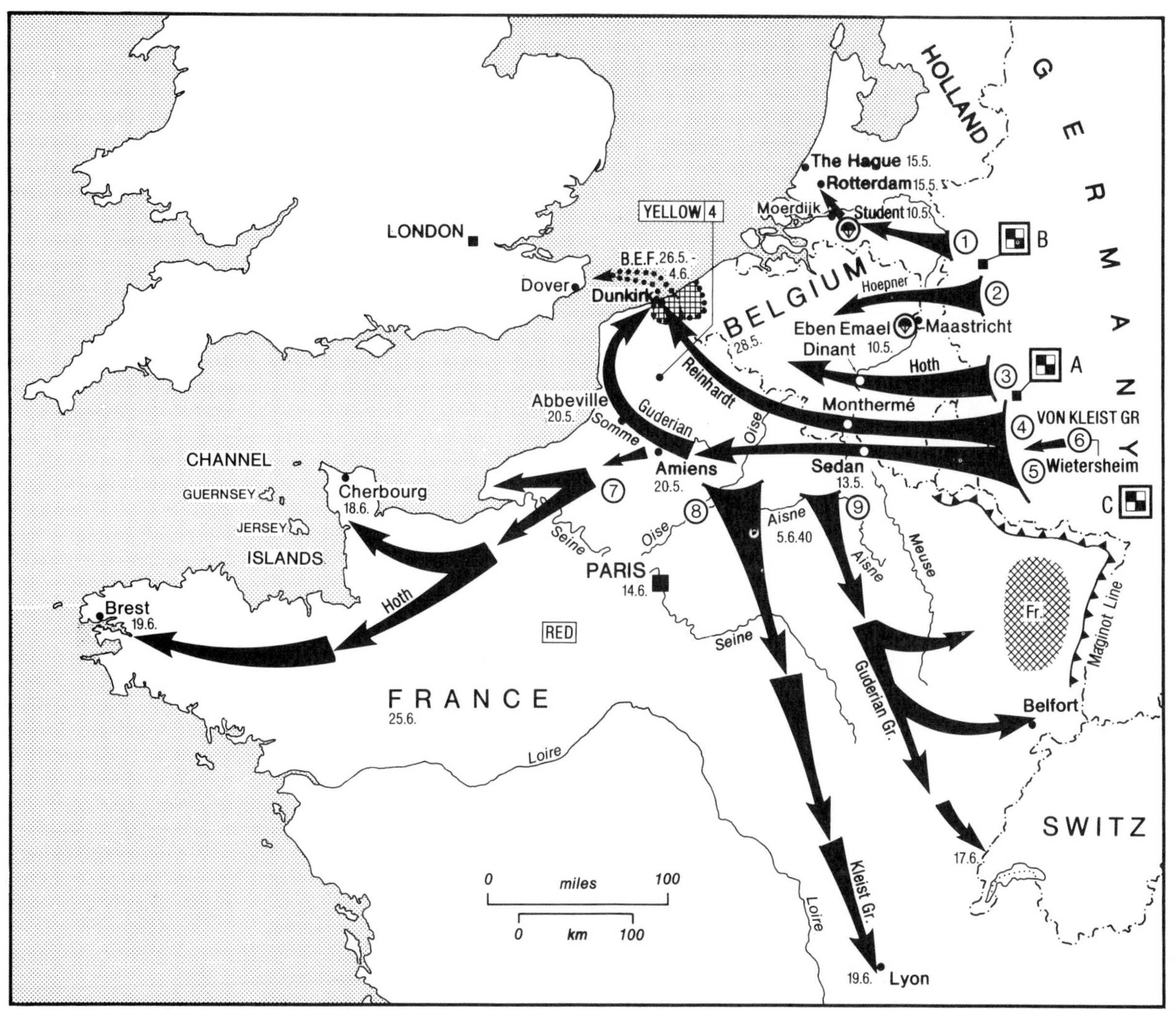

Western Allies Gamelin; 10 Dutch, 22 Belgian, 9 British (plus 1 Inf Tank Bde), 77 French infantry divs, 6 (Fr) mobile divs, 3,600 tanks

Allied Air Forces 2,372 aircraft incl 1,151 fighters.

4. Panzer break-through: France, 1940

Striking west across the Meuse at Sedan and Monthermé, Panzer Group von Kleist (K) – two panzer and a motorized corps – is responsible for the main armoured movement of Operation 'Yellow' (map 3). Weak opposition is concentrated in French Second and Ninth Armies deployed along the west bank of the river.

Orders issued to the leading divisions, especially 1st Panzer Division at Sedan, illustrate the high level of air support required to give effect to *Blitzkrieg*; *see* Part 4.

Panzer Group von Kleist (First Panzer Army) leads the offensive commencing 0530 hours 10 May 1940, when five panzer, three and a half motorized divisions strike through the Ardennes to the east bank of the Meuse, ready to smash all opposition and establish a west bank bridgehead.

Guderian (Second Panzer Army) 13 May 1940. Arriving at Sedan with *three panzer divisions* XIX Panzer Corps leads von Kleist across the Meuse in mid-afternoon; timed for 1600 hours, the assault is initiated by panzer grenadier/engineer battle groups of 1st Panzer Division. Simultaneously downstream at Monthermé, Reinhardt's XXXXI Panzer Corps, attacking westwards with *two panzer divisions*, also secured a foothold on the west bank, while von Wietersheim's XIV Motorized Corps waits in reserve to follow through when called.

Hoth (Third Panzer Army) 13 May precedes the main effort by von Kleist at Sedan with XV Panzer Corps providing flank protection at Dinant. Hoth wins a Meuse crossing with *two panzer divisions* on the morning of the same day and prepares to drive west; Rommel (7th Panzer Division) in the lead.

Hoepner (Fourth Panzer Army) 19 May. XVI Panzer Corps redeployed from Army Group 'B' with *two panzer divisions* joins Hoth to form a Gruppe reinforcing the main armoured effort. N.B. On 24 May, *9th Panzer Division* joins Kleistgruppe from Rotterdam.

Allied counter-attacks – 17 May. A French armoured contingent under General de Gaulle pushes north-east from Laon. On the 21st, a scratch British armoured force led by General le Q. Martel strikes south around Arras. These attacks create concern in higher German headquarters, but

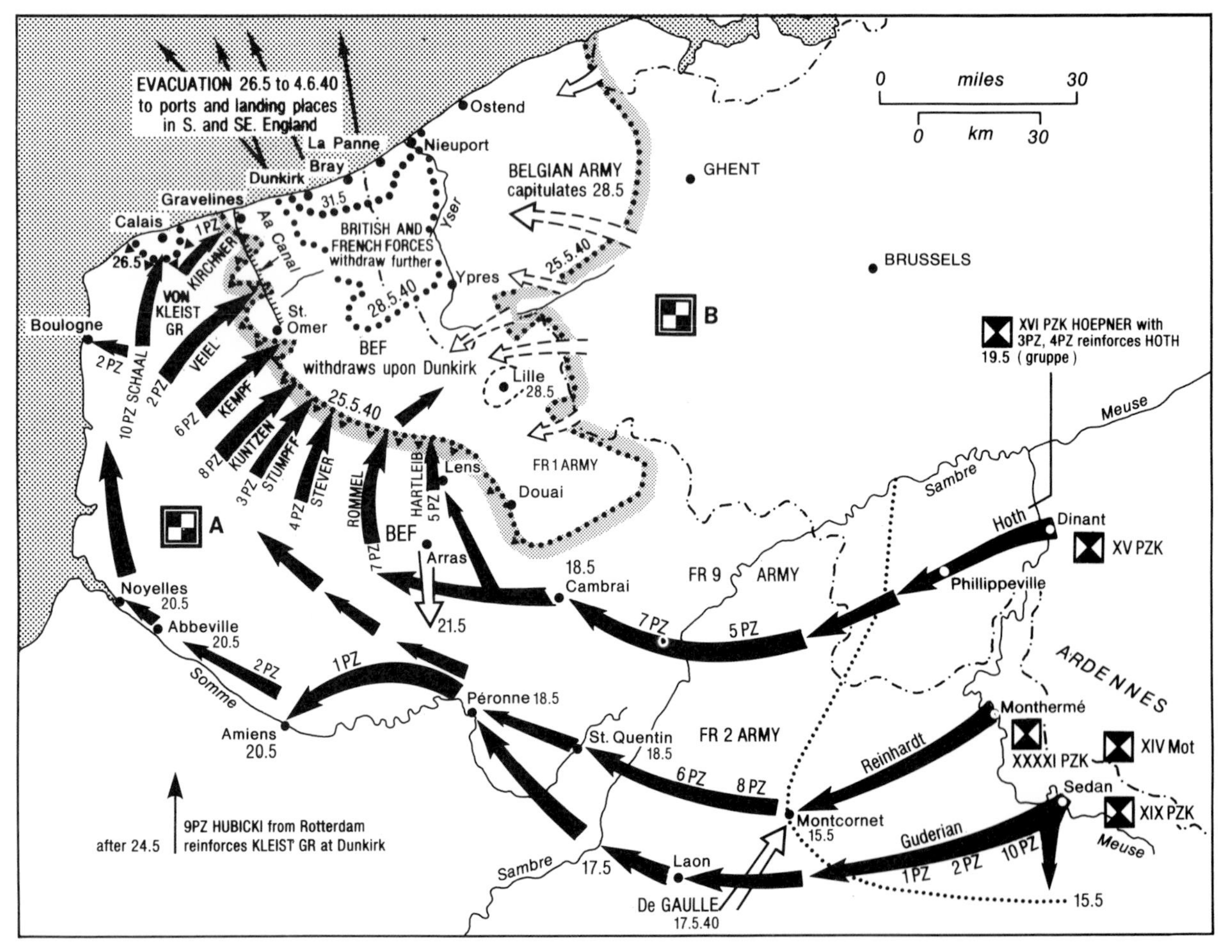

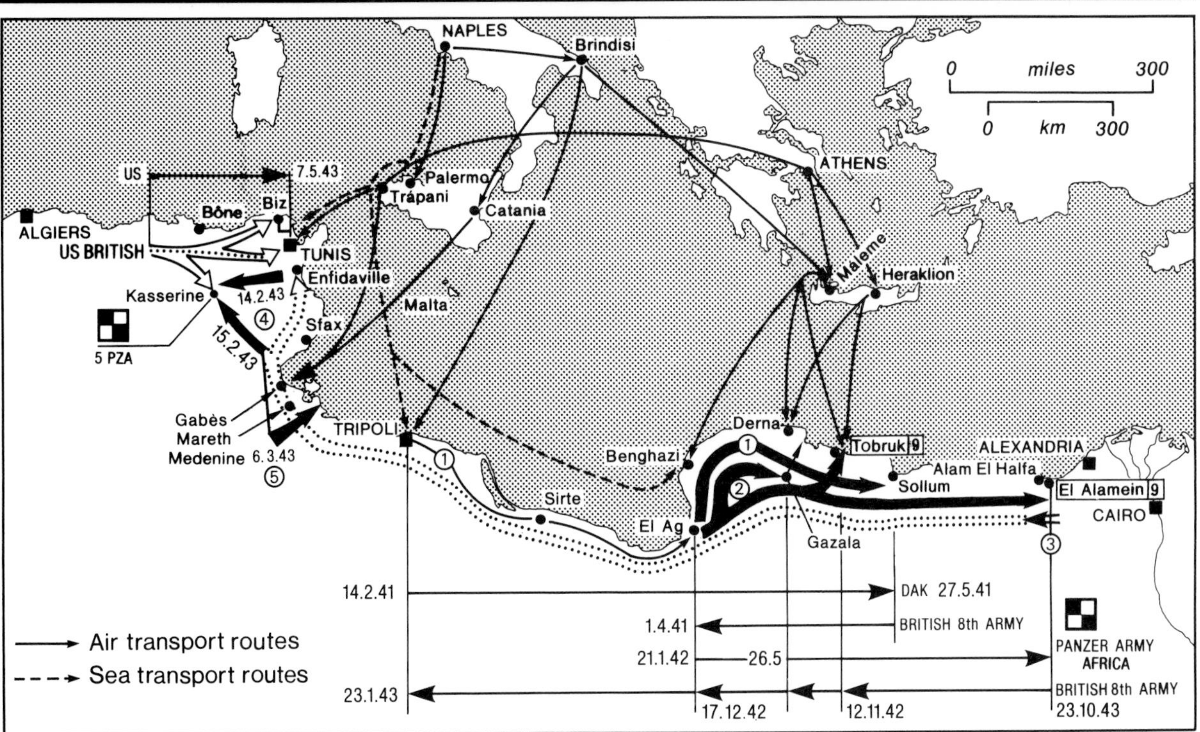

do little to stem the tide of armour which on reaching the coast at Abbeville 20 May, swings north-west and by the 24th, co-operating with Army Group 'B' closing on Ypres, is shepherding the BEF and other Allied troops into a coastal pocket around Dunkirk.

But Hitler's nervousness puts a brake on operations; the thought of danger to an over-extended panzer force operating in unsuitable terrain and the need to conserve armour for the next phase of the offensive – Operation 'Red' – is enough to halt armoured progress at the Aa canal. Slow-moving infantry catch up in forced marches while the Luftwaffe unsuccessfully attempts to finish off defenders besieged in Dunkirk. 330,000 British and French troops evacuated from Dunkirk port and beaches by an armada of small ships, escape to England in Operation 'Dynamo'.

5. Desert side-show: North Africa, 1941–3

Rommel (Panzer Army Africa) 14 February 1941 arrives in North Africa with Deutsches Afrika Korps, abbreviated DAK, to oppose a British desert force (later British Eighth Army) under Field Marshal Wavell threatening Tripoli. Military operations extending over two years involve DAK and Italian units in heavy fighting, developing into a confrontation between Army Groups; Afrika – First Italian Army (formerly Panzer Army Africa) plus Fifth Panzer Army versus British 18th Army Group – First and Eighth Armies plus US (II) and a French Corps.

Despite a nominal military balance, the key to successful panzer action lies in supply facilities, but German-Italian sea and air transports running a Mediterranean gauntlet, rarely escape the punishing attention of naval and air attacks mounted from Malta or Alexandria – notwithstanding the aggressive presence of German 2nd Air Fleet based in Sicily. Hitler's shortsightedness over reinforcements for Rommel, coinciding with an OKW view that the theatre is a side-show, invites disaster and his decision to cancel 'Hercules', a Luftwaffe plan for eliminating Malta by airborne invasion, will prove fatal.

Rommel ❶ (Panzer Army Africa) 31 March 1941. 'Sunflower' slowly increasing in power is Rommel's first offensive with DAK, but instead of 'blocking' Wavell, Rommel outmanoeuvres Eighth Army to reach Sollum on the Egyptian border but is thrown back to El Agheila.

DAK 5 Lt Div vanguard/Ariete, two It inf divs; by 20 November 1941 DAK = 21st, 15th Pz, part 90th Lt Div, 178 Pz Kpfw III-IVs

X AirCorps, 50 Stukas plus fighters.

Rommel ❷ (Pz-Army Africa) 21 January 1942. Rommel's second offensive 'Theseus', as a Gruppe with more Italian units, develops into 'Venezia' capturing Tobruk (map 9) before pushing on to Alam Halfa/El Alamein. A shortage of supplies, offsetting Rommel's often brilliant tactics, cripples panzer operations.

Pz-Gr Africa DAK as hitherto. 'Ariete', 'Trieste', 'Littorio' (arriving) four other It. divs inc. Trento, 560 tanks (320 Pz Kpfws) (see map 9). II Air Corps, 530 aircraft inc. 80 Stukas.

Rommel ❸ Pz-Army Africa 23 October 1942. The 'Desert Fox', promoted Field Marshal after a triumph at Tobruk (map 9), is defeated at El Alamein – and turns about.

Pz-Army Africa at Alamein; DAK plus 164th Lt Div, Para Bde (Ramcke), It. deployment as hitherto plus Folgore

(Para) Div. 285 Pz Kpfws – reduced to twenty by 4 November 1942; 150 German aircraft.

A hazardous withdrawal, almost 2,000 miles via Tripoli into Tunisia, is followed by 'Springwind' an offensive involving both PzAOK5 and DAK in counter-attacks against US forces at Kasserine. PzArmy Africa (Messe) meanwhile faces Montgomery at Mareth; Rommel is now GOC, Army Group Africa – promoted 23 February 1943.

Von Arnim ❹ 'Springwind', Fifth Panzer Army 14 February 1943, involves 10th, 21st Panzer and a DAK battle group in attacks against US II Corps at Kasserine, but suffers from poor co-ordination. After early success against an inexperienced US defence, the attack is called off. A new plan follows.

Fifth Pz-Army At Kasserine (Gruppe Zeigler) 15th, 21st Pz; DAK Battle Group (Liebenstein), 164th Lt, Centauro.

Rommel, Messe ❺ 'Capri', Pz-Army Africa 6 March 1943. At Medenine with Rommel's help Messe's Pz-Army Africa strikes at Eighth Army forming up to assault Axis positions at Mareth. Rommel expects to prevent a British First and Eighth Army link-up, but the attack fails and 'Supercharge II', a British armoured counter-strike turns the defence, forcing Pz-Army Africa into retreat.

At Medenine 15th, 21st, 10th Pz, 90th Lt – 141 Pz Kpfws.

Messe Thereafter Pz-Army Africa renamed Italian First Army withdraws to Enfidaville fighting rearguard battles. All German and Italian forces in North Africa capitulate on 13 May 1943.

Army Gr Africa Rommel, after 9 March 1943 von Arnim; Fifth Pz-Army, and It. First Army: ten German divs (three pz), six It. divs.

Western Desert Force/Eighth Army ❶ Wavell, elements one armd div, three inf divs; by 20 November 1941 (Eighth Army), 6 divs (one armd) plus ind bdes, 577 tanks.

Br Eighth Army ❷ Ritchie six divs (four mot, two armd) plus ind bdes 800–1,000 tanks, see (map 9) 530 aircraft. ❸ Montgomery ten divs (three armd) 1,200 tanks (see map 9) 1,200–1,500 aircraft.

Br First Army ❹ Anderson: II US Corps (Fredendall) part 1st US Armd Div, Fr inf, later Br 6th Armd.

Br Eighth Army ❺ Montgomery three divs (one armd), 300 tanks.

Br 18th Army Gr Alexander; Br First and Eighth Armies, 24 divs inc five US (two armd), four Fr, fifteen Br (four armd).

6. Conflict in the Balkans, 1941

In the aftermath of victory over Western Allies in May 1940 (map 3), a prime German concern is to safeguard Roumanian oil supplies and deter Turkish intervention in the Balkans. The German Army and Luftwaffe are consequently filtered as 'training' units into friendly Roumania and Bulgaria. But Hitler is faced with an unexpected military situation when Axis partner Mussolini, invading Greece from Albania (28 October 1940), fails against the Greek Army and a British expeditionary force lands in Greece in November.

Instructing German Twelfth Army (List) to invade Greece ('Marita') and eliminate opposition to the Italians in Albania ('Alpine Violet'), Hitler also thereby expects to counter British intervention in the region. But anti-German moves in Yugoslavia complicate the issue and Hitler deploys German Second Army (von Weichs) in Austria and Hungary for Operation '25' – the subjugation of Yugoslavia – in which Twelfth Army, invading the southern part of the country, will also participate.

Kleistgruppe (First Pz-Army) 8 April 1941 joins the German offensive. Striking at largely immobile opponents, military operations are concluded in twenty days. The British Expeditionary Force, including a tank brigade deployed in northern Greece, is outmanoeuvred by XXXX PzKorps and withdraws south – escaping mainly to Crete; 5th Panzer reaches Kalamata 28 April 1941.

The Luftwaffe then takes control of the offensive, improvising Operation 'Mercury' at short notice. Enlarging upon the paratroop and glider assault tactics that had taken the west by surprise in May 1940, XI Air Corps (Student) with the assistance of 5th Mountain Division (Ringel) and a panzer detachment, landed late in the campaign, captures the island in twelve days; VIII Air Corps (von Richthofen) in support.

Six panzer divisions, three and two-thirds motorized divisions including SS Das Reich and LSSAH lead the Balkans offensive.

Kuebler ❶ XXXXIX Mtn K; LI AK six infantry inc. 1st MtnDiv

Vietinghoff ❷ XXXXVI PzK: 8th, 14th PzDivs; 16th InfDiv Mot

Von Kleistgruppe ❸ Von Wietersheim XIV PzK: 5th, 11th PzDivs; 60th InfDiv Mot; Reinhardt XXXXI PzK: SS Das Reich Div, Regt Gross Deutschland, Regt General Goering XI AK: 294th InfDiv, 4th MtnDiv

Stumme ❹ XXXX PzK: 9th PzDiv; SS InfBde Mot Leibstandarte AH and after 12 April, 5th PzDiv

Boehme ❺ XVIII AK: 2nd PzDiv; 5th MtnDiv; 6th MtnDiv; XXX AK: three InfDivs

OKH uncommitted Reserve; 4th, 12th, 19th PzDivs, three InfDivs. Twelfth Army reserve, 16th PzDiv (frontier security Bulgaria-Turkey)

German Second, Twelfth Army von Brauchitsch; 23 Infantry, 9⅔ mobile divisions, 1,200 tanks

Luftwaffe Löhr 4th Air Fleet, 800 Aircraft (400 Stukas, 210 fighters)

Yugoslav Army/YAF 28 inf divs, three cav divs, 400 aircraft

Greek Army/GAF 20 inf divs, one motorized division. 80 aircraft

Brit.Exp. Force Greece: 1 Tank Bde, 2–3 inf (Brit. NZ, Aust) divisions, Crete: 2–3 inf (Brit. NZ, Aust, Greek) divisions. No air support

Italian Ninth, Eleventh Armies in Albania: 38 divs (two armd) 320 aircraft.

'Mercury' Student XI Air Corps: 1st Para Div, 1st Assault (glider) Regt, 5th Mtn Div; part 5/31st Pz Regt landed 29 March 1941. 530 Ju 52 transports. Von Richthofen VIII Air Corps 150 Stukas, 180 fighters, 320 other aircraft.

7. The war moves east, 1941

In Operation 'Barbarossa', Army Groups North, Centre and South with powerful Luftwaffe support strike in three directions: Leningrad, Moscow and Kiev–Rostov.

Encirclements of the Red Army are a triumphant feature of the early days, but military operations fanning out over a vast and often trackless interior are soon brought to a standstill. Halted by difficult terrain, bad weather, inadequate supplies and exhausted by an unyielding defence, the panzer divisions after capturing Kiev are driven to unrewarding battles for Leningrad and Moscow.

Hoepner (Fourth Pz-Army) 22 June leads Army Group North (von Leeb) to Leningrad. Guderian and Hoth (Second and Third Pz-Armies) 22 June responsible for the main German effort, lead Army Group Centre (von Bock) in the Moscow direction. Von Kleist (First Pz Army) 22 June leads Army Group South (von Runstedt) to Kiev and Rostov.

The outstanding panzer success of the early weeks is an envelopment of five Russian armies east of Kiev resulting in 600,000 prisoners for which von Kleist and Guderian are responsible. In the course of a subsequent operation, 'Typhoon' (map 8) 2 October 1941, convergent action by Guderian, Reinhardt and Hoepner encircling Bryansk and Vyasma proves equally rewarding.

Seventeen panzer divisions, thirteen and a half motorized divisions lead 'Barbarossa' – but despite optimistic predictions of a three-week campaign, operations are destined to last four years. Expanded and re-equipped, in later campaigns the panzer force will nevertheless fail to match Russian numbers or strategy. Divisions are switched between theatres, fronts, and controlling corps. Four years later on the Central Front in January 1945, when the Red Army pushes across the Vistula (map 18), only four panzer divisions supporting indifferently equipped infantry divisions face 163 Russian divisions. At the conclusion of hostilities the panzer force is totally burned out and only weak battle groups remain at the Army's disposal.

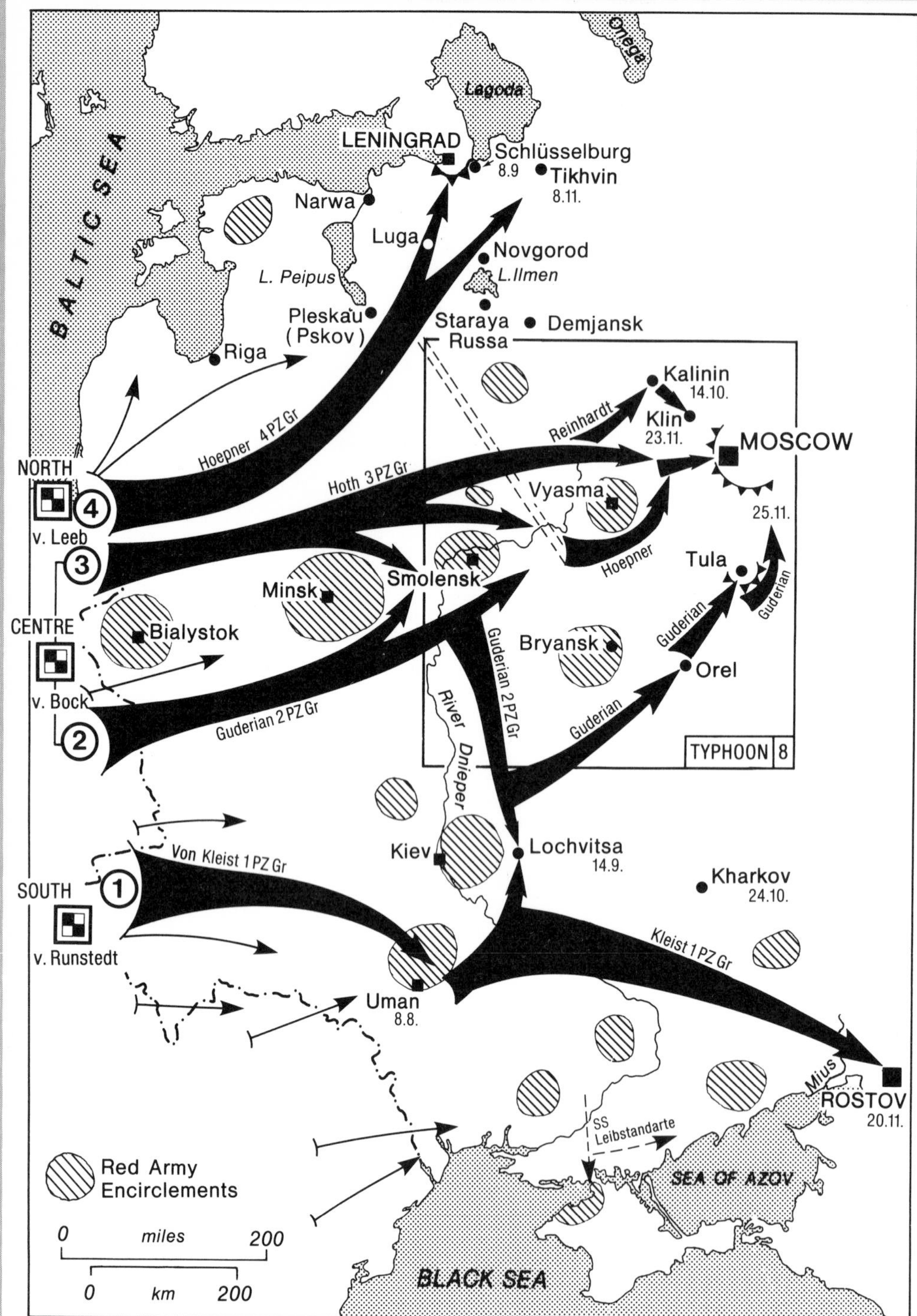

Hoepner ❹ PzGr 4: XXXXI PzK Reinhardt, LVI von Manstein: three PzDivs 1st, 6th, 8th: three MotDivs 3rd, 36th and SS Totenkopf (later trapped with SS 'Polizei', 'Danemark' and others at Demjansk).

Hoth ❸ PzGr3: XXXIX PzK Schmidt, LVII PzK Küntzen: four PzDivs 7th, 12th, 19th, 20th: three MotDivs 14th, 18th, 20th: No SS formations

Guderian ❷ PzGr 2: XXIV PzK Geyr, XXXXVI PzK Vietinghoff XXXXVII PzK Lemelsen, five PzDivs 3rd, 4th, 10th, 17th, 18th: 3½ Mot Divs 10th, 29th, SS Das Reich (later switched to Hoepner for attack on Moscow) and Regiment 'Gross Deutschland'

Von Kleist ❶ PzGr 1: III PzK von Mackensen; XIV PzK von Wietersheim; XXXXVIII PzK Kempf; five PzDivs 9th, 11th,

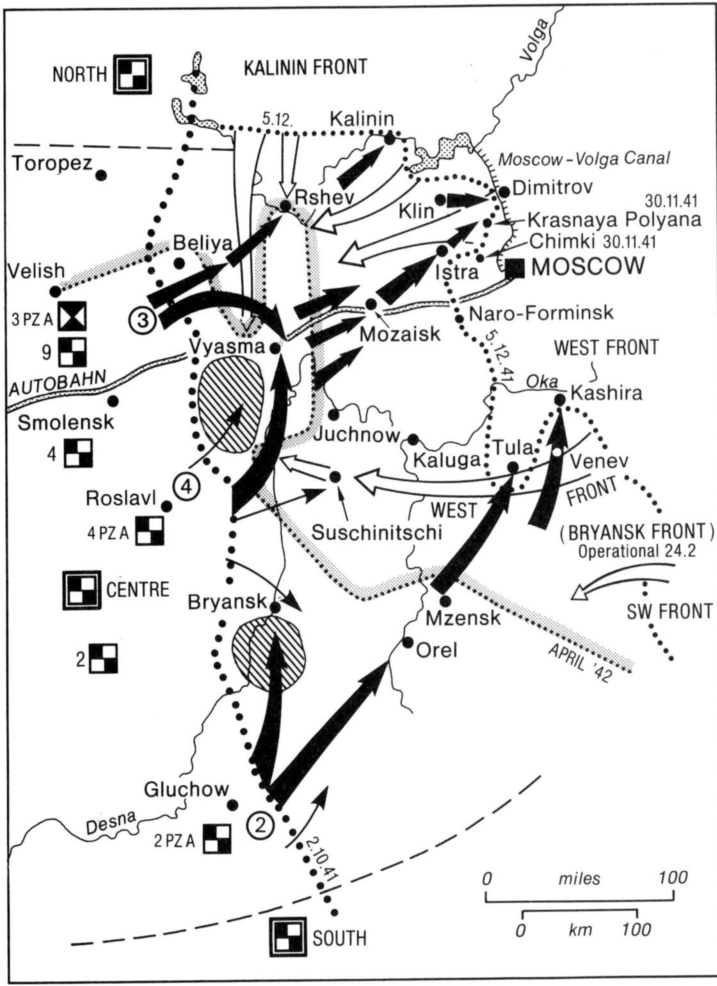

13th, 14th, 16th; four MotDivs 16th, 25th, SS 'Wiking', SS (Brigade) 'Leibstandarte' AH, Regt Gen Goering.

OKH Reserve 2nd, 5th PzDivs: 60th MotDiv

German Army von Brauchitsch 153 divisions (seventeen Pz, + two reserve, 134 mot divs) 3,417 tanks

Luftwaffe Keller, 1st Air Fleet; I Air Corps/A Gr North; Kesselring 2 Air Fleet, II, VIII Air Corps/A Gr Centre; Löhr 4th Air Fleet, IV, V Air Corps/A Gr South; – 3,800 aircraft

Red Army/Air Force 150–180 divs, 20,000 tanks, but only 1,000 T34s and 500 KVs, 10,000 aircraft (2,750 modern types).

8. Paralysis before Moscow, 1941

Operation 'Typhoon'. Despite spectacular gains in territory and *matériel*, the German Army's 'Barbarossa' offensive (map 7) has failed to destroy the Red Army or reach Moscow before the onset of winter 1941. Panzer diversions to the flanks either to assist Army Group South encircling the Red Army at Kiev or assist Army Group North stalled before Leningrad, create delay and all thoughts of a short campaign are ruled out by October when the panzer groups are redeployed for Operation 'Typhoon' – a three-point Army Group Centre (von Bock) offensive to encircle the Soviet capital. Autumn mud slows 'Typhoon' starting early October. Efforts are re-doubled when frost hardens the ground, and the final phase of the attack begins 15–17 November. Attacks in sub-zero temperatures continue until 5 December, but with no winter clothing, short of supplies and air support diverted to the Mediterranean, the advance to Moscow is paralysed.

❸ Hoth/Reinhardt (Third Pz-Army) 2 October 1941. 3rd Panzer Group: – three panzer, two motorized divisions fight north-east to Kalinin before being re-directed on Klin to co-operate with Hoepner in a final attempt to seize Moscow from the north. 1–5 December, 7th Panzer Division forces the Moscow–Volga canal near Dimitrov but is repulsed by fresh Siberian divisions; 1st Panzer in support reaches Belyi-Rast 25 miles from the Soviet capital.

XXXXI Pz Corps (Reinhardt); LVI Pz Corps (Schaal); PzDivs 1st, 6th, 7th; 14th, 36th Inf Divs Mot plus infantry.

❹ Hoepner (Fourth Pz-Army) 2 October 1941. 4th Panzer Group: – six panzer, two motorized divisions responsible to Fourth Army (von Kluge, who replaces von Bock as Army Group Commander 19 December 1944) encircles the Red Army at Vyasma before pushing on to Mozaisk and Istra – assisting Third Pz-Group in a revised plan of operations to assault Moscow from the north. By 5 December 1941, 2nd Panzer Division at Krasnaya Polyana, eighteen miles from the Soviet capital and Army Pz Engineer Bn 62 in Chimki is within sight of the Kremlin. XXXX Pz Corps (Stumme); XXXXVI (Vietinghoff); LVII Pz Corps (Kuntzen); PzDivs 2nd, 10th, 5th, 11th, 19th, 20th; 3rd Inf Div Mot, Das Reich, plus infantry.

❷ Guderian Second Pz-Army 30 September 1941: Five panzer, four and a half motorized divisions strike for Moscow via Bryansk and Orel, but fail to seize Tula, a tightly defended road and rail junction *en route*. The town is bypassed. Counter-attacks by fresh Red Army divisions starting 25 November finally bring Guderian to halt at Kashira, 80 miles south of Moscow. XXIV Pz Corps (Geyr); XXXXVII Pz Corps (Lemelsen); XXXXVIII Pz Corps (Kempf); PzDivs: 3rd, 4th, 9th, 17th, 18th; Inf Divs Mot: 10th, 16th, 25th, 29th IR(Mot)Gross Deutschland, plus infantry.

A Russian counter-offensive under Zhukov with divisions fresh from the interior and far east, all but succeeds in collapsing the German Army on this front – but Rshev in the north and Vyasma in the centre remain bulwarks against the Red Army tide.

Nehring Second Pz-Army 16 January 1942. Infantry units surrounded in December 1941 at Suschinitschi hold out until relieved by 18th Panzer Division (Nehring).

German Army Von Brauchitsch: 46 Inf Divs; fourteen panzer, eight mot, two Ind Pz Bds, 1,700 tanks and assault guns.

Luftwaffe Kesselring: 2nd Air Fleet, II, VIII, Air Corps 1,320 aircraft, by 5 December, reduced to 600–700

Red Army, Air Force Zhukov 92 divs, thirteen tank bdes 700–800 tanks, 1,170 aircraft. By 5 December, 1,200 aircraft.

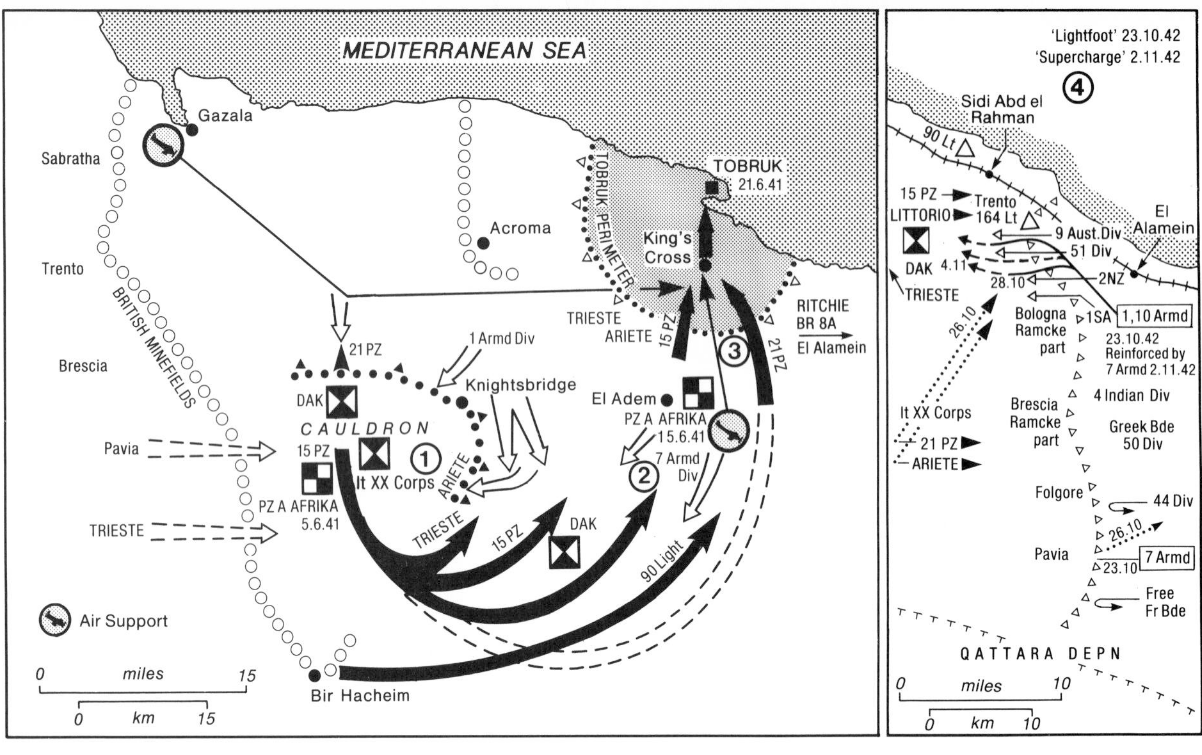

9. 'Victory or Death': Rommel in North Africa, 1942

Developing Operation 'Theseus' (map 5) into Operation 'Venezia' Rommel succeeds at the second attempt in capturing Tobruk on 21 June 1942. This highpoint in the General's career earns him promotion to Generalfeldmarschall and 'Venezia' opens the way for a renewed offensive into Egypt.

Rommel (Pz-Army Africa) within a fortnight, starting 21 January 1942, 'Theseus' carries DAK (Nehring) and three Italian corps – organized into Panzergruppe Afrika – to Gazala – Bir Hacheim.

Rommel Pz-Army Africa 26 May 1942 then develops offensive operations eastwards against Tobruk. 'Venezia' renews the clash of armour.

Nehring ❶ DAK (15th, 21st Panzer and 90th PzGr Divisions with Italian motorized infantry support) fights in the 'Cauldron' with its back to British minefields north of Bir Hacheim. For several days following Rommel's attempt to overcome the defence from the rear, this strong point held by Free French battalions denies every attempt to reduce it. The position is bypassed when a new route is opened through the minefield.

Rommel ❷ Swinging DAK in a right hook towards El Adem, and beating off ineffectual counter-attacks, the panzer divisions prepare for Rommel's second assault on Tobruk from the south-east.

Rommel ❸ Supported by Italian XX Corps including 'Ariete' and 'Trieste', and the Luftwaffe flying from airfields near Gazala and El Adem (80 Stukas), Rommel personally conducts operations to smash the defence. Tobruk, held by 32,000 British and Empire troops, falls 21 June 1942.

On 22 June 1942 Panzer Army Africa captures British fuel and motor transport in unexpected quantities so Rommel decides to pursue British Eighth Army eastwards in the direction of El Alamein and Suez.

Stumme/Rommel ❹ Pz-Army Africa 23 October 1942. Opposed at El Alamein by a reinforced British Eighth Army deployed in conjunction with powerful air support, Pz Army Africa once more short of supplies and outclassed in the air is decisively beaten in a setpiece battle conducted by a newcomer to the desert; General Bernard Montgomery.

Despite a 'victory or death' call from Hitler to the Field Marshal, Montgomery's victory over Rommel at El Alamein precipitates retreat via Tripoli into Tunisia. Panzer battles follow at Kasserine (*see* Pz-AOK5 Africa) 14–19 February, and Medenine, 6 March, before Rommel departs the theatre for Europe on 9 March 1943.

Pz Army Africa ❶–❸ Rommel; DAK (Nehring) – 15th, 21st Pz, 90th Lt. It. XX Corps (Baldassare) Ariete, Trieste. It. X Corps (Gioda) Brescia, Parvia. It. XXI Corps (Navarrini) Trento, Sabratha: Littorio arriving, 320 Pz Kpfws (560 total), II Air Corps 400–500 aircraft inc. 80 Stukas.

Eighth Army ❶–❸ Ritchie; XIII Corps (Gott) 50th, Ist SA, 5th Indian Divs. XXX Corps (Norrie) 1st, 7th Armd, 4th Indian Divs. plus ind. tank bdes 800–1,000 tanks (170 Grants) 530 aircraft.

Pz Army Africa ❹ Rommel at Alamein; DAK (Thoma) as hitherto plus 164th Lt Div Para Bde (Ramcke). It. strength as hitherto plus Folgore (Para) Div. 285 Pz Kpfws – reduced to twenty by 4 November 1942. 150 Ger. aircraft.

Eighth Army ❹ Montgomery at Alamein; XXX Corps

(Leese) 9th Aust, 51st, 2nd NZ, 1st SA Divs. X Corps (Lumsden) 1st, 10th Armd Divs. XIII Corps (Horrocks) 4th Indian, Greek Bde, 50th, 44th, 7th Armd Divs: plus indp. tank bdes. 1,200 tanks (205 Grants, 267 Shermans), 1,200–1,500 aircraft.

10. New Objectives in the East, 1942

Operation 'Blue' ('Brunswick'). Failing with 'Barbarossa' and 'Typhoon' to achieve anything more in 1941 than astronomical numbers of prisoners-of-war and jumping-off points from which to continue the campaign in the east, Hitler assigns new objectives to the Army Groups.

A shortage of armour restricts offensive operations to Army Group South (later divided 'A' and 'B') whose re-equipped panzer force in consecutive stages of Operation 'Blue' renamed 'Brunswick' 30 June, will be expected to trap the Red Army west of the River Don – seize Stalingrad in Operation 'Siegfried' (Army Group 'B') – and in Operation 'Mouse' (Army Group 'A') advance into the Caucasus to occupy Russian oil-producing centres at Grosny, Tiflis and Baku. None of the objectives is attained.

The inclusion of more than thirty non-German formations – sixteen Roumanian, ten Hungarian, nine Italian in the August total of one hundred divisions committed to 'Blue'/ 'Brunswick' will further undermine Hitler's flawed strategy of widely diverging offensives. Deployed north and south of Stalingrad, the relative inability of satellite divisions to withstand attack will be ruthlessly exploited by the Red Army. *See* Part 2, Satellite contributions for the panzer force.

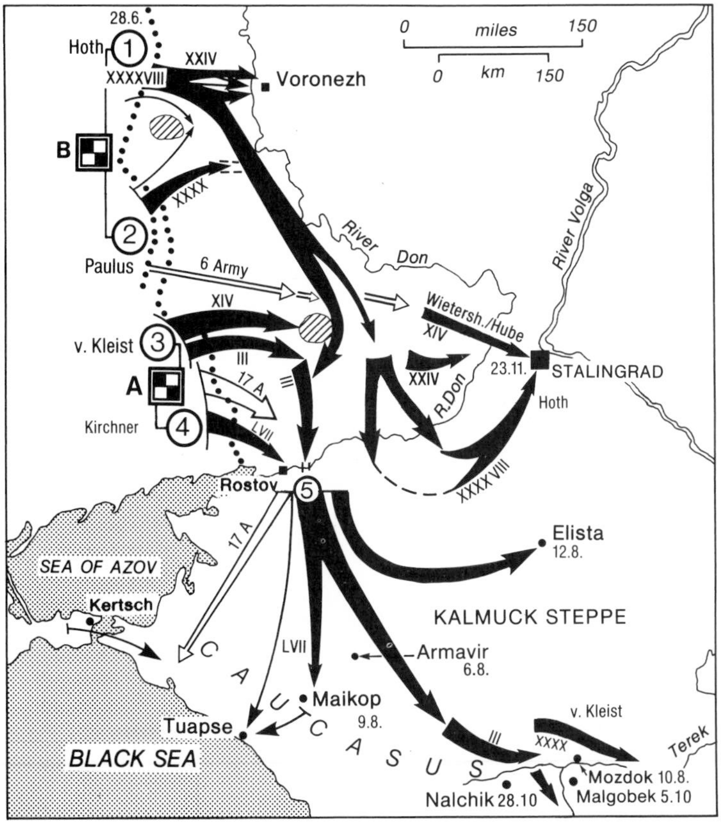

Hoth Fourth Pz-Army 28 June 1942 succeeds in capturing Voronezh on 6 July for Army Group 'B', but disaster follows in action supporting Sixth Army at Stalingrad (map 11).

Von Kleist First Pz-Army 9 July 1942 joins operations that will take the Pz-Army into the Caucasus, but the strenuously resisted offensive is abandoned after supplies and air support are curtailed.

Nine panzer and seven motorized divisions lead the offensive.

Hoth ❶ Fourth Pz Army: XXIV PzK; XXXXVIII PzK; three PzDivs, 9th, 11th, 24th; three mot divs, 3rd, 16th, Gross Deutschland.

Von Weichs Second Army; Hungarian Second Army

Geyr ❷ XXXX PzK: 3rd, 23rd PzDivs, 29th InfDivMot; Paulus Sixth Army

Von Kleist ❸ First Pz Army: XIV PzK; 14th, 22nd PzDivs; 60th InfDivMot, III PzK, LSSAH, 16th Pz; Roumanian Third Army

Kirchner ❹ (von Wietersheim) LVII PzK; 13th PzDiv, SS Wiking; Ruoff, Seventeenth Army: Part Italian Eighth Army

Von Kleist ❺ First Pz Army; Armeegruppe Ruoff, Seventeenth Army and Roumanian Third Army; XXXX, III, LVII Pz Corps, 23rd, 3rd, 13th Pz Divs, 16th Mot, SS Wiking, and GD until August 1942

Army Gr 'B' ❶ von Bock/von Weichs 27 divs inc. three Pz, three PzGr, ten Hungarian, 400 tanks ❷ nineteen divs inc. two Pz, one PzGr

Army Group 'A' ❸ List 16 divs inc. three Pz, two mot, four Roum. ❹ eighteen divs inc one Pz, one PzGr, four Roum., six It. ❺ twenty divs inc. three Pz, three Mot, four Roum. one Slovak (Schnelle), 400 tanks (total Army Grps 'A' and 'B' 1,500 tanks)

4th Air Fleet Von Richthofen: I, Fiebig VIII Air Corps. 2 Pflugbeil IV Air Corps (until 26 July, then 5), 3, 4, 5 = 1,500 aircraft

Red Army, Air Force ❶❷ Golikov Voronezh/Bryansk Fr; five armies (one tank) 1,000 tanks. ❸❹ Timoshenko SW/ Stalingrad Fr seven armies (two tank forming) by 20 July, 38 divs, one air army 400 aircraft. ❺ Budenny N. Caucasus Fr; four armies, one air army 120 tanks, 130 aircraft.

11. Battles for Stalingrad, battles for oil, 1942

Operation 'Blue'/'Brunswick', had made a promising start for Army Gr 'B' by securing Voronezh on 6 July. Operations 'Siegfried' and 'Mouse' were unfolding in reasonably good time (map 10) and by mid-November more than 90 per cent of Stalingrad is in the hands of von Weichs. In the Caucasus, List's Army Group 'A' stands within striking distance of prime Soviet oil-producing centres until a Red Army counter-stroke reverses the double offensive.

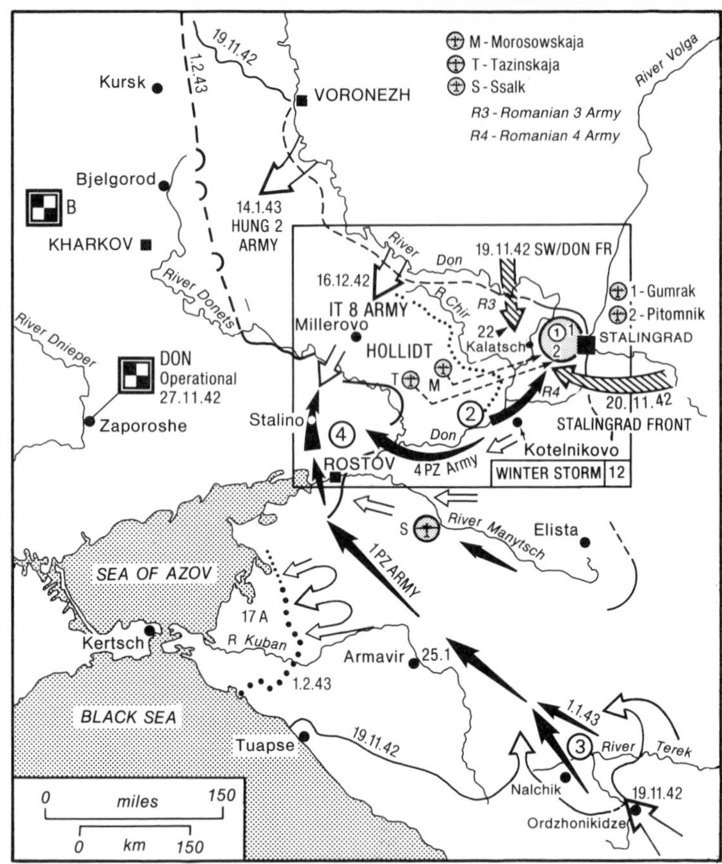

Hoth ❶ Fourth Pz-Army/Sixth Army (Paulus) 19 November 1942 is immediately incapacitated by a Red Army pincer movement breaking through Roumanian positions north and south of the city and uniting at Kalatsch.

Hube, Heim German Sixth Army, XIV Panzer Corps (Hube) and much of Fourth Pz Army is isolated. A mobile reserve – 22nd Panzer bracketed with Roumanian 1st Armd Div in XLVIII Pz Corps (Heim) – supporting the Roumanians is destroyed in abortive counter-attacks.

Trapped in the pocket are 14th, 16th, 24th Pz and 3rd, 29th, 60th Mot Divs.

Hoth, Kirchner ❷ Fourth Pz-Army 12 December 1942 launches 'Winter Storm', a relief operation improvised by A Gr Don with panzer divisions brought great distances; 6th Pz from France, 17th Pz from A Gr Centre, and 23rd Pz from First Pz-Army. The panzer divisions under LVII PzK (Kirchner) brought from Seventeenth Army in the Caucasus, fight to within 30 miles of the city. Relief operations are called off as a new Russian offensive west across the Chir threatening Millerovo exacerbates the situation. *See* (map 12) LVII Pz-Corps action at Stalingrad.

Von Kleist, Von Mackensen ❸ First Pz-Army 22 November 1942 to 1 January 1943 is obliged to release 23rd Pz, SS Wiking and air support to assist Hoth and Paulus at Stalingrad. Von Kleist is further threatened with the loss of Rostov-on-Don – the Pz Army's principal supply and communications centre, 400 miles behind the front. But under von Mackensen, (von Kleist's successor) – First Pz-Army will fight its way to safety.

Von Mackensen, Hoth ❹ Army Group Don (von Manstein) regroups First and Fourth Pz Armies and launches counter-attacks against Red Army spearheads crossing the Donets and exploiting success westwards. But Kharkov is lost and Zaporoshe (Army Group headquarters) threatened.

Hoth Fourth Pz-Army 22 February 1943 leads the recapture of Kharkov (map 13).

Army Gr 'B' ❶ Von Weichs in Stalingrad; 22 divs (three Pz, three Mot, two Roum.) 100 tanks.

Army Gr Don ❷ Von Manstein; thee Pz divs, six Roum. inf divs, 170–200 tanks.

First Pz-Army ❸ Von Kleist (von Mackensen after 1 January 1943) six divs (two Pz).

First, Fourth Pz-Armies ❹ Von Mackensen, Hoth; 17–18 divs (nine Pz) *see* (map 13).

4th Air Fleet Von Richthofen; I Fiebig, VIII Air Corps. 2, 3, 4, Pflugbeil IV Air Corps.

Red Army, Air Force ❶ Stalingrad counter-offensive 19– 20 November; nine armies, forty divs, 979 tanks and SP guns, four air armies, 1,350 aircraft. ❷ Kotelnikovo axis; three armies, 19½ divs, 635 tanks. ❸ N. Caucasus; four armies, 24 divs, one air army, 232 aircraft. ❹ Kharkov *see* (map 13).

12. The agony of Stalingrad, 1942

Hitler's fatally flawed summer offensive continuing into winter 1942 (map 11) is a turning-point in the fortunes of the German Army and its panzer force. 'Citadel' (map 14) and 'Autumn Mist' (map 17) excepted, panzer divisions will henceforth exploit mobility and fire power in a 'fire brigade' role, relieving encircled formations, delaying or containing Russian offensives and generally bolstering unprotected and immobile infantry. This change of emphasis is reflected in the relief of Stalingrad, December 1942.

Hoth, Hube ❶ Fourth Pz-Army/Sixth Army (Paulus) 19 November 1942. 22 divisions including three Panzer (14th, 16th, 24th), three motorized (3rd, 29th, 60th) and XIV Panzer Corps (Hube), more than 220,000 men, are besieged in Stalingrad by seven Russian armies.

Hoth, Kirchner ❷ Fourth Pz-Army 12 December 1942 launches relief Operation 'Winter Storm', spearheaded by 6th Panzer. Urgently railed from France the division leads LVII Panzer Corps (Kirchner) 6th, 17th and 23rd Panzer to within 30 miles of the Stalingrad perimeter. Provisioned by VIII Air Corps from 'Moro' (sovskya), 'Tazi' (nskya) and other airfields, the defenders of Stalingrad offer bitter resistance, but the tonnage received, on average 150 tons daily, is much less than the minimum 550 tons needed to sustain them.

Hoth ❸ Fourth Pz-Army 17 December 1942 faces further difficulty when a new Red army offensive on the upper Chir smashing through Italian Eighth Army threatens to engulf the airfields. The panzer divisions are diverted to the new crisis point. The relief attempt is called off and efforts to stabilize the situation bring another (7th Panzer) division from France. Panzer action is dissipated over a wide area.

North and south of Rostov, panzer divisions are switched between sectors to delay the Red Army's drive on von

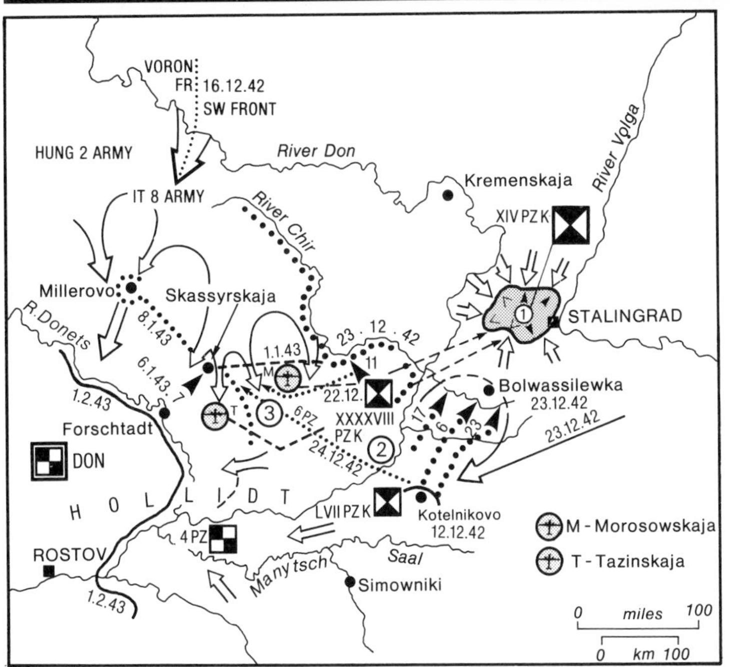

Mackensen's Rostov 'gateway'. A successful panzer defence of Rostov allows First Panzer Army 1 January 1943 to fight its way back from Caucasus – but at catastrophic cost to German Sixth Army and surviving Fourth Panzer Army units in Stalingrad.

Von Manstein By 1 February 1943 both Panzer Armies under control of Army Group Don are relatively safe between the Donets and the Dnieper.

The Army Group commander will regroup much-depleted armour and launch a counter-offensive (map 13), to seal off Red Army spearheads exploiting success westwards. Von Manstein's offensive against an over-extended Red Army is to prove remarkably successful and the situation is 'miraculously' turned to German advantage.

Army Gr 'B' ❶ Von Weichs in Stalingrad; 22 divs (three Pz, three Mot, two Roum inf), 100 tanks.

Army Gr Don ❷ Von Manstein/Armeegruppe Hoth (4 PzA, 4 RomA); three Pz divs, six Roum inf divs. 175–200 tanks (6th and 23rd Pz=141 Pz Kpfw III-IVs).

Army Gr 'B' ❸ Von Weichs; Garibaldi It. Eighth Army, 9–12 It. inf divs; Jány, Hung Second Army, ten inf divs, one Hung Pz div, von Salmuth, German Second Army, etc.

A Gr Don Von Manstein/Armeeabteilung Hollidt; six Roum. inf divs, one Roum. Pz Div, three Ger. inf divs.

4th Air Fleet Von Richthofen; ❶❷ Fiebig VIII Air Corps, ❸ Pflugbeil IV Air Corps.

Red Army, Air Force ❶ Investing Stalingrad 47 divs; ❷ Kotelnikovo axis 19½ divs, 635 tanks; ❸ Stalingrad counter offensive 36 divs, 1,030 tanks.

13. Von Manstein's miracle, 1943

In a bid to outmanoeuvre and complete the destruction of German and satellite armies surviving the onslaught at Stalingrad, the Red Army (Voronezh and South West Fronts) flushed with victory, exploits success across the Donets, thrusting towards Zaporoshe and the Sea of Azov. The offensive is brought to a standstill by First and Fourth Panzer Armies – regrouped and launched into a well-timed

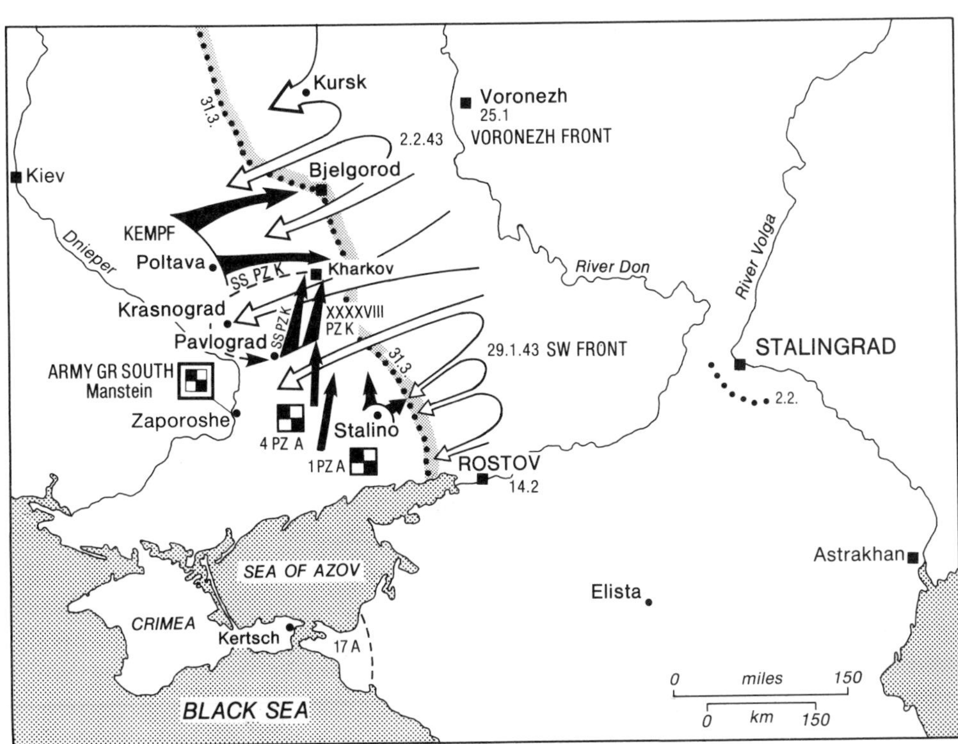

counter-stroke devised by von Manstein C-in-C, Army Group South (formerly Don).

Von Mackensen First Pz-Army 27 January 1943 concludes an arduous retreat from the Caucasus with the task of holding Stalino and, with two Pz-Corps striking north on 22 February, biting into the flank of Russian Sixth Army and its armoured spearheads (Popov) leading SW Front in the drive to the Dnieper at Zaporoshe.

Hoth Fourth Pz-Army 22 February 1943 is allotted the principal role in von Manstein's counter-offensive. Supported by 4th Air Fleet, Hoth pushes two Pz-Corps northwards and on the 22nd is reinforced by a newly created SS Pz-Corps (Hausser) – released by Armeeabteilung Kempf (previously Lanz) after defying Hitler's orders and evacuating Kharkov on the 16th. Hoth aims to slice through Voronezh Front's extended left wing and re-occupy Kharkov, previously lost to Russian 69th Army and Third Tank Army spearheads. The offensive is a success, cutting-off Russian Sixth Army (and Popov) spearheads, recapturing Kharkov on 12 March and continuing on to Bjelgorod, an equally important railway junction falling to Gross Deutschland on the 18th. Bjelgorod, like Kharkov, becomes a spring-board for Hitler's projected summer offensive 'Citadel' (map 14).

Von Mackensen First Pz-Army: XXXX PzK Henrici; 11th Pz, SS PzGrenDiv Wiking, 333rd InfDiv; III PzK Breith: 3rd, 7th PzDivs.

Hoth Fourth Pz-Army: LVII PzK Kirchner; XXXXVIII PzK von Knobelsdorff; 6th, 17th, 19th PzDivs.

Kempf Army Abteilung: II SS PzK Hausser; 1st SS PzDiv Leibstandarte Adolf Hitler, 2nd SS PzDiv Das Reich, 3rd SS PzDiv Totenkopf; PzGrenDiv Gross Deutschland.

Army Gr South Von Manstein Kharkov offensive; nine pz divs (3SS), two mot divs, 6–7 inf divs, 350–450 tanks, mostly deployed in the SS divisions.

4th Air Fleet Von Richthofen; Korten I Air Corps-Kempf, Pflugbeil IV AirCorps-Hoth, Mahnke Air Div Donets-von Mackensen/Hoth.

Red Army, Air Force Vatutin, SW Front 29 January; 29 rifle divs, four armies, 137 tanks (Front Mobile Group Popov) – one air army, 300 aircraft.

Golikov, Voronezh Fr 2 February; three armies (one tank) 120 tanks.

14. Break-point: 'Citadel', 1943

After suffering two disastrous winters in the east, a revitalized panzer force enjoying new weapons and equipment – Tigers, Panthers and Ferdinands – is assembled on sectors north and south of a huge and strongly defended Red Army salient centred on Kursk. Operation 'Citadel' involving Army Groups Centre and South will strike concentrically to eliminate the salient.

Hoth Fourth Pz-Army 5 July 1943 responsible to Army Group South will carry the main weight of the offensive; SS PzKorps (Hausser) providing the cutting edge; Army Abteilung (AA) Kempf in support.

Model Ninth Army responsible to Army Group Centre will co-operate in attacks from the north. But 'Citadel' is not a success.

Losing more than half its armoured strength, 'Citadel' fails to break the deeply echeloned Russian defence and after seven days' fighting when the offensive coincides with 'Husky', the Allied invasion of Sicily, Hitler calls it off. (Panzer Action in Italy, page 201.)

Critically drained of resources, the German Army will never recover the strategic initiative. Fourth Pz-Army, failing to reach Kursk and link up with Ninth Army, is shattered in the attempt; the decimated panzer divisions lose their power and German domination of European Russia is permanently broken.

Twenty panzer/panzer grenadier divisions (including OKH reserve) plus infantry and Army troops assemble for 'Citadel' led by Hoth and Kempf (Army Group South) and Model (Army Group Centre).

Hoth ❶ Fourth Pz-Army, II SS PzK Hausser: 1st SS PzDiv, 2nd SS PzDiv, 3 SS PzDiv: XXXXVIII PzK von Knobelsdorff; 3rd, 11th PzDivs, Gross Deutschland, 167th Inf Div, 10 Pz (Panther) Bde Decker, LII AK Ott, two Inf divs.

Kempf ❷ Army Abteilung, III PzK Breith: 6th, 7th, 19th PzDivs, 168 Inf Div, 503 (Tiger) Bn; XI AK Raus, three Inf divs: XXXXII AK three Inf divs.

Model ❸ Ninth Army, XXXXVII PzK Lemelsen: 2nd, 4th, 9th, 20th PzDivs, 505 Hvy (Tiger) PzBn, 6th Inf Div, XXXXI PzK Harpe: 18th PzDiv, 10th PzGrDiv, 653, 654 Pzjaeger (Ferdinand) Bns; XXXXVI PzK Zorn: Five infantry divisions and Gruppe von Manteuffel: XX and XXIII AK with seven infantry divs.

A Gr South Reserve (uncommitted) XXIV PzK Nehring: 5th SS 'Wiking', 17th PzDiv.

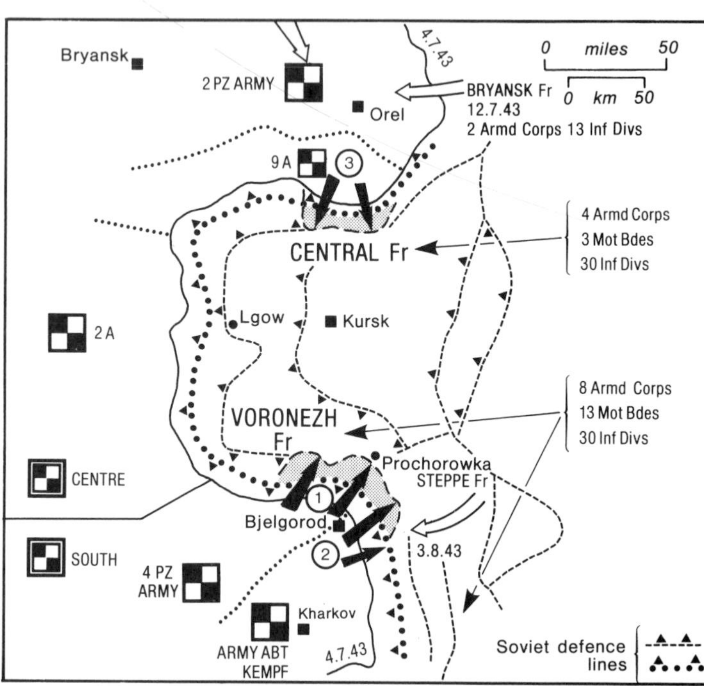

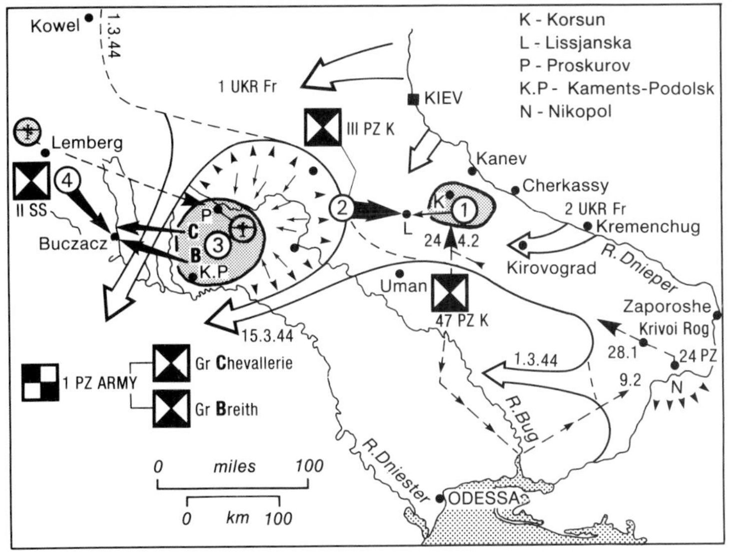

OKH/A Gr Centre Reserve 5th PzDiv (OKH) switched to Second Pz-Army, 12th PzDiv, 36th I.D. Mot.

A Gr Centre Von Kluge; 21 divs inc 6 PzDivs, 2 Pzgr, 700–800 tanks (45 Tigers), 350 assault guns.

A Gr South Von Manstein; 22 divs inc 11 PzDivs, 1 Pz bde, 1,300 tanks (101 Tigers), 250 assault guns. (Total 2,700 tanks/assault guns, inc. 146 Tigers).

Luftwaffe ❶❷ Dessloch, 4th Air Fleet, Seidemann VIII Air Corps – 1st, 4th Air Divs. 1,100 airc. ❸ Greim, 6th Air Fleet, Deichmann 1 Air Corps – 700 aircraft (Total 1,800 aircraft).

Red Army/Air Force Rokossovsky Central Fr; Vatutin Voronezh Fr; Konev Steppe Fr (from 18 July). 100 divs inc five tank armies, 3,306 tanks and assault guns, 2,650 aircraft.

15. A moving pocket in the Ukraine, 1944

Following a disastrous German outcome to 'Citadel' (map 14) the Eastern Front lacks armoured reserves with which to counter powerful Russian offensives aimed principally at enveloping von Manstein's Army Group South. Bjelgorod and Kharkov are lost; disaster threatens on the scale of Stalingrad. Hitler reluctantly sanctions retreat.

Consequently, in September 1943, panzer action focuses upon the Dnieper between Kiev and the Black Sea, where a million German troops struggle to evade encirclement. Success depends on von Manstein's ability to evacuate a 200-mile wide zone east of the river, using crossings at Kiev, Kanev, Cherkassy, Dniepropetrovsk and Zaporoshe.

Von Mackensen, Hoth First and Fourth Pz-Armies August–December 1943 stand with Eighth Army at the centre of the fighting.

Thirteen panzer divisions: 3rd, 6th, 9th, 11th, 13th, 14th, 17th, 19th, 23rd, 24th, SST, SSW, GD and three PzGr divisions: 10th, 16th, 20th, serve at crisis points.

Vormann, Breith ❶ On 28 January 1944 the threat to von Manstein is significantly heightened when 54,000 men of two Army Corps including SS Wiking, are trapped in a pocket at Cherkassy–Korsun on the Dnieper. A relief attempt by Eighth Army devolves upon 24th Panzer – transferred from Nikopol, 150 miles south and temporarily under command of XXXXVII Panzer Corps (Vormann). But even before the attempt is defeated by 2nd Ukr Front, 24th Panzer is ordered to return to Nikopol and counter a renewal of Red Army attacks on the bridgehead there. A fresh attempt to relieve Cherkassy from the west, organized by First Pz-Army (III Pz Corps Breith) will succeed by a narrow margin.

Hube ❷ First Pz-Army 17 February 1944. Reinforced by 503rd Tiger Bn (Pz Regt Bäcke) III Panzer Corps (Breith) approaches within reach of the Cherkassy defence, allowing 30,000 men trapped for twenty days and supplied by air, to break out and join Breith at Lissjanska. SS Wiking, one of the most redoubtable panzer divisions on the Eastern Front, leading the breakout, loses all its heavy weapons and equipment. But von Manstein's problems are far from over.

Hube ❸ First Pz-Army 24 March 1944 with 300,000 men is encircled at Kaments-Podolsk. Air transports from Lemberg resupply the divisions in a constantly moving pocket. Organized into corps-groups and fighting north-west to make contact with an SS relief force (II SS Pz Corps), the Pz-Army is reduced to a handful of tanks in 1st, 6th, 7th, 11th, 16th, 17th, 19th Pz, 20th Pz Gr and battlegroups 1SSLAH, 2SS Reich. Supplies, at first flown into Proskurov, are subsequently delivered by parachute. Transport action continues until 10 April 1944 (*see* Part 4, page 141).

Hube, Bittrich ❹ First Pz-Army and II SS Panzer Corps (Bittrich) unite at Buczacz on 8 April 1944.

Army Gr South ❶ Von Manstein; in Korsun–Cherkassy pocket, (Gruppe Stemmermann) SS Wiking, SS Bde Wallonien, seven inf divs. ❷ Breith relief corps; 16th, 17th Pz Divs, Tiger Bn 503. ❸ Hube in First Pz-Army pocket 22 divs (seven Pz, one pz gren div), Tiger Bns 503, 509.

II SS Pz Corps ❹ Bittrich, 9th SS, 10th SS PzDivs.

4th Air Fleet Dessloch: South of Kiev; August 1943, 1,150 aircraft by March 1944, 165 aircraft.

Red Army ❶–❹ Vatutin 1st UKr Fr; 63 rifle divs, six tank, two mech corps; Konev 2nd Ukr Fr; six armies in action to reduce Korsun, 135 tanks, thirteen rifle divs.

16. The West springs a trap: Normandy, 1944

On 6 June 1944, when 21st Army Group (Montgomery) invades Normandy in Operation 'Overlord', six panzer divisions and a panzer grenadier division stationed in northern France are mostly deployed too far away for immediate intervention. The opportunity for a concerted panzer offensive that might throw 21st Army Group back into the sea is lost. Divided command, faulty Intelligence, an almost total lack of air support and a faulty appreciation of Allied intentions contribute to German failure.

After a weak start the panzer divisions, rising to ten in number also a Pz Gr division, are deployed piecemeal mainly in defence of Caen. They are SS Panzer Divisions: 1st, 2nd, 9th, 10th, 12th and 17th (PzGr); Army panzer

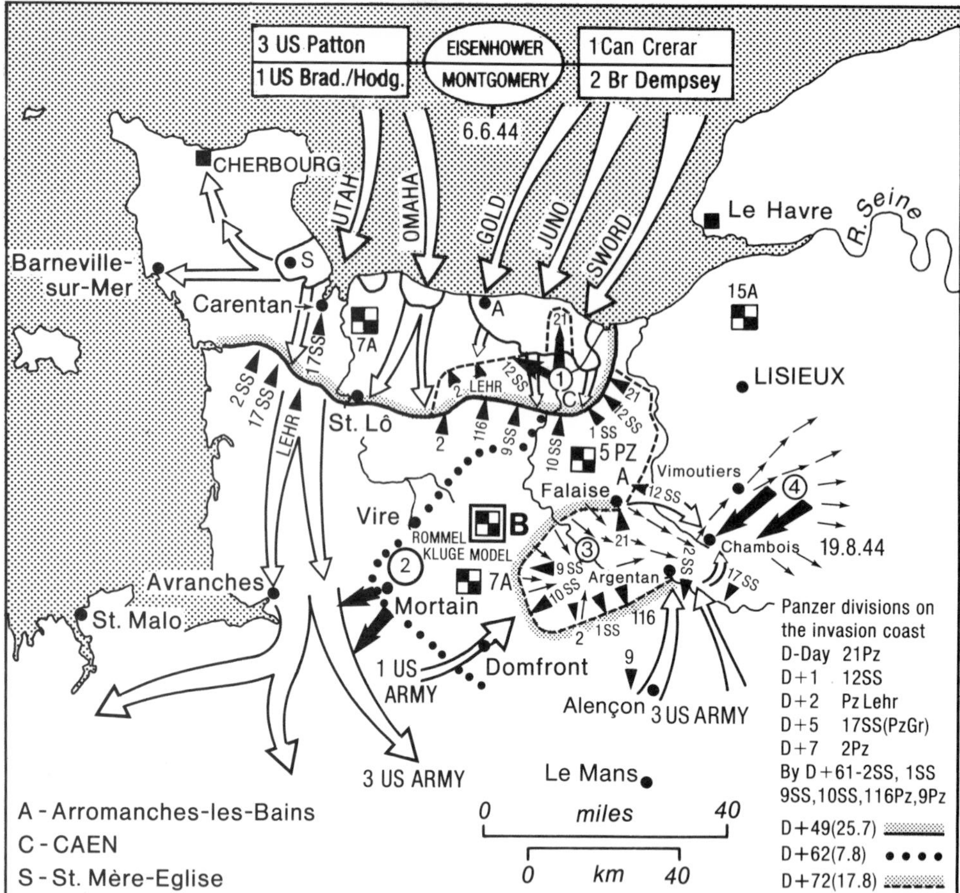

divisions: 2nd, 9th, 21st, 116th and PzLehr. During this time 11th Panzer at Bordeaux is committed in the south against 'Anvil', later renamed 'Dragoon': *see* Fifth Pz Army Europe, 15 August (D+70).

Geyr, Eberbach ❶ Pz-Group West (Fifth Pz-Army) 6 June 1944. 21st Panzer Division counter-attacking the beach-head thrusts to the coast at Lion-sur-Mer. Reinforcements – 12th SS (Hitler Youth), Panzer Lehr and 2nd Panzer Division – are slow in arriving. Hitler is deceived into concentrating most of the available panzer divisions on the German right around Caen to counter continuous British/Canadian offensives, 'Epsom', 'Charnwood', 'Goodwood', 'Totalise' and more. Von Kluge, the German Army Group Commander (after Rommel is wounded 17 July 1944), sees his weak left wing driven in and enveloped by a US armoured thrust lead by General George Patton – Operation 'Cobra', Fifth Panzer Army, Europe [25 July].

Hausser, von Funck ❷ Fifth Panzer Army Europe [7 August] Starting from Mortain with two Panzer Corps, XXXVIII – 2nd and 116th PzDivs; 1st SS PzK – 1st and 2nd SS PzDivs, a German Seventh Army counter-attack 'Lüttich', is shattered by Allied air power and aborted: 9th Panzer, north-west of Alençon, momentarily slows the US advance.

Dietrich, Hausser, Eberbach ❸ Fifth Pz-Army, Europe 19–21 August 1944 is one of two German armies, Seventh and Fifth Pz, also Pz-Group Eberbach, trapped south of Caen. The pocket is resolutely defended by Army and Waffen SS; 12th SS follows a tenacious defence of key points with a notable role in holding open an escape route for both Armies and Panzergruppe

Bittrich ❹ Battle groups from 2nd and 9th SS Pz Divisions counter-attacking under II SS Pz-Corps previously evacuated from the pocket, assist in extricating the trapped divisions. None, according to Model, escape across the Seine 'with more than ten tanks'.

C-in-C West Von Runstedt; 59 divs (nine Pz, one Pz Gr including four SS) two SS Pz arriving.

Western Allies Eisenhower; 86 divs (39 for 'Overlord' 17 in first wave inc. two armd).

Army Gr 'B' ❶ Rommel 41 divs. Pz dispositions D-Day 21 Pz Divs. south of the Seine, 2nd, 116th Pz Divs north of the Seine. By D+7 also includes 12th SS, Pz Lehr, 17th SS from OKW reserve (Pz Gr West). By D+61 (6 August 1944) ten Pz divs, one Pz Gr Division (six SS including 9th SS, 10th SS from A Gr N. Ukraine.

Seventh Army ❷ Hausser; four Pz Divs (two SS), two Pz Div battle groups.

Fifth Pz Army, Seventh Army ❸ Dietrich, Hausser; twelve-thirteen div. battle groups (six-seven Pz).

II SS Pz Corps ❹ Bittrich; 2/9 SS Pz Div battle groups.

3rd Air Fleet Sperrle; 800–1,000 aircraft rising to 1,300 by D+10. Invasion front II Jagd Korps (Junck) 496 aircraft all types – battle-fit 319 inc. II Flieger Korps (Bülowius)

with 75 ground-attack types.

Allied Forces ❶–❹ Montgomery, Br 21 A Gr; Bradley, US 12 A Gr. By 25 August 1944, 39 divs (thirteen armd–four Br, six US, one Fr, one Can, one Pol).

US Third Army Patton seven divs (three armd).

Allied Exp. Air Forces Leigh Mallory; in Britain 12,837 aircraft, 7,774 battle-fit.

17. 'Autumn Mist', autumn disaster: Belgium, 1944

Operation 'Autumn Mist', formerly 'Watch on the Rhine', is Hitler's last offensive in the west. After weeks of secret preparation, two panzer armies are launched west through the Ardennes attacking US First Army resting on the River Meuse. Hitler intends to recapture Antwerp and Brussels, encircle Allied armies deployed between the Ardennes and the German front in Holland and, wishfully, force an Allied evacuation of the continent.

Dietrich and von Manteuffel Sixth SS and Fifth Pz-Army (Europe) 16 December 1944 report early gains when the Allies are once again taken off-guard by an armoured stroke delivered out of the Ardennes. But progress is unspectacular, even less so in the north where, hampered by a staunch American defence squeezing attacking SS divisions into a narrow operational area from which they are unable to break-out, the offensive loses momentum.

Von Manteuffel Fifth Pz-Army (Europe) 24 December 1944 records better progress in the south. But Bastogne, a vital communications centre *en route* to the west, has steadfastly refused to surrender. The SS divisions are redeployed. German efforts are redoubled – absorbing effort intended for the westwards thrust. Bastogne nevertheless remains a thorn in the German side, refusing to surrender. Petrol and ammunition shortages curtail panzer operations and the German offensive is hamstrung. On 26 December 1944 Bastogne is relieved by US III Corps.

Von Manteuffel Fifth Pz-Army (Europe) 3 January 1945. When good flying weather allows Anglo-US air forces to strike at extended panzer supply columns, and Allied armies re-grouped under temporary command of Field Marshal Montgomery are launched into powerful counter-attacks, 'Autumn Mist' has run its course and Hitler calls it off.

Von Manteuffel Fifth Panzer Army 4 January 1945 orders a final effort by I SS Pz Corps (Priess) to capture Bastogne. The action ends in failure.

Sixth SS Pz-Army Dietrich; I SS PzK Priess: 1st SSLAH, 12th SS HJ, two VGDs and 3rd Para Div: II SS PzK, Bittrich: 2nd SS Reich, 9th SS Hohenstaufen LXVII AK two VGDs.

Fifth Pz-Army von Manteuffel; XLVII PzK von Lüttwitz; 2nd Pz, PzLehr, 26th VGD; LVIII PzK, Krüger: 116th Pz, 560th VGD, later FBB: LXVI AK two VGDs, XXXIX PzK Decker arriving 27 December co-ordinates offensive against

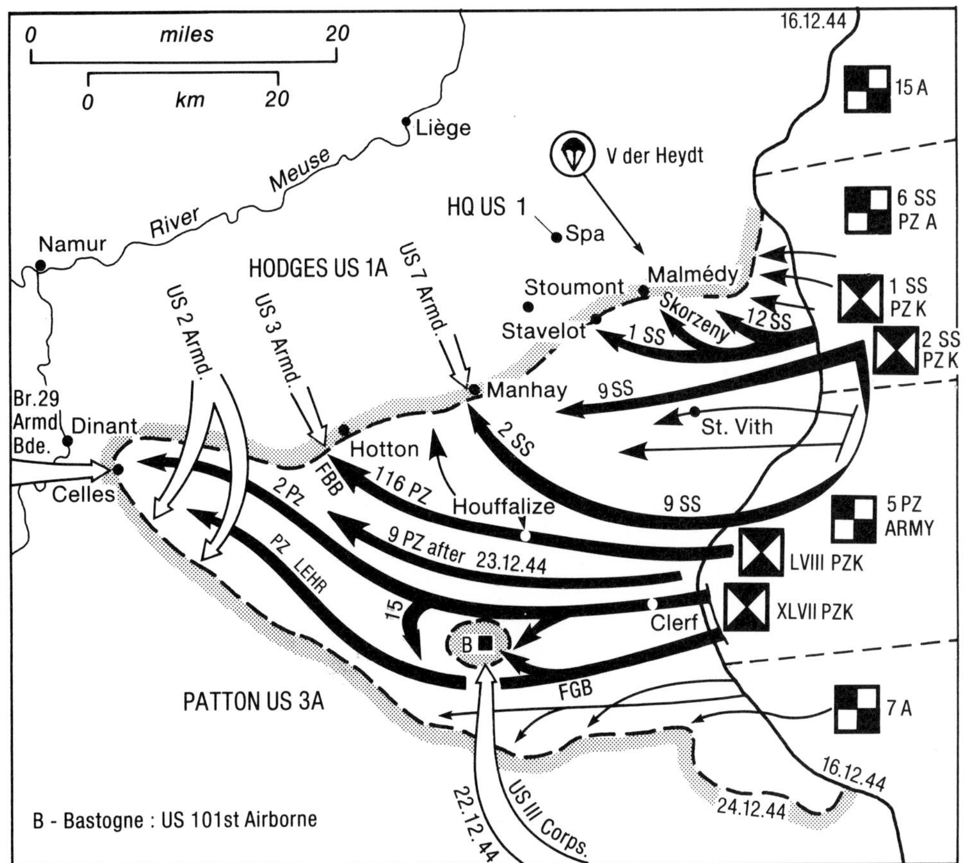

Bastogne with 11th Pz, 3rd, 15th PzGrDivs: thereafter joins *ad hoc* Armeegruppe von Lüttwitz 30–31 December before transferring south to Alsace for 'North Wind'.

Fifteenth Army von Zangen; Four Army Corps including 15th PzGrDiv and 9th PzDiv.

Seventh Army Brandenburger; Three Army Corps with three VGD and 5th Para Div.

OKW Reserve; 10th SS Frundsberg, 11th Pz, 3rd PzGr, 6th SS Mtn Div.

Führer Grenadier Bde FGB – reinforces Seventh Army on 22 December.

Führer Begleit Bde FBB – reinforces Fifth Pz Army on 23 December.

Army Group 'B' Model; nine panzer divisions (inc two reserve), two pz-grenadier divs, fourteen inf divs (inc two para) 1,750 tanks and SP guns inc. 30 King Tigers.

Luftwaffen Kdo West Schmid; II Fighter Corps (Pelz) 1,800 aircraft inc. 91 ground-attack types (Schlacht Geschwader 4) Pickert, III Flak Corps.

US First Army Hodges, six Inf divs, 82nd Airborne, three armd divs.*

US Third Army Patton, six Inf divs, 101st Airborne, two armd divs.*

British XXX Corps Horrocks, 6th Airborne Div, two inf divs, three armd bdes.

*Together rising to 29 divs.

18. Retreat through Poland, 1945

When the Red Army returns to the offensive in eastern Poland, striking west across the Vistula to threaten Berlin, 1st Ukranian Front at Baranov crushes German infantry in Fourth Pz-Army's first line of defence. XXIV Pz corps (Nehring), a mobile reserve comprising two panzer divisions (16th, 17th) and a panzer grenadier division (20th), also a Tiger Bn (424), is deployed to attack the flank of any penetration west of the river, but is instead engulfed in fighting around Kielce and forced to retreat.

Nehring (Fourth Pz-Army) 12 January 1945 fights north-west to Petrikau, seeking contact with Panzer Corps Gross Deutschland (von Saucken).

Von Saucken, Pz Corps Gross Deutschland comprises the powerful Hermann Goering (Fallschirm) Panzer Division (HG1) and the new Panzer Grenadier Division Brandenburg (BR), both diverted from East Prussia for the relief attempt. The move is contrary to Guderian's advice to Hitler and to the detriment of the defence there.

Nehring and von Saucken retain their mobility only with the help of air transports operating from the area north-west of Breslau. Neither Pz Corps will survive without container supplies of fuel and ammunition. *See* Part 4, New Horizons in Transport, page 137.

Two other panzer divisions (19th, 25th) and a 10th Pz-Grenadier battle group deployed in reserve west of Warsaw, none more capable than a regimental Kampfgruppe, face equally devastating Red Army attacks.

These panzer divisions: 16th, 17th, 19th, 25th and the Pz-Gr battle groups deployed in reserve behind infantry of Army Group 'A' are all that can be spared of a burned-out panzer force to oppose the Red Army's direct drive on Berlin (163 divisions, 6,500 tanks and assault guns). Powerless to restore the situation, the depleted formations withdraw fighting to the west.

Army Group 'A' Harpe; 26 inf divs, four Pz divs, two Pz Gr divs includes Kampfgruppe 10th PzGr.

East Front excl. Courland, 145 Inf divs, eighteen Pz divs, ten Pz Gr divs.

6th Air Fleet Greim 1,060 aircraft all types (300 ground-attack) rising to 1,500 aircraft (450 ground-attack).

Red Army/Air Force Zhukov 1st BeloRuss Fr, Konev 1st UKR Fr; ten armies (two tank), 163 rifle divs.

Russian superiority(:) 6,500 tanks and SP guns (5:1), 4,772 aircraft (17:1).

19. Last cauldron: Army and SS in Hungary, 1945

Following an unsuccessful conclusion to 'Autumn Mist' (map 17) Sixth SS Panzer Army (Dietrich) is switched across Europe to reinforce Army Group South (Wöhler) defending western Hungary. There on 26 December 1944 Budapest, the capital city of 800,000 inhabitants housing numerous military agencies and defended by upwards of 70,000 men including 13th Pz Division and Feldherrnhalle responsible to SS General Pfeffer von Wildenbruck (IX SS Mtn Corps), is encircled by two Ukrainian fronts.

Balck, Gille ❶ (Sixth SS Pz-Army) 13 February 1945. Operation 'Konrad' is the first of three attempts by Armeegruppe Balck (Sixth Army) to relieve Budapest. Starting on 1 January with IV SS Panzer Corps (Gille) transferred with Totenkopf and Wiking from Ninth Army/Army Group Centre, 'Konrad' is a failure; despite heavy fighting by SS Wiking to within fifteen miles of the perimeter. Budapest remains besieged. 'Konrad 2' a second

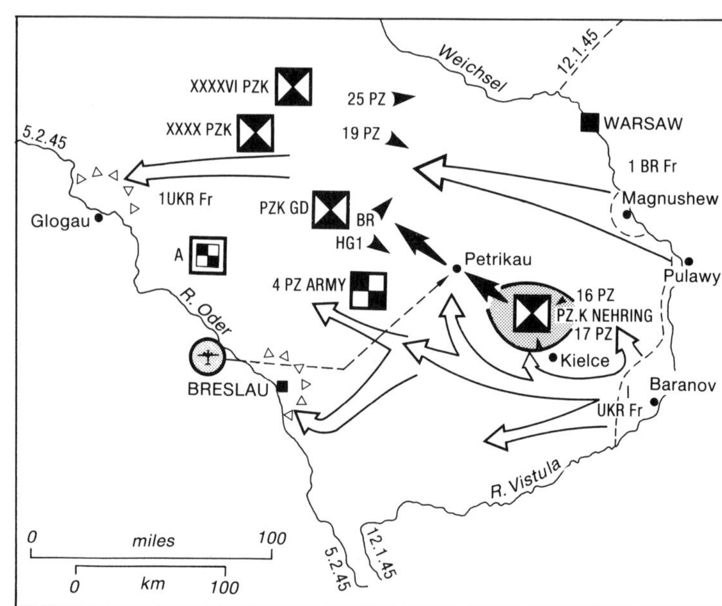

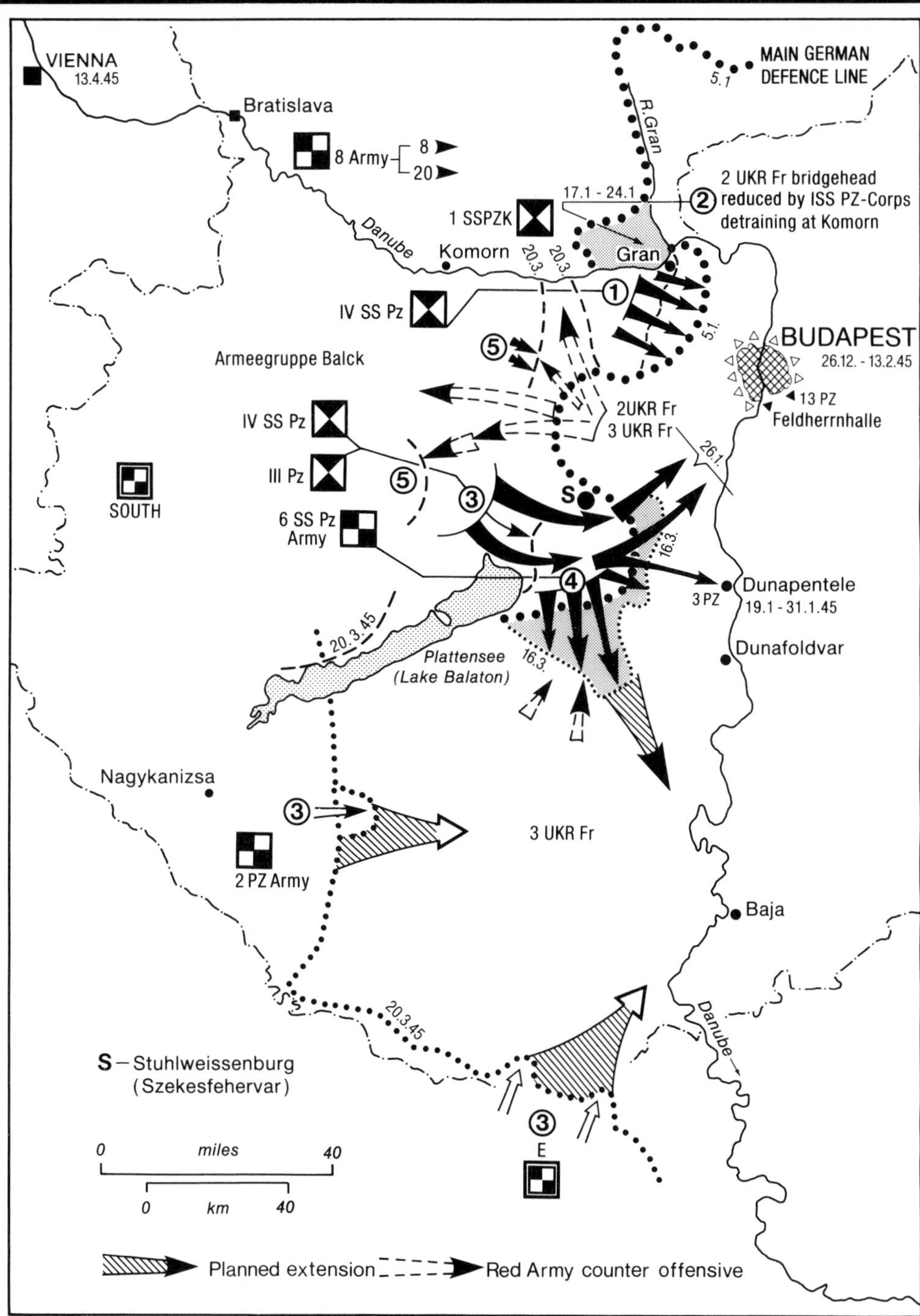

attempt by III PzK (Breith) 9–12 January fares no better.

Priess ❷ Panzer battles next develop east of Komorn where an unexpectedly powerful Operation 'South Wind' lead by I SS Pz Corps – LSSAH and 12 SS HJ – reduces 2nd UKR Front's bridgehead on the River Gran. Pz Corps Feldherrnhalle with remnants of units isolated in Budapest provides mainly infantry support.

Balck, Gille, Breith ❸ Meanwhile Sixth Army's third relief attempt 'Konrad 3' follows on 18 January 1945, from a new direction. But the reinforced SS Panzer Corps (Gille) attacking south around Stuhlweissenburg with 1st and 3rd Panzer Divisions, SS Totenkopf and SS Wiking while flank protection to the north is provided by Breith's III Panzer Corps – 6th and 23rd Panzer Divisions and south by Pz Recce Bns 1st, 3rd, 23rd again fails to relieve the city. A break-out attempt by the defenders on 11 February is equally unsuccessful; Budapest surrenders on 13 February 1945. Hitler's arbitrary diversion of panzer divisions to this secondary front is nevertheless set to continue.

Dietrich, Balck, de Angelis ❹ Sixth SS Pz-Army 6 March

1945 opens a new offensive 'Spring Awakening' in which Sixth Army (Balck), Second Panzer Army (de Angelis) – four infantry divisions and a weak 16th Reichsführer SS Panzer Grenadier Division (Baum) – are also involved in Hitler's plan to encircle the Red Army west of the Danube, recapture Budapest and retain oil-production centres at Nagykaniscza south-west of Lake Balaton. But 'Spring Awakening' falters in waterlogged terrain and when counter-attacked in strength by 3rd UKr Front fails to recover momentum. ❺ A renewal of Russian attacks aiming at Vienna and the Danube valley threatening German communications precipitates a general retreat; by 20 March, panzer rearguards are fighting desperately to defend positions west of their original start-line.

6th Armeegruppe Balck; Sixth Army, Hung Third Army, Gille, IV SS Pz Corps; Breith III Pz-Corps, Harteneck I Cav Corps, SS Wiking, SS Totenkopf, Pz Divs 1st, 3rd, 6th, 23rd, three cav divs, Hungarian tanks, infantry, Army troops. After 14 January, 503, 509 Tiger Bns. By 20 January, 274 Pz Kpfw IV–VIs, Jag Pz and SPs. By 6 March, 138 mixed tanks.

Eighth Army Kreysing (north of Danube) 8th, 20th Pz Divs, remnant battle groups Feldherrnhalle, 13th Pz.

Sixth SS Pz-Army Dietrich; Priess I SS Pz Corps, Bittrich II SS Pz Corps, SS Pz-Divs 1st, 2nd, 9th, 12th. Reinforced 6 March, 23rd Pz and two cav divs. By 6 March, 540 tanks and SP guns (320 battle-fit).

Second Pz-Army de Angelis; Lanz XXII Mtn Corps, Konrad LXVIII Corps, 16th SS PzGren Div, four Inf divs (two Mtn).

4th Air Fleet Dessloch; Deichmann, I Air Corps, by 6 March 850 aircraft.

Red Army/Air Force 1 January 1945, Malinovsky 2nd UKr Front; Tolbuchin 3rd UK Front; 54 Inf divs; five mech corps; three armd corps, two cav corps. By 6 March, 407 tanks, 965 aircraft.

20. Germany in defeat, 1945

Armageddon 1945. Panzer divisions starved of petrol at times to the point of immobility, with few if any towing machines, lacking in ammunition and air support, record local successes against overwhelming odds. All are swept into defeat. The Red Army advancing in overwhelming strength in the east employs tank and motorized forces patterned on the German model and much of its transport supplied by Western Allies. Equally powerful US and British armies close in from the West.

East: First and Fourth Pz-Armies 12 January 1945, face the eastern threat to Berlin, but with only four panzer divisions between them to support an infantry defence of the Vistula and Carpathians south of Warsaw (map 18) collapse under massive attacks. Second Pz-Army March 1945 deployed south of Budapest with no armour at all also gives way under Russian pressure. Third Pz Army 8 February 1945 after failing to protect Königsberg and East Prussia, withdraws to Pomerania and the Oder north of Berlin under command of Army Group Vistula; Sixth SS Pz-Army 6 March 1945, the best-equipped formation, defeated in western Hungary (map 19) withdraws to Vienna. The city falls on 13 April.

North-east: Army Group Courland possesses only two panzer divisions in its order of battle.

South-west: Only a single panzer division opposing Anglo-US armies is left in northern Italy.

West: Fifth Pz-Army, Europe 16 December 1944 follows an abortive joint offensive Fifth/Sixth SS Pz-Army in the Ardennes (map 17), with encirclement and surrender in the Ruhr. Reduced to forty tanks, Fifty Panzer Army capitulates on 18 April.

Berlin is encircled by the Red Army on 25 April 1945 (*see* Third Panzer Army, 16 April). Hitler takes his own life on the 30th. Keitel signs the Wehrmacht's capitulation to the Russians in Berlin on 9 May 1945.

With the last of the panzer divisions contained in East Prussia surrendering to 2nd BR Front on 14 May, the remnant of a once omnipotent panzer force count for little more than flags on Red Army and Allied Intelligence maps. Dispersed far and wide, surviving units serve mostly in the east with Army Groups Centre and South.

Berlin LVI Pz K Weidling; 18th, 20th, 11th SS PzGrDivs. Pz Division Muncheberg.

A Gr Centre Schörner; First PzA Nehring, Fourth PzA Gräser: 6th, 8th, 16th, 17th, 19th, 20th, 21st, HG1, FBD, 2nd SS, 10th SS PzDivs; Brandenburg; 10th PzGrDiv.

A Gr South Rendulic; Second PzA de Angelis, Sixth SS PzA Dietrich: 1st, 3rd, 23rd, 25th, FGD PzDivs; 1st, 3rd, 5th, 9th, 12th SS PzDivs, Feldherrnhalle.

A Gr Vistula Student; Third PzA Raus: 4th SS, 25th PzGr Div.

East Prussia Von Saucken, formerly German Second Army: 4th, 5th, 7th PzDivs: Gross Deutschland.

North-east. A Gr Courland Hilpert, formerly A Gr North: 12th, 14th PzDivs.

West: A Grs 'B', 'G'. 'B', Model: Fifth PzA Harpe, 9th Pz Div, Fifteenth Army: PzLehr, 116th Pz. Seventh Army; 2nd, 11th Pz. 'G', Schulz: First Army, 17th SS.

South west: A Gr 'C' Vietinghoff, Tenth Army; 26th PzDiv. 29th, 90th PzGrDivs.

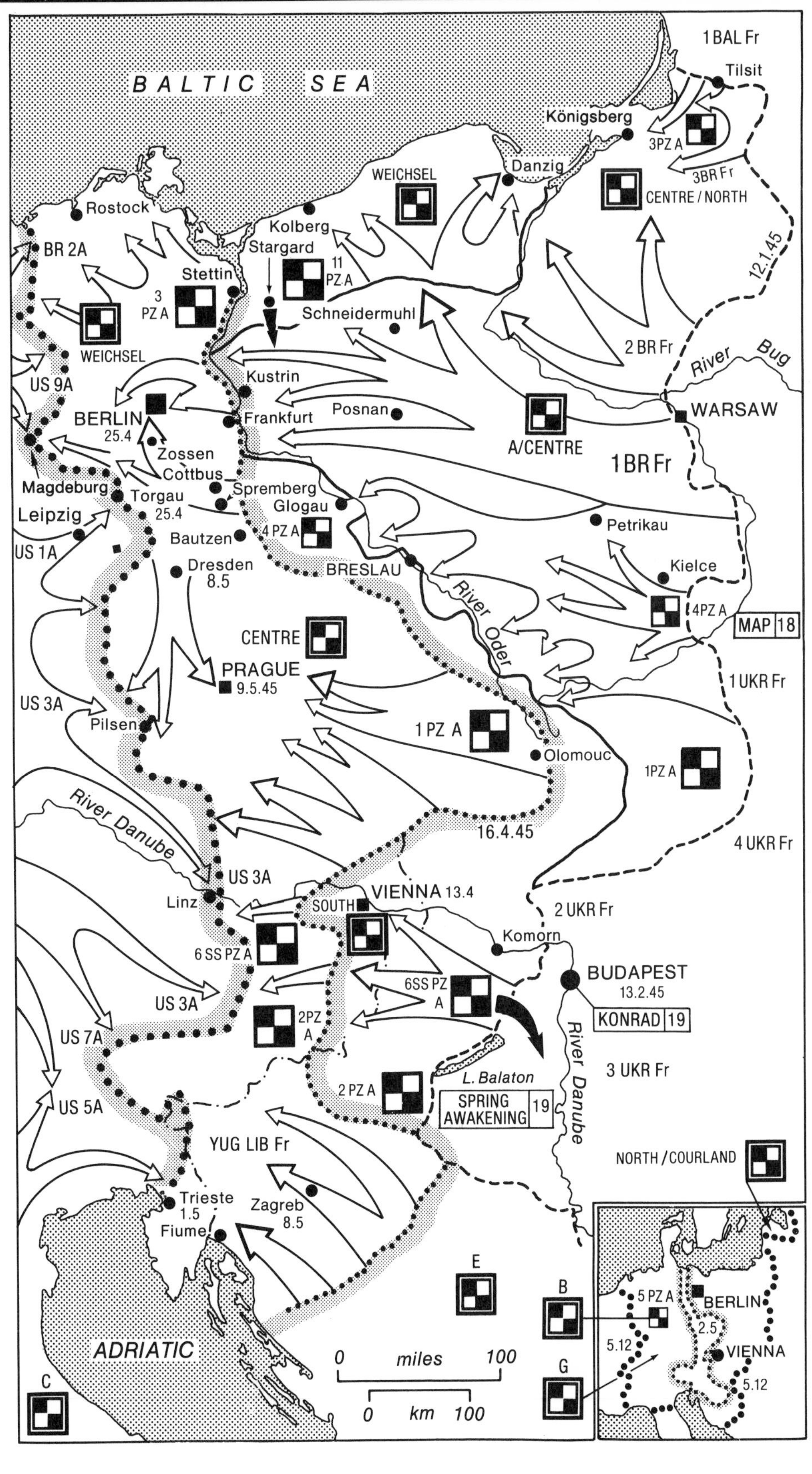
BALTIC SEA
1 BAL Fr
Tilsit
Königsberg
3PZ A
3BR Fr
CENTRE / NORTH
12.1.45
Danzig
WEICHSEL
Rostock
Kolberg
Stargard
11 PZ A
BR 2A
Stettin
3 PZ A
Schneidermuhl
WEICHSEL
2 BR Fr
River Bug
US 9A
Kustrin
WARSAW
BERLIN
25.4
Frankfurt
Posnan
A/CENTRE
Zossen
Cottbus
1 BR Fr
Magdeburg
Spremberg
Torgau
25.4
Glogau
Leipzig
Petrikau
US 1A
Bautzen
4 PZ A
Dresden
8.5
BRESLAU
Kielce
River Oder
4PZ A
MAP 18
CENTRE
PRAGUE
9.5.45
1 UKR Fr
US 3A
Pilsen
1 PZ A
Olomouc
1PZ A
River Danube
16.4.45
4 UKR Fr
US 3A
Linz
VIENNA 13.4
SOUTH
2 UKR Fr
Komorn
6 SS PZ A
BUDAPEST
13.2.45
6SS PZ A
KONRAD 19
US 3A
US 7A
2PZ A
River Danube
L. Balaton
3 UKR Fr
2 PZ A
SPRING AWAKENING 19
US 5A
YUG LIB Fr
NORTH / COURLAND
Trieste
1.5
Zagreb
8.5
Fiume
E
B
5 PZ A
BERLIN
2.5
5.12
VIENNA
5.12
ADRIATIC
0 miles 100
0 km 100
G
C

Part 6. Campaigns and battles, 1939–45

1. First Panzer Army (PzAOK 1)

Originally XXII motorized Infantry Corps, raised near Hamburg in August 1939. Corps Commander General der Kavallerie Ewald von Kleist (Generaloberst 19 July 1940).

Poland, 1939 (map 2) 1–16 September. Spearheading Fourteenth Army (List), concentrated in eastern Czechoslovakia for Operation 'White', von Kleist developed panzer operations on the outer wing of Army Group South. The Corps consisted basically of 2nd Panzer Division (Veiel) and 4th Light Division (Hubicki). On 17 September von Kleist Corps thrusting north-east through Poland to the Bug via Tarnow completed a double encirclement of the Polish Army by joining up with Guderian at Vlodava east of Warsaw (*see* Second Panzer Army, 17 September 1939). 5 March 1940 redesignated Panzer Group von Kleist.

France: Operation 'Yellow', 1940 (map 3). On 10 May at the start of the operation Panzer Group von Kleist, consisting of three motorized corps, XIX, XXXI and XIV, was concentrated east of Luxemburg on the German side of the Ardennes. Initially responsible to Army Group 'A' (von Runstedt), von Kleist's Group would lead the main armoured movement against the Allies, subsequently answering to German Tenth Army (List) and ultimately Fourth Army (von Kluge). Allotted five of the ten panzer divisions committed to the western offensive, von Kleist's leading panzer corps, XIX (Guderian) and XXXXI (Reinhardt), followed by XIV Motorized Corps (von Wietersheim), pushed west through the Ardennes forest towards the Meuse. Brushing aside a weak cavalry screen, von Kleist confronted 1st French Army Group (Billotte) with two of its four armies, Ninth (Corap) and Second (Huntziger), deployed on the west bank of the river north and south of Sedan.

France: Panzer Corridor, 1940 (map 4). On the afternoon of 13 May, von Kleist stormed the Meuse supported by II Air Corps (Lörzer) and Stuka Wings of VIII Air Corps (von Richthofen), the latter having been diverted from Hoepner's decoy offensive under Army Group 'B' at Maastricht (Fourth Panzer Army, 10 May). Overcoming mainly weak infantry opposition, von Kleist built west bank bridgeheads at Sedan (Guderian) and Monthermé (Reinhardt). Guderian was immediately successful (Second Panzer Army, 13 May), but Reinhardt was delayed by spirited opposition and was not ready to move west until the 15th. Starting on that date, von Kleist's Group lead Twelfth Army thrusts to the Channel via St-Quentin and Péronne. Secondary action by Hoth's XV Corps (mot) crossing the Meuse downstream at Dinant and driving in the direction of Arras secured the right flank and reinforced the offensive. In concerted panzer operations, joined by Hoepner on the 19th (*see* Fourth Panzer Army), von Kleist and Hoth Groups thrust west to the Channel coast and created a panzer 'corridor', splitting the Allied front and forcing French armies apart. The British Expeditionary Force was pinned to the coast at Dunkirk (*see also* Second and Third Panzer Armies, 13 May). On 23 May, with von Kleist and Hoth sharing all the panzer divisions between them, and subordinate to Fourth Army (von Kluge), Army Group 'B' prepared for a final offensive. Events turned out differently. On 24 May, in accordance with Hitler's instructions, panzer operations were halted outside Dunkirk. At Goering's prompting the Luftwaffe was left to complete the work of destruction, but failed and allowed the BEF to escape to England in Operation 'Dynamo', ending 4 June.

France: Operation 'Red', 1940. In the 'Red' phase of the Battle for France (map 3), with the panzer force redeployed in three attacking groups facing south along the Somme and Aisne, von Kleist at Amiens, co-operating with XVI Corps (Hoepner) at Péronne, was given the central role leading Sixth Army – Army Group 'B' (von Bock) in the drive to envelop Paris from the west. Lined up with Hoth (Fourth Army) on the Seine to the west at Abbeville, and Guderian (Twelfth Army) – Army Group 'A' (von Runstedt) on the Aisne to the east at Rethel, the Group prepared for action. On 5 June von Kleist's corps, consisting basically of XIV Panzer Corps with two panzer and one SS motorized division, attacked south-west from Amiens with the intention of bypassing Paris to the west and, in conjunction with Guderian, encircling Paris Army and French forces concentrated about the capital. Supportive action devolved upon XVI Panzer Corps attacking south at Péronne, but determined opposition by French 3rd Army Group brought Sixth Army's offensive to a halt. Instead, on the 9th, OKH switched von Kleist eastwards to join Ninth Army close by Guderian serving Army Group 'A' (von Rundstedt).

[*Hoth, meanwhile, working south across the Seine from Abbeville, bypassed Paris to the west before sweeping into Normandy and Brittany.*]

Above: Field Marshal Ewald von Kleist served with distinction in Poland, France and Russia. He was GOC, Army Group South, Ukraine, in March 1943 and died a prisoner in Russia in 1956.

On 11 June in a revised plan of operations von Kleist bypassed Paris to the east after crossing the Marne south of Laon. Incorporating XVI Panzer Corps (Hoepner) Kleistgruppe negotiated Château-Thierry to reach Troyes on 14 June – the day on which 87th Infantry division (German Eighteenth Army) entered Paris. Général Wegand, the French C-in-C, authorized an armistice on 22 June and Hitler followed the army into Paris on the 23rd. Von Kleist reached Angoulême on the 25th – the day on which the armistice became effective. At the conclusion of the battle, the French Government accepted the partitioning of France into occupied (German) and unoccupied (Vichy Government) zones, broadly north and south of Lyon, with an Atlantic coast extension to the Spanish frontier. Lyon itself remained unoccupied until Operation 'Anton' brought II SS Panzer Corps into action (*see* Fifth Panzer Army Africa, 11 November 1942).

Diversion in the Balkans, March 1941 (map 6). Arriving in south-east Europe for action against the Greek Army [*von Kleist's redeployment followed the arrival of a British Expeditionary Force at Volos and Piraeus on the 7th*], von Kleist's Group with two panzer corps was concentrated in Bulgaria north of Sofia. But in a change of plan following anti-German moves in Belgrade, von Kleist was committed instead against Yugoslavia. On 8 April, two days after the start of Operation '25' (von Weichs), with XXXXVI Panzer Corps (von Vietinghoff) pushing towards Zagreb (14th Panzer Division), von Kleist lead the offensive against Belgrade, entering Nish on the 9th and Belgrade (11th Panzer Division, Crüwell) on the 12th – making contact there with XXXXI Panzer Corps (Reinhardt) from the north-east. Thereafter, subordinate to Second Army less 5th Panzer Division, transferred to Stumme, von Kleist's group linked up with 16th Motorized Division (Henrici) following the capture of Sarajevo (15 April). The panzer group was then allotted to Army Group South (von Runstedt) for the invasion of Russia, a hazardous undertaking in which von Kleist's task was to lead the attacking forces in the direction of Kiev.

Russia: Operation 'Barbarossa', South 1941 (map 7). On 22 June, consisting initially of three panzer corps von Kleist's Group, with a total of eight divisions and the motorized SS Leibstandarte Brigade (Dietrich), overcame determined opposition, breaking the Stalin line (16th Panzer Division) and taking Zhitomir on 19 July (19th Panzer Division) and encircling Russian Sixth, Twelfth and Eighteenth Armies at Uman, before crossing the Dnieper at Kremenchug on 11–12 September. The Kremenchug crossing was followed within days by the most rewarding of all 'Barbarossa' encirclement battles. On 14 September 1941, von Kleist's XLVIII Panzer Corps (Kempf), acting in conjunction with Guderian's arrival east of Kiev, pushed 16th Panzer Division (Hube) northwards to meet 3rd Panzer Division (Model) and co-operate in Hitler's plan to envelope five Russian armies (*see* Second Panzer Army, 14 September). Von Kleist followed this move by capturing Stalino (1st Mountain Division, XIV Panzer Corps) and subsequently Taganrog on the Sea of Azov. Thereafter proceeding to the Mius, von Kleist won a bridgehead on the 20th. On 25 October 1941, up-graded and renamed First Panzer Army, von Kleist pressed on to Rostov; III Panzer Corps (von Mackensen) reached the town on 20 November. But weakened by the absence of XXXXVIII Panzer Corps (9th Panzer Division and two motorized infantry divisions), transferred to Guderian for 'Typhoon' (*see* Second Panzer Army, 30 September 1941), von Kleist was unable to retain Rostov and its vital Don crossings won by the Leibstandarte. Therefore, losing Rostov to the Red Army, von Kleist retired behind the Mius for the winter. On 17 May 1942, preceding von Kleist's commitment to a summer offensive leading Army Group 'A' into the Caucasus, two preparatory undertakings yielded profitable results. 'Fridericus I' centred on III Panzer Corps (von Mackensen) – two panzer, one motorized and eight supporting infantry divisions – routing two Russian armies south-east of Kharkov, recapturing Issyum and claiming 214,000 prisoners. 'Fridericus II', taking more prisoners winning Kupjansk, gained a bridgehead on a tributary of the Donets, crucial to the forthcoming summer offensive – Operation 'Blue' (*see* Fourth Panzer Army, 28 June).

Russia: Operation 'Blue', 1942 (map 10) renamed 'Brunswick' on 30 July 1942 (map 10). Operation 'Blue' and its successor 'Mouse' would take von Kleist (from July 1942 to 1 January 1943) from the area south-east of Kharkov to the foothills of the eastern Caucasus. Advancing from Rostov to the Terek in the final stage of the offensive, First Panzer Army extended its communications by more than 400 miles. In the battle for Rostov on 23–25 July, III Panzer Corps (von Mackensen), co-operating with LVII Panzer Corps (Kirchner) – Seventeenth Army made heavy demands on 13th, 14th, 22nd Panzer and SS Wiking Divisions. On 26 July, First Panzer Army/4th Air Fleet (von Richthofen) forced the River Don east of Rostov. The operation was lead by III and LVII Panzer Corps with three panzer and two motorized divisions assisted by four infantry and a Slovak (Schnelle) division. On 2 August von Kleist was reinforced by XXXX Panzer Corps (Geyr) making good the loss of LVII Panzer Corps transferred to Seventeenth Army. The Panzer Group then bypassed Armavir on 6 August, pushing south-east to Maikop (13th Panzer Division) reached three days later. Mozdok (3rd Panzer Division) fell on the 25th and Malgobek (SS Wiking Division) north-west of Grosny on 5 October, but supply shortages halting movement for weeks at a time, relentless opposition by the Red Army and the onset of winter forced von Kleist on to the defensive. Starting on 25 October von Kleist renewed the offensive with immediate success at Nalchik and by 2 November had pushed III Panzer Corps (von Mackensen) to the outskirts of Ordzhonikidze – furthermost point in First Panzer Army's drive to the Caucasus (map 11). But armour attacks lead by 13th Panzer Division (Herr) failed to capture the town, a key road and rail junction at the head of the Georgian Military Highway, giving access to oil-producing regions in the south, and Ordzhonikidze remained firmly in Russian hands. Despite intensive action by 13th, 23rd Panzer and SS Viking Divisions in the vanguard of the offensive, von Kleist's bid to capture Russian oil-producing centres at Baku, Grosny and Tiflis came to a standstill.

Meanwhile, Hitler had dismissed Field Marshal List, C-in-C, Army Group 'A', on grounds of incompetence, and decided to direct operations in the Caucasus himself, from Führer HQ, Rastenburg. But after fourteen days as GOC Army Group 'A', Hitler nominated von Kleist as his successor. Consequently, on 22 November command of First Panzer Army passed to General von Mackensen, but the panzer army's future was soon to be compromised by the loss of major ground and air formations diverted to assist 'Winter Storm' operations at Stalingrad (map 12). (*See* Fourth Panzer Army, 12 December 1942.)

Starting on 1 January 1943, First Panzer Army, abandoning the Terek for Rostov, began a fighting withdrawal to the north-east, firm contact being established with Fourth Panzer Army on the 20th. Armavir was evacuated on the 25th. On 27 January after releasing 13th Panzer Division to reinforce Seventeenth Army defending the Kuban bridgehead, von Mackensen was taken under command of Army Group Don (Field Marshal von Manstein); the panzer army's remaining four divisions continuing north through Rostov or immediately west across the frozen Sea of Azov under pressure from North Caucasus Front.

By 4 February First Panzer Army was safely behind the Don, regrouping in the Don-Donetz triangle. [*On 14 February Rostov, defended by LVII Panzer Corps (Fourth Panzer Army) was evacuated and von Manstein's Army Group Don was renamed Army Group South.*]

Von Manstein's Miracle (map 13). By 22 February, First Panzer Army was regrouped north of Stalino, co-ordinating operations with Fourth Panzer Army in a battle to recover Kharkov. In a series of deftly contrived manoeuvres the Panzer Army first intercepted and then struck back at Popov's armoured group leading South West Front, exploiting Russian success westwards after the victorious siege of Stalingrad; battles in which SS Viking, 7th and 11th Panzer Divisions (XXXX Panzer Corps), outflanking Popov, forced a Russian retreat to the Donets. On 28 February von Mackensen reached the Donets south of Issyum, sealing the fate of Popov's armoured group and destroying South West Front units still south of the river and mostly unable to re-cross to safety.

During the spring and early summer of 1943, Generaloberst von Mackensen and First Panzer Army played no direct part in von Manstein's Operation 'Citadel', the battle for Kursk, unfolding on the army's left flank in the summer of 1943 (*see* Fourth Panzer Army, 5 July 1943). But from August to December 1943, the collapse of 'Citadel', followed by thrusting Russian exploitation westwards greatly endangered First Panzer Army, obliging von Mackensen to retire from the Donets. On 15 September he retreated to the Dnieper, defending Zaporoshe, Dniepropetrovsk and Nikopol, the manganese-producing centre, south of the city. Together with German Sixth Army (reconstituted) and Seventeenth Army, First Panzer Army held an east bank Zaporoshe bridgehead with XXXX Panzer Corps (Henrici), protecting essential electrical power installations. Von Manstein's deployment on the Dnieper blocked a Red Army approach to the Crimea from the Ukraine. On 14 October 1943 von Mackensen evacuated Zaporoshe, a move following months of heavy defensive fighting with only two panzer divisions, 17th and 23rd, on a strength of twenty-one formations. From mid-October until 20 November First Panzer Army struggled to contain Malinovsky's 3rd Ukrainian Front striking south across the Dnieper between Nikopol and Krivoi Rog. The front made deep inroads into the defence, forcing costly action upon the panzer army – now under command of General Hube (appointed 29 October). Bloody November battles defending Nikopol and Krivoi Rog in conjunction with Sixth Army sapped the power of 9th, 13th, 17th, 23rd SS Totenkopf and Gross Deutschland Divisions.

On 29 December 1943, GOC, Army Group South (von Manstein) switched First Panzer Army northwards from the lower Dnieper bend to partner Fourth Panzer Army, creating a strong defensive block north (Fourth Panzer Army) and south (First Panzer Army) of Kiev. Reading Red Army intentions in this area, the Field Marshal anticipated thrusts breaking south-west across the Dnieper into the rear of the Army Group. [***Meanwhile at Nikopol*** *(map 15) where the defence of the city and its manganese installations had been entrusted to Army Group Schörner, 24th Panzer Division (Edelsheim) returning from an abortive journey northwards to lead a XXXXVII Panzer Corps attempt to relieve Cherkassy, arrived too late to save the situation and Nikopol was lost.* ***At Kirovograd*** *on First Army's right flank in January 1944 (map 15), where 2nd Ukrainian Front (Konev)* *advancing west of the Dnieper after breaching the river north of Krivoi Rog had trapped part of Eighth Army's XXXXVII Panzer Corps (Vormann) – 3rd and 14th Panzer Divisions, 10th Panzer Grenadier Division and 376th Infantry Division – 3rd Panzer Division (Bayerlein) defied Hitler's stand-fast order by breaking out of encirclement and linking up with 11th Panzer Division, Gross Deutschland and SS Totenkopf to mount a successful relief action from the south-west.*] The Russian offensive west of the Dnieper nevertheless gained ground, enveloping more of Army Group South.

Russia: The Relief of Cherkassy, North Ukraine (map 15). On 17 February 1944 Hube overcame opposition by 1st Ukrainian Front (Vatutin) and, with a reinforced III Panzer Corps (Breith), succeeded in driving a relief corridor eastwards through Russian forces investing Cherkassy to reach Lissjanska enabling 54,000 men of XI Army Corps (Stemmerman) and XXXXII Army Corps (Lieb) – Eighth Army – to escape encirclement; 1st and 2nd Ukrainian Fronts having trapped the hapless corps at the junction with Eighth Army (Wöhler) since 28 January when their converging thrusts united 30 miles south-west of Cherkassy at Swenigorodka. But a greater shock was in store for Hube than seeing ten flanking divisions encircled. On 4 March 1944, an unexpected Russian spring offensive split First and Fourth Panzer Armies, forcing Hube into giving ground to Ukrainian Fronts under Zhukov and Konev. These Red Army Groups, in powerful westward drives, forced a wedge between Hube and Raus (Fourth Panzer Army) encircling Hube's divisions between the Dnieper and the Bug, cutting them off from all landward communication with Army Group South. Subsequent operations introduced a new dimension into armoured warfare.

Russia: A moving panzer pocket, North Ukraine (map 15). Hube's panzer army of 300,000 men, including elements of Fourth Panzer Army, mainly Leibstandarte Adolf Hitler and 7th Panzer Division, 22 divisions in total, eight panzer – 1st, 6th, 7th, 11th, 16th, 17th, 19th, Leibstandarte – Kampfgruppe SS Reich and 20th Panzer Grenadier Division, but none with more than eleven tanks (16th Panzer Division) became totally enveloped for fourteen days while continuing to fight north-westwards supplied by air transport groups under Major-General Morzik. (Transport action in support of the panzer force is elaborated in Part 4, page 141.) On 24 March, Hube (air-lifted out of Stalingrad before the surrender in 1942 and a key figure in early battles for Sicily and Calabria) organized his much weakened divisions into three separate corps groups two of which, Chevallerie and Breith incorporating III Panzer Corps (Breith), XXIV Panzer Corps (Nehring) and XXXXVI Panzer Corps (Schultz), divided the panzer divisions between them. Expected by the Red Army to turn south the Panzer Army, sustained by air-transported and local supplies, instead moved north-west on von Manstein's orders, fighting off all attempts by Zhukov to destroy the encircled divisions. On 8 April 1944, First Panzer Army made contact with II SS Panzer Corps (Bittrich), a relief force sent from the west via Lodz with SS Panzer Divisions Frundsberg, Hohenstaufen and a Jaeger division in support. All eventually reached the security of the main battle line in eastern Galicia (Army Group North Ukraine).

On 20 April 1944, Hube was promoted Generaloberst for his success in extricating First Panzer Army, but a flying accident immediately afterwards brought about his death, robbing the panzer force of a most able commander – one of the few in whom Hitler evinced much confidence. From the time of the Army's escape from encirclement in the North Ukraine in April 1944 until its surrender on 8 May 1945, defensive operations continued in southern Poland protecting the region west of Tarnopol against encroaching 1st and 4th Ukrainian Fronts. The Panzer Army's run-down order of battle in July 1944 included 1st and 8th Panzer Divisions and 20th Panzer Grenadier Division. Deployed on the southern wing of Army Group Centre (First Panzer Army, Seventeenth Army, Fourth Panzer Army, Ninth Army), First Panzer Army served new commanders: General Raus (22 April 1944), Generaloberst Heinrici (16 August 1944) and finally General Nehring (21 March 1945).

In Roumania during the summer of 1944, Russian progress south of the Carpathians against First Panzer Army's right-flanking neighbour, Army Group South Ukraine (Friessner), threatened catastrophe when German Sixth Army (Fretter-Pico) was encircled by 2nd and 3rd Ukrainian Fronts striking from Jassy and Kishinev (Tiraspol) and uniting on 29 August at Husi.

[***The destruction of Sixth Army at Husi** in August 1944, from which GOC Fretter-Pico, command staff, 13th Panzer Division, 10th Panzer Grenadier Division and elements of Eighth Army escaped, opened the way for 2nd Ukrainian Front (Malinovsky) to strike via Ploesti into western Roumania north of the Danube, penetrating Hungary in the direction of Debrecen and threatening to turn First Panzer Army's southern flank. **Panzer intervention by Sixth Army (Fretter-Pico) at Nyireghyaza** in October 1944, involving panzer divisions in running battles with Russian armour, deferred the impending collapse of Army Group South Ukraine. Starting on 2 October at Grosswardein 40 miles south of Debrecen and culminating 25 miles to the north at Nyireghyaza, LVII Panzer Corps (Kirchner) and then III Panzer Corps (Breith) struck back at 6th Guards Tank Army spearheads, cutting them off from rearward support and destroying the substance of three mechanized corps. By 29 October the efforts of three under-strength panzer divisions (20–30 tanks each), 1st (Thunert), 13th (Schmidhuber) and 23rd (von Radowitz) allotted to Breith (III Panzer Corps) for action against 6th Guards Tank Army rear communications at Nagy-Kallo (22 October 1944) – supported by Feldherrnhalle (Pape) – while 24th Panzer Division (von Nostitz-Wallwitz) and 4th SS Polizei Division (Schmedes) assisted with diversionary attacks elsewhere, successfully concluded three weeks of mobile operations, removing the threat of envelopment from Army Group South Ukraine (re-named South 24 September 1944) and relieving First Panzer Army of much anxiety.*] Army Group South meanwhile claimed 632 Russian tanks and assault guns destroyed and a similar number of anti-tank guns destroyed or captured.

Germany in defeat (map 20) October 1944–April 1945. After a period of respite from major operations, with only 8th Panzer Division serving briefly in reserve during October, First Panzer Army was bypassed on both flanks by Soviet Fronts – North, thrusting to Berlin across the Weichsel on 12 January 1945, and South along the Danube to Budapest (13 February 1945) and Vienna (13 April 1945) – leaving the Army exposed and semi-isolated at the eastern end of a defensive Carpathian wedge. When threatened front and rear by Russian and US Armies converging on Czechoslovakia, First Panzer Army (Nehring), lying east of Olomouc, withdrew into Moravia taking up positions east of Prague. By 5 May a renewal of panzer strength – 6th, 8th, 19th Panzer Divisions and two panzer grenadier divisions (Feldhernhalle, Brandenburg), none more powerful than a regimental battle group was intended as the eastern shield for an Alpine redoubt. Hopes were short-lived. On 6 May concentric Ukrainian Front operations leading to the capture of Prague brought about the collapse of Army Group Schörner. On 9 May 1945, First Panzer Army joined the general surrender.

Career note. After being relieved of his command (Army Group 'A') in March 1944, at the same time that Field Marshal von Manstein was dismissed as GOC, Army Group South, von Kleist surrendered to the Americans in 1945 who handed him over to the Yugoslavs in 1946. They delivered von Kleist into Russian hands in 1948. He died at Vladimirovk in October 1954 during imprisonment in Russia.

Other commanders of First Panzer Army: von Mackensen died on 19 April 1969, Raus at Bad Gastein in 1956, Heinrici on 13 December 1971, Nehring lives in West Germany.

2. Second Panzer Army (PzAOK 2)

Originally XIX Motorized Infantry Corps, raised near Vienna in July 1939, controlling 2nd Panzer Division and 4th Light Division. Corps Commander General Heinz Guderian (Generaloberst 19 July 1940).

Poland, 1939 (map 2). At the start of Operation 'White' on 1 September Guderian's corps, comprising 3rd Panzer Division (Geyr von Schweppenburg) and two motorized divisions, concentrated in Pomerania, spearheaded German Fourth Army (von Kluge) – Army Group North. The Corps faced Pomorze Army deployed in defence of the Danzig corridor. On 5 September pushing east to Graudenz with Geyr von Schweppenburg's 3rd Panzer Division in the lead, Guderian cut the Danzig corridor, encircling and destroying the greater part of Pomorze Army. Guderian's troops included panzer and reconnaissance demonstration (Lehr) battalions from army training schools. On 7 September OKH switched XIX Panzer Corps to the outer wing of the Army Group offensive, instructing Guderian, directly under Army Group control and reinforced by 10th Panzer Division (Stumpff), to push south behind Warsaw in a bid to frustrate possible Polish plans for a withdrawal east of the city. Brest-Litovsk was reached on 15 September. Two days' journey to the south on 17 September, 3rd Panzer Division (Geyr von Schweppenburg), leading the Corps into Vlodava, joined up with von Kleist pushing north from eastern Czechoslovakia. This manoeuvre completed the outer ring of a double encirclement of the Polish Army, bring mobile operations to a successful conclusion.

France: Operation 'Yellow', 1940 (map 3). By 10 May Guderian's XIX Motorized Corps was concentrated east of Luxemburg (Bitburg) on the German side of the Ardennes, in readiness for the battle for France. The Corps was subordinate to von Kleist spearheading the German offensive in the west. (*See* First Panzer Army, 10 May 1940.)

France: Panzer Corridor, 1940 (map 4). On 13 May, deploying three of von Kleist's five panzer divisions, 1st (Kirchner), 2nd (Veiel) and 10th (Schaal), Guderian lead Army Group 'A' across the Meuse at Sedan. Reinforcing 1st Panzer Division (Kirchner) with Infantry Regiment Gross Deutschland (Graf von Schwerin) and heavily supported by corps artillery and air attacks (see Part 2, page 113), Guderian shattered the front of French Second Army (Huntziger), securing a 12-mile deep bridgehead preparatory to pushing west – and disputing with von Kleist over restraining orders received on the evening of the 15th, again on the 17th and finally on the 24th. By 15 May all three of Guderian's panzer divisions were across the Meuse ready to push west. For a short time 10th Panzer Division served behind as left flank guard at Stonne. On 16–17 May at Montcornet Guderian brushed aside an armoured counter-attack by 4ème Division Cuirassée, recently formed under General de Gaulle, and directed against the corps left flank. On the 19th, 1st Panzer Division secured a bridgehead across the Somme at Péronne. On the 20th 2nd Panzer Division reached Abbeville and the Channel. The Corps then directed its divisions northwards against Boulogne, Calais and Dunkirk. (*See* First Panzer Army, 24 May 1940.)

France: Operation 'Red', 1940 (map 3). On 8 June German forces in the west, having been regrouped for the 'Red' phase of the battle for France, faced south along the Rivers Somme and Aisne. Guderian's command, broadened into a Group, was in control of armoured forces concentrated behind Rethel on the upper Aisne north of Reims. Responsible to German Twelfth Army (List) – Army Group 'A', for the task of breaching French 4th Army Group defences, Guderian was allotted four panzer and two motorized divisions which he organized into two motorized (panzer) corps. On 10 June, 1st Panzer Division leading XXXIX Corps pushed out of an infantry bridgehead at Château-Porcien, west of Rethel, bypassed Reims to the east and spearheaded the advance of the Army Group to the south-east; 3rd Air Fleet in support. Von Kleist's Group, also with two panzer corps, redeployed alongside after failing to exploit Somme bridgeheads westwards at Amiens and Péronne, thrust south, bypassing Reims to the west, towards Vichy and Lyon. On 17 June, transferred with Sixteenth Army under command of Army Group 'C', Guderian's push carried to Belfort and the Swiss border south-east of Dijon; 1st Panzer Division making contact with German Seventh Army fighting on the west bank of the Rhine. The arrival of panzer divisions in the Franche-Comté isolated the bulk of the French Army holding the Maginot Line and brought about the surrender of some 500,000 men of French Second, Third, Fifth and Eighth Armies in the Nancy–Belfort area; 250,000 attributed to panzer group

Above: Generaloberst Heinz Guderian, born in 1888, entered the Army Cadet School at Colmar in 1901. He rose through various commands and by 1931 was Chief of Staff, Inspectorate Motor Troops (Kraftfahrkampftruppen). In 1934 he was Chief of Staff at Armoured Troops Command: then GOC, XVI Motorized Corps (1938) where he was promoted to General der Panzertruppen. He served from 1939 to 1940 as GOC, XIX Motorized Corps and then Guderian Gruppe, becoming Generaloberst in July 1940.

action. Von Kleist's arrival at Lyon and Vichy on the 20th completed the isolation of Paris in conjunction with Hoth's advance from the west. The move signalled an end to the campaign in France. On 22 June the French Government signed an armistice at Compiègne. On 16 November, Guderian's command was redesignated Panzer Group 2 (Panzergruppe Kdo 2) followed by training and redeployment for 'Barbarossa'. Subordinate to German Fourth Army (von Kluge), Army Group Centre (von Bock) and with three panzer corps on the Bug at Brest-Litovsk, Guderian lined up with Hoth – 3rd Panzer Group (Ninth Army) – to the north. The panzer groups would spearhead operations in the direction of Moscow. (*See* Third Panzer Army, 22 June 1941.)

Russia: Operation 'Barbarossa', Centre, 1941 (map 7). On 22 June 1941, thrusting to Bialystok, Minsk and Smolensk, 2nd and 3rd Panzer Groups pushed towards Moscow – restricted in radius by OKW fears of over-extended flanks. Guderian's objective with his three panzer corps was to destroy enemy forces immediately opposite and prevent their regrouping or forming a new front further east. The action started briskly. At Minsk 17th Panzer Division, Guderian's leading division at the time, made contact with 3rd Panzer Group, turning aside from its parallel course to complete the encirclement of the city on 27 June. Inside the Bialystok–Minsk pocket 32 Russian infantry and eight tank divisions, 324,000 men, were encircled and destroyed. Smolensk fell to 29th Motorized Division on 16 July. On 20 July, the Group followed this success, with the capture of Elnya and Roslawl (4th Panzer Division), 1 August, bringing in large numbers of prisoners from Russian Thirteenth and Twenty-eighth Armies. For all intents and purposes the road to Moscow was open. Yet instead of regrouping to renew the drive eastwards, the panzer groups were directed north and south [*one of Hoth's panzer corps being taken to assist in the drive to Leningrad (Army Group North) see* Fourth Panzer Army, 15 August 1941]. Guderian was instructed to turn south. Accordingly, on 25 August, Guderian changed direction and with only two panzer corps, XXIV and XLVII, swung south through 90 degrees, thrusting in the direction of Kiev where von Kleist's Group would co-operate in a bid to trap South West Front. Guderian's first objective was Konotop; Gross Deutschland and SS Reich arrived on 2 and 3 September as reinforcements for the drive.

On 14 September Guderian's thrust to link up with von Kleist was successfully completed and the two Groups led by 3rd Panzer (Model) and 16th Panzer (Hube) met at Lochvitsa. The subsequent destruction of South West Front was accomplished with 600,000 prisoners being taken from trapped Russian armies. (*See* First Panzer Army, 14 September 1941.)

Russia: Operation 'Typhoon', 1941 (map 8). On 30 September, 2nd Panzer Group briefly rested and regrouped 360 miles south-west of Moscow in readiness for Operation 'Typhoon' – to be pursued in conjunction with 3rd and 4th Panzer Groups (2 October) – was ready to strike north-east for the Soviet capital. For this task Guderian's command was reconstituted as Second Panzer Army, directly subordinate to Army Group Centre (von Bock). Guderian started his push on Moscow two days earlier than other groups, pursuing a north-easterly route via Orel to Tula – a key road and rail junction south-west of the capital. Despite autumn rains turning the 'going' to mud, 3rd Panzer Division (Breith) entered Orel on 3 October. On 6 October Bryansk fell to 17th Panzer Division (von Arnim). By breaking into the rear of Bryansk Front, Guderian completed the encirclement of three Russian armies, which together with the envelopment of a further four at Vyasma (*see* Fourth Panzer Army, 7 October) yielded 657,000 prisoners. But supply deficiencies and appalling autumn and winter conditions at the front hampered further progress, in particular at Mzensk on the 10th where, for the first time, the superior T34 was encountered, sending a shock wave of consternation through the German military establishment. Immobilized divisions were resupplied by air transports arriving at forward airfields. On 15 November, coinciding with the beginning of winter frost (17 November in the north) the final assault on Moscow was ordered by Army Group Centre. But at the distant end of a long supply line, the offensive stalled in exceptionally severe conditions; 40 degrees of frost being recorded on some sectors. Guderian's objective, taking Tula *en route*, and outflanking Moscow in a wide sweep through hostile and unrewarding country, now looked decidedly ambitious,

On 20 November, after tightening the ring at Bryansk, XXXXVII Panzer Corps thrust eastwards, with 18th Panzer Division (Nehring) protecting the Panzer Army's right flank at Jefremov, the most easterly point in the Moscow offensive. From 25 November until 5 December, with the battle for Tula at its height, Guderian's worn out, inadequately supplied and equipped combat units reduced at times to *panje* (sledge) transport met Russian resistance everywhere determined to exploit winter terrain and harsh campaigning conditions to a maximum. Failing to seize Tula in an outflanking move from the north-east (3rd and 4th Panzer Divisions XXIV Panzer Corps), Guderian's best effort was to secure Venev (17th Panzer Division) and, in deteriorating circumstances, with the same division reach Kashira, 37 kilometres further on the road to Moscow. On 5 December, lacking the necessary power to break the Red Army's defence of Tula or extend his offensive eastwards, Guderian's drive to Moscow ended in mid-winter. *Blitzkrieg* on this front was over and within weeks its prime exponent, General der Panzertruppe Guderian, would be sacked. On 20 December, winter withdrawals to ease the plight of advanced units exposed to the mounting pressure of counter-attacks by new, Siberian divisions brought Generaloberst Guderian into conflict with von Kluge, the new Army Group Commander appointed on 19 December. The result; on 25 December Guderian was dismissed by Hitler, and General Rudolf 'Panzer' Schmidt was appointed in his place.

In opposing the Red Army's Moscow counter-offensive lead by Zhukov, which broke the German defence into 'island' fragments varying from Army-sized areas down to companies and battalions, locked into 'hedgehog' positions, the remnants of panzer divisions would be committed to local action. On 16 January, 1942, on Second Panzer Army's 'front', two battle groups organized by General Walther Nehring around 18th Panzer Division – reduced to twelve tanks – pushed 80 kilometres to relieve Suschinitschi. The town was a communications centre vital to the German defence of the front at a point where Russian Sixteenth Army threatened to turn the Army Group's southern flank. Defended all-round for thirty days by 206th Infantry Division, Nehring's efforts were rewarded with success; the defenders were relieved but the town was evacuated. By the end of February 1942 German tank strength in the east had sunk to 140 battle-fit machines and Second Panzer Army was to remain in Army Group Centre's order of battle only for the next twenty-one months until September 1943. Controlling mainly infantry corps in defensive action south-east of Rshev, where German Ninth Army's bastion opposite Moscow anchored the front, this period in the Panzer Army's declining fortunes was marked by local commitments north and east of Orel and between Belew and Shisdra.

Russian partisans in February–March 1942 and thereafter were a new factor in panzer operations in the east, especially in rear areas north and south of Bryansk where the need to control them brought action from Schmidt. Operations 'Grunspecht', 'Klette' and 'Vogelsang' during the spring of 1942 – and again in April 1943 with 'Ferkel', 'Hamburg', 'Zigeunerbaron' and 'Freischütz', indicate the scale of Moscow-directed guerrilla action – the menace of which, involving more and more active troops in combating the threat to supply lines and dumps, can be gauged from an OKW memoir dated 8 June 1943: '3,000 Russian dead, 2 aircraft and 3 tanks captured, 2,900 bunkers destroyed'; 18th Panzer Division was closely involved in these clearing-up tasks. Despite local successes, the problem of losing supplies to widespread guerrilla action and consequent operational disruption would never be totally eradicated, reaching a peak in June 1944 with more than 10,000 acts of sabotage – two days before the Red Army's 22 June offensive resulted in the total collapse of Army Group Centre. In August 1942 the Army's panzer strength was temporarily renewed for Operation 'Wirbelwind' (whirlwind), a determined attempt at improving Army positions south-west of Moscow, involving 4th, 9th, 11th, 17th, 18th and 20th Panzer Divisions in action around Suschinitschi. But operations failed within days; minefields and heavily defended localities bringing the offensive to a stand-still. Panzer action before Moscow was nevertheless set to continue.

[*At* ***Rshev*** *in August 1942, Stavka was as intent upon capturing the cornerstone of Ninth Army defences west of the capital as Hitler was of holding on to it. Coinciding with the German 'Blue' summer offensive in the south, Red Army attacks tied down 1st, 2nd, 5th Panzer and Gross Deutschland Divisions struggling to prevent a breakthrough; their presence on this front kept them out of the offensive in the south. Averting a crisis at Systchewka, midway between Rshev and Vyasma, 1st and 6th Panzer Divisions parried particularly dangerous attacks disrupting the Army Group front, but Rshev remained German – until the spring of the following year.*

In ***Operation 'Buffalo'****, starting on 1 March 1943, Ninth Army (Model) evacuated the Rshev salient, involving the withdrawal of 29 divisions including 23rd and 5th Panzer, in action at key points along a 300-mile front. The operation was completed on 25 March, shortening the line and releasing the panzer divisions and Ninth Army for Operation 'Citadel'.* (See *Fourth Panzer Army, 5 July 1943.*]

On 15 August 1943, General 'Panzer' Schmidt was replaced by General der Infantry Lothar Rendulic. This change of command followed a critical week in which General Walter Model (Ninth Army) while engaged in the 'Citadel' offensive, was also directing the deployment of Second Panzer Army. Under fierce attack by the Red Army developing offensive operations during and after 'Citadel', and suffering heavy losses in men and material, Rendulic withdrew to the west, seeing Vyasma, Bryansk and Smolensk change hands as the Red Army surged forward. Second Panzer Army was now retained in Army Group Centre reserve until 21 August 1943, when it was transferred to Army Group 'F' (von Weichs) in the Balkans.

The Balkans. After 22 August 1943, the redeployment of Second Panzer Army south of Belgrade would significantly strengthen German presence in a region of south-eastern Europe where Hitler and OKW expected imminent Allied invasion. General Rendulic continued in command until 24 June 1944 when Franz Bohme, a temporary successor, was followed by General der Artillerie Maximilian de Angelis – the Army's last commander, serving from 18 July 1944 until the end in May 1945. Rendulic's first action, coinciding with

Operation 'Axe' across the Adriatic (*see* panzer action in Italy, 9 September 1943) was to disarm Italian troops in Yugoslavia. Then, in a country dominated by partisans, operating in extensive tracts of remote and mountainous country, Rendulic, with no panzer divisions on his strength, engaged Tito's partisans at Brod. From 9 to 18 October 1944, Second Panzer Army moved to hold Belgrade – delaying Red Army and Tito groups converging on the capital long enough to ensure safe passage for German units evacuating Greece and other occupied regions in the Balkan peninsula. Henceforth, until 27 November 1944, the Army was continuously in action against partisans – organized under Russian auspices into four armies – initially in the Danube-Drave area and then on the Dalmatian coast before withdrawing north into Hungary and eventual collaboration with Sixth SS Panzer Army (Dietrich). In **Hungary,** 1945 (map 19) on 6 March, the 'panzer army' deployed south of Budapest and Lake Balaton, co-ordinated offensive action with the Waffen SS (Operation 'Spring Awakening'). But drained of resources and powerless to protect oil-production centres in western Hungary (*see* Sixth SS Panzer Army, 6 March 1945) de Angelis failed to resist Russian pressure exerted in the Vienna direction, and with no forces except infantry, withdrew into Austria.

Germany in defeat (map 20). On 8 May 1945 Second Panzer Army (de Angelis) capitulated in Steiermark (map 20).

Career Note: Generaloberst Guderian died at Schwangau in 1953, 'Panzer' Schmidt at Krefeld in 1957 and Generaloberst Rendulic at Seewalchen in 1971.

3. Third Panzer Army (PzAOK 3)

Originally XV Corps (motorized), raised at Jena on 10 October 1938, in control of 1st and 3rd Light Divisions. Corps Commander General Herman Hoth (Generaloberst 19 July 1940).

Poland, 1939 (map 2). In the battle for Warsaw starting on 1 September, Hoth Corps, basically two light divisions reinforced by 25th Panzer Regiment was deployed in upper Silesia facing the junction between Lodz and Cracow Armies. Under German Tenth Army – Army Group South – the Corps was to play a leading role in the advance to Warsaw, sharing the vanguard with XVI Corps (motorized). (*See* Fourth Panzer Army, September 1939.)

From 9 to 12 September Hoth completed the first encirclement of Polish forces on this front, taking 60,000 prisoners at Radom. The operation was developed in conjunction with XIV Panzer Korps (von Wietersheim). Transferred to the west for Operation 'Yellow', Hoth's Corps, with two panzer divisions under German Fourth Army – Army group 'A' – was accorded a secondary role in the western offensive. From an assembly area east of the Meuse opposite Dinant, Hoth would provide flank protection for von Kleist, the spearhead commander at the point of main effort, 40 miles upstream at Sedan (*see* First Panzer Army, 10 May 1940).

France: Operation 'Yellow', 1940 (map 3). On 13–14 May, supporting von Kleist Group in the advance to the Channel, Hoth Corps in control of 5th (von Vietinghoff) and 7th (Rommel) Panzer Divisions, forced the Meuse at Dinant and consolidated there before pushing west in the direction of Cambrai. Rommel's division, first across the Meuse on the morning of 13 May, exploited a reconnaissance success at Houx by securing the west bank with 7th Infantry Regiment (motorized) lead by Colonel Balck – the first assault formation to breach the barrier. The division's 25th Panzer Regiment (Rothenburg) followed on the 14th. On the 15th, a few miles to the west of the crossing at Dinant, Rommel encountered and brushed aside 1ère Division Cuirassée (Bruneau), counter-attacking at Philippeville.

France: Panzer Corridor, 1940 (map 4). On 19 May, Hoth Corps, temporarily expanded as a Group and responsible to Fourth Army, was deployed on von Kleist's right in the race to the Channel. The combined panzer groups created a panzer 'corridor' with Hoth pushing powerfully to Cambrai in control of 3rd and 4th Panzer Divisions, SS Totenkopf (XVI Panzer Corps) reinforcing his own 5th and 7th Panzer Divisions (XXXIX Panzer Corps). Three days later at Arras, Hoth Group engaged the British Expeditionary Force – making a belated and unrewarding armoured counter-attack south, striking at 7th Panzer Division.

BEF action by Frank Force on 21 May, with two infantry battalions supported by 58 Mk I and sixteen Mk II tanks under General le Q. Martel, was poorly co-ordinated with a French intention to drive south, thereby cutting the panzer corridor. Failing in this intention, the BEF withdrew to the west. The action nevertheless gave rise to OKW fears for the safety of von Kleist's armour at the western end of the corridor, and still pushing north-west along the coast from Abbeville, partly resulting in Hitler's famous stand still order. Outmanoeuvred by the armour of two groups the BEF, penned into Dunkirk, nevertheless escaped to England (*see* First Panzer Army, 24 May 1940).

France: Operation 'Red', 1940. On 5 June, at the start of the Red phase of the German offensive against France (map 3), Hoth, with 5th and 7th Panzer Divisions, was concentrated opposite French Tenth Army (Altmayer) on the Channel wing of the panzer line-up, facing south towards Paris. Crossing the lower Somme east of Abbeville, Hoth drove from Hangest to the Seine at Elbeuf reached on the 9th, diverting Rommel to the channel coast at St-Valéry – entered on the 11th. Rommel was instrumental in taking 46,000 British and French prisoners. Encountering only light opposition at Elbeuf, Hoth crossed the Seine on the 10th (followed by Rommel on the 17th) to push through Normandy and Brittany with his two panzer divisions, overrunning the Headquarters of French Tenth Army at Rennes in the process. On 19 June Rommel reached Cherbourg, and Brest fell to the Corps. Nantes was reached on the 20th. [*On the opposite flank south-east of Paris, von Kleist's simultaneous arrival at Lyon signalled an end to panzer operations in France.*] Général Weygand, the French C-in-C, authorized an armistice on the 22nd and after further easy corps progress to Royan on 25 June, the 'front' stabilized along the line Royan–Angoulême–Grenoble.

Operation 'Sea-lion', July–October 1940. Co-operating with ground-attack units of 3rd Air Fleet, Hoth's

XV Panzer Corps – 4th, 7th Panzer, 20th Motorized Division – prepared to spearhead Ninth Army/Army Group 'A' in Operation 'Sea-lion', OKW's impromptu plan to invade the South of England (*see* page 173). Intended for embarkation at Boulogne in the second (principal) wave of the invasion, D+2, Hoth's Corps, following in the wake of assault infantry and paratroops, would consolidate in the Brighton area shielding the main effort by Sixteenth Army seizing harbours at Folkestone and Dover to the east. Thereafter the corps would swing out northwards in the first phase of an army plan to isolate London and occupy south-east England between the Thames estuary and Portsmouth. [*The main effort of 'Sea-lion' was the responsibility of Sixteenth Army/ 2nd Air Fleet (VIII Air Corps especially) with XXXI Panzer Corps (Reinhardt) – 8th, 10th Panzer, 20th Motorized, Gross Deutschland and the Leibstandarte SS Adolf Hitler – embarking at Rotterdam/Antwerp in second-wave operations. After assisting in the Army task of securing Folkestone and Dover (from the west and north), Reinhardt too would break out northwards in accordance with von Runstedt's plans.*] Because of the failure of the Luftwaffe and the inability of the navy to guarantee a successful crossing of the Channel, 'Sea-lion' was postponed in October, and cancelled early in 1941. Luftwaffe 'difficulties' are elaborated in Part 4, page 120. On 16 November, officially designated 3rd Panzer Group and still under Hoth's command, the Group remained for a time in the west before moving to Germany in December and further training until June 1941, when the corps was allotted to Ninth Army (Strauss) Army Group Centre (von Bock) for the 'Barbarossa' offensive against Russia. (*See* also First, Second and Fourth Panzer Armies, 22 June 1941.)

Russia: Operation 'Barbarossa', Centre (map 7). Serving Ninth Army on 22 June 1941 with two panzer and two infantry corps supported by ground-attack wings of VIII Air Corps, and co-operating with Guderian's 2nd Panzer Group (Fourth Army) to the south, Hoth spearheaded Army Group Centre's northern axis of advance, enveloping three Russian armies to the east of Minsk. Striking for Smolensk on 5 July, 3rd Panzer Group reached Vitebsk (7th Panzer Division), entered five days later by 20th Panzer Division. On 5 August, Hoth and Guderian's combined Panzer Groups pursuing the destruction of opposing Russian armies with undiminished energy, trapped fifteen Russian divisions at Smolensk (XXXIX Panzer Corps), 7th Panzer Division in the lead. On the outer northern flank of Hoth's offensive, 19th Panzer Division reached Veliki Luki on the evening of the same day. The city fell on the 18th. There for a time, while Hoth gave up XXXIX Panzer Corps (Schmidt) for the offensive against Leningrad (*see* Fourth Panzer Army, 16 August) and Guderian was diverted south to Kiev (*see* Second Panzer Army, 25 August), the offensive towards Moscow was at a standstill.

Russia: Operation 'Typhoon' (map 8). By 2 October 1941, Hitler had decided after all to attack Moscow and Army Group Centre (von Bock) was instructed to mount a full-scale offensive – Operation 'Typhoon' lead by three panzer groups. Still serving Ninth Army, but with a change of panzer corps, Hoth was subsequently concentrated north of the Smolensk/Moscow highway, deployed as the northern arm of a three-point – north, centre and south – offensive; 4th Panzer Group (Hoepner) redeployed by OKH from Army Group North being accorded the decisive central role. 2nd Panzer Group (Guderian) was to join the attack from the south-west. Hoth with two panzer corps, XXXI (Reinhardt) diverted from Leningrad, and LVI (Schaal), would launch into the attack against Moscow co-operating with Hoepner (Fourth Panzer Army, 2 October) and Guderian (Second Panzer Army, 30 September). OKW's new plan of offensive was intended to take the Panzer Group far to the north-east and into the rear of Moscow in a wide sweeping movement. Hoth was in command of the Group until 5 October when he was replaced by General Reinhardt; a new appointment taking Hoth to command of Seventeenth Army, South Ukraine. Reinhardt pressed forward against determined opposition by the Red Army. On 7 October snow fell on the Eastern Front. Supply difficulties and over-long routes necessitated air transport assistance for the leading panzer divisions. Nevertheless, in a successful envelopment of Vyasma lead by 7th Panzer Division (LVI Panzer Corps),

Above: Generaloberst Hermann Hoth entered the army as a cadet in 1904 and served with the infantry until 1934. He was GOC, XV Motorized Corps in November 1938; serving in Poland and France before promotion to Generaloberst in July 1940. In 1941 he became GOC, Seventeenth Army and during 1942–3 he was GOC, Fourth Panzer Army.

Reinhardt collaborated with Hoepner on his right swinging north, to take more than 600,000 prisoners from four encircled Russian armies; LVI Panzer Corps (6th and 7th Panzer Divisions) tightened the ring. In the weeks following the occupation of Vyasma, 'Typhoon' slackened in mud and adverse terrain, but on 14 October, despite poor campaigning conditions, Kalinin, north-west of Moscow, a strong point in the outer defences of the capital, fell to 1st Panzer division, XXXXI Panzer Corps (Model). Despite problems with supplies the advance continued broadly in the direction of Moscow.

On 23 November, in deteriorating winter conditions and suffering increasingly from fuel and ammunition shortages, Reinhardt received instructions from von Bock to change direction and move south on Klin (7th Panzer Division) LVI Panzer Corps. Instead of continuing with the enveloping thrust, taking the panzer group far to the north and east behind Moscow, Hitler planned to capture the city by turning them south – despite increasing opposition from Russian Thirtieth Army. The new manoeuvre co-ordinated by von Bock and involving Guderian and Hoepner was intended by Hitler as the final phase in the battle for the Soviet capital. Leading the Army Group's northern arm of the offensive, Reinhardt's LVI Panzer Corps (Schaal) with 6th and 7th Panzer Divisions and 14th Motorized Infantry Division, struck south, beating down determined opposition. On 27 November a 7th Panzer Division battle group (von Manteuffel) won a bridgehead at Yakhroma, crossing the Volga–Moscow canal at Dimitrov. But within hours, and in the absence of follow-through forces, Reinhardt was obliged by fresh Siberian reserves under Russian Twentieth Army to relinquish the vital foothold. LVI Panzer Corps remained on the defensive, alert for signs of a counter offensive. From 1 until 5 December, Model's XXXXI Panzer Corps – 1st and 6th Panzer, 23rd Infantry Division – lead the Panzer Group, pushing on south to reach Belyi-Rast, a suburban settlement within 25 miles of the Soviet capital. But corps progress was blocked by superior forces and in an exhausted state the panzer group offensive ground to a halt.

[*On Reinhardt's inner flank, Hoepner's 4th Panzer Group achieved marginally better results (*see *Fourth Panzer Army, 17 November 1941), but von Kluge's Fourth Army facing Moscow at Naro – Forminsk remained inexplicably inactive – despite the urging of colleagues to press forward.*]

For the German Army, at the limit of its resources and likely to face vigorous (but unexpectedly ferocious) countermeasures, retreat in mid-winter was decidedly in prospect.

The turning-point in the battle for Moscow came on 5 December 1941 with Kalinin Front (Konev), counterattacking boldly in a Stavka three-Front plan to sweep forward against both flanks and centre of von Bock's Army Group, regaining the initiative west of the capital. Reinhardt's spearheads, like Guderian's on the southern wing, were forced to withdraw in hazardous conditions as the Red Army almost succeeded in trapping Army Group Centre in a vast encirclement manoeuvre. Pulling back to less exposed positions the way it had come – via Klin – the Panzer Group was obliged to traverse a single snowbound axis upon which it and its supporting corps relied wholly for supplies and communication. Moves to protect this vital artery in wintry conditions involved 1st Panzer Division and others in exhausting action. Locked waist-deep into snow-drifts and often fighting on foot (Raus's 6th Panzer Division engaged the enemy with its last two tanks), Reinhardt's exhausted formations fought hard at this critical point on the Army Group flank – countering relentless pressure with totally inadequate resources. Frostbite claimed more casualties than battle. In a very short time an ailing von Bock would be replaced as GOC, Army Group Centre by von Kluge. On the Russian side, General Georgi Zhukov, appointed 10 October to direct West Front, continued with responsibility for the Moscow counter-offensive in general. Also on 5 December, Hitler ordered the transfer of the Army Group's supporting 2nd Air Fleet (Kesselring) to the Mediterranean. [*Second Panzer Army advancing to Moscow from the south-west via Tula was simultaneously halted. There too in bleak mid-winter and at the limit of its resources, the German offensive against Moscow was at an end.*]

On 3 January 1942, Hitler reaffirmed a 16 December order ('Not one step back!') and von Kluge's Army Group held on, defying the winter and braving the worst of the Red Army's counter-attacks. Redesignated Third Panzer Army, and for a while after 8 January subordinate to Fourth Panzer Army, Reinhardt's forces continued defensive action on the northern wing of the Army Group, strenuously contesting possession of important railway centres – Velish and Veliki Luki – turned into 'hedgehogs'. Further south, around Rshev and Vyasma, German winter positions west of Moscow remained threateningly within 80 miles of the city. When the spring mud dried-out, compaigning conditions improved. On 1 May 1942, Reinhardt's Third Panzer Army was redeployed forward of Vitebsk, replacing Fourth Panzer Army, transferred South for 'Blue' – the 1942 German summer offensive. (*See* Fourth Panzer Army, 28 June 1942.) Henceforth the action opposite Moscow, where four armies: Third Panzer Army, Ninth Army, Fourth and Second Panzer Armies were deployed (from north to south in Army Group Centre), would become increasingly bitter and the panzer divisions' task of countering local break-ins correspondingly harsh. On this front the Red Army, maintaining a constant pressure to eliminate the German threat to Moscow, was intent upon re-possessing Rshev, the eastward-pointing cornerstone of German Ninth Army defences at the eastern end of a deep salient. Consisting mainly of infantry corps, Reinhardt's panzer strength, diminished by the demands of other sectors, would only occasionally be renewed. Like Model's Ninth Army, the principal formation holding on to Rshev itself, Third Panzer Army would become indistinguishable from others preoccupied with defensive operations west of Moscow. Panzer divisions employed in sealing dangerous gaps in the front around Moscow would later assist Ninth Army to evacuate the Rshev salient. (*See* Operation 'Buffalo', Second Panzer Army, 1 March 1943.)

During the spring of 1943, anti-partisan sweeps co-ordinated with Second Panzer Army in Operation 'Maigewitter' proved only moderately successful. While in the forthcoming July offensive against Kursk (Operation 'Citadel') (*see* Fourth Panzer Army, 5 July 1943) the Panzer Army would play no part.

In the aftermath of 'Citadel', with the Red Army surging powerfully forward to the west, August battles involved Reinhardt in defence of Vitebsk – a railway junction vital to the supply and communications of the central front, and a town which the Panzer Army fought desperately to retain – continuing in action until February 1944 and claiming 40,000 Russian dead and 1,200 tanks destroyed. From 3 to 17 February, the battle for Vitebsk developed into further bitter confrontation with Russian Fronts and a withdrawal to new positions west of the city; but no respite.

Russia: The collapse of Army Group Centre. On 22 June 1944, at the start of the Red Army's decisive 'Bagration' offensive, planned to destroy Army Group Centre (Busch), Third Panzer Army, composed solely of infantry formations, lost an entire infantry corps, cut-off and destroyed in the city. Engulfed in the Army Group collapse and, like other formations, powerless to halt the Russian offensive which was driving a deep wedge through its northern wing, splitting it off with Army Group North while simultaneously exploiting the Army Group's exposed southern flank, Third Panzer Army retreated westwards to the Baltic in the direction of Königsberg and East Prussia.

[*At **Bobruisk**, situated in the far south of the Army Group 'front', at the time of the June catastrophe, only a single division (20th Panzer) (von Kessel) in Army Group reserve was available for immediate counter-attack. Despite brisk action under Ninth Army XXXXI Panzer Corps (Hoffmeister then von Kessel), securing a vital bridgehead for trapped divisions to escape across the Beresina, the lone panzer division could achieve nothing to affect the general situation. But in a remarkably swift redeployment of armour, ordered or requested by Field Marshal Model, Army Group Centre's new commander, appointed 28 June 1944, and successor to Busch (von Kluge's replacement), 4th, 5th, 7th and 12th Panzer Divisions from flanking army groups rushed to the assistance of the defence north and south of Minsk. Divisional tasks, for example under XXXIX Panzer Corps (von Saucken) defending Borisov on the Beresina, north-east of the city, were to secure exit routes, hold bridgeheads and by judicious counter-attacks assist the Army Group's stricken infantry divisions – 28 of which, 350,000 men and 47 general officers, were trapped and lost between the Beresina and the Niemen following the fall of Minsk on 3 July. Without the crisis redeployment of armour and associated heavy anti-tank support to secure escape routes for the Army Group across the Beresina and Niemen, especially at Baranovitchi where 4th and 12th Panzer Divisions were deployed, even greater numbers of German troops would have perished in the east.*]

On 6 August 1944, following the loss of Vitebsk, a new commander was appointed to Third Panzer Army – Generaloberst Erhard Raus. Holding the Red Army's drive to Königsberg in check with Gross Deutschland (Hasso von Manteuffel) – the army's most powerful panzer grenadier division, re-deployed from Roumania (where in May under its same commander at Jassy the division had destroyed Red Army spearheads driving for the oil-fields at Ploesti), Raus was required by Hitler to lead counter-attacks designed to restore cohesion between the shattered Army Group Centre and the ever more tightly besieged Army Group North forced away from Leningrad and pocketed against the Baltic north of Riga.

Lithuania: Two Heads. On 16 August Raus launched Operation 'Doppelkopf', with Gross Deutschland, 4th, 5th, 12th Panzer Divisions and Panzerverband Graf Strachwitz (two panzer brigades) subordinate to XXXIX Panzer Corps (von Saucken). In support, XXXX Panzer Corps (von Knobelsdorff) assisted the progress of 'Doppelkopf' with 7th and 14th Panzer Divisions. In a daring operation Raus succeeded notably in driving north from Tilsit via Schaulen to establish short-lived contact between Army Groups, a junction being effected east of Riga by Graf Strachwitz's arrival at Tukkum. Despite this momentary set-back to its Baltic offensive, the Red Army continued heavy attacks with autumn and winter offensives in massive strength, overwhelming the Panzer Army and penning Gross Deutschland, 7th Panzer Division and others into Memel from which they were fortunate to escape by sea – to be reinserted into the German defence under Fourth Army forward of Königsberg. In the course of the subsequent Red Army drive encircling Königsberg east of the city, Panzer Army Headquarters, sited near the coast, avoided capture by the narrowest of margins. On 8 February 1945, Hitler ordered Raus and his staff to move out of East Prussia and prepare the emergency defence of Pomerania – 2nd BR Front's prime objective. Königsberg, assailed by 3rd BR Front, was left to German Fourth Army and held out until 12 April 1945.

Germany in defeat (map 20). On 25 February 1945, following Steiner's abortive Staargard offensive, Third Panzer Army subordinate to Army Group Weichsel, assumed responsibility for Eleventh Panzer Army's commitments in Pomerania (*see* Eleventh Panzer Army, 15 February 1945). Raus nevertheless failed to make a lasting defensive impression and with other defeated elements of the Army Group retreated east to Stettin. Anchoring the northern wing of the Army Group on the Oder, with an east-bank bridgehead near the mouth of the river at Altdamm, which Hitler intended as a base for future operations, Raus held on grimly; the kernel of the Panzer Army's defence being provided by III SS (Germanisches) Panzer Corps (Steiner), controlling Nordland, Nederland, Wallonien and Langemarck Divisions. With these SS divisions and miscellaneous infantry deployed in the Altdamm bridgehead, Steiner fended off relentless Russian assault. But Third Panzer Army's last commander, General Hasso von Manteuffel, appointed 15 March 1945, relinquished the army's vigorously defended east-bank (Altdamm) bridgehead, and the much diminished III SS (Germanisches) Panzer Corps, formerly at the heart of the defence, was redeployed north of Berlin – where at Eberswalde the Corps was reconstituted as Armee Abteilung (or Gruppe) Steiner.

[***The Battle of Berlin**, 16 April 1945. Drained by battle losses and the transfer of divisions to other fronts (Wallonien destroyed, Nordland allotted to Ninth Army), Steiner's weak and understrength 'Army', consisting of little more than a burned-out 4th SS Polizei Division (Harzer) as its principal formation, a Marine division and later for a time 25th Panzer Grenadier Division, was powerless to contain a massive Red Army offensive crossing the Oder at Küstrin. Reduced to impotency, Steiner watched helplessly as Zhukov, encroaching on the capital, separated von Manteuffel and himself from south flanking German Ninth Army (Busse) blocking direct access to Berlin from the east. Hitler then accorded Steiner the impossible task of relieving Berlin from the north. Nothing came of the plan. No less likely to succeed in conditions of total Russian superiority (6,250 tanks and SP guns, 2,500,000 men) was a relief offensive by a new German Twelfth Army (Wenck), which Hitler* *ordered to approach Berlin from the west at Tangermünde. Progress was slow and the intended link-up was never achieved. The army's only motorized formation, 'Clausewitz', constituted from parts of the Panzer School at Putlos, 233rd Reserve Panzer Division, Feldherrnhalle and others, had been transferred early on to counter US progress in the Ruhr. After 16 April 1945 Berlin was rapidly encircled; 1st BR (Zhukov) and 1st UKR (Konev) Fronts uniting on 25 April west of the city at Ketzin. LVI Panzer Corps (Weidling) comprising Nordland, 20th and 25th Panzer Grenadier Divisions and Muncheberg, defending Ninth Army's front immediately east of Berlin, was instructed to take over the city's defence. Additional battle groups were contributed by 18th Panzer Grenadier Division, 9th Paratroop Division and* ad hoc *units including detachments from SS 'Charlemagne'. The Berlin garrison in the meantime was increased by miscellaneous units to 300,000 men.*

Retreating through the outer suburbs to the city centre, LVI Panzer Corps was reduced to individual vehicles of Nordland and Muncheberg, defying the Red Army until 15.00 hours on 2 May. In the last resort, SS battle groups from Nordland, Charlemagne, Polizei, Hitler Youth and Volksturm units defended the zoo, the Air Ministry and the Chancellery block where, until his suicide on the 30th, Hitler's HQ was located. Here and there around the perimeter desperate battle groups broke out of the city hoping to reach safety. On the southern outskirts in the Potsdam sector local counter-attack groups from 18th and 20th Panzer Grenadier Divisions, after a futile defence of Tempelhof, broke out with others to join the survivors of Ninth and Fourth Panzer Armies seeking contact with Twelfth Army (Wenck) approaching Berlin from the Elbe.]

On 8 May 1945, after retreating through Mecklenburg north of Berlin, Third Panzer Army (von Manteuffel), largely bypassed in the battle for Berlin and including Steiner's Group with barely more than Polizei and 25th Panzer Grenadier Division by way of regular 'divisions' with which to fight rearguard actions, surrendered mainly to the US Army.

Career Note: Raus died on 3 April 1956, Reinhardt on 22 November 1963 and Hoth at Goslar on 25 January 1971.

4. Fourth Panzer Army (PzAOK 4)

Originally XVI motorized Infantry Corps, formed in February 1938 from the Berlin panzertruppe command. The Corps' purpose under General Oswald Lutz and subsequently General Heinz Guderian, was to supervise the raising and training of 1st to 5th Panzer Divisions. On 24 November 1938, after Guderian had been appointed chief of Mobile Troops, command of the corps changed to General der Kavallerie Erich Hoepner (Generaloberst 19 July 1940).

Poland, 1939 (map 2). At the start of Operation 'White' on 1 September, Hoepner's corps, consisting of 1st (Reinhardt) and 4th (Schmidt) Panzer Divisions was concentrated in upper Silesia facing Polish Lodz Army deployed south-west of Warsaw. Pushing north-east in conjunction with XV Corps (Hoth), Hoepner lead German Tenth Army (von Reichenau) through Poland via Petrikau to Warsaw, reached on 9 September by 4th Panzer Division. From 16 to 20 September panzer action by Hoepner's two divisions, fighting on a reverse front, destroyed a determined Polish counter-attack directed from north-west of the city against the River Bzura (northern) flank of German Eighth Army. The Polish threat by twelve or more divisions of regrouped Poznan (Bortnowski) and Pomorze (Kutrzeba) Armies was swiftly disposed of; 170,000 prisoners being taken at Kutno.

France: Operation 'Yellow' (map 3). By 10 May 1940, XVI Panzer Corps was redeployed in Germany serving Sixth Army (von Reichenau) west of the Rhine and opposite Maastricht in readiness for Operation 'Yellow'. In control of 3rd (Stumpff) and 4th (Stever) Panzer Divisions, Hoepner's role in the forefront of Army Group 'B', opposite Allied armies in Belgium and Holland, was to draw the defence forward to the Dyle Line diverting attention from the focal point of panzer action by Army Group 'A' at Sedan. (*See* First Panzer Army, 13 May 1940.) Starting punctually at 0400 hours, preliminary operations by 2nd Air Fleet (Kesselring) and, later in the day, ground-attack wings of VIII Air Corps (von Richthofen) immediately south and west of Maastricht aimed to neutralize key objectives in front of Sixth Army moving against Brussels. Most of the preliminary skirmishing proved remarkably successful, especially the commando use of parachute and glider detachments by 7th Air Division (Student). Committed in surprise action at dawn, the Fallschirmjaeger (85 men carried in eleven gliders) neutralized the fortress at Eben Emael while also capturing intact two of the three bridges spanning Sixth Army's major obstacle – the Albert Canal. Hoepner's Maas crossing-point in Maastrict itself was demolished by Dutch army engineers. The obstacle was swiftly overcome by IV Corps engineer bridging columns. With Stever's 4th Panzer Division temporarily under command, IV Corps was initially responsible for the Maastricht bridgehead, but movement was exceptionally cramped by Allied air attacks, and development was hampered by limited bridging capacity.

[***Airborne attacks across the Maas*** *were launched simultaneously against Rotterdam and The Hague by 7th Air Division detailing other detachments to seize bridges at Moerdijk, Dordrecht and the airport at Waalhaven (Rotterdam). Airborne operations here were part of Student's tactical plan to seize key objectives in surprise action. They were carried into effect in conjunction with the air transported 47th and 65th Infantry Regiments from 22nd Air Landing Division (Graf von Sponeck). Bracketed into Airlanding Corps, Student, the attacking divisions were dependent for survival upon the prompt arrival of ground support in the shape of 9th Panzer Division (Hubicki) XXXIX Panzer Corps (motorized) detailed by Eighteenth Army for the relief task – a crucial element in the general plan of operations. Few of Student's attacks were an outright success, but surprise and confusion, assisting the invasion process, enabled air-transported and paratroops to mount a serious attack on Rotterdam while threatening to capture The Hague.*]

On 11 May at 0430 hours, 5 Panzer Brigade (Breith), initiating Hoepner's deceptive curtain-raiser to Operation 'Yellow' with the full support of VIII Air Corps (von Richthofen), lead Fourth Panzer Army into action while 3rd Panzer Division, preceded by its motorized infantry regiment (von Manteuffel), followed on. Moving out of the Army Group bridgehead on the west bank of the Maas, the panzer divisions were to thrust south-west through Belgium via Hannut and Tirlemont to Gembloux where Hoepner's corps would confront French First Army (Blanchard) and the BEF (Gort) drawn forward to the Dyle Line in anticipation of a major German offensive in this direction. On 12 May at Hannut, Hoepner brushed aside a French counter-attack lead by General Prioux's cavalry corps. The French force, equipped with Hotchkiss and heavy Somua tanks, consisted of two light mechanized divisions; 2nd DCM (Langlois) and 3rd DCM (Bougrain). The engagement brought Stever's 35th Panzer Regiment (Eberbach) into action – the first of the western offensive. Battle was joined next day by 5th, 6th and 36th Panzer Regiments (560 tanks).

[***Victory in Holland*** *where confusing airborne attacks unnerved the defence, drew appreciably closer on 12 May when 9th Panzer Division (Hubicki), pushing towards Rotterdam and The Hague under command of XXXIX Pz Corps (motorized) made contact with Fallschirmjaeger holding the Moerdijk bridge. Thereafter, with 9th Panzer Division proceeding via Dordrecht to Rotterdam, the offensive continued with devastating air attacks on the city, breaking Dutch resistance and concluding with the surrender of the Dutch Army on 14 May.*]

On 14–15 May at Gembloux, where French and Belgian forces under General Blanchard held fortified positions covering Brussels and Flanders, renewed opposition by Prioux's two French light mechanized divisions and the resistance of infantry supported by artillery in fixed defences was swiftly overcome by 3rd and 4th Panzer Divisions clearing the way to Brussels. But in accordance with OKW intentions to reinforce the main armoured movement of Operation 'Yellow' successfully initiated by Panzer Group von Kleist at Sedan on the 13th, a change of direction was imminent. Brussels was instead entered by 14th Infantry Division on the 17th, the day after Allied forces evacuated the Dyle Line and started their retrograde movement in the direction of the Channel.

Above: Generaloberst Erich Hoepner entered the army as a cadet in 1905 and from 1906 to 1938 served in the cavalry. He was GOC, XVI Motorized Corps in 1938, then promoted to General der Kavallerie in 1939. He served in Poland, France and Russia. He was implicated in the Generals' plot to assassinate Hitler and was hanged for treason.

France: Panzer Corridor (map 4). On 19 May, Hoepner's corps was switched from Belgium to Flanders, joining XV Corps in Hoth Group (Fourth Army) (*see* Third Panzer Army, 19 May 1940). Co-operating with Panzer Group von Kleist at the point of main effort, now moving east of Lille, panzer battles developed in expectation of trapping the BEF and its supporters retreating to the Channel. By the end of May, with Dunkirk falling to 18th Infantry Division (Cranz) on 4 June, Hoepner's corps was redeployed with other attacking formations for phase two of the Battle of France.

France: Operation 'Red' (map 3). On 5 June, at the start of 'Red' operations, Hoepner was directly responsible to Sixth Army at Péronne. But when the attack south from the Army's Somme bridgehead at Péronne failed against determined opposition, the corps was redeployed eastwards, reinforcing von Kleist Group (10 June) and preparing for a Marne crossing on the 12th in the direction of Montmirail and Château-Thierry. On 12 June, serving Panzer Group von Kleist – re-directed east from Sixth Army at Amiens to Ninth Army South of Laon (*see* First Panzer Army, 5 June 1940) – Hoepner crossed the Marne south of Soissons, driving south-east via Montmirail and Château-Thierry to negotiate the Seine at Nogent and Romilly before pressing on to Dijon and Lyon, entered by 4th Panzer Division on the 21st. Thereafter, detached from von Kleist and serving Twelfth Army, Hoepner thrust to Grenoble, threatening the rear of French Army of the Alps, which was opposing Italian forces deployed aggressively between Menton and Mont Blanc. Hoepner was promoted Generaloberst on 19 July. His Corps, responsible to Second Army until the end of October, remained at Orléans until returned to Berlin. On 15 February 1941, redesignated 4th Panzer Group and subordinate to Army Group North, Hoepner's command was redeployed east in preparation for a new undertaking; the spearheading of Hitler's 'Barbarossa' offensive in the direction of Leningrad. In the forthcoming thrust of 500 miles to Leningrad via Pleskau, Luga and Novgorod, Hoepner's group would encounter some of the most difficult tank terrain on the Eastern Front; marsh, forest and swamp, hampering panzer movement at critical times.

Russia: Operation 'Barbarossa', North, 1941 (map 7). Initially, the weakest of the four panzer groups leading the invasion on 22 June 1941, Hoepner's two panzer corps, XXXXI (Reinhardt) and LVI (von Manstein), with three panzer, three motorized divisions, including SS Totenkopf, and two infantry divisions, were concentrated on the East Prussia/Lithuanian border in the neighbourhood of Tilsit. On 25 June, thrusting north-east across the Lithuanian border to Leningrad, Hoepner defeated a determined Russian counter-attack launched against his XXXXI Panzer Corps (Reinhardt) by North West Front at Rossieny where heavy Russian KVI tanks, making their first appearance of the campaign, created considerable alarm. Kovno was entered a day later; 8th Panzer division, LVI Panzer Corps (von Manstein) crossed the Duna on the 27th. On 2 July, Hoepner breached an incomplete line of fortifications protecting the former Lithuanian/Russian border. During August battles flared at Staraya Russa and Novgorod on the outer flank of the Army Group offensive, where von Manstein's LVI Panzer Corps repulsed further determined Red Army counter-attacks. On 16 August, 4th Panzer Group was reinforced; XXXIX Panzer Corps (Schmidt) bringing 12th Panzer Division and two motorized divisions from Hoth's 3rd Panzer Group/Army Group Centre. By the 25th the new panzer corps was ready to assist in attacks on Leningrad directed towards Schlüsselburg on the east side of the city. On 8 September, lead by XXXXI Panzer Corps (Reinhardt), Hoepner renewed the Leningrad offensive, involving 1st Panzer Division in heavy fighting to break Russian resistance on the Duderhof hills fifteen miles from the city centre; Schlüsselburg fell and by the end of the month investing forces of Eighteenth Army had closed in from the suburbs, reaching Lake Ladoga in the east. The landward blockade of Leningrad appeared to be complete, but siege proved ineffective, the defenders continuing to receive supplies across frozen Lake Lagoda.

On 17 September Hoepner's attacks were brought to a standstill by unbreakable Russian resistance. Although persistent attacks had carried the panzer group to within an ace of its objective, the Red Army's steadfast defence of the inner city defeated further intentions and 4th Panzer Group was instead transferred to Army Group Centre/Fourth Army to spearhead 'Typhoon', a new German offensive against Moscow. Schmidt's XXXIX Panzer Corps then tightened the blockade by extending operations eastwards and cutting Leningrad's rail connection with the hinterland at Tikhvin on 8 November (12th Panzer Division).

Russia: Operation 'Typhoon' (map 8). On 2 October 1941, Hoepner spearheaded Operation 'Typhoon' striking east for Moscow in conjunction with 2nd and 3rd Panzer Groups (*see* Second and Third Panzer Armies, 30 September and 2 October respectively). Departing from a concentration area east of Roslawl and in control of four Army corps, six panzer divisions, SS Reich and five infantry divisions, Hoepner forced the Desna with infantry before directing XXXX Panzer Corps (Stumme) on Vyasma; 10th Panzer Division (Fischer) in the lead. On 7 October 10th Panzer Division reached the vicinity of Vyasma, uniting with 7th Panzer Division from 3rd Panzer Group to the north. The move sealed the fate of four Russian armies (400,000 prisoners). Notwithstanding this, and Guderian's success at Bryansk which raised the total of prisoners captured by the Army Group to 600,000 officers and men (*see* Second Panzer Army, 6 October 1941), mud, poor 'going' and supply difficulties took the pace out of the German offensive. On 17 November, von Bock's Army Group Centre renewed the attack on Moscow (starting on the 15th in the south where Guderian initiated the winter phase of the offensive). Hoepner's divisions – 10th Panzer and Das Reich (XXXX Panzer Corps Stumme), 5th and 11th Panzer Divisions (XXXXVI Panzer Corps von Vietinghoff) struck hard for the Soviet capital, taking advantage of frost-hardened ground. But with no better clothing and equipment than other groups committed to the offensive, and equally short of supplies in midwinter, the offensive slowly lost momentum. Nevertheless, by 5 December, two important outposts in the central defensive arc around Moscow: Istra, 26 November (Das Reich and 10th Panzer Division), and Chimki, 30 November (62nd Panzer Pioneer Battalion) were in German hands. Hoepner's drive continued with 2nd Panzer Division (V Corps) closing on Krasnaya Polyana and there, within 20 miles of the Kremlin, the German Army's offensive against Moscow in mid-winter failed on this sector as elsewhere along the Front – baulked by the Red Army's unyielding resistance, beset by frostbite, unserviceable equipment and every kind of shortage.

On 1 January 1942, 4th Panzer Group was redesignated Fourth Panzer Army and on the 8th Hoepner was dismissed; never to be re-employed. In his place, General Richard Ruoff was appointed GOC, Fourth Panzer Army. Defensive operations involving the panzer divisions in much hard fighting continued in the area west of Moscow. During May 1942, Ruoff's panzer army headquarters was transferred to Army Group South (von Bock) to serve with German and Hungarian Second Armies under Army Group von Weichs. The Panzer Army under a new commander, Generaloberst Hoth (appointed 31 May) would spearhead Operation 'Blue', a summer offensive taking the panzer divisions on the fatal road to Stalingrad.

Russia: Operation 'Blue', 1942 (map 10). On 28 June 1942, Fourth Panzer Army under its new commander, Generaloberst Hoth, comprising XIV and XXXXVIII Panzer Corps with refreshed and refurbished divisions, concentrated at Kharkov before advancing powerfully to Voronezh with the support of VIII Air Corps (Fiebig). Kempf's Panzer Corps – 24th Panzer, Gross Deutschland and 16th Motorized Infantry Division – provided the spearhead. Russian Thirteenth (Pukov) and Fortieth (Parsegov) Armies of Bryansk Front bore the brunt of violent fighting.

[*Sixth Army joined the 1942 summer offensive, starting 30 June 1942, with Paulus thrusting east lead by XXXX Panzer Corps and co-operating with Second Panzer Army in an Army Group plan to trap Russian forces west of the Don; an expectation destined to go unfulfilled.*]

On 6 July 1942, the ninth day of Operation 'Blue', 24th Panzer Division (Hauenschild) in a renewal of *Blitzkrieg,* driving powerfully across rolling steppe at the head of Kempf's XXXXVIII Panzer Corps entered Voronezh. In conjunction with Gross Deutschland, 24th Panzer Division secured the left flank of an Army Group South claiming 28,000 prisoners, 1,000 tanks and 500 guns destroyed or captured at the conclusion of the first phase of the offensive. Nevertheless, the bulk of Russian defenders succeeded in escaping eastwards in good order. Army Group South was then divided into new Army Groups 'A' (List) and 'B' (von Bock); 'A' would lead the offensive into the Caucasus while 'B' protected the east flank at Stalingrad. On 9 July when Army Group 'A' (List) – First Panzer Army (von Kleist) and Seventeenth Army (Ruoff) – also joined in the summer offensive, panzer operations between the Donetz and the Don were set for expansion. Ordering Fourth Panzer Army to change direction and, together with Sixth Army (General Paulus), thrust broadly south-east following the river Don in the direction of Stalingrad, Hitler planned to trap the Red Army deployed west of the river. On 13 July, Fourth Panzer Army was transferred from von Bock to List and subsequently directed south alongside von Kleist in another effort to trap Russian forces between the Donets and the Don, north of Rostov. Nothing came of the plan except an adverse concentration of panzer divisions mostly removed from the main axis of advance. On 21 July Fourth Panzer Army, on the Don facing south with First Panzer Army to the west, won a bridgehead across the river at Nikolayevskaya. XL Panzer Corps (Geyr von Schweppenburg), controlling 3rd and 23rd Panzer Divisions, led the way south to the River Manych; 3rd Panzer Division (Breith) being first into Asia. [*Sixth Army continued alone in the direction of Stalingrad.*] On 23 July 1942 [*with First Panzer Army entering Rostov, the 'gateway' to the Caucasus*], Hitler directives named Grozny and Baku as List's primary objectives; List's Army Group 'A' (less Fourth Panzer Army) implemented the directive on 25 July. [***Sixth Army progressing** towards Stalingrad from the north-west, and protecting a long open flank on the Don, was assisted by the arrival of XIV Panzer Corps, but suffered protracted delay. Operational plans were again revised.*]

On 30 July, Hoth was instructed to release Geyr von Schweppenburg's XL Panzer Corps to von Kleist (Army Group 'A') and return under command of Army Group 'B' which, with XXXXVIII Panzer Corps comprising 14th and 16th Panzer Divisions and 29th Infantry Division (motorized), followed a new line of march toward Stalingrad along the south bank of the Don. Striking powerfully for the city, a Russian arms-manufacturing and river freight transshipment centre, stretching thirteen miles along the west bank of the Volga, the panzer army encountered strong opposition from 64th (Schumilov) and 57th (Tolbuchin) Armies. General Georgi Zhukov, the master co-ordinator of Moscow West Front defensive operations 1941, and future Stalingrad defence co-ordinator, had yet to be appointed.

[*First Panzer Army meanwhile continued south into the Caucasus, extending divergent operations in the direction of Mozdok – a useful but minor oil-producing centre in the western foothills.*]

[***Sixth Army was beset by problems.** Approaching Stalingrad from the north and west in late July–August 1942, operations were curtailed for eighteen days – XIV Panzer Corps suffering in particular as fuel supplies were diverted to von Kleist whose First Panzer Army's more distant objectives demanded and received a greater (none the less inadequate) measure of support.*

On 7 August, Sixth Army operations against Stalingrad were renewed from the north (XIV Panzer Corps) and west (XXIV Panzer Corps) enveloping Russian First Tank Army (Moskalenko) and 62nd Army (Lopatin), blocking access to Kalatsch – the traditional Don crossing-place leading 70 kilometres east to the city.

On 19 August Paulus ordered a start to the final phase of the attack on Stalingrad. On the 22nd, XIV Panzer Corps (von Wietersheim) supported by VIII Air Corps (Fiebig) crossed the Don north of Kalatsch and pushed 16th Panzer Division (Hube) on to Rynok – a riverside settlement immediately north of the city. On 23 August 1942, 2nd Panzer Regiment (Graf Strachwitz) reached the Volga. Kalatsch fell to LVI Army Corps (von Seydlitz) on the 25th. But Hube's panzer division on the Volga was practically surrounded for a week and obliged to rely upon air-transported supplies.]

Meanwhile, approaching Stalingrad from the south-west, Hoth was delayed by Russian 64th Army at Abganerovo and not until 19 August, co-ordinating operations with Sixth Army, did he move simultaneously to attack Stalingrad from this direction; 24th Panzer Division (Hauenschild) leading XXXVIII Panzer Corps (Kempf). But not without difficulty. Suffering the bitter resistance of Schumilov's 64th and other Russian armies defending Stalingrad, Hoth like Paulus, would be obliged for more than three months to fight for every inch of the city 'mouseholing' residential districts, clearing barricades and assaulting the defence factory by factory and block by block. But German resources would prove totally inadequate for the task. Pushed to the brink of the Volga, six Russian armies, responsible to Zhukov for the defence of Stalingrad since 26 August, retained a slender grip on the city.

Russia: The battle for Stalingrad (map 11) entered a new phase on 19 November when a well-judged Russian counter-offensive, Operation 'Uranus', launched north and south of the city with 1,500,000 men, almost 1,000 tanks and strong air and artillery support, enveloped Sixth and Fourth Panzer Armies– 22 divisions, three panzer and three motorized, Army engineers, Panzerjaeger, signals, flak, bridging columns, supply staffs, corps troops, army troops and administrators, totalling 220,000 officers and men. Fourth Panzer Army, fighting in the southern half of the city, was struck in the flank and split apart. Hoth at Panzer Army Headquarters outside the encirclement was left with little more than Roumanian infantry with which to combat the onslaught. But relief for the defenders of Stalingrad was in prospect.

Russia: Operation 'Winter Storm' (map 12), starting on 12 December, was initiated by LVII Panzer Corps (Kirchner) hurriedly transferred north from Seventeenth Army in the west Caucasus. Conceived by Army Group Don (von Manstein), a new headquarters established on 24 November at Novo Cherkassy north-east of Rostov, the operation was carried out by three panzer divisions, notably 6th (Raus) brought at full strength and in quick time by rail from France to join 23rd (von Senger und Etterlin) and subsequently 17th Panzer Division (Lengsfeld) east of Kotelnikovo. With 6th Panzer Division leading, the relief attempt drove forward supported by Roumanian infantry and IV Air Corps. But to no avail.

After twelve days of bitter mid-winter action, 11th Panzer

Regiment (Hünersdorff), at the centre of operations, was brough to a standstill by Second Guards Army and three armoured brigades, when fewer than 30 miles (48 kilometres) separated 6th Panzer Division from German Sixth Army perimeter. Meanwhile on the Panzer Army's left flank, between the Don and Donets, a new crisis was developing. [***Catastrophe on the Chir*** *materialized on 17 December 1942 when Italian Eighth Army, deployed on the upper Chir, collapsed under pressure from Southwest Front; 22nd Panzer Division, grievously weakened in earlier battles staving off a Roumanian (Third Army) break-up, was virtually eliminated in counter-attacks.*]

Von Manstein's Plan (map 12) for coping with the emergency would require 6th Panzer Division (Raus) to discontinue attacks in the Stalingrad direction (24 December 1942) and instead swing north to join 11th Panzer Division (Balck) in XXXXVIII Panzer Corps (von Knobelsdorff)/Army Detachment Hollidt. Hollidt was charged with the defence of the vital Army Group Don area west of Stalingrad where transport wings of VIII Air Corps, flying mostly from Tazinskaya and Morosovska, linked beleaguered Sixth Army with its only supplies – now under threat from SW Front (Malinovsky) thrusting to the airfields' perimeter. Assisted by 7th Panzer Division (von Funck), dispatched by rail from France, on the heels of 6th Panzer and detraining at Forstadt, von Manstein reinforced Hollidt on the Donets at a point where the division would combat any hostile move across the Donets likely to prejudice plans for shielding Stalingrad air-supply centres and restoring cohesion to the German Army's shattered right wing. In destroying Malinovsky's Second Guards Army spearhead invading the vital airfields and subsequently in holding off the northern arm of a Russian pincer reaching out for Rostov, von knobelsdorff was dramatically successful. Fighting for Ordzhonikidze, 400 miles away, in the eastern Caucasus, von Mackensen was wholly dependent upon Rostov for supplies. South of Rostov, where Fourth Panzer Army was defending the outer approaches to the city, panzer operations between the Don and the Manych would eventually repay the effort involved, but with fewer than sixty serviceable tanks available in 17th and 23rd Panzer Divisions (LVII Panzer Corps), reinforcements for Fourth Panzer Army were an urgent necessity. Consequently, in late December SS Wiking Division (Steiner) was taken from von Mackensen, 11th Panzer Division (Raus) was switched from XXXXVIII Panzer Corps north of the Don, and 16th Motorized Division came in from outpost duty at Elista. With these divisions in aggressive action south-west of Kotelnikovo, Hoth held Rostov against Russian 51st and Second Guards Armies long enough for the fugitive First Panzer Army to slip through to safety.

'Winter Storm' had proved a failure and Sixth Army at Stalingrad was lost, but in subsequent battles across the Donetz between the Don and the Dnieper, where Kharkov fell to Voronezh Front on 16 February, panzer action within the framework of von Manstein's counter-strategy would do much to restore the power and confidence of the German Army. By 17 February 1943, First and Fourth Panzer Armies were regrouped behind the Donets in the triangle north of Rostov, and following a Führer conference at Zaporoshe, counter-attacks to recover Kharkov would soon start in earnest.

Russia: Return to Kharkov (map 13). On 22 February 1943, Fourth Panzer Army, striking north for Pavlograd with the support of VIII Air Corps (Fiebig) and First Panzer Army (q.v.), launched attacks sealing off Voronezh and South West Front spearheads (Popov) exploiting the Red Army's momentum in the Don bend following victory at Stalingrad. In thrusting south-west to the Sea of Azov, in the process of isolating and destroying Army Group Don, the Russian Fronts were dangerously extended. On 7 March, after regrouping north of Pavlograd, Hoth's offensive entered a new phase, aiming directly for Kharkov from Krasnograd. By 12 March 1943, Hoth had destroyed large parts of Russian Sixth Army, re-entered Kharkov with II SS Panzer Corps (Hausser), while Kempf prepared to recover Bjelgorod (Gross Deutschland Division) on the 18th.

Russia: Requiem for a Panzer Army (map 14). After consolidating in spring thaw conditions which inhibited mobile operations, Fourth Army was redeployed north of Bjelgorod for Operation 'Citadel' – the German 1943 summer offensive against the Red Army. The objective of Army Groups South (formerly Don) and Centre was to emasculate the Red Army on the Eastern Front by eliminating an enormous concentration of troops and weapons north and south of Kursk. Fourth Panzer Army/Army Group South, with two panzer corps north of Bjelgorod and supported by Army Detachment Kempf, would strike the main blow from the south. Simultaneous action by Ninth Army (Field Marshal Model) striking concentrically from the north was planned to bring spearheads together in the centre of the bulge at Kursk. Seventeen panzer divisions were committed to the offensive. **Citadel** opened on 5 July with the divisions involved reporting minimal gains north and south. Violent artillery exchanges and a marked increase in air activity by both sides heralded the start of panzer operations on an unprecedented scale. But in attempting to overcome Russian opposition 'Citadel' was doomed to failure. Coinciding on 10 July with Operation 'Husky', the Allied invasion of Sicily, Hitler reviewed progress on the 12th in the wake of ferocious losses and – as the Red Army judged the time right for its own counter-offensive against Second Panzer Army, holding the adjoining Orel sector to the north – halted the offensive next day. From 5 to 16 July 1943, the day on which the attacking panzer divisions finally broke-off the action, 'Citadel' proved a death ride for Fourth Panzer Army. More than 1,200 tanks, more than half the strength of the seventeen panzer divisions committed to the offensive, were lost; individual divisions at the point of main effort being reduced to 20 per cent of their armoured strength.

At **Prochorowka** on Sunday the 11th and Monday 12 July, the heaviest tank fighting of the war developed on the SS front, 25 miles from the start-line and a further 25 miles from Oboyan, Fourth Panzer Army's objective half-way to Kursk. The battle developed at crisis level after the SS Panzer Grenadier Divisions Leibstandarte Adolf Hitler (Wisch), Das Reich (Krüger) and Totenkopf (Priess), had regrouped and side-stepped opposition by Katukov's First Tank Army. Three days earlier, on 8 July, at Teteravino, the SS Panzer Corps had been helped out of a potential crisis by ground-attack wings of VIII Air Corps, breaking-up a threatening flank attack by Russian II Guards Armoured Corps. This VIII Air Corps action is elaborated in Part 4, page 55. At the height of the battle for Prochorowka, Hausser's SS Panzer Corps was engaged by Fifth Guards Tank Army (Rotmistrov) released from Stavka reserve; some 900 Pz Kpfw III/IVs, Tigers, Panthers, Ferdinands and other German armour, clashing head-on with a roughly equivalent number of T34s, KVIs, IIs and SU76 (15.2cm) assault guns. With so great a concentration of armour fighting for supremacy, the Prochorowka battlefield turned overnight into a ferocious malestrom of German and Russian tanks and supporting vehicles swirling in combat while Stormovicks, Henschels and JU 87 tank-busters added weight to the engagement. On the SS right, III Panzer Corps (Breith) – 6th Panzer Division (Hünersdorff) especially – attacking northwards in support of the SS by taking Rotmistrov in the left flank, pushed hard against determined opposition; an 11th Panzer Regimental (Oppeln) battle group winning a Donets crossing at Rschavetz, pointing the way to Prochorowka and contact with the SS armour. But there 6th Panzer Division was stopped. On the opposite flank, supporting action by Gross Deutschland, 3rd and 11th Panzer Divisions, biting into the opposition, helped XXXXVIII Panzer Corps forward. But by nightfall on the 12th, hundreds of wrecked vehicles, 70 Tigers among them, testified to a terrifying defeat for Fourth Panzer Army. [*Ninth Army, battling to reach Olchowtka and Ponyre, less than twelve miles from the northern start-line south of Orel, was even less successful; the progress of 2nd, 4th and 9th Panzer Divisions being delayed by extensive minefields, gun-pits, massed artillery fire and vicious counter-attacks all taking deadly toll of Model's armour.*]

The Luftwaffe's loss of superiority and fruitless efforts by the panzer force to fight through defences organized in depth by a thoroughly prepared opponent were at the root of defeat; skill and courage of those involved, notwithstanding. So, with the Red Army passing to the offensive, attacking first the eastern face of the main battle line held by Second Panzer Army north of the bulge, and then focusing south upon Kharkov where Fourth Panzer Army was deployed, German positions north and south of Kursk would soon prove untenable. The initiative seized by the Red Army would never again be recovered and panzer diaries would henceforth record successes only in retrograde steps as German armies retreated along the entire length of the front; Hitler's plans to halt the Red Army involving the panzer divisions in vigorous, yet more often than not, fruitless counter-action.

From August to December 1943, neither Fourth nor First Panzer Armies (joining Hoth alongside in the New Year) could find the strength to withstand Russian motorized offensives trapping the German Army at all levels. Lacking armoured reserves with which to cope with overwhelming attacks in a rapidly deteriorating situation, Fourth Panzer Army, suffering under remorseless pressure from Voronezh Front (Vatutin), abandoned first Kharkov, complete with depots and war material, and then other key communications centres. On 7 August 1943, at Graivoron west of Kharkov where Hoth was resisting renewed Russian pressure, only the intervention of Gross Deutschland holding firm at Achtyrka saved 11th and 19th Panzer Divisions from encirclement. By 22 August, following the fourth Battle of Kharkov, the city was abandoned despite energetic counter-attacks by 3rd and 6th Panzer Divisions supported by II SS Panzer Corps. Hitler, whose avowed intention it was to hold the city, nevertheless refused to countenance a phased Army Group withdrawal to the Dnieper. On 14 September 1943, with Army Group South's panzer strength amounting to no more than 250 tanks, Central Front broke through the northern wing defended by Fourth Panzer Army east of the Dnieper. The break-through endangered Kiev, Kanev (Bukrin) and Cherkassy. At other Dnieper crossings to the south, pressure mounted at Dniepropetrovsk and Zaporoshe (*see* First Panzer Army, August–December 1943). The Russian thrust aimed at Kiev immediately threatened von Manstein with encirclement. Hitler recanted over withdrawal and the Army Group (from north to south: Fourth Panzer, Eighth, First (Panzer) and Sixth Armies, was belatedly allowed to find sanctuary behind the Dnieper. Russian pressure increased in a race to win crossing-places.

[*At* ***Kanev/Bukrin,*** *22–24 September 1943, XXIV Panzer Corps (Nehring), separated from Hoth during Fourth Panzer Army's retreat from Kharkov to Kiev and attached to Eighth Army (Wöhler), was overtaken fifty miles away, east of the Dnieper, but promptly retired to counter-attack a west-bank bridgehead won by Third Guards Tank Army (Rybalko) at Bukrin on the 22nd. Committing his only regular mobile division (10th Panzer Grenadier) supported by impromptu motorized infantry groups organized from corps infantry divisions and launched into concentric attacks with 19th Panzer Division dispatched from Kiev, Nehring inhibited Voronezh Front's consolidation across the Dnieper. In the ensuing action, XXIV Panzer Group destroyed the greater part of three Russian paratroop brigades landed behind the front on 26 September with orders to widen the bridgehead into a sally-port for Rybalko's armoured brigades. But Nehring's success and the subsequent containment of the bridgehead by XXXXVIII Panzer Corps (Eberbach) proved short-lived with Vatutin redirecting Rybalko northwards on Kiev.*]

During October 1943, Fourth Panzer Army continued its resistance to 1st Ukrainian Front (Vatutin) concentrating on Kiev. But unsuccessful in defending the city, Hoth abandoned it on 6 November and Vatutin pushed 100 miles further west to seize Zhitomir. On 15 November 1943, Hitler replaced Hoth with General Erhard Raus. The new commander would win respite from retreat by mounting energetic counter-attacks. On 19 November, launching powerful Army and SS formations under XXXXVIII Panzer Corps (Balck) north from Fastov, Raus sliced deeply into Vatutin's extended flank; 1st, 7th, 19th, 25th and 2nd SS Panzer Divisions recapturing Zhitomir and shortly afterwards recovering Korosten. The action continued with the Leibstandarte attacking 1st Ukrainian Front at Brusilov and along the River Teterev, destroying sizeable Russian formations. But uncontainable pressure (1,100 tanks, 6,000 guns and 452,000 men) building-up to smash the panzer army forced Raus and south-flanking First Panzer Army (redeployed on 29 December from Krivoi Rog on the lower Dneiper) to yield ground. Retreat was imperative. In January 1944, 7th Panzer Division was roughly handled losing its Co (Schultz) blocking 1st Ukrainian Front moving into Shepetovka. A crucial road and rail centre affording Army communications to the west, the town was for a time resolutely defended by this veteran of campaigns in France in 1940, before giving way to overwhelming pressure.

From 16 to 26 March 1944, a Red Army spring offensive forced Fourth and First Panzer Armies apart, splitting von Manstein's Army Group front wide open; Raus, left with only Balck's XXXXVIII Panzer Corps and sundry infantry defended Tarnopol. Enveloped since 11 March, in the yawning gap between panzer armies, this communications centre, a 'fortress' according to Hitler, and not to be yielded at any price, was one of many lost or threatened at the time. Kowel was another, besieged by 1st Ukrainian Front on the Army Group's northern boundary, and a 'fortress' to be held at all cost.

[***The relief of Kowel*** *on 5 April 1944, was accomplished by 4th (von Saucken) and 5th (Decker) Panzer Divisions, driving south under Second Army/Army Group Centre; heavy losses being reported by investing Russian formations. From 16 March the defence of Kowel had been entrusted to SS General Herbert Gille, GOC, SS Wiking, refitting at Debica after a catastrophic experience at Cherkassy* (see First Panzer Army, 17 February 1944). *Gille was expressly flown into Kowel as commander of the 'fortress' garrison while an SS panzer battle group (Mühlenkamp) incorporated into the relief force was subordinated to 4th Panzer Division.*]

The relief of Tarnopol, at the second attempt, starting on 11 April 1944, was carried out by XXXXVIII Panzer Corps (Balck) fourth Panzer Army. On the 16th, an *ad hoc* panzer battle group (Friebe) with 24 Pz Kpfw Vs, nine Tigers (507th Panzer Battalion) and a 9th SS Panzer Division Hohenstaufen battle group with 30 Pz Kpfw IVs and 30 assault guns got to within seven miles of the town. Their proximity prompted 2,500 of the defenders to break out, but only 55 men, mainly from 357th and 359th Infantry Divisions, survived the attempt. There for a time the front stabilized. On 18 May 1944, when Raus was transferred to First Panzer Army, command of Fourth Panzer Army passed to Generaloberst Josef Harpe. The new GOC would serve until 28 June 1944, after which General Walther Nehring (DAK and XC Corps Tunisia) (*see* Fifth Panzer Army, December 1942) would deputise until 5 August. During this time Harpe was deputising for Model as commander of Army Group North Ukraine – formerly Army Group South. In June 1944, the Red Army's 'Bagration' offensive, overwhelming Army Group Centre (*see* Third Panzer Army, 22 June 1944), forced costly withdrawals upon an increasingly exposed and run-down Fourth Panzer Army. Retreating across southern Poland in July 1944, Fourth Panzer Army withdrew in the direction of Sandomierz (Baranov) and the Weichsel (Vistula); undergoing another change of command on 5 August – to General Herman Balck, a former GOC, 11th Panzer Division, now promoted from XXXXVIII Panzer Corps. Rearguard action in southern Poland was continued by a diminishing and overcommitted number of panzer divisions deployed without respite here as elsewhere east and west, especially in Normandy where 'Overlord' was draining much needed panzer strength, and in Italy.

[***Defending Warsaw*** *on 2 August 1944, Ninth Army launched counter-attacks against a 1st BR Front spearhead moving north-east around the city. The offensive was ordered by Field Marshal Model, commanding both Army Groups Centre and North Ukraine (to which latter headquarters First and Fourth Panzer Armies were now responsible). At the centre of operations XXXIX Panzer Corps (von Saucken) shattered the Front's III Corps vanguard, driving to outflank the defence at Volomin.* ***Panzer intervention by Ninth Army at Volomin*** *involved four panzer divisions – 4th, 19th, 5th SS Wiking and Hermann Goering – in concentric action bringing temporary relief to a weak Army Group front forming east of the Polish capital. The involvement of SS Wiking in the defence of Warsaw presaged action by a new (IV) SS Panzer Corps (Gille); corps composition – 3rd SS Panzer Division 'Totenkopf' (Becker) redeployed from Roumania and 5th SS Panzer Division 'Wiking' (Mühlenkamp), refitted and re-employed after its disastrous experience at Cherkassy. At* ***Magnuschew****, south of Warsaw (map 18) on 8 August 1944, Hermann Goering and 19th Panzer were instrumental in containing a potentially explosive Red Army bridgehead established west of the Vistula by 1st Belorussian (1 BR) Front, threatening Berlin; Panzer action at this point reduced that threat.*]

And there on the Vistula south of Warsaw, as at Baranov (Sandomierz) where Fourth Army was containing a 1st Ukranian (1 UKR) bridgehead, calm reigned for five months before the storm broke and the Red Army swept on to Berlin. During the autumn of 1944, Fourth Army/Army Group 'A' (Harpe) consolidated on the Vistula, building defences against a future Red Army assault. But with barely twelve panzer divisions out of a current total of about twenty armoured or motorized divisions (four for Harpe) to defend the entire Eastern Front against 61 Russian armies (six tank armies with 15,000 armoured fighting vehicles) this was unlikely. The cards, as Guderian would say, were stacked in favour of the Red Army. *[In January 1945, IV SS Panzer Corps (Gille), the mainstay of Army Group Centre's defence of Warsaw, was transferred to Army Group South (Sixth Army). The SS Panzer Corps would drive east along the Danube to relieve Budapest in Operation 'Konrad' (map 19)* (see *Sixth SS Panzer Army, 13 February 1945.)]* On the Vistula the long-awaited Red Army offensive was about to break.

A moving panzer pocket in Poland (map 18). On 12 January 1945, the Red Army opened the way to Berlin with a massive 1st Ukrainian Front (Konev) offensive erupting out of the Baranov bridgehead, shattering Fourth Panzer Army's front, held solely by infantry divisions. Pushing north-west to Kielce in conjunction with 1st Belorussian (1 BR) Front (Zhukov) breaking out from the Vistula at Magnuschew and Pulavy, and in so doing destroying Ninth Army's southern wing, Konev's offensive threatened the Army Group with total disaster. Outclassed in numbers and firepower, Fourth Panzer Army, with more infantry than armour, was scattered in the Red Army offensive. With Ukranian and White Russian Fronts thrusting to the Oder at Glogau and Breslau, more than halfway and less than 150 miles from the capital, the battle for Berlin assumed a grim reality. Within hours of Konev's break-out, Fourth Panzer Army's only mobile reserve, 16th and 17th Panzer Divisions (XXIV Panzer Corps Nehring) retained by the Army's last GOC, General Gräser, for action against the flank of any Russian penetration was encircled at Kielce. Nehring would nevertheless force a way into contact with a Gross Deutschland relief force of two divisions striking south-west from Lodz under von Saucken. The mobility of both formations would be narrowly assured by Luftwaffe resupply wings (*see* Part 4, Transport action, page 143).

During the subsequent defence of Western Silesia by Army Group Centre, called into question on 25 January when the Red Army renewed its Berlin offensive across the Oder north and south of Breslau, Fourth Panzer Army retained Glogau until Gräser abandoned it on 31 March. Unrewarding Fourth Panzer Army counter-attacks then marked Red Army progress westwards to the Neisse, reducing what remained of industrial Silesia.

*[**The last panzer offensive** of the war, by Seventeenth Army on 5 March 1945, involved Panzer Group Nehring – XXXIX Panzer Corps (Decker) and LVII Panzer Corps (Kirchner) deployed in defence of Silesia. Re-occupying Lauban, Decker's 19th Panzer Division and FGD joining Kirchner's 8th Panzer Division and FBD inflicted notable losses on a Russian mechanized corps.]*

Germany in defeat (map 20). On 16 April 1945, when the Red Army struck for Berlin across the Oder-Neisse line, sizeable elements of both Fourth Panzer Army (Gräser) and Ninth Army (Busch) were encircled in a Frankfurt–Guben pocket. The battle for Berlin, from which Fourth Panzer Army was thereby effectively eliminated, can best be followed by referring to Third Panzer Army, 16 April 1945. On 6 May 1945, in Bohemia north of Prague, Fourth Panzer Army pulled surviving units together and with a semblance of 'panzer' divisions – Bohemia, Brandenburg (Grenadier), 2nd SS, 10th SS and 20th Panzer Division, reinforcing Volksturm and *ad hoc* units of all kinds, defied a final Russian offensive employing three Tank and seventeen Infantry Armies directed into the rear of Army Group Centre (Schörner). On 8 May 1945, Fourth Panzer Army, a shadow of its former self, and like other formations in the east lacking basic stores and vehicles, surrendered to the Red Army.

Career Note: Implicated in the Hitler assassination plot of 20 July 1944, Generaloberst Hoepner was one of many conspirators hanged for treason.

5. Panzer Army Africa (PzAOK Afrika)

In common with OKH practice in Europe this Panzer Army HQ, one of two raised in North Africa, the other being Fifth Panzer Army (Africa), evolved by stages to control increasingly complex mobile operations and a burgeoning number of panzer divisions and support units. Yet at the time of the Panzer Army's confrontation with General Bernard Montgomery on 23 October 1942 at El Alamein, the decisive battle of the African campaign, so determined was the High Command to regard Africa as a side-show that Field Marshal Erwin Rommel the army commander disposed of only two panzer divisions (and two Italian armoured formations equipped with much inferior machines), three motorized (one Italian), five unmotorized Italian infantry divisions, one Falschirmjaeger brigade (Ramcke) and support units. Montgomery's strength comprised three armoured and seven motorized divisions plus supporting brigades – with four or more times the number of German tanks. On 10 October 1940, four months prior to the arrival of Deutsches Afrika Korps (DAK), the veteran of Spain, von Thoma, currently Panzer Waffengeneral (5 March 1940), in a report to OKW on the employment of armour in the desert, recommended the employment of four panzer divisions in Africa taking into account the likely supply situation and operational needs.

On 14 February 1941, the first panzer units for DAK arrived at Tripoli. Taken mainly from 3rd Panzer Division to create a new 5th Light Division (Streich) for service in the desert came reconnaissance (AA3) and 39th Anti-tank Battalion (PzJaegAbt 39); a vanguard quickly followed to Africa by 5th Panzer Regiment, 8th Machine-gun Battalion, 605th Anti-tank Battalion, 606th Anti-aircraft Battalion, 75th Divisional Artillery Regiment, and signals – all to be incorporated within weeks into a new, 21st Panzer Division. Following on for DAK from May to August 1941 came 15th Panzer Division (von Prittwitz); tanks and vehicles – the heavy equipment of 8th Panzer Regiment – being shipped to Tripoli while grenadiers of 104th and 115th Infantry Regiments accompanied by light units were ferried forward to Derna in Ju 52s flying from Brindisi. Despite battle losses and frequent changes in their order of battle, these 'African' Panzer divisions were destined to remain in North Africa as core units of DAK until general capitulation two years later in Tunisia. There in May 1943 10th Panzer Division, after serving briefly in conjunction with the Corps, also surrendered to the Allies. The two 'African' divisions were reformed shortly afterwards; 15th Panzer in Sicily as a panzer grenadier division, 21st Panzer in France, March 1944.

Panzer command in Africa. DAK's first and most famous commander was General Erwin Rommel. Regarded by all who knew him as a forceful, highly professional soldier, an infantryman by training but panzer commander by ambition, Rommel won early distinction in action against the Italians on the Isonzo in October 1917. Leading an assault on positions considered by both sides to be impregnable, Captain Rommel's thrusting tactics resulted in the retreat of Italian Second and Third Armies resulting in 60,000 prisoners being taken by German XIV Army. Rommel's ambition to lead a panzer division was fulfilled by Hitler in February 1940 when the Führer, whose escort battalion he had commanded since 1938, gave him command of 7th Panzer Division at Bad Godesberg. Nominally subordinate to Comando Supremo in Rome, via Marshal Bastico, C-in-C, Africa to whom all African armed services were subordinate, Rommel was in practice responsible to OKW and Hitler via Field Marshal Albert Kesselring. [*Transferred from the Eastern Front to Rome on 28 November 1941, Kesselring was followed a week later by 2nd Air Fleet Headquarters under orders to move from Moscow to the Mediterranean. Kesselring's move, coinciding with Rommel's first retreat to El Agheila, was a timely one. In addition to commanding 2nd Air Fleet, co-ordinating Mediterranean air and sea operations with the Italians, Kesselring, as C-in-C, South (Europe) with additional staff, was destined to shoulder an increasing burden of German responsibilities in the theatre until 10 March 1945, his career then changing direction as OB West in succession to von Runstedt.*]

Right: In November 1917 Oberleutnant Rommel led six companies of Württembergers in a heroic action. After 50 hours of fighting, with a battle group that at the outset consisted of barely more than two companies, Rommel, at considerable risk from artillery fire, infiltrated Italian lines along the Isonzo to reach the summit of Monte Matajur and take 9,000 prisoners. For his achievement he was decorated with the 'Pour le Mérite' and promoted to Captain.

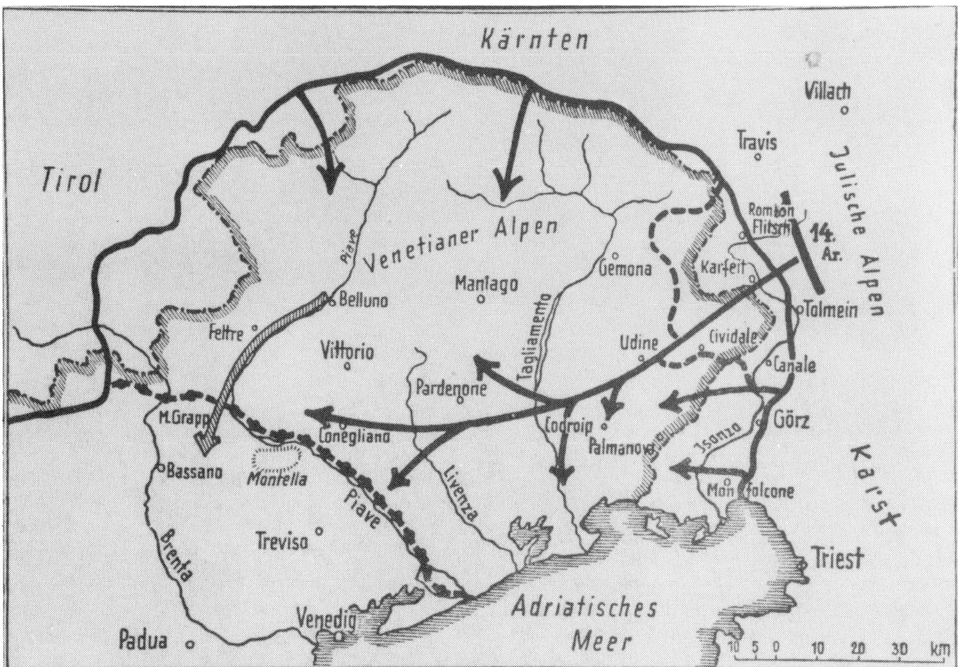

Rommel's career in Africa and his command of DAK started on 15 February 1941 – three days after arriving in Tripoli – when DAK became operational. Thereafter Generalleutnant Rommel, former commander 7th Panzer Division, promoted General der Panzertruppen on 1 July 1941, would serve in Africa for two years with few breaks in service until 9 March 1943 when as Field Marshal he returned to Germany to consult with Hitler. On 15 August 1941, following his promotion to General, Rommel assumed command of both German (DAK) and Italian (XXI) Corps with an expanded HQ – Panzer Group Africa – leaving DAK to General Ludwig Crüwell who, until his capture eight months later on 29 May 1942, when he crashed in his Fieseler Storch, would see the Corps through its first major reverse – British Eighth Army's 'Crusader' offensive to relieve Tobruk, starting on 18 November 1941 (q.v.). Crüwell's successor in command of DAK, General Walther Nehring (18th Panzer Division), appointed 9 March 1942, would follow in time for Gazala battles leading to the capture of Tobruk. But before Nehring could cap this success by participating in the battle of Alamein, circumstances dictated otherwise and he returned wounded to Germany on 31 August 1942; a new appointment following in Tunisia (*see* Fifth Panzer Army, 8 December 1942). Command of DAK then passed briefly to von Vaerst and, during the battle of El Alamein, except for a day as GOC, Panzer Army, to von Thoma. Thereafter for varying

Left: Field Marshal Erwin Rommel entered the army as a cadet in 1910. He served in the west from 1914 to 1916 (Marne, Argonne, Vosges) and the east in 1917 (Austro/ Italian front). In 1929 he became an Instructor at the School of Infantry, Dresden, where he wrote the book *Infantry Attacks.* In 1935, at Hitler's instigation, he was posted to the War Academy, Potsdam, and in 1937 was promoted to Colonel. He subsequently served in several theatres although not in the east. He is best remembered for his leadership of Panzer Army Africa.

Right: Field Marshal Albert Kesselring served in artillery during the 1914–18 war. By 1936 he was Chief of the Luftwaffe General Staff in succession to General Wever. In 1937 he became GOC, Air District 3 (Dresden): then GOC Luftwaffe Group/1st Air Fleet (Berlin) in 1938. He commanded 1st Air Fleet in Poland and 2nd Air Fleet in France, where he was promoted to Field Marshal. He was on the Central Front in Russia in 1941, and then in southern Italy from 1942. In March 1945 he was chosen as the replacement for von Runstedt.

spells, Bayerlein, Fehn, von Liebenstein, Ziegler and finally Hans Cramer served as DAK commanders.

Meanwhile Rommel's career continued upwards. Promoted Generaloberst on 21 January 1942, with a Panzer Group Headquarters expanded and redesignated Panzer Army Africa – the highest level of mobile command in the desert – Rommel controlled both DAK and three Italian corps (X, XX and XXI). Promotion to Field Marshal was Rommel's reward for capturing Tobruk on 21 June 1942. On 2 September, following eighteen months' service in the inhospitable North African climate, Rommel took sick leave in Europe. But when a heart attack at the start of the battle of El Alamein removed his successor, General der Kavallerie Georg Stumme, introducing Generalleutnant von Thoma to Panzer Army command – for the exceptionally short period of 24 hours – Rommel returned to Africa on 25 October, resumed his Panzer Army command and carried on the battle; von Thoma, reverting to his DAK command, was captured on 4 November 1942. The Field Marshal's last appointment in Africa commencing 23 February 1943, bringing him command of Army Group Africa, continued until 9 March when he visited Hitler – never to return. Thereafter Rommel's future as an army group commander was to lie in Europe (*see* career note). Rommel's energy in opposing British desert commanders, Wavell, O'Connor, Cunningham, Ritchie, Auchinleck and eventually Montgomery in two years of mobile operations in the Western Desert, was characterized by thrustful and opportunist tactics, often brilliantly successful – like those of 7th Panzer Division under his command during the Battle of France (*see* Third Panzer Army, 13 May 1940). Briefed solely to block a British threat to Tripoli, the 'Desert Fox', as Rommel was nicknamed by British opponents, would instead lead his Africa Corps to legendary fame – in protracted battles with British Eighth Army.

The need for a German military presence in Africa arose out of successful action by General Wavell starting at Sidi Barrani in December 1940. In sweeping Italian forces five hundred miles out of Egypt to threaten Tripoli, Wavell's Western Desert Force (O'Connor) re-named Eighth Army 26 September 1941, including 7th Armoured Division 'Desert Rats' and Royal Tank Regiments with 50 Matildas taking 130,000 prisoners destroyed ten Italian divisions at Beda Fomm. Mussolini appealed to Hitler. A German 'blocking' force was raised. Subsequent Italian experience in Africa and on the Eastern Front can be followed in Part

2, Satellite contributions for the panzer force. On 31 March 1941, Rommel disregarded his 'blocking' directive, organizing cross-desert battle groups and launching his first offensive, 'Sonenblume' taking the Africa Corps 400 miles from El Agheila to the Italian/Egyptian frontier at Sollum. After a minor setback ('Brevity') DAK consolidated there on 27 May. But having failed to break Wavell's Eighth Army or capture the crucial supply port of Tobruk – the best-developed harbour on the coast midway between Tripoli and Alexandria – Rommel could do no more than sit on the frontier and, in the wake of Operation 'Scorpion', defend Sollum/Halfaya 21–27 May, while simultaneously investing the port. An interesting sidelight on Rommel's failure to reduce Tobruk, Eighth Army's forward supply and communications base, for which he blamed the divisional commander (Streich) and had him transferred out of the theatre, is contained in the following (edited) account of panzer action 10 April–1 May 1941, by a junior officer captured from 2nd Battalion, 5th Panzer Regiment. In this engagement the panzer battle groups suffered heavily, von Ponath's 8th Machine-gun battalion in particular; a staunch defence of Tobruk by a British and Empire garrison (Klopper) thwarting any intention Rommel might have had of extending offensive operations into Egypt.

Readers preferring to follow the course of events eastwards should turn on to 15 August 1941 or alternatively, for a British Eighth Army report illustrating 15th Panzer Division's battle group organization and tactics in the course of 'Scorpion', turn to Halfaya, 21–27 May 1941.

Tobruk, 10 April–1 May 1941. A first-hand account of panzer action in the first battle by 5th Light Division (Streich); this is a junior commander's view of desert warfare on 10–14, 23, 30 April, and again on 1 May 1941.

'Tobruk. 10 April 1941. Towards evening we reached our advanced positions 17½ miles in front of Tobruk. We have covered 100 miles . . . wearily we pitch camp. Vehicles are checked over. I have to force the louvres open with a hammer, the sand having jammed them.'

'Tobruk. 11 April 1941. At 0900 hours we move off into the desert again to the S.E. in order to cut off Tobruk from the south. With us are anti-tank, machine-gun and anti-aircraft units . . . Ten miles south of Tobruk and already the enemy's artillery is giving us an H. E. welcome. . . . As soon as they get the range we withdraw 100–200 yards. Their fire follows us – their observation must be good. At 1630 hours we attack with two half-squadrons. The artillery puts down a barrage, but can make little impression on us. Through! We career on for 1,000 yards and turn carefully through a minefield. As the smoke lifts I see barbed wire and anti-tank trenches. "Halt!" Gun-flashes. "Gun, 9 o'clock. A.P. shell, light-coloured mound, fire!" A hit. Again – 10 yards to the right . . . with six shots we have finished off the anti-tank position. We move along the wire looking for a gap and the leading tank finds one, and in doing so runs on to a mine, of course. Another goes to its rescue, while I give covering fire.'

'Tobruk. 14 April 1941. At 0010 I am called, and ordered to report with the company commander at 0100 hours. Situation: Machine-gunners and engineers have worked a gap through the anti-tank defences; 5 Tank Regiment, 8 Machine-Gun Battalion, anti-tank and anti-aircraft artillery will cross the gap under the cover of darkness and overwhelm the position. Stuka attack at 0645 hours. 0715 hours. Storming of Tobruk. With least possible noise 2 Battalion, Regimental H.Q. Company and 1 Battalion move off completely blacked-out. Bitterly cold. Of course, the enemy recognizes us by the noise and as ill luck will have it, a defective spot-light on one of the cars in front goes on and off.'

'Soon artillery fire starts up on us, getting the range. The shells explode like fireworks. We travel six miles, every nerve on edge. From time to time isolated groups of soldiers appear – men of 8 Machine-Gun Battalion – and then suddenly we are in a gap. Already the tank is nose-down in the first trench. The motor whines: I catch a glimpse of the stars through the shutter, then for the second time the tank goes down, extricating itself backwards with a dull thud, the engines grinding. We are through and immediately take up file in battle order. In front of us 8 Company, then 2 Battalion H.Q. Company, then 5 Company. With my troop I travel left of the (6) company commander. With 2 Battalion H.Q. Company about 60 men of 8 Machine-Gun Battalion with Oberst Ponath are marching in scattered groups. Tanks and infantry? – against all rules! Behind us follow the Regimental H.Q. Company and 1 Battalion plus the other arms. Slowly, much too slowly, the column moves forward. We must, of course, regulate our speed by the marching troops, and so the enemy has time to prepare resistance. The more the darkness lifts, the harder the enemy strikes. Destructive fire starts up in front of us now – 1 – 2 – 3 – 10 – 12 – 16 bursts and more. Five batteries of 25-pounders rain hail on us. 8 Company presses forward to get at them. Our heavy tanks, it is true, fire for all they are worth, so do we all, but the enemy with his superior force and all the tactical advantages of his own territory makes heavy gaps in our ranks.'

'Wireless; "9 o'clock anti-tank gun, 5 o'clock tank!" We are right in the middle of it with no prospects of getting out. From both flanks A.P. shells whizz by. Wireless "Right turn, Left turn, Retire." Now we come slap into 1 Battalion, which is following us. Some of our tanks are already on fire. The crews call for doctors, who alight to help in this witches' cauldron. English anti-tank units fall upon us, with their machine-guns firing into our midst; but we have no time. My driver, in the thick of it, says "The engines are no longer running properly, brakes not acting, transmission working only with great difficulty." We bear off to the right. Anti-tank guns 900 metres distant in the hollow behind, and a tank. Behind that in the next dip 1,000 yards away another tank. How many? I see only the effect of the fire on the terrace-like dispositions of the enemy . . . Above us Italian fighter planes come into the fray. Two of them crash in our midst. The optical instruments covered with dust. Nevertheless, I register several unmistakeable hits. A few anti-tank guns are silenced, some enemy tanks are burning. Just then we are hit, and the wireless is smashed to bits. Now our communications are cut off. What is more, our ammunition is giving out. I follow the battalion commander. Our attack is fading out. From every side the superior forces of the enemy shoot at us.'

' "Retire" There is a crash just behind us. The engine and petrol tank are in the rear. The tank must be on fire. I turn round and look through the slit. It is not burning. Our luck is holding. Poor 8th Machine Gunners! We take a wounded man and two others aboard, and the other tanks do the same. Most of the men have bullet wounds. At its last gasp my tank follows the others, whom we lose from time to time in the clouds of dust. But we have to press on towards the south, as that is the only way through. Good God! Supposing we don't find it? And the engines won't do any more! Close to our right and left flanks the English tanks shoot into our midst. We are hit in the tracks of our tank, and they creak and groan. The minefield lane is in sight. Everyone hurries towards it. English anti-tank guns shoot into the mass. Our own anti-tank and 8.8 cm. guns are almost deserted, the crews lying silent beside them. The Italian artillery, which was to have protected our left flank, is equally deserted! We go on. Now comes the gap and the ditch! The driver cannot see a thing for dust, nor I. We drive by instinct. The tank almost gets stuck in the two ditches blocking the road, but manages to extricate itself with great difficulty. Examine damage to tank. My men extract an A.P. shell from the right-hand auxiliary petrol tank . . . The petrol tank was shot away, and the petrol ran out without igniting!'

'Tobruk. 14 April 1941. At 1200 hours we retire into the wadi south of us . . . We cover up. Heavy cumulus clouds cover the sky. Every 10–30 minutes 2 or 3 English bombers swoop out of them amongst the tanks. Every bomber drops 4 to 8 bombs. Explosions all round. It goes on like this until 1900 hours without a pause. . . . Casualties in 2 Battalion of 5 Tank Regiment, 10 tanks, apart from 5 7.5 cm. guns of 8 Coy.! A few dead, several wounded, more missing. The anti-tank units and the light and heavy A.A. were badly shot up and the 8th Machine Gunners were cut to pieces. The regiment has lost all its doctors – presumably captured. The regiment is practically wiped out.'

'Tobruk. 15 April. Artillery fire from 0700 hours. The bombers repeat yesterday's game. My troop has two heavy tanks again. Tank No. 625 isn't running any more. however. It only serves as a pilbox. According to orders, I report at the brigade commander's office at 1200 hours. Once more the principal subject discussed is the action in front of Tobruk on 14th April. We simply cannot understand how we ever managed to get out again. It is the general opinion that it was the most severely fought battle of the whole war. But what can the English think of us! A weak battalion, only two squadrons strong, bursts through the complex defence systems until it is just on a mile from the town, shoots everything to bits, engages the enemy on all sides, and then gets away again. . . . The war in Africa is quite different from the war in Europe. That is to say, it is absolutely individual. Here there are not the masses of men and material. Nobody and nothing can be concealed. It doesn't matter whether it is a battle between opposing land-forces, or between air-forces, or both; it is the same sort of fighting, face to face, each side thrusting and counter-thrusting. If the struggle was not so brutal, so entirely without rules, you might compare it with the joustings of knights. And now before Tobruk. . . .'

'Tobruk. 20 April. In the afternoon tank No. 623 rolls up with a new engine. Now I have the strongest squadron in the regiment: 4 Pz Kpfw II tanks, 4 Pz Kpfw III. Gradually, however, the job of squadron commander is becoming difficult. I have absolutely nothing to go by, everything is in the desert. Where are the tanks, where are the H.Q. cars and squadron office? And I have no command tank and no motor-cycle – and then the reports and the paper-war which begins as soon as the last shot has been fired!'

'Tobruk. 23 April 1941. The journey I planned has been postponed owing to the arrival of Lieut. Grim with 6 tanks. The engines of the tanks are partly new, partly overhauled in the factory. They have new gears, transmission, brakes, etc. The British do not miss the chance of sharing in the welcome with some well-aimed fire. The faithful 625, which is the only heavy tank of the squadron remaining with us,

Above: Tripoli 1941 and the unloading of Pz Kpfw IIIs for Rommel as part of 8th Panzer Regiment, 15th Panzer Division. They were soon in action with DAK at Tobruk and then throughout the campaign in North Africa (*see* maps 5 and 9).

will now be sent back to have its 6 shell-wounds cured. Whilst in the workshop it will have its engines changed.'

'Tobruk. 29 April. 50 dive-bombers circling over Tobruk. Tank 622 turns up. They tell us about the desert – of hunger and thirst, of Benghazi and of Derna. Since tank No 625 is still in the workshops, I am getting No. 634 as my 5th tank, with Serjeant Schäfer, my driving instructor from Wünsdorf.'

'Tobruk. 30 April. Finishing touches to our preparations for battle. 1745 hours. March to assembly place. Strong Stuka attacks. 2000 hours: our own strong artillery bombards the enemy heavily, 8 Machine Gunners in front. 1 Engineer Battalion and 1 Battalion of Assault Engineers break through and demolish the barriers on either side. The light signals show that the attack has begun. At 2200 hours sleep under the tank.'

'Tobruk. 1 May 1941. We intend to take Tobruk. My 4th attack on the town. Up at 0330 hours, leave at 0430 hours. We lose touch in the darkness and dust – and join up again. We file through the gap where many of our comrades have already fallen. Then we deploy at once, 6 Sqn. on the left, 5 Sqn. on the right, behind H.Q., 8 and 7 Sqns. The regiment is now Hohmann's Mobile Battalion and consists altogether of 80 tanks. The English artillery fires on us at once. We attack. No German patrol goes in front to reconnoitre. Tier upon tier of guns boom out from the triangular fortification before us. The two light troops of the company and my left section are detailed off to make a flanking movement. I attack. Wireless message: "Commander of 6 Coy. hit on track." Then things happen suddenly. . . . A frightful crash in front and to the right. Direct hit by artillery shell. No! It must be a mine. Immediately send wireless message: "Commander Schorm on a mine, will try to get old direction." 5 metres back – new detonation. Mine underneath to the left. Now it's all up – with driving. Wireless message: "Getting back went on mine again." Now mount tank 623. Back through the artillery fire for 100 yards and got in. Wireless: "Tanks active behind ridge. The men of the mined tank all right." '

'Back carefully. Then with the last tank in Company H.Q. and Lieut. Roskoll I give cover to the north. 9 heavy and 3 light tanks of the squadron have had to give up owing to mines. Of my troop, the commander's tank and both of the section leaders' tanks are damaged. Of course the enemy went on shooting at us for some time. A slight change of position: forward – right – backwards – left! With the commander's approval I am to go up in front to salvage tanks. Whilst we are on the way we are fired at by M.G.s and anti-tank guns from about 500 yards. I silence them with H.E. and drive in the tracks of 624. I bring up the rear, and then the laborious work of salvaging begins. The anti-tank gunfire starts up again and has to be kept in check by constant fire. . . . At last I move off slowly with 624 in tow, through the gap and on 800 yards. 250,000 Marks saved. The crew is really delighted to have its tank back. It is now late afternoon. Dive-bombers and twin-engined fighters have been attacking the enemy constantly. In spite of this, the British repeatedly make counter-thrusts with tanks. As soon as the planes have gone the artillery starts up furiously.

It is beginning to grow dark. Which is friend, which is foe? Shots are being fired all over the place, often on your own troops and on tanks in front on their way back. Suddenly a wireless message: "British attacking gap with infantry." It is actually true. Two companies get off their motor lorries and extend in battle order. All sorts of light signals go up – green, red, white. The flares hiss down near our M.G.s. It is already too dark to take aim. Well, the attack is a failure. The little Fiat-Ansaldos go up in front with flame-throwers in order to clean up the triangle. Long streaks of flame, thick smoke, filthy stink. We provide cover until 2345 hours, then retire through the gap. It is a mad drive through the dust. At 0300 hours have snack beside the tank. 24 hours shut up in the tank, with frightful cramp as a result – and a thirst! Tobruk. 2 May 1941. Recovering tanks.' The panzer officer was subsequently captured.

The tactics of desert battle group commanders, reflecting training and experience in early campaigns, are dramatically illustrated in an Eighth Army report discussing Operation 'Scorpion' – the German re-occupation of Halfaya Pass by 15th Panzer Division (von Esebeck) on 27 May 1941. After a setback for DAK – opposing 'Brevity', Eighth Army's first counter-attack seeking to restore contact with Tobruk, and involving the loss and recovery of Sollum and other frontier positions on the 15th – the panzer division organized battle groups to accomplish the task required of it; the re-occupation of the pass (*see* Halfaya, 1–5).

'Halfaya. 1. 21 May 1941. General. Early in the day the division received orders by radio telephone to carry out a surprise attack on the Sollum front coinciding with the attack on Crete by XI Air Corps (Student) starting 20 May.'

'Major-General von Esebeck, GOC 15th Panzer at the time was away wounded and Colonel von Herff was responsible for the German forces in the frontier area. Believing the balance of strength to be sufficiently in his favour, the latter decided to widen the scope of the operation as ordered and, instead of merely keeping the British forces busy in the frontier area, to take Halfaya, the frontier pass giving access to the coastal plain. Von Herff hoped at the same time to force a tank engagement.'

'Halfaya. 2. 24 May 1941. Plan of attack. The actual orders for the operation were issued by the divisional commander; zero day – 26 May. Broadly speaking, the intention was to make a feint attack in the Capuzzo area and cause the British to reinforce their position there, while at the same time giving the impression that German reinforcements of about the strength of one division were moving from the Tobruk area to outflank the British Desert Force from the south (causing them to withdraw from the escarpment to the coastal area without fighting). The method adopted to implement this plan comprised a strong advance south-eastwards by three groups (two lorried infantry and one armoured), while the fourth group made a wide sweep from Sidi Azeiz – first moving south to the area north of Maddalena, and then eastwards to Deir el Hamra. This latter move was to be made in several columns in order to confuse Eighth Army as to the actual axis of advance.'

'Halfaya. 3. Composition of the German attacking force – 15th Panzer Division is divided into four battle groups. The Panzer or Cramer Group (commanded by Oberst Cramer, OC, 8th Panzer Regiment) consisted of:

8th Panzer Regiment less one troop.
Detachments from 5th Panzer Regiment and 33rd Reconnaissance Unit.
Two batteries and a half-troop of 33rd Artillery Regiment.
One battery from the Grati (Italian) Artillery Regiment (which failed to arrive on time).

Of the two lorried infantry groups one was commanded by Major Bach, OC, 1st Battalion, 104th Lorried Infantry Regiment.

The Bach Group consisted of:

1st Battalion, 104th Lorried Infantry Regiment.
The pioneer platoons of 3rd and 33rd Reconnaissance Units.
A mixed platoon from 33rd Anti-Tank Battalion.
One section of 33rd Artillery Regiment.
One troop of 8th Panzer Regiment.

The other lorried infantry group was commanded by Oberst Knabe, OC, 15th Motor-Cycle Battalion. The Knabe Group consisted of:

15th Motor-Cycle Battalion less one company.
The M/C companies of 3rd and 33rd Reconnaissance Units.
One reinforced rifle company of 14th Lorried Infantry Regiment.
One company (less one mixed platoon) of 33rd Anti-Tank Battalion.
Detachments of 33rd Artillery Regiment.

The Wechmar Group under the command of Oberst Freiherr von Wechmar, OC, 3rd Reconnaissance Unit, had

Below: A Pz Kpfw III 'special' with a long, 5cm gun and heavier armour (50mm instead of 30mm) which supplemented DAK's other 'special', the Pz Kpfw IV with a long-barrelled 7.5cm gun. These, together with a 7.5cm short-barrelled Pz Kpfw III, formed the mainstay of Rommel's armour.

sufficient heavy weapons to fight as an independent unit, combining striking force with speed. This group consisted of:

3rd and 33rd Recce. Units (less elements allotted to other groups).

One company of 605th Anti-Tank Battalion.

One troop and two sections of 33rd Artillery Regiment.

One troop of captured field guns manned by personnel of 33rd Artillery Regiment.'

'Halfaya. 4. Individual tasks of the four groups:

i. Panzer Group – The armoured or Cramer Group was to take up a position on the track Capuzzo–Bir Hafid–Sidi Omar. The general direction of advance was to be Bir Ghirba–Qaret el Ruweibit, i.e., south-eastwards. After confusing the British by frequently changing direction, the tanks were to cross the frontier in battle formation at 1600 hours and under cover of artillery fire to make for the first objective, Point 203 (Qaret abu Sayid) and Point 204 (two and a half miles south-east of Sidi Suleiman). This line is at right angles to the general line of advance. Further advance, either in the same direction or north-east towards the rear of the British forces at Halfaya, was to be held back pending the arrival of artillery and orders from divisional battle H.Q. which was to move with the Cramer Group.'

'ii. Bach Group – As the Bach Group was expected to meet strong counter-attacks it was given artillery support to the strength of one half-troop from 33rd Artillery Regiment and one battery from the Grati (Italian) Artillery Regiment. The task of the Bach Group was to follow up the Cramer Group and occupy Halfaya Pass. It was to advance on zero morning through the wadis of the escarpment as far as Qalah and, from noon on, to reconnoitre in the direction of the pass. The British forces at the pass and in the plain were to be pinned down by artillery fire. After 1545 hours fire was to be concentrated on the pass, and from 1600 hours the Bach Group was to be ready to capture Halfaya on foot and to thrust forward as far as Minqar el Shaba as British resistance weakened. Both roads at the pass were immediately to be consolidated by mining the forward slopes. The troop attached from 8th Panzer Regiment was to be used in the attack on the pass until the engineers had removed the mines from the south-western slope. Sollum was to be held by a reinforced troop, and reconnaissance of the coastal plain was to be carried out during the attack on the pass.'

'iii. Knabe Group – The Knabe Group was to form the mobile reserve of the division. It was to be ready from 1500 hours on zero day (26th May) in the neighbourhood of Capuzzo, and was either to follow the Cramer Group in its vehicles, or to go to the support of the Bach Group at Minquar el Shaba.'

'iv. Wechmar Group – The Wechmar Group was to assemble at Sidi Azeiz the evening before zero day, and to start at dawn on zero day for the frontier, north of Maddalena via Gabr Saleh. After crossing the frontier between Frontier Posts 68 and 71 at 1500 hours on 26 May, the group was then to split up into several columns, in order to confuse the British, and to advance on Deir el Hamra feinting in other directions to add to the confusion.

Above: An '88' in desert action. British tank attacks were often defeated by the aggressive presence of the '88' in the forefront of DAK battle lines. Firing over open sights, and at ranges reducing to 500 yards, the '88' was more than a match for the Cruisers issued to Royal Tank Regiments.

Once over the frontier speed was to be the first consideration. The group was to avoid major engagements, and to restrict offensive action to attacking numerically weaker forces. If enemy opposition was not encountered, or was only weak, the Wechmar Group was to push on to Bir Sofafi, and lie up there. Contact with the British forces was to be maintained.'

'Halfaya. 5. German Intelligence – According to an Intelligence appreciation the British Eighth Army had withdrawn some of its forces still disposed in two groups, viz. a desert force and a coastal force. The former was believed to consist of a reinforced reconnaissance unit, about one battalion of tanks, four or five troops of artillery, and anti-aircraft and anti-tank detachments.'

'The British forward patrol line, held strongly by tanks and armoured cars, was thought to run from Halfaya Pass via Points 207 and 205 to Point 204 (Tumuls) whence it ran southwards parallel to the frontier wire. The forward defended locality was believed to have been strengthened by anti-tank guns and a few Mark II tanks.'

'The British artillery was believed to be concentrated in the Sidi Suleiman area, while strong reserves, probably including tanks, were suspected in the Bir Habata district.'

'It was expected that the Desert Force would attempt to hold up the German advance by laying down an artillery barrage. The Germans had little hope of destroying our mobile patrols, but it was considered possible that we might throw in our reserve tanks which would then be destroyed by the joint action of the Cramer and Wechmar Groups.'

'The British Coastal Force defending Halfaya Pass and the coastal plain was believed to consist – approximately – of one infantry battalion, with two or three troops of artillery, and at least one squadron of tanks.'

'Halfaya. 26 May 1941. i. Execution of the attack – The tank attack itself was timed for 1500 hours, and preparations were in full swing in the early morning of the 26 May when the British made two sorties, towards Point 206 and Anza el Qalala respectively, and drove back the German patrols. Further advance was stopped by the Bach Group, which had moved forward during the night to the Wadi Agrab area. The Bach Group, reinforced by a company of lorried infantry and half an anti-tank company, then passed to the attack, and proceeded to carry out its task in the tank-proof country of the escarpment wadis. Elsewhere the German advance was proceeding according to plan. Shortly after 1500 hours the Cramer Group, together with Force H.Q., crossed the frontier, advancing south-east on a broad front, with two tank battalions forward and one echelonned in rear to the right flank. The battalion from 5th Panzer Regiment was sent off to attack in rear the British artillery harassing the German flank from the direction of Sidi Suleiman. The main body of the group continued its advance without pause and reached its first objective at 1700 hours, when the artillery attached to the Cramer Group was ordered up.'

'Command in this sector of the attack was rendered difficult by the lack of armoured fighting vehicles and the breakdown of wireless apparatus, with the result that headquarters received very few, or no, reports from the other attacking columns up to 1700 hours. It was, however, clear from intercepted enemy R/T and aerial observation that the enemy had been completely taken by surprise, though there appeared little likelihood that the enemy's tanks would be brought to battle in co-operation with the Wechmar Group. On the other hand the Bach Group reported by radio telephone that strong enemy tank formations were attacking their right wing.'

'Von Herff decided, therefore, to attack the enemy opposing the Bach Group at 1715 hours; the Knabe Group was accordingly ordered by radio telephone to advance south-east in the direction of Abar Abu Telaq. Verbal orders were given to the Cramer Group to turn north-eastwards in the direction of the escarpment south-east of Minqar el Shaba, and then attack the rear of the British opposing the

Bach column in conjunction with the Bach and Knabe Groups.'

'In execution of this order Cramer called in 1 and 2 Battalions of 5th Panzer Regiment, and wheeled the regiment north-eastwards at 1845 hours, with one battalion forward and two echelonned in rear to either flank. After a short time heavy gun fire was heard from a northerly direction, presumably from the direction of the Bach Group, which reported further heavy enemy attacks by British Mark II tanks against their right wing. The Cramer Group was therefore ordered, in spite of the arrival of darkness, to advance at full speed to Halfaya Pass in order to destroy the enemy opposing the Bach Group, which was given information to this effect by R/T. The Knabe Group was halted north of Abar el Silqiya in order not to leave it exposed to enemy tank attacks without anti-tank and artillery support.'

'The night was moonless, thus increasing the difficulties of keeping direction, and the Cramer Group was held up in the difficult sandy country north-east of Sidi Suleiman. Cramer decided to halt his tanks shortly after 2020 hours, about five miles south of Halfaya Pass.'

'The impression gained by Von Herff from reconnaissance reports and intercepts was that the British had not observed the left wheel of the Cramer Group. It was moreover established that the Wechmar Group had reached its objective for the day in the Deir el Hamra area, and that the British were completely ignorant of its whereabouts. It was also clear from intercepted enemy R/T that the British must have been completely bewildered by the German surprise attack, and had obviously received no reports from its units.'

'ii. 26 May 1941. Orders for 27th – Von Herff decided to make a surprise attack on the enemy opposing the Bach Group using the Cramer, Knabe and Bach Groups in conjunction. In accordance with the orders issued at 2200 hours the Cramer Group was to attack the escarpment at 0430 hours on the morning of 27th May on both sides of Minqar el Shaba, and to open fire from there with all arms on the enemy concentrations in the coastal plain. It was also to hold part of its troops ready for an attack on the Halfaya Pass positions from the rear.'

'The Knabe Group's orders were, first, to take up position by 0430 hours in the area a quarter of a mile north of Abar Abu Telaq and to move forward, with the Halfaya Pass road as its axis of advance, while the Bach Group, which had reached by dusk the height a quarter of a mile north of Halfaya Pass, was to attack Halfaya itself, at the foot of the pass. Lastly, the Wechmar Group was to move off before dawn in a north-westerly direction to reach the area east of Sidi Suleiman and then to cover the main body of the division from the south-east.'

'iii. 27 May 1941. Execution of the attack. The night of the 26th/27th May passed quietly, though the tanks' petrol columns failed to get through during the night. Had they got through, the Germans consider they could have carried the pursuit, after the next day's engagement, as far as Sidi Barrani. In the face of the shortage of petrol a decision had in fact to be taken whether to postpone the dawn attack on the 27th May, and so to lose the element of surprise, or to limit the scope of the tank advance. The latter alternative was chosen.'

'At about 0430 hours the Knabe Group, followed shortly afterwards by the Cramer Group, advanced as ordered, the armoured (Cramer) group moving, as on the previous day, with one battalion forward and one in rear on either flank. In spite of heavy enemy artillery fire the Cramer Group reached the escarpment at about 0530 hours, and brought concentrated fire to bear on enemy movements, gun positions, and tanks in the coastal plain, creating great disorder. The Knabe Group reached Halfaya Pass at 0540 hours, where elements of this group and of 5th Panzer Regiment (Cramer Group) forced their way, in the face of artillery, anti-tank and machine-gun fire, into the British positions. By 0615 hours Halfaya Pass was in German hands.'

'The Bach Group, whose advance was hampered throughout by British tank attacks, reached the foot of the pass at 0630 hours. Under concentric attack by the Cramer, Knabe, and Bach Groups, and suffering violent action by German artillery, Eighth Army withdrew, pursuit being immediately (0630 hours) undertaken by the Knabe and Bach Groups, whose orders were not to proceed with recconaissance beyond a reasonable distance. Subsequently, the Bach Group fell back on Halfaya Pass and later, with a high proportion of the 8.8 cm. guns available to the Panzer Group, took up defensive positions there. The other battle groups alert for counter attack also withdrew to their previous positions along the escarpment.'

Operation 'Battleaxe'. On 15 June 1941, British attacks aimed at restoring contact with Tobruk brought 5th Light and 15th Panzer battle groups back into action. Inflicting a severe defeat on underpowered British forces, Rommel retained control of the strategically important Halfaya Pass. On 15 August, Rommel's command was reconstituted as Panzergruppe Afrika controlling DAK (15th, 21st Panzer Divisions) and two, eventually three, Italian Corps: XX, X and XXI (Ariete, Trieste, Pavia, Brescia, Trento and Sabrata Divisions), 90th Light (incomplete) in reserve; Rommel's Corps appointment was taken over by General Ludwig Crüwell. Regrouping to assault Tobruk, Rommel prepared for action, but to no purpose. Forewarned by signal Intelligence, Rommel's action was pre-empted.

Operation 'Crusader'. Starting on 18 November, a British Eighth Army counter-offensive, under General Sir Alan Cunningham surprised Rommel, driving his Panzer Group back to El Agheila with heavy losses. In the blow and counter-blow following the British initiative, tank battles on Sunday, 23 November ended marginally in Rommel's favour, but on the 28th DAK's HQ was partly overrun, losing cipher and wireless equipment with disastrous consequences. Eighth Army's capture of cipher settings (*see* Part 2, Panzer Signals and 'Ultra') was to enable GC and CS Bletchley soon to listen almost permanently into wireless traffic between panzer groups, corps and divisions which, together with other ciphers being read, would place Rommel at a distinct disadvantage for the rest of the campaign in Africa. General von Ravenstein, GOC, 21st Panzer Division, and Major Bach, resisting the British onslaught at Halfaya until 17 January, were both taken prisoner along with many others. The Panzer Group suffered 38,000 casualties.

Operation 'Theseus' (map 9). On 21 January 1942, Rommel launched 'Theseus', his second desert offensive –

progressively reinforced by 90th Light Division brought up to strength. Rommel's order of battle in addition to DAK included three Italian corps; XX, X and XXI with two Italian armoured (Ariete and Littorio) and two motorized (Trieste and Trento) divisions plus infantry. Benefiting from improved air support and supplies – thanks to Kesselring's endeavours – 'Theseus' recovered some of the ground previously lost; Benghazi and Derna included. By 4 February the offensive had driven Eighth Army back to a line Gazala–Bir Hacheim.

Second Battle of Tobruk (map 9). On 26 May 1942, with a panzer group command broadened into Panzer Army Africa, Rommel initiated 'Venezia', an extension of his second offensive, planned to culminate in the seizure of Tobruk. The port with its coveted supply facilities would fall within three and a half weeks on 21 June. Facing odds of two to one in armour, Rommel more than justified his famous nickname – outmanoeuvring and all but destroying Eighth Army in preliminary battles at Gazala. Panzer army strength consisted in the main of 400 Pz Kpfw IIIs fewer than twenty of which were the up-gunned version, mounting a long, 5cm gun and improved frontal armour. Cunningham's successor, Ritchie, faced Rommel with 843 tanks, slightly fewer than 250 of which, were the formidable new Grants with a 7.5cm gun. In the first round of operations at the end of May with but few of his Pz Kpfw IIIs and IVs re-equipped with long 5cm or 7.5cm guns respectively, Rommel tried by tank v. tank actions to obtain supremacy over British armour. When these actions became expensive German armour was conserved by refusing to engage in tank v. tank combat.

Instead, strong screens of anti-tank guns, including a high proportion of 8.8cm and Russian 7.62cm (Marder III) self-propelled guns positioned to cover the panzer force,

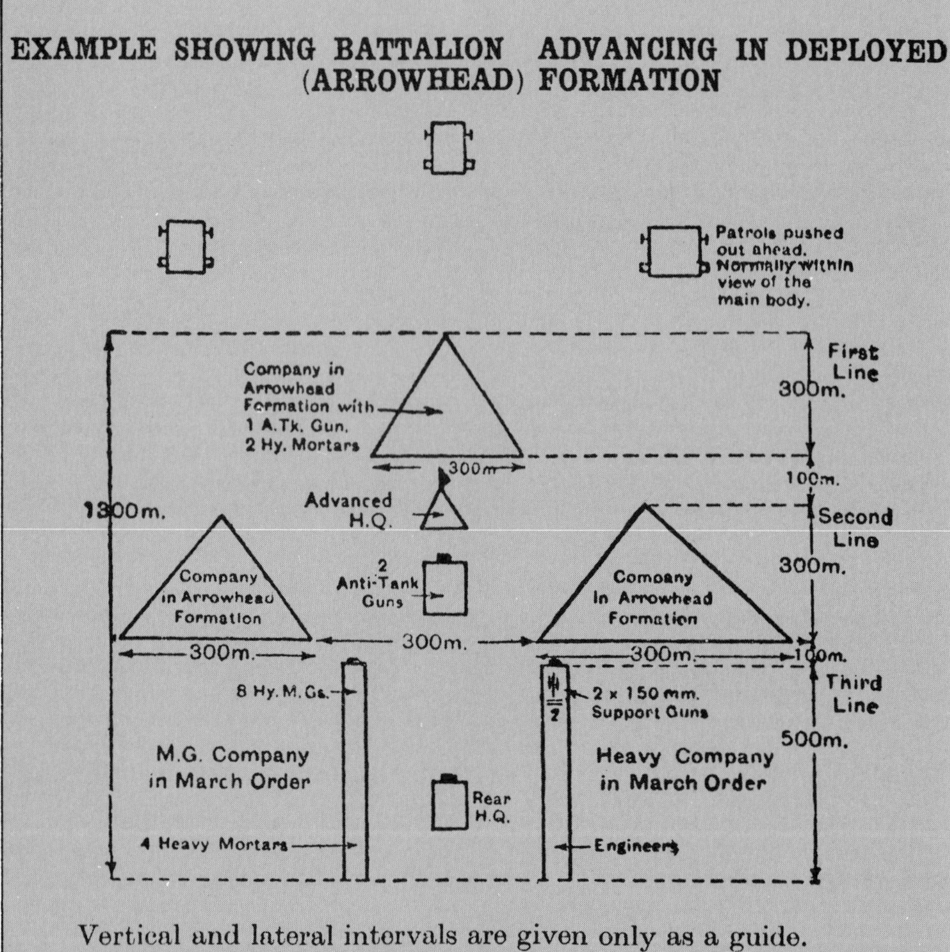

Left: A diagram illustrating the theoretical deployment of tanks and anti-tank guns (2cm, 3.7cm and 8.8cm) by a panzer battalion in Libya, 1941–2; the anti-tank guns following close behind the battalion commander.

prevented the enemy getting tanks into close-range conflict. If they were too heavily engaged by Ritchie's tanks or artillery the panzer companies were withdrawn. The panzer army had a very high proportion of anti-tank guns and could consequently cover its flanks very widely, making outflanking movements extremely difficult. When British tanks attacked, the panzer army subjected them to heavy artillery fire and worked their anti-tank guns forward, using every available bit of ground for cover to get within striking distance. The result was either to force Ritchie to attack at a disadvantage or to withdraw to avoid loss of tanks. The knocking-out of the anti-tank screen by 7.5cm and other artillery fire proved difficult when British tanks and guns had been considerably outnumbered, as they often were.

Eighth Army, caught off balance, out-gunned and out-manoeuvred by Rommel's handling of armour, suffered the loss of Tobruk and considerable stocks of fuel and vehicles. Reporting on its withdrawal after the débâcle at Gazala, the Army commented on its defeat in the following terms:

'Gazala 26 May–15 June 1942. The majority of our actions were of a counter-attack nature and were nearly always held up by anti-tank gun screens, which, because of their numbers and very clever concealment, were difficult to neutralize with the amount of artillery at our disposal.'

'The use of the 8.8 cm gun in the boldest possible manner had a considerable effect on these operations. This gun was often moved into position, particularly on the flanks of armoured formations, to within 1,500 yds of our tanks. German casualties must have been very high amongst crews and many of these guns were knocked out, but the damage they did, even to our Grant tanks, was considerable. The Russian 7.62 cm self-propelled gun was also used in the same way. Another feature of German tactics was continuous shelling of our tanks in their battle positions from Pz Kpfw IVs and guns on self-propelled mountings. This fire had little effect and did minor damage only, but it did cause a certain amount of exhaustion to our crews, who, of course, to avoid unnecessary casualties, could not be allowed to dismount for rest or any other purpose. 'The German tank attacks were usually heralded by very heavy artillery concentrations in order to inflict casualties both on the tanks and supporting artillery, after which the tank attack was pressed home.'

The Free French defence under General Koenig of Bir Hacheim, a strong point at the southern end of the Gazala Line, outflanked by Rommel, was broken by Stuka action after several days and withdrawn sustaining heavy losses. Among the many ruses devised by Rommel's staff to convey an impression of panzer strength being greater than actually was the case – during attacks on Benghazi for instance ('Sonenblume', 31 March 1941) was the trailing of cables behind infantry advancing to the attack in trucks. The resulting dust clouds gave the immediate impression that a tank attack was being launched. At other times captured British trucks, were fitted with concealed anti-tank guns, to the disconcertment of approaching British forces. Telegraph poles were used as dummy 8.8cm guns.

On 22 June 1942, after his success in capturing Tobruk – the high-water mark of a remarkable career – Rommel was rewarded with promotion to Field Marshal. The offensive continued eastwards with the benefit of fuel and transport obtained from vast British stores dumped in the neighbourhood of Tobruk, but against the advice of Kesselring and colleagues who wanted a safer and more dependable build-up. On 1 July Rommel reached Alam Halfa and El Alamein. Panzer army intentions: to renew the confrontation with British Eighth Army, complete its destruction and enter Cairo – an event for which, in addition to urgent military preparations, elaborate processional arrangements were being made to enable Mussolini to ride in triumph through the city. But things turned out differently. Strongly entrenched, progressively strengthened and enjoying swift access to resupply bases in the vicinity of Cairo and Alexandria, British Eighth Army immensely heartened under a new commander, turned at bay, enjoying the protection of an air umbrella that the Luftwaffe, trailing in ground organization and strength, was totally unable to match.

Rommel's (re-named) German–Italian Panzer Army, reinforced by 164th Light Division (von Liebenstein), but suffering endlessly from air attack was, by contrast, progressively weakened as supply arrangements betrayed to Eighth Army and the Desert Air Force in detail by Signal Intelligence faltered and air force support waned. When petrol supplies dried up, at times almost completely, operations were severely curtailed. This aspect of Rommel's desert war is elaborated in Part 4, page 137. On 30 August the panzer army failed to dislodge Eighth Army at Alam Halfa. In steadfastly refusing to expose his armour to Rommel's temporarily ascendent Pz Kpfw IVs equipped with the long 7.5cm gun, a new British commander, General Bernard Montgomery, called Rommel's future into question.

The turning-point for Rommel (map 9) came on 23 October 1942, at El Alamein, a railway halt, 60 miles west of Alexandria. At this unremarkable location, Eighth Army under Montgomery, striking back at Rommel after a massive built-up in artillery support and a four or more to one advantage in armour (1,200 British tanks facing 285 German and 278 Italian tanks) broke the weak German–Italian panzer army into pieces, precipitating a general retreat in the direction of Tripoli. On 3 November, just as the movement was getting underway, Hitler instructed Rommel to stand fast – despite the threat of encirclement. By the 4th, the panzer divisions deployed in the north were down to twenty tanks and DAK's commander von Thoma had been captured. In the south, surviving Italian formations with parachute Brigade Ramcke, found themselves stranded; Littorio and Trieste (XX Corps) fighting hard, were practically wiped-out. For the next three months, starved of supplies, transport and equipment of all kinds, fighting rearguard actions over more than 1,500 miles, desperate German and Italian formations receiving minor injections of strength *en route*, were fortunate indeed to ward-off pursuit. Rain and an unaccountably cautious follow-up saved the panzer army from extinction. On 15 February 1943, the panzer army reached the illusory protection of Fifth Panzer Army outposts in Tunisia. At Mareth the apparent strength of prepared fieldworks – a line of reinforced old French block-houses stretching twenty miles inland from the sea to rest on 'impassable' terrain, backed by Wadi Akarit in the coastal corridor south of Gabes, held promise of sanctuary, but Rommel was not impressed.

A re-organization of Axis forces in North Africa was now due. The presence of Fifth Panzer Army in Africa (q.v.) and a need to satisfy Italian claims to command were primary considerations. But a supreme headquarters – Army Group Africa – to be established in Tunis would fail to stifle strong German–Italian differences of opinion; whether for instance Tripoli, the Italian Army's prinicipal base and a prestigious colonial capital in Africa, with extensive military and stores-handling facilites, should have been evacuated by Rommel in defiance of Comando Supremo instructions. And, worried the Italians, did Rommel deliberately strand their units at El Alamein? Adding to the Field Marshal's problems (and Kesselring's, too) were other impediments to operational efficiency – rivalry between panzer army commanders. Unco-ordinated counter-attacks following Allied landings in Morocco and Algeria (*see* Fifth Panzer Army in Africa, 8 November 1942) led to missed opportunities when the Allies were gathering strength and at their most vulnerable in January and February 1943. This would be followed by Rommel's departure from Africa on 9 March after only fifteen days as Army Group Commander. Despite disaffection between Axis partners and commanders, the war in Africa continued unabated.

Operation 'Spring Wind'. *On 14 February 1943, joint action by Rommel and von Arnim, was intended to drive off mainly US forces threatening Sfax and Gabes – crucial to the security of Rommel's communications. Attacks led by von Arnim's deputy, General Ziegler, from El Faid and later by Rommel himself at Kasserine employing a strong part of 10th Panzer Division (Hildebrandt) and a reassigned veteran 21st Panzer Division (Broich, after Fischer was killed in action 5 February 1943), and working briskly in support of a DAK battle group (von Liebenstein), scattered inexperienced US forces. But exploitation failed when command weaknesses surfaced (see also* Fifth Panzer Army, 14 February 1943). Meanwhile 15th Panzer Division (Borowietz) deployed forward of the Mareth Line, acted vigourously in defensive action there. 'Spring Wind', although a failure, gained time for Axis armies to consolidate in Tunisia and Rommel's appointment to Army Group Command followed on 23 February 1943. Italian First Army, Rommel's former headquarters, reconstituted in the hands of General Messe, then intended a determined stand in the modest fieldworks at Mareth – an intention that, despite the arrival of a new Italian armoured division, Centauro (Calvi) and more infantry, would remain unfulfilled as Eighth Army closed in for the kill. Rommel planned to strike first, upsetting Eighth Army's timetable.

Operation 'Capri' was undertaken on 6 March 1943 by DAK (Cramer), employing 10th (Broich), 15th and 21st (Hildebrandt) Panzer Divisions with 150 tanks between them. But the offensive failed to disrupt Eighth Army forming up at Medenine to attack the German–Italian line. Forewarned of Rommel's intentions by SIGINT and deploying 600 carefully sited 6pdr anti-tank guns (destroying fifty tanks in this costly spoiling attack) helped Montgomery substantially in putting paid to Rommel's plan – his last in Africa. Devised but not directed by Rommel, this abortive panzer action caused little delay to the Allied counter-offensive that was building-up. On 9 March, before British and US Forces could lever the panzer army out of the Mareth Line, and final battles for Bizerta and Tunis would destroy both panzer armies in Africa, Rommel, who was about to benefit (unexpectedly) from a senior appointment in Italy, departed for Europe and a meeting with Hitler.

On 20 March, Montgomery's Eighth Army (XXX corps with heavy artillery support) opened a breach in the Mareth defences. Simultaneous moves to outflank the line via the Tebaga gap to the west were started by the New Zealand Corps which brought 164th Light and 21st Panzer Divisions back into action; A US II Corps (Patton) move behind Messe also drew 10th Panzer Division into counter-attacks.

***Blitzkrieg* in reverse.** On 26 March 1943, employing tactics reminiscent of the best German combined army/air operations, Operation 'Supercharge II' – executed in conjunction with the Desert Air Force (Broadhurst) – turned the Mareth Line, nullifying German–Italian plans for a protracted stand in the former French defensive system. The Mareth Line was consequently abandoned, despite 10th Panzer's success in stalling an American break-through to Gabes on the coast behind Axis defences. On 30 March, when US II Corps renewed its threat to First Italian Army communications (but not in time to prevent the panzer army's ecape), Messe and von Arnim parried the drive with 10th and 21st Panzer Division battle groups. But within days US and British reconnaissance units were uniting to forge a ring securing the panzer armies. On 7 April, following fourteen days of heavy fighting, Messe's Army abandoned 'last ditch' defences at Wadi Akarit, falling back along coastal routes to Enfidaville. Under constant threat from Anglo-US air forces and increasingly short of supplies, Messe was unlikely to stay the course.

The **capitulation** of Rommel's former desert army, which Messe had taken over three months earlier, was accepted by the Allies on 13 May 1943, following four weeks of resistance that Eighth Army twice failed to break. Stripped of armour (transferred west of Tunis where the Allied Commander-in-Chief (Alexander) was directing 'Vulcan' 18th Army Group's main effort at breaking von Arnim's defence of the capital (*see* Fifth Panzer Army Africa, 22 April 1943), Messe was left powerless.

Career note: Field Marshal Erwin Rommel, 1943–4. Rommel left Africa for Europe on 9 March to press with Hitler his case for withdrawing into a mountain sanctuary, Enfidaville–Tunis–Bizerta. Hitler declined the proposal and Rommel was forbidden to return. Instead, Hitler offered Rommel a command in the invasion sensitive Balkans theatre. But on 15 August, in the aftermath of 'Husky' (*see* Panzer Action in Italy, 10 July 1943) Rommel was instead appointed to command Army Group 'B' with headquarters in Munich. Rommel's brief was to plan an Axis defence of the Alps and northern Italy. On 12 September Rommel moved HQ to Lake Garda. On 21 November Hitler resolved the question of who should defend Italy in favour of Kesselring who advised him to stand firm in the south. Rommel, with partly the same staff, was consequently appointed Inspector of Coastal Defences in the west.

In north-west Europe. On 15 January 1944, Rommel's status was changed to C-in-C, Army Group 'B' with an operational command stretching from the Zuider Zee to the mouth of the Loire, but one that was limited to twelve miles inland. By May 1944, with HQ at La Roche-Guyon west of Paris, the Field Marshal shared responsibility for the deployment of armour in Normandy with Geyr von Schweppenburg, GOC, Panzer Group West (*see* Fifth Panzer Army, Europe). Following his adverse experience of the effect of air power on mobile operations in Africa, Rommel planned to dispose the panzer divisions close to the beaches, alert for immediate counter-attack. But, with three divisions only – 2nd, 116th and 21st Panzer at his disposal, and overruled by C-in-C, West (von Runstedt) supported by Hitler – Rommel was instructed not to concentrate them. Instead, at Geyr von Schweppenburg's instigation, these and the other available panzer divisions held in OKW reserve in northern France – Panzerlehr, 1st SS, 12th SS, 17th SS (Panzer Grenadier) were deployed inland. A visit from Guderian on 28 April failed to resolve the problem in Rommel's favour.

On 6 June 1944 when the invasion of Normandy did come and Geyr von Schweppenburg was placed under Rommel on the 7th, the mobile divisions moving to support infantry divisions surviving on the coast were forced under furious air assault into time-consuming detours, delaying them beyond all expectation. Sizeable fighting elements were destroyed by air action before they could come completely into action and those that did, suffered equally from the destructive effect of air and naval gunfire. Disaster threatened and a personal tragedy was in the offing.

Rommel was injured on 17 July, barely five weeks before the Allies would destroy his Army Group. The incident occurred as he was returning from a front-line visit to I SS Panzer Corps on the eve of 'Goodwood' D+42; a low-flying air attack on the Field Marshal's car by 605 Squadron RAF at Ste-Foy-de-Montgommery immediately north of Vimoutiers, causing him severe head injuries and removing him from active service. Von Kluge succeeded him in command of the Army Group which, on 19 August, after losing most of its equipment and armour was encircled and practically destroyed in the Falaise pocket (*see* Fifth Panzer Army, 19 August 1944).

Thereafter, gravely concerned by developments in Normandy and the war in general, Field Marshal Rommel, a popular figure with subordinates and the public in Germany (but less endeared to the Italians who continued to believe that he had deliberately stranded them at El Alamein), was implicated in the Hitler assassination plot of 20 July 1944. Recriminations followed.

Rommel's death by suicide. Taken under escort from Herrlingen, his home town in Würtemburg, Rommel ended his own life on 14 October 1944; an ignominous death by poisoning belieing the trappings of a state funeral attended by Keitel among others in Ulm on 18 October 1944. Thus closed the career of a brilliant and respected panzer tactician, one of the ablest of the war. Rommel's talent for mobile operations – culminating in the capture of Tobruk, a shattering defeat for British Eighth Army – was at times more than offset by the knowledge that his British opponents learned of his intentions and difficulties from Sigint. Despite so unenviable a handicap, Rommel's ability to read the battle moves of his opponents and to counter them with superior tactics until battles of attrition and supply robbed his Panzer Army of vitality proved of the highest order.

6. Fifth Panzer Army Afrika (PzAOK 5, 1943)

Raised in Tunisia in December 1942, by upgrading XC Army Corps. The Corps Commander, appointed on 16 November, was General Walther Nehring. A former DAK commander, wounded and flown home from North Africa in August 1942, Nehring was not retained as GOC Fifth Panzer Army when the Army Corps was upgraded; the post instead being taken by Generaloberst Hans-Jurgen von Arnim, appointed on 8 December. Both commanders were responsible to C-in-C (Oberbefehlshaber, OB), South, Field Marshal Albert Kesselring, whose HQ was located at Frascati twelve miles south-east of Rome. In a command reshuffle on 9 March 1943, von Arnim moved up in the Axis military hierarchy, succeeding Rommel as GOC, Army Group Africa; command of Fifth Panzer Army then passing to General Gustav von Vaerst (15th Panzer Division) who would retain the appointment until Fifth Panzer Army – and all other German and Italian troops in Africa – capitulated during the second week in May. General Walther Nehring would meanwhile lead the Tunis build-up, promoting OKW intentions to establish a strong military presence in Tunisia, a province of Vichy France since June 1940, at a time when Anglo-American forces, after disembarking in North Africa 400 miles west of Tunis, were driving east along the Mediterranean coast, and threatening Sicily.

Allied presence west of Tunis arose out of Operation 'Torch', launched on 8 November 1942, when 107,000 British and American troops unexpectedly pouring ashore in Morocco and Algeria, seized Casablanca, Oran and Algiers before consolidating partially into British First Army (Anderson) and turning east to threaten Tunis and Sicily. At the time of 'Torch', in November 1942, following Rommel's defeat at El Alamein (*see* Panzer Army Africa, 23 October 1942), German–Italian military resources in North Africa were totally exhausted; the value of Rommel's Panzer Army, facing annihilation in Cyrenaica, being negligible. But no less important than helping to save Rommel's forces by establishing a sanctuary in Tunisia, was the overriding need to win time for the defence of Europe with a new, mainly German, build-up in the south. From 8 to 27 November 1942, Hitler's reaction to 'Torch' concentrated upon military and diplomatic action, not only in metropolitan France but also in North Africa where plans to protect this strategically important corner of the Mediterranean with its sea approaches to Italy, would rest upon a strong German led force occupying key points in Tunisia.

The race for Tunis and Bizerta. This started on 9 November 1942, with a build-up of German activity, code-named 'Braun'. Directed by OB South it evolved with great alacrity and proved a remarkably effective counter to the Allied invasion. Disembarking on the North African coast 24 hours earlier, the Allied centre (Oran) and eastern (Algiers) task forces comprising seven divisions, including US 1st Armored Division (Fredendall), consolidated into British First Army (Anderson), were unfortunately slow in getting under way to Tunis.

[***Operations 'Anton' and 'Lila'*** *starting on 11*

November, meanwhile inaugurated a German take-over of Vichy France; OKW's interest focusing in particular upon the maritime regions of the south including Corsica. 'Anton' would be followed on 27 November by 'Lila', a security operation in which 7th and 10th Panzer Divisions serving II SS Panzer Corps (Hausser) seized Toulon harbour, but failed to prevent the scuttling of the French fleet.] The German race for Tunis, starting within hours of the invasion, progressed daily, pulled together after 16 November by XC Corps Commander, General Walther Nehring. Nehring's brief, developed by his successor von Arnim, was to direct the deployment and action of all German/Italian armoured, motorized and support units arriving in Tunisia, to confront the Allies whose post-invasion lodgements at Bougie (11 November) and Bône (12 November) increased the threat to Tunis and compounded the Germans' problem. Notwithstanding the Allies' advantage in disembarking large numbers of troops in comparative safety, Allied planners were to be surprised at OB South's unexpected speed and adroitness in building a bridgehead, securing a strategic prize and keeping the Allies at arm's length from Europe. By midday on 9 November, the first of several Stuka and fighter groups dispatched from II Air Corps, Sicily subordinate to Luftwaffe Colonel Martin Harlinghausen, newly appointed Fliegerführer, Tunis (soon to succeed von Waldau similarly serving Rommel – but whose command would be abolished in favour of unified air force support directed from Tunis) were arriving at Tunis and nearby Djedeida. Over the next five days brisk air-trooping operations between Sicily and Tunis, accelerating the build-up, would involve giant Me 323 transports in hazardous and ultimately suicidal transport operations (*see* Part 4, page 139), combat troops of 5th Parachute Regiment (Koch) and Kesselring's escort battalion flown from Rome landing on the 11th; anti-aircraft and anti-tank detachments following on. So that by the time Walther Nehring arrived from Germany on the 14th, reported back to Kesselring on the 15th and then settled into his appointment on the 16th, after recuperating from wounds suffered at Alam Halfa in August, Tunis and its crucial transport facilities were firmly in German hands.

The build-up continued to gather momentum. From late November panzer units including Tiger detachments from 501st Heavy Tank Battalion, intended for Rommel, would be followed by 10th Panzer Division and Hermann Goering Division (minus its panzer regiment). These came mainly from France where 10th Panzer had been released from occupational duties in Marseille at the conclusion of 'Anton' and Hermann Goering Division at Cognac was interrupted in the early stages of converting to a panzer division. Motorized and infantry support, diverted from Rommel, especially 47th Infantry Regiment, the veterans of air-landing operations in Holland in 1940, joined in the race for Tunis together with both German and Italian artillery, heavy anti-tank, anti-aircraft and infantry units.

On 27 November the first panzer unit – a company of six Pz Kpfw IIIs and three Tigers from 501st Heavy Tank Battalion slipped into Bizerta harbour. Four hundred vehicles and more weapons arrived on the 28th.

Tigers (Pz Kpfw V), eventually no more than nineteen in number, were first used in action on 29 November west of Tunis, securing Nehring's grip on Djedeida; but fared badly. Lacking spares in subsequent operations, they were more often out of action than in. Only the dedicated work of tank crews kept the massive vehicles operational. On 8 December, when XC Corps (or Stab Nehring) was upgraded in Tunisia to become Fifth Panzer Army the army commander appointed from the Eastern Front (XXXIX Panzer Corps) to replace Nehring – whose unpalatable but wholly realistic forecast that Tunisia could not be defended in the supply circumstances branded him defeatist – was Generaloberst Hans-Jurgen von Arnim.

By the end of December von Arnim's tank strength was reported to OKW as 350 – mainly Px Kpfw IIIs, but costly battles by both Nehring and von Arnim, securing key points and blocking Allied thrusts out of the mountains around Tunis, reduced their numbers. Soon only half would be fit for battle. Personnel strength in the theatre amounted to 66,000 by mid December with numbers continuing to rise.

Expanding the bridgehead. January 1943. At Kesselring's prompting von Arnim struck out of the confines of the bridgehead which Nehring had created. The early capture of road junctions Djedeida, Tebourba and Medjez el Bab, west of Tunis, also Mateur covering Bizerta, had

Above: General Walther Nehring served with distinction in North Africa, commanding DAK from March to August 1942 (second Battle of Tobruk, map 9) and XC Corps in Tunis from November to December 1942 before departing the theatre for the Eastern Front and eventual command of First Panzer Army in March 1945.

secured key sectors for OB South, although Medjez was later abandoned. New moves were intended to extend the bridgehead west and south-west.

Operation 'Courier'. On 18 January 1943, von Arnim struck out with 10th Panzer Division (Fischer) and the mixed Tiger-grenadier battle group (Weber), aiming to win time and space in Tunisia with offensive operations 'Courier I and II', executed in conjunction with the Italian Division Superga (Lorenzelli). Von Arnim's battle groups reinforced by paratroops and mountain infantry, supported by flak troops and engineers, pushed outwards, blocking Anglo-US forces advancing against Tunis from Pont du Fahrs, 50 kilometres to the south-west. The stalling effect of 'Courier' on British First Army and the presence of 21st Panzer Division sent back to Sfax by Rommel, whose rear was so obviously threatened by events in Tunisia, enabled Panzer Army Africa to withdraw safely out of Tripolitania and during February 1943 reach prepared positions at Mareth. This revitalized chain of old French block-houses, stretching twenty miles inland from the coast, had been constructed in the 1930s to deter Italian attacks from Tripoli. Now it was hoped by the High Command that the Mareth 'Line' with additional fieldworks would stand up to Eighth Army. Neither Rommel nor Messe, his successor in command of Panzer Army Africa, shared the view.

In February 1943, aggressive panzer action to deter Allied progress all around the 400-mile bridgehead, was undertaken by an incomplete 10th Panzer Division in conjunction with veteran 15th and (refurbished) 21st Panzer Divisions. Operations that were supported by *ad hoc* German and Italian battle groups including an impromptu motorized 'Division' von Broich (later von Manteuffel) – composed of any number of different units as they arrived in North Africa.

Operation 'Spring Wind', starting on 14 February 1943, was launched to counter US forces pushing deeper into central Tunisia. At Sbeitla the Americans threatened to extend their drive eastwards slicing across the Tunisian bridgehead between Mareth and Enfidaville to Sfax on the east coast; a move that would close the escape route of Panzer Army Africa. Should Rommel decide to retire northwards via the coastal defile at Gabes, German retention of Sfax was essential; counter-action was imperative. Deploying battle groups from 10th and 21st Panzer Divisions under the direction of General Ziegler (von Arnim's deputy), operations against US II Corps (Fredendall) east of Sbeitla were pursued in conjunction with a DAK battle group led by Colonel von Liebenstein pushing north from El Guettar – bringing immediate results. On the first day, Zeigler won a resounding success, scattering green US troops. On the 19th, following a regrouping under Rommel, 'Spring Wind' culminated in the capture of the Kasserine Pass – a crucial sally-port for extending 'Spring Wind' into an encirclement manoeuvre reaching to the north coast behind British and US forces facing Tunis. Yet after further limited success the idea of wider action was abandoned and the pass was given up. In Kesselring's view, neither of the two commanders demonstrated much faith in exploiting 'Spring Wind' or evinced confidence in the other.

Rivalry between commands had quickly surfaced. Rommel favoured a deep thrust to capture Tebessa, the Allied supply base well behind the front and a significant staging-point *en route* to the coast at Bône. Comando Supremo and von Arnim preferred more limited action directed on Le Kef immediately to the Allied rear. Opportunities were lost through indecision; Tiger support promised by von Arnim was withheld for action in the north, fuel and ammunition continued in short supply. Rommel, disillusioned over the course of events in general, would anyway have preferred to withdraw into defensible mountain territory north of Enfidaville, but continued towards Le Kef as instructed. On 22 February, Kesselring called a halt. The result was to lose forever the greatest opportunity the Germans would have to defeat First and Eighth Armies in turn, and achieve a stalemate – however short-lived – in North Africa. Rommel, appointed Army Group Commander on the 23rd, planned instead to strike in the south at British Eighth Army, forming-up to attack the Mareth Line.

Operation 'Oxhead'. On 26 February 1943, panzer action was renewed in northern Tunisia with Fifth Panzer

Right: Generaloberst Hans-Jurgen von Arnim (left) with Generalmajor Wolfgang Fischer of 10th Panzer Division. Von Arnim served in Poland and France as GOC, 52nd Infantry Division. He was GOC 17th Panzer Division in 1940; GOC XXXIX Panzer Corps in 1941; GOC, Fifth Panzer Army in 1942; and in 1943 he became GOC, Army Group Tunis.

Army launching Operation 'Oxhead'. Lead by Corps Group Weber comprising 501st Battalion (Tigers) and three mixed infantry battle groups of regimental size, helped forward by strong air support, 'Oxhead' was intended to improve army positions around Medjez el Bab. The town controlled access to Tunis by the direct route from the east and was securely held by the Allies. Reinforced by an impromptu motorized 'division' under the battle-experienced Colonel von Manteuffel – the future Commander, Fifth Panzer Army in Europe 10 September 1944, and with the Italian Division Superga also participating, but all suffering heavy losses in vehicles and men, the offensive made only limited gains and was called off within two days. Unrelenting Allied pressure in March and early April, directed by Field Marshal Alexander, the new 18th Army Group commander who took up his appointment immediately after the US débâcle at Kasserine, drove the panzer armies relentlessly back upon their main areas Enfidaville, Bizerta and Tunis – there to conduct a tenacious but abortive defence. Attempting the best possible use of inadequate resources skilfully deployed to take advant-age of difficult mountainous country, in much the same way that the panzer divisions would operate in the forthcoming campaign in Italy, Fifth Panzer Army and Messe's First Italian Army – formerly Panzer Army Africa – suffered endless supply deficiencies; their petrol, ammunition and supplies tightly rationed as one supply-ship after another, identified by British Sigint and attacked by the Royal Navy and Air Force were sent to the bottom of the Mediterranean.

Operation 'Vulcan'. By 22 April 1943, when Alexander's 18th Army Group launched Operation 'Vulcan' aiming directly at Tunis from the west, 10th, 15th, 21st and Hermann Goering Panzer Divisions were ready to defend the front, but suffering like all others from a shortage of crucial stores, disposed of fewer than 150 tanks against an estimated 1,400 possessed by 18th Army Group.

From 22 April to 6 May 1943, the burned-out divisions of Army Group Africa, ceaselessly attacked from the air, especially on the Central Sector west of Tunis between Medjez el Bab and Goubellat where DAK was now concentrated, were penned into an ever-shrinking bridgehead and reduced to impotence; in the case of 15th Panzer Division making a last-ditch stand in the path of British First Army's main effort – IX Corps (Horrocks) with 6th and 7th Armoured Divisions driving straight for Tunis on 6 May – to the point of destruction. By nightfall on 6 May 1943, the collapse of both German and Italian armies – subordinate to Army Group Tunis, successor to Army Group Africa – was imminent. Unable to resist Alexander's overwhelming pressure and desperate for ammunition (had it arrived it could not have been distributed because of lack of fuel), von Arnim lost control of the situation. The panzer divisions fought to the last round, but Tunis and Bizerta were yielded on the 7th.

Capitulation of Fifth Panzer Army in Africa followed on 13 May 1943 when the seniormost German commanders in the theatre, von Arnim and von Vaerst, were both taken prisoner. German military operations in North Africa

Below: Ju 52 wings from Sicily crossing the Mediterranean at wave height in airbridge operations to supply Rommel and von Arnim in North Africa.

concluded with the surrender of 230,000 German and Italian effectives; fewer than 700 officers and men escaped the Allied sea and air blockade to reach Europe. Three Army divisions, 10th, 15th and 21st Panzer, four motorized divisions and most of the Hermann Goering (Fallschirm Panzer) Division, minus its panzer regiment, were lost. Some, like HG and 15th Panzer were reformed, the latter as a panzer grenadier division (*see* Panzer Action in Italy, 10 July 1943). 21st Panzer Division, rehabilitated by Panzer Group West in March 1944, would have an important role to play in the defence of Normandy (*see* Fifth Panzer Army in Europe, 6 June 1944). The war in Africa was over, but new battles in Sicily were about to exact a further toll of the panzer force.

7. Panzer action in Italy, 1943–5

German reaction to the Allied invasion of Sicily, Operation 'Husky', in July 1943 – followed for almost two years by the demands of a gruelling campaign on the mainland of Italy, would absorb the energies of Hermann Goering, 16th and 26th Panzer Divisions and five panzer grenadier divisions. Until their numbers were reduced by transfers to other fronts, these powerful mobile divisions with supporting arms and services would provide a core of German resistance in Italy continuing until capitulation on 2 May 1945. Two panzer corps, but no panzer army headquarters served in the theatre. Responsibility for providing ground attack support for the panzer divisions and the air defence of Sicily lay with the fighter and Stuka Wings of II Air Corps (Bülowius).

The Panzer division commonly associated with the defence of Sicily and mainland Italy after suffering heavy losses in Tunisia (*see* Fifth Panzer Army, Africa, 13 May 1943) was the Hermann Goering Fallschirm Panzer Division. Reforming at the time of 'Husky' in the neighbourhood of Taormina, the division would operate in Sicily by forming two battle groups for mobile operations; basically the panzer regiment under the divisional commander General Conrath, and the other comprising divisional panzer grenadier units lead by Oberst Schmalz, the Brigade Commander. Later, on the mainland, two more panzer divisions, 16th (Sieckenius) and 26th Panzer (von Lüttwitz), redeployed from France, would join Hermann Goering in defending Calabria, Italy's southern-most province, separated from Sicily by the Straits of Messina. The five panzer grenadier divisions deployed in the theatre defending Sicily or mainland Italy, comprised 15th (Rodt), reforming on the island between Marsala and Trapani from remnants of 15th Panzer destroyed in Africa; 90th (Lungershausen), rebuilding in Sardinia after a similarly disastrous experience; 16th Reichsführer SS (Gesele), a new formation raised to brigade strength from a regimental nucleus stationed in Corsica; and two other first line divisions, 3rd (Gräser) and 29th (Friess), which, like the two panzer divisions, would be brought south from France. In northern Italy for a time during August 1943, following Mussolini's downfall, and prior to the exit of Italy from the war on 8 September, two other panzer divisions would be involved in security duties including sweeps against partisans. They were the Leibstandarte (Adolf Hitler) and 24th Panzer. The presence of these and other valuable divisions so far from main fronts would become a blight on German resources. Most would have been better employed in critical situations elsewhere, and with pressure mounting east and west the 'Italian' divisions were inevitably drawn off for action there. Eventually fewer than half of the panzer or panzer grenadier divisions committed in Italy against superior Allied land, sea and air forces would remain in support of a growing number of infantry divisions.

Defending Sicily, 10 July 1943. When General Patton's US Seventh and General Montgomery's British Eighth Armies, lead by airborne troops, initiated Operation 'Husky' at Gela and Pacino in the south-east corner of Sicily, nothing but incomplete German armoured formations were on hand to stiffen Italian Sixth Army (Guzzoni) resistance. The German divisions, Hermann Goering Division and 15th Panzer Grenadier, were divided in support of Italian formations; Italian Sixth Army consisting of four divisions of immobile infantry and miscellaneous coastal protection units with a German liaison officer, General von Senger und Etterlin serving at Army Headquarters at Enna. But on 14 July 1943, the picture changed rapidly with the arrival of German reinforcements in the shape of 1st Paratroop (Fallschirmjaeger) Division (Heidrich) followed soon afterwards by 29th Panzer Grenadier Division (Rodt) and, on 17 July, to take control of all German troops in Sicily, XIV Panzer Corps Headquarters (Hube). 2nd Parachute Regiment (Heilmann), the advance guard of 1st Paratroop Division, airlifted via Rome out of OKW reserve at Avignon, was parachuted into Catania airfield then transported into action by road. Under Hermann Goering command, these battle-seasoned paratroops formed by HG units into mixed battle groups, incorporating Tiger detachments of 504th Heavy Tank Battalion, fought aggressively in defence of key points. So unexpected was this development that Anglo-US planners were obliged to revise their strategies and reconsider formerly optimistic views on the chances of a swift and easy passage northwards through Sicily. Allied pressure on German ground and air forces defending the island nevertheless continued to mount unrestrainedly.

On 25 July, with the battle for Sicily approaching its height, Benito Mussolini, Il Duce, was dismissed by the Grand Council. As a result of this development Hitler issued orders to accelerate a German build-up in Italy; 16th and 26th Panzer Divisions followed by 3rd and 29th Panzer Grenadier Divisions moved swiftly into northern Italy from France, pushing down to Rome or to Calabria. On 26 July, also in response to developments in Italy, Hitler ordered 2nd Paratroop Division (Ramcke) with General Student's I Parachute Corps HQ, to be flown from the OKW reserve at Avignon to the neighbourhood of Rome; the order being executed next day. On 31 July, Italian Sixth Army, responsible for defending Sicily, was formerly subordinated to XIV Corps (Hube), and the German liaison staff under von Senger und Etterlin was disbanded. On 17 August, the evacuation of Sicily, in Operation 'Lehrgang' under Hube's direction, resulting in 40,000 German troops with 10,000 vehicles (47 tanks) evading encirclement, was concluded with all involved crossing the Straits of Messina to Calabria in good order; the bulk of their equipment being trans-shipped intact and Luftwaffe anti-aircraft protection playing a key role in the operation.

In **northern Italy** during August 1943, where a new Army Group, 'B', under Field Marshal Rommel, established on the 17th with headquarters in Munich, was expecting to take command of mainland operations, six infantry and two panzer divisions – Leibstandarte Adolf Hitler and 24th Panzer, responsible to II SS Panzer Corps Headquarters (Hausser), redeployed from the Mius to Reggio after failing with 'Citadel' – were involved in security sweeps; Operation 'Feurstein' especially. Rommel's first move as GOC, Army Group 'B' was to review the security of transalpine routes affording German access to central and southern Italy. In this respect the situation improved immediately with General Feurstein, a mountain warfare specialist from the Bavarian mountain training school at Mittenwald and a former commander of 2nd Mountain Division, leading mixed Tiger and infantry battle groups to gain control of vital arteries, the Brenner Pass in particular. Feurstein's command was subsequently expanded into LI Mountain Corps and played an important role in the defence of Cassino early in 1944. These and subsequent moves to safeguard the German position in Italy, code-named 'Axe', were executed with small loss and by the time the Allies carried the war to the mainland on 3 September and the Italian Government, following a secret armistice, openly surrendered to the Allies on 8 September, the German order of battle in Italy totalled eighteen divisions; ten of which were responsible to Field Marshal Kesselring OB (C-in-C), South, where a new Tenth Army was created under General de Panzertruppen von Vietinghoff, and eight in the north serving another new, Fourteenth Army (von Mackensen), answerable to Rommel.

In **Calabria** on 3 September 1943, military operations on the mainland of Italy began to take firm shape. A British landing under Montgomery at Reggio was contested by 29th Panzer Grenadier and 26th Panzer Divisions although the latter's armour was retained in Rome for contingency action. German reaction to the British landing at Reggio was followed six days later by Tenth Army concentrating Hermann Goering, 16th Panzer, 3rd and 29th Panzer Grenadier Divisions against a fresh incursion into Calabria lead by US General Mark Clark at Salerno 150 miles to the north. On the same day German reaction to Italy's break with the 'Axis' (broadcast the previous day) set in train Operation 'Axe', the occupation of Rome and the disarming of Italian forces.

The occupation of **Rome** on 9 September 1943 was initiated by General Student who garrisoned the city with 2nd Parachute Division brought from Ostia and 3rd Panzer Grenadier Division redeployed south from Bolsena. Securing Rome against Regular Italian forces, Student disarmed Centauro, Ariete and other divisions of General Carboni's Motorized Corps; a move that he followed by organizing the capture of Italian Army HQ at Monte Rotondo (by airborne assault), and on the 12th released Mussolini from detention at the Campo Imperatore Hotel, a resort residence in the mountains south of Rome. The operation was carried out by Obersturmbannführer Otto Skorzeny. In northern Italy, corresponding security moves by Army Group 'B' would take the Leibstandarte from Milan via Turin to Mont Cenis where divisional battle groups were deployed to break the resistance of Alpini and partisan units threatening German communications. At the conclusion of 'Axe' resulting in the seizure by Army Group 'B' of at least 230 tanks, 24th Panzer Division was stationed in Verona while the Leibstandarte stood guard over alpine communications. In the South two panzer corps headquarters, Hube's XIV evacuated from Sicily to Calabria and in Hube's leave of absence led by General Hermann Balck, and a new LXXVI Panzer Corps commanded by General Herr, both responsible to von Vietinghoff's Tenth Army, were on hand to direct operations against Anglo-US landings at Reggio and Salerno.

At **Salerno** on 13 September 1943, the US lodgement 30 miles south of Naples was counter-attacked by 16th and 26th Panzer Divisions supported by 29th Panzer Grenadier Division. Not withstanding vigorous action by the troops involved, the offensive was a failure and although renewed on the 14th panzer attacks were again defeated with the help of naval firepower. Baulked in this endeavour, Kesselring ordered Tenth Army back to the Volturno; the last 16th Panzer Division rearguards leaving the city on 30 September. Despite losing Naples to the Allies, OKW's determination to protect the southern flank of Europe by opposing every mile of Anglo-US progress through Italy was to be amply demonstrated in the months to come. During October 1943 on the Adriatic coast, LXXVI Panzer Corps (Herr) retreating from Foggia (abandoned 27 September) opposed British Eighth Army advancing northwards to Termoli and the Sangro; 29th Panzer Grenadier, 1st Paratroop and 16th Panzer Divisions bearing the brunt of heavy fighting. In November 1943, a new Army Group 'C' under Field Marshal Kesselring, changing his title from OB, South to OB, South West and pursuing a rewarding defensive strategy, was encouraged by Hitler at Rommel's expense. Accompanied by the staff of Army Group 'B', Rommel was consequently transferred to the west (*see* career note, Romel, concluding Panzer Army Africa). Notwithstanding the defection of the Italian Government from the German cause, and the relatively short distance from Salerno to the Reich's frontier north of the Po, there would be no easy push by Allied C-in-C, Field Marshal Alexander, through alpine passes to Vienna. By exploiting the natural strength of mountains extending almost from coast to coast and the delaying effect of swift-flowing rivers south of Rome, like the Sangro (LXXVI Panzer Corps) and Garigliano (XIV Panzer Corps), Kesselring converted Italy to a bastion that would require all the power the Allies could muster to dispose of it; the Sangro – Cassino – Garigliano (Gustav Line) defences especially.

Fighting for twenty months at a cost of 300,000 casualties, and not without the greatest of determination, would the Allies thread their way forward, every route barred by a steadfast defence. Deployed first on one sector and then another, panzer and panzer grenadier battalions proved their worth time and again in responding to Anglo-US pressure by conducting prolonged rearguard actions – holding off the enemy until the last possible moment and

Above: Italy, September 1943, and Tigers supporting the 'Leibstandarte' are guarding the alpine routes visible in the background. Deployed on security duties from headquarters in Milan, SS armour (here of II SS Panzer Corps) helped Rommel to contain partisan attacks intended to disrupt the flow of supplies and reinforcements to the south.

then slipping away to new positions from which to dominate the battlefield. Panzer grenadiers employing these tactics in SPWs, supported by mountain troops or paratroops committed in ground roles, imposed frustrating delays from commanding ridges and strong points. With little or no Luftwaffe support to offset the air power ranged against the ground forces, German casualties soared; 500,000 by the close of hostilities. But an orderly front was always maintained – nothwithstanding a surprise Mediterranean coast offensive by US VI Corps (Lucas) landing at Anzio – Nettuno, 70 miles behind the main German battleline centred on Cassino.

Panzer action at Anzio–Cassino began on 22 January 1944 when the US-British lodgement (US VI Corps), 25 miles south of Rome and 70 miles to the rear of the main German battle line, was seen to threaten disaster to Tenth Army anchored at Cassino.

A cornerstone of the defence stretched across Italy since December 1943, Monte Cassino dominated the Liri valley, a north-south branch of the Garigliano, through which passed primary routes to Rome. Defended initially by 15th Panzer Grenadier Division (Rodt) and units of 5th Mountain Division (Schrank), battles for possession of this strong point would continue for four months with Tenth Army throwing back all attempts at its capture. Kesselring's reaction to the new threat to Cassino posed by the Anzio landing – anticipated by a contingency plan 'Richard' – would be as effective as it was swift.

All exits from the beachhead were sealed off by alarm units rushed from Rome. These emergency battle groups of motley character were followed into action by paratroops and panzer grenadier units under Paratroop General Schlemm (I Fallschirm Korps); Schlemm being responsible for the Roman hinterland into which US VI Corps was intruding. In a supporting move, Fourteenth Army HQ (von Mackensen) was brought from the north to handle a concentration of Kesselring's best divisions – Hermann Goering (Schmalz), 26th Panzer (von Lüttwitz), 3rd (Gräser) and 29th (Rodt) Panzer Grenadier Divisions.

On the Garigliano/Cassino front, where US Fifth Army (Clark) was exerting maximum pressure, a reinforced 90th Panzer Grenadier Division (Baade) supported by Fallschirmjaeger units was moved to the centre of operations defending Cassino (XIV Panzer Corps), while to the north 5th Mountain Division (LI Mountain Corps) held on to the flanking massive, dominating the Rapido, an inland tributary of the Garigliano.

Operation 'Sunrise'. Starting on 16 February 1944, two experienced corps commanders – Schlemm, I Fallschirm Korps and Herr, LXXVI Panzer Corps (switched from the Sangro) – would lead the Anzio–Nettuno counter-offensive 'Sunrise' devised by Hitler. Yet despite powerful support provided by assault units issued with Tigers, heavy assault guns and a new weapon, Goliath – a radio-controlled demolition tank filled with high-explosives for use against fixed defences 'Sunrise' failed to make the expected progress. Notwithstanding the élan of battle groups mounting attacks against a strongly entrenched enemy while enduring violent assault by naval and air bombardment, all attempts to eliminate the Allied invasion force failed – although attacks were pressed home on the 16th, 18th and again on 22 February, then continued intermittently for four months. Von Mackensen's efforts came to nothing. Against a staunch defence 'Sunrise' proved fruitless. None of the

Goliaths reached their objectives; and the defenders shrugging off weeks of siege warfare made preparations to resume the offensive.

Last Battle for Cassino. Starting on 11 May 1944, XIV Panzer Corps (von Senger und Etterlin), holding the main German battle line at this point with 1st Paratroop Division (Heidrich), was heavily engaged in repulsing, powerful and repeated Allied ground and air assaults. Bombing attacks during February aimed at dislodging the paratroops around Cassino had resulted instead in the destruction of the Benedictine Abbey which, in crowning Monte Cassino, commanded strategic views of the Liri valley. Despite Tenth Army's profoundly admired powers of resistance (1st Paratroop Division in particular) Allied forces pushing north – French Moroccan troops in the lead – finally turned the defence. On 17 May 1944, Tenth Army engulfed in a new wave of attacks (Operation 'Diadem') instructed battleweary panzer crews, panzer grenadiers, mountain, paratroop and infantry battle groups to disengage from the fourth and final battle of Casino.

On the 22nd, the Anzio bridgehead too erupted with a US Division threatening Tenth Army communications at Valmonte. Hermann Goering Division, released by Kesselring from reserve on the 23rd to meet the threat of encirclement, suffered grievously in air attacks while moving up in daylight. In the retreat from Cassino, XIV Panzer Corps was redeployed to the rear of Tenth Army, leap-frogging most of the available panzer grenadier divisions in flank protection moves north. On 25 May, US Fifth Army units striking from the bridgehead at Anzio united in the coastal area at Terracina with those from the front at Cassino, while Alexander's other troops continued their efforts to destroy the retreating German Army.

In the **US race for Rome,** entered by Fifth Army on 4–5 June 1944, General Mark Clark, breaking free of Fourteenth Army constraints at Anzio, pushed into an empty city; a move that allowed Tenth Army, retreating from Cassino, to bypass the town and, together with Fourteenth Army, occupy new defences north of Florence. Stalemate ensued and following Kesselring's evacuation of Rome and retreat north to the Green Line, Hermann Goering Division was ordered out of the theatre; 26th Panzer Division being left alone to work with three remaining panzer grenadier divisions, 29th, 90th and 16th SS, also 1st and 4th Paratroop Divisions (the latter raised in action at Anzio) and 23 other formations bringing German fighting strength in Italy up to 29 divisions by October 1944. These, and nineteen other divisions deployed in the Balkans, were left to delay British, US, Russian and satellite forces advancing towards Germany until Army Groups South West and South East capitulated officially on 2 May (Tenth and Fourteenth Armies having surrendered to Alexander on 29 April 1944). Panzer action in Italy never aspired to the dramatic scale of movement and deep penetration characterizing panzerarmee operations in North Africa and in the east. Instead, hull-down tanks revetted into reverse slopes exploited terrain opportunities to a maximum or, when lying concealed in maize fields and the masonry ruins of provincial Italian towns and villages, worked with panzer grenadiers in devising ambush tactics. Perhaps for a week or so in the retreat from Cassino (17 May 1944), when the mainly panzer grenadier divisions subordinate to XIV Panzer Corps played a key role in the escape of Tenth Army, was there a semblance of manoeuvre providing a basis for tactical success. Thereafter, when fighting vehicles were lost in action or abandoned for want of fuel, panzer crews and panzer grenadiers would fight long and hard on foot – exacting a heavy toll of advancing Allied armies, much as they would do elsewhere in Europe as the tide of military operations edged remorselessly towards Germany and Berlin itself. (*see* Third Panzer Army, 16 April 1945).

Right: Oberstgruppenführer and General der Waffen SS Paul Hausser served the army as a career officer from 1914 to 1918 and the Reichswehr until 1932. In 1933 he joined the SA (Sturmabteilung) and subsequently became Director of the SS Junkerschule at Braunschweig. In 1936 he was Inspector Verfügungstruppen and in May 1939, GOC, SS Verfügungs Division (Das Reich). From June 1942 to June 1944 he served as GOC, II SS Panzer Corps, fighting at Kharkov and Buczac (*see* maps 13 and 15). Late in the war he was GOC, Seventh Army in Normandy where he was wounded escaping from the Falaise pocket. In January 1945 he was appointed GOC, Army Group Upper Rhine in succession to Himmler, followed by Army Group 'G' in succession to Balck.

8. Fifth Panzer Army Europe (PzAOK 5, 1944–5)

Originally Panzer Group West, raised in December 1943 from the staff of Panzer General, West, Leo Geyr von Schweppenburg; Headquarters at Paris Auteuil. Geyr's appointment to OB West Headquarters, Paris (St-Germain-en-Laye), serving von Runstedt as panzer adviser, began in July 1943.

Command in the west. On 3 July 1944 (D+27), Geyr was succeeded as GOC Panzer Group West by General Heinrich Eberbach. On 5 August (D+58), after two days as Armeegruppe or Panzerarmee West, Eberbach's Headquarters, was upgraded and redesignated Fifth Panzer Army with Eberbach ccontinuing as GOC until Hitler required him to undertake more pressing employment on the invasion front, leading a new formation (Panzer Group Eberbach) against US Third Army [D+66]; SS Obergruppenführer Sepp Dietrich (I SS Panzer Corps) meanwhile assuming Eberbach's responsibilities as GOC, Fifth Panzer Army. But in a subsequent change of command on 12 September 1944, General Hasso von Manteuffel was appointed GOC to lead the army in the battle of the Ardennes, starting on 16 December. The change was not permanent, however, and in March 1945 with new employment taking Manteuffel to Third Panzer Army, General Josef Harpe assumed the role of Panzer Army Commander, continuing until capitulation on 18 April 1945. *Bracketed dates starting [D+34] refer to Seventh Army which on D-Day, and subordinate to Army Group 'B' (Rommel), was the command body responsible for the coasts of Brittany and Normandy between the Loire at Nantes and the Orne north of Caen; HQ, Le Mans. After conceding Cherbourg to US First Army (Bradley) on D+23, Seventh Army continued in action at St-Lô south-east of the city, opposing a new US offensive leading to 'Cobra', the decisive break-out in Normandy [D+49]. On 2 July (D+26) following GOC Dollmann's death by suicide, command of Seventh Army passed to SS Oberstgruppenführer Paul Hausser – the first General of the Waffen SS to hold Army command; Dietrich and Steiner, Sixth and 11th SS Panzer Armies, reaching equivalent rank in due course.*

Panzer operations in Normandy are consequently split between Panzer Group West or its successor Fifth Panzer Army, and Seventh Army; distinctive phases being marked by block-dates in the following sequence with a D-Day

equivalent provided until D+85 (30 August 1944) when the last substantial bodies of German troops were crossing the Seine in flight.

PANZER CONTROVERSY AND 'OVERLORD'

The invasion of north-west Europe, Operation 'Overlord' on 6 June (D-Day) 1944, was undertaken by an Allied expeditionary force under the supreme command of General Dwight D. Eisenhower. The plan of assault and subsequent development was, however, the responsibility of 21st Army Group; Army Group Commander, General Bernard Montgomery. Eight weeks later on the invasion front, 'Overlord' was to give rise to a new Fifth Panzer Army; Army Commander, General Heinrich Eberbach. Following two months of intensive tank–infantry operations in a bitter struggle for supremacy in Normandy, the long overdue move by OKW was intended to correct a fatal flaw in command arrangements for panzer divisions in the west. Not in fact until 5 August (D+60) would Panzer Group West (Geyr/Eberbach) in control of panzer divisions since D+1 and responsible to Army Group 'B' (Seventh Army, Panzer Group West, Fifteenth Army) be up-graded and re-designated Fifth Panzer Army. During this crucial period Allied operations had reached their peak, with US forces operating in the western half of the invasion zone, initiating break-out operations on 25 July 1944 [D+49], breaching Seventh Army defences and moving into exploitation. Unfortunately for von Kluge, the Army Group commander who succeeded Rommel when he was injured on D+41, the headquarters and divisions best suited to handle the crisis – Panzer Group West with most of the available armour – was at the time deployed at the opposite end of the battle zone defending Caen; a consequence of 21st Army Group's skilfully applied strategy of attracting German resources away from the critical US break-out sector.

OKW's belated tightening of control of panzer action in Normandy – characterized by a frequent and calamitous loss of initiative – four weeks earlier when Eberbach was brought in to replace Geyr. A cavalry officer with a long history of professional appointments – Geyr was military attaché, London 1933; GOC, 3rd Panzer Division, 1937–40; GOC, XXIV Panzer Corps, 1940–2 – and the General who in July 1943, prior to inaugurating Panzer Group West (December 1943), created a rehabilitation and training command for panzer divisions re-fitting under OB, West von Runstedt. Geyr's training programme was noted for paying special attention to the role of mobile divisions in action against large enemy airborne formations, expected in the hinterland of the invasion front in conjunction with a seaborne assault. Concurrently with its training role, Panzer Group West was intended by OKW to serve as a panzer reserve controlling I SS Panzer Corps (and an incomplete XXXXVII Panzer Corps) with four panzer divisions, 1st SS, 12th SS, 17th SS and Panzer Lehr – the intended hammer in an OKW counter-invasion strategy. But Geyr's views on the operational employment of panzer divisions in the west, a subject upon which he tendered much advice to OB West, differed considerably from those of Field Marshal Rommel, GOC, Army Group 'B'. In Rommel's opinion, based upon personal experience of Allied air power in the Western Desert (*see* Panzer Army Africa, 1 July 1942), if panzer divisions were to retain their mobility serving in a counter-attack role, undue exposure to Allied air supremacy, such as might be encountered in a lengthy approach march to the invasion front, must be avoided at all costs; the crux of Geyr's argument being that the panzer divisions should be retained well clear of the coast and consequently outside the range of naval artillery, in central, well-camouflaged locations where they would be on hand to counter either sea or airborne invasion. The issue was never resolved to the satisfaction of the parties involved in the controversy. There were in any case too few under-strength panzer divisions deployed in the west, too little equipment and not much of an air force flying in support.

A compromise solution, in which three of the ten panzer divisions currently deployed in the west were allotted to Army Group 'B' (2nd, 21st, 116th), three to Army Group 'G', on the Mediterranean coast (9th, 11th, 2nd SS) and the remaining four to Panzer Group West (1st SS, 12th SS, 17th SS Panzer-Grenadier and Panzer Lehr) failed to provide adequately for any one of the options. In the event Rommel gained limited control of only three panzer divisions with which to support a front stretching from the Loire into Belgium and Holland. Geyr was denied the full orthodox deployment of a powerful mobile reserve considered essential by von Runstedt to his 'hammer' policy, and he himself needed permission from OKW to commit any of the (strategic) reserve panzer divisions allotted to Panzer Group West – the strongest of which was Panzer Lehr. Geyr's eventual replacement by Eberbach, nine years his junior with an equally impressive record of panzer service – CO, 35th Panzer Regiment, 1937; GOC, 4th Panzer Division, 1942; Commander, XXXXVIII Panzer Corps, 1942 and thereafter important professional appointments including a spell with the Inspector-General of Armoured Troops (Guderian), was expected to promote vigorous action halting the slide of Army Group 'B' into disaster. But all too late.

The Allies spring a trap (map 16). By 5 August 1944 (D+60), when Fifth Panzer Army (Eberbach) was inaugurated by up-grading Panzer Group West, ten first class divisions, most of which were superior Waffen SS panzer or panzer grenadier divisions, had been committed to the invasion front piecemeal and burned-out in local action generally contesting Anglo-Canadian (British Second Army) initiatives devised by 21st Army Group holding the panzer divisions around Caen. The ten panzer/panzer grenadier divisions committed in Normandy by D+60 included two (9th SS, 10th SS) withdrawn from the Eastern Front where the majority were deployed in action against the Red Army. Those involved in Normandy were the Army's 2nd, 21st, 116th and Panzer-Lehr, and those of the Waffen SS, 1st, 2nd, 9th, 10th, 12th Panzer and 17th SS Panzer Grenadier Divisions. Of two other Army panzer divisions in the west, as yet uncommitted and re-fitting in the south under Army Group 'G' (Blaskowitz) – 9th Panzer Division (Jollasse) at Nîmes and 11th Panzer Division at Toulouse – 9th Panzer would arrive at the front within hours to re-inforce Seventh Army (Hausser) resisting US First Army at Domfront, while 11th Panzer remained at Toulouse before moving into the Rhône valley and opposing Operation 'Dragoon', a second Allied invasion of France on 15 August 1944 (D+70). Despite so impressive an assembly of panzer divisions in Normandy, including a rare concentration of the best SS panzer divisions, their commitment under unified command to hammer the Allied expeditionary force and push it back into the sea – although this, as the following account illustrates, was intended by Hitler and OKW from the outset – never materialized. Indeed by D+60, Fifth Panzer Army, sharing the invasion front with Seventh Army, was already outmanoeuvred and committed in desperate counter-attacks trying vainly to hold together a rapidly disintegrating front as US forces, exploiting their opportunity for mobile operations after [*D+49*], swept south and then east, jeopardizing the future of von Kluge's Army Group.

In fact, such was the Army Group's plight following the US break-out [*D+62–D+71*] that Eberbach's command, by this time a 'Gruppe' acting independently of Fifth Panzer Army and counter-attacking US Third Army closing the ring on a Seventh Army and Fifth Panzer Army pocket forming south-west of Caen, was in imminent danger of annihilation; fortunate battle groups, looking to escape in the direction of the Seine, being sent scrambling for safety under horrendous conditions. The vexed question of how best to integrate the deployment of ten panzer divisions with that of fifty or so infantry and static divisions to form an effective defence against cross-Channel invasion of France, had generated deep-seated controversy in German command circles. Arising largely out of Geyr's limited eastern experience, the problem had been compounded by Hitler's equally paranoid refusal to allow either flexibility or responsibility to any single individual in handling the panzer divisions; a 'difficulty' that was resolved all too late in the day when Geyr was subordinated to Rommel on 7 June (D+1). But Hitler's dissatisfaction over developments in Normandy would lead not only to his replacing Geyr with Eberbach as noted, but on that same day, 3 July, retiring OB West, von Runstedt and substituting von Kluge. Two weeks later in consequence of an injury to Rommel on 17 July (D+41), von Kluge would assume the added responsibility of Rommel's Army Group 'B', an unsatisfactory arrangement soon to give way to another change of command in Normandy. Suspected of disloyalty to Hitler, von Kluge was recalled by OKW on 16 August (17th in practice, D+72); command in the west then passing to Field Marshal Walter Model, former GOC, 3rd Panzer Division in 1941, XXXXI Panzer Corps Commander in the battle for Moscow, 1941–2, and thereafter, still on the Eastern Front, GOC, Ninth Army in 1942. Model's subsequent commands, carrying promotion to Field Marshal (1 March 1944), were as GOC, Army Group North Ukraine and finally Army Group Centre. But not even Model, the 'Führer's fireman', could save the situation.

By 20 August 1944 (D+75), the shattered remnants of more than forty of the divisions committed by OKW to the defence of the west, including eleven panzer and panzer grenadier divisions, six of them SS – escaping from the battle zone with fewer than 45,000 effectives – were of little military consequence. Senior commanders such as Model, Hausser and Eberbach, would evade capture by the narrowest of margins – only temporarily so in Eberbach's case, taken prisoner by British Second Army on 31 August 1944. Half a million casualties in the west, including 200,000 effectives abandoned in coastal 'fortresses' and the Channel Islands, by the end of August, testified to the scale of destruction consuming the Wehrmacht. Evidence of the failure of Hitler's military direction and its consequences for the panzer force is nowhere better exemplified than in the mis-management of panzer divisions in France, particularly those of Panzer Group west in control of I SS, II SS and eventually XXXXVII Panzer Corps (or that Group's successor, Fifth Panzer Army) which from the earliest days of 'Overlord' was committed piecemeal against 21st Army Group lodgements 'Gold', 'Juno' and 'Sword' on the Calvados coast north of Caen.

Panzer Group West and Seventh Army facing invasion 6 June–10 July (D-Day–D+34). At 0330 hours on D-Day, 6 June, British airborne landings (commencing

Below: This photograph by an RAF reconnaissance flight over Normandy in 1944 reveals the scale of destruction which had laid waste Panzer Group West and Seventh Army's communications in the run-up to 'Overlord'.

at 0015) to secure Ranville and other key localities on the east bank of the Orne – sealing the outer flank of a seaborne lodgement – were subjected to preliminary assault by II/192 Panzer Grenadier battle group found from 21st Panzer Division (Feuchtinger) which the divisional commander on his own initiative deployed against the airborne troops consolidating east across the river. Feuchtinger's division, stationed south of Falaise (HQ St-Pierre-sur-Dives) and nearest of all to the Calvados beaches, was not however released by Seventh Army (Dollmann) to LXXXIV Corps (Marks) for action against British 6th Airborne until 0700 hours, by which time Army Group headquarters (Speidel, deputising for Rommel, absent on 48 hours' leave) was receiving reports of amphibious assault craft supported by massive naval and air strikes disembarking tanks and infantry on the Calvados coast north of Bayeux. The reaction of OB West (von Runstedt) to 'invasion' in the early hours of D-Day was to alert Panzer Group West (1st SS, 12th SS, Panzer Lehr, 17th SS Divisions) and on his own initiative move 12th SS Division (OKW reserve) from Evreux towards the coast at Lisieux, while at the same time urging OKW (Jodl and Keitel) to release these panzer divisions for offensive action. By 1000 hours the full extent of the Normandy landings, but not their true significance as the main effort of 'Overlord', was being recognized at Army Group HQ; Speidel then moving 116th Panzer Division (von Schwerin) forward to the coast north of the Seine where, in common with 2nd Panzer Division at Abbeville, it was retained in expectation of further assault. But not until 1440 hours on D-Day was Seventh Army (Dollmann) advised by Army Group 'B' that OKW was at last releasing 12th SS Division (Witt) and Panzer Lehr Division (Bayerlein) for offensive action in the Normandy battle zone. Shortly afterwards OKW decided that I SS Panzer Corps (Dietrich) would assume control of these formations.

Meanwhile, on the invasion front two Allied armies – First US (Bradley) and Second British (Dempsey) – were disembarking assault formations along a 50-mile stretch of the Calvados coast between the Orne at Ouistreham and Quinéville ten miles south of Barfleur. 21st Panzer Division (Feuchtinger), regrouping during the day north of Caen with the revised intention of engaging the seaborne lodgement immediately west of the Orne, (Sword), recalled units *en route* to attack the British airborne troops east of the river – a move that attracted the attention of Allied fighter-bombers; a bad augury for the future of panzer operations in Normandy. Nevertheless, by 1600 hours 21st Panzer had assembled two strong battle groups ready to strike to the coast north of Caen. The most successful of these was a reinforced panzer grenadier battalion I/192 (Rauch) which reached the sea north of Caen at 1900 hours and luckily split 'Juno' and 'Sword' between Luc- and Lion-sur-Mer, but despite Rauch's good fortune in finding a gap between beach-heads the attack failed either to disrupt or deter Montgomery's eastern build-up. Stronger action by a more powerful concentration of tanks and infantry – both panzer battalions of 22nd Panzer Regiment (Oppeln-Bronikowski) and 1/125 Panzer Grenadier Battalion, intended to assist Rauch in the push north – resulted instead in the first armoured clash of the campaign in Normandy, at Biéville where armoured squadrons of the Staffordshire Yeomanry deployed in support of British 3rd Division drew 21st Panzer on to a north-easterly axis leaving Rauch's panzer grenadiers on the coast without heavy support and thereby unable to make further progress. (The Luftwaffe was nowhere to be seen, having flown fewer than 320 sorties against an estimated Allied 14,000 D-Day missions.)

Panzer action to reduce the airborne lodgement on the east bank of the Orne, where Feuchtinger deployed 125th Panzer Grenadier Regiment (Luck) re-inforced by the 21st Divisional Reconnaissance Unit and 200th Assault Gun Battalion continued purposefully with attacks against strongly defended positions. At 2100 hours when a fresh wave of airborne landings – 6th Airborne's remaining parachute battalions, armoured reconnaissance and light artillery units – threatened the safety of his division, Feuchtinger recalled the panzer grenadiers on the coast and regrouped with the panzer regiment north of Caen, preparing for action next day in conjunction with 12th SS Hitler Jugend Panzer Division (Witt) arriving from Lisieux and taking up positions on the division's left flank north of Carpiquet where a usable airfield two miles west of the city had recently been evacuated by the Luftwaffe. At about the same time on the evening of D-Day, Rommel was returning to his headquarters on the Seine at La Roche-Guyon west of Paris, following 48 hours' leave of absence celebrating his wife's birthday at Herrlingen, near Stuttgart. Panzer action on D-Day – 21st Panzer Division striking in regimental strength at invasion forces east and west of the Orne with no advantage in Luftwaffe support and a lack of unified direction – suffered the additional handicap of OKW fears in releasing crucial reserves too early in the battle.

Such inhibition was above all the consequence of a brilliant Allied deception plan, Operation 'Fortitude', which even before the invasion began was successful in focusing OKW attention on the Pas-de-Calais, 150 miles to the north-east, where the main assault by a phantom force of forty divisions was expected hourly by Fifteenth Army (von Salmuth) and continued to be expected until late July, inhibiting the movement of 2nd and 116th Panzer Divisions that would otherwise have certainly intervened more quickly and powerfully in the Normandy battle-zone (2nd Panzer, D+7; 116th Panzer, D+43). The D-Day intentions of 21st Army Group (Montgomery) passing responsibility for action on the eastern flank of the invasion coast to British Second Army (Dempsey) – 6th Airborne Division (Gale) three assault divisions (50th, Canadian 3rd, British 3rd) and three armoured brigades – required spearheads from 'Gold', 'Juno' and 'Sword' to drive eight miles inland on the first day, seize Caen, a strategic communications centre with Carpiquet airport adjoining to the west, and then push on south in a bid to win good 'going' for armour and suitable terrain for airfield construction – an essential pre-requisite for future offensive support. Thirty miles to the west of the Anglo-Canadian (British Second Army) effort, US forces in simultaneously phased operations would pursue broadly comparable objectives. Deploying two US airborne divisions, 82nd (Ridgway) and 101st (Taylor) for the capture of Ste-Mère-Eglise and beach exit defiles, US First Army (Bradley) was struggling with reduced armoured support to establish 4th and 1st Infantry Divisions on 'Utah' and 'Omaha' Beaches north and east of Carentan.

On the US flank of the invasion coast, Montgomery's intentions were focused principally upon the port of

Cherbourg – which like Caen at the time was defended by German Seventh Army (Dollmann). Prompt US capture of the stores-handling facilities of Cherbourg was considered top priority by the Allies in order to link the US invasion force direct to the United States by sea. On the German side, Field Marshal Rommel's plan to counter invasion on this stretch of the Normandy coast was initially to eliminate the US threat by panzer intervention; a proposal vetoed by Hitler who instead directed that all available resources be concentrated in the east against British Second Army.

On **7 June (D+1)**, 12th SS Panzer Division Hitler Jugend (Witt), the first of four OKW reserve panzer divisions to reach the invasion battle zone – the others being Panzer Lehr (D+2), 17th SS (D+5) and SS Leibstandarte Adolf Hitler (D+22) – arrived west of Caen, secured Carpiquet and prepared to assist 21st Panzer concentrating for a renewed attack northwards to the coast. Moving to the attack in bounds via Lisieux, to reduce the danger of air attack between Evreux west of Paris and the division's assembly area, initially south-east of Caen, Hitler Jugend's 25th Panzer Grenadier Regiment (Meyer) and II Panzer Battalion/12th SS Panzer Regiment (Wunsche) would be followed into action by 26th Panzer Grenadier Regiment (Mohnke) and the Panzer Regiment's I Panther Battalion delayed at the Orne by a fuel shortage. But pre-emptive pressure exerted by Anglo-Canadian forces renewing offensive operations against Carpiquet and Caen was to rob the panzer divisions of their first opportunity to launch a co-ordinated counter-attack. The planned offensive evolved instead as independent action by Hitler Jugend's reinforced 25th Panzer Grenadier Regiment (Meyer) ambushing Canadian (3rd Division) spearheads at Authie a mile or so north of Carpiquet, while 21st Panzer (Feuchtinger) resisted British (3rd Division) attacks threatening Caen south of Biéville.

On **8 June (D+2)**, Panzer Lehr (Bayerlein), filtering into the battle zone from Le Mans 100 miles to the south, arrived on the left of Hitler Jugend at Norrey–Brouay twelve miles west of Caen, under orders from I SS Panzer Corps (Dietrich) to prepare for an offensive to the coast – in conjunction with HJ. Bayerlein's exceptionally well-equipped panzer division included 901st Panzer Grenadier Regiment (Scholtz) and 902nd (Gutmann), all four battalions riding in armoured personnel carriers; the division's panzer complement, however, lacked the Panther Battalion of 130th Panzer Lehr Regiment (Gerhardt) which at the time of OKW's order releasing the division to Seventh Army (Dollmann) was entrained for the east. During the night of D+2 Rommel shifted Panzer Lehr into positions opposite British XXX Corps (Horrocks). A war-experienced formation, XXX Corps comprised the veteran 7th Armoured Division (Erskine) and 50th Highland Division (Graham) consolidating Bayeux and preparing to outflank Caen in a powerful drive south. Moving in broad daylight from Le Mans to the invasion front on orders from Seventh Army, Panzer Lehr had been obliged to negotiate rubble and crater obstacles deliberately created by Allied bombers attacking key road and rail routes and centres. Like Hitler Jugend and other units arriving in the battle zone, Panzer Lehr suffered continuous air attacks resulting in unacceptable delays and casualties. Rommel at La Roche-Guyon on the same day – following his return there on D-Day evening – was meanwhile regrouping surviving infantry and the new panzer divisions, entrusting the defence of Caen, currently in the hands of 21st Panzer and 716th Infantry Division with Carpiquet firmly secured by 12th SS HJ, to Geyr von Schweppenburg's Panzer Group West. But Geyr's Group, with I SS and eventually II SS and XXXXVII Panzer Corps, would all too soon suffer in battles of attrition with British and Canadian armies implementing Montgomery's plan to seize Caen and drive south.

On **9 June (D+3)**, Panzer Lehr, instead of participating with HJ in a I SS Panzer Corps offensive to the coast – for which available forces were inadequate – deployed two regimental-size battle groups (901st and 902nd Panzer Grenadier Regiments) astride the Tilly–Bayeux road, launching attacks to recover Bayeux held by 50th Infantry and a 7th Armoured support group. Conducted with orthodox precision, Bayerlein's attack failed under intensive artillery fire and air strikes. When an exposed flank was threatened attacks were halted and the division recalled; a setback followed next day by an altogether more shattering blow for Rommel preparing for decisive action against the Allied invasion force.

On **10 June (D+4)**, Panzergruppe West HQ at la Cain, four miles north of Thury-Harcourt (revealed by 'Ultra' intercepts), was destroyed in air attacks and Rommel's planned counter-offensive with Panzer Lehr, HJ and 21st Panzer Division was temporarily, and as it turned out fatefully, postponed. Thirteen staff officers died in the attack and Geyr was wounded. The crisis was resolved in part by substituting 'Sepp' Dietrich's I SS Panzer Corps HQ and making it responsible to Seventh Army; Geyr's own HQ would remain out of action until 26 June when a new staff was assembled.

On **11 June (D+5)**, 17th SS Panzer Grenadier Division (Ostendorff), arriving from Poitiers on the western (US) flank of the invasion coast, assembled defensively south of Carentan.

Deployed in conjunction with a Fallschirmjaeger battle group (FJR 6), the divisional commander was instructed to disrupt US First Army's build-up around Carentan, but with no assault guns – the division's only armour delayed by harassing air attacks – 17th SS Division (GvB) made little headway in splitting 'Utah' and 'Omaha' which undisturbed proceeded to join up eastwards with 'Gold', 'Juno' and 'Sword' to form a strongly held and continuous Allied front.

On **13 June (D+7)**, Panzer Lehr, the westernmost of three panzer divisions (Pz Lehr, HJ, 21st Panzer) deployed opposite British Second Army in defence of Caen, was subjected to an outflanking move by 7th Armoured Division seeking to bypass Caen as a result of which occurred one of the most celebrated panzer actions of the war. Unable to reach Caen via Tilly where Bayerlein's division, firmly in control of the locality since D+2, was fighting off heavy attacks, British XXX Corps (Bucknall) was instructed to change direction and, instead of confronting Panzer Lehr from this direction, swing south-west and as part of a pincer movement involving British I Corps in attacks north-east of the city, approach Caen from the west via Villers-Bocage; the vanguard of XXX Corps being provided by 22 Armoured Brigade/7th Armoured Division (Erskine). Unfortunately for XXX Corps the British offensive was brought to an abrupt conclusion by the action of a single section of four Tigers (No. 2 Company) lead by Obersturmführer Wittmann from

101st heavy SS Panzer Battalion. Deployed on Height 213 north-east of Villers, Wittmann's Tigers covered the same high ground that 7th Armoured had been given at its objective. The SS Tigers, corps troops of I SS Panzer Corps, had suffered both technical and tactical losses from air attacks, arriving behind the left wing of Panzer Lehr with only thirteen fit Tigers, brought from Beauvais, 40 miles north-east of Paris. The weakness of Panzer Lehr's left flank connecting with 352nd Infantry Division, a much depleted survivor of gruelling battles with the invasion forces, was clear to both sides and it was here that British Second Army planned to break through to Caen – until Wittmann and advance elements of 2nd Panzer Division (von Lüttwitz), brought unknown to 21st Army Group from Fifteenth Army north of the Seine to reinforce the threatened sector, forestalled the move.

Alerted to the approach of 22 Armoured Brigade – a powerful battle group of tanks, motorized infantry and support weapons – Wittmann moved into action at 0800 hours. Directing the fire of his own Tiger's powerful 8.8cm gun, the 55-ton vehicle's main armament, Wittmann destroyed the rear and leading vehicles of the British column caught napping at Montbroque effectively blocking the Villers–Caen road and preventing British withdrawal or reinforcement. Stalking the remaining vehicles in the space of a few minutes Wittmann and his section picked off twenty Cromwells, four Fireflies (SP 17pdrs) six light armoured cars and most of the infantry halftracks, leaving a trail of smoking wrecks and burning vehicles that a few minutes earlier had constituted the vanguard of 22 Armoured Brigade. Reinforced by a Panzer Lehr battle group (including Tigers from No. 1 Coy) and, during the afternoon, 2nd Panzer Division's reconnaissance battalion, Wittmann's aggregated battle group continued the action for a further three days; abandoning Villers-Bocage, 7th Armoured Division (Erskine) withdrew north-east to regroup. This unexpected check to British progress south around Caen was to leave Panzer Lehr at least temporarily in possession of the hotly contested Tilly-Villers sector, and 2nd Panzer Division (with no panzer regiment until D+12) in possession of Caumont. Diversionary British attacks north-east of Caen faring no better against a 21st Panzer Battle Group (Lucke) were discontinued.

During the course of seven days' heavy fighting, 21st Army Group brought ashore 326,000 men, 54,186 vehicles and 104,428 tons of supplies. Rommel, disadvantaged by Anglo-US air forces destroying road and rail bridges across the Seine and Loire, received next to no replacement *matériel* or personnel. For whereas Allied armies continued to receive stores at an accelerating rate across open beaches or at temporary ports (Mulberries) towed 60 miles across the Channel and then anchored at Arromanches and St-Laurent – unhindered by the German Navy or Luftwaffe – the battlefield was largely sealed aganst increment for the panzer divisions. Suffering relentless assault by fighter-bombers picking off vehicles in daylight while heavy bombers of US 8th Air Force shattered road and rail centres by night, Rommel's transport communications were enormously hampered; reinforcements and supplies were forced into ever-widening detours and time-consuming night marches. Yet despite the theatre-wide strain imposed by Allied air attack – which full-scale offensive was compounded by the Maquis interfering with operational traffic at every possible opportunity – troop movements were soon recovering to the point where new divisions were reaching the invasion zone – 2nd Panzer Division (Lüttwitz) from Fifteenth Army at Amiens on D+7, SS Das Reich (Lammerding) from First Army at Toulouse on D+9 and various Army or SS heavy panzer battalions/Werfer brigades from home stations in Germany or occupied territories in the west. Although these improved the German order of battle in Normandy, Rommel's power to sweep the Allied invasion force back into the sea would remain inadequate; Hitler's aspirations were to go unfulfilled and the 'Overlord' armies unchallenged by any serious attempt to evict them from beach-heads consolidating into a continuous line between the Orne estuary in the east and Montebourg, fifteen miles short of Cherbourg in the west.

On **15 June (D+9)**, panzer reinforcements arriving for Rommel from Army Group 'G' included SS Panzer Grenadier Regiment Der Führer (Weidinger) bringing I/Der Führer and

Above: Hauptsturmführer Michael Wittmann, leader of a Tiger company from 101st SS Heavy Panzer Battalion, led his forces in the ambush on 13 June 1944 D+7 of 7th Armoured Division who were spearheading an attempt to outflank Panzer Lehr.

I/Deutschland while leading 2nd SS Panzer Division Das Reich from Toulouse to the battle zone south-east of St-Lô. Placed on stand-by for action at Caumont supporting 2nd Panzer Division (Luttwitz) opposite the junction of British Second and US First Armies, Der Führer prepared for action. Unhappily for those involved in transferring Das Reich from Army Group 'G' to the battle zone in Normandy, the move was surrounded by much notoriety; shameful reprisals taken by the division against civilians and Maquis at Tulle and Oradour-sur-Glane in the Dordogne north-west of Limoges during a four-day SS security operation (D+2–D+6) defaming the combat reputation of the Waffen SS from that day onwards. [*And not for the first or last time. During 'Autumn Mist' (see Sixth Panzer Army) Kampfgruppe Peiper's execution of American prisoners at Malmédy was a massacre no less criminal*]. At the centre of events in the Dordogne was the disappearance of Major Helmut Kämpfe, Der Führer's Panzer Grenadier (III) Battalion commander, ambushed by Maquis and at first believed imprisoned at Maquis headquarters in Oradour. It was this loss of a trusted leader and the discovery of German corpses at Tulle that provoked the infamous killing of local French men, women and children by the Waffen SS.

The involvement of Das Reich in internal security duties at a time when every available panzer division was needed in action at the front – whatever the short-term benefit to the Wehrmacht of inhibiting Resistance action in the Dordogne and perhaps beyond – was to exemplify the unsatisfactory and disjointed use of Das Reich in Normandy. Forced by events into providing battle groups for other divisions on widely separate sectors of the front, Das Reich more than any other panzer divisions was to fall victim to the piecemeal commitment of armour in Normandy forced upon the High Command by the unrelenting pressure of 21st Army Group operations. [*Not in fact until 27 July (D+51), in the aftermath of the US break-out west of St-Lô would Das Reich serve under united command, by which time it was too late for the division to influence events in Normandy by more than the slightest degree.*]

On and after **16 June (D+10)**, more of Das Reich was reaching the front. Moving in separate tracked and wheeled vehicle march columns, Der Führer (under a new commander, Weidinger, appointed on D+8 when Stadler was promoted GOC, 9th SS Panzer Division) was followed by 2nd SS Panzer Regiment (Tychsen) arriving 20 June (D+14) and assembling south of St-Lô opposite US First Army (Bradley). Nevertheless, a substantial part of Das Reich – two battalions of Deutschland (II and III), the division's second Panzer Grenadier Regiment – would remain for the time being incomplete and refitting in Toulouse–Montauban. During the period 17–24 June (D+11–D+18), following a Führer conference at Margival (D+11), Army Group 'B' (Rommel) initiated the planning phase of a boldly conceived counter-offensive against 21st Army Group. Employing three panzer corps, I SS (Dietrich), II SS (Hausser-Bittrich) and XXXXVII (Funck) to be concentrated in the area of Caumont, the offensive would be lead by Panzer Group West (Geyr). Panzer divisions already in the line, 2nd, 21st and Panzer Lehr, were to be replaced by infantry divisions from Britanny and the South of France. Two new SS Panzer divisions, 9th Hohenstaufen and 10th Frundsberg (II SS Panzer Corps) were confirmed *en route* from the east, and 1st SS Leibstandarte Adolf Hitler was confirmed moving from OKW reserve in Belgium. Convened in former 'Sealion' headquarters at Margival (Soissons), the Führer conference there had ended with no clear-cut decision on the future conduct of the battle. But within days of the meeting attended by Rommel, von Runstedt, Jodl and chiefs of staff, an Army Group plan was being shaped over a Seventh Army study envisaging an offensive northwards at the junction of US (First) and British (Second) Armies in the centre of the front at Caumont. The Army Group's intention was to strike for the coast at Bayeux and then according to circumstances expand into a single or double encirclement manoeuvre rolling up the exposed flanks of, it was to be hoped, a surprised and outwitted defence.

The shock formation in Rommel's projected offensive was to be II SS Panzer Corps (Hausser-Bittrich) switched from the east front to the west with two SS Panzer divisions after effecting the relief of First Panzer Army in the Ukraine (*see* First Panzer Army, 8 April 1944). Having entrained for Normandy on 12 June (D+6), the SS Panzer Corps was bringing two fairly strong panzer divisions, 9th SS Hohenstaufen (Bittrich) and 10th SS Frundsberg (Harmel). By nightfall on 24 June (D+18) GOC, Panzer Group West Geyr and Corps commanders Dietrich, Funck and Hausser were in agreement over inter-corps boundaries, start-lines, ammunition, stores and fuel replenishment programmes; the minutiae of a panzer offensive confidently expected to start early in July, following the arrival of replacement infantry and new assault divisions to join those released from the line. A night start was intended as the surprise element in the plan of attack. But OKW arrangements for concentrating armour under Panzer Group West and striking a decisive blow at the invasion force were then betrayed to 21st Army Group by 'Ultra'. Warned of the movement to Normandy of II SS Panzer Corps and others including the Leibstandarte *en route* from OKW reserve in Belgium, Montgomery accelerated plans for a new offensive.

On **25 June (D+19)**, British Second Army (Dempsey) launched Operation 'Epsom' – referred to in German military literature as the third battle of Caen. Overcoming delays by storms of rare violence raging through the English Channel and wreaking havoc on Mulberry harbours, the new British offensive was intended to isolate Caen from its hinterland by hooking around the city from north-west to south-east and securing a bridgehead astride the Orne at a point where the river approached the city from the south. Attacking on a two-corps front between Tilly and Carpiquet where Panzer Lehr (Bayerlein) and 12th SS HJ (Meyer) were still in the line under I SS Panzer Corps (Dietrich), Dempsey would be assisted by I Corps distracting 21st Panzer north-east of Caen.

In its principal phase timed for day two, **26 June (D+20)**, 'Epsom' intended slicing through 12th SS Panzer Division (Meyer) in the line north of Cheux, breach the Odon close by Gavrus and Baron-sur-Odon, and then exploit to the Orne via Hill 112, a prominent feature dominating routes between rivers. In order to provide a strike force for actions against 12th SS Panzer Division, Dempsey deployed the newly landed British VIII Corps (O'Connor) controlling 11th Armoured Division (Roberts), 15th Scottish, 43rd Wessex Infantry Divisions, and 4 Armoured Brigade. British XXX Corps (Bucknall) cast in a supporting role opposite

Panzer Lehr, west of HJ, would open the proceedings on D+19 by committing 49th Infantry Division and supporting armour in the direction of Rauray – HJ's connecting locality with Panzer Lehr. British tank strength, including 7th Armoured Division (Erskine) waiting in reserve behind XXX Corps, stood at 600 against an estimated 102 of 12th SS and 150 of Panzer Lehr (plus Panzerjaeger). Maximizing air and artillery support, including offshore 16in batteries of HMS *Rodney* and the monitors *Roberts* and *Erebus*, the British offensive recorded early success but then stalled in the face of determined resistance; that of 12th SS HJ Panzer Division (Meyer) in particular. Tearing a 3-mile gap in the front of I SS Panzer Corps (Dietrich) where HJ battle groups of 25th (Müller) and 26th (Mohnke) SS Panzer Grenadier Regiments defended the outermost localities of the main German battle line, Dempsey pushed hard with 11th Armoured Division exploiting to the Odon and Hill 112, but failing to break the defence.

Concealing half of his panzer strength (II/12th SS Panzer Regiment) in company localities, hull-down behind the forward panzer grenadier battle groups – as an immediate counter-attack reserve and anti-tank screen – while deploying I/12th SS Panzer Regiment and III/26th Panzer Grenadier Regiment (Olboeter) as a regimental panzer battle group (Wunsche) on the left wing at Rauray – Meyer soon dashed British hopes of a decisive breakthrough. Over the next few days until 28 June (D+22), confrontation on the Odon between two British corps and two much depleted panzer divisions of I SS Panzer Corps, HJ and Panzer Lehr (reinforced on D+21 and again on D+22) would develop into the costliest armour-infantry battle in the short history of Panzer Group West; HJ's defence of Rauray, Cheux and Hill 112 against British XVIII Corps attacks meriting well-deserted acclaim in the military histories of both sides.

On **27 June (D+21)**, a reinforced Das Reich regimental battle group, Der Führer, consisting of two SS panzer grenadier battalions and an Army panzer company under Otto Weidinger joined the action south of Rauray. Redeployed from the division's assembly area south of St-Lô, Weidinger's objective was to close a gap between HJ and Panzer Lehr, the result of British pressure splitting the defence. Next day on the other side of the British break-in, at Verson, two more SS panzer grenadier battalions – 1st SS Panzer-Grenadier Regiment (Frey) leading 1st SS LAH Panzer Division (Wisch), risking the journey through France from Belgium, also a 22nd Panzer Regiment panzer battle group, transferred to the crisis point from 21st Panzer Division, still guarding north-east Caen – joined in operations to constrict the British penetration which by the third day of the battle (D+21) had won through to the summit of Hill 112. At this point 'Epsom' failed; counter-attacks by 12th SS Panzer Regiment (Wunsche) redeployed from the defence of Rauray holding the offensive in check. Meanwhile on 27 June (D+21) II SS Panzer Corps (Hausser) with SS Panzer Divisions Hohenstaufen (Bittrich) and Frundsberg (Harmel), intended for Rommel's Caumont offensive, was assembling north-west of Alençon on urgent recall from the east; a three-weeks' journey from Lemberg spent mostly *en route* through France via Nancy or Epinal where the corps detrained at the conclusion of a four-day rail journey starting 12 June (D+6). When committed on the Odon (D+23) by a despairing Seventh Army commander (Dollmann), anxious to relieve the pressure on German divisions suffering heavy losses in continuous action since D-Day, II SS Panzer Corps would succeed in taking the remaining momentum out of 'Epsom', changing the tactical picture temporarily to Panzer Group West advantage.

On **28 June (D+22)**, Panzer Group West, controlling four army corps, three of them panzer – I SS Panzer Corps (Dietrich), II SS Panzer Corps (Hausser) and XXXXVII Panzer Corps (Funck) – twelve divisions in all, became directly subordinate to Army Group 'B' (Rommel); Panzer Group responsibilities between the Seine and the Drôme (Caumont) focusing upon the defence of Caen. On this sector of the invasion front, no fewer than eight panzer divisions or significant elements of the Leibstandarte (1st SS LAH), 2nd SS (Der Führer only), 9th SS, 10th SS, 12th SS, 2nd, 21st and Panzer Lehr, subordinate to Panzer Group West (Geyr), were now drawn into battle on Montgomery's east flank. Only 17th SS Panzer Grenadier Division, reinforcing weak infantry formations deployed south of Carentan, opposed US First Army in the west, although the mass of 2nd SS Panzer Division retained in Army Group reserve south of St-Lô was soon to become involved (D+29), contributing battle groups to threatened sectors, e.g., Der Führer subordinated to 353rd Inf Division (Mahlmann) at La Haye-du-Puits.

[*This imbalance in the deployment of panzer divisions in Normandy was to continue mostly unchanged even after the fall of Cherbourg on 29 June (D+23); the release of US forces after gaining control of the base then causing Rommel to redeploy Panzer Lehr (Bayerlein) west to assist 17th SS Division at Pont-Hébert on 9 July (D+33) by which time 2nd SS Panzer Division would be strengthening GvB and Seventh Army at Sainteny (Périers). Thereafter, one or other of these panzer divisions, serving Seventh Army with the support of regular parachute and infantry battle groups responsible to LXXXIV Corps (von Choltitz) would be committed in counter-attacks opposing US First Army (Bradley) expanding south of Carentan; Bradley's aim thrusting south via St-Jean-de-Daye to St-Lô being to gain a start-line (St-Lô–Périers) from which to commence a future if somewhat delayed break-out on 25 July (D+49).*]

On **29 June (D+23)**, four days after the start of British Second Army's 'Epsom' offensive, counter-attacks by II SS Panzer Corps serving Wilhelm Bittrich – a new corps commander replacing Hausser promoted GOC, Seventh Army (Dollmann's suicide being reported at the time as a heart attack) – finally frustrated 21st Army Group's plan for isolating Caen by thrusting around the city from the north-west. Co-operating with I SS Panzer Corps (Dietrich) assaulting the eastern flank of the British penetration at Verson, II SS Panzer Corps (Bittrich), converging on nearby Cheux from the west and south-west, sealed the fate of 'Epsom' forcing Dempsey on to the defensive and leaving Panzer Group West (Geyr) temporarily in control of the battlefield. But whatever hopes OB West or Rommel entertained of extending the II SS Panzer Corps offensive into a strike northwards, splitting the Allied front around Caumont as Rommel originally intended – until 21st Army Group pressure had forced Seventh Army (Dollmann) into asking Rommel for the immediate and unscheduled use of II SS Panzer Corps in the Odon battle – were dashed by the crushing weight of Allied artillery and air power brought

Right: Hedgerow fighting in Normandy intensified as 'tank-hunters' armed with the Panzerschreck lay in wait to ambush Allied armour. Firing an 88mm hollow-charge missile, this Bazooka-type rocket-launcher proved to be a devastating weapon. Here, a Fallschirmjaeger of II Paratroop Corps (Meindl) demonstrates its handling.

to bear on the attacking divisions. Notwithstanding HJ's check to 'Epsom' occasioned by a staunch defence of Rauray and Cheux, the deep penetration achieved by 11th Armoured Division (eventually withdrawn from Hill 112 through fear of encirclement by the converging SS panzer corps) created deep German concern for the safety of the sector, consequently involving 12th SS Panzer Division, the Corps Werfer Regiment, 101st SS Tiger Battalion and 8.8cm Flak from III Flak Corps in heavy fighting to retain a grip on the key features of the Odon battlefield; notably Hill 112.

However, such were the losses sustained by the panzer divisions in the Odon battles – particularly from 16in naval guns offshore – that the commander of Panzer Group West (Geyr) and subsequently von Runstedt himself proposed withdrawing out of naval artillery range and evacuating parts of the front north of the Orne including Caen where the river divided the city north and south. Following their replacement by infantry as earlier planned, Geyr would have redeployed the panzer divisions as a strong mobile reserve on the east flank of the front, ready to take advantage of any Allied thrusts eastwards in the direction of Paris. Rommel disagreed; stressing the danger of exposing armoured concentrations to air attack.

On **3 July (D+27),** Hitler's predictable reaction to Geyr's suggestion of surrendering ground in Normandy, freely supported by von Runstedt – who also advised making peace with the Allies – quickly surfaced; both men were dismissed. In Geyr's place Hitler appointed Eberbach and in von Runstedt's, von Kluge. For the panzer divisions fighting in Normandy the outlook was one of increasing bleakness; Hitler's obstinate refusal to countenance reality condemning them to operate at a disadvantage within range of naval artillery while also enduring day and night attacks by Allied air forces. There was also little chance of reinforcement or improvement in a deteriorating supply situation, sapping panzer confidence in a successful outcome to the struggle in Normandy – even more so when on 17 July (D+41) (q.v.) a low-flying air attack would remove Rommel from the scene of battle. From **4 July (D+28)** to **20 July (D+44),** during which time Rommel was wounded, Panzer Group West (Eberbach) was to face 21st Army Group offensives growing in power and momentum. Operations

'Windsor' (D+25), 'Charnwood' (D+32), 'Jupiter' (D+34), 'Green-line' (D+39) and above all 'Goodwood' (D+42), were all designed by General Montgomery to fix the panzer divisions in the east, destroying their material basis, allowing neither rest nor respite to panzer grenadiers, crews or personnel of any kind – frustrating all Rommel's hopes of effectively strengthening the western flank of the invasion front where US First Army (Bradley) after celebrating the capture of Cherbourg on D+23 was pressing forward with renewed vigour south of Carentan, posing a serious threat to St-Lô, the western anchor of the German battle line. In this sector west of St-Lô, before Panzer Lehr joined Seventh Army (D+33), a handful of infantry formations reinforced by 17th SS Panzer Grenadier Division (Ostendorf) served LXXXIV Corps (von Choltitz) or, directly responsible for the town and the battlezone to the east, II Parachute Corps (Meindl).

In the meantime British initiatives west of Caen: Operation 'Windsor' **4 July (D+28)** extended on **8 July (D+32)** into Operation 'Charnwood', was bringing 12th SS HJ Panzer Division (Meyer) under renewed pressure defending Carpiquet and adjoining localities at Rots, Buron and Authie. Directed by British Second Army (Dempsey), Operation 'Charnwood' was preceded by a bombing offensive in which 2,000 tons of bombs were dropped on German positions in the northern half of the city – the built-up area containing Anglo-Canadian assault objectives defended by HJ or, when 21st Panzer Division was withdrawn a short distance into rest, 16th Luftwaffe Division (Sievers).

By **10 July (D+34)** 12th SS Panzer Division's resistance to 'Charnwood' had been broken by bombing and a ground assault led by 3rd Canadian Division. The same offensive crippled the neighbouring Luftwaffe Field Division. Threatened with encirclement, Meyer relinquished control of Carpiquet (I/25th Panzer Grenadier Regiment), evacuating the battle zone north-west of Caen and retiring through the city and across the Orne into Vaucelles. On the same day Hill 112 was lost to 43rd Infantry Division. In new positions south of the river, HJ would exploit the defensive potential of war-wasted streets until 11 July (D+35), when the division was relieved by 1st SS LAH (Wisch) and, in turn, 272nd Infantry Division which continued to deny Caen to Canadian II Corps (Simmonds) until D+42 when the city fell to Montgomery in the course of Operations 'Goodwood' and 'Atlantic'. Meanwhile, leaving Vaucelles and its other Orne sectors south of the river to Wisch, HJ was redeployed south of Caen to Potigny, five miles north of Falaise. Meyer then formed emergency battle groups around 25th and 26th Panzer Grenadier Regiments, and 12th SS Panzer Regiment (Wunsche). HJ's battle-fit tank strength stood at nineteen Pz Kpfw IVs and 25 Panthers with four Pak 7.5cm guns in support.

Seventh Army taking the strain *10 July [D+34] to 24 July [D+48]. The reaction of Army Group 'B' to US First Army (Bradley) attacks savaging Seventh Army (Hausser) south of Carentan, had necessitated the urgent redeployment of Panzer Lehr (Bayerlein), released from Tilly on 5 July (D+29) to reinforce 17th SS Panzer Grenadier Division (Baum), the mainstay of a sagging Seventh Army infantry defence north-west of St-Lô. Despite the pressures of 'Epsom' during which time it was replaced in the line at Tilly by 276th Infantry Division, Bayerlein's division had served from 26 June to 5 July as XXXXVII Panzer Corps reserve. In its new location, right of the much weakened 17th SS Panzer Grenadier Division struggling north and west of St-Lô to contain US First Army spearheads probing south from St-Jean-de-Daye and threatening Pont-Hébert, Bayerlein was instructed to launch an immediate spoiling attack and then prepare a strong divisional offensive northwards. Following the collapse of Seventh Army resistance in Cherbourg on 29 June (D+23), eliminating a 20,000-strong mixed infantry battle group von Schlieben (709th Infantry Division), an intensification of US pressure southwards had long been expected by Army Group 'B', but effective counter-measures to reinforce surviving Infantry Divisions 77th, 91st, 243rd and 353rd (from Brittany) fighting south of the town had failed for want of resources to progress beyond the arrival on D+5 of 17th SS Panzer Grenadier Division (Ostendorf, Baum after 18 June) and starting on 5 July (D+29) Das Reich battle groups of varying size and power, including Der Führer (Weidinger) returning to the division from employment west of Caen since D+21.*

Us First Army intentions in this the preparatory phase, of the break-out battle 'Cobra' scheduled by Bradley for 20 July (D+44), but deferred by Channel conditions delaying crucial supplies and reserves until 25 July (D+49), focused upon the capture of St-Lô and its associated network of roads. Possession of St-Lô, currently Seventh Army's forward communications and supply base, and in particular the St-Lô–Périers highway crossing the Vire to the west, with subsidiary routes (from Pont-Hébert) running south, was a pre-requisite for mobile operations by US Third Army (Patton) planning to attack out of the high hedgerow bocage country of Normandy and into Brittany. But for the arrival of Panzer Lehr, ejecting US spearheads from Pont-Hébert on 8 July (D+32), this Allied objective would have been realized. The defence of Seventh Army's battle line east and west of St-Lô was shared by two German army corps; LXXXIV (von Choltitz, former panzer corps commander, Anzio) covering the area west of St-Lô to the sea at Bretteville, and II Parachute Corps (Meindl, veteran assault regiment commander, Crete) responsible for the town itself and the line east to Caumont.

Panzer Lehr, 17th SS Goetz von Berlichingen and eventually 2nd SS Das Reich, deployed between St-Lô and Périers, were subordinated to LXXXIV Corps, whereas II Parachute Corps relied principally upon 3rd Parachute Division (Schimpf) and Infantry Battle Group 352 reinforced by the panzer reconnaissance battalion of 17th SS Panzer Grenadier Division. The first counter-attack of any significance developing after D-Day against US First Army in the western sector of the invasion front, and lead by 17th SS Division (Ostendorf) with the help of FJR6 (von der Heydte) had penetrated into the centre of Carentan but failed to adhere there. US 82nd Airborne and 2nd Armored Division, benefiting from heavy air cover, remained firmly in control while further counter-attacks, sapping the strength of 17th SS Panzer Grenadier Division, required the support of a Das Reich panzer battle group – II/2nd SS Panzer Regiment (Kesten) – to restore temporary stability to the line at Bois Grimot on 9 July (D+33), but failing to deter US progress southwards.

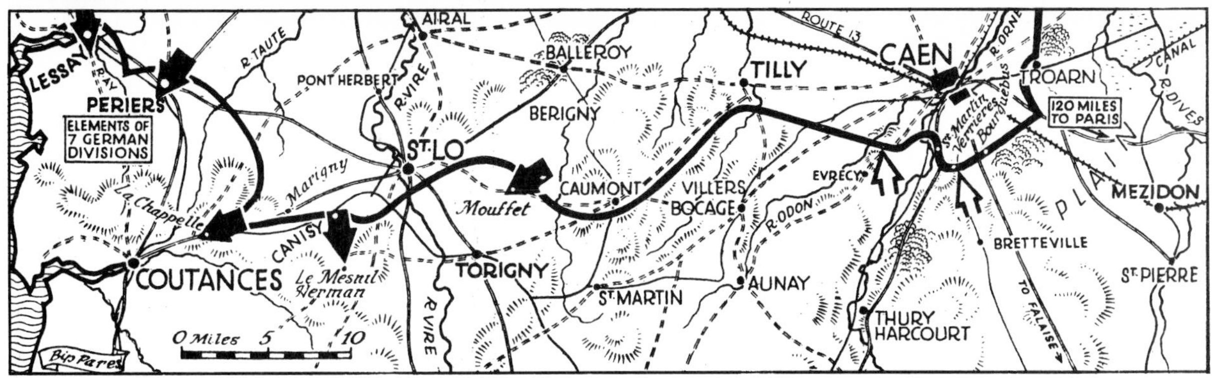

Above: 20 July 1944 was D+44. The main German battle line, following the Allied offensives code-named 'Epsom'. 'Charnwood' and 'Goodwood', was broken and the strong points of Carpiquet, Caen and Bourguébus had fallen to the Allies at a time when most of the panzer divisions were concentrated in their defence.

Heavy casualties on both sides (40,000 Americans) testified to the extreme bitterness of fighting in the close bocage country where armour was disadvantaged by limited vision, narrow lanes and high-banked hedgerows. On the German side too, casualties soared; 28 General officers and more than 90,000 other dead, wounded or missing to date. Supply deficiencies, particularly in petrol, oil and lubricants hampered the movement of even individual vehicles while ammunition shortages curtailing artillery barrages reduced the effectiveness of artillery support and ceaseless American air interdiction delaying unit assembly times destroyed operational groupings.

On ***11 July [D+35]****, Panzer Lehr's (Bayerlein) offensive under LXXXIV Corps (von Choltitz), striking northwards from an assembly area between Pont-Hébert and le Hommet, followed preliminary action by a Das Reich battle group (Wisliceny) attacking towards le Dézert, also Panzer Lehr ejecting spearhead units of US 3rd Armored Division from Pont-Hébert; the recovery of this Vire crossing west of St-Lô thereby improving the security of the Corps sector. Bayerlein's instructions were to strike north, thrusting for St-Jean-de-Daye south of Carentan, recover Airel and similar key points facilitating US access to St-Lô, and then establish blocking positions on high ground overlooking the Taute–Vire Canal. Regimental panzer grenadier Battle Groups 901 (Scholtze) and 902 (Welsch), deployed two-up in the style of a panzer division attack in close country, opened the way forward. Neither battle group was equivalent (in SPWs) to more than five or six panzer grenadier companies, a panzer battalion of twenty – thirty Pz Kpfw IVs or Panthers, and an engineer company. The Das Reich battle group (Wisliceny), formed from a reinforced III Battalion Deutschland previously deployed like II/2nd SS Panzer Regiment (Tychsen) supporting 17th SS Panzer Grenadier Division, an FJR 14 battle group and other reinforcements assisted Panzer Lehr in the offensive. All in vain. After recording limited success against US infantry surprised at le Dézert and Bahois, less than halfway to St-Jean-de-Daye the offensive stalled. Subsequent US counter-attacks were immediately effective in eliminating an over-extended subordinate battle group – I/901st (Philipps) with ten Panthers encircled north of le Dézert.*

[D+35–D+48]. *For the next thirteen days the best that Panzer Lehr could do as US First Army (Bradley) preparing for 'Cobra' squared-up to the St-Lô–Périers highway, was to conceal its armour hull-down in twos and threes, fighting off powerful US armour and infantry attacks – culminating on 25 July in Operation 'Cobra' (see Seventh Army, [D+49]). During this period of intensive operations by Seventh Army in the west, the panzer divisions suffered the loss of irreplaceable material and manpower including the commanders of 17th SS – Ostendorff, succeeded on 18 June by Baum (ex-38th SS Panzer Grenadier Regiment) and 2nd SS – Lammerding replaced on 24 July by Tychsen (ex-2nd SS Panzer Regiment). With divisional strengths declining to 40 per cent or less effectiveness, 17th SS Panzer Grenadier battalions were reduced to 120 men. 130th Panzer Lehr Regiment (Gerhardt), by the time that St-Lô fell to US First Army (after pushing through II Para Corps) on 18 July (D+37), had declined to 30 per cent of its D-Day establishment of 103 Panthers and 79 Pz Kpfw IVs. The divisional panzer grenadier battalions returned equally reduced strengths. But perhaps the greatest loss to Seventh Army lay in the unexpected way in which 2nd SS Das Reich was rendered impotent through seconding battle groups to other divisions at crisis points – Weidinger (Der Führer) to reinforce 353rd Infantry Division (Mahlmann) at La Haye de Puits, Wisliceny (Deutschland) to 17th SS and later Panzer Lehr at Pont-Hébert, also I/2nd SS Panzer Regiment with artillery support deployed east of St-Lô as a II Parachute Corps reserve (uncommitted). Consequently in Das Reich's own sector around Sainteny on 7 July there had remained only 2nd SS Panzer Regiment (Tychsen) with a single (II) Panzer Battalion; artillery support being provided by IV Battery/AR Das Reich assisted by II SS Werfer Battalion. Heavy anti-tank support for two weak panzer, one panzer grenadier and five infantry divisions deployed in the Sainteny sector was provided by Army 657th Panzer Jaeger Battalion equipped with Jagdpanzer IVs.*

Meanwhile, in the South of France, desperately needed panzer grenadiers – II (Deutschland) and II (Der Führer) also III Panzer Artillery Regiment were still undergoing training. Other support units brought in to lace Seventh Army defences included Army Engineer Battalion 'Angers', 8 Werfer Brigade and various Army artillery battalions. The Luftwaffe was little in evidence. More powerful support for the critical St-Lô wing of Seventh Army facing Bradley's pre-'Cobra' build-up to fourteen US divisions (one motorized, two armoured) was in the offing, but Montgomery's strategy of attracting the panzer divisions to the Caen sector claimed 2nd Panzer (von Lüttwitz) withdrawn from the line at Caumont and 116th Panzer (von Schwerin) redeployed south of Caen from Fifteenth Army north of the Seine. Both panzer divisions under XXXXVII Panzer Corps (von Funck)

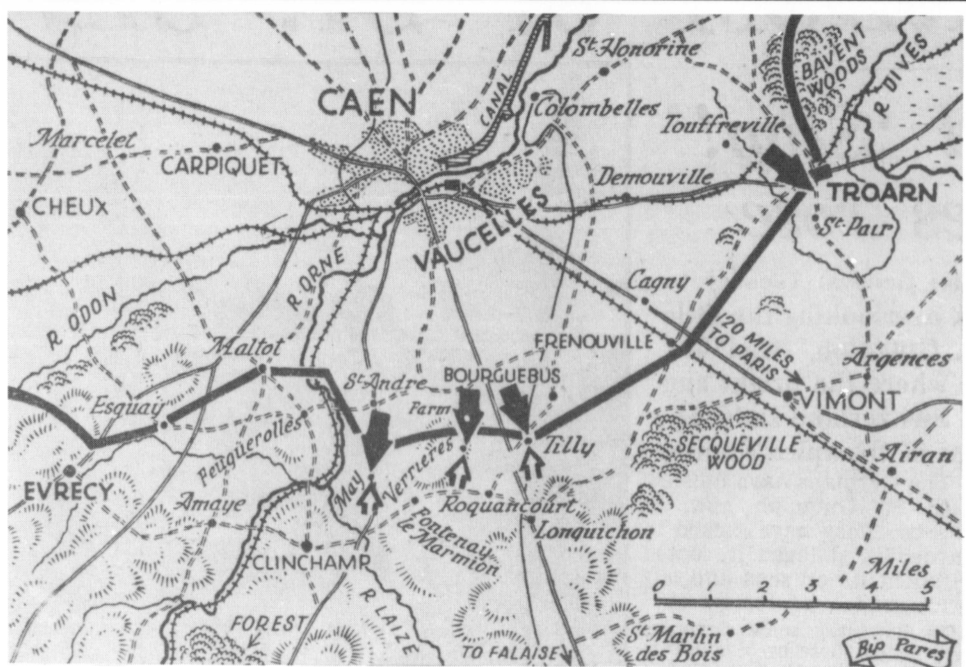

Left: D+34 to D+48.

were intended for action west of the Vire, but with action flaring around Caen on D+42 found themselves instead opposing Montgomery's Operation 'Goodwood'.

Panzer Group West Defending Caen 10 July (D+34) to 24 July (D+48). In the aftermath of 'Charnwood' driving 12th SS Panzer Division (Meyer) out of Carpiquet across Caen and into the suburbs south of the Orne at Vaucelles – followed by redeployment north of Falaise – the focus of panzer action on the invasion front returned initially to the battlefield west of Caen where II SS Panzer Corps (Bittrich) blocked British Second Army (Dempsey) working south of the Odon.

10 July (D+34) to 16 July (D+40). Countering British VIII Corps (O'Connor) offensives 'Jupiter' (D+34) and 'Greenline' (D+39) striking south at Evrecy and Maltot or other points of tactical importance along the Odon, especially Hills 112 and 113, was to make heavy demands on 9th SS Hohenstaufen (Stadler) and 10th SS Frundsberg (Harmel). Other units drawn into the bitter second phase of conflict on the Odon included SS Corps' 102nd Tiger Battalion in action with a panzer battle group (I/12th SS Panzer Regiment) and advance elements of 277th Infantry Division relieving Hohenstaufen. But in a future and more vigorous clash of armour involving I SS Panzer Corps (Dietrich) in action on the battlefield east of Caen starting on 18 July (D+42), no fewer than six of the seven panzer divisions deployed around Caen – 1st SS LAH, 12th SS (HJ), 21st, 9th SS (switched from the Odon), 2nd (redeployed from Caumont), 116th (uncommitted at Creil) – were to face their greatest challenge yet, engaging Anglo-Canadian armour and infantry implementing Montgomery's grand slam Operation 'Goodwood'. Montgomery's strategy of fixing the panzer divisions in the east at a time when US First Army (Bradley) was preparing break-out operations opposite Seventh Army (Hausser) in the west was unfolding in heavily orchestrated actions around Caen inflicting maximum damage on Panzer Group West and its subordinate SS Panzer Corps – I SS (Dietrich) and II SS (Bittrich). These SS panzer corps deployed east and west of the city – with SS Corps Tiger Battalions (101 and 102), Werfer and Army troops in support – constituted the mainstay of the panzer defence of Caen. Montgomery's intention was to engage them in the strongest possible way, bringing them to action defending sensitive localities on the axes of Anglo-Canadian thrusts wrongly interpreted at all levels of German command as 21st Army Group's attempt at breaking free of the Caen cauldron and, in conjunction with fresh landings in the Pas-de-Calais, heading for Paris.

Farther west, XXXVII Panzer Corps (von Funck), less troubled by British Second Army operations in the immediate vicinity of Caen diverting pressure from US First Army west of St-Lô, held the connecting Panzer Group/Seventh Army sector at Caumont. The relative inactivity of the Allies at this point was to persuade Rommel into withdrawing 2nd Panzer Division (von Lüttwitz) into reserve, replacing it with 326th Infantry Division (Drabich-Waechter) taken from Fifteenth Army north of the Seine. Together with 116th Panzer Division (von Schwerin), also on the move from Fifteenth Army, Rommel now proposed to reinforce the Seventh Army front west of St-Lô (*see* Seventh Army [D+34–D+48]. In the event, neither panzer division would be moving west in support of Seventh Army, their presence being considered essential in the east reinforcing Panzer Group West against a renewal of Anglo-Canadian operations expected any day ('Goodwood').

On **17 July (D+41)** the day before 'Goodwood' – with Panzer Group West (Eberbach) poised to meet the challenge of a new offensive out of the British airborne bridgehead east of the Orne – Field Marshal Rommel was seriously wounded in a low-flying air attack. The incident followed Rommel's visit to I SS Panzer Corps headquarters at Urville. Returning by road to La Roche-Guyon the Field Marshal's staff car was overturned by Spitfires of 602 Squadron RAF patrolling at Ste-Foy-de-Montgommery. From the neighbourhood of the attack between Livarot and Vimoutiers, Rommel was evacuated to the Luftwaffe hospital at Bernay north-east of Paris. But so serious were his head injuries and so extraordinary the circumstances of his subsequent death by suicide (three months later) that Rommel was to play no further part in the war (*see* career note at the conclusion of Panzer Army Africa).

With Rommel in hospital, another Field Marshal, von Kluge (OB West) would assume the extra duties of GOC, Army Group 'B' – continuing in the dual role until 17 August (D+72) when, on Hitler's instructions, Walter Model arrived to take command in the west.

On **18 July (D+42),** Panzer Group West (Eberbach) faced 'Goodwood' a British Second Army (Dempsey) offensive directed south around Caen from the outer north-east quarter of the city where Montgomery had chosen to concentrate three armoured divisions: 11th (Roberts), Guards (Adair) and 7th (Erskine) in the 6 Airborne bridgehead east of the Orne. Lead by VIII Corps (O'Connor) redeployed from the Odon, the British armoured divisions with 750 tanks and more than 7,000 other fighting and support vehicles, were given as their main objective the Bourguébus Ridge; a plateau of high ground some eight miles to the south. Whether Montgomery intended to convert a break-through at Bourguébus into an exploitation battle south across the Caen–Falaise plain – as declared to SHAEF and others beforehand – is questionable. The Bourguébus Ridge, a commanding feature on the way to Falaise and the tank-country beyond, held obvious attractions for any south-bound expeditionary force, and its significance as an operational objective was not lost upon Panzer Group West (Eberbach) or other senior German commanders who were quick to incorporate it in defensive arrangements. Rommel's ill-fated visit to I SS Panzer Corps on D+41, the headquarters in control of the critical sector east of the Orne, was a consequence of Bourguébus-related planning. Panzer Group West's dispositions to meet the new offensive are considered later.

Canadian II Corps (Simmonds) would co-operate with the British 'armoured corps' by launching armour-supported infantry attacks on the inner (city) wing of the offensive; code-name for the Canadian operation – 'Atlantic'. On the other side of Caen, British I Corps was also preparing to co-operate in 'Goodwood' by launching armour-supported infantry attacks southwards. Canadian objectives were the industrialized eastern sectors of Caen and the south Orne suburb of Vaucelles from which 1st SS LAH Panzer Division had meanwhile withdrawn – relieved by 272nd Infantry Division – to be relocated in reserve west of Bourguébus. The success of 'Goodwood' was to be 'guaranteed' by Allied air forces unloading an unprecedented 7,000 tons of high-explosives on key targets throughout the battle zone – timed to commence less than two hours before the armoured start-time at 0745 hours. Yet despite the initial shock to the defence of 'the greatest bombing offensive ever undertaken in support of ground operations', 'Goodwood' was destined for a premature conclusion. When the British armoured divisions faltered in deeply echeloned defences established by Panzer Group West, Montgomery would call a halt. Panzer Group West dispositions to meet the long-awaited attack – known to be in preparation at least four days previously – started in the forward line with the two infantry divisions, 16th Luftwaffe and 272nd holding well-defended localities. 16th Luftwaffe (Sievers), already reduced to a regimental-size battle group by bombing in support of 'Charnwood' (D+32) was to suffer the brunt of British Second Army's offensive – reinforced by 192nd Panzer Grenadier Regiment detached from 21st Panzer Division.

Behind the two infantry divisions stood the armour of 21st Panzer Division (von Lüttwitz) – less 192nd Panzer Grenadier Regiment supporting the Luftwaffe division – while I SS LAH (Wisch) in I SS Panzer Corps reserve stood behind 272nd Infantry Division. 21st Panzer Division's battle groups, especially von Luck's 125th Panzer Grenadier Regiment with both panzer grenadier battalions – reinforced by thirty SP Jagdpanzer IVs (7.5cm), SP artillery (10.5cm) and the divisional Panzer (IV) Battalion plus 503rd (Tiger) Battalion, were allotted strong points in the depth of the battlefield, creating numerous defended localities while providing a mobile reserve to deal with break-ins. Further south, more units of 21st Panzer Division, the reconnaissance and engineer battalions, were protecting divisional and corps artillery deployed on the Bourguébus Ridge. Still further to the rear stood an (8.8cm) panzerjaeger battalion and (8.8cm) flak. Other flak units, under Luftwaffe command (III Flak Regiment) and amounting to ninety (8.8cm) guns sited at tactically important points in the battlefield, at Cagny in particular, protected the Caen–Lisieux road. They were to present Allied armour with a formidable challenge. Werfer and Army artillery units too were brought in to reinforce divisional firepower. In Panzer Group reserve at Potigny, south of Caen, stood the much depleted 12th SS Panzer Division Hitler Jugend (Meyer) ready to intervene if required. Much to the surprise of HJ's commander, 'Panzer' Meyer, orders arriving on the 16th had given the division a new assembly area north-west of Lisieux requiring 12th SS Panzer Regiment (Wunsche), comprising I Mixed Panzer Battalion, II/26th Panzer Grenadier Regiment (Krause) and III/26th Panzer Grenadier Regiment in SPWs (Olboeter) to move out immediately. Others prepared to follow.

Promptly at 0745 hours on **18 July (D+42)** in the wake of a bombing offensive led by 1,500 heavy bombers of US 8th, 9th Air Forces, and RAF Bomber Command, 11th Armoured Division rolled forward against negligible opposition. Pushing through German infantry and supporting panzer grenadiers shocked and disarrayed by the bombing, 11th Armoured pressed on towards Bourguébus, bypassing the 125th Panzer Grenadier battle group (Luck) surviving in Cagny, a key mid-battlefield position, gateway to Lisieux and the east. This strong point organized by von Luck incorporating Luftwaffe 88s employed in an anti-tank role, a Tiger detachment and others, defied 11th Armoured Division and follow-up waves of 7th Armoured Division until late afternoon. By mid-evening, Roberts's division was brought to a standstill in action against a powerful I SS LAH battle group (Peiper) comprising I (Panther) Battalion and I SPW Panzer Grenadier Battalion – counter-attacking in defence of Bourguébus; 126 tank wrecks, more than half of 11th Armoured Division's Sherman establishment being left to litter the sector. Supporting Guards and 7th Armoured Divisions fared no better against 21st Panzer and HJ defending Cagny and the communications point leading east at Vimont. It was the undeniable tenacity of panzer battle groups echeloned in depth with powerful anti-tank support protecting a battle front stretching from the Orne south of Caen (272nd Infantry Division) to Bourguébus (I SS LAH) and on to Cagny and Vimont (12th SS reinforced by Battle Group Wunsche recalled from Lisieux) to Troarn (21st Panzer) that denied the British offensive all chance of a dramatic break-through.

18 July (D+42) to 20 July (D+44). During the course of battle over the next few days Erskine's 7th Armoured Division, following Roberts's and then coming into action alongside at Bourguébus, gained a foothold on the disputed ridge while Guards Armoured secured the outer flank of the penetration opposite 12th SS but short of Vimont turned by HJ into a formidable strong point. In Operation 'Atlantic' the Canadians cleared Vaucelles and advancing south attacked 272nd Infantry Division – eventually bringing 9th SS Panzer Division across the Orne in support while 2nd and 116th Panzer Division moving up behind I SS LAH remained there until their redeployment in consequence of crisis developments in the west (*see Seventh Army [D+51]*). From the German point of view Panzer Group West's apparent success in containing the British offensive and limiting progress to Bourguébus, while also denying exploitation in the direction of Falaise masked the real success of Montgomery's initiative evident in the violent reaction of OKW and Panzer Group West. By aiming in massive strength at the high ground south of Bourguébus, threatening rupture to the main German battle line along the Caen–Falaise or Caen–Cagny–Lisieux axis, Montgomery deliberately fostered erroneous German appreciations predicting the new offensive as a prelude to a second landing north of the Seine. Even at this late stage OKW, deceived by Operation

Below: Casualties in the clash of armour at Villers. On the left a knocked-out Pz Kpfw IV and, to the right, a Tiger bear witness to the ferocity of the fighting.

'Fortitude' (p. 58), was convinced that forty Allied divisions waited in Britain to carry out invasion tasks. In consequence of Montgomery's action OKW had moved 12th SS Division to Lisieux, *east* of Caen (and back again), diverted 2nd Panzer Division to the Caen battlefield (behind 272nd Infantry Division) therefore away from its intended course in support of Panzer Lehr at St-Lô, retained 116th Panzer Division after the 19th in the same general locality, while Panzer Group West transferred 9th SS Panzer Division across the Orne on D+46 reinforcing I SS Panzer Corps while also committing ! SS LAH and 21st Panzer to front-line action.

21 July (D+45)–25 July (D+49). For the next five days II SS Panzer Corps was obliged to retain 10th SS Panzer Division on the Odon west of Caen implementing plans to contain the pressure of British XII Corps' subsidiary attacks at Maltot.

Seventh Army shattered by 'Cobra', *25 July [D+49] to 6 August [D+61]. At 1100 hours on 25 July, US First Army (Bradley) initiated the ground assault phase of Operation 'Cobra'. The new American offensive boasted powerful resources; three army corps (VII, VIII, XIX), fourteen divisions (one motorized, two armoured with a third arriving) and the unfettered use of US 8th and 9th Air Forces. 'Cobra' aimed once and for all to break the cordon of Seventh Army (Hausser) infantry and panzer divisions barring US progress out of the bocage. Lead by US VII Corps (Collins), three infantry divisions formed up on a narrow front to open the way west of St-Lô; US 2nd and 3rd armored divisions supported by motorized infantry (US 1st) waited to exploit the expected breach. The panzer and panzer grenadier divisions forming the backbone of the defence remained unchanged; Panzer Lehr (Bayerlein) deployed opposite US VII Corps blocked all approaches to*

the network of roads immediately west of St-Lô; 17th SS (GvB) Panzer Grenadier Division (Baum) stood firm around Marchésieux and, next in line to the west, 2nd SS Panzer Division Das Reich (Tychsen) maintained an unshakeable grip on Périers. As has been noted [D+34–D+48] none of these divisions were at anything like full strength; their depressed state being reflected in correspondingly weak infantry support – 353rd Infantry Division, 1,500 effectives; 243rd Infantry Division no more than a 700-strong battle group; FJR 6 reduced to a half-company of 60 men, etc. Moreover, the 2nd and 116th Panzer Divisions, intended to reinforce Seventh Army, were instead fixed south of Caen by OKW fears of a renewed British Second Army offensive aimed at Falaise (see Panzer Group West (D+49)).

German LXXXIV Corps (von Choltitz), responsible to Seventh Army for the area west of St-Lô between the town's western outskirts and the coast at Lessay, controlled all three panzer/panzer grenadier divisions and their supporting infantry. This was the sector where the full weight of 'Cobra' was to be unleashed – preceded by a massive air bombardment with US 8th and 9th Air Forces unloading 4,000–5,000 tons of high-explosives and Napalm, mostly upon Panzer Lehr. The result of the US bombing offensive and the follow-up assault by US VII Corps was to destroy all cohesion of Panzer Lehr, reducing Bayerlein's division to a 'restgruppe' symbol on LXXXIV Corps' situation map. Of the 188 Pz Kpfw IVs and Panthers with which Panzer Lehr entered the Normandy battle zone on D+2, fewer than fifteen Pz Kpfw IVs (II Panzer Lehr Regiment 130) of the forty remaining to 130th Panzer Lehr Regt (Gerhardt) at the start of 'Cobra' had constituted Bayerlein's sole counter-attack reserve opposing US armour and infantry striking south. Bayerlein's other panzer battalion, I/6th Panzer Regiment, with a broadly equivalent number of Panthers, was divided in support of 902nd Panzer-Grenadier Regiment (Welsch) split into battle groups holding forward defended localities about Hébécrevon – the division's principal defensive position west of St-Lô. On the Division's left flank around La Chapelle the divisional Panzerjaeger Battalion (7.5cm SP anti-tank guns) served 901st Panzer Grenadier Regiment (Hauser) in much the same support capacity as the panzer battalion on the right. Divisional flak (8.8cm towed and SP weapons) lay farthest back, well concealed and, like the divisional artillery, ready to meet the challenge of Shermans, Honeys or other US armour penetrating the main battle line. All to no avail.

Horrendous concentrations of high-explosives and Napalm hurled down upon Panzer Lehr by the US Air Force, reinforcing the destructive effect of VII Corps artillery fire, destroyed 50 per cent of Panzer Lehr units standing west of St-Lô; reducing Bayerlein's 'division' to 2,500 officers and men with only handfuls of tanks and guns. Despite this débâcle, Panzer Lehr faced US First Army with unexpected opposition, but with no reserves to call upon, Seventh Army was about to collapse, Collins's VII Corps achieving remarkable results over the next forty-eight hours driving through Panzer Lehr. Pushing south through Hébécrevon, Marigny and St-Gilles towards Coutances, US armour and motorized infantry – enjoying full tactical air support directed by forward air controllers – shattered all remaining opposition. At other points along the front – east and west of St-Lô where fewer than seventy Pz Kpfw IVs and Panthers faced subsidiary attacks by US VIII and XIX Corps, Das Reich, Goetz von Berlichingen and supporting infantry stood their ground; new orders followed.

On **27 July [D+51]**, *obeying orders from von Choltitz,*

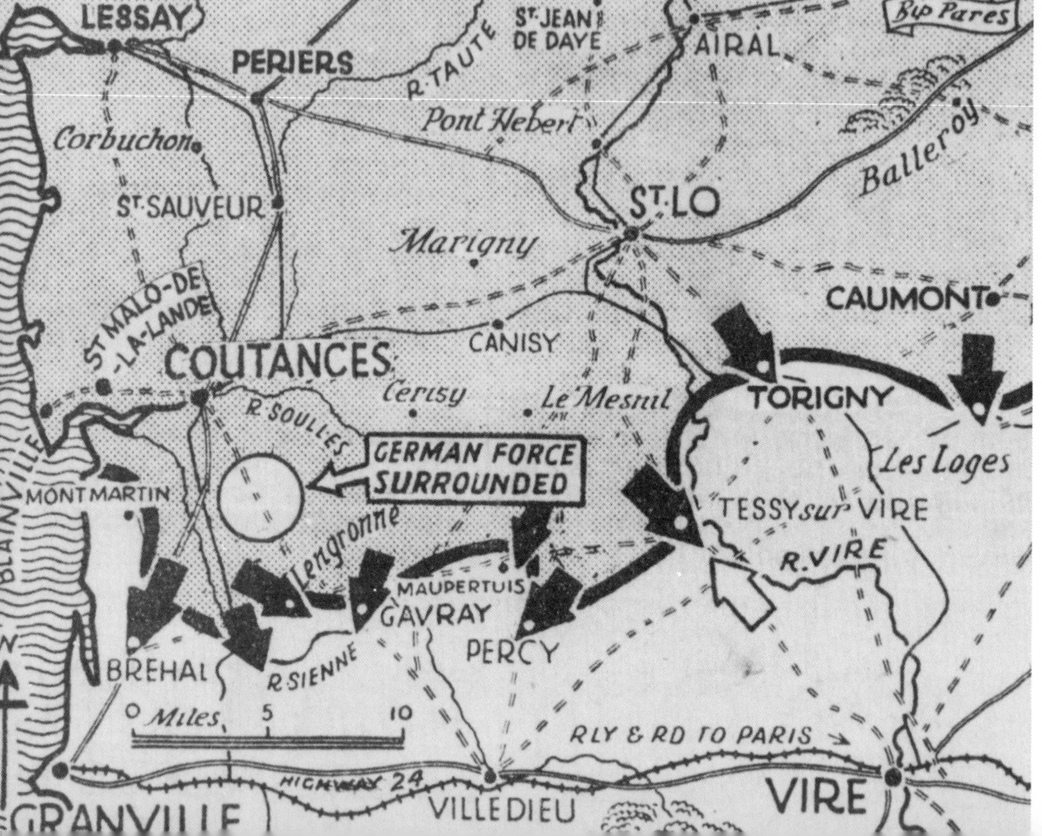

Left: Operation 'Cobra' swept onward from D+51 to D+53 creating the first of the Normandy pockets. In Roncey, 5–10 miles south of Coutances, elements of seven German divisions – including Panzer Lehr, Das Reich and Goetz von Berlichingen are trapped. The resultant break-out battles were very costly.

the defending divisions serving LXXXIV Corps west of St-Lô evacuated their positions and in phased operations degenerating into confused fighting as US armour sweeping towards Coutances threatened the retreating columns from the rear, sought to rally at Roncey, ten miles south-east of Coutances. Many panzer and infantry units caught up in the Seventh Army withdrawal were cut-off from parent formations, others engaged by marauding US armour were destroyed in bitter fighting. Acting upon their own initiative as communications failed, panzer battle groups varying in size and ability rallied as instructed in the neighbourhood of Roncey; Panzer Lehr to the east of the town, Das Reich, GvB and mixed infantry battle groups – the survivors of 275th, 353rd, 243rd and 91st Infantry Divisions also smaller combat and administrative units – were swept along in the crisis. OKW moves to restore the situation would come to depend upon panzer divisions transferred from the Caen wing of Panzer Group West (Eberbach) to the crisis sector south of St-Lô. In this area, between Tessy and Percy, 2nd Panzer Division (von Lüttwitz) and, twenty-four hours later, 116th Panzer Division (von Schwerin) bracketed into XXXXVII Panzer Corps (von Funck), were to launch heavy but unrewarding counter-attacks westwards. None of these attacks directed against US XIX Corps (Corlett) would translate into anything more than a local defensive success; the flow of US armour to the south continuing without interruption.

On the same day OKW ordered Army Group 'G' (Blaskowitz) to release 9th Panzer Division (Jollasse) reforming at Nîmes and dispatch it north to Alençon. Once there 9th Panzer could expect to join LXXXI Corps (Küntzen) moving in from Rouen. In control of 708th Infantry Division, taken from the Atlantic coast at Royan, local security battalions and 9th Panzer (elements), LXXXI Corps would form an offensive 'truppe' for the protection of Seventh Army's soon dangerously at risk southern flank [D+62–D+71]. Alençon's value to Seventh Army lay in its position at the centre of the Army's Normandy communications. Service installations of all descriptions packed the area; supply, engineer, workshop and signals units in particular. As a further measure in strengthening crisis command arrangements south-east of Mortain, a reserve Panzer Corps LVII (Krüger) was ordered north from Toulouse.

*On **28 July [D+52]**, 2nd Panzer Division (von Luttwitz), redeployed by Panzer Group West from the Caen battlefield at Bretteville, arrived west of Tessy. After establishing blocking positions forward of Tessy, 2nd Panzer prepared to counter-attack XIX US Corps (Corlett) by striking west in the direction of Villebaudon and Coutances. On the same day Das Reich, retreating south of Coutances, lost its Commander (Tychsen); the divisional HQ battle group being overrun by US 4th Armored Division at Trelly. Das Reich was then taken over by Otto Baum commanding GvB 17th SS Panzer Grenadier Division. Baum was also given command of all LXXXIV Corps units rallying between Coutances (lost during the day) and Roncey ten miles to the south-east – a superficially small area fast assuming the character of a pocket as US armour (2nd, 3rd and 4th Armored Divisions) sealed every escape route.*

*On **29 July [D+53]** GOC LXXXIV Corps (von Choltitz) ordered the defenders of the Roncey pocket to break out south-east. Forming* ad hoc *battle groups at the expense of many heavy weapons, particularly artillery, the encircled infantry and panzer/panzer grenadiers, seeking to bypass US blocking forces, struggled to comparative safety around Percy. Not all were to succeed in reaching XXXXVII Panzer Corps facing west with 2nd and (arriving) 116th Panzer Divisions; von Funck incorporated survivors of Panzer Lehr in defence of Percy. At St-Denis-le-Gast a particularly violent clash occurred when break-out units of Das Reich and GvB encountered 2nd US Armored Division. Casualties mounted. All too soon 2,500 German dead and 5,000 prisoners were testifying to the bitterness of the break-out battle while renewed attacks by II/116th Panzer Division west of Villebaudon failed against XIX US Corps (Corlett).*

*On **30 July [D+54]**, armoured columns of Patton's US Third Army, officially activated on 1 August (when Bradley stepped-up to command US 12th Army Group and Hodges assumed command of First Army), seized Avranches at the base of the Cotentin Peninsular. Next day Patton's armour would cross the Sélune to Pontaubault. The US break-through, which started six days earlier west of St-Lô, was complete; and while US First Army (Hodges) continued to press German Seventh Army battle groups further away from the Cherbourg–Avranches corridor, US Third Army (Patton) VII, XV and XX US Army Corps prepared for unrestricted mobile operations. The American's scheduled goal was Britanny, where the Atlantic coast ports (still strongly defended) were needed to supplement the limited stores-handling capacity of Cherbourg; but US Third Army's dynamic commander relished the prospect of breaking-out to the east. Driving for the Seine towards Le Mans (entered 10 August) through Seventh Army's open flank south of Mortain, Patton's hussar performance would precipitate the disastrous collapse of Army Group 'B' much feared by German commanders at the front. At this stage in the battle Montgomery devised a new plan for hastening the process of German disintegration.*

*Starting on **30 July [D+54]** and continuing until 6 August [D+61], whilst the panzer divisions south of St-Lô, 2nd, 116th, Battle Group Panzer Lehr, 2nd SS and 17th SS subordinate to XXXXVII Panzer Corps (von Funck) were striving to contain US First Army seeking to widen its corridor eastwards in the direction of Tessy, Vire and Mortain – British Second Army's 'Bluecoat' offensive (D+54) would threaten Vire from the north, creating fresh problems. Launched south-west of Caumont on an axis converging with US V Corps approaching Vire from the north-west Montgomery's new offensive struck 326th Infantry Division threatening to unhinge German defences at the junction of Seventh Army (Hausser) and Panzer Group West (Eberbach). Von Kluge's response to the dangers of 'Bluecoat' was immediate – Panzer Group West must further reduce its panzer commitment south of Caen concentrating instead for counter-action on the opposite flank south of Caumont – for which purpose Bittrich's II SS Panzer Corps headquarters was to quit the Odon, moving immediately to the area* (see also *Panzer Group West.)*

31 July [D+55] to 1 August [D+56]. *On 31 July, 21st Panzer (Feuchtinger) reinforced by 503rd (Tiger) Battalion, arrived south-east of Caumont, reinforcing 326th Infantry Division, unsettled by 'Bluecoat'; 10th SS Division Frundsberg (Harmel) meanwhile joined the action south-west of Villers-Bocage. They then launched counter attacks.*

On **2 August [D+57]**, *9th SS Panzer Division Hohenstaufen (Stadler), the kernel of the counter-attack forces assembling under II SS Panzer Corps to oppose 'Bluecoat' south-east of Caumont, came into action east of Vire reinforced by 102nd SS (Tiger) Battalion. More transfers and a panzer battle group (Olboeter) raised by 12th SS Panzer Division Hitler Jugend joined the battle for Vire, striking at Chênedollé east of the town. Aiming concentric blows at British armoured and infantry divisions (11th Guards Armoured and 15th Scottish) driving south-west from Caumont under VIII Corps (O'Connor), II SS Panzer Corps would win the race for Vire, averting the threat to Seventh Army's rearward communications. But despite the success of the SS Panzer Corps in stalling the British offensive north of Vire and slowing subsidiary operations by XXX Corps immediately to the east, Vire would be lost to US V Corps (Gerow) on 6 August. Mortain would also fall, with US VII Corps (Collins) entering the town on D+58.*

Simultaneously on **2 August [D+57]** *OKW was communicating Hitler's own counter-attack proposals to OB West. The proposals required von Kluge to mount a major offensive westwards across the Cotentin Peninsular, starting east of Mortain and aiming for Avranches; at least four panzer divisions would be needed for the twenty or so miles thrust to the coast and these, OKW argued, could be found by reducing Seventh Army/Panzer Group West commitments to a shorter line in general. Operation 'Lüttich' was intended once and for all to sever US Third Army's communications, bringing to an end the supplies and reinforcements flowing south to Patton. In the course of 72 hours this resourceful General had succeeded in passing no fewer than seven divisions across the Sélune bridge at Pontaubault. Sweeping aside a battle group rushed from St-Malo and ignoring attacks by the Luftwaffe, Patton turned XV Corps (Haislip) east into the practically undefended Seventh Army flank south of Mortain threatening Laval (7 August) and Le Mans (10 August). Other US (Third Army) Corps entering Britanny by way of Rennes (3 August) and St-Malo (18 August) pushed for the Atlantic ports – encountering determined resistance from 'fortress' garrisons. Hitler's counter-attack proposals, meanwhile developed by von Kluge, demanded the concerted effort of all the available panzer divisions under the command of a specially qualified panzer operations staff (Eberbach). Such proposals were not only unrealistic in the circumstances of total Anglo-US air supremacy – but suicidal.*

Hitler's map-table plans for an all out panzer offensive east of Mortain, redressing the strategic picture in the west came too late. There was no spare panzer capacity for operations on the grand scale envisaged by 'Luttich' – Montgomery's new offensive on the Vire had seen to that; for whatever panzer divisions von Kluge might have freed for a strategic offensive in the west in hope of destroying American chances of a rapid break-out, were (once again) absorbed in local fighting on the northern front. Furthermore, Eberbach's commitment to panzer group operations on the Vire, reacting to 'Bluecoat' and rumbles east of the Orne where I SS Panzer Corps (1st SS, 12th SS Panzer Divisions) was facing renewed Canadian interest in driving for Falaise, was clearly an overriding consideration. In the circumstances von Kluge decided that XXXXVII Panzer Corps (von Funck) alone should lead Hitler's offensive against US First Army, employing whatever panzer divisions could be assembled in quick time east of Mortain, and not as Hitler proposed in a comprehensive build-up waiting for relieving infantry and suitable (unsuitable for US air operations) weather.

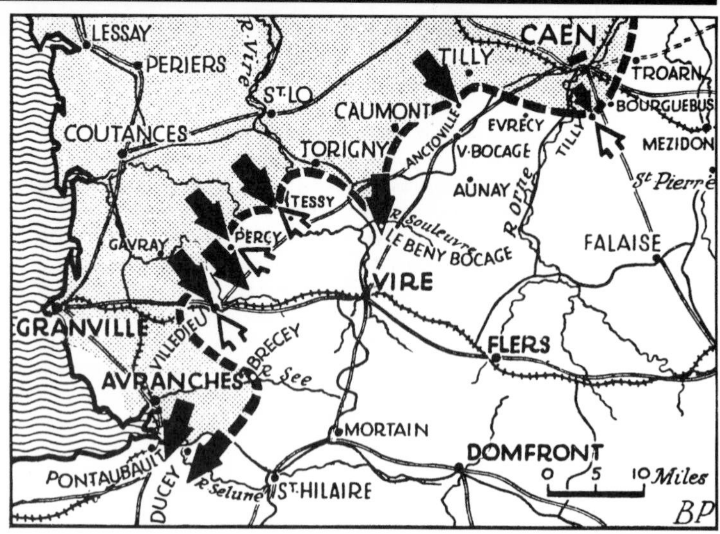

Above: On 31 July 1944 (D+55), General George Patton led the break-through to Pontaubalt; the panzer divisions escaping from Roncey retreated south-east. When Patton traversed the Sélune with seven divisions the enemy opposition was minimal. A week later Hitler ordered a suicidal counter-offensive to cut US lines of communication, but it ended in failure having been betrayed by 'Ultra' and brought to a standstill by superior Allied air power.

3 August [D+58] to 5 August [D+60]. *Patton's drive east in the direction of Paris and the Seine continued unopposed.*

6 August [D+61]. *By late evening of 6 August, 1st SS Pz Division en route from the Orne south of Caen (relieved by 89th Infantry Division) and 2nd SS Panzer Division disengaging from Seventh Army's front at Courson were assembling with 2nd and 116th Panzer Divisions east of Mortain. Supporting the projected panzer offensive were additional panzer battle groups – 17th SS (Fick) allotted to Das Reich, the assault formation at the centre of the counter-attack line-up east of Mortain, and 130th Panzer Reconnaissance Battalion taken from Panzer Lehr to protect the southern flank. Bayerlein's decimated division meanwhile contributed a small but effective battle group (Hauser) to the western defence of Vire where II Parachute Corps (Meindl), finally prised out of St-Lô, was fighting to ward-off converging US and British attacks.*

The effective panzer strength of 'Lüttich' was probably no more than 150 battle tanks; Pz Kpfw IVs and Panthers serving the panzer regiments involved, i.e., 3rd Panzer Regiment (2nd Panzer Division), 16th Panzer Regiment (116th Panzer Division), 1st and 2nd SS Panzer Regiments. The responsible Luftwaffe command (II Jagd Corps) had promised air cover and ground-attack support for the panzer divisions, with three hundred Me 109 and Fw 190 fighters flying from airfields around Paris. Other preparatory arrangements for 'Lüttich' involved the transfer of reserve infantry divisions, 363rd (Dettling) and 84th (Menny) from Fifteenth Army north of the Seine to LXXXIV Corps immediately north of the 'Lüttich' area. Under a new commander (von Elfeldt) LXXXIV Corps was to protect the right flank of the offensive. Zero hour was set for 0100 hours, 7 August [D+62]. But to the totally unexpected disadvantage of 'Luttich', the operation was fatefully compromised by another 'Ultra' coup. Forewarned on the eve of operations by 'Ultra' reporting tank concentrations north of Mortain, and air-support requests by the Leibstandarte (I SS) naming possible targets in the same locality. Allied Army and Air Force chiefs were given ample time in which to initiate counter-measures. The crucial element of surprise that might have carried the day for von Kluge was irretrievably lost and 'Lüttich', by which Hitler set much store would, by thrusting west away from the focal point of action by US Third Army driving east towards Le Mans, be turned instead to Allied advantage. The Mortain counter-offensive and von Kluge's crisis continued [D+62–D+71]. At this point we return to the northern front and action by Panzer Group West.

Too little, too late for Eberbach. 25 July (D+49) to 16 August [D+71]. Known as Panzer Group West until 2 August (D+57), Eberbach's HQ was redesignated, Panzer Army West 3–4 August (D+58–59), thereafter (D+60) Fifth Panzer Army. With Seventh Army in disarray as US First and Third Armies punched south, exploiting the breach west of St-Lô [D+49–D+61], British Second and Canadian First Armies were maintaining pressure to hold the panzer divisions in the east by bringing them into action south of Caen or, after D+54, south of Caumont. Montgomery's strategy of drawing the panzer divisions away from the American sector, enabling Bradley and Patton to break out of the Cotentin Peninsular and, with the least possible opposition, drive into Brittany, was to prove the positive factor in Allied success. At the time of the US break-out, with events at their most critical, there were more panzer divisions retained by Panzer Group West opposing the Anglo-Canadian armies on the Caen–St-Lô sector than facing US First/Third Armies on Seventh Army's sector between St-Lô and Lessay. A measure of the crisis gripping OKW and Army Group 'B' (von Kluge) as US armies developed 'Cobra' is evident in the changing ratio of panzer divisions deployed on the three main fronts; west and south opposing US First/Third Armies or north and east resisting British Second and eventually Canadian First Armies.

[*D+49*] Day one of the US break-out; west 3 : east 7

[*D+52*] Day four (Tessy counter-attack); west 4 (excluding Panzer Lehr 'destroyed') : east 5

[*D+61*] Day thirteen (Mortain counter-attack); west 5 (excluding Panzer Lehr 'destroyed') : east 4

[*D+69*] Day twenty (Alençon counter-attack); south 8 (excluding Panzer Lehr 'destroyed') : north 2

Tank deployment on [*D+49*] confirms the imbalance of panzer strength east and west; west facing US First Army, 110 tanks east facing British Second Army, 600 tanks. Thus seven of the ten panzer/panzer grenadier divisions deployed by OKW in Normandy on D+49 – 1st SS, 12th SS, 21st, 9th SS, 10th SS, 2nd and 116th – were in action with Panzer Group West, opposing British Second or Canadian First Armies or, in the case of 116th Panzer, in OKW reserve at Creil. Three other panzer divisions – Panzer Lehr (destroyed day one), 2nd SS and 17th SS (Panzer Grenadier) – opposed US First Army in the west, while the last of the panzer divisions to be committed in Normandy, 9th Panzer arriving Alençon [*D+61*] was at the time still *en route* from Nîmes. Of the seven panzer divisions detained in the east by Montgomery around Caen, where Panzer Group West was preparing for a renewal of Anglo-Canadian pressure following 'Goodwood' D+42–D+44 and OKW was expecting the main threat in Normandy, 1st SS, 12th SS, 2nd, 21st and 9th SS were serving I SS Panzer Corps (Dietrich) south of the town, leaving 10th SS on the Odon under II SS Panzer Corps (Bittrich) and 116th in OKW reserve.

The need for additional infantry divisions to free panzer divisions from front-line service had been recognized by Rommel and OKW soon after D-day, but Hitler's insistence upon maintaining the strongest possible force in the Pas-de-Calais, protecting V-1/V-2 sites or available to repulse an expected second landing, would deprive Army Group 'B' of its best source of reinforcement – Fifteenth Army, north of the Seine. When all too late at the end of July Hitler perceived the true threat to Seventh Army/Panzer Group West in the weight and direction of Allied attacks, OKW speeded the release of infantry divisions from Fifteenth Army to Normandy. Incoming infantry divisions – no fewer than eleven by 12 August (D+67) – were to be deployed along the northern front serving Panzer Group West or its successor, Fifth Panzer Army (D+60) on the Caen–Caumont sector especially. The panzer divisions freed by relieving infantry would then be expected to regroup for action under Eberbach at Mortain, but in practice failing to assemble in time would achieve success neither there [*D+62*] nor subsequently at Alençon [*D+66*].

25 July (D+49)–26 July (D+50). On 25 July with 'Cobra' west of St-Lô destroying Panzer Lehr [*D+49*], I SS Panzer Corps (Dietrich) in the east was subjected to renewed pressure by Canadian First Army (Crerar) pushing south towards Falaise.

Operation 'Spring' launched by the Canadians south of Caen from positions gained at the conclusion of 'Atlantic' – the Canadian counterpart to 'Goodwood' (D+42) – continued for 24 hours until the power of the defence, particularly by battle groups from 1st SS Panzer Division, proved unbreakable. But Allied pressure exerted simultaneously to the east by British XII Corps (Ritchie) on the Odon in Operation 'Express' D+46 and thereafter would result in bitter fighting for Maltot, a strong point eventually wrested from II SS Panzer Corps (Bittrich).

27 July (D+51) to 29 July (D+53). By 27 July, US success with 'Cobra' [*D+49*] was prompting Montgomery to re-assess Anglo-Canadian options for expediting the collapse of German Seventh Army (Hausser). Swinging VIII Corps west across the battlefield from Caen, where the Corps had stood at the conclusion of 'Goodwood', to Caumont where Panzer Group West linked up with Seventh Army, Montgomery proposed in Operation 'Bluecoat' to launch two armoured and three infantry divisions across the rear of German Seventh Army; Vire being selected as VIII Corps' objective. Subsidiary attacks by XXX Corps (Bucknall) would focus upon tactically important ground to the south-east. In the meantime, von Kluge's reaction to 'Cobra' was resulting in rapid panzer redeployment; 2nd and 116th Panzer Divisions being switched from Caen to a new concentration area south of St-Lô. 2nd Panzer (von Lüttwitz) leading the way west over the River Vire south of Vire itself on the night of the 27th made preparations for an immediate counter-attack westwards from Tessy; XXXXVII Panzer Corps (von Funck) in control (*see* [*D+52*]).

30 July (D+54). Operation 'Bluecoat', commencing on 30 July, with the intention of getting VIII Corps (O'Connor) into Vire, a point in the main battle line where Panzer Group

West (Eberbach) connected with Seventh Army (Hausser) – while XXX Corps (Bucknall) was making for Montpinçon the tactically important high ground to the east – provoked immediate response from von Kluge.

On **31 July (D+55)** II SS Panzer Corps (Bittrich) with Hohenstaufen (Stadler) and Frundsberg (Harmel) was ordered west from the Odon to Caumont; 21st Panzer Division (Feuchtinger), already under orders to move west from Caen where it had held the line in near continuous action since D-Day, leading the way. Feuchtinger's task was to restore the situation to von Kluge's advantage north of Vire where 11th Armoured Division (Roberts) driving for le Bény-Bocage had penetrated the defences of 326th Infantry Division. Hohenstaufen (Stadler) and Frunsberg (Harmel), trailing 21st Panzer Division in the race for Vire, where II Parachute Corps (Meindl), prised out of St-Lô by XIX Corps (Corlett), was holding the town with 3rd Parachute Division (Schimpf) and a Panzer Lehr battle group, were soon on the move. Other reinforcements for the defence of the threatened sector including a recce unit battle group (Olboeter) from 12th SS Panzer Division Hitler Jugend were also on the way. For the panzer divisions charged with neutralizing 'Bluecoat', speed was the order of the day. For von Kluge the 'Bluecoat' threat posed a grave dilemma. Coming as it did at a crucial moment, when the battle to contain the damage caused by the US break-out at Coutances [*D+54*] would require the commitment of at least four panzer divisions in counter-attacks expected of him by Hitler [*D+57*], Montgomery's powerful blow by three armoured and three infantry divisions striking at the hinge of Seventh Army and Panzer Group West while US Third Army punched east seemed likely to precipitate the kind of disaster predicted by Rommel.

31 July (D+55) to 2 August (D+57). Much to von Kluge's relief the counter-action started by 21st Panzer (Feuchtinger) and developed by II SS Panzer Corps (Bittrich) defending Vire – best viewed in the context of Seventh Army operations south of St-Lô [D+55–D+61] lifted the immediate threat to that Army's rear communications running eastwards south of the town. Despite this success by II SS Panzer Corps at a time of mounting tension occasioned by US success with 'Cobra', events on the northern front were moving towards no less a traumatic phase in the fortunes of Panzer Group West. Hitler's destructive influence on events in Normandy at this point is reflected in new orders from OKW reacting to 'Cobra' and its consequences – a Führerbefehl (directive) to von Kluge requiring him to mount a (suicidal) counter-attack east of Mortain (*see* Seventh Army [*D+62*]).

3 August (D+58)–4 August (D+59). Although Hitler intended that Eberbach should lead the action at Mortain, code-named 'Lüttich', von Kluge dissented, insisting instead that Eberbach should continue directing critical operations in defence of Vire and equally sensitive positions to the south-east of Caen. A renewal of British/Canadian pressure at these danger points could but not fail to snap an over-taut Army Group battle line, but as a first step towards improving command arrangements Panzer Group West was upgraded and redesignated Panzer Army West.

On **5 August (D+60),** however, a further change of name converted Panzer Army West into Fifth Panzer Army. But stripped within days by the Führerbefehl for 'Lüttich' [*D+62*] of all but two panzer divisions, 21st and 12th SS HJ, the Army would then consist of fewer than ten–eleven infantry divisions with which to defend a battle line stretching from the Channel coast at Cabourg south around Caen and on to Caumont 70 miles inland.

6 August (D+61)–7 August (D+62). British Second Army, exerting pressure north and east of Vire on 6 and 7 August, continued the task of holding II SS Panzer Corps (Bittrich) in action, closing a gap driven into II Parachute Corps lines at le-Bény-Bocage. In this sector 11th Armoured Division had breached the main battle line while other forces were assaulting Montpinçon, the tactically important high ground to the east. There, more British armour and infantry divisions including Guards and 7th Armoured Division supported the operation; II SS Panzer Corps, reacting to the threat, involved 9th SS, 10th SS, 21st Panzer and a HJ battle group in heavy defensive fighting. When a renewal of Allied pressure shifted the action once more to Caen, Canadian First Army offensives 'Totalise' (D+62) and 'Tractable' (D+67) would bring 12th SS Panzer Division Hitler Jugend back into the line with the support of 21st Panzer redeployed from Vire. This sequence of Allied attacks was to be largely successful in denying von Kluge an opportunity for massing all but four panzer divisions for the Mortain counter-offensive *[D+61–D+62]. While Fifth Panzer Army was juggling with panzer units in a bid to prevent a decisive break-through in the north, Seventh Army was launching Operation 'Lüttich', first mooted [D+57] and finally unfolding [D+62] under XXXXVII Panzer Corps (von Funck). In control of 2nd, 116th, 1st SS, 2nd SS Panzer Divisions and supporting battle groups, von Funck's offensive was not a success; Allied air attacks, 'Ultra' and a staunch US defence bringing the offensive to a standstill (see* [D+57–D+62].)

New orders were soon forthcoming from Rastenburg. On 9 August Hitler would demand that Eberbach renew 'Lüttich' with the additional power of II SS Panzer Corps and panzer divisions taken from Caumont (21st, 9th SS and 10th SS) and Caen (1st SS, 12th SS). *But in a rapidly deteriorating situation, with US Third Army racing east to Le Mans and threatening to isolate both Normandy armies, OKW was to re-shape its plans, directing Eberbach eastwards instead to counter Patton swinging an armoured corps (XV, Haislip) north from Le Mans [D+65] and threatening Alençon [D+66]. Situated 50 miles behind Seventh Army's front at Mortain and protected only by an emergency defence force, the Army Group's supply and communications centre at Alençon was directly in line with Patton's advance.* Retention of the base was crucial to the maintenance and supply resources of the German Army in the west. More significantly, Patton's radical change of direction northwards at a time when 'Totalise' D+63 was threatening to break up Fifth Panzer Army's holding positions south of Caen, thereby threatening Falaise, engendered well-founded High Command fears of encirclement – the gap between Allies converging on Falaise and Alençon being no more than 55 miles. Faced with this prospect OKW would soon be demanding the release of panzer divisions from Caen, Caumont and Mortain, all to be regrouped under a new command, Panzer Group Eberbach. The force so assembled was to be launched against US Third Army spearheads striking north from Le Mans. Alençon

Above: SS Standartenführer Kurt 'Panzer' Meyer, GOC, 12th Panzer Division HJ. A career SS officer, Meyer entered the Leibstandarte in 1932, served in Poland, France, the Balkans and Russia. He was transferred to Hitler Jugend in 1944 as CO, 25th Panzer Grenadier Regiment. In June of that year he succeeded Brigadeführer Fritz Witt, HJ's commander, who was killed in action. Meyer was subsequently taken prisoner at Amiens that September and command of HJ passed to Hugo Krass who was GOC at the time of operations in the Ardennes ('Autumn Mist', *see* map 17) and Hungary ('Spring Awakening', *see* map 19).

would be saved and conditions restored for a renewal of 'Lüttich' westwards.

Such were Hitler's intentions. The actual course of events, culminating in the total defeat of the panzer divisions in Normandy, is best followed in the context of Seventh Army operations on the southern front *[D+62–D+71]*. On the northern front at this critical juncture Fifth Panzer Army continued in control of the main battle line stretching from the Channel coast at Cabourg to the Seventh Army boundary south of Caumont and on to Vire, but battle lines generally were being shortened to allow panzer divisions to disengage and provide the necessary strength for Panzer Group Eberbach. With Fifth Panzer Army confirmed in a static role (under Dietrich after D+64), Panzer Group Eberbach would prevail as the principal armoured formation in Normandy – responsible to Seventh Army until 18 August (D+73) and thereafter directly to Army Group 'B'. Notwithstanding Fifth Panzer Army's almost total dependence upon infantry with which to combat Allied armour continually probing for brittle points along a 70–80-mile front, future action by the Army's sole remaining reserve, 12th SS HJ Panzer Division (Meyer) opposing Canadian First Army between Caen and Falaise would rank as a major episode in the Normandy history of the panzer force.

7 August (D+62). Operation 'Totalise' launched by Canadian II Corps (Simmonds) south of Caen, coinciding with German Seventh Army's Mortain offensive *[D+62]* faced I SS Panzer Corps (Dietrich) with unexpectedly powerful opposition. The Canadian force included in its order of battle two armoured divisions landed mostly within the previous fortnight, three infantry divisions and two independent armoured brigades.

Starting shortly before midnight on 7 August, in the wake of a powerful bombing offensive (3,500 tons of high-explosives on key targets), two assault infantry divisions breached the Panzer Army front at a point where 89th Infantry Division (Heinrichs) held the Caen–Falaise road south of Bourguébus, more or less where 'Goodwood' had left off on 20 July 1944 (D+44). Heinrichs' forward infantry and flanking units of 271st and 272nd Infantry Divisions were unable to resist Allied ground and air offensives tearing a five-mile gap in the German front and were overwhelmed. Nothing more than the nub of 12th SS HJ Panzer Division (Meyer), resting with emergency battle groups in reserve north of Falaise, stood between the Canadians and their objective – Falaise; the Leibstandarte (I SS LAH), hitherto the main stay of Fifth Panzer Army's defence south of Caen – now in the hands of 89th Infantry Division – having meanwhile been transferred (5–6 August) to Mortain for Seventh Army's 'Lüttich' offensive.

8 August (D+63). At midday on 8 August, main force 'Totalise', including 4th Canadian (Kitching) and 1st Polish (Maczek) Armoured Divisions with 400–500 tanks, formed up in columns facing south on each side of the Caen–Falaise road waiting to exploit any breach won by the infantry. Despite support from yet another wave of bombers unloading high-explosives on the defence, the Canadian drive, opposed at this point by 12th SS HJ Panzer Division, fell apart. Although further attacks south would continue spasmodically over the next 48 hours, by evening the tempo of the offensive had been lost. By D+66 'Totalise' had been abandoned. This unexpected check to the Anglo-Canadian offensive is attributable to the handling and élan of HJ battle groups co-ordinating defensive action with the firepower of 101st SS (Tiger) Battalion; the German Army's battle skills, always a positive factor in the Normandy campaign, being seen here at their best despite the handicap of total air inferiority and the absence on other fronts of two sizeable battle groups; a Schnellgruppe (Olboeter) – one SPW and one pz coy with Wasp and Recce units at Vire, and one Panzer Regiment (Wünsche) with three panzer companies, a Tiger Company and two panzer grenadier battalions on a neighbouring front at Grimbosq. Grossly outnumbered in tanks and infantry, Meyer assembled HJ's remaining divisional and support units into a battle group (Waldmüller) comprising II Panzer Battalion (39 Pz Kpfw IVs), an anti-tank battalion (Jagdpanzer VIs), a Tiger Company (10 Pz Kpfw VIs), a panzer grenadier battalion (I/25), two other companies, ancillary flak (8.8cm) and Werfer troops.

The SS corps/divisional plan of defence was simple. Instructing Battle Group Wünsche to return immediately from Grimbosq where it was reinforcing 271st Infantry Division opposing a dangerous British incursion on HJ's left flank, Wünsche on arrival later in the day was deployed as a mobile reserve and second line of defence on high ground overlooking the Caen–Falaise road north of the River Laison

– the last defensible Fifth Panzer Army position between Caen and Falaise. In a blocking move closer to the enemy, a detachment of Tigers under Michael Wittman, commanding 101st SS Tiger Battalion, with 138 tank destructions to his credit (*see* D+7), also panzerjaeger and flak troops – used in a ground role – would advance to Cintheaux blocking the Caen–Falaise road directly in the teeth of the expected Canadian armoured attack. HJ's main counter-attack battle group Waldmüller, with the remaining armour and support units, would be committed right flanking against Polish armoured spearheads rolling south in support of the Canadians. The resulting clash of armour, putting an end to Canadian hopes of a swift and decisive break-through to Falaise, was marked by the death of Michael Wittman – in action against a superior force of Shermans seeking to force a way through Cintheaux. The Canadians were nevertheless denied their objective until early evening. At other points along the sector Waldmüller halted Polish progress, later breaking free of encirclement. Regrouping after dark in new positions north of the Laison, the division prepared for yet another Canadian offensive.

On **9 August (D+64)** with the battle for Falaise reaching new heights of violence, Canadian and Polish armoured divisions struggled to push south against HJ battle groups including panzer Kampfgruppe Wünsche now firmly established in blocking positions north of the Laison. At Fifth Panzer Army headquarters during the afternoon, orders arrived to the effect that Hitler required Eberbach to lead a renewal of 'Lüttich' [*D+62*]. Intending to take panzer divisions from Caumont and Caen – resisted in the case of HJ, totally unable to disengage – 'Lüttich' was now an unalterable Führerbefehl; Eberbach being Hitler's chosen executive. Bittrich's II SS Panzer Corps with 9th and 10th SS was to move immediately from Caumont to Mortain, joining 2nd, 116th, 1st SS and 2nd SS in a counter-offensive aimed at Avranches across the rear communications of US Third Army (Patton) stretching back to Cherbourg. But to the concern of OKW and von Kluge, US Third Army spearheads identified north of Le Mans driving in the direction of Alençon 40 miles south of Falaise changed the picture completely and within days Eberbach would be preparing instead to save Alençon by counter-attacks against US Third Army (Patton) pushing north from Le Mans [*D+65*].

10 August (D+65)–11 August (D+66). On the Falaise front more heavy fighting was developing as Hitler Jugend inflicted severe losses on Polish/Canadian armour attempting to work south; HJ battle groups reinforced by 102nd SS Tiger Battalion (released by II SS Panzer Corps moving to Mortain where the Corps' heavy weapons would be less effective in the attack) and a bicycle battalion from 85th Infantry Division finally breaking the Canadian offensive. Counter-attacking a Canadian battle group (Worthington) occupying Hill 140, a key feature north of the Laison – HJ's last line of defence – a concentric attack by Panthers, IVs and Tigers destroyed 47 Shermans or other Canadian tanks. By the end of the day in the battle for Falaise with the advantage going to the defence, German tank strength opposing Canadian First Army stood at seventeen Panzer IVs, seven Panthers, eleven Tigers and perhaps ten Jagdpanzer IVs. When replaced in the line north of the Laison by 85th Infantry Division, HJ in its weakened state was withdrawn into corps reserve and at the end of D+66 prepared for the next Canadian onslaught.

12 August (D+67) to 16 August (D+71). Starting on 12 August, Operation 'Tractable' culminating on the 16th (D+71) in the capture of Falaise, renewed Canadian First Army's (Crerar) efforts to win the objective that had so long escaped its grasp. Assisted by air attacks launched against the defence in massive strength and the co-ordinated

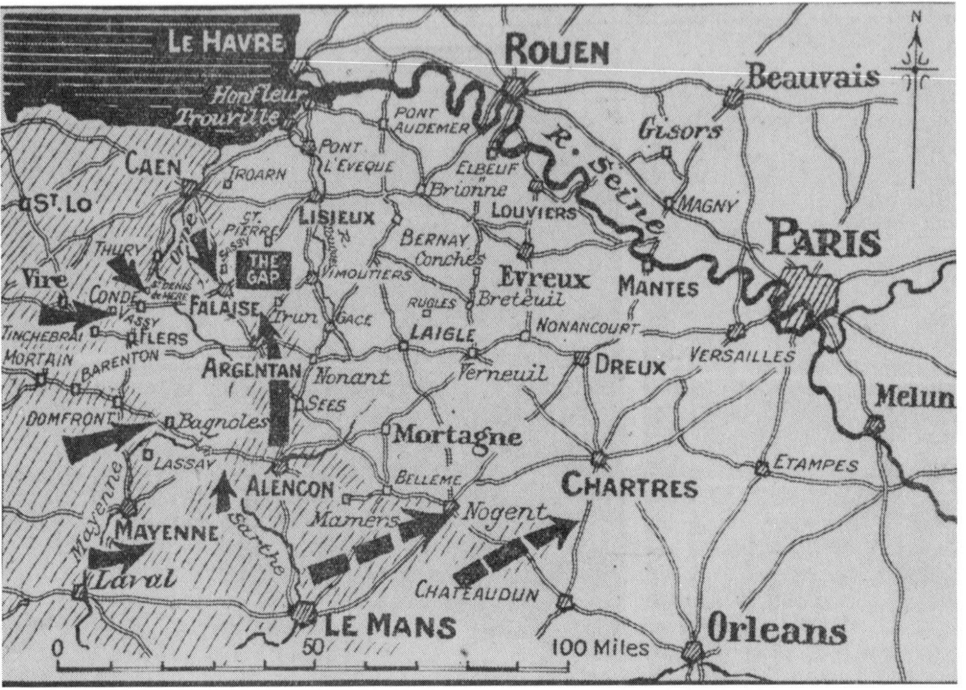

Left: 15 August 1944. D+70. Patton's Third Army swung north from Le Mans to threaten von Kluge with encirclement. When contact was established between the Anglo-Canadian and US Forces at Chambois (1st Polish Armed Division, US 90th Infantry Division) the 'gap' was closed until a relief attack by II SS Pz Corps, previously evacuated from the pocket, re-opened the escape route.

Above: 17 August 1944 D+72. Pictured here is a battle group of the Hitler Jugend (Hitler Youth) Division changing positions after defending the northern shoulder of 'the gap'; through this gateway Model evacuated the Falaise pocket, leaving behind 10,000 dead and 40,000 prisoners-of-war. Hitler Jugend was largely responsible for the Allied failure to push quickly into Carpiquet, Caen and Falaise.

pressure of British Second Army pushing from the north-west, 'Tractable' would bring HJ and the only other panzer division available to Fifth Panzer Army, 21st Panzer, back into action, holding off the northern arm of an Allied pincer closing inexorably behind two German armies and a Panzer Group. The gap between Allied armies was now less than 40 miles separating Canadians at Falaise from Americans north of Alençon. Neither HJ nor 21st Panzer Division in battles to ward off encirclement were to escape increasingly bitter fighting in defence of Falaise and eventually the northern shoulder of the pocket when Allied pincers closed on [D+74]. In this critical situation HJ Panzer Division reduced to three panzer grenadier battalions of two companies (two in SPWs), 24 Pz Kpfw IVs a handful of Jagdpanzers, flak and ancillary troops – the equivalent of no more than a single regiment – yet the mainstay of I SS Panzer Corps on the Laison, resumed defensive operations against Canadian First Army. The German infantry divisions holding the Panzer Army line north of Falaise, 85th, 89th, 270th, 271st, notably under-provided with anti-tank weapons, were swamped in the Canadian attack; HJ battle groups reduced to fifteen Pz Kpfw IVs could no longer restore the situation for Fifth Panzer Army.

By **15 August (D+70),** HJ battle groups supported by 21st Panzer Division were fighting either in the ruins of Falaise or defending tactically important ground to the east. 21st Panzer (Feuchtinger), forming two battle groups (Luck) and (Rausch) but no better equipped than HJ to stem the Canadian offensive, was to be set against 1st Polish Armoured Division redirected eastwards on Trun, a key communications point on the Panzer Army's main east-west route and still open to the defence in an increasingly constricted pocket. But for OKW the impending loss of Falaise was only one of several issues exercising staff minds. The southern arm of the pincer was closing fast. Alençon was lost, Argentan, hitherto regarded as a firm base for the defence of the southern front, going the same way; the entire Normandy campaign was a disaster with Seventh Army, Fifth Panzer Army and Panzer Group Eberbach virtually a write-off. And, to Hitler's consternation, von Kluge was missing. After setting out on a visit to Hausser and Eberbach at Nécy nothing more had been heard of him.

But the most pressing of problems besetting OKW in the west at this time of crisis was the landing of US and French forces in the area of Army Group 'G' (Blaskowitz) on the Mediterranean coast between Cannes and Toulon. In Operation 'Dragoon', aimed at the Rhône valley, the Allies were pouring ashore 86,000 men, 12,250 vehicles and 46,000 tons of stores – the *matériel* strength of US Seventh Army (Patch) with which French 1st Armoured Division (Vigier) was included. An Allied thrust north along the Rhône valley was clearly intended to bypass German First and Nineteenth Armies deployed in the south and still protecting Mediterranean or Atlantic coasts and hinterlands. At Toulon and Marseilles, 244th and 242nd Infantry Divisions stood firm as ordered; other garrisons were similarly expected to defend key Atlantic ports. For the rest, retreat was in prospect with 11th Panzer Division (von Buttlar) acting as rear and flank guard for Nineteenth Army departing from the Mediterranean coast and First Army making its way north-east from the Atlantic to the Rhine as best it might.

On **16 August (D+71)**, with the battle for Normandy degenerating beyond recovery, Hitler sanctioned the withdrawal of Army Group 'B' while simultaneously ordering the withdrawal of Army Group 'G' from the Mediterranean. Von Kluge – despite his belated reappearance at Fifth Panzer Army Headquarters, now operating outside the pocket at Meulles, was to be 'recalled' for consultation with Hitler.

In von Kluge's place Hitler appointed Field Marshal Walter Model, a panzer general whose loyalty and adroitness in defence of the Eastern Front had greatly impressed him.

Walter Model – 3rd Panzer Division; XXXXI Panzer Corps; Ninth Army and latterly Army Group North Ukraine – would arrive at La Roche-Guyon the following day, too late to change the course of events in Normandy, but in time to conduct the escape of ruined divisions in phased withdrawal. Retreating from encirclement in the Argentan–Falaise pocket before crossing the Seine and withdrawing through France and Belgium was to become a horrendous undertaking, one that would bring the German Army back to the frontiers of the Third Reich. This traumatic development of the war in Normandy, obliging II SS Panzer Corps to launch relief attacks from outside the pocket (D+75), would be followed by the capture of Eberbach on 31 August (*see* D+74–D+76). Here, panzer action in Normandy returns to Seventh Army's critical southern front [*D+62–D+71*], tracing the failure of Hitler's counter-attack at Mortain where 'Lüttich' proving ill-conceived would culminate in the encirclement of Army Group 'B' on 19 August (D+74) – the German Army's least glorious day in France.

Crisis in Normandy *7 August [D+62] to 16 August [D+71].* ***7 August [D+62].*** *Hitler's intelligently conceived but in the circumstances suicidal plan to halt the flow of US armour and infantry pouring into Brittany and penetrating east behind Seventh Army, code-named 'Lüttich', was about to trigger an Army Group crisis of the first magnitude. Intended as a 20–25-mile thrust west from Mortain to the coast at Avranches to sever American First Army communications, but compromised from the outset by another 'Ultra' coup alerting the defence and allowing counter-measures to be initiated before midnight on [D+61], even as the first spearheads of XXXXVII Panzer Corps were crossing the start-line, 'Lüttich' was doomed to failure. With skies clearing and giving access to the battlefield on the morning of D+62, Allied air forces were soon inflicting serious delay on the panzer divisions: right, 116th and 2nd Panzer; left, 1st SS and 2nd SS Panzer. Launching round the clock air attacks against exposed panzer columns, US Air Forces brought 'Lüttich' to a standstill – the first time that a panzer offensive had been rendered wholly ineffective by the concentrated use of air power. Elsewhere, in ground action, US units moving into blocking positions prepared the defence of strong points. But the crisis factor in 'Lüttich' was its timing and direction. Thrusting west with the best available panzer divisions at a time when US Third Army was driving powerfully and virtually unhampered in the opposite direction, 'Lüttich' was actively encouraging envelopment. And in the mean time at Mortain, where prolonged resistance by US 102nd Infantry Regiment (30th Division) was blocking Das Reich and delaying the movement of subordinate battle groups assaulting from the east (Battle Group Fick, 17th SS Panzer Grenadier Division), the offensive was fast losing momentum. At the same time other factors were giving rise to von Kluge's concern over slow progress – the late arrival of 1st SS Panzer Division from Caen (delayed when a crashed fighter aircraft forced the division to find a new and time-consuming route to the battlefield); a panzer battalion from 116th Panzer Division 'otherwise engaged', but above all the total absence of the Luftwaffe. Kept away from the battlefield by Allied air forces striking at II Jagd Corps (Pelz) on support airfields in the vicinity of Paris, the Luftwaffe was incapable of mounting a single sortie in support of the panzer divisions.*

During the afternoon, the arrival at von Kluge's headquarters of a special courier (General Buhle, OKH chief of staff at OKW) bearing a Führerbefehl would require the Field Marshal to release panzer divisions immediately from other fronts and renew the offensive under General Eberbach (Fifth Panzer Army). The Führerbefehl raised more difficulties for von Kluge. Facing intense pressure at Caumont and Caen where the panzer divisions under Fifth Panzer Army (Eberbach) were fully committed – 9th SS, 10th SS and 21st Panzer at Caumont, 12th SS at Caen – the best that he could do for the moment was to get 10th SS moving from Caumont to Mortain and plan a follow-up with II SS Panzer Corps (Bittrich) bringing 9th SS and 21st Panzer south; 12th SS was also put on notice to move. Both II SS and XXXXVII Panzer Corps were then to be responsible to Eberbach. Most worrying to von Kluge was the openness of Seventh Army's southern flank, penetrated by US Third Army (Patton) as far as Le Mans – 50 miles to Seventh Army's rear. The arrival of 9th Panzer Division (Sperling) 24 hours earlier at Alençon, reinforcing 708th Infantry Division and security battalions contriving a south-facing front under LXXXXI Corps (Küntzen), gave rise to minor satisfaction, but immediately on arrival 9th Panzer Division's Panther battalion was redirected north, strengthening I SS Panzer Corps left with only 12th SS Panzer Division at Caen. The battalion was later returned uncommitted to cope with the mounting crisis in the south. By the end of the day von Kluge was advising OKW of his intention of renewing 'Lüttich' with the addition of II SS Panzer Corps. Subordinate to Eberbach as required by Hitler, a new start was planned for 10 August [D+65].

8 August [D+63]–9 August [D+64]. *'Lüttich' was meanwhile less than halfway to its Avranches objective, held in check by US ground and air forces and virtually at a standstill. At the centre of operations defending Hill 307 were four companies of US 102nd Infantry Regiment enveloped by Das Reich but denying the tactically important high ground east of Mortain to the SS and persistently inhibiting the westward movement of attacking units through the town. On other sectors too attacking divisions, for example 2nd Panzer Division (von Lüttwitz), farthest* *ahead at le Mesnil-Tôve, was failing against mounting opposition while being constantly hammered in low-flying attacks which robbed the offensive of energy and strength. Later in the week, with the tide of battle receding, US observers were to count more than a hundred panzer wrecks on the battlefield. For the Allies in Normandy D+63 was to prove a day of momentous decision. The beckoning opportunity for encircling Seventh Army and Fifth Panzer Army presented by Patton's unstoppable thrust to the east was not to be missed. Bradley proposed the motion; Montgomery concurred. Allied plans to envelop Army Group 'B' by uniting an Anglo/Canadian/US pincer movement on a north/south Falaise–Argentan–Alençon axis were agreed; Patton would swing north from Le Mans.*

*On **10 August [D+65]**, Intelligence reports reaching von Kluge confirmed US Third Army's change of direction; Haislip's XV Corps was identified swinging north from Le Mans threatening Alençon and the Army Group's vital east-west supply route Alençon–Flers. The move was correctly interpreted for what it was – the southern arm of an Allied pincer closing on Army Group 'B'. The Mortain offensive was called off. The panzer divisions were to be redirected. Panzer Group Eberbach [D+66] would instead launch a counter-attack into the flank of US Third Army threatening Alençon. On the outcome of Eberbach's action was to depend the future of the Army Group.*

***11 August [D+66].** The crisis gripping Army Group 'B', suffering pressure on three fronts, north, east and south, was a trial of strength for the Normandy High Command and its front-line leadership. Unable to find a strategy to match the situation, Hitler's orders were to stand firm here, shorten a line there, move panzer divisions and bring in the infantry, but served more to confuse than clarify the issue. The Luftwaffe's absence from the battlefield; petrol and ammunition stocks dwindling to the point of exhaustion because the area was largely sealed against replenishment by Allied air forces compounded the problem. The panzer divisions now faced tasks well beyond their powers. 9th SS Panzer Division, for instance, reported its strength as ten Pz Kpfw IVs, thirteen Panthers, fifteen assault guns and ten Pak 7.5cm. Inside the pocket, slowly closing but not yet sealed, motorized movement of troops and transport in daylight on roads swept by artillery and air strikes was time-consuming and hazardous; infantry supply columns choking the roads with horse-drawn vehicles added to the trauma. Night moves presented traffic control and transport staffs with endless problems deciding priorities, sorting traffic and handling units of all descriptions vying for the use of a decreasing number of roads in a slowly constricting pocket.*

***11 August [D+66] to 14 August [D+69].** Building Panzer Group Eberbach by redeploying panzer divisions from the north and north-west to meet the crisis at Alençon in the south was Army Group priority. But Alençon fell on 12 August [D+67] before Eberbach had gathered the strength necessary to choke-off American progress. The defence of Alençon, Seventh Army's supply base, enveloped by US XV Corps (Haislip) had been entrusted to LXXXI Corps (Küntzen), deploying 9th Panzer (Spurling) since 6 August [D+61], 708th Infantry Division, four security battalions and the rump of Panzer Lehr (Bayerlein). Much too weak to withstand the relentless pressure of US armour and infantry enjoying continuous air support in their drive toward Falaise and a junction with Montgomery, the defence collapsed and fighting moved forward in the direction of Argentan where 116th Panzer Division, switched from Mortain and at first deployed south of the town, would reinforce the defence. Provoked by the loss of Alençon and the danger threatening Argentan, next in line and no more than twelve miles short of Falaise, Hitler issued fresh orders. Panzer Group Eberbach (LVIII Panzer Corps, XXXXVII Panzer Corps) was to be reinforced and US XV Corps was to be counter-attacked from the west. Starting from the area of Carrouges north-west of Alençon (where 2nd and 116th Panzer Divisions, redeployed from Mortain, stood their ground with the help of units from 9th Panzer), the offensive was to be supported by attacks from the opposite flank delivered by II SS Panzer Corps; the resulting pincer closing at Sées, midway between Alençon and Argentan, cutting off Haislip's XV Corps from US Third Army. Reinforcements for Eberbach, 9th SS, 10th SS and 21st Panzer Divisions were to move immediately.*

In the event, demands for reinforcements elsewhere by I SS Panzer Corps defending Falaise against 'Tractable' [D+67–D+71] was to claim 21st Panzer; 10th SS, unable to break free of commitments under LVIII Panzer Corps (Krüger) arriving east of Mortain from Toulouse (originally a reserve Panzer Corps HQ) eliminated Frundsberg; 9th SS Hohenstaufen, on the other hand, was able to disengage from battle south-east of Vire, proceeding on 13 August [D+68] to join 2nd SS Das Reich, assembling for Eberbach's offensive in the Forêt de Petite Gouffern east of Argentan. But air attacks, delaying the movement of panzer divisions to assembly areas flanking US XV Corps driving north on its Alençon–Argentan axis, west (2nd, 9th, 116th) or east (2nd SS, 9th SS), and short-falls in ammunition and petrol supplies forced Eberbach on to the defensive. The unremitting efforts of US 12th Army Group (Bradley) to narrow the Falaise–Argentan gap by exerting pressure all along the front, compounded German problems. And, unknown to OKW or those in command at the front, US and British forces were warned by 'Ultra' of the dangers threatening US XV Corps on its crucial north-bound axis. Their reaction was to halt progress north of Argentan and shift the axis of envelopment eastwards from Argentan–Falaise to Chambois–Trun. This change of emphasis in OKW strategy departing from cordoning to belated armoured riposte, engaging US Third Army (Patton) on the Alençon–Argentan–Falaise axis, is illustrated in Panzer deployment.

> ***14 August [D+69].** Day twenty of the US break-out.*
> *Seventh Army and Panzer Group Eberbach.*
> *10th SS (LVIII Panzer Corps), 2nd, 9th, 116th (XXXXVII Panzer Corps) 1st SS, 2nd SS, 9th SS (II SS Panzer Corps) plus Panzer Battle Groups Lehr and 17th SS.*
> *Fifth Panzer Army: 21st, 12th SS (I SS Panzer Corps).*

*On **15 August [D+70]**, Hausser contracted Seventh Army battle lines in the west and north-west, allowing the panzer divisions to disengage for action at Alençon. US First Army (Hodges), extending its grip on operations at the conclusion of 'Lüttich', pushed east reinforcing the pressure of US Third Army probing north-east around Argentan (without Patton). On the opposite side of the pocket, attacking from north and north-west, British Second and Canadian First Armies stepped up the drive to enter Falaise. At this critical time for von Kluge and the panzer divisions in Normandy,* *a fresh problem was creating anxiety for Army Group 'G' in the South of France where Operation 'Dragoon' involving a second Allied expeditionary force was disembarking men, vehicles and stores on beaches between Cannes and Toulon (see Fifth Panzer Army [D+70]). On this day of crisis von Kluge went missing. Travelling to Nécy, Eberbach's headquarters between Falaise and Argentan, contact was broken and although the Field Marshal reappeared early the next day at Fifth Panzer Army Headquarters, Meulles, outside the pocket, Hitler appointed a new OB West/GOC Army Group 'B' – Walter Model [D+71].*

***16 August [D+71].** At this point, much to the surprise of his subordinates, Hitler ordered Army Group 'G' (Blaskowitz) to evacuate the South of France while also agreeing to the evacuation of the Falaise (Morteaux–Chambois) pocket by Army Group 'B' where command still rested with von Kluge who pulled II SS Panzer Corps (Bittrich), Das Reich and Hohenstaufen out of the pocket and into Army Group reserve east of Vimoutiers, a communications centre twelve miles to the east. On the same day, at Führer Headquarters in East Prussia, Hitler briefed Walter Model, OB West designate, on the situation in Normandy. Too late to change the course of events there, Model would preside over the escape of ruined divisions and a phased withdrawal of Army Group 'B', now perilously close to finding itself sealed into a pocket east of the Dives.*

Model takes over. 17 August (D+72)–18 August (D+73). By **17 August (D+72),** the plight of Army Group 'B', defending a pocket on the Dives extending seventeen miles west to Briouze and 12–15 miles deep between Morteaux and Chambois, was so desperate that nothing the new OB West, Field Marshal Walter Model could do was likely to turn the situation to German advantage – despite Model's distinguished record of defensive operations in the east. An evening conference with von Kluge and staff at Army Group 'B' Headquarters (La Roche-Guyon) followed a morning briefing by chief of staff von Blumentritt at OB West Headquarters (St-Germain-en-Laye) putting Model in the picture. Next day (D+73) for a close-up of operations in Normandy, the Field Marshal proposed to visit Fifth Panzer Army Headquarters at Fontaine-l'Abbé. There Hausser, Dietrich and Eberbach stated their views on the chances of survival for whatever remained of eleven panzer divisions, a comparable number of infantry and two parachute divisions facing an uncertain future in or about the Falaise pocket. Now closed to escape on three sides, there remained on the Dives to the east a gap of 12–15 miles between Morteaux and Chambois where exhausted divisions with their last vestige of strength held the Allies apart. Through this corridor, dominated by heavy artillery and tactical air forces operating at full power in support of American, British and Canadian armies re-directed to converge on Chambois, the remnants of two German armies and a Panzer Group would seek escape from envelopment on the scale of Stalingrad. But the state of the panzer divisions – key to any successful break-out operation – whose deterioration was daily more evident in strength returns to higher headquarters, and fuel and ammunition stocks diminishing to the lowest ever level following the loss of Alençon [D+67] allowed Model little optimism for believing that the 80,000–100,000 men still inside the pocket could be evacuated to safety behind the Seine as initiated by von Kluge on [D+71].

For the troops at the front, artillery fire and air strikes launched by the besieging ground and air forces against every vehicle movement, troop concentration, bridge and cross-roads within the pocket were a constant danger. By inhibiting the use of traffic centres and forcing motorized columns into competing with infantry on back roads, sharing the protection of forest and woodland, assembly times and operational grouping were at all times significantly compromised. Nevertheless, the redeployment of panzer divisions in the crisis inherited by Model, starting with the pattern established by von Kluge [*D+71*], was set to continue. Hohenstaufen and Das Reich, already on the move out of the pocket into Army Group reserve at Lisieux, were halted by Model at Vimoutiers. Accompanying II SS Panzer Corps (Bittrich) eastwards the move was not without incident. When Hohenstaufen unexpectedly encountered Polish armour on the Trun–Vimoutiers road, the SS division was lucky to force a break-through, collecting evacuated units in a new assembly area west of Vimoutiers. At the same time, 12th SS HJ and 21st Panzer serving Fifth Panzer Army (Dietrich) defended the northern shoulder of the pocket. Standing their ground south and east of Falaise, 12th SS (Meyer) and 21st Panzer (Feuchtinger) battle groups persisted in bitter action, delaying Canadian 4th

Below: 17 August 1944. D+72. Field Marshal Walter Model took over Army Group 'B' and command in the west. He had served in the offensive against Moscow earlier in the war (with Third Panzer Army, December 1941) and before his arrival in Normandy had earned a reputation for ruthlessness as GOC, Ninth Army in their defence of Rshev and Army Group North Ukraine after Operation 'Citadel' in July 1943. Model led Army Group 'B' through 'Autumn Mist' (*see* Sixth Panzer Army, December 1944) before his suicide in the Ruhr pocket at the end of the war.

Opposite page, left: General Leo Geyr von Schweppenburg entered the army in 1904 with the 26th Light Dragoon Regiment. He served the Reichswehr as CO of the 14th Cavalry Regiment and from 1933 to 1937 he was Military Attaché in London and Brussels. In 1937 he became GOC, 3rd Panzer Division and in early 1940 he was GOC, XXIV Panzer Corps. After spells with XXXX and LVIII Panzer Corps he was appointed Panzer General West, based in Paris, in 1943. He then led Panzer group West until replaced by General Eberbach.

Opposite page, right: General Heinrich Eberbach joined the army in 1914 and served in the western (at Champagne, where he was disfigured) and south-eastern theatres (in Macedonia), ending it on the staff of the Turkish Eighth Army. After a post-war period in the police, he enlisted in the Wehrmacht in 1935 where he gained experience in an anti-tank battalion before rising to command 35th Panzer Regiment. In 1941 he was OC, 5 Panzer Brigade/4th Panzer Division during its time at Tula in Russia. In March 1942 he became GOC of the division and in November, GOC, XXXXVIII Panzer Corps until he was wounded at Stalingrad. In 1944 he was appointed GOC, Panzer Group West (subsequently renamed Fifth Panzer Army), before serving briefly as GOC, Seventh Army prior to his capture at Amiens in August 1944.

(Kitchner) and Polish 1st (Maczek) Armoured Divisions directed south of Morteaux on a Trun–Chambois axis. The defence of this critical sector was the responsibility of I SS Panzer Corps (Krämer); other Fifth Panzer Army sectors between the coast and Condé being left to infantry divisions. Away to the south, separated from Dietrich by a 12–15-mile gap in which the hamlets of Trun, St-Lambert, Moissy and Chambois collected escape routes taking retreating columns nose to tail out of the pocket, Panzer Group Eberbach retained the strongest concentration of panzer 'divisions'.

Forced on to the defensive by the rapid advance of US Third Army pushing north from Alençon (on routes leading to Chambois) Eberbach sought to block American progress north of Carrouges and also at Argentan where 116th Panzer Division was turning the town centre into a strong point to be held until the last day of the break-out [*D+76*]. Weakened by failure at Carrouges [*D+66–D+69*], Panzer Group Eberbach comprised 2nd, 9th, 116th (plus 9th Panzer's Panther Battalion), Panzer Lehr remnants split and waiting release for refitting, 17th SS (mostly outside the pocket, forming battle groups for the defence of Dreux and St-Germain) and I SS LAH. The controlling headquarters was that of von Funck's XXXXVII Panzer Corps. In resisting the pressure of US Third Army intensified by air attacks and 2ème Division Blindee (Leclerc) thrusting north-west of Alençon through the Forêt d'Ecouves, 9th Panzer Division (Sperling) was practically destroyed. The American drive north from Le Mans, seeking contact with British and Canadians south of Caen had been led by French 2nd (Leclerc) and US 5th Armored Divisions, responsible to XV Corps (Haislip); but this situation was about to change following standstill instructions issued by Bradley to Patton on 13 August [*D+68*]. A new plan for closing the 'gap' would require a specially constituted US 'provisional' infantry corps (Gerow) to lead the operation.

Freed from the Argentan sector, Haislip's XV Corps would instead lead Patton on a 'long' envelopment of Army Group 'B', reaching the Seine at Mantes–Gassicourt [*D+74*].

At the western end of the pocket, where Seventh Army was retreating step by step under immense pressure, 10th SS Panzer Division – reduced to eight tanks and one-third of its normal strength, but reinforced by a 9th Panzer battle group – resisted all attempts by British and American divisions to collapse the Army's rearguard. Withdrawing north-east from Domfront, 10th SS imposed frustrating delays on both US First Army (Hodges) striking for Briouze, and British Second Army (Dempsey) squeezing a way east around Flers; control of the panzer divisions in the extreme western sectors rested with LXXXIV Corps (Elfeldt) and LVIII Panzer Corps (Krüger). Altogether some seventeen Allied armoured and infantry divisions were directly engaged in

the task of sealing the Falaise pocket – delayed for a while by a bomb-line controversy and minor confusions – but in the circumstances, a foregone conclusion.

On **18 August (D+73),** at Model's morning conference with senior commanders outside the pocket at Fifth Panzer Army Headquarters (Fontaine–l'Abbé), crucial decisions were taken in respect of a relief operation by II SS Panzer Corps (Bittrich). The meeting was attended by von Gersdorf, deputising for Hausser who at his own request remained behind at Panzer Army HQ (Villedieu); Dietrich and Eberbach both being present. Instructing Eberbach to supervise the operation using for the purpose Bittrich's HQ at Vimoutiers, Model proposed to block the jaws of the powerful Allied pincer closing on Chambois. Success would depend upon the speed with which Bittrich's two SS panzer divisions could collect sufficient strength west of Vimoutiers for the three–five-mile push to Trun–Chambois on fuel to be delivered by air transports to forward airfields. Within 48 hours, Seventh Army, Fifth Panzer Army and Panzer Group Eberbach would be across the Dives, regrouping behind the Toucques ten miles to the rear. Divisions fighting inside the pocket including Eberbach's Group (while he remained outside at Vimoutiers) were placed under the orders of Seventh Army (Hausser). For the relief thrust, Eberbach was allotted II SS Panzer Corps (Bittrich) comprising 2nd SS and 9th SS Panzer Divisions pushing to Trun (the northern shoulder of the pocket) and XXXXVII Panzer Corps (von Funck) deploying 2nd and 116th Panzer Divisions around Argentan (the southern shoulder of the pocket). But by mid-afternoon despite selfless action by HJ and 21st Panzer battle groups, Trun had fallen to Canadian 4th Armoured Division assisting the Poles of 1st Armoured Division pushing south to Height 262 above Coudehard and then on to Mont Ormel dominating the vital Vimoutiers-Trun relief/escape route. An alternative passage Chambois-Vimoutiers four miles south was not so threatened.

By late evening, Army Group 'B's escape corridor was at best no more than a 4–5 mile enfiladed gap separating encircling Allied armies. US progress with 90th Infantry Division striking north for Chambois with flank protection provided by 2nd French DB (Battle Group Langlade) had now carried to the southern edge of the village, leaving only St-Lambert and Moissy in the centre of the corridor to offer the best chance of escape. The pocket was all but closed. The disgraced OB West, von Kluge – recalled by Hitler 'for the sake of his health' – had started earlier that morning from La Roche-Guyon for Germany. News of his death by self-administered poisoning *en route* from Verdun to Metz arrived at La Roche-Guyon late in the day.

Break-out from the Falaise pocket 19 August (D+74) to 21 August (D+76). On **19 August (D+74),** Allied armies closed the Falaise pocket. In the event this set-back to Model's plans for an orderly evacuation of Army Group 'B' as agreed with the Army Commanders (D+73) was not the outright disaster that might have been expected. Break-out groups, encouraged by the relief operation mounted next morning by II SS Panzer Corps (Bittrich), would succeed in escaping until D+76 when the relieving SS panzer divisions (2nd SS/9th SS) started their own phased withdrawal to the Seine. Previously withdrawn into Army Group reserve, Das Reich and Hohenstaufen pushing forward to the Dives from the east and north-east would establish a corridor in the space of a morning, making contact with escape columns fighting their way out across the river between St-Lambert and Chambois. By the time of the break-out the Falaise pocket had assumed the character of an embattled bridgehead, box-shaped and with an area of less than 25 square miles; its escape side on the Dives to the east. Bounded by the river meandering four miles between Trun and Chambois, but nowhere more than five feet deep although in parts steeply banked and wooded, the Falaise pocket included the forested acres of Gouffern sheltering a mass of exhausted units: wheeled transport, horse transport, armoured fighting vehicles, ancillary services and headquarters constituting the embattled remnant of Army Group 'B'. At 1700 hours, when closure was effected by US 90th Division (Maclain) uniting with 1st Polish Armoured Division (Maczek) in Chambois, the area contained the headquarters of two armies (Fifth Panzer Army, Seventh Army) a Panzer Group (Eberbach, who personally remained outside the pocket at II SS Panzer Corps Headquarters Vimoutiers–Meulles, directing the relief operation), four army corps (LXXIV, LXXXIV, II Para, XXXXVII Panzer) six infantry divisions, six or seven panzer divisions and 3rd Parachute Division.

Certain panzer units and higher headquarters were already on their way out of the pocket, released by Model

Above: Obergruppenführer Wilhelm Bittrich served in the 1914–18 war as a pilot and from 1932 to 1933 as an air force officer. He then transferred, in 1934, to the SS Verfügungstruppe and by 1938 he was Battalion CO II/SS Deutschland. In 1939–40 he was a Standartenführer in Poland and France; then he served on the Moscow sector of the Eastern Front in 1941 before leading 'Hohenstaufen' at Tarnopol in 1944, and then at Caen. He succeeded Hausser as GOC, II SS Panzer Corps and led the Falaise relief attack on D+75. He was subsequently prominent at Arnhem, the Ardennes, and Hungary.

for refitting (Panzer Lehr) or re-employment in defensive positions between the Dives and the Seine (17th SS, 21st Panzer, I SS Panzer Corps, LVIII Panzer Corps) where Patton's 'long' thrust – to the Seine at Mantes via Dreux – was threatening a second envelopment. Negotiating the chaos in the pocket due to a totally inadequate road system and artillery fire pouring in from all sides, evacuating units crossed the Dives between St-Lambert and Chambois; retreating transport, individual vehicles even, suffering the unavoidable hazard of marauding rocket-firing Typhoons and fighter-bombers. The Luftwaffe, long since vanquished and rarely appearing in its close-support role for the Army, occasionally provided some Ju 88s to assist the ground forces in difficult situations, but air-transported supplies of fuel brought to forward airfields for the panzer divisions (Eberbach) was the principal evidence of Luftwaffe battlefield activity. Timed for 2230 hours and phased to coincide with the relief operation by II SS Panzer Corps (0500 hours [D+75]), two break-out columns: left, II Para Corps (Meindl) moving via St-Lambert; right, XXXXVII Panzer Corps (von Funck) moving via Chambois, were to strike east in the direction of Vimoutiers. Meindl's column, mostly on foot, was to cross the Dives at St-Lambert protected by a vigorous rearguard defence of Magny delaying Canadian progress south of Trun. The column was to be lead by 3rd Parachute Division (Schimpf) and a small HJ detachment.

Von Funck's column, allotted the superior bridge and road facilities leading east via Chambois, incorporated panzer elements still mobile in the pocket; the Leibstandarte (1st SS LAH, 116th and HJ (tracked units)) leading. A key objective for both relief and break-out columns was Hill 262. (Overlooking Coudehard straddling the escape route five miles east of the pocket, this tactical feature, like Mont-Ormel east of Chambois, was already dominated by Maczek's armour.) A rearguard, basically 12th SS HJ (Meyer) and a 21st Panzer battle group (Rauch), would be responsible to LXXXIV Corps (Elfeldt). Such were the Army Group plans for breaking free of encirclement.

In the event, with communications failing, units whose movements were dictated by hostile artillery, tank and anti-tank fire, followed at dawn by air-attacks destroying the cohesion of most break-out groups, direction was often lost and units reduced to diminishing numbers. Many units planning to join 'organized' columns or making their own arrangements when communication with superior headquarters was lost, failed to make good their escape. Hausser, the Seventh Army Commander, escorted by II Para Corps, was wounded; Elfeldt, the rearguard commander, with his HQ was captured. Wisch, the Leibstandarte's CO was among the severely wounded and Wünsche, the commander of 12th SS Panzer Regiment taken prisoner. Many others were killed, wounded or captured in break-out battles. Meindl's column was pinned down by fire from the Poles on Hill 262 and holed-up for much of D+75. Contact with the relieving panzer divisions pushing to Coudehard via Champosoult and Hill 262, where the Polish Armoured Division was taken under fire from all sides, was established at midday but not until dusk was the corridor properly secured. The mobile escape column directed on Chambois, including units of 1st SS, 12th SS, 2nd, 9th, 116th and 10th SS Panzer Divisions, found Chambois unshakeably held by Polish/US units. Break-out groups searching for alternative ways across the Dives resorted to Moissy and St-Lambert, bringing out little more than battalion handfuls of men and vehicles; most heavy weapons, tractors and towing-machines being destroyed or abandoned beforehand.

The Dives was a killing-ground. Enfiladed by Canadian armour and artillery, the river banks, particularly in the key escape area of St-Lambert, proved a strong disorganizing factor for break-out groups; smashed transport and war *matériel* encumbering every possible crossing-point turned a comparatively minor obstacle into a hazardous hindrance.

The relief attack by II SS Panzer Corps had started on schedule at 0500 D+75, twelve miles east of the Dives. From positions south-west of Vimoutiers, where Bittrich had collected units of 2nd SS Das Reich and 9th SS Hohenstaufen, the relief attack would rely mostly upon surprise and stamina pushing with minimum support (Corps Werfer and Tiger detachments) into contact with the break-out columns. But Bittrich's attack in the direction of Trun and St-Lambert triggered a major confrontation between Das Reich and Polish armour; controlling Hill 262, the Poles dominated the break-out/relief route at this point. With panzer grenadiers of III SS Panzer Grenadier Battalion (Werner) mounted in SPWs, a handful of Pz Kpfw IVs and a Panther leading Der Führer (Weidinger) west, the SS isolated Polish strong points before making contact with Meindl's column at midday.

In the ensuing tank/anti-tank action around Boisjos, a defended helmet blocking the use of the Trun–Chambois road to escape groups, Polish and German casualties were particularly heavy. Hohenstaufen, in action north of Das Reich and attacking the Polish flank in the direction of Les Champeaux, was least successful and shortly after midday D+75 the offensive was discontinued.

Notwithstanding this check to the northern attack, Bittrich's escape corridor, won at heavy cost to both break-out and relief groups, was held overnight and well into next day. At 1600 hours on 21 August, D+76, orders for Der Führer to retire were received and acknowledged by the regimental commander (Weidinger); the battle of Normandy was entering its final phase – retreat to the Seine. Estimates of the numbers breaking-out and crossing Der Führer's lines vary from 8,000 to 10,000 of an estimated 20,000 'freed' by Das Reich; leaving 10,000 dead and 40,000 prisoners in the pocket. A lesser cause for satisfaction was the pitifully small number of armoured fighting vehicles brought out by the panzer divisions – fewer than seventy Pz Kpfw IVs and Panthers, a handful of SP flak and some personnel carriers (SPWs). The last panzer division to leave the pocket was 2nd Panzer Division (von Lüttwitz), defending St-Lambert where undestroyed bridges helped escape groups searching for east-west escape routes. At 2100 hours on D+76, calling in his west bank units, von Lüttwitz retired east across the Dives moving in the direction of Coudehard. Less fortunate was a 116/9th Panzer battle group blocking US progress through the town centre at Argentan. Unable to disengage in time to prevent encirclement, the battle group surrendered. In the subsequent and final phase of the Battle of Normandy, with fighting in the neighbourhood of the Dives subsiding as fewer escape groups filtered east or ended their resistance in isolated rearguard pockets, panzer divisions would be organized into heterogeneous battle

Above: Self-propelled anti-tank guns continued their dominant role in tank battles, serving heavy Army anti-tank battalions east and west. Among the latest and best examples serving in Normandy was the Jagdpanther Sdkfz 173 mounting an 8.8cm Pak 43 which was effective at 1,000 yards.

groups defending a Seine bridgehead at Elbeuf–Rouen. At the highest level of command, OB West's difficulties were multiplying, Paris was threatened and the chances of an orderly Army Group withdrawal west of the Seine diminishing. Equally at risk were joint OKW/OB West plans for the defence of northern France. The underlying cause of these problems was the unstoppable progress of Patton's US Third Army developing a 'long' envelopment to the Seine – sixty miles east of the Dives.

Escape across the Seine. 22 August (D+77) to 30 August (D+85).

Starting on 22 August (D+77) and continuing until 30 August (D+85), panzer operations in Normandy constrained by the loss of equipment in the Falaise pocket were restricted to defensive measures protecting Army Group 'B' withdrawing from the Dives to the Seine. Local counterattacks culminating in defence of Rouen were all that panzer divisions could manage in the aftermath of the disaster at Falaise. Driven into a bridgehead of 200–300 square miles west of the Seine, protected on the north side by the Channel coast, in the west by the Toucques but with an inland flank stretching back 70 miles from Gacé via Dreux and Evreux to the Seine at Mantes, the future of Army Group 'B' was only marginally less precarious than at the time of its recent encirclement. In the fighting already described, the Western Allies had destroyed in less than three months the power of two German armies (Fifth Panzer Army and Seventh Army) and a Panzer Group (Eberbach), eliminating in the process three times more panzer divisions than were lost at Stalingrad – three (plus three motorized infantry divisions). A new danger also threatened the retreating Army Group – the 'long' envelopment by US Third Army (Patton) thrusting to the Seine at Mantes–Gassicourt, a crossing-place giving access to north-west Paris. At this point on the river, Patton had already crossed to the north (east) bank, posing a threat to Paris while re-directing two army corps including XV (Haislip) north along the west bank of the river towards Elbeuf and Rouen – which if successfully concluded would finally choke-off all escape routes for Army Group 'B'. Outmanoeuvred yet again by the speed of Patton's advance, Fifth Panzer Army was forced into defending bridgeheads north and south of Rouen where inclusive of Duclair and Elbeuf sixty ferries were evacuating escape groups with their vehicles and equipment to the north (east) bank.

Only the presence of emergency battle groups formed from rear or reconstituted units of burned-out divisions – like that of 12th SS (Battle Groups Wahl and Mohnke) and 17th SS (Battle Group Fick) prevented the threatened US break through to Elbeuf. Defending bridgehead approaches at Vernon and Louviers (where Battle Group Fick was overrun), improvised battle groups incorporating replacement transport and artillery personnel held back the enveloping wing of US Third Army until I SS Panzer Corps could bring a contribution to reinforce the threatened flank. Much of this burdensome rearguard action, the key to

Model's programme of phased withdrawal to the Seine, exploiting natural obstacles in the west such as the Toucques 4–5 miles east of Vimoutiers, lay with II SS Panzer Corps (Bittrich). Collecting units that by filtering or fighting their way around Polish, Canadian, US and French armour, had run the gauntlet of escape routes leading out of the Falaise pocket, II SS Panzer Corps added 21st and 10th SS Panzer to 2nd SS and 9th SS Panzer Divisions previously employed in the relief attack (D+75). As other divisions – reduced to material levels equivalent to depleted panzer companies – were collected in viable numbers, notably 1st SS, 2nd and 116th Panzer, they too were employed in defence of important centres *en route* to the Seine where ferries, pontoon bridges, assault boats and local river craft transported all they could to the safety of the north (east) bank. With pressure increasing on the Elbeuf flank, II SS Panzer Corps was moved back in defence, bringing 2nd SS with twelve Pz Kpfw IVs and little more than two panzer grenadier battalions; Battle Groups 21st Panzer and 9th SS, remaining in the west would protect Orbec, Bernay and Lisieux (LXXXVI Corps) for as long as circumstances permitted.

Defending a contracting bridgehead until the night of 29/30 August (D+84/85) when 9th SS in Rouen crossed to the north bank, Army Group 'B' succeeded in transferring totally unexpected numbers of men and material across the river. Ignoring day and night attacks by Allied air forces, 25,000 vehicles were saved for the next phase of operations taking Fifth Panzer Army (Dietrich) and Seventh Army (Eberbach) over the Somme and Maas to the German frontier – but at the cost of more transport, tanks and heavy weapons (mainly flak) saved during the retreat from the Falaise pocket but now abandoned on the south bank. OB West was later to report that 'None of the panzer divisions crossing the Seine could muster more than ten tanks.' A total of eleven panzer divisions: 2nd, 9th, 21st, 116th, Panzer Lehr, 1st SS, 2nd SS, 9th SS, 10th SS, 12th SS and 17th SS (Panzer Grenadier) – (about one-third of the panzer force) caught in successive envelopments or near envelopments had been virtually eliminated from the German order of battle, and whereas they would nominally reappear in the west, notably in the Ardennes (Fifth Panzer Army, Sixth SS Panzer Army) on 16 December, their élan and fighting power had ended in Normandy.

Retreat through France and Belgium 31 August to 16 September. The consequences to Army Group 'B' of its loss of eleven panzer divisions in Normandy was an enforced retreat from the Seine north and east of Paris (entered 24 August by US 4th Infantry Division and 2DB Française, Leclerc) to the western borders of Germany; a movement simultaneously matched by Army Group 'G' retiring from Atlantic and Mediterranean coasts to the Rhine. With no panzer reserves to speak of and lacking the battlefield support expected of the Luftwaffe, Model was deprived of any of the crucial resources for turning retreat into victory – in the way that Manstein had shown possible in the Ukraine (Fourth Panzer Army) in February 1943. Such a telling riposte as Manstein's would have required no less than the total rehabilitation of the panzer divisions eliminated in all but name from OKW's order of battle – a re-equipment programme entrusted in fact to a new General der Panzertruppen West, General Horst Stumpff. Not surprisingly a counter-offensive on this scale, involving Fifth Panzer Army (von Manteuffel) and a new Sixth SS Panzer Army (Dietrich) was already taking shape in Hitler's mind. Code-named 'Autumn Mist', Hitler's last offensive in the west would start shortly before Christmas (*see* Fifth Panzer Army and Sixth SS Panzer Army, 16 December). Meanwhile, whatever the state of battle groups recovering from defeat west of the Seine, panzer operations in the first week of September would continue in desultory fashion north and east of Paris, but without General Eberbach, taken prisoner (31 August) in circumstances described later. Battle groups brought together under temporary command, like those of Mohnke and Fick west of the Seine before evacuation, included Gruppe von Schwerin built out of 1st, 2nd, 12th SS and 116th Panzer, while other Battle Group 'divisions' – 9th SS, 10th SS and 21st Panzer provided I and II Panzer Corps with a modicum of strength, counter-attacking at crisis points as they developed on the line of retreat through France and Belgium.

Fifth Panzer Army (Dietrich) and Seventh Army (Eberbach in succession to Hausser, wounded escaping across the Dives with 3rd Paratroop Division) retreated across northern France and Belgium to Aachen, Germany's gateway to the Ruhr, closely pursued by 21st Army Group implementing a broad front strategy devised by General Eisenhower. North of Aachen a new headquarters, First Paratroop Army (Student) close by Tilburg, extemporized defences between the city and the coast north of Antwerp whilst First Army (Chevallerie von Knobelsdorff), redeployed from south of the Loire to south of Trier, established a grip on the Rhineland, separated by a short gap from Nineteenth Army (Wiese) arriving from the Mediterranean on the upper Rhine north of Basle. On the Channel coast, Fifteenth Army (von Zangen) filtering its remaining infantry divisions northwards across the Scheldt into Holland was bypassed by 21st Army Group thrusting to Antwerp. The Army was fortunate in escaping disaster on the Normandy scale. Meanwhile, on 31 August General Eberbach's Seventh Army Headquarters, temporarily located at Albert north of the Somme, was surprised by British Second Army (Dempsey) and overrun. Eberbach was taken into captivity. Other commanders and staffs had narrow escapes. Model (OB West) and Dietrich (Fifth Panzer Army and Seventh Army in succession to Eberbach), also threatened by the pace of the Allied advance, moved swiftly out of the area.

On the Allied side three Army Groups implementing Eisenhower's 'broad front' strategy while fanning out north and east of Paris, captured Antwerp (4 September) with its port installations undamaged (British Second Army, 21st Army Group) but unusable on account of Fifteenth Army's defiant retention of the Scheldt estuary – and a week later thrusting for the Ruhr, threatened Aachen (US First Army, 6th Army Group, Devers) and Metz (US Third Army, 12th Army Group, Bradley). By 12 September, when command changes and new dispositions were taking effect in the west, the majority of the 'Normandy' panzer divisions were deployed under Seventh Army (Brandenburger) aligned north to south: 9th, 1st SS, 12th SS, 2nd SS, 2nd and 116th – between Aachen and Luxemburg.

Seventh Army's primary role was the defence of Aachen (116th and 9th Panzer) where arterial routes via Jülich and Düren allowed access to Cologne, gateway to the Ruhr and a major concentration of German defence industries. Protected by the Siegfried Line (Westwall) – constructed before 1939 and now undergoing emergency rehabilitation – Aachen was rightly considered a vital post in the German scheme of defence in the west. Fifth Panzer Army also serving a new commander General der Panzer Truppe Hasso von Manteuffel (Seventh Panzer and GD) responsible to Army Group 'G' (Blaskowitz) was directed by OKW to prepare a new Hitler-inspired offensive. Manteuffel's task would be to assault the right flank of US Third Army (Patton) moving against Metz, jeopardizing production in the Saarland and indirectly threatening the Ruhr. These tasks thrust upon Fifth Panzer Army and Seventh Army by Hitler and OKW, were wholly inconsistent with their disastrously depleted strengths. With fewer than 100 tanks, 600 aircraft and no reserves in the west, OKW scraped together training units – whatever their state of readiness – drafted naval ratings, police units, Luftwaffe and SS personnel into *ad hoc* battalions of all kinds to reinforce depleted formations such as Fifth Panzer Army with 17,000 effectives (less than the strength of a single division), infantry formations reduced to company strength – about to face 2,000 Allied tanks backed by 14,000 aircraft.

RAD construction battalions and army engineers acting under the supervision of western Gauleiters with instructions to slave in restoring 'Siegfried' defences – linked with stretches of the Maginot line into a somewhat illusory Westwall – discovered that vital maintenance equipment and artillery had been extracted for installation on the Atlantic coast. New panzer brigades, heavy (Army) anti-tank and assault gun battalions, Volksgrenadier infantry divisions (VGD) and VG support units – raised by Himmler in his capacity as OC, Replacement Army, would do little to regenerate the western Army Groups commanded once again by von Runstedt, recalled to serve as OB West (effective 5 September 1944). Troop transfers from other fronts, notably two panzer grenadier divisions, 3rd (Denkert) and 15th (Rodt) from Italy, deployed (26 August) west of Metz, were reinforcing First Army (von Knobelsdorff), Army Group 'G' (Blaskowitz), while certain of the panzer divisions, mostly burnt-out in Normandy, Panzer Lehr, 11th, 21st Panzer and 17th SS Panzer Grenadier Divisions, were falling back through Lorraine defending the Saar. In addition to these reinforcements, First Army would also receive 25th Panzer Grenadier Division (battle group) rebuilding in the west after returning in June from Army Group Centre.

Among other measures taken by OKW to rehabilitate the panzer force in the west (22 August) was the appointment already noted of a General der Panzertruppen West (Stumpff), supervising the refitting of the Normandy panzer divisions – especially those deployed along the German frontier Aachen–Trier where Army Group 'B' (Model) held

Left and right: Tank-hunting at close quarters was greatly assisted by a new generation of hand-held recoilless anti-tank weapons. The Panzerfaust could penetrate six or more inches of Allied armour at 50 yards with its hollow-charge grenade, whilst the Panzerschreck was used to strengthen the protective power of infantry and panzer grenadiers.

the line. A later OKW directive (11 September) would name 'Sepp' Dietrich as the general responsible for refitting the (six) SS Panzer divisions west of the Rhine (*see* Sixth Panzer Army). These developments, assisting Hitler's plans for continuing military operations for the next eight months, would frustrate all Allied hopes of putting an early end to hostilities entering their sixth year. Despite chronic shortcomings in the Army's stocks of motor transport, armoured fighting vehicles, weapons, munitions, vehicle fuels and spares – compounded by massive Allied air attacks against targets deep in Germany – there was to be no collapse in the fighting spirit or command apparatus of the Wehrmacht. Nowhere was German refusal to countenance defeat more apparent than in Holland, north of the Albert Canal, where First Paratroop Army (Student) blocked a British Second Army thrust into north Germany. Reinforced with a single battalion of 25 Jagdpanzers and a company or two of mixed flak, Generaloberst Student's 'Army' with HQ south of Tilburg (Goirle), consisted of Luftwaffe recruits organized into five parachute regiments, reserve (convalescing) infantry regiments, local defence militia and a martial miscellany of all kinds with a handful of regular paratroop battalions (FJR 6, 1/FJR 2) deployed in support.

Forming mixed battle groups with these and two low-grade infantry divisions, Student proceeded to establish a remarkably effective defence of a hitherto unprotected northern flank and, in a later Command move, was given Army Group 'H' (18 November) with responsibility for defending Holland between the North Sea coast and Venlo. The Army Group comprised First Paratroop Army (Schlemm) and Fifteenth Army (von Zangen) withdrawn from Belgium across the Scheldt into South Beveland. But a greater surprise in store for Allied planners than Student's improvised defence of Holland was the presence there of panzer divisions redeployed from Normandy. Lying north and east of Arnhem in Army Group 'B' reserve behind First Paratroop Army were the northernmost of the panzer divisions refitting under II SS Panzer Corps (Bittrich) – 9th SS Panzer Division (Harzer) and 10th SS Panzer division (Harmel). It was to be the unconfirmed presence of these SS divisions in Holland and their reaction to airborne invasion that would compromise the forthcoming British offensive 'Market Garden'.

Panzer reaction at Arnhem 17 to 26 September. The remarkably swift reaction of II SS Panzer Corps (Bittrich), deploying emergency battle groups against British 1st Airborne Division (Urquhart) striking for the more distant of five bridges needed to provide a passage for British Guards armour thrusting for the Ruhr was to result in the destruction of all Montgomery's hopes of shortening the war by an imaginative although mishandled airborne operation 'Market Garden'. First Airborne's objective in Montgomery's

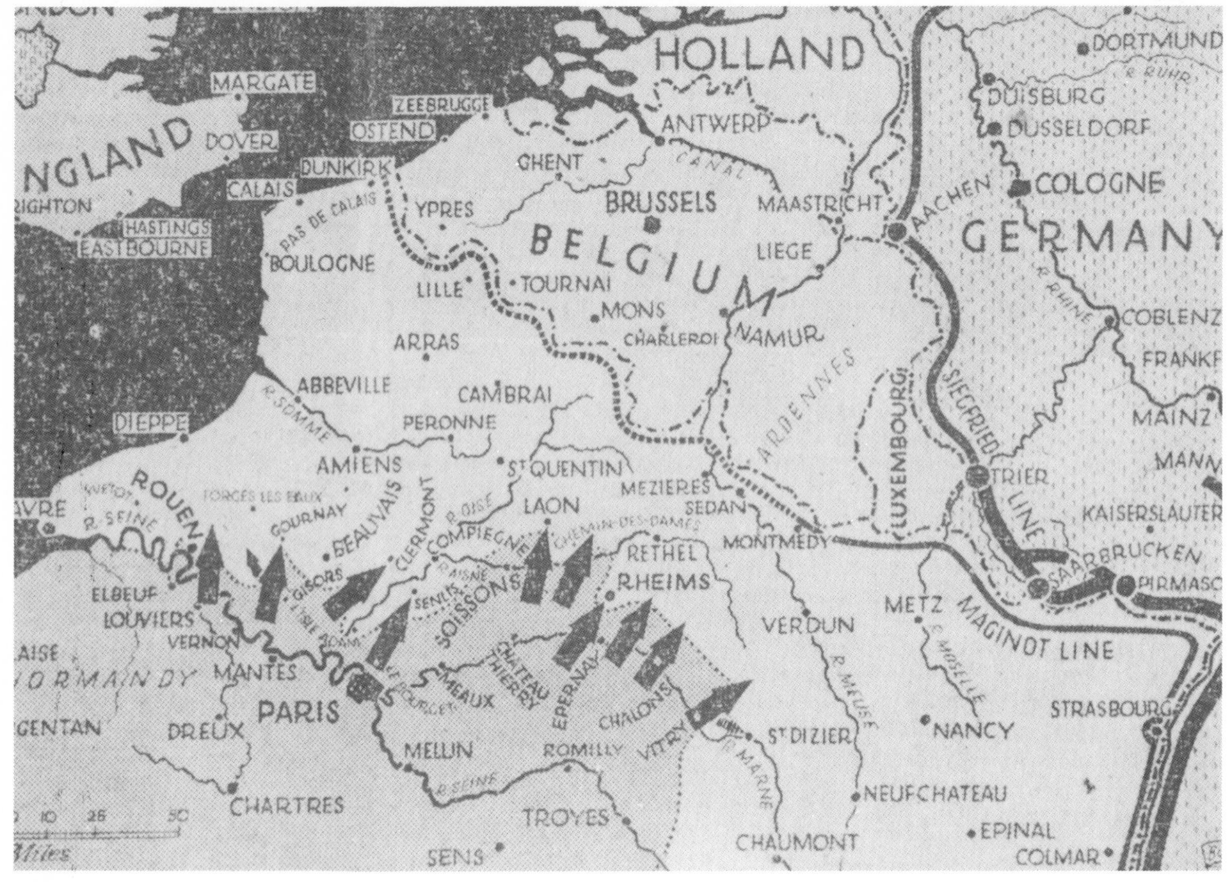

basically five bridge plan to pass Anglo-Canadian forces (21st Army Group) through Holland, and north Germany into the Ruhr, was the capture of Arnhem road bridge intact while simultaneously two US airborne divisions 101st (Taylor) and 82nd (Gavin), dropping south between Eindhoven and Nijmegen, seized others. The resulting Grave–Arnhem corridor was to have given British XXX Corps (Horrocks) an easy ride to the north and relief contact with 1st Airborne. But whereas the US paratroops, benefiting from collaboration with British armour at Nijmegen and twice fighting off 107 Panzer Brigade attacking from the west and cutting the corridor, secured their objectives, General Urquhart's men struggling to reach the bridge from a dropping zone located (in Student's view) too far west, and by a twist of fate close to Model's HQ in Oosterbeek – failed to win through in strength. And, once Model's appreciation of Montgomery's intentions was confirmed by orders recovered from a crash glider, their relief was to prove beyond the resources of British Generals. The consequences are well known. In ten days of violent battle, emergency action groups formed by 9th and 10th SS Panzer Divisions, bringing depleted units up to strength with local contingents and then progressively reinforced with Werfer, flak, MG and King Tiger (SS) battalions, destroyed the prospects of Urquhart's men (9th SS) and XXX Corps advancing north of Nijmegen (10th SS).

Notwithstanding the success of 2nd Paratroop Battalion (Frost) in reaching the northern end of Arnhem road bridge, the firepower and battle-craft of reinforced SS battle groups deployed at speed against 1st Airborne, was to prove decisive. Frost's men, isolated from Division at Arnhem, while holding the northern end of the great bridge against assault by Battle Group Brinkmann (10th SS Reconnaissance Battalion) and Knaust (SS Panzer Grenadier School) were overrun (20 September); further British resistance by 1st Airborne elements cordoned off by Harzer at Oosterbeek ended six days later with 6,000 prisoners and 17,000 Allied casualties (3,300 German casualties). Co-ordinated action in the south by XXXXVII Panzer Corps (von Lüttwitz) – 9th Panzer, 15th Panzer Grenadier Division, attacking the British XXX Corps' corridor from the east at Meijel, but bringing little success was soon abandoned. Thereafter 116th Panzer arriving in the Arnhem area released the SS panzer divisions for refitting under Sixth Panzer Army (Dietrich) q.v.

Panzer battles on the upper Rhine 18 September to 13 October. In contrast with the success won by SS panzer battle groups deployed against 21st Army Group's airborne spearheads at Arnhem – shortlived once Montgomery reasserted his grip on Allied operations clearing the Scheldt estuary and opening Antwerp – were German failures on the upper Rhine where Fifth Panzer Army (von Manteuffel) was concentrating divisions in the Vosges for an offensive against US 12th Army Group thrusting to Metz and threatening the Saar. The weight and direction of von Manteuffel's offensive, Hitler decided, should lie primarily

Above: North-west Europe 1944. The Allies had broken out of Normandy that August and were pursuing a broad front strategy which led to battles for the Ruhr, north of Brussels in September, Aachen in October, and Saarbrucken the same month – all with Fifth Panzer Army. In December Hitler's Ardennes counter-offensive 'Autumn Mist' proved a costly failure and the Siegfried Line an illusory barrier. Fifth Panzer Army was driven back across the Rhine and encircled in the Ruhr area, north-west of Cologne, where it surrendered on 18 April 1945.

with new panzer brigades (106, 108, 111 and 112), 3rd and 15th Panzer Grenadier Divisions, 11th and 21st Panzer striking northwards from the neighbourhood of Epinal into the flank of US Third Army driving east at Lunéville. From 18 to 25 September, when Fifth Panzer Army's Vosges offensive finally got underway, with much less than Hitler's intended strength and later by far than he originally proposed (3 September), scant progress was recorded by XXXXVII Panzer Corps (von Lüttwitz) committing 11th Battle Group (von Wietersheim) and 21st Panzer Division (Luk) reinforced by 111, 112 and 113 Panzer Brigades. Von Manteuffel's under-powered offensive was soon in trouble, petering out with little to show for the gruelling effort involved. The panzer brigades for the most part were subsequently incorporated into the panzer divisions and the Army Group Commander, General Blaskowitz, relieved of his command. In his place as GOC, Army Group 'G', OKH posted General der Panzertruppen Hermann Balck (11th Panzer, XXXXVIII Panzer Corps). Balck's tenure of command over Fifth Panzer Army, First and Nineteenth Armies (regrouped 29 November in favour of creating an SS Upper Rhine command out of Nineteenth Army) and two SS Corps would continue until 23 December when a new appointment on the Danube involving the relief of Budapest (map 19) (*see* Sixth Panzer Army) took him out of the theatre. Expected to conduct a vigorous defence of Alsace-Lorraine with woefully inadequate resources, the new GOC was to recall that at this critical time following defeat in Normandy, 30–70 German tanks were faced daily by more than 700 US tanks in action on key sectors.

For Balck's impoverished Grade IV infantry defending Metz (Saarburg) and Strasbourg against a rising flood of US armour, panzer support for the time being would rest with depleted battle groups of 17th SS Panzer Grenadier (Müller), 11th Panzer (von Wietersheim), 21st Panzer (Luk), 3rd (Denkert) and 15th (Rodt) Panzer Grenadier Divisions. Only the presence of Panzer Lehr (Bayerlein) reforming but as yet incomplete in OKW reserve and released for action in Lorraine south of Saar Union, prevented a premature collapse of the defence and a breach in the Westwall as US Third and Seventh Armies clearing Alsace-Lorraine closed up to the west bank of the Rhine.

The eventual loss of west bank Rhineland including Strasbourg (22 November), entered by 2nd French Armoured Division (Leclerc), working with US Seventh Army pushing north along the Rhine from Belfort, reflected not only the feebleness of OB West's order of battle arising out of defeat in Normandy, but marked a significant decline in critically important munitions-producing facilities which, in the case of Strasbourg, meant the loss of much of the Army's anti-tank ammunition.

Defending Aachen 14 October to 15 December. On 14 October, before further disasters on the upper Rhine could rebound to the discredit of Fifth Panzer Army or its commander, Hasso von Manteuffel, the panzer army was relieved of responsibility there and returned under command of Army Group 'B' (Model). OKW's intention in switching Fifth Panzer Army close to Aachen where US First and Ninth Armies were exerting heavy pressure in thrusts via Cologne to the Ruhr, was to prepare for a new Hitler offensive 'Watch on the Rhine' to be launched west out of the Ardennes against US First Army. But on 22 October, following a renewal of American attacks culminating in the capture of Aachen – threatening to breach the Westwall uncovering the defence of Cologne – Fifth Panzer Army was returned to the line between Jülich and Düren controlling 9th Panzer (von Elverfeldt) and six or more infantry divisions subordinate to XII SS, LXXXI and, with more armour on the 29th, XXXXVII Panzer Corps (von Lüttwitz). Von Manteuffel's responsibilities at the heart of the defence included the key Hurtgenwald and Roer river sectors where over the next seven weeks gruelling operations by Fifth Panzer Army would pull 9th, 116th, 10th SS Panzer, and 3rd and 15th Panzer Grenadier Divisions into action against US Ninth Army pushing forward with massive air support and determined to improve its positions, around Düren especially. Fighting in the panzer army's sector continued until 16 December when more important events taking taking place in the Ardennes, 60 miles south, brought relief, but not to Fifth Panzer Army.

Von Manteuffel's part in 'Autumn Mist' 16 December 1944 to 2 January 1945. Formerly 'Watch on the Rhine' (*see also* Sixth SS Panzer Army) was at first concealed in a series of OKW measures planned to deceive Allied Intelligence. Fifteenth Army HQ was brought out of Holland on 14 November, replacing Fifth Panzer Army and designated Gruppe von Manteuffel; Fifteenth Army's place being taken by Wehrmachtsbefehlshaber Niederlande while similar measures were taken to disguise the true nature of Sixth Panzer Army, the SS Panzer Army (q.v.) with which von Manteuffel would share the operative employment of the panzer divisions allotted for the offensive (map 17).

At 0530 hours 16 December, the first phase of 'Autumn Mist' unrolled with Fifth Panzer Army in control of seven divisions (three panzer) concentrated east of the Ardennes between Bitburg and Prum. Von Maneuffel's three panzer divisions were divided unequally between panzer corps; XXXXVII (von Lüttwitz) with 2nd (Lauchert) and Panzer Lehr (Bayerlein), while LVIII (Krüger) controlled only 116th Panzer (von Waldenburg). Infantry support for the panzer divisions, in addition to one VG division allotted to each panzer corps, was provided by two VG divisions subordinate to LXVI Corps (Lucht). Army troops allotted to von Manteuffel included eight heavy artillery units, three Volkswerfer brigades, two Volks artillery corps, an artillery observation battalion, thirteen engineer and bridging units and four OT (construction) regiments. Two anti-tank support units, Panzerjaeger Abteilung 653 and Assault Gun Brigade 244 were released by OKH to serve as reinforcements for the panzer divisions, while air support (II Jagd Corps) and anti-aircraft protection (III Flak Corps) despite limitations on flying imposed at the time by fuel and equipment shortages would be provided by Luftwaffe OB West (Schmid) (*see also* Part 4, page 129).

Launching bold attacks from this quarter of the Ardennes four years earlier (map 3) (First Panzer Army, 10 May) the German Army had surprised and then defeated Allied commanders, but in December 1944 the new offensive constrained by a system of narrow and easily congested roads threading snowbound uplands would succeed by the barest of margins in advancing fewer than 60 miles to the river Meuse at Dinant. Directed by OB West, von Runstedt, returning to active duty on 5 September 1944, and OB Army Group 'B' Walter Model – both of whom had tried unsuccessfully to persuade Hitler into adopting more limited objectives than Antwerp and Brussels 120 miles across the rear of two powerful Allied Army Groups (21st, Montgomery and 12th US, Bradley) – the offensive was destined to fail as in Normandy on [7 August] in the face of a steadfast US defence and Allied airpower. Profiting from the absence of Anglo-US air forces held at bay by poor flying weather, von Manteuffel's panzer divisions pushed over the Our at Gemund and Dasburg, closing on the distant Meuse where a crossing between Fermoy and Namur would it was hoped, lead 60 miles on to Brussels, the Army's objective. Unfortunately for 'Autumn Mist', any such hopes of a break-through to Brussels were soon dashed by American resistance prolonged at St-Vith (106th Infantry/7th Armored) until 21 December, requiring the intervention of 9th SS Panzer Division re-deployed from Sixth Panzer Army and the release of Führer Begleit Brigade from OKW reserve; opposition followed by an even greater set-back at Bastogne, where the US Army would thwart not only von Manteuffel but Dietrich and German intentions in general. Bypassed north and south by 2nd Panzer and Panzer Lehr driving west, Bastogne, in the hands of US 101st Airborne Division (Mcauliffe – 'Nuts!' to a truce offer), would in consequence absorb much of the energy that should have taken the offensive forward, but was instead committed to futile operations intended to mask or reduce it.

On the 24 December 'Autumn Mist' reached its zenith at Foy-Notre-Dame (2nd Panzer, Lauchert) – three miles short of Dinant; the hitherto dismal weather clearing from the west allowing Allied air forces to sweep into action. Equally disastrous for chances of success was the arrival of a relief column (US 4th Armored Division) from US Third Army striking from the south through Seventh Army and raising the siege of Bastogne on the 26th. Counter-attacks by FGB and subsequently 1st SS failed to disrupt the relief movement. On 27 December XXXIX Panzer Corps (Decker) arrived from Army Group Centre (Fourth Army) in a redeployment plan to tighten control at Bastogne. On the 29th, the Corps was bracketed with XXXXVII Panzer Corps (von Lüttwitz) into Armeegruppe von Lüttwitz, setting action in train to resolve the problem of Bastogne by concentric attack (east 1st SS, 167th VG, and west FBB, 3rd, 15th Panzer Grenadier). But to no avail. On 30 December, following a day's postponement, von Manteuffel's offensive to reduce Bastogne, unlocking communications to the west, failed completely; the panzer corps involved then reverted to Fifth Panzer Army followed in the case of XXXIX Panzer Corps by a transfer to Alsace. Redeployed north of Strasbourg, Decker was to reinforce a slackening diversionary offensive 'North Wind' (*see below*, 1 January 1945). On this front by 2 January, problems of road congestion, fuel and ammunition resupply compounded by devastating Anglo-US air attacks were delaying by hours if not days the movement of attacking battle groups and reserves. Despite a belated switch of the main effort from Dietrich and the release of OKW reserves, including 9th Panzer, 15th Panzer Grenadier Division and the 'Führer' Brigades (FBB) and (FGB), 'Autumn Mist' was all but dead.

1 January 1945. 'North Wind', a diversionary First Army (Obstfelder) offensive in Alsace, south of Pirmasens with seven divisions (three corps) attacking US Seventh Army deployed north of Strasbourg, relied principally upon

Left: General Hasso von Manteuffel entered the army in 1916 with the 3rd Hussar Regiment at Rathenow. He served in the Reichswehr as an instructor at the Panzertruppen school, Wünsdorf, and saw action in France as CO of 3rd Motor cycle Battalion and 3rd Schützen Regiment. In 1941 he was CO of 6th Schützen Regiment of 7th Panzer Division on the Moscow sector at Dimitrov. In 1943 he went to Tunisia as GOC, Division von Manteuffel, then east as GOC, 7th Panzer Division. He was transferred to Gross Deutschland in 1944 and was GOC, Fifth Panzer Army in the Ardennes; his final war action was with Third Panzer Army in Mecklenburg in 1945 (*see* maps 8, 17 and 20).

XIII SS Corps (Simon) led by 17th SS Panzer Grenadier Division (Lingner). Infantry battle groups were contributed by 36th Infantry Division. Spearheaded by 17th SS Panzer Grenadier Division, 'North Wind' made local gains north of Strasbourg between Rimlingen and Achern, but after running into heavy opposition, soon faded out. Renewed on 6 January by XXXXIX Panzer Corps (Decker, released from 'Autumn Mist' dying in the Ardennes), the new attack thrusting to Hagenau and creating momentary panic in Strasbourg also ended with nothing to show for it. The Seventh Army offensive north of Strasbourg where 21st Panzer and 25th Panzer Grenadier Divisions were involved under Decker, was supported by Nineteenth Army (Rasp) assaulting the defence concentrically from positions south of Strasbourg where Armeegruppe Oberrhein (Himmler), directly responsible to Hitler, was holding a west bank bridgehead at Colmar–Guebwiller. The efforts of those involved were in vain. At the conclusion of these abortive operations, draining panzer strength and manpower, Himmler's Armeegruppe (OB and Headquarters) was transferred to Pomerania (*see* Eleventh SS Panzer Army), leaving the upper Rhine and future operations under Ninth Army to Army Group 'G' (Hausser). In the north, where Fifth Panzer Army was fighting a rearguard action, events were moving to a similarly dismal conclusion.

'Autumn Mist' fade-out 3–31 January 1945. On 3 January Anglo-US forces subordinate to Field Marshal Montgomery – British XXX Corps and US First Army (north), US Third Army (south) – started concentric operations to squeeze the panzer armies out of their Ardennes bulge. When the converging armies united at Houffalize on the 16th, 'Autumn Mist' had run its course, but not before making one last attempt at reducing Bastogne. On 4 January a final attempt at breaking the US hold on Bastogne by I SS Panzer Corps (Priess) controlling 9th and 12th SS Panzer Divisions – reduced to 25 per cent tank strength – and panzer grenadier battalions less than 150 strong, also a weak 340 VGD, failed totally in its purpose. On 8 January when Hitler begrudgingly authorized limited withdrawals, the depleted panzer divisions 2nd, 9th, 116th (reduced to the effectiveness of a panzer grenadier regiment), Panzer Lehr, 3rd and 15th Panzer Grenadier Divisions, rallied to rearguard duties in circumstances made doubly difficult by the absence of Sixth Panzer Army (Dietrich) progressively withdrawn (8–24 January) and under movement orders to transfer east. Brisk action on 10 January by the Führer Grenadier Brigade (Kahler) subordinated to Seventh Army (Brandenburger) at Wiltz south-east of Bastogne, helped a shaky defence in resisting US Third Army pressure which was destroying 5th Paratroop Division (Heilmann). The action helped in preventing the collapse of an all too weak southern flank. By 31 January, after three weeks of hard fighting, von Manteuffel's divisions had reached the temporary security of the Westwall (Prum–Schleiden); retaining bridgeheads over the Our at Vianden and Dasburg, the divisions of Army Group 'B' were otherwise back at their start-line.

Crisis Point Rhine February to March 1945. In the aftermath of 'Autumn Mist' incurring 70,000 German casualties and the loss of 500 tanks and assault guns, defensive prospects for the German Army west of the Rhine looked distinctly bleak, with eighty British, Canadian, US and French divisions, including 24 armoured (fifteen US, six British/Canadian, three French) deploying 6,000 tanks in three Army Groups – 21st (Montgomery), 12th US (Bradley) and 6th US (Devers) – resuming operations to clear the Rhineland, encircle the Ruhr and drive into Germany beyond. The strength of the Wehrmacht in the west – sixty much depleted divisions (nine panzer/panzer grenadier) organized into three Army Groups standing west of the Rhine: 'H' (Student) lower Rhine, 'B' (Model) middle Rhine and 'G' (Blaskowitz) upper Rhine – was spread 500 miles from the North Sea south of Rotterdam to the Swiss frontier at Basle. Fewer than 450 tanks and assault guns, supported by Jagdpanzers (Heerestruppen) deployed in company strengths stood at their disposal. Model's Army Group 'B', in action on the middle Rhine between Roermund and Trier, was appreciably weakened by panzer transfers to the east – Sixth Panzer Army (Dietrich), two SS panzer corps, four SS panzer divisions switched to Western Hungary, and the Führer Brigades, FBB and FBG, sent to Cotbus for expansion and then posting to Army Group Weichsel – retaining fewer than 170 battle-fit tanks and approximately the same number of heavy anti-tank guns serving 29 divisions (five panzer/panzer grenadier) holding left bank positions. Army Group 'G' was to be similarly weakened, losing panzer divisions to the east (*see* 24 March–1 April 1945).

A resumption of Allied pressure in the west brought panzer divisions into action at crisis points – in the case of Army Group 'H' (Student) defending the Reichswald between the Rhine and the Maas, in counter-attacks to delay 21st Army Group (First Canadian, Second British, Ninth US Armies) clearing the left bank south-east of Nijmegen where First Paratroop Army (Schlemm) held the line.

*[**8 February 1945. Reinforcing First Paratroop Army in the Reichswald.** On 8 February, XXXXVII Panzer Corps (von Luttwitz), withdrawn into OB West reserve at the conclusion of 'Autumn Mist' with 116th Panzer (von Waldenburg) and 15th Panzer Grenadier Division (Rodt), counter-attacked the Anglo-Canadian advance at Kleve in a sector where II Paratroop Corps (Meindl) called for assistance in containing overwhelming attacks. When XXXXVII Corps (von Lüttwitz) failed to restore the situation in the Reichswald, Geldern was lost on 3 March and Canadian First Army was able to link up with US Ninth Army (Simpson) converging from the south. By 12 March the left (west) bank of the Rhine south of the Reichswald, including a substantial First Paratroop Army bridgehead at Wesel, had been surrendered – notwithstanding the intervention of Panzer Lehr (Niemack) drawn into battle at various stages in the Allied offensive. And in the battle for Cologne on the adjoining sector to the south the panzer divisions were equally powerless.*

*[**23 February 1945 [Reinforcing Fifteenth Army on the Rhine.** On 23 February, when US First Army (Hodges) aiming for Cologne secured a bridgehead over the River Roer (Linnich–Jülich–Düren) the Westwall was decisively breached at a crucial point, affording access to the Ruhr. Neither 9th Panzer (von Elverfeldt) nor 3rd Panzer Grenadier Division, deployed under LVIII Panzer Corps (Krüger), challenging American progress could halt the offensive. Reinforcements drawn into the battle from south flanking Army Group 'G', 11th Panzer (von Brandenfels)*

failed equally in stemming the American onrush while 9th Panzer would soon be reporting the loss of its commander, von Elverfeldt. By 7 March Cologne city centre was in the hands of US First Army, and the great Hohenzollern bridge destroyed by retreating battle groups.]

At **Remagen** in Fifth Panzer Army's sector, where LXVII Corps held the line, an undamaged (Ludendorff) bridge fell unexpectedly into the hands of US First Army/9th Armored Division (Leonard); the Army commander (Hodges) seizing his chance promptly, developed a right (east) bank bridgehead. The corps adjutant, Major Scheller, arriving only hours before to organize the defence of the Ludendorff bridge was, with others, judged neglectful of his proper responsibility and on Hitler's orders he and they paid with their lives for the mishap. More positive measures to combat the threat to trans-Rhine defences posed by Hodges's expanding bridgehead at Remagen were initiated by Model, GOC, Army Group 'B' and (von Zangen) GOC, Fifteen Army; the defensive measures set in train involved panzer divisions in more abortive counter-attacks. Vigorous action over the next few days by 3rd Panzer Grenadier, Panzer Lehr, 9th and 11th Panzer Divisions serving LIII Panzer Corps (Bayerlein) and LXXIV Corps (Puchler) would all fail in eliminating the danger. The US bridgehead remained a thorn in German flesh. Fifth Panzer Army's strength on the right bank of the Rhine between Bonn and Duisberg, with an extension eastwards along the Ruhr north of Cologne, lay in nothing more than five VG and 3rd and 5th Paratroop Divisions deployed north and south of Cologne. On 10 March OB West, von Runstedt was relieved of his post for the last time and Field Marshal Kesselring, hitherto OB South West (succeeded by von Vietinghoff from Tenth Army), was installed in his place. On 12 March GOC, Fifth Panzer Army, von Manteuffel, was succeeded by General der Panzertruppe Harpe. Transferred to the Oder north of Berlin, von Manteuffel replaced Raus at Third Panzer Army (q.v.).

17–31 March. During the last fortnight in March, Allied armies were consolidating their hold on the west bank of the Rhine before mounting new offensives in reasonably quick time and winning Rhine crossings in strength: north, 21st Army Group at Wesel (23–24 March); centre, US 12th Army Group at Oppenheim (22 March); south, US 6th Army Group at Darmstadt (25 March) and Speyer (French First Army 31 March).

*[**17 March. Seventh Army on the Middle Rhine** faced preliminary US tidying-up operations east of Trier (4 March) as US Third Army (Patton) thrusting along the Moselle engaged 2nd Panzer (Lauchert) and 11th Panzer (von Brandenfels) before reaching Coblenz on the 17th and swinging south into contact with US Seventh Army (Patch).*

***19 March. First Army defending the Saarland** where US Seventh Army (Patch) was clearing the west bank and, penetrating the Westwall between Zweibrucken and Pirmasens, watched the Army's only remaining motorized formation, 17th SS Panzer Grenadier Division (Bochmann) flushed out of strong points on the River Blies and into Germesheim, the last German bridgehead standing west of the Rhine. Bochmann's division, reduced to 800 effectives, would then hold Germesheim until the bridgehead, swollen with retreating troops and civilians, was evacuated on the 25th].*

24–31 March. A decisive factor in the collapse of German resistance in the Saar, as elsewhere along the Rhine, was the absence of mobile divisions (drawn off for action on the Eastern Front) and the relative weakness of the remainder. Panzer divisions surrendered to the Eastern Front by Army Group 'B' (Model) at the conclusion of 'Autumn Mist' (SS 1st, 2nd, 9th, 12th) were followed soon afterwards by 21st, 10th SS and 25th Panzer Grenadier, withdrawn from Army Group 'G' (Blaskowitz) principally for the benefit of Army Group Weichsel (Himmler) preparing a new offensive in the east. All that remained on the upper Rhine was 17th SS Goetz von Berlichingen. On the middle Rhine serving Army Group 'B' stood Panzer Lehr, 11th Panzer, 3rd Panzer Grenadier, 2nd and 9th Panzer Divisions; and on the lower Rhine (Army Group 'H') 116th Panzer and 15th Panzer grenadier Divisions. On 24 March, when 21st Army Group (Montgomery) incorporating two airborne divisions, launched a powerful three Army offensive (Canadian First, British Second, US Ninth) across the lower Rhine at Wesel, destroying First Paratroop Army in the process, only a single panzer division battle group (von Waldenburg), 15th Panzer Grenadier Division (Rodt) and 106 Panzer Brigade, were on hand to bolster infantry and paratroop divisions scattered in overwhelming attacks. By the time these battles were concluded, with the loss of 10,000 men a day, surviving panzer divisions were reduced to regimental-size battle groups with few if any tanks, their mobility impaired by shortages of fuel, spares and vehicles, and their firepower severely curtailed by a lack of heavy weapons and dwindling ammunition supplies. Most would, nevertheless, continue in action at one crisis point after another as the Western Allies, thrusting into the heart of Germany, encircled the Ruhr and fanning out north, centre and south threatened Hamburg, Magdeburg and Munich. Eventually (24 April) on the Elbe south of Magdeburg, US First Army (Hodges), pushing hard for Leipzig, made contact with Russian Fifth Guards Army (Schadov) 30 miles north-east at Torgau. The move divided Germany into two battle zones (map 20).

Encirclement in the Ruhr By 1 April, with US Ninth Army (Simpson) and US First Army (Hodges) uniting 60 miles north-east of Cologne at Lippstadt, Harpe's Fifth Panzer Army and von Zangen's Fifteenth Army were encircled in the Ruhr with the remaining nineteen divisions of Model's Army Group 'B'. The Ruhr pocket created east of the Rhine by fast-moving US spearheads and at first broadly rectangular in shape, embraced within its northern limits the Ruhr-side industrial districts of Duisberg, Essen (Krupp), Bochum, Dortmund and Hamm – all for the most part located north of the river. Over to the south lay Düsseldorf and Wuppertal with their satellite industrial suburbs, but the greater part of the encircled area consisted of Sauerland countryside open to the east but limited in the south by the River Sieg. In the centre of the southern front stood Siegen, a communications centre affording good road and rail links northwards to Dortmund via Olpe, HQ Army Group 'B' (Model) and Witten. An Army Group in better shape than Model's 80 per cent Grade III formations, reinforced by urban defence volunteers raised by neighbourhood defence chiefs, might have been expected if adequately supplied and equipped to stage a protracted resistance. But despite the presence of four panzer/panzer grenadier divisions – 9th (Zollenkopf), 116th (von Waldenburg), Panzer Lehr (Hauser) and 3rd Panzer Grenadier (Dankert) – this did not happen. The formidable task of countering pressure from all sides of the pocket, especially north and south at Witten and Siegen, was to prove too much for an Army Group imperilled by shortages of every kind and fatally weakened by counter-attacks at Remagen (7–25 March) and Wesel (24 March).

8 April 1945. By 8 April, Fifth Panzer Army's dispositions in the Ruhr pocket fronting the Rhine lay north and south of Cologne (XII SS Corps, 3rd Paratroop Division and Volksturm) and eastwards along the Sieg via Siegburg to Siegen where LVIII Panzer Corps (Botsch) (Battle Group 9th Panzer and five infantry divisions) constituted the best of Harpe's meagre resources.

[***Fifteenth Army, encircled with Fifth Panzer Army*** *and meanwhile reduced to three infantry divisions, held the country east of Siegen, driven into the pocket by US First Army thrusting from the Remagen bridgehead (25 March). The Army Group Commander then released Panzer Lehr (Hauser) and his only other reserve motorized formation, 3rd Panzer Grenadier Division (Dankert), for counter-attacks east of Winterberg. Supported by infantry of LIII Panzer Corps (Bayerlein), Model's intention was to use the mobile divisions at Madebach for breaking through US First Army, preventing Fifteenth Army from uniting with Lucht's new Eleventh Army (q.v.) forming to the east. But the rigorous opposition of US armour to any attempt at breaking through the daily widening corridor, pushing German Eleventh and Fifteenth Armies farther apart, defeated Panzer Lehr's purpose and those of supporting formations, executed from 30 March to 5 April. Forbidden by Hitler to make further break-out attempts, operations were closed down and there for a day or so the front stabilized – Bayerlein transferring to the north where another crisis was developing.*]

Armeegruppe von Lüttwitz, in the Ruhr and responsible to Army Group 'B' for the defence of war industries established since 1850 along the River Ruhr between Duisberg and the Mohne Dam, was an impromptu formation supervising XXXXVII Panzer Corps (von Lüttwitz) and LXIII Corps (Abrahams). Separated from First Paratroop Army (Schlemm) at the time of 21st Army Group's thrust east of Wesel, von Luttwitz retained 116th Panzer (von Waldenburg), some worn-out infantry, paratroop, Volksturm, flak and artillery units with which to assist neighbourhood forces defending industrial production crucial to the prosecution of the war. Despite the welcome arrival of Bayerlein's LIII Panzer Corps, taking over 116th Panzer and infantry support in the critical Castrop/Witten sector of the front, where US (Ninth Army) pressure to split the Ruhr pocket north and south was at its maximum, the outcome of this unequal struggle was never in question. Nothing that Bayerlein – or anyone else – could do, was to affect American progress. By 12 April 1945, Ruhrland industrial districts north of the river, including the giant Krupp works at Essen and the military complex at Sennelager, had been lost – many districts, including Essen, Duisberg and Bochum, going undefended for lack of resources, others like Castrop being bitterly fought over. On 14 April, the Ruhr pocket was split by US armour, driving south from Witten and north from Olpe. The result of this American action on Army Group 'B' was to create a western enclave surrounding Düsseldorf and Wuppertal (HQ Army Group 'B' transferred from Olpe) enclosing Fifth Panzer Army (Harpe), 9th Panzer (Zollenkopf) and the mass of Armeegruppe von Lüttwitz.

Isolated eastwards around Iserlohn was a small pocket containing Fifteenth Army (von Zangen) with Panzer Lehr (Hauser), 3rd Panzer Grenadier (Denkert), 116th Panzer (von Waldenburg) and depleted Jagdtiger companies (Ernst and Carius). The battle state of Ruhr panzer/panzer grenadier divisions at the time of capitulation is typified by the strength returns of Denkert's 3rd Panzer Grenadier Divisions: 0 per cent panzerjaeger, 0 per cent panzer/sturmgeschützen, 0 per cent pioneers, 10 per cent panzer grenadiers. By 18 April 1945 Army Group 'B' had officially surrendered 325,000 effectives, but not its GOC, Field Marshal Walter Model; his suicide followed three days later at Wedau on the southern outskirts of Duisberg.

Panzer Battle Group Divisions in the west. 19 April to 9 May 1945. With surrender in the Ruhr pocket claiming Fifth Panzer Army (Harpe), LIII Panzer Corps (Bayerlein), 9th, 116th, Panzer Lehr and 3rd Panzer Grenadier Divisions, fewer than a handful of regular – but severely depleted – panzer battle groups, 2nd Panzer, 11th Panzer, 15th and 17th SS Panzer Grenadier Divisions, survived in the west, pursuing near purposeless operations. The profitless employment of the four battle group divisions and impromptu formations such as 'Clausewitz', incorporating depleted Panzerjaeger battalions and *ad hoc* Panzer Verbande, created out of local resouces, would continue until 9 May when the unconditional surrender of the German Army in the east brought hostilities officially to an end (map 20). Facing west in the weeks prior to capitulation, battle groups were deployed in widely separated engagements between the North Sea and the Swiss frontier.

[***First Paratroop Army south of Bremen*** *(Student, – Straube) committed Panzer Grenadier Division (Rodt) and Panzer Verband GD in counter-attacks to slow Second Army (Dempsey) thrusting to Hamburg.*]

[***Eleventh Army (Lucht) encircled in the Harz Mountains*** *(see page 247), surrendered 9th/116th Panzer Division remnants and SS Panzer Verband Westfalen.*

A new Twelfth Army *(Wenck)* ***raised on the Elbe*** *in early April, south-east of Magdeburg with HQ at Dessau, assembled Kampfgruppe Panzer Division Clausewitz (Unrein) from many and divers units collected south-east of Hamburg. The division was subordinated to XXXIX Panzer Corps (Decker), switched to the Elbe from the Oder (Ninth Army east of Berlin), and seconded to OB North West. Decker's task with Unrein's 'Clausewitz' and Heun's 'Schlageter' (motorized infantry division) was to drive a corridor south from Uelzen through British Second and US Ninth Armies investing Eleventh Army encircled in the Harz.*

By 21 April, the relief attempt that had begun in fine style five days earlier on the 16th, south of Uelzen, failed short of Brunswick. Overwhelmed by Allied superiority, notably in the air, destroying the attacking formations, neither Clausewitz nor XXXIX Panzer Corps survived the engagement as viable military entities; the depleted corps staff being amalgamated for a time with other staffs to form XXXXI Panzer Corps (Holste).

On 22 April, Twelfth Army (Wenck) was directed by OKW to relieve Berlin from the south-east (see also Third Panzer Army, 16 April). Possessing no more than a handful of RAD units, infantry teaching cadres, one or two panzer school units, HJ and Volksturm organized into impromptu divisions like Schlageter, Scharnhorst, Ulrich von Hutten and Theodor Korner, the attempt was unlikely to succeed although contact was affected with Ninth Army/Fourth Panzer Army elements retreating from Frankfurt (Oder) on the opposite (east) front. See also Pz AOK 3, 16 April 1945.

***Seventh Army** (Obstfelder) **east of the Rhine,** shattered in battles for the Saar and retiring south-east through Hesse and Thuringia, retained Kampfgruppe 2nd Panzer (von Berg) and 11th Panzer (von Bradenfels) at the centre of an otherwise feeble order of battle – mostly local infantry, flak and Wehrkreis emergency formations. Flank attacks by these 'divisions', directed south from Eisenach against US Third Army (Patton) advancing powerfully via Erfurth towards Chemnitz and the Tyrol during April, would do nothing to deflect Patton from his objectives.*

***First Army** (Fortsch) **in Bavaria,** retreating from the upper Rhine through Wurtemburg and Bavaria, carried along 17th SS Panzer Grenadier Division (Bochmann) for action north of Heilbron (3–12 April), around Nuremberg (17–20 April) and Munich (24–28 April) and finally with few if any heavy weapons remaining to it in the area south of Bad Tolz. The Army's order of battle, inclusive of 17th SS, 2nd Mountain, six other infantry divisions and local defence units – only marginally superior to Obstfelder's east flanking Seventh Army or Brandenburger's west flanking Nineteenth Army devoid of all regular motorized formations with which to hold Stuttgart (surrendered 22 April) or the Black Forest against French First Army (Tassigny) – precluded all but the most local of offensive operations in southern Germany. By 9 May 1945, Franco-US forces driving into southern redoubts – French First Army (Tassigny), US Seventh Army (Patch) and US Third Army (Patton) – were occupying the Tyrol and alpine foreland including Innsbruck, Salzburg and Linz, uniting with US Fifth Army (Truscott) from Italy at the Brenner Pass (Patch) and 3rd Ukrainina Front (Tolbuchin) from Hungary at Linz (Patton).*]

9. Sixth SS Panzer Army (SS PzAOK 6)

Raised in September 1944 to lead a Hitler-inspired Ardennes counter-offensive – 'Autumn Mist' (formerly 'Watch on the Rhine') – ordered by OKW on 10 November 1944. Army Commander SS Oberstgruppenführer and Generaloberst der Waffen SS 'Sepp' Dietrich. Panzer Headquarters, Münstereifel. In control of I SS Panzer Corps (Priess), II SS Panzer Corps (Bittrich) and 150 Panzer Brigade (cover-name for a 2,000-strong SS sabotage commando led by Obersturmbannführer Otto Skorzeny), the Panzer Army was concentrated west of the Rhine on the German side of the Ardennes only three days prior to the offensive planned for 16 December 1944.

In **Operation 'Griffon',** Hitler required Skorzeny by means of infiltration with American-looking vehicles and personnel to create alarm and confusion among US forces deployed on the battle front opposite the SS Leibstandarte spearhead. Skorzeny was further charged with assisting the spearhead (Peiper) to secure bridges at Huy and Liège on the axis of advance to Antwerp. Two assault gun brigades (394) and (667) a Panzerjaeger battalion (653) and an assault panzer battalion (217) were allotted to Dietrich as Army troops in addition to three Werfer brigades and three Volks artillery corps. LXVII Army Corps (Hitzfeld) with two VG divisions (272nd) and (326th) would provide infantry support for the offensive.

The Panzer Army's objective, under the supervision of Field Marshal von Runstedt, called out of retirement on 5 September and reinstated as OB West, was to recapture the recently opened Allied supply port of Antwerp while Fifth Panzer Army (von Manteuffel), also on 16 December, secured Brussels, the Belgian capital. Both Armies were subordinate to Model's Army Group 'B'. Neither von Runstedt, Model nor von Manteuffel were optimistic about Hitler's plans which they received in 'do not alter' form. Once across the Meuse, the two attacking panzer armies were expected to swing 125 miles north-west, enveloping and destroying four US, British and Canadian armies trapped between them and Army Group 'H' (Student) in Holland. The role of Seventh Army (Brandenburger) to the south and Fifteenth Army (von Zangen) to the north was to provide flank protection, but as events were to prove, Seventh Army operating within striking distance of Patton's US Third Army was much too weak for its role.

Operation 'Autumn Mist' (map 17). 'Autumn Mist' started on 16 December 1944 at 0535 hours, with bad weather keeping Allied air forces at bay. Of the four newly equipped SS panzer divisions, two, 1st SS Leibstandarte Adolf Hitler (Mohnke) and 12th SS Hitler Youth (Kraas) would lead I SS Panzer Corps (Priess), while two other SS panzer divisions in II SS Panzer Corps (Bittrich), 2nd SS Das Reich (Lammerding) and 9th SS Hohenstaufen (Stadler) prepared to follow on. Air support for the attacking divisions by II Jagd Corps was negligible.

Operation 'Stosser', a supporting parachute drop by 800 Fallschirmjaeger (von der Heydte) on the northern flank of the offensive was planned to confuse the defence and, by securing traffic points on the Hoher-Venn, block the advance of US reinforcements from this direction; but the operation was delayed for want of transports. Results on the first day were far less than expected with only limited gains being reported. US First Army, standing fast on the northern shoulder of the offensive, hemmed the attacking divisions into a narrow operational area from which they were unable to break out. The offensive consequently failled at a critical time and at critical points; defeated as much by a steadfast US defence of key communication centres as the constricting effect of ravines and forest terrain inhibiting off the road movement particularly at Butgenbach (12th SS, 12th VGD), Elsenborn and Monschau (326 VGD). At these points on the SS front and also in the south where Fifth Panzer Army was blocked at St-Vith and Bastogne, the offensive stalled never to recover momentum.

The spearhead of 'Autumn Mist', Kampffgruppe Peiper, a 4,000-strong Leibstandarte armoured battle group (I SS Panzer Regiment, Jochen Pieper with 72 Pz Kpfw IV/Vs and 30 Pz Kpfw VIs) pushing for the Meuse at Huy in

Right: SS Oberstgruppenführer and Panzer Generaloberst der Waffen SS, 'Sepp' Dietrich. A Bavarian, he entered the army in 1911, serving from 1914 to 1918 in the 42nd Infantry Regiment and the 5th Bavarian Panzer Detachment. In 1928 he joined the SS and rose rapidly through the ranks to become the OC Hitler's bodyguard in 1932, which was officially renamed Leibstandarte Adolf Hitler in 1933. From 1939 to 1943 he commanded an expanded Leibstandarte in Poland, France, the Balkans and Russia before moving, in July 1943, to head I SS Panzer Corps. In June 1944 he fought in Normandy and from September he was GOC, Sixth SS Panzer Army (*see* maps 16, 17 and 19).

conjunction with 40–50 Skorzeny commandos, four to a jeep, was rendered totally ineffective when trapped at La Gleize in the Ambleve valley east of Stourmont. Fitfully re-supplied by air, Peiper's battle group abandoned much of its equipment including 28 Pz Kpfw IVs and Panthers after all relief attempts had ended in failure. Reduced to 800 men by 24 December, the Kampfgruppe withdrew to the east. On 17 December, von der Heydte's scratch force of 800 paratroops was finally dropped a day late and mostly off-course. Fewer than 200 of the Fallschirmjaeger, descending ahead of the supposedly advancing 326th VG Division, reached the neighbourhood of their objective – a cross-roads on the Hoher-Venn giving enemy access to the area from the north. Instead, rallying under von der Heydte, the group moved east in a bid to escape, but within seven days most were in captivity at Monschau. On 20 December OB West decided to switch the main effort of 'Autumn Mist' from Sixth SS to Fifth Panzer Army while a second and equally futile attempt by the SS divisions of II SS Panzer Corps to break through to the Meuse in the centre of the front at Vielsalm (9th SS) was rebutted. Here, as elsewhere to the north, a staunch American defence of the sector denied the SS the use of roads and bridges essential to progress.

[*Fifth Panzer Army pushing forward in the south on 21 December, also suffered an unwelcome reverse with US resistance at Bastogne and St-Vith delaying or halting the leading Panzer divisions.*]

On 24 December, eight days after the start of 'Autumn Mist', skies cleared above the battle-field allowing Allied air forces to operate at full power. The offensive was then swiftly brought to an end. By this time too, Skorzeny's mission ('Griffon') using mocked-up Panthers and personnel disguised as American troops to spread confusion in disruptive commando type operations, had proved largely ineffective and after a spell of more regular employment assisting Peiper with attacks on Malmédy, on 21 December, was withdrawn.

[*On 26 December US Third Army (III Corps) drove a corridor through German Seventh Army, raising the siege of Bastogne (*see *Fifth Panzer Army.)*]

On 3 January, Anglo-US counter-action was directed by Field Marshal Montgomery starting with operations against the northern flank of Sixth SS Panzer Army. On 4 January, following a last-minute switch of 1st, 9th and 12th SS Panzer Divisions (I SS Panzer Corps) to von Manteuffel, a new offensive failed to eliminate resistance at Bastogne. Consequently the town, reinforced from the south by US Third Army, continued to tie-down offensive capacity needed by Fifth Panzer Army for the drive to the Meuse. On 8 January, while obstinately refusing to acknowledge defeat, Hitler authorized limited withdrawals. The attacking panzer divisions, whose progress had fallen well short of major objectives – on fuel so limited that operations were at times brought to a standstill – withdrew under punishing air attack to the relative security of the Westwall. A new directive followed. On 21 January Hitler instructed OKW to switch Sixth SS Panzer Army to western Hungary, a sector of the Eastern Front where on 26 December Budapest had been encircled by Russian 2nd and 3rd Ukranian Fronts. Two days later, Hungary changed sides, joining Bulgaria and Roumania in declaring war on Germany. Into this dangerous military vacuum in an economically sensitive area the Wehrmacht's last significant panzer reserve was sent by Hitler to join Army Group South (Wöhler) – ignoring Guderian's view that panzer reinforcement was most desperately needed on the Oder (*see* Fourth Panzer Army, 12 January 1945).

[*On the* ***Danube*** *(map 19) until 2 January 1944, when the transfer of IV SS Panzer Corps (Gille) from Army Group centre brought 3rd SS Totenkopf (Becker) and 5th SS Wiking (Ullrich) to Komorn, only LVII Panzer Corps (Kirchner) deployed north of Budapest and III Panzer Corps (Breith) to the south served Army Group South.*

*Despite the success of panzer divisions eliminating Russian spearheads at Nyireghyaza (*see *First Panzer Army, October 1944), Army Group South's seven divisions, 1st, 3rd, 6th, 8th, 13th, 23rd, 24th and Panzer Grenadier Division Feldhermhalle supported by 109 and 110 Panzer Brigades with a handful of infantry divisions, fighting south of the Carpathians had proved too weak and too few to stem the tide of Russian armour and infantry sweeping west and enveloping Budapest.*

Defending Budapest. *By 13 February 1945, when Buda fell to 2nd Ukrainian Front, the defence of Budapest lead by Pfeffer von Wildenbruck (IX SS Mountain Corps) had swallowed up five German divisions including 13th Panzer and Panzer Grenadier Division Feldherrenhalle (60th Motorized). In an attempt to relieve Budapest on 1 January with IV SS Panzer Corps (Gille) using 3rd and 5th SS Panzer Divisions to assault the defence on the Danube east of Komorn, and again from the south-west on 18 January when reinforced by 1st (Thunert) and 3rd (Phillips) Panzer Divisions, Sixth Army (Balck) approached to within fifteen miles of the Hungarian capital, but there the attempt failed. On 11 February a break-out led by 13th Panzer Division ended in disaster. On the 13th, Budapest surrendered 70,000 military effectives; Hitler at once devised a new scheme for re-occupying the town.*]

Operation 'Spring Awakening' (map 19) on 6 March 1945 required Dietrich with his two SS panzer corps – I SS (1st SS Leibstandarte AH and 12th SS HJ), also II SS (2nd and 9th SS), to co-operate with Sixth Army (Balck) – III Panzer Corps (Breith), 1st, 3rd, 6th and 23rd Panzer Divisions plus IV SS Panzer Corps (Gille) – in a powerful thrust east. Starting east of Stuhlweissenburg (Szekesfeharvar), 'Spring Awakening' aimed to blunt Ukranain Front spearheads threatening Hungarian oil production at Nagy-Kanisza, also related refineries and essential war industries in Vienna. But no less crucial in Hitler's view was the need for Dietrich to re-take Budapest, and, in conjuction with Second Panzer Army to the south, establish bridgeheads across the Danube for future operations. Involving thirty divisions, eight of them panzer, 'Spring Awakening' secured early gains in the face of determined 3rd Ukranian Front opposition. But hampered by adverse terrain bogging armoured vehicles and restricting movement, the offensive slackened and failed; no more than local advantage accruing from the operation leaving the panzer army with only 185 battle-fit tanks and assault guns. Giving 'Spring Awakening' no more than a moment's consideration, Stavka could see few strategic problems arising out of Hitler's counter-attack conducted so far from its own primary objective – Berlin.

Germany in defeat (map 20). Gravely weakened by its abortive action at Stuhlweissenburg, reducing the Army's meagre tank strength to even less meaningful proportions, Dietrich ('Sixth Panzer Army means six tanks') in control of I and II SS Panzer Corps, was forced back on Bratislavia in mid-April giving more ground before fighting rearguard battles in Austria yet failing to hold Vienna. At the beginning of May 1945, prior to Sixth SS Panzer Army's surrender to US or Russian forces, Hitler's rage over SS 'failures' resulted in orders that the SS divisions under Dietrich's command, Leibstandarte, Totenkopf and HJ, the pride of the Waffen SS, should be stripped of their cuff titles. In refusing to comply with the Führer's directive, Dietrich told his divisional commanders, 'There's your reward for all that you've done these past five years.' No words are more suited than Dietrich's to express the futility of Hitler's war direction, or to summarize more succinctly a barren political ideology which, in aspiring to a thousand-year Reich, betrayed the faith of the German Army and people.

Right: SS Oberstgruppenführer and General der Waffen SS, Felix Steiner. A Prussian, he entered the army in 1914, serving with the 5th Infantry Regiment at Tilsit before seeing action in the east at Tannenberg and the west in Flanders. From 1921 to 1934 he was a member of the Reichswehr Infantry, undertaking staff and police training duties, becoming Training Director. In 1935 he moved to SS-Verfügungstruppe as battalion commander, serving in Poland and France as OC, Deutschland. In December 1940 he was appointed GOC, SS Wiking Division and in 1941–2, during the Russian campaign, he led it at Malgobek (*see* map 10). In May 1943 he raised III Germanisches Panzer Corps which comprised Nordland and Nederland. He was posted to Leningrad that December where he later fought at Narwa. In 1945 he was GOC, Eleventh Panzer Army but, with no divisions left to speak of, Steiner only theoretically pariticipated in the battle for Berlin (*see* map 20).

10. Eleventh SS Panzer Army (SS PzAOK 11)

Raised in Pomerania in January 1945, from the staff of SS Headquarters Upper Rhine. Army Commander appointed on 28 January 1945 from command of III SS (Germanisches) Panzer Corps was General der Waffen SS Felix Steiner. Prior to Steiner's appointment, at the conclusion of the third Battle of Courland, OKH had withdrawn III SS Panzer Corps Headquarters from Eighteenth Army by sea across the Baltic, followed by SS Brigades Nordland and Nederland. The SS Brigades would be refitted as panzer grenadier divisions. Steiner's (Germanisches) SS Corps was swiftly relocated south-east of Stettin, responsible to Himmler's Army Group Weichsel and in control of mainly SS divisions committed to the emergency defence of Pomerania.

*[**Defending the Narwa bridgehead.** In July 1944, six months prior to Corps battles in Courland, Steiner had conducted a vigorous defence of Eighteenth Army's Narwa bridgehead. A land corridor strategically situated south-west of Leningrad between the Baltic and Lake Peipus, this neck of land with Narwa at its head connected the city's hinterland with Estonia and Baltic regions to the south. In blocking Lenningrad Front (Govorov) attempts to crash through the corridor, Steiner gained time for Army Group North (Schörner) – Sixteenth and Eighteenth Armies, to withdraw to the south-west in safety and consolidate in the Baltic peninsular (Courland) west of Riga.]*

The battle for Arnswalde. On 15 February 1945, Eleventh SS Panzer Army/Army Group Weichsel launched Operation 'Sonewende' southwards from Stargard to Arnswalde. Although strategically unrewarding, Steiner's counter-offensive into the northern flank of the Red Army Fronts driving for Berlin nevertheless liberated Arnswalde for four days before pressure from 2nd BR Front forced the Army into retreat. At Guderian's insistence General Wenck, until a motor accident on the 17th prevented him from continuing, assisted Eleventh Army staff in the preparation of the offensive. At the centre of the Stargard attack stood III SS Panzer Corps lead by General Martin Unrein, promoted from command of 14th Panzer Division (retained by Eighteenth Army in Courland). The attacking formations included SS Panzer Grenadier Divisions Nordland, Nederland, Langemarck and the Army's Führer Begleit Division. Two other corps participated in 'Sonewende'; XXXIX Panzer Corps (Decker) and Corps Munzel with Holstein, SS Polizei, SS Wallonien and the Führer Grenadier Division shared between them. With these worn down and incomplete formations organized into weak battle groups, the 'Panzer Army' won local success and, as noted, recaptured Arnswalde, but there the offensive petered out. On 25 February 1945 – General der Panzertruppen Erhard Raus with Third Panzer Army (HQ) arrived in Pomerania from East Prussia, assuming responsibility for Eleventh Panzer Army operations – leaving the defence of Königsberg and East Prussia to Fourth Army (Hossbach).

In the **general retreat** to the Oder following Russian attacks which split the defence in Pomerania into isolated fragments, Steiner returned to his (Germanisches) Panzer Corps, withdrawing with it into the Altdamm bridgehead on the Oder east of Stettin. Thereafter the Corps was redeployed north of Berlin (*see* Third Panzer Army, 25 February 1945). With responsibility for the defence of Pomerania handed over to Raus, OKH posted Eleventh Army (HQ) to Mecklenburg north of Berlin – to be rebuilt there for operations in the west.

A **new Eleventh Army** under General Walther Lucht, responsible to C-in-C, West (von Runstedt), would subsequently resist British progress on the Weser and in the Hartz Mountains. On 4 May 1945, when operations in north-west Europe concluded with German surrender to Field Marshal Montgomery, 9th and 116th Panzer Division battle groups were serving Eleventh Army as a mobile reserve.

Source Notes and Bibliography

In the process of tracing armoured facts and philosophies for discussion in the present work I have extracted a certain amount of material from previous publications thereby incurring a debt of assistance to the following authors (and publishers):

1. To Rudolf Steiger (Rombach Verlag) for kind permission to quote from *Panzertaktik*; Dr Gerhard Hümmelchen (Bernard and Graef) whose work of joint authorship with Fritz Morzik – *Die Deutschen Transport Flieger in Zweiten Weltkrieges* provided me with the basis for New Horizons in Transport, Part 4, also the late editor B. H. Liddell Hart (Collins) whose Rommel Papers in translation by Paul Findlay with the assistance of Lucie-Maria Rommel, Manfred Rommel and General Fritz Bayerlein provides a valuable insight into Rommel's problems in North Africa; to Dr David Kahn (Hodder and Stoughton) for permission to quote from *Hitler's Spies* and to incorporate extracts into Part 4, The Army's Eye in the Sky.

2. Intelligence publications (used with caution) summarizing the organization and methods of the German Army and Air Force:

Current Reports from overseas, War Office 1944–5.
Brief Notes on the German Army in War, War Office 1940–3.
Periodical Notes on the German Army, War Office 1941–2.
Pocket Book on the German Army, War Office 1943–4.
War Information Circular, GHQ India, 1941–4.

3. British post-war Intelligence publications:

Hinsley F. *British Intelligence in World War II*, vols I-III, HMSO, 1979–88.
March, C. (ed). *Rise and Fall of the German Air Force 1933–45.* Arms & Armour Press, 1983.

4. Publishers in the Bundesrepublic of Germany whose military lists include many unit and campaign histories:

Bernardt and Graefe, Frankfurt (Main): Studien und Documente zur Gesichte des Zweiten Weltkrieges.
DVA Stuttgart: Schriftenreihe des Militärgeschichtlichen Forschumgsamt.
Motorbuch Verlag, Stuttgart.
Musterschmidt Verlag, Gottingen, Frankfurt (Main).
Munin Verlag, Osnabrück.
Podzun-Pallas Verlag, Bad Nauheim: notably the works of Dr Werner Haupt.
Verlag Rombach, Freiburg (Breisgau): Einzelschriften zur Militärischen Gesichte des Zweiten Weltkrieges.
Kurt Vowinckel, Osnabrück: Die Wehrmacht in Kampf.

5. Works consulted to advantage but excluding those of authors named above; the list is by no means a definitive one and is limited by considerations of space to fifty-two authors:

Barnett, Correlli. *The Desert Generals.* George Allen & Unwin, London, 1983
Belchem, David. *Victory in Normandy.* London, 1981
Bennett, Ralph. *Ultra in the West.* London, 1979.
Bond, Brian. *Liddell Hart: A Study of his Military Thought.* London, 1976
Carell, Paul. *Invasion. They're Coming!* London, 1962
Carver, Michael. *The Apostles of Mobility.* London, 1979
Cooper, Matthew. *The German Army: Its Political and Military Failure.* London, 1978
— *The German Air Force: An Anatomy of Failure.* London, 1981
D'Este, Carlo. *Decision in Normandy.* Collins, 1984
Diest, Wilhelm. *The Wehrmacht and German Rearmament.* London, 1981
Erickson, John. *The Road to Stalingrad.* London, 1975
— *The Road to Berlin.* London, 1983
Fleming, Peter. *Invasion 1940.* London, 1957
Fulgate, Brian, I. *Operation 'Barbarossa', 1941.* Presidio Novato, USA, 1984
Fuller, J. F. C. *Armoured Warfare: An annotated edition of FSR III (1932).* Harrisburg, 1943
— *The Second World War: 1939–45.* London, 1948
Forty, George. *German Tanks of World War II 'In Action'.* London, 1987
Grandais, Albert. *La Bataille du Calvados.* Paris, 1973
Guderian, Heinz, *Die Grundlagen des Panzerangriffs.* Berlin, 1938
— *Die Panzerwaffe (Achtung! Panzer)*, 1943
– Panzer Leader. London, 1952
De'Guingand, Francis. *Operation Victory.* Hodder & Stoughton, London, 1947
Hamilton, Nigel. *Montgomery: The Making of a General.* London, 1981
Hastings, Max. *Overlord.* Joseph/Guild Publishing, London, 1984
Irving, David. *The Rise and Fall of the Luftwaffe.* Boston, 1973

Keegan, John. *Six Armies in Normandy.* London, 1982
Keitel, Wilhelm. *Memoirs.* Kimber, 1965.
Kesselring, Albert. *Memoirs.* Kimber, 1953
Lewin, Ronald. *Rommel as Military Commander.* London, 1971
— *The Life and Death of the Afrika Korps.* Batsford, 1977
Liddell Hart, Basil H. *The Remaking of Modern Armies.* London, 1927
— *The Other Side of the Hill.* London, 1948
Macksey, Kenneth. *Kesselring: The Making of the Luftwaffe.* Batsford, 1978
— *The Tank Pioneers.* London, 1981
Manstein, Erich von. *Verlorene Siege.* Bonn, 1955, published as *Lost Victories.* London, 1958
Martel, Giffard, le Q. *Our Armoured Forces.* London, 1945
Mellenthin, F. W. von. *Panzer Battles.* Cassell, 1956
Montgomery, Bernard L. *Memoirs.* London, 1958
Mueller-Hillebrand, Burkhart. *Das Heer 1933–45.* E. S. Mittler, Frankfurt, 1956
Munzel, Oscar. *Gepanzerte Truppen.* Herford, 1965
Nehring, Walther. *Die Geschichte der Deutschen Panzerwaffe 1916–45.* Stuttgart, 1974
Ogorkiewicz, Richard M. *Armoured Forces.* Arms & Armour Press, London, 1960
Piekalkiewicz, Janusz. *Unternehmen Zitadelle* and other works. Lübbe, 1983, onwards.
Pipet, Albert. *La Trouée de Normandie.* Paris, 1966
— *Mourir à Caen.* Paris, 1974
Rosinski, Herbert. *The German Army.* London, 1939
Ruge, Frederick. *Rommel in Normandy.* London, 1979
Schramm, Percy, E. (ed). *Kriegstagebuch des Oberkommandos der Wehrmacht 1940–41.* Bernardt and Graef Pawlak, 1982
Seaton, Albert. *The German Army.* London, 1982
— *The Russo-German War, 1941–45.* Praeger, 1971
Senger und Etterlin, Frido von. *Neither Hope nor Fear.* Macdonald, 1963 Technical works, 1957 onwards.
Shirer, William, L. *The Rise and Fall of the Third Reich.* London, 1964
Speidel, Hans. *We Defended Normandy.* London, 1951
Stanley, Roy M. *World War II Photo Intelligence.* Charles Scribner's Sons, 1979.
Stoves, Rolf. *Die Gepanzerten und Motorisierten Deutschen Grossverbände 1935–45.* Bad Nauheim, 1986
Strawson, John. *The Battle for North Africa.*
— *Hitler as Military Commander.*
— *The Battle for Berlin.* London, 1969–74
Tessin, Georg. *Verbände und Truppen der Deutschen Wehrmacht und Waffen S.S. 1939–45.* Biblio Verlag, Osnabrück, 1974
Trevor Roper, H. R. *The Last Days of Hitler: Hitler's War Directives 1939–45.* London, 1947, 1964
Warlimont, Walter. *Inside Hitler's Headquarters.* London, 1962
Westphal, Siegfried. *The German Army in the West.* London, 1951
Wheatley, Ronald. *Operation Sea Lion.* London, 1958
Young, Desmond. *Rommel: The Desert Fox.* London, 1950

Photographs and reproduction maps, unless otherwise stated, are from private archives. The author acknowledges the assistance received in this way from Rolf Guttermann and Oswald Finzel; other photographic sources to which credit is due are the Bundesarchiv Coblenz, Daily Express Newspapers, London and the Imperial War Museum, London.

Index

1. Index of German military formations and units

2. Index of German personalities

3. Index of places